W9-AEW-194

HOW SCHOOLS WORKED

How Schools Worked

Public Education in English Canada, 1900–1940

R.D. GIDNEY AND W.P.J. MILLAR

Carleton Library Series 224

McGill-Queen's University Press

Montreal & Kingston • London • Ithaca

© McGill-Queen's University Press 2012

ISBN 978-0-7735-3953-2 (cloth)
ISBN 978-0-7735-3990-7 (paper)

Legal deposit first quarter 2012
Bibliothèque nationale du Québec

Printed in Canada on acid-free paper that is 100% ancient forest free
(100% post-consumer recycled), processed chlorine free

This book has been published with the help of a grant from the Canadian
Federation for the Humanities and Social Sciences, through the Aid
to Scholarly Publications Program, using funds provided by the Social
Sciences and Humanities Research Council of Canada.

McGill-Queen's University Press acknowledges the support of the Canada
Council for the Arts for our publishing program. We also acknowledge
the financial support of the Government of Canada through the Canada
Book Fund for our publishing activities.

Library and Archives Canada Cataloguing in Publication

Gidney, R. D. (Robert Douglas), 1940–
    How schools worked : public education in English Canada, 1900–1940
/ R.D. Gidney and W.P.J. Millar.

(Carleton library series ; 224)
Includes bibliographical references and index.
ISBN 978-0-7735-3953-2 (bound). – ISBN 978-0-7735-3990-7 (pbk.)

    1. Education – Canada – History – 20th century. 2. Education and state
– Canada – History–20th century. I. Millar, W. P. J. (Winnifred Phoebe
Joyce), 1942– II. Title. III. Series: Carleton library ; 224.

LA411.8.G535 2012   370.971   C2011-907194-0

Typeset by Jay Tee Graphics Ltd. in 10/13 New Baskerville

Contents

List of Figures*

* All figures produced by Cheryl Wituik, Vortex Visual Concepts.

List of Tables

List of Abbreviations

AR	*Annual Report* of provincial department of education or city board of education (titles vary)
ATAM	*Alberta Teachers' Alliance Magazine* (succeeded by *Alberta Teachers' Association Magazine*)
CEA	Canadian Education Association*
CSJ	*Canadian School Board Journal* (succeeded by *Canadian School Journal*)
CTF	Canadian Teachers' Federation
DBS	Dominion Bureau of Statistics (subsequently, Statistics Canada)
DM	deputy minister
JEdNS	*Journal of Education for Nova Scotia*
King Report	British Columbia, *School Finance in British Columbia*
Murray Report	Manitoba, *Report of the Educational Commission*
Ontario Blue Book	Ontario, Department of Education, *Schools and Teachers in the Province of Ontario*
PAA	Public Archives of Alberta
Proceedings, OEA	*Proceedings of the ... Ontario Educational Association*
Putman-Weir Report	Province of British Columbia, *Survey of the School System*
RCDPR	Canada, Royal Commission on Dominion-Provincial Relations
SD	School District
UAA	University of Alberta Archives
WSJ	*Western School Journal*

---

* For a brief period in and around the Second World War, the Canadian Education Association modified its name to incorporate Newfoundland and was known, in abbreviation, as CNEA. We use the more familiar short form, CEA.

Acknowledgments

Debts need grateful acknowledgment. Ann and Don Gutteridge listened patiently over many meals to interminable monologues about this book and answered our endless questions about their own experience as pupils and teachers in a still largely unreconstructed mid-century school system; Don read the entire manuscript and offered ever-helpful advice and encouragement. We also had the benefit, rarely encountered in academe, of the always supportive but blunt, perceptive, and productive criticism of some early drafts by a congenial team of Canada Department of Justice lawyers: John McManus, Ursula Tauscher, Jason Brannen, and Maria Green. Between them, they provided us with a different form of "going back to grad school." Two anonymous readers contributed welcome support at a critical time in the publication process. The staff at the Education Library, the University of Western Ontario, have for many years provided wonderful assistance with interlibrary loans and borrowing privileges generally. Our thanks as well to Cheryl Wituik, Vortex Visual Concepts, for her work on the illustrations and figures; to Judith Turnbull for her meticulous copyediting; and to Don Akenson, Mary-Lynne Ascough, Joan McGilvray, and Ryan Van Huijstee at McGill-Queen's University Press. Finally, there are no errors and omissions in this book. Unless we're wrong.

Introduction

Between the 1880s and the 1940s, several generations of children in English Canada encountered a school system where the principles and practices, customary assumptions and institutional structures, were profoundly different than they are today. Dropped back, indeed, by the proverbial time machine into the classrooms of 1900, or even 1940, nearly all of those born after mid-century would find themselves in an environment that was, at the very least, disconcertingly unfamiliar, if not forbiddingly alien. Our aim is to map the main contours of that system. In doing so, we hope to rescue it from an increasing degree of obscurity and opacity, the inevitable result not only of the passage of time but of fundamental shifts in the organization of Canadian school systems, in the pedagogical values most Canadians espouse, and in beliefs about the role of public education in Canadian society.

I

There is already a substantial literature on education in the later nineteenth and early twentieth centuries. But with some notable exceptions, it tends to be circumscribed by an exclusive focus on particular provinces, by restricted time frames, and by spotty coverage of the full range of interlocking assumptions and structures that gave the system its operational momentum. We hope to offset some, if not all, of these limitations. There is also a persistent bias that bestows undue attention on the emergence of a reform agenda variously known as "the new education" or "progressive education." While it is not possible to write about the period without taking some account of the abundant rhetoric this movement generated, we have given it short shrift in the pages that follow. This book is *not* about schools as they should be, or might be in the best of all possible worlds. It is about schools and school systems at work – schools as they actually operated within the opportunities the world around them provided and the constraints that world imposed.[1]

We want to know, for example, how many children went to school, how often, for how long, and the range of their educational attainments. What and how were they taught? How were they assessed and promoted from grade to grade? What were the qualifications and experience of their teachers? What were their school buildings like? Who paid the bills and how much did they pay? What consequences, intended or not, followed from the way in which schooling proceeded? And how did the answers to these questions change over time?

A more formal way of explaining our objective is to borrow a template proposed by the political scientist Ronald Manzer. "The provision of elementary and secondary education," he writes, "involves four distinct problems of public policy making": the *scope* of provision, which includes the ages at which children are to attend school and the range of educational services to be offered; the supply of *resources*, which measures the depth and priority of public commitment; the *substance* of educational provision, which refers to what is to be learned, when, and how; and the *distribution*, which refers to who benefits from the existing scope, resources, and substance of educational provision and who pays for them.[2] Manzer is primarily concerned with policy issues and their resolution, while we concentrate near-exclusively on describing the main features of educational provision; but Manzer's four categories nicely capture the broad areas we propose to explore.

A relentless focus on the schools at work does not mean that we are disengaged from the ideas generated by the reform agenda or by the issues raised in the extant historiography. Rather the reverse. For example, Neil Sutherland has offered a distinguished account of how a consensus took shape that would guide policy in several areas crucial to the future welfare of Canadian children.[3] We want to examine the extent to which that consensus was translated into routine practices in the schools – to assess its progress beyond a handful of early adopters and more particularly to ask when (or even if) it began to percolate into the nooks and crannies of the wildly diverse provisions for schooling characteristic of the first four or five decades of the twentieth century. Gender issues, a staple of the recent literature, comprise important sections of those chapters dealing with pupils, teachers, supervisors, and programs of study; in the latter case, for example, we are at some pains to disentangle the evidence about levels of gender segregation in Canadian classrooms. There are also competing claims about the role of the school in promoting class reproduction or, alternatively, equality of educational opportunity and occupational mobility. Among other things, we want to probe the extent to which working-class children were streamed into dead-end programs and hence into subordinate roles in the occupational and social order. Similarly, the period is often seen as one of increasing bureaucratization for teachers; again, we want to see when and where this was actually the case, and to try to assess as well the degree to which the supervision that did exist was effectively exercised. More generally, to those who have tended to dismiss the early twentieth-century school as the home of mindless rote, drill, and irrelevance *or*, under the spell of a romanticized afterglow, who cast it as a model of focused purpose, high academic standards, public accountability for achievement, and communal solidarity, we want to invite contemplation of more tempered and nuanced assessments. Our focus on the schools at work is meant, in other words, not only to contribute to a richer understanding of the period itself but also to dissect some of the major interpretive issues in the pertinent literature.

Our text, on the other hand, does not pretend to be comprehensive. It is in fact quite selective in its coverage, ignoring a wide variety of deserving subjects, great and small. From the 1880s onwards, as we have already noted, an emerging reform agenda for the schools would constitute an important part of any full account. This includes sub-topics such as pedagogical reform, the testing and special-education movements, and many related developments. Some of these subjects have been dealt with exceedingly well by historians, while others remain to be explored; but they are, we think, best pursued as aspects of the reform agenda, which is not our intention here. Despite its importance in determining what actually happens on the ground at both provincial and local levels, the politics of education is entirely missing. We devote a chapter to the supervision of teachers' professional work by provincial inspectors, principals, and local superintendents, but ignore the considerable literature on the regulation of teachers' lives outside the classroom routinely exercised by trustees, parents, and other interested parties. Again, there is now a very large and accessible literature on the assimilative aims of schooling in the period, and for that reason alone we do no more than touch on the subject. For a similar reason, and also because our focus is on provincial school systems, we do not include Native education. There are plenty of other examples, some of which we note as we go along, but to reiterate, the book is not intended to be, nor is it, an exhaustive survey. Our aim, rather, is to explore central tendencies – to describe some of the main structural features and operating procedures characteristic of provincial school systems, and, above all, to illuminate the patterns of learning and work the majority of pupils and teachers in English Canada might experience. That means, in turn, that minorities of various kinds, most exceptional cases, and many pertinent issues have been left to others or to future work of our own.

II

Having explained what we are attempting (and not attempting) to do, we turn now to a number of other preliminary matters that demand attention: an explanation of our time frame; the reasons for our decision to exclude Quebec; the nature of the research base; and a clarification of some confusing terminology.

Our account begins with the turn of the twentieth century and not earlier. It is only during the first decade of the century that there is anything like published and usable national-level statistical data, the source for much of our analysis throughout the text. Similarly, it is only then that we begin to get a reasonably representative set of other published sources to draw upon. We believe, nonetheless, that we are describing a mode of governance, administration, finance, and educational policy put in place between the 1840s and the 1880s in eastern Canada and adopted holus-bolus across the West. We think that the two decades between 1900 and 1920 are best understood as the apogee of a system constructed by the mid-Victorians; despite some modifications after that, the main lineaments remained in place until the 1940s. While there are developments in the period that can certainly be read as the roots of the modern, in our own view the system is best understood as reflecting, in its essential features and tendencies, its Victorian origins.[4]

Our terminal dates are more varied. Generally, the narrative concludes around 1940, when a thorough-going reconstruction of governance and finance began to take shape across the country, marking the commencement, in effect, of another story, one that signals an impending rupture with the Victorian past. For a similar reason, however, our account of curriculum and pedagogy ends about 1935, just before the impact of new initiatives began to challenge more traditional principles and practices. On the other hand, the chapters on patterns of attendance extend to mid-century in order to follow the children born in the later 1920s and 1930s through to the end of their schooling.

Though for convenience we will, often enough, resort to phrases like "Canadian," "Canada-wide," "national," "the nation," or "across the country," we can hardly claim that, without Quebec, this is a genuinely national study. The exclusion is, in any case, incomplete: there are statistical series where it proved impossible to separate out the figures for Quebec, and we have occasionally drawn an example from Montreal or some other part of the province. But in the main Quebec is not part of this study. One reason is that the province's distinctive administrative structure, institutional organization, and cultural milieu for education would have made all of our arguments much more complex and necessitated even more qualifications than now litter the text.[5] But the compelling factor was that this book draws extensively for its research base on quantitative data and demands provincial-level statistics that can be compared and contrasted systematically. On this point, Quebec posed serious difficulties. From the time the Dominion Bureau of Statistics (DBS) began to compile statistical records on education, it warned about the special problems presented by the figures from Quebec.[6] Carl Goldenberg summed up the problem judiciously in the late 1930s: "Quebec financial statistics, particularly with respect to education, but also for public welfare and public health, are not comparable with those for other provinces, owing in large part to the services provided by the Roman Catholic Church and religious orders; these services in many instances provide in Quebec what is provided by governments (municipal and provincial) in other provinces." He went on, "Exact attendance figures, for publicly controlled schools only, are not obtainable for Quebec," and he added that the Quebec figures he did use were to be considered only rough approximations.[7] It was mainly for this reason that we abandoned any attempt to incorporate Quebec, even though it might have made for a much more productive and interesting study.[8] (Since this study ends before 1949, when Newfoundland became a part of Canada, that province is also excluded.)

Because one of our aims is to analyse national and provincial patterns of pupil attendance, course enrolments, teacher qualifications, levels of expenditure, and a variety of other system characteristics, we use a lot of numbers. As with any piece of work based on quantitative data, there is a need for technical explanations about the sources, quality, and interpretation of the data. We also want to make the evidentiary base for our conclusions as transparent as possible and to ensure that our data are accessible to others. At the same time, we want to avoid cluttering the text and references with an excessive amount of quantitative data or extending even further what is already a lengthy book. Our compromise is to try to minimize the amount of data in the text itself and to include within the chapters only the most pertinent tables, consigning the rest to several appendices on the Internet.* These include a description of the sources we have exploited,

---

* The appendices are available on the Internet at http://mqup.mcgill.ca/HowSchoolsWorkedAppendices.pdf. This format unfortunately makes it more difficult for readers to access them and evaluate, more or less immediately, the basis for much of our reasoning. Still, we chose this compromise because it makes for a far shorter book with fewer tables and long explanatory references, and it provides the opportunity to include supplementary material that may be of interest only to specialists or to those interested only in this or that particular topic.

critical analysis of the problems they raise, and supplementary tables and other documentation we felt essential to the project. Those who are content to take us at our word can ignore this necessary but cumbersome exercise; those with specialist interests can consult the appendices as they see fit. The tables included in the text are identified by chapter and table numbers (e.g., Table 2.1 or Table 3.5); references to the additional tables included in the appendices are designated as, for example, "Table A.2" or "Table B.8." We have avoided reproducing tables that are easily accessible in other published sources even when they are important to arguments in our text. Appendix A begins with a general introduction to and commentary on the key sources: see sections 1 to 3.

Aside from a substantial body of quantitative data, there are other indispensable sources that we have read through for each province: perhaps the two most important examples are the various provincial department of education *Annual Reports* and the annual surveys of education produced, from 1921 on, by the DBS. On the other hand, one simply cannot read everything written about schooling in the period.[9] Aside from the variations in the quality and quantity of the sources, it would be impossible to delve deeply into the records in each provincial archive or to read systematically through all the education-related publications produced over half a century in each province. Thus we have necessarily been selective, probing one set of archival records in some depth,[10] reading several different types of magazine drawn from the professional press of various provinces, and using a variety of other sources to illustrate this or that development by examples representative of circumstances widely, if not universally, shared. We have also selected a handful of communities for intensive study, not only offering detailed portraits in chapter 4, but also drawing on these repeatedly throughout the text to illustrate particular issues. We could just as well have picked Vancouver or Toronto, Woodstock (NB) or Woodstock (ON), Salmon Arm (BC) or Canning (NS), or any one of the rural school districts in Ontario or Manitoba where the surviving records provide good sources to illustrate our arguments. We decided upon Winnipeg, Fredericton, Blairmore (AB), and Kipp SD No. 1589, just outside Davidson (SK). They are not necessarily more "typical" than any other place, but these four communities offer an opportunity to describe in some depth, and to allow comparisons between educational developments in one big city, one more modest urban community, one medium-sized village, and one rural school district.

In chapters 6 and 7 especially we make extensive use of the "Rowell-Sirois Report," so named after the two chairs of the Royal Commission on Dominion-Provincial Relations. This commission, an important investigation of the arrangements governing federal-provincial relations, was established in 1937 and issued its final report in 1940. The standard abridgement of the report, by Donald Smiley, focuses near-exclusively on its main subject and drastically excises a wealth of material on provincial and municipal finance.[11] Moreover, besides the report itself, the commission generated thousands of pages of hearings, submissions, associated studies, and appendices, all of which constitute a remarkably rich and largely unexploited source for understanding the political economy of educational finance and its setting within the municipal and provincial framework. The full version of the report is accessible in many university libraries; we have also made extensive use of the related material located in the government documents section of the Robarts Library at the University of Toronto and elsewhere.

In various parts of the text and in several tables we cite figures relating to educational expenditure. But what do they mean in modern terms? Is $3 million spent in 1900 in building a new high school, or $3,000 invested in 1920 in school libraries, a lot of money or only a little? Does a $1,000 salary earned in 1925 make a teacher rich or poor? Is a $10,000 reduction made between 1930 and 1933 in a city's education budget a modest or crippling cut? To grasp the significance of expenditure figures in the past, it is useful to be able to convert dollar amounts into today's values. Though not a foolproof guide, the Bank of Canada includes on its website an inflation calculator that is very helpful in equating past and present dollar values.[12]

Our sources include, as well, a wide range of theses, reports, articles, and monographs, local, provincial, and national, by historians and other scholars interested in education in twentieth-century Canada, some of which are of the highest quality and much of them indispensable for this study.[13] We have, in other words, benefited enormously from the work of others, and in this regard we want particularly to acknowledge the exceptionally rich trove of scholarship on the period produced by historians in British Columbia.

Legal terminology varied from province to province; to avoid confusion we have adopted standard usage for a number of commonly recurring terms. Despite the use of "school section" in rural Nova Scotia and Ontario, we invariably use the phrase "school district" common to other provinces. By the 1930s some provinces had abandoned the term "inspector" in favour of "superintendent"; we will maintain "inspector" throughout, reserving "superintendent" for local supervisory officers. An Ontario "public school" or "separate school," or a Nova Scotia "common school," is, in this book, an "elementary school." But "public schools," "the public system," or "public education" encompasses both elementary and secondary schools funded and controlled by provincial governments. "Mechanic arts" (Nova Scotia) or "industrial arts" (in several provinces at some points in time) is usually "manual training" here, while "household arts," or "home economics" and a couple of other variants, is usually "domestic science." The phrase "ungraded school" (or, in some provinces, a "miscellaneous" school or classroom) was commonly used as a synonym for the one-room school and as an antonym for the "multi-graded school." We will also use that conventional terminology even though the one-room school was anything but "ungraded" – children were still classified by age or attainment and then assigned to particular grade levels.

Public education in each province is governed by statutory laws passed by the provincial legislature. There may be several pertinent statutes or a single comprehensive one called "The School Act" or "The Education Act." But the schools are also governed by sets of "regulations." These are published policies or rules made by the department of education under authority of one of the school acts, and they have the same force of law as the act itself. Regulations are usually identified by an assigned number, as in "Regulation 17." In the early decades of the century the bureaucratic locale of provincial officialdom was still, in some places, "the Education Office" or some similar nomenclature; we will always use "Department of Education." Its senior non-political head might be "superintendent of education," "chief superintendent," or "deputy minister." His annual reports to the provincial cabinet, the Council of Public Instruction, or the minister of education had various titles; regardless, we will refer to them uniformly as, for example, Ontario or Nova Scotia, *Annual Reports* (i.e., Ontario, *AR*; Nova Scotia, *AR*; "Department of Education" inferred but not explicitly noted). "Schoolmen" are senior provincial officials, inspectors, superintendents, education academics, and the like – influential participants in the enterprise but not teachers or principals.

The word "average" is imprecise because technically it can refer to three different quantitative dimensions. Because of its familiarity, we will use it throughout the text in the sense of "mean." It is important, however, not to confuse "average" with "median," which is the mid-point of a frequency distribution of cases, with an equal number falling above and below it.

We observe one other important terminological convention. Though it may drive to distraction those who have never learned to count in Roman numerals, these were used in nearly all provinces throughout the period to identify grade levels. Since we think it would be not only confusing but anachronistic to shift to Arabic numerals, we will preserve grade designations in their original form.

HOW SCHOOLS WORKED

1

Essential Contexts

We begin with three necessary "prefaces" that together provide the scaffolding upon which the rest of the text is built. The first focuses on the institutional infrastructure for public education in the early twentieth century. The second confronts the problem of accounting for provincial differences. And the third constitutes a brief overview of the kind of society that provided the context for schooling in the period.

By the turn of the twentieth century, there existed a well-established legal framework common to most provincial school systems, and it would undergo few changes before 1940. Since all the chapters that follow assume some basic knowledge of how these systems operated, an elementary introduction may be helpful.[1] The Confederation agreements of 1867 made education the "exclusive jurisdiction" of each province; with only a handful of exceptions, that included *all* education of whatever kind the provinces chose to establish or allow to develop – public or private, academic or technical, from early childhood to university-level studies, and anything else that might be defined as "education." Constitutional responsibility for education, in other words, rested with the provinces and not the federal government; accordingly, Canada had not one but nine distinct provincial education systems, each with its own body of law and regulation, its own peculiar nomenclature, and its own administrative arrangements.

Despite real differences from province to province, there was nonetheless much common ground. Provincial legislatures created education laws. The government of the day, either through cabinet as a whole or through a minister of education, shaped general policy. Departments of Education, headed by a deputy minister or superintendent (or both), offered policy advice to the government, implemented its decisions, encouraged the development of schools and other educational institutions, administered the acts and regulations, and carried out the routine work of record-keeping and financial auditing. In some provinces, policy advice was lodged in the hands of an advisory council, but whatever the exact arrangements, the collective powers of these provincial (or central) authorities were extensive: they determined the means by which local schools were established and maintained, the curriculum to be taught, the textbooks to be used, the qualifications required for a licence to teach in the public schools, and a remarkable variety of other system-wide rules. Each central authority also employed a corps of school inspectors to see that law and policy were enforced, even in the most remote corners of the province.*

The actual operation of the schools, however, was delegated to local authorities we would now call boards of education. These consisted of groups of "trustees" who presided over geographical units known as "school districts," which might include a few square miles and a single one-room school or all of the schools of a city, town, or enlarged rural unit such as a township or, in British Columbia, a "rural municipality." In rural areas the board was usually made up of three trustees; in larger units, usually more. Though there were some exceptions in urban eastern Canada, trustees were normally elected to office by local ratepayers – those who paid property taxes or some other form of local tax, which identified them as residents of the school district. There were certain duties all school boards had to perform: build and maintain schools, hire licensed teachers, set school tax rates, and generally meet the minimum requirements of the law. But beyond that, the education acts also allowed trustees a good deal of latitude over such things as the organization and administration of their schools, the kind and quality of buildings, the facilities and equipment they contained, the qualifications of the teachers, the levels of instruction a local school system might offer.

The "exclusive jurisdiction" of the provinces had few constitutional limits, but there were some. For example, the constitution gave the federal government, and not the provinces, responsibility for the education of Native Canadians. By 1905, with the creation of Saskatchewan and Alberta, modern provincial boundaries were more or less established across southern Canada, but Ottawa continued to govern a vast northern territory where education remained within its jurisdiction; by 1914 the territorial council of the Yukon had created its own small education system, funded by federal money. The federal government also bore broad responsibilities for national economic development, and under that rubric, during the second

---

* Many observers have remarked on the highly centralized nature of Canada's provincial school systems. In this respect as in many others, the organization and timing of changes were quite different from the American experience, and while we should always be informed by the rich American literature that exists, we should be cautious about generalizing from American precedents.

decade of the twentieth century, it began to fund (though not control) programs to encourage the growth of agricultural and technical education.

The most significant limitations on the powers of the provinces in education, however, were the constitutional guarantees to denominational schools that no province could abridge.[2] In English Canada, such schools existed in Alberta, Saskatchewan, and Ontario. In those provinces, local minorities of either Protestants or Roman Catholics had the right to form their own schools independent of the majority in the school district. In Saskatchewan and Ontario, that right extended to elementary education only. In each of these three provinces, it should be emphasized, the separate schools were part of the *public* education system: they were government-funded, and they operated under nearly all the same acts and regulations as any other public school. Private schools existed in all provinces, but separate schools were not (and are not) private schools. Because they are part of the public system, and because before mid-century their numbers were relatively modest, we make no attempt in this book to distinguish them from other public schools. In other parts of English Canada, the public schools were officially non-sectarian, but "gentlemen's agreements" in Nova Scotia and New Brunswick allowed school boards to organize classes or entire schools that served religious minorities to one extent or another. Halifax, for example, had a well-established system of Roman Catholic elementary and high schools that operated under the aegis of the city's common school board. And anywhere in Canada where there was bloc settlement by groups of Catholics or Protestants, the local public school tended to reflect that reality whatever the official regulations might say about the matter.

Like governance, finance was a shared responsibility between central and local authorities. Provincial governments gave grants to local schools intended to subsidize teacher salaries or assist more generally in the operation of the schools. Commonly, there were additional special-purpose grants – for maintaining secondary education, for example, hiring better-qualified teachers, establishing libraries, providing transportation in rural areas, or encouraging the introduction of innovative practices. Local funds were raised by school boards, which levied a tax on the property within their district, whether residential, commercial, or industrial. Unlike the situation in most provinces today, however, where provincial governments make the key decisions about local tax rates, school boards in the early twentieth century were usually free to raise whatever amounts they needed for operating costs, subject only to the tolerance or prior approval of those who elected them. In some provinces this source of revenue was supplemented either modestly (as in New Brunswick and Nova Scotia) or substantially (as in Manitoba and Ontario) by a township, municipal, or county levy that was then apportioned out to each school district. Capital costs tended to be subject to far greater scrutiny or control by provincial or municipal governments, or were approved by special vote of the ratepayers.

Because education in Canada is a provincial jurisdiction, and because so many of the published and unpublished sources are organized by province, there is an almost intuitive tendency to write as though provincial boundaries defined the subject or to draw comparisons between individual provinces. In the chapters that follow, we try to resist both tendencies because we think they are mostly (though not always) misleading. First and most obviously, some differences were simply artifacts of history. It is not very surprising that, in the first two or three decades of the century, rates of increase in enrolments were higher in Alberta than in Nova Scotia or that regularity of attendance might be worse in Saskatchewan than in Ontario. All such statistics do is reflect differences between new and long-settled provinces. Second, some of the significant variations are regional, not provincial, in nature. For some of the most important questions we raise in this book, the three Maritime provinces, taken together, differ quite dramatically from Ontario and the West. Whatever the differences among the three Prairie provinces, there is as much, if not more, common ground among them. Similarly, the "resource belt" stretching across the northern parts of Ontario and the western provinces has a degree of coherence – in education as in other things – that transcends provincial borders and differs in many respects from the settled agricultural and industrial heartlands of Canada.

There are also variations that at first glance may appear significant but are nothing more than the result of minor or idiosyncratic policy differences. In 1951, for example, Nova Scotia appeared to have far higher rates of irregular school attendance than Alberta. That year, however, Nova Scotia enrolled 15% of its 5-year-olds and 74% of its 6-year-olds; the figures for Alberta were, respectively, 1% and 42%. Since 5- and 6-year-olds tended to have very high rates of absenteeism and seasonal irregularity, they inevitably made Nova Scotia's attendance record look worse than Alberta's. Similarly, since more children in Nova Scotia completed their education earlier, that province's retention rates for adolescents also looked worse. Do these figures turn Nova Scotia into an educational laggard, a backwater in the story of educational progress? Obviously not. Both results are simply a function of the fact that Nova Scotia allowed children to start earlier than did Alberta. Allowing little children to attend school was a sure invitation to higher levels of irregular attendance, but if children started school earlier, they were also more likely to complete their schooling earlier.[3]

Or take another example: local education officials (and some historians after them) were quick to note that on many conventional measures British

Columbia tended to score considerably better than most other provinces. British Columbia was also one of the most highly urbanized provinces in Canada, and its urban population was highly concentrated. In 1931, for instance, 59% of the population lived in only two metropolitan centres – Greater Vancouver and Greater Victoria.[4] A few years later, the education department's *Annual Report* would note that 48.3% of British Columbia's total enrolment was to be found in these two metropolitan areas.[5] That is to say, nearly 50% of British Columbia's children attended "big-city" schools – and big-city school systems were the lighthouses for everything up-to-date in Canadian education. In 1931, on the other hand, the total urban population of the Maritimes stood at 40%; 14% lived in a metropolitan centre, and presumably a rough equivalent of that 14% attended "big-city" schools. Thus one has to pose the question, are comparisons between provinces little more than comparative measures of urbanization? And if so, does this make a difference in interpreting apparent differences between provinces?

"What should be stressed in comparing the school statistics of one province with another is not their points of difference but points of resemblance," the head of the Dominion Bureau of Statistics (DBS) remarked in 1921: "In spite of differences in programmes of study, provincial aims and conditions, the actual standing at a certain age in different provinces is roughly the same. Indeed there would seem to be at least as much difference in attainments in different types of schools in the same province as there is between the attainments in one province and another."[6] A few years earlier, describing the country's education system for an international audience, Peter Sandiford wrote that "theoretically speaking, there is no such thing as a Canadian system of education: there are nine provincial systems. Such, however, is the unanimity of spirit and ideals possessing the whole, that in spite of local differences in detail ... one is justified in speaking or writing of a Canadian system of education."[7] We are not saying that provincial differences didn't exist or don't matter; sometimes they did, and sometimes they mattered a lot. All we want to suggest is that for many pertinent issues there are more fundamental categories of analysis, that there are national patterns that transcend provincial ones, and that provincial comparisons may mask more than they illuminate. These at least are the assumptions underpinning the chapters that follow.

Our third "preface" is intended as a reminder of the social structure within which provincial school systems operated. Canada in the early twentieth century was a very different country than it is today. In 1901 its population was 5,371,000. By 1931 the figure had doubled to 10,367,000, only about a third of the country's present population, yet spread across very nearly the same vast expanse of territory. Even in 1951, there were still little more than 15 million people. Whenever one is attempting to understand Canadian patterns or compare them to developments elsewhere, one has to take into account the relatively modest size and wide dispersal over an enormous territory of the country's population. The same might be said about the population, size, and geographical diversity of individual provinces.

Nor should we simply assume that the country could mobilize the kind of fiscal resources necessary to underwrite the expansion of education that took place after the Second World War. As a people, Canadians could hardly be described in the interwar years as part of the world's poor, but in one 1936 estimate, Canada, with a per capita income of $347, ranked seventh out of thirteen countries; it stood far below the United States ($508) and well below the United Kingdom ($457), Australia ($409), and Germany ($389). Moreover, there were vast disparities within Canada: in 1928, for example, national per capita income was $471; in British Columbia, the most prosperous province, the figure was $613; in Ontario, $555; in Saskatchewan, $412; and in New Brunswick, $317.[8] Ultimately, the quality and quantity of education that communities could collectively provide, or individual adults could provide for their children, depended on the fiscal resources available to them, and for Canadians these resources were considerably more limited in the decades before 1940 than in some other jurisdictions or than they would be only a decade or two later.

While urbanization was not a new phenomenon in the early twentieth century, the growth of towns and cities was gradually turning the nation into a predominantly urban society. In absolute numbers, both urban and rural populations increased across the period, but the former grew at a far faster rate: between 1901 and 1951 the rural population increased by 173% and the urban by 389%.[9] In 1911 only 42% of Canada's population was classed as urban; by 1931 the figure was 53%, and by 1951, 63%.[10] For perfectly good reasons, historians of the period have filled books and articles recounting the sheer rapidity of urbanization, the vast increase in the scale of urban society, and the stresses urbanization created. But too exclusive a focus on the pace and scale of urbanization can also mislead, and it is important to remember, as we proceed, both the modest size of most urban communities compared to today and the very large proportion of the population that lived in rural Canada.

In 1921 there were seventy-nine "cities" of at least 7,500 people in Canada. Seven of them had over 90,000; eight, between 30,000 and 90,000; twelve, between 20,000 and 30,000; twenty-eight, between 10,000 and 20,000; and twenty-four, between 7,500 and 10,000.[11] A decade later, in 1931, Canada still had only eight "metropolitan" cities – that is, cities and their suburbs with more than 100,000 people. Montreal was by far the largest but was still below a million people. Toronto was only just nicely above half a million, Vancouver just below 250,000, and the other five less than that.[12] Most urban Canadians lived in yet smaller centres. London in 1931 had 71,000 people; Regina and Halifax, between 50,000 and 60,000; Saint John, 47,000; and Saskatoon, 43,000. Victoria trailed along at 39,000, and Brantford at 30,000. *And these were still among the top twenty cities in the country.*[13] Even in 1941 Canada still had only eight cities with over 100,000 people; far more had populations between 5,000 and 10,000, and 76% of those urban communities of 5,000 or more people had fewer than 30,000.[14] That is to say, even among those classed as genuine urban communities, most were, by any modern standard, of modest size.

Substantial numbers of Canadians lived in even smaller communities – in villages and small towns scattered across every province. Despite some limited definitional changes, indeed, the census definition of "urban" was essentially any incorporated community of a thousand people or more; and one can legitimately ask whether the smallest "urban" centres, with populations of, say, 1,000 to 5,000, were urban or rural in their orientation and social structure.[15] Even among these small communities, moreover, there was an enormous degree of diversity. As Rex Lucas notes, they included "market-towns, fishing villages, pulp and paper towns, railway towns, mining communities, manufacturing towns, county seats, agricultural villages, tourist resorts, small communities with several industries, and so on. This variety incorporates different types of social patterns."[16]

While residents of rural Canada constituted a slowly decreasing proportion of the total population, national totals or percentages obscure the differences among provinces and regions. In 1931 Ontario, Quebec, and British Columbia were relatively highly urbanized, with just over 60% of their people living in towns, cities, and villages. But in Saskatchewan and Prince Edward Island, 80% of the people were classified as "rural"; in New Brunswick the figure was 65%. In the three Maritime provinces combined, 60% were rural dwellers; in the three Prairie provinces, 70%.[17] That is to say, in large swathes of the nation, the population was predominantly rural. And while the figures had changed by 1951, nearly 30% of Ontario's population still lived in rural communities; in the Maritimes and on the prairies, rural people still constituted, by small margins, the majority of the population.[18] In raw numbers, about half the Canadian population was classed as rural in 1931 – about 5 million people. By 1951 the balance had shifted but the proportion was still relatively close – nearly 9 million urbanites and just over 5 million rural dwellers.[19]

Just as "urban" cannot be read to mean "big cities," a homogeneous economic base, or a common social structure, so "rural" cannot be equated with "farmers" or "agriculture." Beginning in 1931 the census drew a distinction between the "farm" and the "rural non-farm" populations. In that year fully 70% of the rural population was classified as non-farm, though provincial tallies varied enormously. In British Columbia, 86% of rural people were non-farm; in Prince Edward Island and Saskatchewan the figure stood at just under 40%.[20] As the DBS statistician described it, "rural non-farm" people "reside in suburban districts near satellite cities,[21] in unincorporated hamlets, police villages, and country parishes. They are engaged less in farming than in selling and distributing goods, in rendering professional and other services, or in lumbering, fishing, trapping and other occupations."[22] As well as growing wheat, breeding cattle, or tending orchards, rural people fished, doctored, preached, taught, cobbled shoes, cut timber, sold groceries, and repaired cars and tractors.

Even adding "rural non-farm" to the category doesn't do justice to the complexities of the social structure. Writing in the late 1930s, Leonard Marsh, then one of Canada's leading social scientists, had this to say:

> Canadian conditions ... really require a threefold rather than a twofold classification: urban, rural, and frontier. It would be of great help towards the better sociological description of Canada to be able to separate the sections of each region which were rural in the positive sense of that word – "countryside" rather than merely "non-urban," including a settled agriculture well past the stage of the first clearing, with at least some villages and a minimum development of community-institutions. On tiny farms around some of the fishing ports the population may properly be regarded as rural. Elsewhere fishing, and even more commonly logging or trapping, is conducted in more or less isolated territory, where it may or may not be dovetailed with some restricted agriculture. Most miners and some loggers work in a distinctly industrial environment, but they may be returned for census purposes as rural residents. The exact weight of these frontier or intermediate sections is difficult to measure, but at a reasonable guess they account for at least 10% of the Canadian population. Strictly speaking, also, they mark off an appreciable percentage of farm residents from the present total. In spite of this, however, farming offers a more definitive index of rural conditions of work and status than the statistical "rural."[23]

We introduce these issues here because they are of central importance for much of the rest of this book. Today most Canadians live in urban communities, most of them in far larger towns and cities than in the first half of the twentieth century; rural people now constitute about 20% of the population; and the farm population amounts to no more than 2.2%.[24] The frontier areas have receded geographically, and the distinctive cultures of frontier, farm, and urban life have been substantially homogenized. But to get at the character of Canadian society before 1950 and to grasp many of the issues that dominate the chapters that follow, modern preconceptions have to be set aside. Though the frontier was steadily in retreat, nearly every province had, along with its urban and settled rural communities, extensive frontier regions within its borders. In the interwar years – more so before that, only somewhat less by mid-century – nearly *half* the population lived in rural Canada – more than half if we added in the villages and small towns that serviced that population and were rural rather than urban in outlook.

Even more important for our purposes is one last set of figures. When they finished their schooling and began looking for work, young people tended to migrate citywards, thus swelling the total juvenile population of urban Canada. But in 1921, 54% of those between the ages of 5 and 14 were rural residents; in 1931 the figure was 51%.[25] Thus fully half of the age group that constituted the vast majority of school attenders during the interwar years – and substantially more than half in the years before that – lived in rural communities. While we would hardly be justified in giving less than due attention to the dynamic growth of big-city school systems, the sheer size and importance of the numbers of those who lived, went to school, and taught in Canada's small communities, both urban and rural, demand our careful attention in the chapters that follow.

Patterns of Attendance

Between 1900 and 1951, the number of Canadian children and young people increased from about 1,760,000 to over 3,500,000. Even in the first decade of the century most of them went to school for a few years, and in the years that followed, more and more stayed in school for longer periods of time. Thus school enrolments increased substantially, from something like a million in 1900 to nearly 2,400,000 at mid-century.[1] Most of this growth took place in the early decades of the century and was concentrated, indeed, in the first twenty-five years. In English Canada, from 1910 to 1915 alone, the rate of enrolment increase hit 20%; in the next five years it was close to that, at over 18% (Table 2.1). These figures incorporate growth rates that were extreme in the new Prairie provinces and more modest else-where: in Saskatchewan, starting from a very low population base in 1900, enrolments increased by nearly 1,700% to 1925; and in Nova Scotia, in the same twenty-five years, by only 14%. In British Columbia the figure was 325%, and in Ontario, 36%.[2] But everywhere the same two developments would shape the educational enterprise and provide the main issues that will engage us in the various chapters of this book: in absolute numbers, more children to be educated, and more children staying in school longer.

We begin this chapter by exploring three major dimensions of school-going during these decades: the points at which children started and left school and the length of time they spent there; the regularity with which they attended; and the levels of educational attainment they achieved. Having tackled these three questions, we will turn to some of the important differences among urban and rural children, boys and girls, and children of different ethnic groups. The chapter is, however, descriptive rather than explanatory. In chapter 3 we probe causes and begin to account for the patterns encountered here.

I

Tables 2.2 and 2.3 provide the basic data for school-going in English Canada by age group and individual ages, 1911 through 1951.[3] In the main, 5-year-

Table 2.1

Enrolment and full-time teachers, public elementary and secondary schools, Canada (excluding Quebec), 1900–1970

	Enrolment ('ooos) N	Rate of growth every 5 years %	Teachers N	Rate of growth every 5 years %
1900	778		19,000	
1905	831	6.8	21,009	10.6
1910	967	16.4	27,586	31.3
1915	1,162	20.2	34,896	26.5
1920	1,376	18.4	40,577	16.3
1925	1,493	8.5	44,718	10.2
1930	1,556	4.2	49,274	10.2
1935	1,545	–0.7	49,518	0.5
1940	1,487	–3.8	50,078	1.1
1945	1,482	–0.3	51,015	1.9
1950	1,750	18.1	63,031	23.6
1955	2,256	28.9	80,534	37.3
1960	2,899	28.5	107,346	33.3
1965	3,534	21.9	141,672	32.0
1970	4,072	15.2	184,479	30.2

Notes: Newfoundland is included after 1945; Yukon, Northwest Territories, and overseas, after 1955. The number of teachers in Saskatchewan in 1965 is an estimate in the original table. The introduction to Series w150–191 notes that the figures for Ontario and British Columbia teachers are "questionable" to 1900 and 1910 respectively because they were under-reported.

Sources: Leacy, *Historical Statistics*, w67–93 and w150–191. The 1900 figures for enrolment and teachers in Saskatchewan and Alberta are estimated from Urquhart and Buckley, *Historical Statistics*, 589, 594.

Table 2.2

Percentage in school of population 5–24, by age groups, Canada (excluding Quebec), 1911–1961

Canada	5–9 %	10–14 %	15–19 %	20–24 %
1911	51.0	80.1	20.7	1.2
1921	64.6	90.5	27.3	2.4
1931	70.1	95.6	37.8	3.1
1941	68.6	95.8	40.1	4.0
1951	67.6	94.7	45.4	5.0
1961	77.7	97.4	62.6	8.2

Notes: 1911–1941: eight provinces, not including Quebec. 1951 and 1961: nine provinces including Newfoundland but not Quebec. Percentages are based on total population aged 5–24.

Sources:

1911–1941: Calculated from *Census of Canada 1941*, vol. 1, 734ff. (Table 54).

1951: Calculated from DBS, *Education, Census, 1951*, Reference Paper #84, 14–15.

1961: Calculated from *Census of Canada 1961*, Series 7.1, General Review Bulletin 7.1-10 (Ottawa, 1965), pp. 10–35/36.

Table 2.3
Percentage in school of population 5–19, by single years of age, Canada (excluding Quebec), 1911–1951[a]

Age	1911 %	1921 %	1931 %	1941 %	1951 %
5	11.7	12.3	11.9	8.0	6.1[b]
6	42.8	50.6	55.8	49.7	53.6
7	70.2	81.4	88.3	89.7	94.0
8	80.0	90.1	94.8	96.0	97.4
9	83.8	92.7	96.4	97.5	94.1
10	84.4	93.8	97.3	97.3	97.6
11	85.7	94.4	97.5	97.6	93.0
12	83.7	93.6	97.1	97.8	96.5
13	79.8	91.1	95.9	96.5	95.0
14	67.2	78.9	89.8	89.7	92.3
15	47.4	56.6	74.0	74.7	82.7
16	27.9	36.1	51.5	54.6	62.4
17	15.6	21.6	32.0	36.9	40.8
18	8.6	12.6	19.1	23.4	25.9
19	5.0	7.7	11.1	13.8	14.7

[a] Percentages for 1951 include Newfoundland, Yukon, and Northwest Territories.
[b] Before 1951 those attending kindergarten were counted among those attending school, but not in 1951. See statement in *Census of Canada 1961*, Bulletin 7.1-10, General Review of Educational Levels and School Attendance, p. 10-3.

Sources:
1911–41: Calculated from *Census of Canada 1941*, vol. 1, 734, 737 (Table 54).
1951: Calculated from DBS, *Education, Census, 1951*, vol. 12, appendix, 82–3 (Table 1, school population), and *Census of Canada 1951*, vol. 2, appendix A, pp. A-4, A-5 (population).

olds did not go to school at all. In 1911 and again in 1921, about 12% of these children were in school, and the percentage actually declined thereafter, to 8% in 1941.[4] Between 1911 and 1951 only about half the 6-year-olds attended school. By the second decade of the century, the key years of school-going were ages 8 through 13: in 1911 over four-fifths of children 8 to 13, 70% of 7-year-olds, and 67% of 14-year-olds were enrolled in school. By 1921, most of those between 7 and 14 were enrolled. Between 1921 and 1951, this group – ages 7 through 14 – constituted the core age group for universal schooling. To put it another way, in 1911 nearly all children attended school for six or seven years (ages 7 or 8 to 13), and by 1921 something like eight years (ages 7 to 14), though more attended for the shorter rather than the longer period. By 1931 the span was generally eight years, and it would remain at that level through 1951.[5]

In most provinces, compulsory attendance ended at a pupil's birthday so that, for example, compulsion from ages 7 to 14 meant from a child's seventh to fourteenth birthday (not, as is often assumed, *through* the fourteenth year).[6] Once children reached the end of compulsory attendance, some-where between 14 and 16 depending on the period and province, they left school in increasing numbers, though each decade a larger percent-age stayed in school. In 1911 only 47% of 15-year-olds, and in 1921, 57%, remained in school; in 1941 the figure had risen to 75% and in 1951 to 83%. Twenty-eight per cent of 16-year-olds and 16% of 17-year-olds were in school in 1911; the figures for 1941 were 55% and 37% respectively, and for 1951, 62% and 41%. Even in 1951 only a quarter of 18-year-olds were in school.

Although Canadian children were universally in school for only a lim-ited number of years, the average length of schooling was somewhat more extended than the previous two paragraphs would suggest. While all (or nearly all) children were in school for the minimum period of time, an additional number of children aged 6 or 16 were also in school, so that nationally (including Quebec) the average length of schooling extended from just under seven years in 1911, to eight years in 1921, eight and a half years in 1931, and by 1941, ten years.[7]

The number of years of schooling attained by the adult population mir-rored these changes. The median (*not* average) years of schooling for all those 15 years of age and over who were not at school in 1951 was 8.2, up from 7.7 in 1941; that is, half the population had eight years or more of schooling and half had less. But the data can also be divided by age groups, which provides a fix on generational differences. For those 45 or older in 1951 (born before 1905), 63% had less than nine years of schooling. Of those between 30 and 44 (born between 1905 and 1920), 48% had less than nine years. The youngest group, born between 1920 and 1935 (age 15 to 29 in 1951), improved on that figure only marginally, with 46% having less than nine years.[8]

We thus have two related trends over the first half of the century: an expanding range of ages at which nearly all children were in school – from about 8–13 to 7–14; and more of those aged 15 to 17 staying in school.

Once children began school, how regularly did they attend? There were three conventional measures of regularity of attendance during the school year. One drew on the census of Canada. For several decades parents were asked two school-related questions by census enumerators: did their child attend school during the past year; and how many months did he or she attend.[9] These data are useful because the questions were the same across Canada and because the answers can sometimes be correlated with other socio-economic variables – the latter rarely possible with the provincial data. But the census data have these disadvantages: they are decadal only, so that they don't measure in any precise way when changes took place; the question about months in school was not posed after 1931, so the continuity is broken; and the reliability of data is subject to the estimates of respondents. Generally, the census figures for regular attendance are higher than the figures in provincial reports and, in any case, are not exactly comparable because they include attendance at all schools, not just those funded through provincial school systems.[10] We occasionally make use of the census figures when they are more helpful than provincial figures, but we prefer, where possible, the annual figures provided by provincial Departments of Education that were based on school registers kept by teachers.

Provincial departments used two different (though overlapping) measures, collated from the school registers. The first was to record the number of days attended per month and then to produce interval tables – that is, the number of children attending up to 60 days (or three months), 60 to 119 days (or four to six months), and so on. Writing just before the First World War, James Miller combined the figures for Alberta, Manitoba, and Nova Scotia (at the time the only three provinces with published data) and estimated that 45% of children attended 100 days or less (under five months) and 67%, 150 days or less (under about seven and a half months).[11] Our own data are based on the only three provinces that produced comparable figures from the early 1920s to 1950 (Table A.5 in appendix A). In 1922 something like 37% of Alberta children attended school for six months or less, and 18% – nearly 26,000 children – attended for less than three months. Only 61% attended for seven months or more. The percentages are a little better for Nova Scotia and worse for Saskatchewan. In all three cases the figures are high enough to suggest that a significant number of children were not in school regularly enough to benefit from instruction.

The second measure was a calculation called "average daily attendance" (ADA), which produced a single percentage for the entire school year. Canada-wide, it stood at 64% of enrolment in 1910 and 73% in 1920.[12] Again, this suggests considerable irregularity. Both indicators, however, show rapid improvement during and after the 1920s. By 1930, for example, Canadian ADA stood at 86%. By 1941, 89% of Alberta's children attended 7–10 months a year and by 1951, the figure was 93%. Nova Scotia and Saskatchewan showed similar improvements. Thus the official figures tell us two things: a lot of irregular attendance in the first two decades of the century, and rapid improvements from the 1920s onwards.

The gap exposed in the official record between enrolments and ADA in the nineteenth and early twentieth centuries has provoked interest among students of Canadian educational history, including suggestions that it constitutes evidence of widespread indifference or outright resistance to state schooling. How real was the gap in the first two decades of the twentieth century?

In 1919 Ontario's official ADA was 66.52%. "On the face of it," wrote Peter Sandiford, a professor of education at the University of Toronto, "the figure seems to show that on any given school day only two-thirds of the pupils were in school. The writer has never yet met an Ontario teacher who believed that one-third of the pupils are, on an average, absent from school each day. 'There is something wrong with that figure,' they said, and shook their heads. Obviously! What is wrong is the method of obtaining and calculating the percentages."[13] Sandiford and two teachers, one in Toronto and another in a very ordinary, very rural school in Rainham Township near Cayuga, conducted their own survey. The official Toronto figure was 70.1%; in the 1,300-pupil Toronto school they studied, the figure was actually 84.1%. In the rural school section it was 77.2%, ten points above the official average for the province.[14]

The problem was a combination of crude measures and inadequate record-keeping. Calculating percentages from the interval tables assumed a school year of 200 days or more, which was often the legally defined number of days in the school year. But in the early twentieth century a substantial number of schools weren't open anything like that long; pupils couldn't attend a school for 200 days if it was open only 100 or 150 days. ADA, the most common and familiar method, was even more problematic. To arrive at ADA, one divided the total number of days attended by all pupils during the year by the number of days in the legal school year – normally 200 days; one could then calculate the attendance percentage by dividing this figure by the percentage of pupils who actually attended.[15] Not only did this method use an unrealistically high figure for days in the school year, but it took no account of various other factors. Children entered or left school during the school year for any number of reasons. Whether they began late or left early, their names remained on the roll and they were counted as absent. Children aged 5 or 6 were notoriously irregular, often beginning school in April or May with the return of good weather.[16] Throwing up his hands at the state of the provincial reports that lay before him in 1921, M.C. MacLean, the new education specialist at the Dominion Bureau of Statistics, sputtered over the obvious: "If a pupil begins school a few months before the end of the school year, it is not possible for him to have attended the full year."[17] Moreover, children aged 5 to 6, and in Ontario, 5 through 7, were allowed but not compelled to attend school; consequently, they could (and did) come and go as they or their parents pleased without fear of retribution, contributing noticeably to the attendance/enrolment gap.[18] Nor did the reports take adequate account of "excusable absence" such as illness or other exigencies that kept children out of school for days or weeks. Most provinces had no "transfer cards" to track children who moved, with their parents, from one school district to another; each move might add a new pupil to one school register but the child would still remain on the rolls of the old school and be marked absent for the rest of the year.

Ontario used a calendar year to measure ADA for a school year that ran from September to June. In 1917, after polling a group of school inspectors, one observer concluded that the provincial ADA was probably 10% below the average attendance calculated month by month, "due of course, to the fact that many pupils attend only part of the year"; grade VIII pupils who finished school in June "attend for only 6 months, and new pupils entering in September only four months of the year covered in the report."[19] Nor was Ontario alone in this peculiarity. Alberta did the same, leading Calgary's superintendent of education to remark in 1920 that "the annual enrolment is much larger than the largest monthly enrolment, the difference for 1920 being ... about 20% of the total enrolment. This represents the number of pupils enrolled who left school or moved out of the school district during the year. The fact that the school year, September to June, is different from the calendar year, for which [provincial] returns are prepared, makes the discrepancy between enrolment for the year and for any month of the year more marked. I am informed that plans are being made to have all Annual Returns in future prepared at the end of the school year in June."[20] Surveying the three provinces for which he had good figures, MacLean estimated that in Alberta, as in Ontario and Saskatchewan, "it is clear that ... the time lost by irregularity pure and simple is not over half of that lost by pupils entered late in the year or leaving early."[21]

At the beginning of the century, provincial officials were already aware of the flaws in their methods of calculating ADA, though they were slow to introduce improvements. One reform was to limit the unit of measurement to a shorter period; another was to work the percentage against only those days when it was actually possible for the child to attend. When, in 1911–12, Nova Scotia authorities broke down "the percentage of those on the roll during the quarter [year] in daily attendance," average attendance jumped a full 10%: "[W]ere the percentages on the roll in attendance calculated for each month, or each week, as is done in some countries [sic: cities], it would show a correspondingly higher rate of regularity in attendance."[22] When Saskatchewan modified its calculations, the results were similar: under the old method, in 1921 average attendance was 63.73%; under the new one, 87.38%. Counting the number of days attended, the old method had Saskatchewan children missing 72.7 days or nearly four months; under the new method, days missed fell to 21.4.[23] When New Brunswick recalculated its figures for 1920–21 using school terms rather than a full year, its average attendance rose from 67.3% to 74.1% – just by eliminating those students who left school at the end of fall term and thus did not appear on the register in January.[24] In 1920 Ontario's average daily attendance was

70.7%. A decade later it was 89.4%. The "improvement" was mostly the result of better methods of calculating attendance.[25] The introduction of transfer cards or some other means of eliminating duplicate enrolments also made a significant difference. Indeed, it was one of the reasons that British Columbia's ADA looked so much better than that of most other provinces in the 1920s.[26]

In the Prairie provinces especially, provincial average attendance figures in the first three decades of the century incorporated large numbers of students in newly opened districts where road conditions and tracts of undeveloped lands hindered attendance. Said one Manitoba report in 1922, "When it is considered that there are so many outlying districts in the province which would have a low average attendance, and thus bring down the average for the whole province, a percentage of attendance of 70 is remarkably high."[27]

More modern standards are a helpful corrective as well. By 1960, for example, Alberta had overcome most of the constraints that kept children away from school in earlier decades. But two different methods of measuring attendance yielded two different results: based on "the number of legal school days" – 200 days – average attendance was 91% and children were absent, on average, 18 days; based on the "number of days individual schools were operated and term of enrolment of individual pupils," the respective figures were 95% and 10 days.[28] In the early twentieth century, attendance in Ontario was judged against a standard of 200 days. At the end of the century, the province had 185 legal school days; set against that standard, attendance for 150 days looks somewhat less ominous.

We are not intimating that irregularity was a trivial matter in the first two or three decades of the century. Even the more accurate assessments of the 1920s and 1930s indicate rates of irregularity in the range of 10 to 20%, and province-wide figures mask variations between town and country and between rural school districts, with their widely different geographic and economic circumstances. Irregularity of attendance, indeed, was viewed by much of officialdom as one of the more urgent problems facing education in the early twentieth century. All we want to suggest here is that attendance was a good deal better than the official provincial and national reports indicate, and improvement in the interwar years was as much a function of better ways of record-keeping as it was of official efforts to ensure ever greater degrees of regularity.[29]

There is an understandable, near-intuitive, assumption that if children attend school for seven, eight, or nine years, they will complete the equivalent number of grades. While that notion holds true for a majority of children in the first half of the twentieth century, there was a far greater

discrepancy between age in school and educational attainment than one
would encounter today. To explore this aspect of attendance patterns, we
draw on the "age-grade" tables produced in the era and the "retention"
tables constructed from them.[30]

An age-grade table tells us how many pupils are in each school grade
and their ages. Since children have birthdays at different times of the year
and start school at different ages, "modal" ages for each grade have to be
decided upon: for example, in the early twentieth century, a typical or
modal age for grade I was usually considered to be 6 and 7, or 7 and 8,
depending on the province. Once the modal ages are established, one can
then determine how many pupils are progressing through the grades at
what is considered a normal rate – one grade a year – and how many are
under-age or over-age for their grade. The conventional terminology for
those over-age was "grade retarded," usually elided to "retarded." Those
who were under-age for their grade were usually described as "accelerants."
Nearly all the retention tables in the period were constructed from the age-
grade tables, and their purpose was to identify the grade levels attained by
the time children left school. Used together, age-grade and retention tables
provide a portrait of educational attainment in the first half of the twentieth century, indicating, among other things, how many attended school to
age 14 or 15 but never reached grade VIII, how many took more than eight
years to complete the public school course, and how many continued their
schooling into the high school grades.

In Canada, age-grade tables date back at least as far as the first decade of
the century. Generated initially by a few of the larger urban school boards,
they were available for most provinces by the mid-1920s.[31] We doubt they
told teachers or school inspectors much they didn't already know by experience and anecdote, but what they did do was provide contemporaries (and
historians) with city- or province-wide data that were systematic and quantitative. Throughout the analysis that follows, however, one central point
needs to be kept clearly in mind. In most pre-Second World War cases,
modal age groups incorporate at least two and in some instances three specific ages. If, say, the modal ages for grade V are 10 and 11 – or even more,
10, 11, and 12 – then children who appear in our commentary or tables as
two or three years under- or over-age, or even one year under or over, were
substantially younger or older than the mean age for the grade. That is to
say, such children were not simply lagging slightly owing to a very late birth
date; rather, we are referring to large differences in ages and to differences
in grade placement that would mostly be considered intolerable today.

If most children proceeded through the school system at a grade a year,
we should expect to find approximately the same proportions in each grade.
If, for example, a hundred 7-year-olds start grade I in any given year, then

eight years later we will have, more or less, a hundred 14-year-olds in grade VIII. What the early age-grade tables revealed was something quite different – a disproportionate number of children below and especially above the normal age range in certain grades. Grade I classes often had twice as many pupils as those in grade II. In 1915, 25% of Alberta's *total* enrolments were in grade I.[32] Between grades I and IV or V in Nova Scotia in 1919, there were very large numbers of over-age children, though much less so in grades VII and VIII.[33] In 1922, and depending on the grade, anywhere from 25% to 40% of Ontario's elementary pupils were over-age; the worst figure – 40.4% – was for grade III, but the percentages in grades II through VI were all above 33%.[34] When, in 1922, M.C. MacLean had enough good figures to account for a million pupils – about half the total elementary enrolments in Canada – he found that 24% were retarded by one full year, 10% were two years behind, and 4% were three years or more.[35] Further analysis showed that of the *10- to 14-year-old age group*, 2.7% were in grade I, 5.3% in grade II, 9.8% in grade III, and 15.6% in grade IV.[36] Comparing progress through the grades to provincial curriculum documents, he drew what he considered to be an obvious conclusion. When pupils left school with no more than a grade IV or V education they had "just covered the four simple rules [of arithmetic] and a smattering of fractions, but had not had time to apply their knowledge to practical problems, thus being deprived of the practice by which alone knowledge of the fundamental values is retained. A large proportion of schoolchildren drop out at a stage very little better than total illiteracy."[37]

The age-grade tables also showed that many pupils were under-age for their grade. In two provinces for which the figures are available before 1920, the percentages of "accelerants" varied considerably: Nova Scotia had substantial numbers of under-age pupils in most grades, while Alberta had far fewer, though in both cases the numbers increased as one progressed through the grades. By grade VII, for example, about 26% of Nova Scotia pupils in 1919 were one or more years under the three-year modal age, and in Alberta in 1915 the figure was about 9%.[38] For Ontario in 1922, percentages varied from 7% in grade I to 21% in grade VII.[39] In the case of MacLean's million pupils, 19.4% were accelerated one year, 6.5% two years, and 2.3% three years or more.[40]

Together, the retardation and acceleration figures reveal very large age spreads in early twentieth-century classrooms. Of Nova Scotia's 29,000 grade I pupils in 1919, 6,600 were age 5 and another 1,000 were under 5; 8,000 were 6, 6,000 were 7, 3,600 were 8, and another 3,500 ranged from 9 to 16 years of age.[41] In Saskatchewan (1916) and in Nova Scotia, the modal ages for grade IV were 8 to 10: 34% of grade IV pupils in Saskatchewan and 20% in Nova Scotia were 12 years or older.[42] In British Columbia in the early 1920s, the estimate was that something like 35% of pupils were over-age for their grade placement.[43]

During the 1920s and after, children's ages and grades gradually became more closely matched. To the extent that the figures can be compared, there appears to have been a very sharp decline in the number of accel-erants between 1920 and 1950. The retardation rate declined somewhat as well. Consider just two indicators from our analysis of the 1929–30 combined age-grade tables for seven provinces (Table 2.4). Some 72% of 13-year-olds were in the modal grades for their age (grades VI, VII, and VIII), but 16% were in grade V and another 10% in grades IV or III. And over a thousand 13-year-olds were in grade I. Altogether 28% were below the modal grades for their age.[44] Or take a particular grade: in grade V, for example, something like 25% of children were one year or more older than the modal ages. Though the rate of retardation appears to have declined during the 1930s and again during the 1940s, one needs to take care not to underestimate its extent even by mid-century.[45] In a national sample carried out in 1948, 18% of boys had repeated one grade and 5%, two, while 12% of the girls had repeated one grade and 2%, two.[46]

Thus far we have drawn on provincial or national-level age-grade tables to illustrate the changing patterns of educational attainment. But the same trends are apparent from an analysis of the age-grade tables for one large city, Winnipeg, for 1901, 1921, and 1951 (Table 2.5). While these don't indicate with any precision the timing of changes, they do make it sim-pler to compare the kinds of changes that took place across the period.[47] Over the course of half a century, the extreme ranges in age that marked the city's classrooms declined. In 1901, for example, 6-year-olds in grade I shared their classroom with 11-, 12-, or even 13-year-olds; by 1921 that range had narrowed; and by 1951, the oldest grade I pupils, who were now between 8 and 9, formed a very small percentage of the total grade I class, 84% of whom were between 6½ and 7½ years old. Overall, Winnipeg's ele-mentary school classrooms had been age-homogenized. Indeed, progress through the grades had become so regularized that by 1951 the modal age group had shrunk from two years to one. Across the grades, there were still considerable numbers who were under-age (accelerants) but almost all by one year only – yet another sign of homogenization. There had also been a clear decline in the amount of retardation; by 1951, very few children were retarded by more than one year. Still, those retarded by a single year constituted a large proportion of children in some grades: in 1951, apply-ing a one-year modal age, almost a third in grade IV and 40% in grade VIII.

Retention tables, as we said, were constructed from the extant age-grade tables. In 1931 the DBS combined the age-grade tables "for 7 provinces [British Columbia and Quebec were excluded] for the past 8 or 10 years,"

Table 2.4
Age-grade distribution of pupils, Canada (7 provinces[a]), 1929–1930

				Grade				
	I	*II*	*III*	*IV*	*V*	*VI*	*VII*	*VIII*
More than 2 years under-age	–	–	1	10	16	35	32	123
								0.1%
2 years under-age	147	62	237	337	454	635	722	1,297
	0.1%		0.2%	0.2%	0.3%	0.4%	0.6%	1.1%
1 year under-age	6,486	4,418	3,815	6,192	7,179	6,967	6,456	8,277
	2.5%	2.5%	2.9%	4.0%	4.6%	4.5%	5.5%	6.9%
Modal ages[b]	212,316	135,721	98,301	114,330	109,829	97,971	85,705	91,149
	82.6%	77.4%	75.1%	73.3%	70.6%	70.5%	72.4%	76.2%
1 year older	21,842	19,876	14,503	17,852	19,995	19,313	17,558	13,378
	8.5%	11.3%	11.1%	11.4%	12.9%	13.9%	14.8%	11.2%
2 years older	8,960	8,061	7,221	9,547	11,007	9,482	5,742	4,478
	3.5%	4.6%	5.5%	6.1%	7.1%	6.8%	4.9%	3.7%
3 years older	3,449	3,747	3,719	4,811	4,878	3,299	1,822	740
	1.3%	2.1%	2.8%	3.1%	3.1%	2.4%	1.5%	0.6%
4 years older	1,797	1,946	1,869	2,026	1,512	1,019	247	216
	0.7%	1.1%	1.4%	1.3%	1.0%	0.7%	0.2%	0.2%
5 years older	1,074	872	801	648	450	120	72	–
	0.4%	0.5%	0.6%	0.4%	0.3%	0.1%		
6 years older[c]	1,015	669	397	281	185	49	–	–
	0.4%	0.4%	0.3%	0.2%	0.2%			
Total in grade	257,086	175,372	130,864	156,034	155,505	138,890	118,356	119,658
	100%	100%	100%	100%	100%	100%	100%	100%

[a] Data unavailable for Quebec and British Columbia.
[b] Modal ages: grade I: 6, 7, and 8; grade II: 7, 8, and 9; etc.
[c] Also includes those more than 6 years older than modal ages.

Note: Percentages below 0.1% are omitted from the table.

Source: DBS, *Annual Survey 1930*, 18 (Table 8).

Table 2.5
Age-grade distribution of elementary school pupils, Winnipeg

a) 1901

				Grade				
	I	II	III	IV	V	VI	VII	VIII
2 years under-age	–	–	–	–	1 0.1%	1 0.2%	1 0.3%	1 0.3%
1 year under-age	–	4 0.4%	30 3.2%	26 3.3%	22 2.8%	26 4.3%	9 2.5%	31 9.0%
Modal ages[a]	1,223 76.6%	654 68.5%	497 52.4%	395 50.6%	283 36.7%	249 41.5%	196 53.7%	184 53.2%
1 year older	170 10.6%	165 17.3%	228 24.1%	197 25.3%	230 29.8%	155 25.8%	93 25.5%	85 24.6%
2 years older	98 6.1%	82 8.6%	131 13.8%	110 14.1%	142 18.4%	130 21.7%	47 12.9%	37 10.7%
3 years older	16 1.0%	40 4.2%	46 4.9%	43 5.5%	72 9.3%	32 5.3%	15 4.1%	8 2.3%
4 years older	27 1.7%	15 1.6%	13 1.4%	8 1.0%	19 2.5%	7 1.2%	4 1.1%	–
5 years older	2 0.1%	1 0.1%	3 0.3%	1 0.1%	3 0.4%	–	–	–
6 or more years older	11 0.7%	–	–	–	–	–	–	–
Total in grade	1,597 100%	955 100%	948 100%	780 100%	772 100%	600 100%	365 100%	346 100%

[a] Modal ages: 2-year modal – grade 1, ages 6 and 7; grade 11, ages 7 and 8; etc.

Source: Wilson, "Education in Winnipeg," 153 (Table IV-3).

Table 2.5 (continued)

b) SEPTEMBER 1921

	I	II	III	IV	V	VI	VII	VIII
								Grade
2 years under-age	–	–	2	1	1	12 0.4%	6 0.2%	32[b] 1.7%
1 year under-age	8 0.2%	117 2.7%	172 4.3%	195 5.7%	175 5.2%	186 6.1%	219 9.0%	279 14.4%
Modal ages[a]	3,161 81.4%	3,273 74.8%	2,898 71.9%	2,252 65.4%	2,085 61.6%	1,847 60.3%	1,556 63.7%	1,264 65.3%
1 year older	500 12.9%	654 14.9%	600 14.9%	570 16.6%	632 18.7%	614 20.0%	447 18.3%	279 14.4%
2 years older	120 3.1%	217 5.0%	205 5.1%	266 7.7%	330 9.7%	288 9.4%	178 7.3%	64 3.3%
3 years older	58 1.5%	66 1.5%	93 2.3%	109 3.2%	126 3.7%	100 3.3%	31 1.3%	17 0.9%
4 years older	15 0.4%	29 0.7%	38 0.9%	34 1.0%	30 0.9%	14 0.5%	5 0.2%	2 0.1%
5 years older	3	14 0.3%	20 0.5%	13 0.4%	4 0.1%	2 0.1%	2 0.1%	–
6 or more years older	17 0.4%	7 0.2%	2	2	2	1	–	–
Total in grade	3,882 100%	4,377 100%	4,030 100%	3,442 100%	3,385 100%	3,064 100%	2,444 100%	1,937 100%

a Modal ages: 2-year modal – grade I, ages 6 and 7; grade II, ages 7 and 8; etc.

b Includes one pupil three years under-age.

Source: Winnipeg School Board, *AR 1921*, 37.

Table 2.5 (*continued*)

c) 30 JUNE 1951

	Grade							
	I	*II*	*III*	*IV*	*V*	*VI*	*VII*	*VIII*
1 year under-age	86 2.7%	8%	9%	9%	10%	10%	8%	8%
Normal[a]	2,707 83.6%	69%	65%	59%	57%	54%	52%	52%
1 year older	392 12.1%	18%	20%	22%	22%	24%	26%	28%
2 years older	52 1.6%	4%	4%	7%	8%	9%	10%	10%
3 years older	–	1%	1%	2%	2%	2%	3%	2%
4 years older	–	–	1%	1%	1%	1%	1%	–
Total in grade	3,237							

[a] "Normal": the largest age group in the grade – a one-year cohort.

Note: Ages in source are as follows: grade I, 5½–6½, 6½–7½ (mode), 7½–8½, 8½–9½; grade II, 6½–7½, 7½–8½ (mode), 8½–9½, 9½–10½; etc. For grade I, our calculations are from the figures. For grades II to VIII, percentages are given in the source.

Source: Manitoba, *AR 1950–51*, Report of Superintendent, City of Winnipeg. 97.

Table 2.6
Retention of children in school, Canada, 1920s

	Boys	Girls	Boys and girls
		N attaining	
Grade I	100,000	100,000	100,000
Grade II	99,168	99,401	99,284
Grade III	97,924	98,624	98,274
Grade IV	95,368	96,956	96,112
Grade V	90,895	93,579	92,237
Grade VI	83,543	88,328	85,936
Grade VII	73,413	80,914	77,163
Grade VIII	61,845	71,812	66,829
Grade IX	42,684	53,798	48,241
Grade X	28,762	37,895	33,329
Grade XI	17,382	23,000	20,191
Grade XII	5,020	6,397	5,708

Note: The table was compiled by the DBS in 1931 from the age-grade tables for seven provinces "for the past eight or ten years." No data existed for British Columbia or Quebec Protestant schools, "but the number of their pupils is insufficient to affect seriously the validity of the figures ... The number shown in Grade XII ... does not fully represent the proportion taking the post-graduate high school year, for it is also taught as 'first year' in the universities."

Source: DBS, "The School Standing Attained by Canadian Children," 1.

giving us a group portrait of those attending school during the late teens and twenties. Table 2.6 shows the results, including the substantial dropout rate occurring every year after grade V. Only 67% reached grade VIII and 48% entered grade IX. At each high school grade, numbers dwindled rapidly. A second Canada-wide retention table, for those beginning school in the mid- to late 1930s and enrolled in grade VI in 1942, suggests a somewhat lower elimination rate.[48] Of every hundred students enrolled in grade VI that year, 82% reached grade VIII in 1944, 51% reached grade X in 1946, and 37% were enrolled in grade XI in 1947.

Retention figures consistent over several decades are rare. One student of Nova Scotia education has calculated that in 1895, 32% of pupils failed to complete grade VI before leaving school, and that figure hardly budged over the next twenty-five years. Writing about the early 1920s, indeed, she would paraphrase MacLean's conclusion: "Assuming grade five to be significant as the level of attainment necessary for the permanent achievement of literacy, about one in three Nova Scotians would have been classified as near-illiterate."[49] A more extended set of figures, covering the years 1921 through 1950, comes from Alberta (Table A.10 in appendix A). It measured the grade levels achieved by those who left school at age 15. In 1921 nearly 40% left school with grade VI or less, and only 8% had completed more than a grade VIII education. By 1950 the figures were quite different: only 9% had grade VI or less, and some 57% had more than grade VIII.

What, then, can we say about levels of educational attainment in the first half of the twentieth century? We have already pointed out two overlapping trends about age in school: more children stayed in school for longer periods of time, and more adults had acquired more years of schooling. However, we have tried to emphasize that more years of schooling do not easily translate into more grades completed. Most children were in school between the ages of 7 and 14 or 15, long enough to complete eight grades of school. But high retardation rates meant that many did not. Consider just two examples. The Dominion Bureau of Statistics used its 1930 age-grade tables for seven provinces to indicate the percentage of 14-year-olds ("generally the last year of compulsory attendance") by grade. Some 25% of the 14-year-olds were in grades V or VI, and another 7% were in grades I to IV. Only 45% were in grades VII and VIII, approximately appropriate for their age. (Another 22% were spread across grades IX to XII.)[50] In 1935–36, 4.1% of Canadian children 10 years and older were in grade I and 14.2% of those 14 years and older were in grade VI. Neither group was likely to complete grade VIII. Of those in grade VIII, 8.7% were 16 years or older; these young people were unlikely to continue into high school.[51] Contemporaries, indeed, assumed that any child retarded more than one year was likely to leave school at the end of compulsory schooling without completing grade VII or VIII.[52] To that group have to be added the substantial numbers who were over-age in grades VII and VIII and thus unlikely to continue into high school.

Leaving school by grade VIII, however, was not simply the result of grade retardation. Even if a pupil made normal progress through the grades, that did not guarantee passage into high school. The barrier of the high school entrance examination, or being above the age of compulsory attendance, or the expectations and aspirations of students and their families – as well as a host of other reasons – all conspired to end schooling at grade VIII. For example, the DBS retention table for seven provinces in the 1920s showed 66,829 enrolled in grade VIII and only 48,241 enrolled in grade IX, a drop of 27.8%.[53] By 1931 the decline was 30.5%.[54] In some provinces in some years, the drop was precipitous. In Ontario in 1930, enrolments between Senior Fourth (VIII) and Lower School First Year (IX) fell by 55% (though by less than that, 27%, in 1931, and 44% in 1934).[55] In the middle of that decade, New Brunswick enrolments from grade VIII to IX fell by 58.7%.[56] DBS statistics tell us that as late as 1951 a quarter of 14- and 15-year-olds who made normal or accelerated progress through the grades and who completed a full eight years of schooling left school as soon as the law allowed.[57]

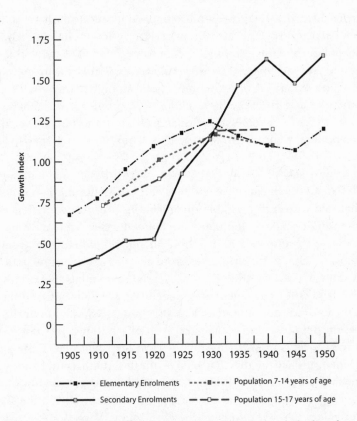

Fig. 2.1   Elementary and secondary enrolments, 1905–1950, and selected populations, 1911–1941. For an explanation of the growth index, see note 58, p. 373. Newfoundland in 1950 and Quebec are excluded.

Yet another signal characteristic of the period, nonetheless, is the sharp upturn in the number of adolescents attending high school. Figure 2.1 charts this change: rates of increase no greater than population growth between 1905 and 1914, the stifling effect of the Great War, and then the takeoff, beginning about 1920 and extending right through the interwar years.[58] Taking note of these growth rates, W.F. Dyde would remark in his 1929 study of Canadian secondary education that "it is scarcely possible that the sudden rise of the high school population is a temporary phenomenon. Probably, almost certainly, the second decade of the present century will come to be recognized as an important turning point in the history of the Canadian high school."[59] By the time the DBS created its 1931 retention table, just under 50% of Canadian boys and girls were remaining in school into grade IX, and by the mid-1940s the figure was pushing toward 60% in English Canada.[60]

Some of the provincial growth rates in secondary education are startling. Between 1916 and 1936, while Alberta's total enrolments increased by 66%, high school enrolments grew by 410% – from 5,700 to 29,300 students.[61] During the decade of the 1920s, Manitoba experienced an increase of 39.2% in elementary enrolments and 174.1% in high school enrolments.[62] Between 1921 and 1950 the high school population of Ontario rose from 42,500 to 136,200 (220%). For British Columbia the figures during the same years were 7,200 to 33,300 (363%). The totals for English Canada were 84,400 in 1921 and 291,700 in 1950 (246%).[63]

Rising high school enrolments, then, were one of the hallmarks of English-Canadian education in the first half of the twentieth century. But with that said, two indispensable qualifications are necessary. The first is that while high school attendance was indeed rising, only a minority of adolescents ever attended high school in the years before mid-century. Confusion on this point originates from the census question itself. The data in Table 2.3 record "attendance at school," and it has sometimes been assumed that adolescent school attendance (say, students between the ages of 14 and 17) indicates attendance at a secondary school. Given the tight fit in recent decades between age and level of schooling, it is understandable why historians might make that logical leap; but it is, quite simply, wrong when applied to the first half of the twentieth century and especially to the years before 1940. In fact, a substantial proportion of those adolescents recorded as attending school were not enrolled at the secondary level; *rather, they were attending elementary school.* When, for example, the DBS produced its combined age-grade table for seven provinces in 1931, it revealed that, of all children in grades I to XII, almost three-quarters of 14-year-olds (73.4%), over half of 15-year-olds (53.6%), and a third of 16-year-olds (32.4%) were in elementary grades. Or to put it another way: in seven provinces, 54% of all 14- to 17-year-olds enrolled in grades I to XII were in elementary grades; that is, only 46% were in secondary grades.[64] The percentage in elementary school dropped through the decade of the 1930s; nevertheless, *of those in school* in 1939–40, 70% of 14-year-olds, 42% of 15-year-olds, and 19% of 16-year-olds were still in elementary grades.[65] In Alberta, to take yet another example, department of education officials tracked annually the grade level attained by those who left school at 15: in 1921, 39% left school with grade VI or less, 58% with grade VII or less, and fully 92% with grade VIII or less; in other words, more than nine out of ten 15-year-olds left without entering high school. By 1930 those figures were 19% with grade VI or less, 40% with grade VII or less, and 73% with grade VIII or less; that is, almost three-quarters of Alberta's 15-year-olds left school before the secondary level.[66]

What we actually have, then, is three distinct groups of adolescents: those still in elementary school, those enrolled in high school, and those not in school at all. Nationally, in 1931, students aged 14 through 17 made up about 79% of all those enrolled in the secondary grades; that is, they constituted the overwhelming majority of secondary school pupils. But they represented only 28% of the total population of those aged 14 through 17. The rest – nearly three-quarters – of that age group were either still in elementary school (32%) or not in any school (40%). In 1939–40, out of the same age group, 37% were in the secondary grades, but 26% were still in elementary school and 37% were not in school.[67] The majority of Canadian adolescents, in other words, were not touched by the high school experience at all.[68]

The second qualification focuses on retention levels for that minority who did enter high school. In 1910–11, for example, of the total grade VIII students in Halifax, 53% entered grade IX, 33% grade X, and 17% grade XI.[69] In British Columbia the percentage of students completing high school in 1916–17 was about 12% and by 1921–22 about 17%.[70] In one Vancouver high school in 1920, 38% failed or left in the first year, 45% in second year, 38% in third year.[71] Using the 1923 age-grade tables for four provinces – Nova Scotia, Manitoba, Saskatchewan, and Alberta – W.F. Dyde calculated that about 33% of those who entered grade IX had left by grade X, and 58% by grade XI.[72] In two provinces in which the "school careers of the [elementary] pupils who were eleven years of age in 1924" were followed, there were steep declines in the number enrolled in each high school grade: in Alberta, enrolment in grade X was 37% of the grade IX enrolment and decreased a further 23% by grade XI; in Nova Scotia, the corresponding figures were 25% and 41%.[73] Pointing to the dropout figures from 1927 to 1935 in Ontario, the editor of the *Canadian School Journal* noted that grades IX and X "constitute the finishing point of a great majority of our [high school] students, especially in small urban and rural districts."[74] At the beginning of the 1940s, about a third of the province's grade IX students were likely to remain in school into grade XII; by the end of the decade, the proportion still stood at only 38%.[75] A mid-century national study estimated that out of 100 pupils enrolled in grade VI in 1942 (and thus born *c.*1931), 51 reached grade X in 1946 and only 37 remained to attend grade XI a year later. The figure was even lower for those entering grade XII.[76]

Thus, even for those who actually entered grade IX, a large cohort left school during or at the end of their first year, and another left during or at the end of grade X. Given that the majority of its students were present for only one or, at most, two years, their high school experience was, at best, fleeting.

While there were important changes over the period, we have, then, what might be described as a parsimonious pattern of school-going. Few 5-year-olds went to school and only about half the 6-year-olds. Between ages 7 and 14 or 15 nearly all children were in school and attending more regularly, but until at least the 1940s large numbers did not complete elementary school. Only a minority of the age group 15–19 attended high school, and only a minority of that minority proceeded far enough to complete their studies. Both in terms of age range and educational attainment, schooling was markedly more limited than it would be by the end of the twentieth century, indeed even by 1965 or 1970. Three graphics illustrate this state of affairs nicely. On the one hand, there is the steady growth in high school enrolments, illustrated for British Columbia in Figure 2.2; still, the same graph indicates the limited reach of the high school, even in the mid-1930s. Figures 2.3 and 2.4, on the other hand, are mute testimonies to what one social scientist described as "the steep curve of educational mortality" in Canadian schools typical of the first four or five decades of the last century.[77]

II

Having offered this review of general patterns of school attendance during the first half of the twentieth century, we now propose to turn to some of the significant variations that characterized those patterns. We begin with the differences between children in urban and rural Canada. As Table 2.7 indicates, virtually all children, rural and urban alike, were in school from the ages of 8 through 12. But in 1921 rural children were somewhat less likely to be in school at age 7 or 13 than their urban counterparts. That is to say, universal schooling in rural areas extended from ages 8 to 12, and in urban areas from 7 to 13 or 14. In 1931 and again in 1941, rural 7-year-olds were still less likely to attend school but the gap at 13 had largely been closed. During the interwar decades, the most noticeable difference in the core ages of school attendance was at age 14. Rural 14-year-olds left school in much larger numbers than urban youngsters; in 1941, for example, 96% of urban but only 85% of rural 14-year-olds were in school. It was only in the decade between 1941 and 1951 (and probably in the postwar years) that rural attendance levels for all those 7 to 14 reached levels comparable with those in urban areas.[78] During the interwar years, the gap between rural and urban school attendance for those 15 to 18 was substantial, and it remained so right through to 1951. Thus, even at mid-century, rural youngsters tended to have shorter school lives than their urban counterparts, though by that point the difference was largely confined to the high school years.

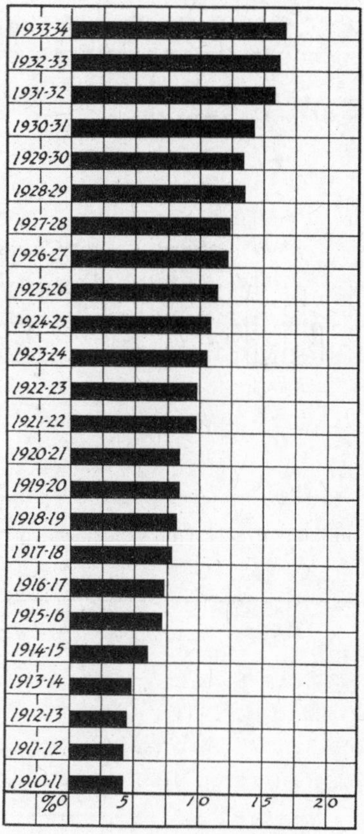

Fig. 2.2   High school enrolment
compared to total enrolment, British
Columbia, 1910–1934

There is, moreover, good reason to believe that these census figures underestimate the extent of the gap. Referring specifically to the age group 15–19, M.C. MacLean explained the discrepancy this way in 1934: "Some boys raised in the country find employment in town or city before they reach the age of 20, thereby swelling the total number reported as city and town dwellers, and reducing the number reported as rural boys to a figure probably considerably smaller than the actual number raised in rural communities. If allowance could be made for this movement, it is probable that less than one-fifth of country-raised boys aged 15 to 19 would be found in school, and nearly half of city-raised boys."[79] Demographers have since agreed with MacLean's analysis, emphasizing the importance of taking into account the migration effect.[80] When one looks at the figures for the adult

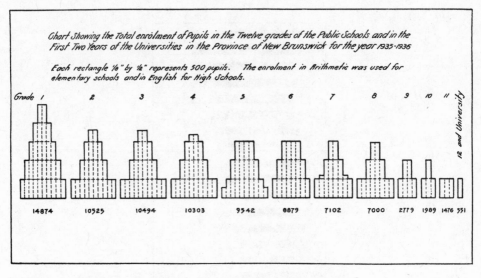

Fig. 2.3   Enrolment distribution by grades, New Brunswick, 1935–1936

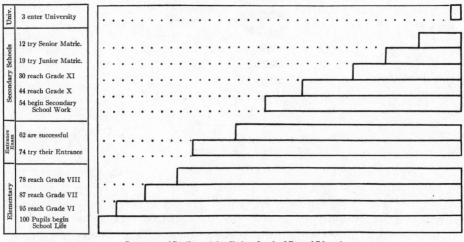

Percentage of Pupils attaining Various Levels of Formal Education

Fig. 2.4   Educational attainment, Ontario, 1939

population, the rural education deficit is much more striking than the census figures for school enrolment suggest. In 1951 the adult population in urban areas with less than nine years of schooling was 46%; in rural areas that figure was 67.8%.[81]

In 1911 and 1921 the census measure for regularity of attendance – those in school for seven to nine months – suggests that a large gap existed

Table 2.7
Percentage of rural and urban population in school, selected years of age, Canada (excluding Quebec), 1921, 1931, 1941

	1921		1931		1941	
Age	Rural %	Urban %	Rural %	Urban %	Rural %	Urban %
6	45.7	58.0	49.4	63.9	40.3	62.2
7	77.4	88.1	84.5	92.9	85.2	95.3
8	88.1	94.5	92.9	97.0	94.5	97.6
12	92.2	96.9	95.9	98.6	97.0	98.3
13	88.5	95.7	94.0	98.2	95.2	97.9
14	74.4	85.8	84.5	95.8	84.6	95.7
15	50.4	65.1	62.3	87.2	64.0	87.1
16	29.0	45.1	38.2	65.7	44.0	66.3
17	15.8	28.5	22.1	42.4	28.3	45.8
18	8.7	17.2	12.5	25.7	17.9	28.6
19	5.1	10.7	7.0	15.1	10.7	16.6

Sources: Our calculations.
1921: Census of Canada 1921, vol. 2, 702ff. (Table 108).
1931: Census of Canada 1931, vol. 1, 1136ff. (Table 72).
1941: Census of Canada 1941, vol. 3, 618ff. (Table 44).

between urban and rural areas: in 1911, for example, 80% versus 64%.[82] By 1931, however, the difference was more modest, and by 1951 it had virtually disappeared.[83] A set of figures for the province of Ontario also suggests that the 1920s saw sharp declines in the difference in rates of regularity. In 1930, using the improved accounting system for average attendance, the province's chief attendance officer provided a graph that covered the years 1921 to 1929. Urban attendance rose from 87.2% to 91.6%, and while better than the rural figures, the difference was not large. Southern Ontario's rural schools rose from 81.4% to 89%, and more remarkably, the rural schools of Northern Ontario rose from 78.9% to 84.7%, so that by 1929 the difference between urban Ontario and the newer and more isolated rural schools of the north was not much more than 6% or 7%.[84]

The differences in rates of progress through the grades, and in educational attainment, are more striking and more persistent. In the national age-grade tables for 1929–30, rural schools tended to have higher rates of repeaters, in grades I to III especially (Table 2.8). Generally, there were fewer pupils in the modal age group in rural areas, and there were both more under-age and more over-age children in rural schools. Or to put it another way, age-grade homogenization was much less common in rural than in urban schools. In the 1940s, 12.5% of urban children left school between grades VI and VIII, while the figure for rural children was 25.7%;

Table 2.8
Age-grade tables, Canada (6 provinces)[a], 1929–1930

a) DISTRIBUTION OF PUPILS, GRADED SCHOOLS

	Grade							
	I	II	III	IV	V	VI	VII	VIII
More than 2 years under-age	–	–	–	6 0.2%	3	15	9	63 0.1%
2 years under-age	31	22	138 0.2%	173 0.2%	222 0.2%	320 0.4%	312 0.4%	667 0.9%
1 year under-age	3,006 1.9%	3,391 3.0%	2,423 3.0%	4,047 3.9%	4,448 4.4%	4,221 4.6%	3,670 4.8%	4,749 6.2%
Modal ages[b]	132,486 85.5%	92,875 81.0%	63,767 78.1%	77,942 75.8%	73,088 72.5%	65,147 71.6%	57,439 74.6%	58,494 76.9%
1 year older	11,839 7.6%	10,790 9.4%	8,168 10.0%	10,751 10.5%	12,299 12.2%	12,265 13.5%	10,149 13.2%	8,591 11.3%
2 years older	4,271 2.8%	4,123 3.6%	3,768 4.6%	5,599 5.4%	6,528 6.5%	5,988 6.6%	3,851 5.0%	2,951 3.9%
3 years older	1,499 1.0%	1,864 1.6%	1,850 2.3%	2,607 2.5%	2,892 2.9%	2,208 2.4%	1,313 1.7%	429 0.6%
4 years older	831 0.5%	903 0.8%	889 1.1%	1,115 1.1%	932 0.9%	690 0.8%	160 0.2%	153 0.2%
5 years older	430 0.3%	391 0.3%	411 0.5%	369 0.4%	302 0.3%	91 0.1%	49 0.1%	–
6 years older[c]	484 0.3%	334 0.3%	215 0.3%	176 0.2%	140 0.1%	32	–	–
Total in grade	154,877	114,693	81,629	102,785	100,854	90,977	76,952	76,097

[a] Prince Edward Island, Nova Scotia, New Brunswick, Ontario, Manitoba, and Saskatchewan.
[b] Modal ages: grade 1, 6, 7, and 8; grade II, 7, 8, and 9; etc.
[c] Or more; to and including age 19.

Source: DBS, Annual Survey 1930, 22 (Table 16).

Table 2.8 (*continued*)

b) DISTRIBUTION OF PUPILS, RURAL SCHOOLS

	Grade							
	I	II	III	IV	V	VI	VII	VIII
More than 2 years of age	–	–	1	4	13	20	23	60 / 0.1%
2 years under-age	116 / 0.1%	40 / 0.1%	99 / 0.2%	164 / 0.3%	232 / 0.4%	315 / 0.7%	410 / 1.0%	630 / 1.4%
1 year under-age	3,480 / 3.4%	1,027 / 1.7%	1,392 / 2.8%	2,145 / 4.0%	2,731 / 5.0%	2,746 / 5.7%	2,786 / 6.7%	3,528 / 8.1%
Modal ages[a]	79,830 / 78.1%	42,846 / 70.6%	34,552 / 70.2%	36,388 / 68.3%	36,741 / 67.2%	32,824 / 68.5%	28,266 / 68.3%	32,655 / 75.0%
1 year older	10,003 / 9.8%	9,086 / 15.0%	6,335 / 12.9%	7,101 / 13.3%	7,696 / 14.1%	7,048 / 14.7%	7,409 / 17.9%	4,787 / 11.0%
2 years older	4,689 / 4.6%	3,938 / 6.5%	3,453 / 7.0%	3,948 / 7.4%	4,479 / 8.2%	3,494 / 7.3%	1,891 / 4.6%	1,527 / 3.5%
3 years older	1,950 / 1.9%	1,883 / 3.1%	1,869 / 3.8%	2,204 / 4.1%	1,986 / 3.6%	1,091 / 2.3%	509 / 1.2%	311 / 0.7%
4 years older	966 / 0.9%	1,043 / 1.7%	980 / 2.0%	911 / 1.7%	580 / 1.1%	329 / 0.7%	87 / 0.2%	63 / 0.1%
5 years older	644 / 0.6%	481 / 0.8%	390 / 0.8%	279 / 0.5%	148 / 0.3%	29 / 0.06%	23 / 0.06%	–
6 years older[b]	531 / 0.5%	335 / 0.6%	182 / 0.4%	105 / 0.2%	45	17	–	–
Total in grade	102,209	60,679	49,235	53,249	54,651	47,913	41,404	43,561

[a] Modal ages: grade I, ages 6, 7, and 8; grade II, 7, 8, and 9; etc.
[b] Or more; to and including age 19.

Source: DBS, *Annual Survey 1930,* 23 (Table 17).

the loss between grades VI and XI was 44.2% and 77% respectively.[85] In another study, the authors note that across the first half of the twentieth century high school completion rates appear to be much lower for farm children than those with fathers employed in urban occupations.[86] Adult educational attainment as of 1951 shows what one might expect from the census enrolment figures: across the generations, adults in both urban and rural areas increased the years of schooling they acquired. But even for those in the youngest age group – those 15 to 29 not in school in 1951 (born c. 1920–35) – 37.3% of urban adults and 61.9% of rural adults had less than nine years of schooling.[87]

But rural people were not a homogenous entity. An analysis by M.C. MacLean begins to identify one type of differentiation for schooling. Drawing on the 1931 census, he drafted a map of Canada designed to illustrate patterns of school attendance in different parts of the country (Figure 2.5). In Canada's agricultural heartlands, his map tells us, nearly all children 7 to14 went to school, but in the country's resource belt, and in areas where farming communities were new or marginal, school-going was less common. This does not mean that 20% of children in the north *never* went to school; rather, most of those not attending were either 7 or 14 years of age – those just beginning school and those nearest the school-leaving age. But what the map does suggest is a shorter school life in the north and probably a certain number escaping the net altogether. Though it is speculation on our part, our guess is that regularity, retardation, and retention levels could be superimposed on the map without unduly changing the pattern it displays. Thus, while significant differences existed between rural and urban Canada, in the interwar years at least there were also important differences between heartland and fringe, between the settled south and the agricultural or resource frontier.

According to the 1951 census, the adult "rural non-farm" population tended to be better educated than the farm population, though considerably less well educated than those living in urban areas.[88] But what needs to be done here is to break down the rural non-farm population by occupational group so that it reflects the differences within that particular segment of the rural population. In the agricultural heartlands of Canada this population included numbers of professionals and proprietors selling services to farm communities, as well as urbanites living in "rural" satellite suburbs near the cities. These were people more likely to have been schooled as long as or above the median number of years for the entire population. But in other parts of the country they included miners, fishers, or loggers, who had shorter periods of schooling. In 1941, for example, the median for fishers was 5.9 years and for loggers 5.2 – well below the 7.7 for the population as a whole.[89] In other words, adult educational attainment among the

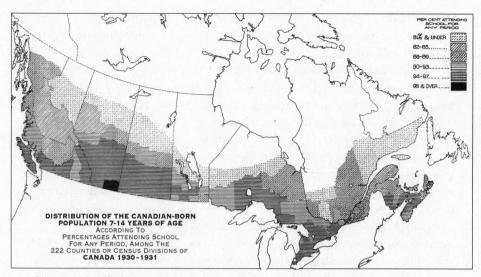

PER CENT ATTENDING
SCHOOL FOR
ANY PERIOD

8% & UNDER
82-85
86-89
90-93
94-97
98 & OVER

DISTRIBUTION OF THE CANADIAN-BORN
POPULATION 7-14 YEARS OF AGE
ACCORDING TO
PERCENTAGES ATTENDING SCHOOL
FOR ANY PERIOD, AMONG THE
222 COUNTIES OR CENSUS DIVISIONS OF
CANADA 1930~1931

Fig. 2.5   Map: distribution and percentage of Canadian-born population, ages 7–14,
attending school, 1930–1931

rural non-farm population can also be superimposed on MacLean's map to
match the differences in the patterns of rural school attendance.

One way or another, in any case, our review of the data on rural/urban
school-going reveals two broad tendencies. By 1931 the nineteenth- and
early twentieth-century gap in regularity of attendance had largely closed,
and during the decade of the 1940s rural children began to attend school
for nearly as long as their urban counterparts, so that by 1951 school-going
between ages 7 and 14 was near-universal in rural and urban Canada alike.
But even at mid-century rural youngsters were far less likely than urban
youngsters to be in school during their mid-teens. And the figures for adults
across three age groups also confirm the persistent gap between rural and
urban educational attainment.

Finally, here, a word about urban communities themselves. While differences between them did exist, there were at least as many commonalities.
From late in the nineteenth century, Ontario had legal provision for publicly funded kindergartens and some of the nation's school-going 5-year-
olds can be accounted for that way. By 1911, for example, Ottawa had
nearly as many children in kindergarten as it did in grade II; Toronto was
the same.[90] In three Canadian cities that W.L. Richardson, just before 1920,
considered roughly representative of the rest – London, Montreal, and
Winnipeg – 6-year-olds, though not quite as numerous as 7-year-olds, were
mostly in school.[91] Within the core age group, the urban pattern in 1921
was a common one: nearly all children 8 to 13 attended school and only

slightly fewer of the 7- and 14-year-olds. After 14, the numbers in school declined sharply each year,[92] but the percentage of urban teenagers staying in school also rose decade by decade.

Drawing on the 1921 census, MacLean compared the school attendance of those aged 7 to 14 in Canada's seventy-nine cities with populations greater than 7,500, and found attendance varied according to the types of dominant industries. But the amount of variation was modest, differing by a matter of only a few percentage points from that in smaller urban centres.[93] Alberta statistics for 1920 list all of the province's urban centres by average monthly attendance: while they range from 79.5% to 90%, fourteen of the eighteen communities were between 85% and 90%, and that included centres as different as Edmonton and Pincher Creek.[94]

In the early twentieth century, age spreads in particular grades and retardation rates appear to have been as wide in the larger cities as in the provincial figures generally, and though retention rates in the early twentieth century varied, large numbers of children left school at age 14 or 15 in Vancouver, Winnipeg, Toronto, London, Ottawa, and Halifax alike.[95] An analysis of eleven large Canadian cities in the 1940s showed that all but three were holding nearly all their children through grade VIII, and most of them through grade X, so that dropouts began when we might expect them in Canada generally during that decade – in the mid-teens and in the higher grades of high school.[96]

One suggestive indicator that appears in the 1951 census concerns levels of adult educational attainment in urban communities of different sizes. In towns and cities from 10,000 to over 100,000 population, there was no great difference between the number of adults with less than nine years of schooling (or with nine to twelve years of schooling), but communities of under 10,000 had a somewhat higher percentage of those with less schooling. And this may bear on the argument that small towns and villages had more in common with their rural counterparts than with larger, more distinctly urban communities.[97]

Gender constitutes a second category of analysis. For the core school-going ages, 7 to 14, there were no important differences between 1911 and 1951 in enrolments for boys and girls; indeed, there were also few differences at age 15. During these decades, however, there were more 16- and 17-year-old girls than boys in school. Census figures on months in school suggest little difference in regularity of attendance, though most observers thought girls attended more regularly.[98]

To the extent that greater regularity determined normal progress through the grades, observers were probably right. Girls were less likely to be grade-retarded, and more likely to be accelerants, than boys. Said one

Alberta official in 1922, "[I]t is noticeable that 39% of the boys are below Grade VI [at age 13] as against only 34% of the girls, and only 36.5% of the boys are above Grade VI as against 41.7% of girls, and that in general the girls at this age seem to be more advanced than boys by about one promotion."[99] The earliest age-grade tables also reveal more girls in the higher elementary grades and more going on to high school.[100] Our analysis of the 1929–30 age-grade table for seven provinces confirms the persistence of the differences (Table A.11 in appendix A). In all the elementary grades (with the exception of grade VIII), there were more girls than boys in the modal age group and girls were less likely to be two or three years over-age in their grade. The DBS retention table for the 1920s testifies to the much larger numbers of girls proceeding through the senior elementary and high school grades (Table 2.6). And for those going through elementary school between the late 1930s and 1940s, the figures tell a similar tale. Twenty-five per cent of boys and 12% of girls left school between grades VI and VIII.[101]

Thus, the "discovery" of the "boy problem" that has provoked so much hand-wringing in recent years – the failure of many boys to keep up with the academic progress made by girls – is yet another case of the historical amnesia commonly afflicting those engaged in the educational enterprise. That a boy problem also existed across the first half of the twentieth century is not only apparent from any retrospective analysis but was also obvious to observers at the time. Boys simply did less well through elementary school and were more likely to leave school earlier than girls. And this was especially true of rural boys, whereas rural girls tended to persist into high school at rates roughly equal to their urban sisters.[102] A striking graphic created for the *Historical Atlas of Canada* nicely illustrates the pattern, including the regional differences.[103] In 1911 the gap between female and male secondary enrolments was remarkably wide, though over succeeding decades it narrowed everywhere. In the early part of the century it was most extreme in the Maritimes, where it remained substantial to 1951. Less wide everywhere else in the early twentieth century, it began to narrow earlier, in the decade between 1941 and 1951.

Total secondary enrolments for males and females, however, mask one important trend. While boys were less likely than girls to complete elementary school, if they made it to high school, they were as likely, or somewhat more likely, to persist through to the senior high school grades. Our analysis of three different cohorts of students passing through the Ontario high school system in the 1920s, 1930s, and 1940s indicates that in the academic stream boys were slightly more likely than girls to remain in school if they got as far as grade IX – or, in the 1920s, grade X. The differences were marginal and sometimes favoured girls, however, until grade XIII, at which point boys were more likely to remain and their numbers were larger. What the figures suggest, in other words, is that generally in high school, compared to elementary school, gender differences in attainment were much less marked.[104] A second study has a much narrower time frame but is Canada-wide. It followed those children who began grade VI in 1942 through senior elementary and high school.[105] Girls were more likely than boys to proceed through grades VI to VIII, but retention from grade VIII to grade X was just about the same for both boys and girls. The boys who made it that far, however, were more likely by a modest margin to progress from grade X to XI, and in British Columbia and Ontario, from grade XI to XII. In other words, while girls were more numerous overall than boys in Canadian secondary schools, boys who reached high school were more likely to stay in school into the senior grades – the grades that were critical for obtaining matriculation and other leaving certificates that led on to the universities and professions. Hence the origins of the long-standing "girl problem": ahead of the boys virtually from the beginning of elementary school, they now reached a stage where, in the main, there was less incentive to complete studies at the matriculation level. Rather, social expectations and restricted opportunities encouraged them to lower their sights and settle for something less than the higher reaches of the post-secondary sector.[106]

In the two decades before 1914, large numbers of immigrants, many of them from continental Europe, arrived in Canada and settled in its larger urban centres and in the rural West.[107] They brought children with them or, more commonly, began raising families in their new homeland. How did these children fare in school, and did their patterns of attendance differ from the more general patterns we have described thus far?*

These are not easy questions to answer. Provincial departments of education did not produce statistics on school attendance by ethnic origins. For our purposes, the published census is badly flawed. It provides detailed evidence about ethnic origins every ten years, but the data are not always usefully linked, or linked at all, to school attendance. There are, moreover, inconsistencies in reporting from one census to the next that make long-term comparisons difficult. But the most serious problem is that before 1931 the census did not report school attendance by ethnic origin at all. Its

---

* Readers will note that while we deal extensively with ethnicity in the pages that follow, we have almost nothing to say about race. There is now a considerable historical literature on racial minorities, though much less on their schooling; but more important for this chapter, there are almost no statistical data that will allow us to isolate these minorities and then draw comparisons with the general pupil population or other segments of it. For that reason we decided that any discussion of racial minorities in provincial school systems would be out of place here. See, however, our brief commentary on blacks in appendix A, section 11.

Table 2.9
Selected ethnic groups in Canada, 1961: percentage whose highest level of education
attained was elementary education[a]

Age 65+		Age 45–64		Age 25–44	
	%		%		%
German	76.6	Ukrainian	70.1	French	55.8
French	74.9	French	66.4	German	40.0
Dutch	70.0	Polish	63.9	Ukrainian	39.6
Italian	68.3	German	61.1	Dutch	39.0
Scandinavian	68.1	Other European	57.8	Russian	38.5
Other European[b]	66.8	Italian	57.7	Italian	36.5
Ukrainian	65.9	Dutch	56.0	Polish	34.9
Polish	63.6	Russian	54.1	Other European	33.1
Russian	62.4	Scandinavian	46.1	Scandinavian	26.3
British	58.8	Asiatic	44.4	British	26.0
Asiatic	57.0	British	40.4	Asiatic	22.6
Jews	42.4	Jews	21.3	Jews	8.4
Average[c]	64.9		52.0		38.3

[a] Canadian-born, 25 years of age and over. Table includes Quebec.
[b] Category used in source.
[c] Includes "others and not stated."
Note: Ethnic groups are ranked in descending order of elementary education as highest level attained.

Source: Calculated from Census of Canada 1961, 7.1-6, General Review: Origins of the Canadian Population, p. 6-64 (Table 10).

only categories were attendance by "Canadian-born," "British-born," and "foreign-born." That last category is indiscriminate: it includes immigrants from continental Europe but also very large numbers born in the United States; moreover, the foreign-born, even in 1911 or 1921, constituted only a very small percentage of the children at school.[108] What we really want to know is something different: the patterns of attendance among the far larger numbers of children born in Canada of recent immigrant descent.

Our best evidence from the published census on schooling and ethnicity is a tabulation for 1961 of the educational attainment, by ethnic origin, of all those 25 years and older who were born in Canada. Since these adults were born no later than 1936, it identifies those who received all of their schooling in Canada during the first half of the twentieth century. More important, it divides this population into three age groups: those aged 65 and older who, as the census puts it, "would have completed their schooling before 1915"; those aged 45–64 "who had completed their schooling during the period 1915–1935"; and those aged 25–44 who attended school from the mid-1930s through the mid-1950s.[109]

Tables 2.9 and 2.10 provide our analysis of the census data and tell us two things. The first is what one might expect from preceding parts of this

Table 2.10
Selected ethnic groups in Canada, 1961: percentage whose highest level of education
attained was secondary education[a]

Age 65+		Age 45–64		Age 25–44	
	%		%		%
Jews	44.9	Jews	62.1	Scandinavian	65.8
British	34.1	British	50.8	Jews	65.6
Scandinavian	26.0	Scandinavian	47.5	Asiatic	64.0
Other European[b]	24.3	Asiatic	47.1	British	64.0
Italian	24.3	Dutch	38.0	Other European	59.0
Dutch	24.2	Italian	38.0	Italian	57.7
Russian	22.8	Other European	35.9	Polish	57.6
German	18.8	German	33.9	Ukrainian	54.2
French	18.5	Polish	30.1	Dutch	54.1
Asiatic	18.4	Russian	28.3	Russian	51.1
Ukrainian	13.0	French	28.3	German	51.1
Polish	12.5	Ukrainian	23.3	French	40.4
Average[c]	27.7		40.4		53.5

[a] Canadian-born, 25 years of age and over. Table includes Quebec.
[b] Category used in source.
[c] Includes "others and not stated."
Note: Ethnic groups are ranked in descending order of secondary education as highest level
attained.

Source: Calculated from Census of Canada 1961, 7.1-6, General Review: Origins of the Canadian Population,
p. 6–64 (Table 10).

chapter: with few exceptions, educational attainment in each ethnic group
rose for each generation, so that fewer adults had only an elementary education (and more attained some secondary schooling). Second, there was
a relatively stable ethnic hierarchy of educational attainment across the
generations. Within any of the three age groups, British Canadians were
more likely to have some secondary education than those of East European
descent; Scandinavian and Jewish adults were more likely to have some secondary education than those of Italian or Dutch origin. Equally, French
and German adults were more likely to have attained only some elementary
education, whatever their age in 1961, than all other ethnic groups. Thus,
the pattern that existed by mid-century – John Porter's "vertical mosaic" in
educational attainment – was well established, and persistent, from the first
decade of the twentieth century.[110]

Measuring the educational attainment of adults in 1961 is not the same
thing as analysing patterns of school-going among children decade by
decade. The published census data do not allow us to do the latter in any
systematic way. The very limited evidence that does exist, however, suggests
parallels. We know from one study of the unpublished household census

of 1901 that children of eastern European immigrants were far less likely to attend school regularly than children of English origin.[111] Yet another analysis of the same source shows that the children of recent immigrants (those who had been in Canada for five years or less) were much less likely to attend school than the children of longer-settled immigrants; the latter group were likely to attend school at nearly the same rate as the children of Canadian-born parents.[112] We also know that in 1911 both enrolment and regularity of attendance were much lower among foreign-born children – a group that would include large numbers of migrants from continental Europe – than among the Canadian-born.[113] Though much diminished, these differences persist through the 1921 census and help account for the differential levels of adult educational attainment of those over 65 in 1961 and probably of those who were a decade or so younger than that.[114]

In 1931, for the first time, the census provides us with the school-going record, by ethnicity, of all Canadian-born children age 7 to 14. By that point, regardless of ethnic origin, most of these children were enrolled in school, but there were still some differences among ethnic groups in the regularity of attendance (Table 2.11).[115] In 1941 and again in 1951, we are able to distinguish between those within and those above the age of compulsion: while about two-thirds of all young people age 15 to 19 (that is, those above the age of compulsion) were still in school and the differences among ethnic groups were not great, the hierarchy of ethnic educational attainment is apparent and the same ethnic groups as in 1961 appear at the bottom – or the top – of the scale.[116]

The provincial-level age-grade and retardation tables we have put to use in earlier portions of this chapter do not exist for ethnicity, and so we can say little about this aspect of patterns of attendance. There are a handful of very limited studies that may be suggestive, though no more than that. As part of his larger 1916 analysis of rural schools in Saskatchewan, Harold Foght created age-grade tables for 150 "slavonic" schools and contrasted these to the combined data for some 2,000 rural schools. The slavonic schools had much higher levels of retardation, with most pupils concentrated in the first three grades; the amount of retardation diminished in the higher elementary grades, suggesting that the minority of slavonic children who remained in school were progressing through the grades at rates comparable to the other rural schools.[117] A decade later another Saskatchewan study compared thirty-one schools in "non-English districts" with thirty-one predominantly English schools. In the former, children tended to be clustered in the lower grades and comparatively fewer remained in school through the senior elementary grades.[118]

In a mid-1930s study of rural schools in western Manitoba, Ivan Hamilton analysed differences in retardation rates between pupils of "English" and of

Table 2.11
Regularity of school attendance, selected ethnic groups, 1931

		Not at school (%)	Attending 7–9 months (%)	N
PEI	English	5.1	85.1	3,848
	French	10.2	82.4	2,435
NS	English	5.9	88.8	32,060
	French	8.4	86.1	10,965
	German	8.8	84.8	4,675
NB	English	5.9	88.7	21,478
	French	15.8	76.0	29,264
ON	English	3.5	94.7	179,906
	French	7.2	89.9	57,315
	German	5.3	92.6	25,200
MAN	English	3.0	94.8	25,646
	French	9.3	85.2	9,189
	German	5.6	91.2	5,788
	E. Euro[a]	6.6	89.9	9,835
	Ukrainian	6.9	89.0	16,019
SK	English	3.8	91.7	34,361
	French	8.1	84.1	10,137
	German	4.9	89.4	23,893
	E. Euro	6.3	84.2	13,013
	Ukrainian	5.3	81.9	13,292
AB	English	2.8	94.4	28,287
	French	9.6	84.7	6,915
	German	3.4	93.0	11,684
	E. Euro	5.3	90.6	6,269
	Ukrainian	4.6	91.4	10,688
BC	English	3.1	95.3	33,804
	French	4.0	93.8	1,937
	Chinese/Japanese	4.0	87.3	5,060
Canada	English	3.7	93.4	359,390
	French	9.6	85.3	128,157
	German	5.1	91.0	73,554
	E. Euro	6.4	88.5	40,900
	Ukrainian	5.5	88.1	44,766

[a] East European: Polish, Romanian, and Russian.
Note: Canadian-born population, 7–14 years of age, excluding Quebec. "English" is used as a proxy for "British"; percentages for Irish and Scottish are very similar to those for English.

Source: Census of Canada 1931, vol. 1, 116off. (Table 74). Our calculations.

"foreign" ethnic origins. The difference across the elementary grades was relatively modest – 8% versus 15% – but he also found that children of Scandinavian origin did nearly as well as their English counterparts, while children of Ukrainian, Polish, and Ruthenian background scored worse.

In high school, however, the situation was reversed. Though many more English children continued on to high school, they tended to have higher retardation rates than those from foreign ethnic groups.[119] This probably tells us that while the foreign ethnic groups were less likely to attend high school, those who did were more able and ambitious than the bulk of their English peers. A second Manitoba study, by D.S. Woods, concluded that by the mid-1930s "increasing numbers of children of all racial origins are moving to the top of the available educational programme." On the other hand, he also found sharp differences between predominantly British and European areas; in the former a higher proportion of young people remained in school through the senior grades of the elementary school and into the high school grades.[120]

All four of these studies focus on schools in rural areas. Was the situation similar in the cities? D.L. Mandeville's examination of schooling in Victoria in 1901 reveals that between the ages of 7 through 13, 81% of "white" children (the census designation for "Caucasian") attended school, while 54% of Japanese and Chinese children and about half of "Indian" children did so. In terms of ethnic groups, there was little to choose between British, French, and continental Europeans, except for children of German or Austrian descent, who came close behind, a high proportion, about 80% or more, attending school. However, the highest percentage of attendance, over 90%, was by Jewish children, while only 69% of Aboriginal children attended school.[121] In an analysis of Vancouver in the 1920s, Jean Barman finds that in the city's East End a third of the residents were Chinese, another 15% Japanese, and almost a quarter continental European. Less than 12% of the pupils in its elementary schools were "of Anglo-Saxon extraction." East End pupils were far less likely than those in other wards to reach grade VIII and comparatively very few of those 15 to 19 were in school.[122]

The data for French Canadians living outside Quebec is no better and in some respects worse. The 1961 statistics on adult educational attainment, for example, can't be used in this case because these national-level data include the population of Quebec, and thus we cannot distinguish between Quebec francophones and those who lived in other provinces. Moreover, since the published census data don't address school attendance by ethnic origin before 1931, they tell us nothing about earlier developments. By 1931, in any case, the vast majority of those francophone children aged 7 to 14 and living in English Canada were, like their peers, attending school for seven to nine months of the year. Almost everywhere, however, they were somewhat more likely to be attending for shorter periods of time or to be listed as "not in school." This is equally true when they are compared to either the British or other non-British ethnic groups (see Table 2.11). The differences are relatively modest, but the gaps exist nonetheless and

probably tell us that French-Canadian children were somewhat more likely
to be irregular in attendance and somewhat more likely to start school later
and/or leave earlier than their counterparts in other ethnic groups.[123]

The only available data on the educational attainment of francophones
outside Quebec come from the 1936 Prairie census. Consistently in all
three provinces, francophones had somewhat lower proportions of adults
with more than eight years of schooling and larger proportions of those
with only five to eight years, or no schooling at all, than those of British
descent. Again, however, the key word is "somewhat," since the differences
are small, never exceeding 10%. As one might expect, moreover, urban
francophones living on the prairies were substantially better educated than
those in rural areas.[124]

While the national-level data are exceedingly limited, there is a modest
amount of illuminating provincial data, especially for Ontario. The difficulties that Franco-Ontarians encountered within the Ontario school system
during the early twentieth century are well documented in the province's
educational history. While some of these difficulties can be explained by
socio-economic and cultural characteristics, as well as by settlement patterns, a large part was due to the attempt by the government of Ontario,
backed it must be said by enthusiastic support from many Anglo-Ontarians,
to suppress, or later to restrict, French as a language of instruction. Ontario's
infamous Regulation 17 is the most familiar example.[125] One would think
that this prolonged and poisonous conflict would at least have produced a
wealth of statistical analysis to document claims on either side, but beyond
the two Merchant Reports of 1912 and 1927, there is very nearly nothing that is helpful here. It is only after 1927 that we begin to get a flow
of useful annual data, published in the department of education annual
reports, from the newly established sub-department headed by the director
of French instruction.

F.W. Merchant's first foray, in 1912, has some very problematic statistics,
but his conclusion is probably sound: a disproportionate number of francophone children were concentrated in the lower grades. While he couldn't
document the corollary, he noted that "it is evident that if an unusually
large proportion of the pupils are in the lower forms many of the children
are leaving school before the completion of the Public School course."[126]
In 1927, perhaps for political reasons, Merchant discounted differences
in grade retardation between French and English, suggesting they were
relatively modest: "There are," he writes, "no striking differences between
the average ages of the French-speaking pupils in the various Forms in
the schools and the average ages of pupils in corresponding Forms in all
the rural and urban public and separate schools ... On the whole it may
safely be said that there are no more 'over-age' pupils in the schools in
which French is taught than in the other schools of the Province of similar

grade."[127] The appendix to his report, however, belies this claim, revealing quite substantial differences in the lower forms; moreover, the lack of difference in the senior grades can plausibly be explained by numbers of francophones leaving school before they reached the fourth form of the elementary schools.[128] Whatever the problems or ambiguities in the two reports, it seems reasonably certain that across the first three decades of the twentieth century Franco-Ontarian pupils lagged well behind their counterparts in anglophone schools.

After the 1927 Merchant Report, compromises emerged that put francophone pupils in a better position to benefit from the publicly funded school system. And as part of the effort to track their progress, the department of education began to collect distinct age-grade tables for them. These tables reveal very high levels of both grade retardation and early school-leaving – retardation rates well above those of the pupil population generally and far higher drop-out rates in elementary and early high school.[129] As useful as the age-grade tables are, however, the summary commentary in 1937–38 by Ontario's director of French instruction is even more telling:

> While the foregoing statistical tables show some progress over the situation reported in 1937, it is evident that much remains to be done yet in order to bring about a satisfactory age-grade distribution of pupils and to check the excessive drop in enrolment in the senior grades of the elementary school. It will be observed, for instance, that while 11,216 pupils were enrolled in Grade I classes of all elementary schools attended by French-speaking pupils in 1938, only 2,913 were found enrolled in Grade VIII classes ... This great discrepancy between the Grade I and Grade VIII enrolments would appear to be due largely to the fact that more than 50 per cent of the pupils enrolled in Grades II, III, IV and V are too old for their respective classes, and are likely to drop out before reaching the higher grades of the school.[130]

The director then went on to comment on pupil progress into and through the secondary grades. His estimate was that no more than 3,000 francophones were enrolled in high school programs: "If this number of 3,000 is compared with the approximate French-speaking school population from Grades I to XIII, say 50,000, we find that about 6 per cent of the French-speaking pupils in Ontario remain at school beyond Grade VIII. This picture is not brightened when one ... observes that only 20 per cent of those entering secondary schools reach either Grade XII or Grade XIII and that less than 4 per cent attain Grade XIII."[131]

Two other provinces provide enough additional data to suggest that our conclusions for Ontario represent trends at work everywhere in English Canada. In New Brunswick a 1929 report by the Moncton school trustees showed that francophones were disproportionately clustered in the lower grades, noting that "there is a considerable loss each year due to pupils failing to obtain promotions and to many leaving school ... it must be borne in mind that very few of our French-speaking children remain in the city schools even to complete Grade VIII. The two chief reasons for this are the very difficult course of study which includes both English and French and the fact that many children are sent away to boarding schools and colleges."[132] A province-wide 1940 study by the Acadian activist Calixte Savoie arrived at much the same conclusions. Drawing on department of education data from across the 1930s, he found that the higher the percentage of francophone children in each county, the higher the level of grade retardation and early school-leaving; something like 82% of Acadian pupils left school before finishing elementary school and 60% didn't even get to grade V.[133] Two years later, as if more proof were needed, Fletcher Peacock, at the time New Brunswick's director of educational services, confirmed Savoie's conclusion through an analysis published in the department of education's *Annual Report.*[134] And in his massive study of education in Manitoba, D.S. Woods was able to compare educational attainment in two rural municipalities with large francophone populations to that in municipalities where other ethnic groups dominated. Again, compared to students of British origin, francophones exhibited less progress through the grades; indeed, they made less progress than children in some municipalities where eastern Europeans and their descendants were in the majority.[135]

Despite serious inadequacies in the data, then, there are some tolerably useful indicators of the impact of ethnicity on school attendance. Across the first half of the twentieth century, more and more children of all ethnic origins attended school during the core school-going ages and more continued on to secondary school. But grade retardation and early school-leaving were more common among those of non-British descent. And the ethnic hierarchy of educational attainment evident before 1914 would persist in the decades that followed. Pupils of French-Canadian origin, however, exhibited more grade retardation than most other ethnic groups, were less likely to complete the elementary grades or enter high school, and tended to leave school earlier. All this was more true of rural than of urban francophones, and more true of boys than of girls. Once again, everywhere the statistics permit a judgment, francophone girls outperformed the boys in school.[136] But generally speaking, francophones appear to have fared relatively poorly in the publicly funded schools of English Canada.

3

Explaining the Patterns

We have, then, patterns of attendance that included substantial though diminishing levels of grade retardation; early school-leaving and limited levels of educational attainment for the majority of Canadian children; significant differences between boys and girls, rural and urban children, and various ethnic groups; and, for a growing minority of youngsters, some exposure to secondary education. How are these patterns to be explained? They arose, in part, from internal characteristics of the school system itself, and some of the changes can be best explained that way.* Here, however, we want to focus on the social context – the circumstances of people's lives and the assumptions they brought to bear about school-going in the first half of the twentieth century. We begin with those children who fell between the ages of 6 or 7 and 13 or 14; then we turn to those outside that core school-going age group.

I

By the second decade of the century, virtually everyone engaged in the educational enterprise was convinced that once individual ability was taken into account, the chief cause of retardation and early school-leaving was irregular attendance. Typically, there was this comment by Winnipeg's school board in its annual report for 1923: "The importance of regularity of attendance and its bearing on the success of the school work is quite strikingly brought out by the close correspondence between the number of pupils promoted during the year ... and the number who attended upwards of

---

* We will take up these school-caused features in chapters 8–10. By "school-caused," we mean not only the actual ways in which school was organized, but collateral sets of beliefs and practices about educating children, customary notions about educational values, and more formal articulations of something approaching an educational philosophy or coherent visions of exemplary pedagogy. These all influenced the patterns of attendance and the educational outcomes children experienced.

two-thirds of the time the school was open."[1] The more time lost month by month, year by year, the more likely it was that children would fall behind their peers. The result was that large numbers of pupils spent seven or eight years in school but got only to grade v or vi by the time they were 13 or 14. "They are now able to go to work," as a Dominion Bureau of Statistics (DBS) report put it in 1920, "and their progress in school has not been such as to induce them to stay."[2]

Some of the irregularity the schoolmen wrote off as frivolous on the part of pupils and parents alike. In 1919 Peter Sandiford analysed the various reasons for absenteeism in two schools, one in Toronto and the other in rural Rainham Township. In the city, he listed, among others, "[a]muse-ments (chiefly picture theatres), down-town attractions (shop-gazing etc.), down-town stores (wandering about aimlessly)." In the countryside, "on May 21 three boys spent the afternoon fishing with the consent of their par-ents. A week or two later two of the three got consent for another half-day's fishing ... Neither parents or pupils seem to regard attendance at school as a serious duty ... Apparently any excuse is sufficient for a day's holiday. The trial of a new Ford car, a sheep washing, a housecleaning, a visit to town with parents, shopping etc., are found among the excuses."[3]

Frivolous absenteeism could be left to the work of an efficient truant officer. But most causes of absenteeism would prove more obdurate. In an era when children commonly walked to school, the Canadian climate was obviously a factor – in rural Canada particularly, severe cold, blizzards, deep snow, and spring or autumn rains that turned roads into quagmires. "The winter of 1933–34," Ontario's provincial attendance officer remarked, "was almost without precedent in its length and severity, and blocked roads and temperatures so low as to carry an element of risk which wrecked regularity of attendance and closed many schools."[4] "Mud," Sandiford noted laconi-cally, as a cause in Rainham Township.[5] The climate, indeed, was one major reason for the notorious irregularity of 5- and 6-year-olds who clogged up grade 1 in the first two or three decades of the century. As a DBS report explained in 1920: "They begin school as soon as winter breaks up ... They learn but little before the summer vacation ... Then they come back into Grade 1 together with a new crop of beginners. When winter comes these young children are likely to drop out until the spring and then they come back again into Grade 1 together with another new crop. In this way we have three crops in Grade 1 ... We thus have from two to three years represented in this Grade 1, although it is really only the work of one year."[6]

Sheer distance from the nearest school was another cause of absentee-ism. Even in well-settled areas of the countryside, two, three, or even four miles of daily travel between home and school contributed to irregular attendance and thus higher rates of retardation.[7] But distance was often combined with bad roads or no roads at all. "The absence of roads in the unorganized territory along the Winnipeg River and in that north of the Municipality of St. Clements," a Manitoba school inspector remarked in 1924, "makes travelling to the schools very difficult, and thus accounts largely for the irregular attendance in some of the schools located in that part of the division."[8] "There are many school sections," wrote Nova Scotia's attendance officer in 1933, "where an appreciable number of pupils live from two to four miles from the schoolhouse, on roads which are frequently tertiary, and sometimes are mere wood tracks. In one extreme case 80% of the pupils live over two miles from the schoolhouse. It is a fairly good building, and the teacher is capable; but as far as these being any benefit in the winter time, the schoolhouse might just as well be situated on the Moon."[9]

Higher rates of retardation and early school-leaving in the countryside could also be explained by a shorter school year; especially in newly opened or poor school districts, children might attend regularly at a school open for only a few months a year, a period too short to cover the work of an entire grade. Writing just before the First World War, James Miller calculated for the only three provinces where the data were available – Nova Scotia, Alberta, and Saskatchewan – that 34% of the schools were open for fewer than 150 days (roughly, seven months), and of these, nearly 10% for fewer than 100 days.[10] In Alberta in 1925, "recently organized schools and those in remote areas are still unable to operate for a full year. The average number of days in operation in ungraded schools was 178.73 and in graded schools 195.1. The shorter school operation in ungraded schools is due to the pioneering conditions existing in the outlying districts."[11] Over the next ten years Alberta (and other provinces) largely eliminated this difference between rural and urban schools, and as a school year of nine or ten months became near-universal, presumably more children were able to progress through the grades at normal rates. Still, even as late as 1945–46 a handful of schools in all provinces were closed for significant parts of the school year.[12]

In some newly settled or remote areas there was no school to attend. One woman of Ukrainian origin growing up in the first decade of the century near Arborg, Manitoba, remarked that "while Father hauled the wood to Arborg, I, though only 10 years old, went into the bush with Mother to cut wood. I did not go to school until I was about 12 years old – there was no school. I was fortunate to get a year in school ... that was all."[13] In northern Ontario, school sections much larger or more irregularly shaped than those in the south, along with discontinuous road patterns, made school attendance difficult for many, and beyond that, "there were children tucked into communities too small, too remote, or too transient to be served by any school section."[14] In Rudy Wiebe's pioneering Mennonite community of

Speedwell, Saskatchewan, first settled in 1925, there were already thirty-five or forty school-age children before an accessible school opened in 1930.[15] But even older communities might lack a school because of resistance to the school tax from those who had no children, because a handful of rate-payers living permanently on the edge of subsistence couldn't raise enough cash to pay a teacher's salary, or because depopulation had reduced a rural school district to below the fiscal threshold required to maintain a school. In the early twentieth century, writes Katherine McLaren, farmers and fishers in Cape Breton flooded into the coal-mining centres around Sydney with results that could leave children without schools in both rural and urban communities. "In 1903 rural Cape Breton county had 48 vacant schools or over one-third of all schools in the county. At the same time Sydney added 11 departments to the city's schools. In Inverness people moved to the mines in Port Hood, Mabou, and Broad Cove where rapid population expansion left 250 children without schooling ... Amherst, Springhill, Parrsboro, and Acadia Mines had grown quickly before the turn of the century, with schools being built too slowly to house the inflow."[16]

Everywhere, however, there was one overriding cause of absenteeism: illness. It is almost impossible for anyone born after 1945 to imagine the threat posed by the ill health of children in earlier generations. Children missed school because of contagious disease in a world without antibiotics or most other modern medical miracles, where often the best that could be done was to quarantine a child (formally or informally) for weeks at a time, and where parents commonly kept children home for similar periods out of fear that they might contract diseases that could maim or kill. Measles, whooping cough, chicken pox, mumps, scarlet fever, typhoid fever, diphtheria, and tuberculosis were perennial menaces, able to terrify parents and reduce doctors to impotence.[17] By the 1920s and 1930s, some of these were being tamed, but only some. Nationally, the influenza pandemic of 1918–19 singularly depressed the upward curve of average daily attendance during the first half of the century, but there were less devastating attacks year in, year out, in one part of the country or another.[18] There were recurrent outbreaks of poliomyelitis.[19] And beyond that there were the more mundane childhood illnesses: colds, sore throats, ear infections.

The impact on attendance was remarked upon over and over again. In Sandiford's Toronto school, illness was by far the largest cause of absenteeism, accounting for 1,348 out of 1,644 days; the same was true in Rainham Township.[20] A British Columbia report of 1924 noted that illness "extending over several months or a longer period results in pupils having to repeat the work of one or more terms."[21] In 1928 Ontario's provincial attendance officer reported that illness accounted for 46% of irregularity in the rural schools.[22] In Manitoba in 1935–36, "the attendance has been seriously interfered with by numerous diseases and epidemics of all kinds which seemed to be rampant during the winter months."[23] "The flu has certainly played havoc with school attendance during the past month," wrote one Alberta columnist in February 1937. "Absences of up to 50% have been common and some rural schools have had to shut down completely. Teachers have been hit just as commonly as their pupils, and in Edmonton all available substitutes have been called into action. The pupils present one week are away the next, consequently no progress can be made with school work. We wonder if it would not be better to close down our schools until the epidemic had run its course."[24] In 1946–47 a committee of doctors and educators conducted a large-scale nationwide analysis of absenteeism. They divided the causes into two categories: medical and non-medical. In the cities, "the proportion of days lost to medical reasons to days lost for non-medical reasons was approximately 4 to 1"; in the rural schools, "the proportion of days lost for medical reasons was approximately equal to that for non-medical reasons."[25] This didn't mean that rural children were healthier; rather, other factors, including inclement weather, affected them more than urban children. But whatever the reason for absence, in urban and rural areas alike, the survey found that retardation levels were directly related to levels of absenteeism.[26]

Less quantifiable, but a near-certain cause of retardation, were chronic health conditions that went undiagnosed or unremedied, especially in rural areas, where health services were far less developed than in urban areas: eyesight or hearing problems, chronic toothache, physical disabilities of other sorts, or the diversity of learning problems we now lump into "special education."[27] And beyond that there was the high incidence of childhood accidents, in the home, on city streets, and during farm work.[28]

Children also missed school because of the economic circumstances of their families. In some cases this was the result of what can only be described as abject poverty. A report on the Halifax city schools in 1911–12 remarked that "frequently the one or two dollars that the older boys, still of school age, can earn, is absolutely needed to prevent starvation at home," adding that in other cases absenteeism was due to "want of warm clothing in winter, especially of footwear."[29] In his 1919 study Sandiford found, in both Toronto and Rainham Township, that poverty ranked second only to illness as a cause of absenteeism.[30] Children were kept out of school because they lacked shoes, suitable clothes, adequate coats in the winter, or the cost of basic school supplies – pencils, paper, or books.[31] There may have been some diminution of this in the mid- to late 1920s; Ontario's provincial attendance officer estimated in 1928 that no more than 0.1% of absenteeism was caused by "indigence."[32] But like their parents, not all children

benefited from the modest prosperity of these years. "I find that a great
deal of the 'absence of pupils' is created by the want of proper clothing,"
London's school attendance officer noted in 1925.[33] In the same year, mine
closures in the Crowsnest Pass "created signs of destitution" in communities
like Blairmore and Coleman, "one in particular being children compelled
to wear parents' old clothes and boots to attend school."[34] Drawing on
interviews with teachers and pupils who had lived in the Okanagan Valley
during the 1920s, Penelope Stephenson describes how

> family impoverishment sometimes drove parents, often through shame
> or embarrassment, to keep their children at home when they could not
> afford to provide them with appropriate clothing or footwear, or with
> a lunch for noon hour. To quote Alice Laviollette ... "The reason why
> I quit going to school was because we had nothing to eat in the house,
> absolutely nothing. We were just starving ... We had nothing to make
> lunch with ... We had no clothes and we were very, very poor." Thus
> rural teachers had to cope with children who were often hungry, under-
> nourished and poorly clothed. Lloyda Wills, who taught Alice and some
> of her siblings at Hilton School, recalled the desperate situation of the
> family. On one particular occasion, after they had been absent from
> school for three days, she decided to go to their home to ascertain the
> reason for their truancy, whereupon she found them "playing outside in
> their bare feet." Lloyda quickly realized why they had not been attend-
> ing school: "They didn't have very much. They didn't have very much to
> eat either. They were quite poor. They didn't even have enough bread
> in the house for their lunches and that's why the mother didn't send
> them."[35]

Not surprisingly, such circumstances were more common during the
1930s.[36] Nor were they only a phenomenon of the interwar years. Studies
of the introduction of family allowances in 1945 show that poverty was one
good reason why children were not sent to school or were sent for only
a few short years.[37] "Absenteeism is greatest," the Committee for School
Health Research reported in 1948, "among people from homes which are
below the average economic level."[38]

While poverty contributed to irregular attendance, it almost certainly
had other effects on school performance. One Toronto analysis of a hundred low-income families in the 1930s concluded that "most of the families
studied were not being properly fed" and that both women and children
were receiving 80% or less essential nutrients than the prevailing standard prescribed.[39] A 1930 Saskatoon survey identified a small number of
children who had "an extremely deficient diet at home due to financial

stringency"; they were, however, receiving "hot lunches at school during the
winter months. Needless to say a noticeable improvement followed, both
as to physical appearance and scholastic achievement."[40] Just how widespread the problem was, we don't know, but if it existed among children of
low-income families in Toronto or Saskatoon, it probably existed in many
other communities. Nor was it something that occurred only in the Great
Depression. Jean Barman notes that in the 1920s, school personnel repeatedly referred to children's "undernourishment" in Vancouver's poorest
area, the East End.[41]

Surveys of housing conditions across the period, moreover, repeatedly
indicate that many families lived in overcrowded or even "wretched" conditions.[42] And while overcrowding is often associated with urban slums, the
problem was widespread in rural areas, especially on the prairies. Perhaps
one summary of the situation, based on data from the 1931 census, gives
some indication of the extent of the problem:

> Although one room per person is considered satisfactory, there was at
> least 25% of the population in Canadian cities of over 30,000 living in
> less than one room per person in 1931 and in some cities the propor-
> tion was probably over 40%. The clearest evidence of urban crowding
> was shown for tenants paying $15 or less per month in rent. A marked
> degree of crowding apparently exists also in the rural districts of the
> Prairie Provinces as indicated by the following rural average numbers of
> rooms per person: Manitoba 0.93, Saskatchewan 0.84 and Alberta 0.88.
> More than average numbers of children were associated with crowding
> only when incomes were relatively low ... There was convincing evidence
> of a close relationship between the amount of earnings and adequacy of
> accommodation.[43]

Again, it needs to be said that such conditions were not merely a
Depression phenomenon – in many communities the situation was worse,
not better, in the 1940s owing to the desperate shortage of housing during and after the Second World War.[44] Overcrowding meant, at the very
least, that children were less likely to have their own bedroom and thus
less likely to have regular, undisturbed sleeping hours, or quiet places for
homework. Moreover, where parents could not afford to heat a bedroom,
homework had to be done at the kitchen table or some other place busy
with distractions.[45] Because of the lack of evidence we cannot assess the
impact that malnutrition or poor housing conditions had on Canadian children's academic performance. But more recent research makes the link
a certain one, and there is no good reason to think it would not apply in
earlier periods.

Family transiency could also disrupt children's schooling. As one British Columbia report put it, "another cause for retardation is the frequent moving of families from place to place. The education of children suffers as a result of the broken attendance and change from one school to another."[46] In Winnipeg in 1930, by far the single largest reason given for "Withdrawal from school" was "Removal from the city," which accounted for 2,112 of 3,742 withdrawals.[47] Mobility was also a feature within the city: "The family of James Gray ... moved a dozen times in his childhood," writes Gerald Friesen, "and, as a result, Gray attended 12 different Winnipeg public schools in nine years."[48] In the mining communities of British Columbia, explained one school inspector, "there is a constant shifting of pupils from one mining camp to another. Unless grading in the various schools is similar, time must be lost by these pupils."[49] In some frontier areas where farming was combined with other occupations, families might move seasonally. As one school inspector in northern New Brunswick described it in 1927, "a deplorable state of affairs exists in some parishes where whole families spend a winter in the lumber camps, the children being thus deprived of school privileges for nearly half a year."[50]

Absenteeism, however, was not simply a product of poverty or the exigencies of family mobility. Large numbers of children from families above the economic margin, often well above it, missed school because their labour was needed at home. Even in the late 1940s, the National Committee for School Health Research found that this was second only to illness as a cause of absenteeism.[51] In town and country alike, children were kept at home to run errands, to help out in medical emergencies, or to mind younger siblings when mothers had to be away from home.[52] But the most common non-medical reason in the countryside was the high cost or absolute shortage of hired help on the farm. And the complaints on this score were heard from one end of the country to the other. "We cannot overlook the fact," one 1910 report on education in Prince Edward Island commented, "that in some parts of the province it is difficult if not impossible to hire help; that parents are forced much against their will to depend upon their children for assisting in planting and saving crops."[53] Employment at home, wrote Ontario's school attendance officer in 1928, was responsible for 32% of irregular attendance at rural schools. "Farm life has radically changed in the last decade. The machine age is upon us, the 'hired man' has largely disappeared, and hand-help at urgent times must fall upon the school girl and boy. Ontario is peculiarly situated in this respect. The simple and more uniform procedure of grain growing in summer, and wood-cutting in winter has given place to specialized production such as truck-farming and sugar-beet, potato, tobacco, tomato and fruit culture on a farm-wide scale. These demand concentrated effort during a few weeks to plant and especially to harvest the crop without loss, and, in his dilemma, the farmer turns to the growing child for available help."[54] In fact, Ontario was hardly "peculiarly situated in this respect." As a 1930 federal Department of Labour report on the employment of children observed, "Potatoes in Prince Edward Island, New Brunswick, Quebec and Ontario, sugar beets in Ontario and southern Alberta, onions, tomatoes and other fruits and vegetables in Nova Scotia, Ontario and the Okanagan district of British Columbia and on Vancouver Island, and tobacco in Ontario and Quebec are among the particular crops affecting the school attendance of children in Canada."[55] But children were also "engaged intermittently in general agricultural work including plough-ing, seeding, harrowing, gathering in crops, herding cattle and caring for livestock."[56] The result of irregular attendance, the report went on, "appears in the poor progress made by such children in school work, their lack of interest in and dislike of it, and, finally, leaving school before they have completed the elementary grades ... Retardation may be due to other causes than poor attendance but the direct relation between the two is obvious."[57]

One related cause of retardation, contemporaries believed, was a late start at school. While children were generally allowed to begin at ages 5 or 6, in most provinces they were not required to attend school until they were 7 or, in Ontario, until their eighth birthday. Some late starters lived in urban areas, but far more of them in the countryside. It wouldn't have mattered very much if those beginning school at 7 or 8 had stayed on an extra year or two in order to "catch up" with those who began at 5 or 6. In most cases, however, they also left school as early as they could. Allied to irregular attendance, this was a sure recipe for low educational attainment. As one Nova Scotia report summed the problem up in 1942, "it is entirely possible for a child in the country to come to school old and leave young and through poor attendance during his school years to enter on his after-school life not indeed illiterate, but semi-literate, in short to enter the world with a severe handicap."[58]

Thus far we have been discussing absenteeism and early school-leaving among children *enrolled* in school. But there were also children aged 7 to 14 who failed to make normal progress through the grades because they were not in school at all. Some of these were already employed in full-time work. From the late nineteenth century onwards, children in the core school-going age group were gradually squeezed out of the labour mar-ket by changes in the nature of work and by increasingly effective enforce-ment of child labour and compulsory attendance laws. Still, in 1911, 4.9% of boys and 2.3% of girls aged 10–14 were recorded in the census as "at work."[59] By 1921 these numbers were substantially reduced: only 1.2% of those aged 10–13 were considered to be gainfully employed – just under

9,000 children – while 11.8% of those aged 14 were employed, amounting to some 20,000 14-year-olds.[60] A substantial proportion of these working children were in Quebec; the figures for the other eight provinces were much lower. But across the country, most of the employed were boys, and very few were in urban occupations; the vast majority worked on farms, and the largest percentage of these were employed on "home farms." Thus, by 1921 the employment of school-age children, like irregular attendance, was increasingly seen as a rural rather than an urban problem.[61]

According to the census, between 1911 and 1931 there were always more children aged 7–14 identified as "not in school" than children listed as employed in full-time work.[62] This was partly because the census count was almost certainly an underestimate of the number of child workers: it did not include those girls working full-time at domestic duties at home, and it failed to take into account other reasons why children might not be present in school in any given census year.[63] But employed or not, there is good reason to think that socio-economic circumstances helped account for those children not enrolled in school.

Using data from the 1931 census, M.C. MacLean, of the DBS, undertook a national-level statistical study of those children listed as "not in school." As he had in an earlier report on the same subject, MacLean argued that levels of adult illiteracy were one key predictor of absenteeism – one of "the most important features of home environment influencing school attendance."[64] Marital status of parents was another factor of some significance: attendance of children aged 7–14 was higher if they came from families in which both parents were present and lower when one parent was absent or deceased, or both were.[65] He also found that size of family mattered: "Clearly the larger families show more non-attendance than the smaller ... there are apt to be more children at the age of 14 in the larger families, and we know that one of the major causes of non-attendance is dropping out before the age of 15."[66] But more important was the link to parental occupation. In 1931 there were some 99,400 children aged 7–14 years living with a single parent, both parents, or a guardian, and who were recorded on the census as not attending school.[67] Out of that total, MacLean concluded, there were "82,530 children who are not at school and whose absence *cannot* be associated with the illiteracy or marital status of parents. There are many other social or anti-social conditions ... responsible for the absence of these from school ... One of the anti-social conditions is likely to be poverty. While there are no direct data to enable us to measure the results of this condition, there are means of approach in the data on occupations."[68]

MacLean went on to link income and occupational category of families to children's school attendance. The latter, he found, was higher among children of wage-earners than among those of non-wage-earners.[69] In the category of wage-earning heads of families "living with wife," the national average for the per cent of their 7- to 14-year-olds not at school was 4.35, but for certain specific occupations the figure rose to as high as 14%. While the occupational categories are somewhat murky, most of the occupations with non-attenders above the national average can be identified as unskilled labouring jobs or at least as primary sector occupations (fishing, hunting, trapping, logging, mining and quarrying, farm labour). And not surprisingly, in families where the wage-earners were in identifiable white-collar jobs, the percentage of non-attenders dropped to 2%. MacLean then went on to match occupations with illiteracy rates and found a near-parallel hierarchy where non-attendance of children and adult illiteracy could both be correlated with type of occupation, thus showing that "the occupation has an influence apart from the illiteracy of the parent, e.g. farm labourers show greater non-attendance than other labourers although the parents are less illiterate," and occupations of an itinerant nature, such as water transportation, that involved moving families from place to place showed higher rates of non-attendance than expected by the literacy of parents.

In his earlier report, published in 1926 and based on the 1921 census, MacLean devoted a chapter to an analysis of non-attenders in Canada's seventy-nine cities and towns with populations of 7,500 or more.[70] Other than to assign them each a number, he did not identify the communities, so one cannot compare them. He found a "decided" or "strong" correlation between levels of manufacturing activity and levels of non-attendance. But he also found that the type of industrial activity was more important. Where industries employed only adult males, non-attendance tended to be low. It was higher in seaports, in those communities with a high percentage of foreign labour, in those with a high percentage of adult illiterates, and in textile towns or wherever there was a larger proportion of females employed. "It was seen in the last chapter," he remarked, "that school non-attendance has a stronger connection with the illiteracy of females than of males." Similarly, on examining his list of cities, he found the same relationship between attendance and "the employment of female labour." But he didn't think the employment of children under 15 had much to do with it. Generally speaking, communities where children left school at 14 "have also a very strong tendency both to keep children of 7 away, that is to be late in sending their children to school; also to keep from school children from 8 to 13 ... Partly at least it is due to want of recognition of the value of school attendance; partly, perhaps, to inability to equip children for school [i.e., poverty], partly again to inability on the part of the mother to supervise the attendance of children owing to her being employed in certain classes of industries."[71]

MacLean's 1931 study and, far more so, his 1926 report have their limitations.[72] Still, they represent the first attempt on a national scale to analyse the determinants of non-attendance, irregular attendance, and early school-leaving among those aged 7–14. More to the point, his second study probes causes of absenteeism that, once stripped of some archaic language and moralizing, sound remarkably congruent with more recent research, above all the clear linkage of educational attainment with socio-economic circumstances.

By 1941, in any case, the number of those 7–14 not attending school had shrunk even further, as had the employment of children under 15 or 16. At age 14, only 2,509 Canadian boys were entered in the census as "wage-earners," though another 8,000 were listed as "no-pay workers," children "mainly employed on the family farm or helping in their parent's business, but not receiving a fixed rate of pay."[73] (Once again, however, their sisters who were engaged in full-time domestic work at home were not counted as working.)

II

When we turn to our second group, those who had reached the age of 14 or 15, we confront two overlapping questions: why did the majority leave school as soon as the law allowed? and why did a growing minority remain in school into their mid-teens or beyond? We begin here with economic circumstances and then turn to the related question of expectations and aspirations.

"It is an old saying," an Ontario school inspector remarked in 1924, "that 'hard times fill the schools.'"[74] Presumably it followed that "good times empty them." Though obvious hyperbole, the waxing and waning of the economy clearly did affect enrolments for those above the legal school-leaving age: job opportunities pulled young people out of school; a contracting labour market kept them in or sent them back to the classroom. Secondary enrolments declined during the First World War when jobs were plentiful and rose sharply during the Great Depression.[75] The extant national statistics mask the effects of the post-First World War depression or the more prosperous years of the later 1920s, but observers thought both had some impact. In the early 1920s a British Columbia report noted "the falling off of labour for young people under 18 years of age. This sent thousands of young people back to secondary schools."[76] The same phenomenon was noted in Alberta and Ontario.[77] A DBS report of 1927 commented on "a movement away from school of older pupils as a result of better employment conditions," though mainly in the towns and cities where employment opportunities were greatest.[78] Craig Heron's analysis of Hamilton, Ontario, suggests a very tight linkage from 1900 to 1920 between working-class enrolment in the high schools and economic conditions, although it weakened in the later 1920s because of the declining number of job opportunities for young teenagers.[79]

The labour shortages of the Second World War pulled adolescents out of school in large numbers. Nationally, high school enrolment dropped by approximately 20% between 1939 and 1942 alone.[80] In Ontario the number of work permits issued to those between 14 and 16 years of age shot up from 1,907 in 1938 to 9,416 in 1941 and to 12,500 in 1943.[81] Because Ontario's rural youth in that age group didn't require a permit to leave school, we have no statistics for the total level of early school-leaving in that province during the war. But it became enough of a concern for the Canada-Newfoundland Education Association to demand that both provincial and federal authorities take action to keep all young people in school until 16 years of age.[82]

Regardless of the state of the economy, however, many young people left school as soon as possible to work on the farm or find what other employment they could in order to contribute to the welfare of the family. Commenting on a historiography that has celebrated the invention of adolescence, Rebecca Coulter writes, in her close study of working-class teenagers in Edmonton during the 1920s, "they did not enjoy the 'invented' adolescence of which historians speak, or a prolonged, dependent and protracted childhood. Rather, in large numbers, they faced the harsh realities of the work world at an early age."[83] To a greater or lesser extent this was true across the first half of the twentieth century. A generation of scholars have demonstrated that most working-class families lived close to the economic edge. Family incomes were commonly at or below the minimum necessary to provide a decent living; teenage children contributed significant amounts to total family incomes, and parents needed their labour.[84] Contemporary observers were aware of that hard reality as well. When in 1912 a Manitoba Royal Commission sampled a group of working young people, it found that many, girls and boys alike, had left school at 13 and some younger than that; few had completed elementary school and many had reached only grade III, IV, or V. "With very little variation the reason for leaving school was given as the need for earning money for the support of the home, and it would be misleading to say that the occupations were selected from choice. Necessity and opportunity govern."[85] It was very little different in the purportedly "roaring twenties."[86]

Obviously, conditions deteriorated during the Great Depression. When Leonard Marsh investigated family incomes in the 1930s, he found large numbers of Canadian families where the earnings of the household head alone could not provide a remotely adequate standard of living. "In these circumstances, children go to work as soon as they can, many of them before they have properly finished school. This resource in 1930–31 kept

many families above the subsistence level ... For the greater proportion of
unskilled workers and labourers, both breadwinners' and family resources
are inadequate, and this is the largest occupational class." Marsh added,
"The number of farm families with no certainty of a bare living income can
only be guessed at, but it would be a moderate estimate which placed the
proportion at one-fifth."[87]

Keeping a youngster in school in these circumstances demanded large
sacrifices. Even aside from the opportunity costs involved, schooling was
never, in any literal sense, cost-free. Generally speaking, the Canadian high
school, like the elementary school, was tuition-free, but not everywhere.
Until 1921, for example, local high school boards in Ontario had the
option to impose modest tuition fees on resident pupils.* Even though
the number of tuition-free high schools had grown steadily since 1900, in
the school year 1918–19 just over half the schools still levied such fees.[88]
Saskatchewan's high school boards were allowed to charge resident fees,
and in the early 1930s at least, nearly all did so.[89] In other provinces, school
boards were also allowed to charge fees but did so only for the senior
matriculation year, since it was an optional year qualifying for entry to second-year university.[90] By the interwar years, most provinces had introduced
free textbook policies for the elementary grades, but high school textbooks
usually had to be bought, as did pencils and pens, scribblers, geometry sets,
gym suits, and other supplies for school.[91] According to one estimate, for
example, the cost of a set of grade IX texts in Saskatchewan was $14.00,
while for grade XI, costs varied by province from a high of $13.25 in British
Columbia down to $7.10 in Ontario.[92] In most provinces, fees had to be
paid to write any of the provincial examinations, beginning with the high
school entrance examination. Daily transportation costs might be involved
as well. In the 1930s, Leonard Marsh remarked, "the average cost of four
years of high school has been estimated at around $500."[93] This was hardly
the kind of outlay that any low-income family could afford. Even at mid-
century, one large-scale sample of Canadian youth found that "inadequacy
of family income is well above the norm for drop-outs of age 15, or in
grade IX."[94]

The death of a breadwinner could reduce even middle-class families
to penury. In her study of Halifax in the 1920s, Suzanne Morton writes
that "the poverty that most women without access to an adult male wage
endured made them particularly dependent on their children's earnings,
no matter how meagre ... Not surprisingly, few children of female-headed
households continued in school beyond the age of fifteen. In 1931 only

* Resident and non-resident fees are two different issues. We describe the additional
burden of non-resident fees for rural parents in chapter 4.

225 of the 1,850 children of widows in Halifax, fifteen or over, or about 12%, attended school. This was significantly different from the rate for the total population, in which approximately 25% of the children 15 years of age or older who lived with a parent remained in school."[95] While the burden of unemployment during the 1930s fell most heavily on those at the bottom of the economic pecking order, the middle class did not escape unscathed and the loss of a white-collar job could also mean a girl or boy forced out of high school.[96] Similarly, the collapse of agricultural prices could cut short or interrupt the education of young people from hitherto modestly prosperous farm families.[97]

On the other hand, we also have a pattern of more young people staying in school longer. In part this was due to negative factors – those which pushed young teenagers out of the labour market. The reorganization of production and technological change in business and industry had, since the late nineteenth century, put more of a premium on skilled labour or simply eliminated many jobs done by older boys and girls.[98] Employers preferred to hire adults even for unskilled jobs tending machines, and the work that was available to those aged 15 or 16 was increasingly described as "dead-end," condemning those who took it to a life of unskilled labour and low and erratic wages.[99] Drawing on the 1931 census as well as on his analysis of occupational trends in earlier decades, Marsh had this to say about the plight of early school-leavers: the urban occupations available to them, "of which store delivery boys and young domestic servants are the chief examples, begin to lose members rapidly as early as the age of seventeen. This is a clear indication of either a 'blind-alley' or a 'stop-gap' occupation. Some of the youths and lads leave this employment of their own accord to take up other kinds, particularly as store assistants and factory workers. But demand itself ceases. At 17 or 18 when a higher wage than 'boys rates' is sought, it is cheaper to replace the growing delivery boy from the fresh crop of youngsters just out of school. Messengers, bell-boys, and similar workers are liable to the same fate." Though some might move into better jobs, in the main "the largest recourse is to unskilled industrial work"; but it was also this older group of juvenile workers that had "the largest number of unemployed." With only some modification, Marsh added, the same fate awaited girls who were early school-leavers.[100] During the Great Depression, the decline in unskilled work became even more precipitate.[101] Thus there was increasingly less work available – and less remunerative work – for early school-leavers and therefore less reason to leave school at the earliest possible moment. Moreover, as the supply of jobs for younger teens dried up, it is at least plausible to think that some parents concurred with this assessment in 1926 by the superintendent of Winnipeg's schools: "It must be remembered too, that more than 80% of the children who complete the elementary school do so before they are old enough to enter upon permanent occupations, and that the parents are keenly alive to the evil results of two or three years of idleness at this formative period."[102]

Across most of the period, large parts of the adult male labour force benefited from rising real incomes.[103] For those who were fortunate enough to remain fully employed (or who were not devastated by the collapse of farm incomes), this was true even during the 1930s, when prices fell faster than wages. A rising standard of living meant more parents could afford to keep their children in school longer. And there was good reason to do so. There was a growing number of attractive "blue-collar" jobs that required something more than an elementary school education – jobs in manufacturing and related service industries, mainly those associated with the second industrial revolution (electrical, chemical, and petroleum industries, communications, and other new technologies).[104] But staying in school was also a requisite for access to nearly all forms of white-collar work, the fastest growing sector of the labour force. In 1901 this sector represented 15.3% of the labour force; by 1921, 25.3%. Between 1911 and 1921 alone, it grew by almost 75%. Though it remained at about 25% of the labour force during the interwar years, it increased to 32% between 1941 and 1951.[105] Especially early in the century, not all white-collar jobs required more than a completed elementary education, but many did. In the first decade of the century, for example, entry to the lowest categories of clerical work in the federal civil service was open to those at least 15 years of age who had completed "the eighth or any of the high school grades."[106] Preference, on the other hand, was likely to go to those with at least some high school education, and as the years passed, that was increasingly expected. A survey of Toronto businesses in 1922 found that the large retail stores took beginners only at age 16, "and they must have at least high school entrance standing." In the financial houses and the public utilities, "the usual junior 16 or 17 years old with a year or two of high school is accepted." Stenographers were wanted in most businesses: "It may be noted that the stenographer with only entrance standing can scarcely hope to obtain to the degree of efficiency that is generally required."[107] Commenting in 1931 on the best preparation for commerce, a prominent Winnipeg office manager urged young people, if family circumstances allowed, to complete the full academic high school course: "As you are no doubt aware, a matriculation standing is necessary before an applicant will be considered by the larger offices in the city."[108]

Young people were repeatedly told that staying in school was advantageous in obtaining good jobs with good salaries, which, generally speaking, was true. Even most lower-echelon white-collar work paid better than the unskilled labouring jobs available to early school-leavers.[109] For their part, even when the education or skill requirements for a job were low (retail sales, for example), employers used school credentials as a surrogate for "good character" – evidence of "certain qualifications other than academic ones. Among these are neatness, cleanliness, ambition, self-reliance and industrious attitude."[110]

Boys who left school early, even with an incomplete elementary education, still had a variety of employment opportunities. For girls the options were much more limited, and as late as 1931 domestic service was still "the dominant occupation in which women find employment."[111] But the flow into white-collar work was far greater for girls than for boys. "As compared with 7.4% of male workers, no less than 21.3% of all female employees seek clerical employment," wrote Leonard Marsh in the late 1930s. "The professional sector bulks even larger (14.8% of the total compared with 4.8% among men), and at first sight is surprisingly large; but it must be remembered that teachers and nurses account for nine-tenths of that sector."[112] The number of trained nurses (including nursing students) rose from 5,600 in 1911 to 30,500 in 1931.[113] In 1910 there were 32,600 female teachers in Canada; by 1930 the figure had risen to 56,000 and by 1950 to 65,600.[114] Between 1901 and 1931, writes Graham Lowe, "the meteoric growth in clerical jobs" that accompanied the administrative revolution "ushered out the traditional male bookkeeper … and marched in battalions of routine female functionaries."[115]

To one extent or another, these were jobs tied to formal or informal educational credentials. In the 1920s elementary school teaching increasingly required something like three years of high school education. Although there were considerable variations for entry into nursing, the Canadian median in 1930 was two years of high school, and the larger, prestigious training schools required more than that.[116] The educational prerequisites for clerical and other lower-level white-collar work were even more variable and more subject to the law of supply and demand.[117] But when and where employers could choose, they preferred those with higher levels of general education. That is not surprising. Typing and shorthand may well be easily and quickly learned in a term or two, but both require the ability to spell and punctuate correctly. Moreover, to translate a dictated letter into serviceable business prose demanded a certain facility with English composition, which required, minimally perhaps, at least the high school entrance standard, and for the better jobs probably more than that.[118]

Using the 1936 census of the Prairie provinces, Marsh analysed the educational background of male and female workers in Manitoba, a province he thought was roughly representative of the nation as a whole. "The most striking feature which these measurements reveal when applied to gainfully employed women is the much higher standard of schooling among them. Over 60% are shown ... to have continued their education or training in some form beyond the elementary grades, and 8.4 of this upper portion (as compared with 4.8 out of 36.0 per cent among men) represents higher education beyond the ages of seventeen or eighteen."[119] Marsh went on to comment that the reasons lay largely in the structural differences between male and female labour markets. But the point that should be emphasized here is simply that for those girls who were seeking employment, staying in school was more important than it was for boys, and thus, proportionately, they tended to stay longer and have higher levels of educational attainment. This was true even of the jobs that didn't require large dollops of formal education. Most Manitoban "shop assistants," for example, had between nine and twelve years of schooling. For young women, the route to the limited array of good jobs available to them lay through the schoolhouse door.

Economic circumstance alone cannot explain everything about patterns of attendance or levels of educational attainment; social, cultural, and academic influences might have an autonomous impact or act in concert with it.[120] Children left school because they lacked the ability to meet promotion standards that, in the early decades of the century especially, remained demanding. As late as 1950, "early dropouts" – those who left at ages 15 or 16 without completing elementary school – "have repeated grades frequently: up to 70% of dropouts in Grades VII and VIII have repeated one or more grades."[121] When asked about the reasons for leaving school as early as possible, many boys and girls cited "lack of interest." For some, leaving school at 14 or 15 was an assertion of adulthood, the signal step in becoming a man or woman, the moment when they put away childish things.[122] Others stayed in school because they found it easy or because they just "liked school."[123] Some young people left school because of what Richard Sennett has termed "the hidden injuries of class." Initially, Hugh Garner's *Cabbagetown* anti-hero had looked forward to attending "the big tech" in east-end Toronto, but "almost immediately he had run head-on into social consciousness. The social and economic divisions erected in a class of forty boys were of fine complexity but nevertheless clearly marked. He was bitter at the memory of having to turn down invitations because his clothes were not good enough; of being left out of the cliques which revolved around the possession of a Model T Ford."[124] On the other hand, some children adapted quickly to the social standards of their high school peers and were happy to escape from what they increasingly saw as the constricted culture of their working-class parents.[125]

Language barriers could pose a major obstacle to children's academic progress. "The children of foreign parents are usually retarded owing to their lack of familiarity with the English language," a British Columbia report noted in 1924.[126] Though there were exceptions, the common practice was simply to start them in grade 1 regardless of age, or at the very least place them in one of the lower grades.[127] Unlike immigrant children, French Canadians might have their own schools, but a raft of pressures worked against their success at school: among a people predominantly rural, the meagre resources available for schooling in any rural community, the vagaries of weather, and the periodic need for children's labour that promoted irregular attendance; a desperate shortage of well-qualified teachers; and the overt hostility of many anglophones, which led to official or unofficial policies restricting French as a language of instruction or imposing bilingual instruction at an early age so that neither French nor English was learned well.[128]

More generally, we cannot even begin to assess the advantages urban young people in the interwar years might have had over their rural counterparts just because electric lighting was near-universal in urban homes. In Canada, after all, homework is largely done during the long dark evenings of fall, winter, and early spring. According to the census of 1941, in four provinces less than 10% of "occupied dwellings in farm areas" had electric lights, and the highest percentage, in Ontario, was only 37%.[129]

Educational attainment, in any case, improved across the decades because of changes in attendance patterns themselves. By the early 1920s, most provinces had increased the age of compulsory attendance to 15 or 16. Improving rates of regular attendance and declining rates of grade retardation meant more children progressed through the grades at normal rates, so that they reached grade IX or X before they were old enough to leave school. Between 1922 and 1928, for example, the median age in grade VIII dropped by nearly a full year, and between 1921 and 1927, the percentage in grade VIII of those over 15 declined as well.[130] Though large numbers left school as soon as possible, noted the Winnipeg School Board in 1929, at the start of the decade "approximately half of them had left before reaching the eighth grade; the present [school] census shows that at least two-thirds had reached the eighth or a higher grade before leaving, while about 40% had reached at least the ninth grade."[131]

Parental expectations and aspirations were also critical. One basic predictor of school success, "parental interest," was important then as always. Some parents encouraged their children to stay in school as long as possible for cultural or utilitarian reasons; others did not.[132] Some parents made great sacrifices to keep their children in school; others feared an extended education would break the ties that bound young people to family and community, expose them to alien values, or encourage them to leave home for greener pastures elsewhere.[133] Parents might keep a girl in school a little longer than her brother to obtain the skills for office work but baulk at a less vocationally focused academic education. They might want to ensure that a boy began learning a practical skill as early as possible and opt for an apprenticeship rather than additional formal schooling. They might assume an elementary education was a sufficient preparation for adulthood and expect a young teenager to get on with the business of living. They might, on the other hand, want a son or daughter to stay in high school long enough to enter teaching or nursing, or even aspire to see a child make it as far as university. They might send an older child out to work in order to keep younger children in school that much longer. "Family values" might also bestow a higher value on home ownership than prolonged schooling, or vice versa.[134]

Schoolmen were wont to blame a good deal of absenteeism and early school-leaving on "parental negligence" or "parental indifference," but much of it was probably due to differing assessments of the appropriate role of the child in the family economy – in Viviana Zelizer's phrase, to the cultural conflict over the priceless and the useful child.[135] Writing about the attitude of immigrant parents in the first decade of the century, Kenneth Sylvester comments that "parents, who quite logically saw their best chances of material improvement in farm ownership and in maintaining tightly woven family networks, were not yet prepared to see the benefits promised from investments in education. They came from a world that had been defined for centuries by unbending social hierarchy, where education served the purposes of others. It was therefore rational to avoid an expense long seen as unnecessary to making a living, particularly given the immediate bounty of acquiring land in lots sixteen to twenty times larger than traditional peasant holdings. As one farmer put it in 1914: 'If we feed freeloaders [teachers] to play with our children, we will never make our fortune here.'" Sylvester goes on to comment that "in time, as the farm economy grew crowded and public lands fell into short supply, the attitudes of succeeding generations grew less sceptical."[136]

Before either young people or their parents were prepared to invest in education, they had to see the pertinence of schooling over other forms of patrimony, or as a complement to them.[137] Throughout the first half of the twentieth century the linkage between education and work was more tenuous than it would later become. Making one's way in the world might depend far less on educational credentials than on social capital – entering or inheriting the family business, apprenticing oneself to relatives or close family friends, or being able to exploit some related form of kin sponsorship. As late as mid-century some 30% of boys and 20% of girls from "high economic status" families were among those who left before completing high school.[138] Some of them might not have been able to meet the requisite academic standards, but many others simply did not need high school to ensure their futures. And even those without this sort of social capital, or much in the way of education beyond the age of compulsion, could ferret out promising opportunities for getting ahead in life.[139] Among rural boys, moreover, joining one's father in the fishery, the artisanal shop, or on the farm were all plausible and often much-preferred alternatives to sitting in a classroom. In a 1942 study of educational attainment in King's County, Nova Scotia, Alexander Mowat, a Dalhousie University education professor, found sharp differences between the sons and daughters of farm families. The boys were much more irregular in attendance, scored lower in standardized reading and arithmetic tests, and left school earlier than their sisters. Speculating on the causes, Mowat thought it "not unlikely that farmers' sons aim to be farmers, and the present curriculum at least in the higher grades does not offer them much help in this, while farmers' daughters, at least, aspire to other occupations towards which success in school work provides a definite stepping-stone."[140] Futures were to be secured, in other words, by means of two different stepping-stones, and the necessary skills acquired in two different ways: the boys learned at home on the job; the girls learned through schooling.

The pertinence of schooling might also mean, as Gerald Friesen has suggested, the extent to which a family was engaged in a world largely dominated by print culture. Elizabeth Goudie, born in 1902, spent much of her life trapping, gardening, and fishing in an isolated part of Labrador. Drawing on her memoir written late in life, Friesen offers this account of the schooling of Elizabeth and her children:

> Elizabeth "had the privilege of going to school two winters ... I spent three years in school in Mud Lake but really I had about four years in school if it were all put together. I got as far as the fourth grade in the old English readers and the Kirkland Scott Arithmetic Book." Her husband, Jim, "never went to school in his life but he learned to read and he could look after his own affairs. He loved to read." In the year before the arrival of her first child, Elizabeth "had lots of time on my hands. I would go hunting and fishing and in the long evenings I would read a book if I had one." In their family years, however, they never had time for such activities. Her two eldest children had little more exposure to books: "Horace and Marie both went to school for a while. Horace was only eleven years old when he started going out into the country on his trapping lines. He only had about three years of school. Marie was kept

in school longer ... Horace wanted to go with his father so much that I
let him go ... He would go to school in the fall and go into the country
in the spring with his father ... Jim was beginning to find the work hard
and Horace could help him with camping in the evening. He was good
company for him so I never tried to keep him home after that. I saw
what he meant to his father, as Horace grew older. When Horace could
stand the hard work, he went with him all year round."

"These," adds Friesen, "are statements about the formal arts of literacy and
the inescapable necessities of life; they demonstrate that the Goudie family understood the value of books and print but, in the years before 1939,
rarely had the opportunity to work within the world created by print except
through the Bible, their domestic accounts, and a few randomly selected
volumes of literature."[141] But as more and more people became enmeshed
in that world, the uses of schooling appeared more relevant for broader
portions of their daily lives. Patterns of school attendance were not determined simply by economic circumstance; they were also a quite complex
nexus of cultural tradition, parental expectations and aspirations, and individuals' interpretations of how the world worked.

The salience of economic circumstance, nonetheless, is not to be gainsaid.
In the previous chapter we noted that the median level of educational
attainment in 1941 was 7.7 years. Medians or averages have their uses, but
obviously differing levels of educational opportunity were not distributed
randomly among the population. Indeed, Leonard Marsh remarked on
"how unrepresentative a measurement of educational level averaged for
all [occupational] classes can be." While it is possible to say that 36% of
employed males had some secondary education or more, "this statement
tells little or nothing of the realities of the educational situation when class
percentages vary from 90 to 20."[142] Ranking the occupational order into
twelve broad categories, from management and professional down to farmers, farm workers, and the unskilled, he demonstrated that, for both men
and women, the acquisition of nine years or more schooling was mainly
the preserve of those on the upper rungs of the hierarchy, that income was
similarly distributed, that the contribution of children to the family income
rose as one moved down the hierarchy, and that the percentage of young
people in school decreased accordingly.[143] Levels of educational attainment
contributed substantially to individuals' placement in the labour force, but
access to education was substantially shaped by social class.[144] Whereas at
mid-century 29% of boys and 20% of girls whose parents were of "high economic status" dropped out of school at some point, for those whose parents
were "below average in economic status" the figures were 78% and 74%.[145]

One of the first Canadian analyses of differential access to a high school education was carried out in 1942 under the direction of M.E. LaZerte, at the time dean of education at the University of Alberta. The children whose fathers were employed in "clerical and commercial service" had, the study revealed, an 87% chance of attending high school; for "trade and industry," the figure was 82%; for "public and personal service," 81%. "Children of ... unskilled laborers have a 21% chance. The percentages of children of high school age in high school in Edmonton from each occupational group show that children of parents in the unskilled occupations do not have educational opportunities equal to those of children of parents in other groups."[146]

Moreover, while it would be a mistake to belittle the role that ethnicity or cultural differences played in shaping patterns of school attendance, it can hardly be divorced from economic circumstance. French Canadians living in anglophone provinces were predominantly rural, in itself a constraint on educational achievement, but they were also predominantly poorer than those of British descent. Similarly, in 1931, Leonard Marsh noted that "no less than 65% of the Poles, Russians, Finns, and other urban Eastern Europeans are labourers or unskilled workers and 78% of the smaller and more mixed group of Central Europeans ... Italian immigrants include the second largest quota of unskilled men (64.6% among the 1921–1931 entrants)."[147] Unskilled labour ranked at the bottom of the income scale, well below the average earnings of the male labour force but highest among the parents of early school-leavers.[148] In his survey of education in rural Manitoba in the 1930s, D.S. Woods, at that point an academic but also an experienced school inspector who knew the territory, wrote that "since large numbers of our rural people of non-Anglo-Saxon origin are settled on secondary lands, slowness to take advantage of schooling which may appear attributable to racial background may be explained, in no small degree, on the basis of recency of settlement and limited income."[149]

To say that economic circumstance was a fundamental determinant of educational opportunity is not to say that there was no such thing as individual mobility. Elementary education was tuition-free, and by the interwar years, secondary education mostly free. Aspirations and economic circumstance may have allowed a minority of working-class young people to continue on to secondary school, giving them a wider array of vocational choices.

The hard evidence for this, however, is very limited and ambiguous. Only Ontario collected province-wide data on the occupational origins of high school students, and then only between 1896 and the early 1930s; the data, moreover, are flawed by crude groupings of occupational categories and by the substantial numbers who were categorized as "other" or unknown. But the numbers suggest that it is quite wrong to see the Ontario high school as the distinctive preserve of the most prosperous portions of society.* Even in 1900 the sons and daughters of manual workers made up about 25% of the high school population; by 1921–22, 30% were from families in manual occupations, and by 1929–30, 37%.[150] Far more of these youngsters were from the homes of skilled rather than unskilled workers, and taken as a whole, they were under-represented in comparison to their families' share of the labour force. Still, there was a steady increase in the proportion of young people from working-class backgrounds in the Ontario high school.[151]

In his singular study of secondary enrolments in Hamilton, 1900 through 1930, Craig Heron traces the gradual, though far from linear, rise in the number of working-class students and remarks that "during the late 1920s and early 1930s ... the percentage of high school students whose fathers worked in a trade or labouring occupation increased in the academic schools to between 30 and 45%, and in the vocational courses hovered between half and two-thirds. The substantial increase in the participation of labourers' children was particularly striking."[152] In a second local study, in this case of London's Technical School, Ivor Goodson and Christopher Anstead show that attendance resulted in substantial levels of social mobility: "38% of males and 49% of females increased their position on the social scale," though another 38% of boys and 45% of girls remained in the same social stratum as their parents.[153] While addressing a somewhat different topic, we ourselves have been impressed by the success of large numbers of Jewish youngsters who were able to use the public schools as a means of achieving social mobility from working-class backgrounds into the University of Toronto's professional schools – youngsters, it is worth adding, who often arrived in Toronto with no fluency in English and some of whom didn't enter the city's school system until they were nine or ten.[154]

The Ontario evidence, however, is also open to alternative interpretations or, at the very least, substantial qualifications. The fact that working-class children constituted an increasing proportion of high school students *before* 1920 might attest to growing opportunities for upward mobility, but after that the evidence is more equivocal. Once urban young people were required to attend school until they were 16, it is entirely possible that the presence of a growing cohort of working-class children was nothing more than the result of compulsory education. The data do not tell us which

* Some readers may assume that while a growing number of working-class young people were indeed entering the secondary schools, they were also being systematically channelled into dead-end vocational programs. In the main, this was not the case. We take this matter up in chapter 10. Here we are interested only in one aspect of the question: the degree to which students continued on to secondary education of any kind.

grades these pupils were enrolled in or how old they were, but the bulk of them may have been 14- or 15-year-olds enrolled in grades IX and X. They couldn't leave school even if they didn't want to be there, and the high rate of school-leaving as soon as they turned 16 doesn't suggest that most of them were taking advantage of new avenues for social mobility.

We also know that, Canada-wide, working-class youngsters were less likely to make the transition from elementary to secondary school and that children from families with low economic status were far more likely to drop out of school early. That is to say, an increasing number of working-class children got to high school but they left in disproportionate numbers before reaching the upper grades. At the same time a growing number of middle-class students were attending high school and staying for ever longer periods of time. In a rare Canada-wide historical analysis of social origin and educational attainment, Neil Guppy and his colleagues conclude that during the first half of the twentieth century there was no gradual reduction in educational inequalities: "It appears no reduction whatever occurs in socioeconomic differences in years of schooling attained until the [birth] cohort of 1938–42 is considered, a cohort that entered high school after World War II."[155] Indeed, if the Ontario data are to be believed, there may actually have been no more social mobility in the interwar years than in the last quarter of the nineteenth century. In 1861 the number of secondary pupils from families in manual occupations was negligible, but by the turn of the century it had risen to somewhere between a quarter and a third of total enrolments. Yet it was still only about 37% in 1929–30.[156]

The meaning of upward (or downward) mobility, in any case, is itself ambiguous. There are always instances of educational Horatio Algers, those who rise, through schooling, from cobbler's son to eminent lawyer or doctor. But when a farm-owner's daughter becomes an elementary school teacher, or the son of a skilled worker in one of the better-paid crafts becomes a salesman, do we have an example of upward or lateral mobility? At least one thing seems certain: the high school was a powerful mechanism for moving young people off the farm and into white-collar occupations. "Out-migration" is a familiar theme in Canadian population history; it has been mainly viewed, however, as a geographical phenomenon in which people move from one part of the country to another, or across international borders. But there was also such a thing as "educational out-migration" – movement, by means of schooling, from the old to the new economy, from declining to new or expanding occupational opportunities, from blue-collar to white-collar work – and the shifts in cultural perspectives that entailed. It may not have been "*up* and out" but it was indubitably "out."[157]

This was particularly true for young women. When G.M. Weir conducted his study of nursing education in 1930, he found that farmers' daughters

comprised, by far, the largest of his occupational categories.[158] Much the
same was true of elementary school teachers.[159] Drawing on the 1941 census for his data, John Robbins, the DBS's education specialist, concluded
that "one out of every five country young people have migrated to the cities and towns of recent years. The movement has been much more pronounced among the girls than the boys – one girl in four, one boy in seven
... The girls, one supposes ... are remaining in school longer than the boys
to prepare themselves for positions in towns and cities."[160] In a study of one
small Manitoba town and its rural environs, the author was able to trace
the subsequent destination of 256 students who reached grade XI or XII
between 1930–31 and 1943–44. Only 96 were boys. "Of the 160 girls, 14
went on to university ... 20 took nursing courses, 24 went to Normal School,
and 34 took business courses ... The majority," the author noted, "of those
who reach the upper grades leave the community ... at least in part because
it has only a limited market for specialized skills."[161]

Schooling seems also to have been a portal of opportunity for girls of
non-British ethnic origin. Franco-Albertan girls, like their German immigrant counterparts, had greater difficulty obtaining jobs in sales and clerical work than the Canadian-born, notes Anne Gagnon, "but teaching
drew Francophone women in almost equal proportions as their English-
speaking sisters."[162] Royden Loewen has drawn attention to the movement
of Mennonite young women from the farm, through the high school, into
teaching, nursing, and secretarial work.[163] And on the prairies, at least,
teaching was clearly an avenue from farm to white-collar work; normal
school records during the interwar years in all three Prairie provinces
point to a growing number of young women of non-British origin flooding
into teaching.[164]

Across the first half of the twentieth century, the number of years children
were in school increased, attendance became more regular, levels of educational attainment rose, and more and more youngsters attended high school
for some period of time. Still, it was a gradual process, uneven in its geographical reach, and for much of the country things were hardly different
in 1910 or 1920 than they would be three or four decades later. Reporting
in 1922 on the state of his inspectorate, a mixed area of new settlement,
poor school districts, and struggling farm folk, one Manitoba inspector
succinctly summarized the manifold causes of irregular attendance. "The
people generally are anxious to give their children an education," he wrote.
"Bad roads, long distances to and from school, the lack of proper food and
clothing, the lack of medical attention and the prevalence of contagious
and infectious disease, all tend to make attendance at school irregular.
Owing to economic stress at home there is a tendency to keep children

home as soon as they are able to be of any service there."[165] Continuities persisted even as the country approached mid-century. Consider one example – the "truancy" files from rural Pincher Creek School Division No. 29, in southwestern Alberta, between 1946 and 1949.* These reflect, in part, the ongoing effort to enforce the provincial attendance laws, but also to supervise the distribution of the "baby bonus" introduced by the Federal Family Allowance Act of 1945. Parents were eligible to receive this if their children were in attendance at school to age 16 – one year longer than the province required them to attend – so that many of the cases involved children at or above the legal school-leaving age. The records consist of investigations of absence from school carried out jointly by the school superintendent of the division and the regional office of the federal Department of National Health and Welfare. In the process, parents were required to explain why their children were not in school.[166]

From a parent:

My child has been absent from school, for the following reasons are, that he had chicken pox, then to follow his mother had to go to the hospital and my child had to go and stay with his grandparents which is quite a ways to school and he was unable to attend school regular. Then when his mother did come home he took sick and was away from school again.

From the superintendent to the regional director of family allowances:

I have not been able to get any direct trace of where these people are living. It may be that they are at one of the lumber camps out from Blairmore, but my usual sources of information for this sort of thing did not know about them. I do not think the children are at any school nor receiving any equivalent training. It seems doubtful, however, if they are resident within any school district.

From a parent:

I kept John home to help seed the grain and seed the garden ... To my knowledge I have only kept John home one day at a time so he would not miss too much school work. So in all he only missed 6 days this spring during our very busy season.

   I do regret myself to see my child away from school, because I do know what it means to a child, because it is the one thing that he needs most. I'm sure that in the future he will attend school regularly.

* The school division did not include the town of Pincher Creek.

From a public health nurse:

I called at the home of Mary X ... Mary has not been ill but her mother said she has been unable to buy her a pair of rubbers or overshoes in her size to wear during the winter months and so she has not sent her.

From a parent:

Suzie can't attend school as for my health. No one is at home. The children father has not live with us for years and hasn't help support the children. I was due to go to an operation but can't as know one here to look after thing so that is why Suzie can not attend school anymore.

From the superintendent to the regional director following an RCMP investigation of the above case:

... the child is urgently needed to keep the home going and that the mother has no income whatever with which to hire other help.

From a parent:

In answer to your letter about my son ... who you say didn't go to school in the month of February. My son was ordered out of school for not having his homework done and was told not to come back until it was done. How is he going to do homework at home when his teacher knows he can't do the work at school. Who is supposed to do it, me?

Willie won't be fifteen years until August and I think it is about time the teacher quit throwing children out of school just because they can't seem to learn the children. They take spite out on them. Willie and a few more children has been in the grade seven three years. What do you think about it? Isn't it time they learned something?

The teacher is teaching grade seven and eight and he says they're not fit for grade four. Can we help that we are not the one who is teaching them and why did the teacher just write about *my* son.

I could name you two or three children that quite before they were fifteen and are still getting their allowance. When I asked the principal about that he had the nerve to say they were glad to get rid of such children.

I'd like to know just who he thinks he is, not that I worry about the family allowance. You may as well stop sending it for my other child too if that is the way you feel about it. I asked the Bank Manager here about it and he said he didn't know the family allowances had anything to do with school.

From the superintendent to the regional director of family allowances, responding to the above letter:

This boy has not returned to school since the suspension of allowances in February. He has now been suspended from school for conduct injurious to the welfare of the school and pupils. It would therefore appear to me that the suspension of allowances should be continued.

Regarding [the mother's] letter to you ... The incident she mentions regarding homework was one of the many difficulties arising from the gross non-attendance of the boy. Any one or all of these incidents could have been adjusted quite easily if it had not been for the unfavorable attitude of the parents. I would judge that they had already decided that the boy should be allowed to stay home from school whenever he wished. On the occasion to which [the mother] refers, the boy was sent home to get a note to explain why he had been absent for the two previous days (as well as several scattered half and whole days during the two weeks before that).

I may say that it appears to me that the chief reason the boy has been slow to learn is that the parents have encouraged him in his attitude of dislike and defiance toward the school.

Finally, not all parents were prepared to sacrifice an adolescent's labour for the family allowance. In one case the superintendent scribbled at the bottom of the "Family Allowance Unsatisfactory School Report": "Father needs him for 'pipe-fitting' – says he doesn't care about Family Allowance."

Why, then, as late as mid-century, did a few children in Pincher Creek School Division absent themselves from school? Weather, illness, transiency and distance from a school, poverty, the demands of the family economy, the expectations and aspirations of parents, conflicts with school authorities, and the irreconcilable differences in outlook or understandings between at least some parents and the norms that schoolmen took to be representative of the good school and the good pupil. Was Pincher Creek School District Canada writ small? Perhaps not. But these extracts from its truancy files are remarkably congruent with the causes of irregular attendance, early school-leaving, and the limited levels of educational attainment we have canvassed throughout the first half of the twentieth century in all parts of English Canada.

4

Schools

I

When children went off to school in the early twentieth century, what kind of schools did they attend? What kind of buildings and classrooms could they expect to learn in? What other facilities and services were available to them, and what were the variations they might encounter?

Consider, first, the character of one big-city school system throughout the first half of the twentieth century. In 1901 the population of Winnipeg was a modest 42,340; by 1921 it had swollen to 179,087. In the first decade of the century it had risen from Canada's sixth to its third largest city, smaller only than Montreal and Toronto. While by 1931 it had ceded third place to Vancouver, its population continued to grow through the interwar years and it would remain the nation's fourth largest city for decades to come.[1] By 1920, like other large Canadian cities, Winnipeg had already created a sophisticated, complex school system.[2] The school board's operating budget that year was something over $2 million, and it spent close to another million on capital costs. It enrolled 33,500 children, it was managed by a board of fifteen trustees, and it was administered by a large staff variously responsible for business and finance, school plant, and academic matters. It employed 771 teachers in fifty-five elementary schools and three high schools. The size of its schools had increased steadily since its major building program had begun in the 1890s. Until 1912, ten classrooms had been typical, but that year the board had opened a new elementary school with twenty-six classrooms, and the next year one with thirty-two. In the main, the elementary schools contained between 300 and 500 children, but seven had 900 or more, and the largest, Strathcona, in the North End, housed 1,260. Most of the buildings were two- or three-storey brick piles with classrooms stacked one above the other and basements that accommodated play spaces as well as storage areas and heating systems. But by 1920 Winnipeg was also experimenting with a new architectural style – the single-storey "bungalow school" that would become increasingly common in Canada's suburbs in the interwar years. From the beginning, the city had provided generous grounds for its new schools and had been engaged in "beautification" programs to make them attractive spaces.[3]

Unlike most of Canada's eastern cities, Winnipeg had the advantage of starting fresh late in the nineteenth century. In 1920 its physical plant was recently built, incorporating the newest, most modern designs in classroom facilities and other conveniences: heating and ventilation systems able to maintain a constant temperature and an adequate supply of fresh air, the latest approved levels of electric lighting, centrally operated electric bells, modern plumbing that included not only washroom and toilet facilities but water fountains as well.[4] By 1920 Winnipeg also had a well-developed system of administration and supervision. While the elected school trustees made broad policy decisions, the daily work of the schools rested with the city's superintendent of schools, Daniel McIntyre, a highly experienced administrator who had held the post since 1885. At head office there was also an assistant superintendent and a group of specialist "supervising teachers" for primary work and other subject areas who moved from school to school maintaining uniform standards, helping teachers with problems they encountered, and bringing fresh instructional ideas into play. Though only in the initial stages by 1920, the organization of a few of the largest schools included "supervising principals" – the traditional "head teacher" given part- or full-time relief from teaching to supervise, coordinate, and guide the work of the rest of the staff.

Winnipeg was also among Canadian leaders in introducing all the hot new ideas of the era that together constituted the curricular, pedagogical, and related services known as "the new education." In the 1890s, music, drawing, and military drill (already morphing into a more broadly conceived program of physical training for both girls and boys) had become regular parts of the school program, each with its own specialist director. Physical training was supplemented from at least the turn of the century by a highly organized system of school and interschool sports for both boys and girls, and classroom music instruction fed into the city-wide school music festival. In 1900 Winnipeg was one of a handful of school systems to take advantage of Sir William Macdonald's initiative (and seed money) to establish manual training in Canada; shortly afterwards, sewing classes and then home economics were added for girls; by 1920 twenty-three teachers were employed in the manual training and domestic science departments. In the city's heavily immigrant North End, W.J. Sisler, principal at Strathcona, had been pioneering special classes since the turn of the century in what we would now call instruction in English as a second language (ESL).[5] During the second decade of the century Winnipeg established its first classes for "backward" children and in 1919 created one of Canada's earliest junior high schools, specially designed to encourage children to stay in school beyond grade VII or VIII and to offer a variety of learning opportunities to the recently discovered "adolescent."

In 1892 Winnipeg had opened its first special-purpose ten-room "collegiate institute," an academic high school. In 1920, swamped by numbers, the school board began planning a thirty-classroom replacement with an estimated enrolment of 1,200 that would incorporate the best of secondary school models, including a substantial library, gymnasium, auditorium, science laboratories, and workrooms of various kinds. The spanking-new Daniel McIntyre Collegiate Institute opened its doors in 1923.[6] A decade before that, however, Winnipeg had embarked on another signal innovation of the era, opening two fully equipped technical schools, one in the North and one in the South End. By 1920 their combined enrolment was 1,500. And in the same year Winnipeg's well-established evening school program enrolled 4,200 students in a remarkable panoply of departments and courses that included elementary subjects for young people who had left school early to go to work, ESL instruction and elementary subjects for adults, a wide range of commercial and shop courses taught at the secondary level, and even a substantial academic upgrading program for teachers from Winnipeg and nearby communities.

New ideas flourished in other areas. In 1920 one school was experimenting with the "Gary Plan," an innovation in school organization and pedagogy that had taken the continent by storm over the previous decade. Winnipeg was also experimenting with an organized audiovisual service for the schools, including motion pictures. In 1920 alone the board spent over $3,000 on supplementary readers for the elementary and high schools and invested in another $1,000 worth of educational materials for use by its subject supervisors. It bought $1,100 worth of "scientific apparatus" and spent $8,520 on typewriters for its high schools. The trustees also decided to supply free textbooks "beginning September next. It will ensure in the first place that each child will have all school requisites immediately on entering school while, in the case of large families, it will materially lessen the effort required to keep the older children in school and thus tend to lengthen attendance."

In 1909 the school board had begun a program of medical inspection. By 1920, under its chief medical inspector, Dr Mary Crawford (who held the job from 1909 until she retired in 1941), it employed five part-time assistant doctors and thirteen full-time nurses.[7] By that point it had added a dental department with a full-time chief inspector and five part-time dentists. The job of these departments was to examine all Winnipeg schoolchildren on a regular basis; identify individual problems that needed remediation (and supply a good deal of it); prevent, or at least isolate, contagion; promote and administer vaccination; and in concert with classroom teachers, maintain a program of health education that included the basics of hygiene, diet, and good health habits generally. From 1914 limited financial assistance was available to secure eyeglasses at a free clinic, and in 1916 similar provision was made for dental treatment. From at least 1915 the medical department began to branch out into psychological services by identifying 152 backward children through IQ testing, and in 1920 the department hired its first trained psychologist, "a specialist in mental tests and measurements."

During the interwar years Winnipeg consolidated and extended the new departures of the three decades between 1890 and 1920. Although its enrolment increased only modestly compared to the explosive growth of earlier decades, its budget had increased by more than a million dollars – from $2 million in 1920 to just over $3 million in 1940.[8] By 1939 close to a thousand teachers were employed, 200 more than in 1920. In an extended overview of the system that year, drafted for a royal commission on municipal affairs, the school board described the programs and services that had developed in the previous two or three decades.[9] All of the larger schools now had supervising principals (twenty-eight in number). The teaching staff included "43 teachers of practical (industrial) arts for the boys and 31 teachers of practical arts for the girls." There were also teacher-supervisors at the central office, including four for the primary schools and one each for music, household arts, physical training, and mechanical arts. The elementary schools were now defined as covering grades I to VI and organized "to make more adequate provision for individual differences" – a regular program for "the average student," thirty-five "opportunity classes" for those "who had dropped behind their age group in academic achievement," and thirty-nine ungraded classes "for children definitely below average." Seventeen junior high schools were organized (though not all in separate buildings) for those in grades VII through IX, offering a core of academic subjects and a variety of options as part of their regular program, plus special "industrial classes" – a continuation of the elementary opportunity classes. Though they were not free, the board ran "vacation schools" in the summer for pupils "whose promotion was conditional" in order to reduce "a certain amount of retardation and repetition." The senior high schools, now five in number, offered a mix of academic and vocational programs leading on to university, normal school, commerce, and the trades. "Physical education programs" (notice the new term) were in place for all grades, and in the junior and senior high schools were conducted by specialist teachers. Vocal music was a standard part of the curriculum, twenty-six schools had school orchestras, and students from thirty-eight schools "have been given the opportunity of some training in the use of musical instruments."

While no bigger than in 1920, the medical department had added two part-time oculists, and there were special "sight-saving" and "lip reading" classes for children with serious sight or hearing problems. Mental testing had expanded to identify children with special needs. The dental department inspected children's teeth and offered instruction in dental care; "all necessary dental treatment ... is done for needy children in the lower grades," and the school dental clinic offered "emergency service in the case of any children suffering ... tooth trouble which requires immediate relief." Free eyeglasses were available to the needy, and a half-pint of milk a day was offered free to those aged 6, 9, and 12 who were 10% or more underweight.

How typical was Winnipeg in creating and then consolidating its schools into a mature twentieth-century urban school system? Particular innovations varied by date; not every big city did things the same way; and financial resources mattered as well. But Winnipeg was no exception among Canada's largest cities and towns. Even by 1920 there was little to distinguish between Winnipeg, Vancouver, Toronto, or, one might add, the Protestant school system of Montreal.[10] Aside from sheer scale, moreover, there wasn't much to distinguish this handful of big cities from smaller cities or larger towns anywhere in the country. With a population of 61,000 in 1921, London was Canada's ninth largest city, a little smaller than Calgary and a little larger than Edmonton, cities that ranked eighth and tenth respectively. All three were much smaller than Toronto or Winnipeg. Yet in terms of London's programs, facilities, or services, its school system was as up-to-date and as innovative as in any of the country's largest cities. Indeed, like several other Ontario cities, London was ahead of Winnipeg or Vancouver in its adoption of kindergarten classes and the specially designed kindergarten rooms built into its newest schools.[11] Writing in 1922, Alberta's chief inspector of schools would remark that "the school systems in Calgary and Edmonton have assumed many of the activities peculiar to complex city school systems. In addition to their responsibilities in connection with fundamental requirements, special educational services have been developed, and these have shown considerable expansion and progress since their organization. In the public schools these include Art, Household Arts, Manual Training, Music, Physical Training, classes for sub-normal children, classes for pupils of exceptional ability, pre-vocational classes, continuation classes and night schools. Special supervisors are engaged to direct these special branches."[12] He could just as well have added junior high schools, secondary school technical and commercial departments, and, in the case of Calgary particularly, thorough-going medical inspection and health programs.[13]

As one moved down the urban hierarchy, as cities and towns became smaller and their tax base constrained accordingly, school systems became more modest. In 1925 the city of Fredericton had a population of about 8,500 and its school board worked within an operating budget of just under $92,000, a far cry from Winnipeg's $2 million. Its enrolment in 1928 was 1,885 pupils (to that point an all-time high).[14] It had six elementary schools, including the "model school" operated in conjunction with the provincial normal school. The largest, Smythe Street, had twelve teachers; a second school had ten teachers and a third, five; but the system also included two smaller schools on the edge of the city, one with three teachers and the other with only one. Fredericton, nevertheless, was as *au courant* as its size and budget would allow. From at least the turn of the century its school board had hired a full-time manual training instructor, and from 1907 a full-time specialist for music, a teacher who served for decades and gradually developed a sophisticated music program that reached all pupils, from grades I through XI. By 1915 the board had added, at a cost of $1,000, "a well-equipped Domestic Science Department" and hired a Mount Allison graduate to conduct it. Both the manual training and domestic science departments were located centrally in the York Street School, and boys and girls in grades VI through VIII from the other city schools travelled to it for regular instruction in these special subjects. The following year the board organized its first classes for "backward" children – which would become, by the 1920s, "opportunity classes" in the lower grades and "pre-vocational classes" in the senior grades. In contrast to places like Winnipeg or Calgary, the Fredericton board did not run its own school health service, but this vital auxiliary service was provided by provincial and city authorities.

Agitation for vocational training had begun as early as 1913, and the board had established evening vocational classes for school-leavers in 1917, covering a variety of commercial and industrial subjects along with general education courses. Once the province had passed legislation to encourage the establishment of day vocational schools in 1919, the board began planning for this innovation. In the two or three years that followed, however, progress was delayed by opposition to the anticipated expenditure. Before the mid-1920s the only new feature in this respect was the introduction in the high school of a small-enrolment commercial course.

Fredericton High School, a long-established and academically distinguished institution, had been housed for decades as the senior department of the York Street School and, like similar institutions everywhere else, was under constant pressure from rising numbers.[15] Though there had been talk of a new high school for years, planning began in earnest in 1923 after a successful bond plebiscite, and by 1925 the school board's proudest boast was the near-completion of a new high school with twenty-three classrooms ("besides a boardroom and secretary's office"), a library, private rooms for principal and teachers, an assembly hall (with a stage) that would seat 750 (obviously built to serve the town as well as the school), and, under it, a gymnasium. Thirteen rooms were to be devoted "exclusively" to vocational education. By 1928 the new high school had an enrolment of 459 students, including 317 in the academic department and 76 in commercial. The vocational classes tagged along behind at a mere 17, but the school also offered a "pre-vocational program" (at one point described rather grandly as a junior high school), with an enrolment of 50 in grades VII and VIII, "designed for those who are handworkers, who must, at a comparatively early age, earn their own living." Initially the regular technical program was limited to two years, but by the mid-1930s, as numbers increased, the board was contemplating adding grade XI so that students could qualify for the engineering program at the University of New Brunswick.

Aside from the introduction of these various special courses and program innovations, there were the more mundane developments that character-ized other urban school systems. By the mid-1930s, for example, the board had at last supplied all schools with good pianos and was in the process of purchasing a 16 mm movie projector "together with a number of films illus-trative of travel and scientific subjects" that might be shared among the dif-ferent schools for instruction in history, geography, and science. A decade earlier it had bought a phonograph and records to be placed in the high school assembly hall as an aid to music instruction. There were music and sports competitions among the elementary schools and, at the high school, various extracurricular clubs, an orchestra and chorus, and the usual run of high school athletics. Given its size, Fredericton could hardly expect to match all the programs and services available to larger communities. But it was no laggard merely following where others led; rather, it was a partici-pant, from the beginning of the century, in fashioning the urban style in Canadian education.

The modernizing school systems of urban Canada were not without their problems. The momentum of urbanization meant that, despite all the build-ing and rebuilding, enrolment pressures were intense and overcrowding was ubiquitous at times. Winnipeg's enrolment stood at 7,500 in 1900 and 17,700 in 1910, and at its peak in 1931, it reached nearly 42,000; in 1900 the board owned sixteen buildings, and in 1931, sixty-eight.[16] In Calgary between 1911 and 1930 "the increase in the public schools was 220% and in the high schools 1,300%"; between 1925 and 1930 alone "93 rooms have been built, 28 of them for public school and 65 for high school use at a total cost including buildings, sites and equipment of $1,274,224."[17] Vancouver's school enrolment had risen from 4,600 in 1901 to nearly 20,000 in 1921, and the number of schools from eight to thirty-six; in 1919–20 the accom-modation crisis was so severe the board had to resort to opening "a num-ber of one-room cottage schools."[18] In 1913–14 Fredericton had opened

Smythe Street School, a building with six classrooms and an assembly hall, but by 1918 the school board reported that "the new and commodious Smythe Street building is already full, and we found it necessary ... to temporarily open a second department in the Assembly Hall and the school is thus deprived of a meeting place for all grades." During the following years, "so congested has become the classroom space, that we have found it necessary to appropriate a portion of each Assembly Hall in the city for classroom work." And continuing pressures forced the board to add annexes to both of its largest schools.[19] "As noted in previous reports for the last few years," wrote the chairman of the Halifax board in 1929, "attention has been drawn to the overcrowded conditions of the schools ... During the last year there were 26 classes on half-time. These classes represent 1,475 pupils, being 12% of the total attendance."[20] Half-time for some children was one expedient; others, all across the country, spent years learning in unsuitable rental accommodation, in badly dated annexes, or in classrooms converted out of auditoriums or school basements. (That modern curse, the school portable, had yet to be invented.)

The pressures were most extreme in the secondary schools. Writing in 1926, the editor of the ATA [Alberta Teachers' Association] Magazine would claim that overcrowding was a serious problem "in all the cities and larger centres of the Province ... we have arrived at the stage where there is not one really modern high school building in the Province; school boards are at their wit's end to provide sitting room for students even with the 'bee-hive' adjuncts to the larger buildings; high school principals are driven frantic in their endeavours to distribute the students over the classes and apportion them to teachers; and the teachers have a class load at least fifty per cent higher than it should be if justice is to be done to the student."[21] The sharp increase in secondary enrolments during the Depression made matters worse. Many boards were desperate, asserted Ontario's minister of education in 1932, "to discover where they are going to house their pupils. Two methods have been favoured. First, the rotary plan, by which all the accommodations of the school are used to their utmost capacity every period of the day – the classes move from room to room, the science laboratories, the assembly hall, the gymnasium, are in use all the time ... Second, the so-called 'staggered' classes ... This plan has been adopted with good results in the Central Collegiate in London, and is to be tried in the Sudbury High and Vocational School next year, where it is expected that accommodation sufficient for about 700 students will, by lengthening the school day and shortening the noon recess, be sufficient for the expected enrolment of 1,000."[22]

Individual classrooms, indeed, were jam-packed throughout the period. Commenting in 1914 on recent changes in school architecture, an article in *The School* claimed that "where 15 years ago it was not uncommon to find as many as 60 pupils per teacher the number today is from 40 to 50."[23] In 1917 the average number of elementary pupils per teacher in Ottawa and Hamilton was 46, in London 45, and for all of Ontario's cities 47.[24] In 1920 the pupil-teacher ratio in Toronto's kindergarten classes, "where the work takes the form of play," was 30:1, but in the primary classes, "where the important subjects of reading, writing and formal number work are begun," it was 52.[25] In the mid-1930s Winnipeg's regular classes averaged 44 students in grades I to VI (though half that in its auxiliary classes); the high school average for compulsory subjects like English was 40 in grade X and 39 in grade XI.[26] In 1929 Vancouver averaged 37 per class in its elementary and junior high schools and 34 in its senior highs.[27] That same year Edmonton had a total of 110 high school classes: all had over 40 pupils and 58 had enrolments between 45 and 68.[28] In 1909 Glace Bay, according to its superintendent of schools, James Bingay, averaged 65 pupils to a teacher, but since pupils attended school in their own part of town, "even when the best arrangement possible was made, there were many departments in the most populous districts which were grossly overcrowded – where the teacher had, not 65 pupils, but 70, 80 and in two cases over 100." A more even distribution and new school buildings kept the average in 1930 at 48; Bingay thought this was still too high, though he was prepared to settle for something between 40 and 45.[29] In 1929 there were on average 50 pupils in Truro's 26 classrooms.[30] In the early 1930s the average pupil-teacher ratio in Fredericton's high school was 39:1, and in its elementary schools, 33.5; Saint John's average for elementary schools was 37:1 and Moncton's, 40:2.[31] In 1914 London's average class size stood at 43 (though nine of its twenty-three schools were above that). In the 1920s the board was able to maintain average class sizes around 35 or 36 (though there were particular schools where the average was 50 or more). By 1939, however, the figure had risen back into the mid-40s.[32]

While the pressure of numbers created plenty of problems, it was not all bad news. Throughout the first three decades of the century (and even occasionally in the 1930s), new schools had to be built, and as previous paragraphs suggest, many boards took advantage of the opportunity to construct buildings that incorporated the newest designs and provided for a wide variety of pedagogical innovations. This was true, moreover, not just of the largest communities but of smaller towns and cities as well.[33] But school plant that was on the cutting edge in 1900 or even 1920 could also be found old-fashioned and dated two or three decades later. Moreover, the Depression, and even more so the Second World War, severely restricted both new construction and renovation. As a result, school buildings were generally in much worse shape in the late 1940s than they had been twenty or thirty years earlier. By 1939 the Winnipeg board was already complaining about the unduly high cost of maintaining and heating its older buildings.[34] And a decade later a report commissioned by the board was highly critical of most of its older schools, declaring some to be beyond repair and others to be badly lit and inadequate across a range of basics, from plumbing to classroom equipment. Altogether, the report concluded, "teachers cannot fully compensate for the sub-standard learning environment of outmoded school buildings, restricted school grounds and antiquated equipment."[35]

Winnipeg was not alone in this; similar assessments applied in other cities and towns as well. Between the turn of the century and the 1940s, nonetheless, there was a common pattern and a distinctively urban style among the schools of Canada's cities and larger towns; whatever the differences, there were shared criteria that identified "the good school" and the "good school system."

But what about the nation's far more numerous small towns and villages – urban centres with populations of a few hundred, or two or three thousand? Blairmore, Alberta, was one of a series of small communities, mainly dependent on the coal-mining industry, that stretched across the Crowsnest Pass from the Alberta foothills to Fernie in British Columbia. First settled at the turn of the twentieth century, Blairmore had a population of 1,100 by the time of the 1911 census, stood at just over 1,500 in 1921 and, at its peak in 1941, at just over 1,700.[36] Its first school was a log cabin, quickly replaced by a more substantial one-room schoolhouse that remained in use until 1923.[37] In 1908 a new two-room frame building was erected, and with an extension added in 1923, it was termed "the Main School" throughout its history (which lasted down to 1960). In the early 1920s the local coal company built and leased to the school board a two-room annex intended to serve the smaller children of "West Blairmore," an area close to the mine and a fair distance from the Main School. It too had a modest extension added in the 1920s. Both buildings had indoor plumbing (we know this only because, as the school board minutes noted, the pipes froze up now and then in winter). From 1922 both were lit, like the town, by hydroelectric power. Sporadically pressed for accommodation, the school board usually had at least one and sometimes two or three additional classrooms rented in private commercial buildings, the "Presbyterian Church Mission," the "United Church Hall," or the "Miners' Union Hall." In the early 1920s the board also had to build a classroom in the main building's basement (which was subject to recurrent flooding). Altogether, during the interwar years, the board had at its disposal somewhere between nine and thirteen or fourteen classrooms that had to accommodate both elementary and high school grades. The school had no auditorium or gymnasium. In 1920 Blairmore's school enrolment stood at about 330; between the mid-1920s and the mid-1940s it oscillated from a peak of 500 in 1925 to just over 300 in 1945, but generally the school accommodated 350 to 450 children.

The board's budget was $31,000 in 1924; a decade later it was just about the same.[38] The five trustees ran their operation in a "hands-on" fashion with very little additional assistance beyond a secretary-treasurer and a truant officer, both part-time. Academic leadership, such as it was, fell to the principal, who, until the mid-twenties, had no release time for supervision. In most years the school operated with nine teachers for the public school grades, usually eight in the Main School along with an additional primary teacher in the west annex.

While Blairmore didn't experience pressure from overall enrolment growth, the oscillation in numbers caused constant log-jams as cohorts of different sizes passed through the elementary grades. In 1920, for example, there were 41 pupils in grade I and 46 in grade IV but only 37 in a combined class of grades V and VI; in 1925 there were 52 in grade VIII and 57 in grade IV but only 25 in the primary class at the Main School (though a combined class in the west annex had 37 in grades I and II). Year after year the board shuffled its teachers and pupils around, rented an additional classroom, or created "split classes" (two grades in one room) to try to cope with the "congestion" in this or that classroom. What it didn't do was hire additional teachers. The number of elementary school teachers stayed stable across the entire period. The only significant expansion in the staff – from a single teacher (the principal) to two, three, and then four – occurred at the high school level, where provincial inspectors were making it clear that the high school department had to be improved or else. Nor could the trustees simply drop the high school department; they themselves, like public sentiment in general, held that a town of Blairmore's size had to have a high school and preferably one that not only covered grades IX to XI but grade XII as well.

One problem the Blairmore board faced, in common with most other small urban communities, was a limited tax base. The town had to raise its school and municipal revenues from just under 800 ratepayers, and "extravagance" was something neither the board nor the ratepayers took lightly. The board was also constrained by the instability of the coal-mining industry. According to the local newspaper in 1925, "the majority of ratepayers of the district are members of the miners' union," and the industry was in constant crisis during the interwar years. High rates of unemployment were frequent and destitution among some miners' families recurrent – not just during the depression of the 1930s but in the mid-twenties as well.[39] The board also ran into bad luck: the 1923 extension to the Main School cost $7,000, and the money to pay for it was invested in the Home Bank, which collapsed that same year.[40] The board had to beg a loan from the Alberta Department of Education to cover its debts and pay it off at 6% interest in the years that followed.

Within these constraints, nonetheless, the teachers in the elementary grades seem to have functioned in a tolerably effective manner. The board kept a close eye on pupil progress through monthly reports from the principal and its own visitations, and had occasion only twice in twenty years to fire a teacher for what it deemed incompetence. During the 1920s and early 1930s the few surviving reports by provincial elementary school inspectors (as opposed to those of the high school inspector) were generally modestly favourable about the quality of teaching in the core subjects, the general organization of the school, and the state of the buildings.[41]

What didn't get taught were the "extras." Music, according to one inspector in the mid-1920s, was badly neglected, as was physical training. The latter couldn't be done in the classrooms and the weather was hardly conducive to regular classes in the playground. Between 1916 and 1925 the school had a cadet corps but cancelled it after a student was accidentally shot in the hand. There appears to have been little in the way of organized sports or other group activities, though this may not have mattered much, since the Crowsnest Pass towns, individually and collectively, had no shortage of organized youth and adult activities ranging from a major annual music festival to church-run scouts, guides, and a variety of field days and sports teams, organized, among others, by the miners' unions.

The school board did what it could on matters it considered within its fiscal capacity. In the 1920s it made modest purchases of equipment for physical training in the playground. In 1926 it bought "the new volumes of the Encyclopedia Britannica ... so as to bring our present library up to date. The same to cost no more than $49.50." But so far as we can see, the board made few additional book purchases for the library. In the late twenties, under pressure from the inspector and principal, it considered investing in supplementary readers but apparently failed to take action in the matter. In late 1932 and early 1933 the trustees debated the purchase of a piano but abandoned the idea: while its acquisition was considered of great value, "the question of finance for the present was a serious one in the opinion of all." The introduction of manual training and domestic science, or vocational and commercial subjects for high school pupils, was not even bruited. Nor was there any provision for individual differences or special needs. Reporting on the grade III class of 1934, the principal noted that six of its thirty-seven pupils were "repeaters." Twelve pupils "rank very good, 16 average and 9 slow. Of the slow ones 2 are subnormal, one has a fair concept of number but has failed entirely to make any progress in English. The other is able to read somewhat painfully but shows no number appreciation. Besides the 37 enrolled, there is also ... a boy who is almost totally blind. He attends fairly regularly at times and is then absent. When there was some hope of him being removed I advised Miss North not to enter his name on the register. It is tragic for the boy, the teacher, and the pupils that we have no other way of handling a case such as this. School must be a perfect prison for the boy."

During the interwar years the Main School was sometimes used for evening classes; mostly these were funded by the department of education's Technical Education Branch and student fees, the board being "willing to supply housing, light and fuel but no other expense." Enrolments were small enough that in some years classes were cancelled altogether, and in 1940 the board decided "not to carry on night classes for adults"; to mid-century there is no evidence that they were resumed.

In the 1920s a majority of the trustees resisted proposals to supply texts and supplies (scribblers, pencils, and the like) free to all pupils, but they did pay for these (along with grade VIII examination fees) for orphans, widows' children, and, early in the Depression, the children of those on relief. Beginning in 1933, however, they began to cover the costs, for all pupils, of texts and supplies through grade VIII, and in 1937, to grade IX. Health services were sporadic. In 1924 the trustees had imported the Calgary board's eye doctor to examine the entire school and to fit glasses for those who needed them – at a total cost of nearly $500, the equivalent of half the annual salary of one of the junior teachers. The same year there was a thorough-going medical and dental inspection, but during the rest of the decade not much beyond that. Initial decisions about medical matters were left to the staff. In 1930 the board interviewed a local doctor concerning medical supervision in the school: "among the other suggestions made by the Doctor was one that every teacher report to the Doctor any noticeable physical defect in a pupil." Occasional entries of modest payments for doctors' fees suggest that the board was paying for medical services in emergencies or where parents couldn't bear the cost themselves. This began to change only in the mid-thirties. In 1935 an annual contract was struck with a local dentist to provide regular dental examinations and treatments for those who needed them.[42] At about the same time the town council and the school board apparently began to share the salary of a district health nurse, and she continued regular medical inspections until she resigned in 1948; board and council jointly decided not to replace her. In 1946 the trustees also decided "that all dental services by the board be discontinued except in necessitous circumstances."

Though the Blairmore school was judged a tolerably good village school in the twenties and early thirties, serious shortcomings in its program of studies began to arise in the late 1930s when the Alberta Department of Education mandated a new pedagogy that emphasized activity methods and a reorganization of grades VII to IX (the Intermediate Division) that required a broader range of subjects as well as the availability of options. The school board did its best. Under pressure from both principal and inspector, it began the purchase of some necessary equipment, supplementary texts, and reference books. But it needed constant prodding. In the early 1940s an inspector would comment that "Blairmore school is singularly lacking in the equipment recognized as essential to the new activity program. Each room should have at least one long work table and a few chairs. The junior rooms need sand tables. Most schools of this size have completely equipped the primary rooms with tables and chairs. There is also an urgent need for [classroom] reference libraries."[43] The principal likewise made reiterated calls for reference materials. "This is the only school in the Pass," he remarked on one occasion, "that has not made progress in placing these tools within reach of teachers and pupils." Otherwise, he went on, the teachers could not carry out the Intermediate program and, he warned, the department of education "will not approve of this kind of work."[44]

To give some substance to organized music instruction, the board finally bought a piano and shared the costs of a specialist teacher with the nearby town of Coleman. It added a teacher to the high school department, which enabled it to improve instruction in art and introduce "Junior Business" in grade IX. Investigating the costs of introducing manual training and domestic science, it quailed initially at the estimates, but by 1939 it was sharing the salary of a teacher for each subject with Coleman. A basement room in the Main School was fitted up (after a fashion) for domestic science, and the boys were sent off for manual training for a half-day a week to Coleman, which had already set up a well-equipped manual training room.[45] By 1940, probably because the war brought renewed optimism about the future of the local economy, the trustees took the plunge and committed themselves to building an annex on the grounds of the Main School to house properly equipped classrooms for manual training and domestic science. Then came a second stroke of bad luck: in early 1941, the new building, costing $14,000 and virtually completed, including the installation of the necessary equipment, burned to the ground. To make matters worse, it had been inadequately covered by builders' insurance, so the board couldn't even recoup its losses. Briefly, domestic science continued to be taught in the school basement and the boys resumed their trek to Coleman. But in the immediate postwar years, at least, neither subject was being offered to Blairmore's young people.[46]

So by mid-century the Blairmore school looked rather as it had in the early 1920s, teaching the core academic subjects without some of the extras that officialdom had increasingly come to see as *de rigueur* for the good

school and lacking the kind of auxiliary services for health or special education that had become the norm in larger communities. Children, indeed,
still went to school in the same two buildings, now increasingly decrepit.[47]
Worse still, after a temporary respite in the late 1930s and early 1940s, the
problems of serious overcrowding emerged once more as Blairmore began
to experience its version of the postwar baby boom.[48] Said the board chairman at the annual ratepayers meeting in early 1948, "[A]ll realised the need
for a new school. Start should be made this year [though] the estimated
cost of a one storey, brick building would be $210,000. Present building
should be condemned." But Blairmore's problems were not unique: they
were mostly shared by other communities in the Pass. And, as department
officials were wont to point out, the real solution was not just a new building
or a few more teachers to relieve overcrowding, but a general reorganization of education in the Pass that would provide a modern education for its
children and young people.[49]

We are not claiming that this review of the Blairmore school, in its particularities, can adequately represent all the circumstances and experience
in villages and small towns across Canada. Even aside from unusual bad
luck, the nation's small communities were far too diverse to be captured in
one case study. Yet we will go on to argue in other chapters that there was
much common ground as well: in the difficulties of sustaining good schools
with a limited tax base; in the consequent limits to introducing a broader
range of subjects in the elementary schools; in the strains imposed by the
state of the Canadian economy during the period; and in the difficulties,
above all, in meeting the growing demand for secondary education. What
the Blairmore story points to, at the very least, is the widening gap between
schooling in Canada's larger and smaller urban communities. Even in the
late nineteenth century there was indisputable difference between the two;
but as the 3 Rs and a primarily academic focus ceased to be taken as the
natural limits of the curriculum and as the school took on a growing variety
of ancillary services – services, indeed, increasingly seen not as ancillary
but as essential to the task – the small-town school fell further and further
behind the big-city models of what a modern school system should be.

II

Consider now, by way of contrast to Winnipeg, Fredericton, or even
Blairmore, Saskatchewan's Kipp School District No. 1589. Situated halfway
between Saskatoon and Regina, Kipp's one-room school, overseen by its
three trustees, was in a prosperous farming community not far from the
village of Davidson. The total budget in the late 1920s was something over
$1,200, most of which was spent on the teacher's salary.[50] The trustees held

four meetings each year. The entire business for 1929–30 included setting
the levy on property taxes to support the school; hiring a new teacher when
the previous teacher resigned in June 1929; insuring the piano; purchasing
six new desks; joining the school fire insurance pool; and putting out ten-
ders for cleaning the building four times a year, hauling coal and wood, and
painting the school floor. The school already had one of the more modern
types of school stoves, and the major innovation in 1929–30 was to spend
$250 to replace the outdoor privies with indoor toilets, installed within an
addition to the entry porch. "These were of the non-flush type, which had
underground tanks containing chemicals, and had to be pumped out about
twice a year."

The Kipp trustees employed one teacher, normally a woman, but from
1929 to 1931 it happened to be a young man. He taught all the children in
the school district all the subjects prescribed by the provincial curriculum,
from grades I through VIII. Except for the occasional visit by the provincial
inspector, the teacher had no professional colleagues and no supervision
or support. The school offered no special services, either to enrich the curriculum or to provide for individual differences. If a pupil wished to pursue
a high school education, he or she would have to travel to the nearest town
or village high school, which was, as likely as not, a modest two- or three-
teacher school, and she would have to provide her own accommodation.
Occasionally, a parent would request that the Kipp teacher guide a boy
or girl through one or two of the high school grades. There were no such
pupils in 1929–30. But in 1925, when there were only "6 pupils between
Grades 1 to 8," the trustees agreed "to ask the teacher to teach Grade IX
also" and at a second meeting agreed "to give the teacher a bonus of $50"
for that additional task. In 1932, however, "parents of a girl applied to [the
school] board to have her take Grade XI at the school with use of correspondence course, teacher to correct papers. Board decided against putting any responsibility on our teacher. No teacher could be expected to do
this satisfactorily, and the lower grades would be neglected. Desk room only
was offered this pupil."

Just how many schools like Kipp were there in early twentieth-century
Canada? How many children attended them? And what was the physical
plant like? We begin with the numbers and then turn to the physical infrastructure itself. Finally, in this chapter, we survey the provision for secondary education outside of Canada's larger cities and towns.

Until at least mid-century, the one-room school was, by far, the most common type of school building in Canada. There was good reason for this.
Most rural children walked to school, rode their ponies, or were driven by
a family member in a horse-drawn carriage or wagon. Though reality often

intervened, the ideal maximum distance children were expected to travel in eastern Canada tended to be set at two miles; in the Prairie provinces, where farms were larger, distances might be greater. In 1941, for example, fourteen children attended the one-room school at Alberta's Chipman Creek: three lived within a quarter-mile of the schoolhouse; seven more had to travel between two and two-and-a-half miles; three children, three miles; and one, four miles.[51]

Since schools had to be physically accessible, there was a high density of school buildings everywhere in rural Canada. In 1920, 2,584 out of a total of 2,826 Alberta schools – or 91.6% – were "one-department" schools.[52] One-room schools in 1923 comprised 79% or more of the school buildings in six provinces, and the national average was nearly 84%.[53] As late as 1944 there were, in Ontario, 6,847 elementary schools, of which 5,081, or 74%, had but a single classroom.[54] Tallying the number of one-room schools does not provide a total count of all rural school facilities. Many two-room schools, established in hamlets or small villages, were also classed as rural.[55] But the main vehicle for rural education was the one-room, one-teacher school. The sheer number of these schools compared to the number of graded schools is nicely illustrated by a map of Alberta in 1931 (Figure 4.1).[56]

While something like 80% of the schools were one-room buildings in 1923, only 43% of Canadian children were enrolled in rural schools (see Table 4.1). Even at that time, the effects of urbanization, and in some provinces of rural depopulation, were obvious. As one Ontario report put it, "the exodus from the country communities is reflected in the attrition in the rural schools. In 1903, of all pupils attending the elementary schools, 58% were in the rural schools and 42% in the urban schools. In 1920, the figures were practically reversed, 40% of the pupils being rural and 60% urban."[57] Much the same was true of New Brunswick. In 1910, 58% of enrolments were in ungraded schools, but by 1930 that had fallen to 46%.[58] By 1923, in Ontario and Nova Scotia about a third of total enrolments were classified as rural, in four other provinces the percentage was somewhere in the forties; in Prince Edward Island and Saskatchewan the majority of enrolments were in rural schools. By the early 1920s, then, children who attended rural schools constituted a minority of Canadian pupils. But that minority was large. In several provinces the percentage approached nearly half of all pupils or constituted an outright majority. And this pattern changed only modestly through to the end of the Second World War. In 1945, 51% of Alberta's pupils were still educated in rural schools.[59] Even in Ontario, the numbers in ungraded schools remained substantial, at close to 30%.[60]

Fig. 4.1   Map: Alberta schools, 1931

We noted earlier in the chapter that urban schools tended to have large numbers of children in each classroom. What of the rural schools? In 1938 the DBS produced its first national frequency distribution of enrolments in one-room schools. Canada had at that point approximately 2,000 one-room schools with fewer than 10 pupils, and 800 with 35 or more (see Table 4.2). Fifty-nine per cent of Ontario's one-room schools had fewer than 20 pupils, a figure that was roughly approximated across much of the country.[61] In their close study of one rural region in north-central British Columbia, Paul Stortz and J.D. Wilson sum up class size in the 1920s this way: "In general, the district's one-room schools were tiny, individual entities. In the 1920s, the average [enrolment] was 13.6 students, one-quarter less than the mean enrolment of all other assisted schools in the province and just over one-half (51.2%) of the average class size of all rural and assisted schools. Moreover, between 1920 and 1930, the one-room schools in the district lost students. The average school enrolment in 1919 was 16.7 pupils; in 1921, 15.9 pupils. The enrolment fluctuated for five years until 1927, when

Table 4.1
Rural and urban enrolments, 1923

| | Rural | | Urban | | Total |
	N	%	N	%	N
PEI	11,132	62.7	6,610	37.3	17,742
NS	40,892	35.7	73,566	64.3	114,458
NB	34,588	47.6	38,084	52.4	72,672
ON	241,086	36.4	420,734	63.6	661,820
MB	70,492	49.5	71,877	50.5	142,369
SK	111,474	57.4	82,839	42.6	194,313
AB	67,760	45.7	80,315	54.3	148,045
BC	44,494	46.9	50,394	53.1	94,888
Total, 8 provinces	621,888	43.0	824,419	57.0	1,446,307

Source: DBS, *Annual Survey 1923*, 53.

Table 4.2
Enrolments in one-room schools, 1936–1937

	N and % with under 10 pupils	N and % with 10–19 pupils	N and % with 35+ pupils	Total N schools	Median enrolments
Prince Edward Island	57	220	5	409	16.57
	13.9%	53.8%	1.2%		
New Brunswick	247	501	182	1,358	18.66
	18.2%	36.9%	13.4%		
Ontario	680	2,438	260	5,269	18.12
	12.9%	46.3%	4.9%		
Manitoba	214	601	114	1,406	18.07
	15.2%	42.7%	8.1%		
Saskatchewan	584	1,923	239	4,227	17.95
	13.8%	45.5%	5.7%		
British Columbia	230	276		601	11.88
	38.3%	45.9%			
Canada	2,012	5,959	800	13,270	
	15.2%	44.9%	6.0%	100%	

Note: Schools with "unspecified" class size were excluded.

Source: DBS, *The Size Factor in One-Room Schools*, 2, 6–7 (Table 2).

an average school size was 13.9 pupils, and then steadily declined to the 1930 figure of 12.8."[62] In 1920 Alberta's High River Inspectorate included 84 school districts; 40% had 10 pupils or less enrolled. Two decades later the Pincher Creek School Division, which consisted of thirty-five one-room schools and one with two rooms, had an average attendance for all schools in the division of 11.8.[63] In 1922, 55.3% of Ontario's one-room schools had an average attendance of fewer than 20 pupils, and 13% had an average of fewer than 10. Nearly a third of all the rural schools had an average attendance of fewer than 15.[64] In 1928 some 46% of Nova Scotia's rural schools had between 20 and 39 pupils; but nearly as great a percentage, 36%, had fewer than 20, and the average enrolment in these schools was 13.4, while the average daily attendance was 9. At the other extreme, nearly 20% had enrolments of 40 pupils or more.[65]

Four conclusions follow from the last few paragraphs. First, until at least mid-century, the prototypical rural school was an ungraded one-room building. Second, a substantial minority of Canadian children attended such schools and the number increases if we include the rural two-room schools. Third, there was a wide range in enrolments in individual schools, including some with only a handful of pupils and others where large numbers were present. Finally, there was an overriding disparity between the size of city school systems and the rural school district. Nova Scotia's superintendent of education produced tables for 1920 which, among other things, recorded enrolments in the city of Halifax of 11,000 pupils; he contrasted that to the two-teacher school in Middle Musquodoboit with 64 pupils and to another Halifax County school with one teacher and 74 pupils. Grade III teachers in the city taught some 2,000 pupils in grade III and taught only that grade. In Middle Musquodoboit there were just three grade III pupils that year, but the teacher in the junior department had to teach 28 other pupils spread across grades I through V. In the second rural school there were 17 grade III pupils; that left the teacher with 57 others, stretching through grades I to VIII.[66]

In 1951 *Maclean's Magazine* published an article provocatively titled "The Shacks We Call Schools." "We're so busy boasting about the handful of new schools we've built since the war," the subheading proclaimed, "that we forget about the thousands which have no lights, no indoor toilets, no drinking fountains, no maps and no libraries. Experts quote figures to prove that these primitive conditions threaten to make a mockery of modern education." In the body of the piece, the author wrote of "the thousands of Canadian schools [that] are dilapidated, dungeon-like, draughty, ill-furnished shacks that no progressive farmer would keep his milk herd in." Inadequate urban schools received their share of attention, but most of the opprobrium was heaped upon the one-room school.[67] Across the first half of the twentieth century it's not hard to find similar jeremiads about the state of the physical plant.[68] Nor is it hard to find more generous interpretations, often written in the fond afterglow that followed the demise of the one-room school. To what extent is either view a judicious assessment? The answer is "sometimes." Or, "it all depends." The quality of the rural school varied depending on the amount of taxable land that ratepayers in the school district possessed, which defined the fiscal resources available to the local school district; on the age of the building, often determined by whether or not the local child population was growing or shrinking; on the number of bachelors and elderly ratepayers in the school district versus the number of those with young families; on the particular region within any given province; on the particular moment in time (the physical plant in rural Canada, like its urban counterpart, was probably in better shape in 1929 than it was in 1945); and on a lot of other considerations besides.

In the settled countryside or anywhere a modest degree of prosperity had been achieved in rural Canada, the first generation of crude log school buildings had been abandoned – in the older provinces, often well before 1920. By then, for example, Ontario had only 120 log schoolhouses left, nearly all of them in isolated parts of northern Ontario; the vast majority of one-room schools in the province were brick or frame.[69] Across the country the quality of the building depended largely on what local trustees and ratepayers felt they could afford. As Harold Foght found in his survey of Saskatchewan schools in 1918, there were "schools of every degree of variation from the best architectural model, set in large well-fenced grounds, to small insanitary structures in bleak, neglected fence corners."[70] In a questionnaire sent a few years earlier to a broad sample of school inspectors across Canada, James Miller got a similar response: the school buildings and facilities ranged from excellent to wholly unsatisfactory.[71]

In 1937 the Alberta inspector responsible for the Camrose district drafted a composite portrait of "the average school" in the area, based on the written responses of his teachers to a questionnaire covering buildings, equipment, supplies, and other features of each school.

> The average school in the Camrose Inspectorate is a one-room frame building, without a basement, in a reasonably good state of repair, painted white, standing in a two-acre plot which is clear of weeds, underbrush, and rubbish. The yard is surrounded by a smooth wire fence and there is a good gate. There are a few trees, probably native, but no shrubbery. There is no flagpole.
>
> There is a barn holding eight horses ... The toilets are outdoor. No chemical is used and no toilet paper is supplied. There is a ball diamond, and one, but not more than two, of the following: swings, teeters, basketball ground, sand box, volleyball court.
>
> The building was built in 1908 and has not been remodelled. There are windows on both sides of the building. No windows are screened and there are no storm windows.
>
> There will be foot scrapers on the platform at the entry. There will be shelves for lunch pails, a washstand, a wash basin, individual towels

provided by the pupils, but no mirror. The water, carried from a neighbour's well, will be contained in a water pail.

The classroom is 28" x 12" with a good floor. No sweeping compound is used. Ordinary brooms are used for sweeping. The room is heated by a stove, surrounded by a metal screen. The blackboard is of Hyloplate, and is in fairly good condition. There are no book shelves along the walls, no magazine racks, and no bulletin boards. Cupboard space is limited.

The desks are single desks fastened to strips. There is a desk and chair for the teacher, but no chair for the visitor. There is a sand table or a work table. No hot lunch equipment is provided, but there is the minimum equipment for the teaching of General Science. This is kept in a locked cupboard.

The chances are even that there will be no framed pictures. There is a flag, but no waste basket, clock, telephone, or thermometer. There is a pencil sharpener and a handbell, but no fire extinguisher, no first aid equipment, no hectograph, no printing press, no lamp, no set of measures, no blackboard compasses, no blackboard set-square, no music ruler. There is a yard stick.

There is a dictionary and perhaps an encyclopedia. There will be a globe, usually old. There is no health chart, no physiology chart, no bird chart, no primary reading charts. Plasticine and scissors are provided. There are no building blocks.

There is an organ, a gramophone, or a piano.

There are maps of Alberta, Canada, the World, and North America, and two of the following: Europe, South America, Asia, British Isles, Africa, Australia.

There are 135 books in the library – 27 suitable for Division I, 43 suitable for Division II, 38 suitable for Division III, and 27 unsuitable for the pupils.

There are 22 pupils distributed among eight grades, one of which may be Grade IX.[72]

From the other side of the country comes this description, provided by one Nova Scotia woman who taught in several one-room schools between 1936 and 1941:

In most cases the country one-room school was approximately 20 feet by 30 feet. The entrance was divided into two porches, one for the girls, and one for the boys. In the centre of the room there was a rectangular box-type cast iron stove (wood-burning). Attached to the back of the

school room there was a shed with a slanted roof. This is where the
wood was stored for the winter months ... out back there were two small
buildings commonly called "outhouses" – one for the girls and one
for the boys ... Most schools had two rows of seats on either side of the
stove. Each seat or desk accommodated two pupils. These desks were
on metal frames which were fastened to the floor with screws. Under
the top of the desk was a divided compartment where the pupils kept
their scribblers, books, pencil boxes, etc. ... As there was no electricity,
the school room had three large windows on two opposite sides. The
blackboards were between the windows and were just ordinary boards
painted black. The cross-lighting caused a glare which made it difficult
for the pupils to copy assignments for the next day, for the younger
ones to see their math questions, or any other work that was taught
from the board.[73]

Even in well-established rural communities, pupils or teachers could
encounter extremes. Norman High prefaced a Cornell doctoral thesis
on educational provision in rural Haldimand County, Ontario, with this
explanation of the origins of his interest in Ontario rural schools. He had
been a pupil in a two-room rural school outside of Beamsville and then at
Beamsville High School; after attending Hamilton Normal School, he had
taught for three or four years in a one-room school in Pelham Township, an
old and prosperous part of the Niagara Peninsula. His elementary education, he wrote, took place

in an area characterized by resources sufficient to support a reasonably enriched school learning environment. That is, the elementary
school had a well-stocked library, a school shop, hot lunches during the
winter, gardens, spacious landscaped grounds, community auditorium
and a museum. The high school, although not so varied and complete, did compare favourably with the elementary school in plant and
programme.

  In the second instance, an entirely different situation existed. Here
was a school with double seats and desks, traditional platform at the
front of the room, small bookcase, narrow windows, crowded classroom, meagre antiquated equipment and small inadequate grounds.
Community resources were by no means negligible but had not been
used to extend and enrich the school programme. The teacher's
outlook wavered from one of discouragement coincident with the
professional isolation and material handicaps of the situation to one of
inspiration that came from meeting the challenge of a difficult task.[74]

As High's comment suggests, bucolic settings did not ensure adequate playgrounds. Whereas Winnipeg and other urban communities usually made provision for large playgrounds, rural schools were often carved out of some portion of a farmer's field, and a none-too-generous portion at that. Commenting on the situation in Annapolis County, Nova Scotia, the local inspector complained that "most of the school buildings are built on grounds that do not give the children opportunity to engage in organized games. No doubt this is true throughout the province ... In many sections if the children wish to play ball they must use the public highway. This condition needs remedying. Children should have opportunity to play and to play in safety. Some sections are enlarging their grounds by lease or purchase. Other sections where conditions are the worst, stubbornly oppose the recommendation of the inspector and district board and refuse to provide proper playgrounds."[75] The sheer volume of reminiscences or contemporary accounts by teachers or pupils gives some ground to think that these quotations present a roughly typical picture of the physical plant in Canada during the interwar years, wherever there were stable rural communities.[76]

In those parts of the country that are better described as frontier regions, or in isolated and poor settlements, some new but some not, conditions were much more variable. Good modern schools, often urban in size and quality, might be found in very isolated company towns located on the resource frontier, often built and sometimes maintained by the company itself.[77] But that was unusual. Indeed, the "school" might not be a building at all, at least in the conventional sense. In 1919 J.B. McDougall recalled his experiences as the school inspector for "New Ontario" during the first decade of the century, organizing schooling for the children in lumber, mining, and railway construction camps across northern Ontario. "The accommodation," he wrote,

was of a most primitive kind. Sometimes an unused camp-building might be available, but in the early stages there is rarely a surplus of these. At times, it was a box-car shunted to a temporary siding at the end of steel or at some wayside gravel-pit. The latter is the usual shelter at a Construction camp, for the school must shift with the camp, and be literally a "school on wheels." Usually it is a tent, and it harmonizes well with the mushroom growth of tents and "shacks" about it. Securely poled and staked it forms a safe and comfortable shelter against wind and weather.

The interior equipment is of the same simple type – home-made benches hewn from the native spruce, and with the skill only such axe-men can muster, a table of similar material and make, about which the children and adult learners gather when they wish to write, etc., a hylo-plate blackboard hung on a home-made easel or attached to the main centre-pole, a stand of books supplied from the Travelling Library branch of the Department of Education, and smaller equipment such as school text books, maps, brushes, chalk, etc.[78]

On British Columbia's coast there were "floating schools" – a cabin that, along with other small buildings, floated on a raft of logs to accommodate a logging camp where the shoreline was too steep to place it on terra firma. When the time came to move on, the "school" along with the rest of the camp was simply towed to a new location up or down the coast.[79] "A school was again maintained on Seal Island during the fishing season," one Nova Scotia inspector reported in 1931. "The teacher ... conducts a school in her own house for twenty children (all of whom are temporary residents from Cape Sable Island sections) during four months."[80] Between the mid-1920s and the late 1940s, the Ontario government maintained, in northern Ontario, a small fleet of railway cars equipped as classrooms – better equipped than many of the country's rural schools – that travelled regular circuits, gathering in, for a few days at a time, small groups of children from isolated homes and camps.[81]

More conventionally, however, schoolhouses were established and maintained in whatever kind of building was available or constructed in whatever manner local people could afford. "There being no school-building" in 1909 when the school board of The Pas was first organized, "school was taught in various places, such as Halcrow's pool-room ... and the old Hudson Bay Company Store."[82] As late as 1946 the Alberta Teachers' Association would complain that "in [school] Divisions North and West of Edmonton, at least 5,000 children are attending school in log buildings which outrage all present ideas of decent living conditions, which are a menace to the health of teachers and pupils and a disgrace to the province of Alberta."[83] A decade earlier, a school inspector arrived in British Columbia's Peace River district to find schools

of the crudest possible structure – usually built of logs – consisting of four bare walls with no ceiling, no ventilation except through doors and windows, and no heating apparatus except an unjacketed stove which provided excessive warmth in some parts of the room and insufficient warmth in others. There were no blinds and in most cases it was impossible to open the windows. The blackboards usually consisted of painted beaver-board, or in some instances, just plain tarpaper. There were no cloakrooms and the back of the room was used as a storage place for coats, hats, rubbers and surplus stove-wood. No screen doors or windows were provided. For this reason one was usually unable to see across the classroom during the mosquito season, because of the smoke from the smudge that was used to keep out the mosquitoes.

Toilet facilities were of the worst imaginable kind. In the winter the children were forced to use open toilets in temperatures of thirty or forty degrees below zero; in the summer, the open toilets provided a gathering place for all the flies and mosquitoes of the neighbourhood. No toilet paper was supplied, and it was usual to find in place of this a Simpson's or an Eaton's catalogue.

Drinking water was in almost every case provided by the melting of snow during the winter and from unsanitary scoop-outs in the summer.

In all schools there was a general scarcity of equipment. In most schools there were few supplementary text-books, and the reading library usually consisted of two or three battered or obsolete novels that were unfit for juveniles to use. In the majority of schools no playground equipment was supplied, and no attempt was made to provide for extra-curricular activities.

In many of the school districts no barns were supplied for the horses which the pupils rode to school, with the consequence that the horses had to be tied to the school fence, or allowed to wander at will around the school-yard.[84]

Conditions on the frontiers of settlement might be worse, sometimes far worse, than in well-established rural communities, but the gap between urban and rural schools was apparent everywhere. When, in 1942, the Ontario government carried out a province-wide assessment of its school facilities, it didn't even attempt to rate urban and rural schools on the same scale, and the sheer gap in what officials considered to be pertinent mea-sures of quality is testimony to the abyss that separated the two kinds of schools. The contrast is evident in the graph the department of education provided to illustrate the differences (Figure 4.2). The same graph, more-over, provides insight into the material conditions in Ontario's rural public schools: 20% lacked a safe water supply; 50% lacked inside toilets; 60% lacked electricity.[85]

In 1947 Canadians got their first nationwide snapshot of the physical state of the schools. The report, carried out by a joint committee established by the Canadian Education Association and the Canadian Public Health Association, was based on data collected in 1945.[86] This is of special value for three reasons. First, the report presents the data for a critical moment – just before prosperity provided the material base for the rapid changes that would occur in the postwar decades. Second, it provides a point-by-point comparison of rural and urban schools and, equally important, compares

SCHOOL FACILITIES

Percentage of schools having certain accommodations, facilities, and services. June 1943.

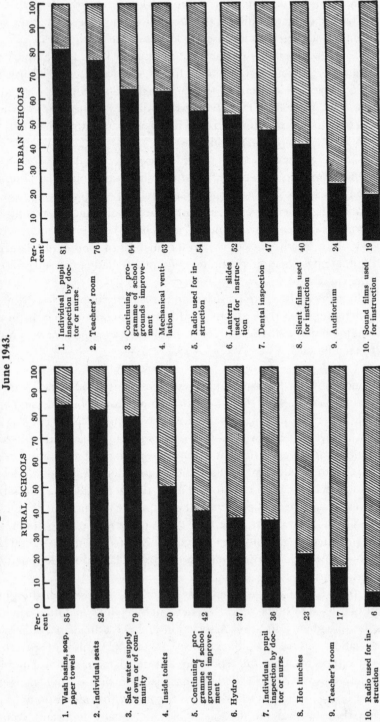

Fig. 4·2   Rural and urban public school facilities, Ontario, 1943

one- and two-room schools, mostly rural, to schools of three, or four or more, rooms, the last of which, in the committee's view, represented the schools of larger villages, towns, and cities. This allows us to see the one-room school in sharp comparative relief and helps avoid singling it out for peculiar condemnation. Third, the report takes us beyond the element of sensationalism in the *Maclean's* article: "thousands" of awful facilities there might have been, but there were also thousands that were not. Thus it offers a more balanced perspective.

The study provides a very detailed tabular analysis of sixteen major categories and nearly sixty subcategories covering lighting, heating and ventilation, provisions for sanitation (toilets, handwashing, and the like), source and quality of water supply, caretaking facilities, and teaching and related accommodation facilities. On most counts, the three-room schools did somewhat better than the smaller schools, and not all of those with four or more rooms were deemed satisfactory. But it is quite obvious that one- and two-room schools fell far below the standards for urban multi-grade schools. In some cases one can probably agree that potentially dangerous or damaging conditions existed in many one- and two-room schools (regarding sanitation, lighting, or screening for fly and mosquito control, for example). In other cases, judgment is necessarily more subjective and depends on what one considers essential to a good pedagogical environment. However, it's still worth remarking that, *as of 1945*, 80% of Canada's rural schools had no artificial lighting; 71% had toilet facilities only outside the school building; 73% did not have running water for handwashing (and 20% had no facilities at all); 44% got their water from "wells, springs and streams not on school site"; in 44% of cases, water was tested "seldom or never."

In 1949 the Canadian Teachers' Federation asked a sample of teachers from across the country to assess their working conditions, including the state of the school plant.[87] The results showed that rural teachers were not uniformly dissatisfied with their working environment. Still, the responses are revealing. Seventy-three per cent of schools had no indoor play space; 48% had no indoor toilets; 26% used a pail and dipper for drinking and washing;[88] one-quarter of the rural schools were judged to be poorly furnished with basic pedagogical equipment; 40% had inadequate lighting. And the "paramount needs" identified by teachers were the kind of educational facilities and services commonly available in urban but not in rural schools.

In making any assessment of the state of the rural schools, one has to set them in the context of their communities. Aside from the large differentials in the tax base that urban and rural schools could draw upon, urban schools had access to a well-developed municipal infrastructure: water and

sewage facilities, electrification, paved streets, public transportation systems, and the like. Until after the Second World War, rural Canada lacked
the amenities that even relatively small towns could provide. Rural electrification proceeded painfully slowly; many rural roads were impassable for
parts of the year; rural water supplies or sewage disposal remained much
the same as a century earlier. Urban and rural homes differed as well. In
1941 the Dominion Bureau of Statistics (DBS) carried out a thorough-going
survey of the nation's housing stock.[89] Of farm houses, 79.2% were without electric power; 86.8% of farm homes used stoves rather than furnaces
for household heating and 82% cooked on a wood stove; 67% drew their
water from wells or other sources outside the house, another 21% from
an inside pump, while only 12% had indoor running water; 93% had no
bath or shower; 89% used an "outside privy"; 79% had neither icebox nor
refrigerator; less than 30% had a telephone; and 28.7% of houses in farm
areas were judged to be in need of "major external repair." There is not a
category in this list where rural homes had facilities that equalled those in
urban areas, and in nearly all categories the gap was wide indeed.

All that is simply to say that rural schools were like the rural communities they were embedded in. The tax base of rural schools *also* varied
enormously, and what one community could afford without undue strain,
another could only dream of. Pioneer conditions or perennial poverty
begat primitive school buildings; if the schools were built of logs, chances
were that most homes in the community were not much better. A safe and
plentiful supply of drinking and wash water was hardly a problem for the
rural school alone; it was shared by the farm families who supported the
school.[90] Outdoor toilets were a fact of life, taken for granted by adults
and children alike. If schools were badly heated or uninsulated, so were
the homes.[91] Innovations to improve the conditions in the school might
only come as a gap began to appear between the physical plant and the
family home. Writing in 1937 about the introduction of electric lighting
in a school not far from Toronto, the author notes, almost in passing, that
"at first, there was considerable opposition; but, after some of the ratepayers had installed electric lighting in their own houses, they withdrew their
opposition."[92] Taxes to maintain or improve the local school and to pay
the teacher's salary came out of the pockets of ratepayers and their families; the amounts had to be weighed against other demands on the family
purse, including the taxes to maintain or improve local roads and other
municipal services. During the first half of the twentieth century, extract-
ing a living from the land (or the sea) was hard and often ill-rewarded, and
the value placed on the education of children, including everything from
teachers' salaries to the state of the physical plant, has to be understood in
the context of the family economy and the variety of pressing priorities that

families had to address. To conclude otherwise is to assume that parents would willingly allow their children to be placed in environments that they themselves would not tolerate at home.

III

In town and country alike, as more and more children completed the work of the elementary grades, a growing number continued their studies into the high school grades. As they did so, provinces extended their legislation to provide opportunities deep into the countryside beyond the traditional urban base for secondary education.[93] What emerged was a pattern of provision substantially different from the kind of arrangements we take for granted today. In all provinces there were "stand-alone" institutions designed exclusively for secondary education. Not all were in the cities and larger towns but most were. These included the county academies of Nova Scotia, the grammar schools of New Brunswick, and, in Prince Edward Island, Prince of Wales College, which until the 1930s was virtually the only school in the province that offered secondary education beyond grade x. Legislation in Nova Scotia and New Brunswick provided that the larger urban areas could establish additional high schools; in Nova Scotia, for example, along with the academy in each county seat, there were also high schools in other towns. Ontario had its "collegiate institutes" and its "high schools," the former almost all located in the cities and large towns, the latter in a variety of settings, including many of the province's more populous villages.[94] In the West, the larger urban communities established their own collegiate institutes or high schools, either as outgrowths of a developing urban public school system or as a distinct sector by special legislation.* Across the country these schools were almost always housed in their own buildings, were generously staffed (usually by university graduates), and taught an academic curriculum extending from grade ix (or in some places grade viii) to university entrance.

Specialized vocational education was not entirely new in 1900. Commercial training was already a well-established part of the program of studies in many of the larger urban high schools.[95] But both commercial and technical training would take off in the early decades of the twentieth century. It was not, it must be said, a universal phenomenon in Canada's secondary schools: before mid-century, for example, Nova Scotia had no day vocational programs, and on the prairies the movement barely reached beyond a handful of the largest urban areas.[96] But by the mid-1920s nearly all of

* In Manitoba and Saskatchewan the larger urban high schools were identified as collegiate institutes; in Alberta and British Columbia the term, universally, was "high school."

those cities with populations over 50,000 had established vocational day and evening classes, and 57% of urban communities with 10,000 to 50,000 people had organized them as well.[97]

Initially, the preferred model was the stand-alone school, an institution with its own building and staff, and sometimes with a distinctive or quasi-separate system of local administration. The rationale was this. A good technical school had to shape its program of studies, including its academic courses, to industrial ends, and this was best done by isolating it, physically and administratively, from the overweening influence of the traditional academic high school.[98] Such schools were in most cases large and impressive institutions. Even before the First World War, Winnipeg had erected two technical high schools, one in the North, the other in the South End. "These," a note in *The School* recorded, "have forge and machine shops, wood-working, pattern-making and electrical shops, mechanical and plumbing rooms, household science room, gymnasium and running track, library, commercial and typewriting classrooms, museums, and other departments."[99] Some smaller communities followed suit: by the late 1920s, already in possession of a good collegiate institute, Port Arthur, Ontario, established its "Technical and Commercial High School," with a total floor space of 65,000 feet. "The building consists of sixty-one rooms, twelve of which are standard classrooms. There are two science laboratories, two household arts rooms, a household science room, model dining room, typewriter room, library, draughting room, five specially equipped shops, administration offices, an auditorium with gallery, stage, dressing rooms and projection room; a gymnasium with apparatus room and gallery; 2 locker rooms with shower rooms adjoining, first aid room, and a cafeteria."[100] A few of the country's big cities even had separate high schools for technical and commercial instruction (Toronto and Vancouver are two examples).

As the movement spread into smaller communities, however, vocational facilities were more commonly attached as departments of existing high schools. One obvious reason was costs: per-pupil expenditure could be kept down through shared facilities and especially by a staff that taught the academic subjects to both academic and vocational pupils or, where enrolments were modest, by staff qualified to teach both academic and vocational subjects. Thus, in Ontario, for example, by the end of the 1920s the most common arrangement was the joint "high and vocational school."[101] But this arrangement was not simply driven by costs, nor was it confined to smaller communities. By the 1920s both of Winnipeg's technical schools (Kelvin and St John's) had become, in effect, composite schools offering academic and technical programs and preparing pupils for matriculation or normal school entrance as well as commerce and industry, as indeed was the newly built McIntyre Collegiate Institute (though its male pupils had to trek to Kelvin for their shop classes).[102]

The collegiate institutes, high schools, and vocational schools or departments in Canada's larger towns and cities represented the modern face of secondary education – large, well-equipped facilities, many of them new and many still in use today. Though different in some important respects, these were institutions that any adult educated in the second half of the last century, indeed any modern teenager, would instantly recognize as schools providing a secondary education. They were not, however, the only or even the most common means of meeting the demand for secondary education in the first three or four decades of the twentieth century.

Trying to explain the variety of institutional arrangements in 1922, one DBS report began with the disclaimer that "secondary education should not be confused with secondary schools."[103] That, indeed, is a critical distinction, not only for the present chapter but for others to follow. In his own analysis of Canadian secondary education written at the end of the 1920s, W.F. Dyde gave the distinction particular emphasis: "In Canada, a secondary pupil is *not* to be defined as a member of a distinct type of institution but rather as one who is pursuing a certain course of study. Secondary education in many parts of the country is closely interwoven with elementary education."[104] Writing a few years later for an English audience, Fred Clarke would emphasize that "the most important fact to grasp" about Canadian secondary education "is that, in practice, the term 'secondary' refers not necessarily to a school, but to a *group of grades* within the whole series of grades."[105] As the demand for something more than the 3 Rs increased, rural and small-town elementary schools, higgledy-piggledy, pushed their programs of study upwards into the high school grades. One result was the development of an entire category of schools often identified, formally or informally, as "continuation schools" – schools or classes that were secondary only but not quite full-scale high schools in terms of enrolments, the qualifications of their staffs, the range of the curriculum or extracurriculum, the number of grades taught, or the facilities available for instruction. The other was the growth, in both graded and one-room elementary schools, of instruction in the high school grades.

In late nineteenth-century Ontario, for example, "continuation classes" had developed in many of the larger village elementary schools, and in 1907 legislation provided for the conversion of these into a distinct sector, the "continuation school" – in effect a small rural high school, organized where no regular high school existed, offering instruction in grades IX through XI or XII, but not grade XIII. The minimum qualification for a continuation school grant was that there had to be at least one teacher engaged full-time in secondary school work. Most commonly located in the smaller villages and hamlets, they could also be established by the combined efforts of three or four contiguous rural school districts.[106] By the 1920s, under various names such as "intermediate school" or "superior school," this type of institution could be found in all provinces, sometimes lodged in its own building, though more often as a "department" (i.e., one or two separate classrooms) within a graded school that taught the elementary curriculum as well.[107] In such cases the principal of the entire school was usually the senior (or only) high school teacher.

In the early 1920s Manitoba had one of the more fine-grained categorizations of its secondary school arrangements, the Murray Report describing the system as one where "opportunities for secondary school training are provided in High School departments attached to the elementary schools and in Collegiate Institutes, which are specially organized for Secondary School purposes. The departments attached to elementary schools are classified according to the number of teachers doing Secondary School work. Schools with one Secondary School Teacher are known as 'Intermediate,' with two Secondary School Teachers as 'High Schools,' with three as 'Collegiate Departments.' Collegiate Institutes may have any number from four upwards."[108] By way of contrast, Nova Scotia operated with a simple dichotomy. There were "pure" secondary schools – the county academies and other urban high schools – on the one hand, and, on the other, the "common schools."[109] But, as one student of the province's school system put it, common schools were not, strictly speaking, elementary schools: "There is no distinct line of demarcation between the elementary and the secondary school. Every 'common' school is a potential high school, and in rural sections it is the rule rather than the exception for some high school work to be done in the section. In other words, every elementary school may do 'continuation' work if it so chooses."[110] Located in rural and village school sections, the common schools were usually ungraded one-room schools, though hamlets and villages might have schools with two, three, or more rooms and an equivalent number of teachers. All common schools, regardless of their size, were required to teach not only grades I to VIII but, where demand existed, grades IX to XI.[111] In a community with a two- or three-room school, one room might be set aside as a continuation class with a teacher specially qualified to handle high school work, though one or two pupils doing secondary work could be found in one-room schools as well. Prince Edward Island's variant was Prince of Wales College for senior high school; "first-class" elementary schools with two or more departments located in the towns and larger villages, required to teach up to grade X; and one-room rural schools, which were allowed to teach up to grade X if there were pupils who sought it.[112]

Teaching the higher grades in a one- or two-room rural school was not, however, unique to these two provinces. Ontario had its "Fifth Classes" – a term originating in the nineteenth century when a few pupils would persist into the "Fifth Reader," which required a year or two beyond the "Fourth Reader," roughly the equivalent of grade VIII. Qualified pupils had a right to receive this instruction in any school district except those that had a continuation or high school.[113] New Brunswick and the three Prairie provinces also permitted high school instruction in one-room schools; indeed in 1930 Saskatchewan mandated grades IX and X in the rural schools anywhere demand warranted, and Manitoba followed suit in 1934.[114] In Alberta it remained optional, although until 1933 those one-room schools that did offer a grade or two of high school work earned an additional grant by doing so.[115] The only exception was British Columbia, where instruction in the secondary grades was confined, near-exclusively, to its high schools or in classrooms attached to elementary schools that the province labelled "superior schools" and where grades VII to X were taught by a teacher qualified to do so.[116]

Given these kinds of arrangements, some form of secondary education was widely available in rural and small-town Canada. In 1907, when the category was first created, Ontario had 97 continuation schools. By 1922 there were 181, and by the late 1920s, 207; to this number has to be added 192 high schools, many of which were in villages not much larger than those with continuation schools.[117] In the early 1930s Saskatchewan was providing continuation grants to 632 schools, and "such schools were to be found in practically every town, village and hamlet in the province."[118] In 1935 Alberta's Legislative Committee on Rural Education could count 62 consolidated school districts and 16 rural high schools offering secondary education to the end of grade XI, plus an additional 250 rural two-room schools teaching grades IX and X, some of which also taught grade XI. Additionally – and this was also true in most other parts of Canada – "the towns and villages all minister to the high school needs of their respective rural communities."[119] Beyond that, there were the one-room elementary schools. In Alberta, the Legislative Committee noted, "one or more high school grades ... are attempted in 1,470 one-room schools" – about half the one-room schools in the province.[120] In rural Nova Scotia, secondary work in the early 1920s was done in 1,200 common schools.[121] At the beginning of the 1920s Ontario had 431 rural schools offering fifth classes; by 1930 the number had mushroomed to 1,316.[122] Though the proportion of high school enrolments in one-room schools varied by province, nearly all had schools where one teacher tried to cope with a range of grades stretching from I to IX or X.

Secondary education might be widely available, but by any modern standard, much of it was conducted in remarkably small units. As W.F. Dyde

would put it in 1929, "The median enrolment of the 49 Ontario collegiate institutes is 415, of the 126 high schools is 133. The median enrolment of both types of school is 165, and the school most commonly found
has between 100 and 150 pupils." Dyde added that the medians for high
schools in other provinces were even lower.[123] Ontario's typical continuation school in the period had two teachers and 50 pupils.[124] At about the
same time in Nova Scotia, 472 of the rural elementary schools had fewer
than 20 pupils, but "here and there, even these schools ambitiously undertake high school work" and many others only slightly larger did so as well.[125]
Describing Manitoba's secondary school provision in the mid-1930s, D.S.
Woods noted that outside of Winnipeg, its suburbs, and three other large
communities, there were 234 "regularly constituted high schools ... These
comprise 126 one room [one-teacher] high schools, 41 two room [two-
teacher] high schools, 17 collegiate departments [three teachers], and 14
collegiate institutes, some of which have large teaching staffs. In addition,
there are approximately 36 two- and three-room schools, not rated as high
schools, doing the work of Grade XI ... In those not rated as high schools,
the one teacher not infrequently, in addition to the high school grades IX
to XI, teaches one or more senior elementary grades; this is true also of a
number of the one-room high schools in which all the pupils of Grades
IX to XI are housed in one classroom and instructed by a single teacher
regardless of the breadth of the curriculum." Enrolments in the "rated"
high school classes, Woods found, ranged from 9 to 42 in the one-teacher
schools, 26 to 71 in the two-teacher schools, and 43 to 96 in the collegiate
departments (three teachers).[126] British Columbia might claim that nearly
all its secondary pupils were taught in distinct high school departments,
but in 1923, 30 of its 67 high schools had only one teacher, while another
15 had two.[127] In 1928–29 that same province had 41 "city high schools"
– schools located in its largest urban communities. Only four communities had high school enrolments over 300 students; 27 communities had
under 300, 15 under 100, and 6 under 50.[128] The high schools in the rural
municipalities and rural districts were, on average, smaller still. As Maxwell
Cameron pointed out, this meant that very nearly *half* (49%) of all schools
offering the secondary grades had total enrolments of 50 or less; 64% had
enrolments below 100; and 71% below 150.[129] Even by 1939–40, half of
British Columbia's rural district high schools had only one or two teachers,
and 39 out of 51 schools had enrolments of 50 or fewer pupils.[130] Indeed, as
late as 1945, 51% of all high school classrooms in Alberta were to be found
in one- or two-room high schools.[131]

Alberta rarely allowed grades higher than IX or X to be taught in its one-
room elementary schools and tried to restrict them to grade IX only, but in

1941 "approximately half" of its two-room schools taught, in addition to the elementary grades, grades IX through XI.[132] According to Prince Edward Island's 1930 Royal Commission on Education, "Last year 750 pupils were enrolled in Grades nine and ten in the 414 rural one-room schools, about 5% of the total enrolment, [not quite] an average of two pupils per school ... 152 [schools] had no pupils enrolled in grade nine and ten; 68 had only one each; 61 had two; 55 had three; 38 had four; 18 had five; 8 had six; 10 had seven; 2 had eight; and 2 eleven."[133] Between 1919–20 and 1940–41, enrolments in Ontario's public school fifth classes averaged no more than seven pupils.[134]

But what *proportion* of Canadian pupils received their secondary education in these small schools? At one end of the scale lay British Columbia. "The number of small high schools is relatively very large," wrote Maxwell Cameron, "but the total number of pupils attending these schools is relatively small," with 16.7% of the total high school population in schools with enrolments of 150 or less. Even so, Cameron added, "The secondary training of nearly 17% of our students is of very great importance."[135] Elsewhere, much higher proportions of students doing secondary-level work in very small schools were common. "There are 4,676 pupils enrolled in Intermediate schools with one secondary teacher," wrote D.S. Woods of Manitoba in the mid-1930s, "and 1,029 in Elementary schools taught by teachers not recognized as qualified for secondary school work. Practically half of the pupils in the Province doing secondary work receive their instruction from but one teacher."[136] In 1922 Nova Scotia had 11,039 secondary pupils, 2,837 of them in eighteen county academies and another 5,400 in sixty-four other "pure" high schools; "The remaining 2,802 high school pupils [about 25%] were accommodated in 1,586 common schools ... Of these, 1,242 were one-teacher schools, 220 were two-teacher schools, and 124 three- or more teacher schools."[137] A few years later, in 1929–30, that province's superintendent of education estimated that there were "6,889 high school pupils in the urban schools and 6,226 in the rural and village schools."[138] Numbers in the high school grades of Saskatchewan's rural schools had risen from 11% of total high school enrolments in 1914 to 36% in 1935. Another 37% were to be found in "town and village schools," many in the one- or two-teacher continuation classes in small communities.[139] In Ontario during the 1920s and 1930s, something like 25% of its secondary pupils were in fifth classes or continuation schools.[140] Nationally, close to 18,000 secondary pupils were enrolled in one-room schools in 1922; by 1940 the figure was more like 40,000. While the figures were much higher in some provinces than others, this represented 15% of all students in the secondary grades and doesn't even include the large number attending one- or two-teacher high schools.[141] We will return in chapter 10 to consider the implications of the large numbers of small schools and small enrolments for the high school curriculum and extracurriculum.

Secondary school instruction was carried on in buildings similar in range and character to the elementary schools. Surveying Blairmore's high school facilities in 1942, one high school inspector noted that

> the three high school classrooms are situated on the second floor of the school building. One of them is of good size and in fair condition. The other two have evidently been formed out of one classroom and two adjoining cloakrooms; they are separated by a large folding partition. The last two mentioned rooms are distinctly unsatisfactory, chiefly because sounds carry so plainly from one to the other that when classes are being conducted in both at the same time, the resulting confusion makes quiet and orderly work impossible.
>
> Natural lighting from east windows is fairly good; there are a few electric light outlets but no suitable fixtures ... Chemistry experimental work is carried on in a basement room which at the time of my visit had several inches of water on the floor due to recent flood conditions. Science supplies for the courses on this year's programme have been adequate.

Reference books for social studies, however, were not adequate, and the inspector included a gentle reprimand: no recent book purchases had been made, and in a school of this size "it is essential for progressive work for the library to be kept up to date."[142] Ewelme High School, deep in rural Alberta, was a one-room extension to the ungraded elementary school which, in 1935, the high school inspector labelled a "tar paper shack." Summarizing his report in a letter to the trustees, the chief inspector of schools tartly observed, "I note that Inspector Balfour finds you have no equipment, that your building cannot be called a classroom, that good work under these conditions he finds is impossible, and that he recommends that your board provide a suitable building for high school work or that they close the high school room and have the students take correspondence courses from the Department of Education."[143]

The growing demand for secondary education resulted in much new construction across the country, in small and large communities alike. When the Blairmore trustees were contemplating the construction of a large annex in 1940, they received a proposal from the Edmonton-based "Waterman-Waterbury MFG Co., Complete School Contractors," which included a description of a four-room high school the firm had just completed for the Turner Valley School Division: "The building contains four full-sized class-

Fig. 4.3   A classroom in a brand-new high school, Nova Scotia, 1931 (count the desks!)

rooms, typing room, teachers room, and a large library on the main floor. A large science room and shop were provided in the basement, with ample lighting. The school has complete air conditioning and is equipped with our latest purifier septic toilets."[144] The high school building that opened in New Glasgow in 1931 was, according to Nova Scotia's chief inspector of schools, "the last word in school construction in the Atlantic Provinces," incorporating "a large, handsome assembly hall," effective sound insulation, excellent laboratories for science teaching, "a good library room," a teachers' room, principal's office, and other improvements.[145] An accompanying photograph of a new model classroom suggests an impressive amount of blackboard space on all three interior walls, a highly valued innovation at the time; but the number of desks indicates class sizes that would make today's high school teachers quiver (see Figure 4.3). One Ontario inspector noted in 1919 that three new buildings in small towns had just been completed "upon the most approved modern principles of school architecture. Special provision has been made in them all for the practical teaching of science. All are provided with Assembly Halls and Gymnasiums. Lighting, heating and ventilation have been carefully provided for, and excellent provision has been made for lavatory accommodation."[146]

But there were also high school departments in older elementary schools where there was no accommodation beyond ordinary classrooms and where conditions generally were "very poor": ill-lit classrooms and glossy blackboards; inadequate ventilation; inadequate provision for science teaching;

and poor sanitation, including "the common drinking cup and the common towel."[147] Somewhere in between, perhaps, was the four-teacher Dutton High School in rural southwestern Ontario, described with acerbity by John Kenneth Galbraith. The building "was a gaunt two-story building of white brick and hideous aspect. It stood in a small yard in which only ragweed and plantain reliably survived the dense foot traffic ... The school had a front door that was reserved for girls and a back door that was available to either sex ... Beyond the back door was a well and pump. There was no baseball diamond, no basketball hoop, no football posts, not even a pond for ice hockey ... The only relief from the barrenness of the yard and the board fences that surrounded it was provided by nice trees which provided some shade and two outdoor toilets."[148]

Depending on where they lived, parents and their children might be able to choose between alternatives for secondary education, though all the choices had their drawbacks. In rural sections close to an urban community, or when parents had the resources to pay for board, children could be sent there. This was often a preferred choice. In 1923, for example, the DBS estimated that 14% of all rural pupils were in attendance at urban schools, and most of those would be high school pupils.[149] In 1924 Manitoba's Murray Commission calculated that "in Secondary Schools in the towns and villages about one-sixth of the Secondary School pupils are non-resident, in the Secondary Schools in rural districts about one-fourth, while in three of the cities about a tenth, and in Winnipeg about one-twentieth are non-residents."[150] The principal of one small-town Ontario high school remarked in 1936 that "we have an attendance of 150. An analysis of the records for the past seven years will show that approximately 55% of the pupils live outside the high school district, that is, live on farms," adding that he thought this "truly representative" of the province's smaller high school districts throughout the province.[151] At 50% the figure was only slightly lower at Aurora High School, and even in London, a much larger urban community, some 25% of its technical and commercial students were "from the country."[152]

   In nearly all parts of the country, non-resident tuition fees were charged when children attended school outside their own school district. However, it is impossible to determine the extent to which these fees were paid directly by non-resident parents to host school districts. Many rural parents were defined as residents of a host school district for high school purposes. By law, for example, the county academies and grammar schools of Nova Scotia and New Brunswick provided tuition-free instruction to all secondary school pupils residing in the county. But other town high schools in these two provinces could charge tuition fees to non-residents. In Ontario, towns and villages were often united with part or all of a surrounding county, rural taxes contributed to the maintenance of an urban high school, and thus rural children attended free of charge. But not all rural areas were covered by such arrangements. In other parts of the country, non-resident fees could be charged not to individual parents but to the school district they resided in. About all we can say with any degree of certainty is that some parents had to pay non-resident fees to send their children to urban schools, or at least to the school they preferred.[153]

Rural parents who opted for an urban education for their children, in any case, still faced the inconvenience and costs of daily transportation or, more serious, the expense of board and lodging. Some pupils, presumably, were able to stay free, or at modest cost, with grandparents, other relatives, or family acquaintances. But a 1922 estimate suggests that, for Ontario at least, the full cost "of sending one child to the town school until he has obtained his junior matriculation standing [i.e., four years of high school] will be about $1,000."[154] And that was assuming that reasonably priced board and lodging was even available. Especially in the Depression, when taking in a boarder might bring welcome revenue, there was likely to be plenty of space available. But 'twas not always thus: in 1943, in correspondence with the secretary-treasurer of the Pincher School Division for advice on the matter, one parent was told, "At the moment I can think of only Mrs. Cook who might take high school students to board. The oil survey people seem to be occupying most of the available accommodation at present."[155] The extra cost of obtaining secondary education, indeed, was one major reason why rural parents had to spend a substantially larger portion of family income on educating their children than did those who lived in urban Canada.[156]

Psychic costs might be involved as well. The precocious Woodrow Lloyd, a future Saskatchewan education minister and premier, just turned 11, left the family farm in 1924 to attend high school, and board five days a week, in a nearby town. "It was a painful wrench for all the family," Lloyd's daughter records. "Emotionally, Woodrow was launched into an independence that he wasn't ready for. Although there were never long stretches of time when he didn't see some member of the family, it was a lonely little boy who enrolled in Webb High School that fall."[157] A no less precocious farm boy in southwestern Ontario, John Kenneth Galbraith, finished elementary school at age 11 and the next year went off to nearby Dutton High School, where, according to his biographer, he struggled for the first two years partly because of the recent death of his mother but also because he "hadn't been well prepared by his one-room [school] experience." Moreover, "[b]ecause the Galbraith children travelled the six miles to school by horse and buggy, they were frequently late, which resulted in routine punishment."[158] In his own account of those years, Galbraith intimates that he also suffered, like other rural children, from urban condescension towards those from the countryside (*urban* condescension, the reader will note, from the renowned metropolis of Dutton).[159]

Wherever there were local continuation classes, however named, they provided a second option. Since the costs were borne by all the ratepayers in the unit, fees were not an issue. But because many small high schools didn't offer grade XII (or in Ontario, grade XIII), students who wanted to finish their high school education still had to leave home and attend an urban school. Again, Woodrow Lloyd, having completed the course at Webb High School, had to finish his secondary education in Regina before he could qualify to enter the University of Saskatchewan, and J.K. Galbraith had to switch to St Thomas Collegiate Institute for his fifth year of high school.[160]

The third option was the one-room rural school. Anywhere there was no alternative available, the demand that the one- or two-room rural school offer some or all of the high school grades was near-universal.[161] Most parents wanted their children to stay close by, for all kinds of good reasons; aside from that, as a Saskatchewan commission pointed out in 1933, those who advocated the preferred alternative of the rural high school often forgot one key factor: "Children cannot be expected to walk more than about 2 miles, and with ordinary conveyance the distance limit might be said to be 8 miles. The problem then becomes one of bringing high school facilities within 8 miles of all schoolchildren."[162] Possible in some circumstances – in populous areas where there were enough candidates to justify it and where the extra cost per ratepayer would be modest – the rural high school was no alternative in other parts of the country where these conditions didn't apply. So, willy-nilly, parents turned to the only available source, the one-room school.

While the number of one-room schools offering high school instruction had grown steadily in the two decades after 1910, the depression of the 1930s saw their numbers, and enrolments, sharply increase. By 1934, David Jones writes of Alberta, "about 50% of one-room schools offered instruction above grade VIII"; in the drought areas, however, "the percentage approached 75%. There was no money to pay farm help, there was nothing to harvest anyway, people were getting into the high school habit, and destitute parents could not afford education outside the district. As one woman told [the local inspector], 'I will have two children to take Grade X this term and as there is no crop or even feed in this district again this year it will be impossible for me to send them away to board.'"[163] Nor was Alberta alone in this. Ontario's fifth classes increased sharply during the interwar years, but more particularly in the 1930s, as did the equivalent classes in other provinces.[164]

The other pressure that emerged from the Depression was for greater access to the senior high school grades. "Parents living in rural districts, in villages and small towns find themselves financially unable to send their boys to the larger centres," the Alberta high school inspectors reported in 1932, and "in many cases they are requesting their trustee boards to add a grade XII class to the local school. In a number of cases their wishes have been acceded to through the engagement of a second teacher and the division of the work of the four high school grades between two instructors."[165] This was exactly what happened in Blairmore. After a dismal set of departmental exam results in 1923, and the judgment of the high school inspector that trying to carry on instruction in grades IX through XII with only two teachers was "ill-advised," the Blairmore trustees abandoned grade XII for the rest of the decade.[166] But in 1930 "several ratepayers" with eight youngsters ready for grade XII petitioned the board to reinstate it, adding that "probably three students from Frank District [a nearby village]" would attend as well. Although it was a split decision (3 to 2), the trustees agreed and an additional teacher was hired, raising the high school staff from three to four.[167] The next year the board cancelled grade XII and laid off the new teacher because of "the prevailing economic conditions and the uncertainty as to the number of students likely to apply for Grade XII instruction in 1931-2."[168] Once again the trustees confronted a petition from nine ratepayers, "each ratepayer having at least one child ready to take some or all of Grade XII." They rejected the request in July but reversed themselves in August and hired another new teacher.[169] Whether they wanted it or not, the trustees were stuck with it: starting with those nine teenagers in 1931-32, the numbers in grade XII rose to 23 in 1934-35 and stayed within that range into the early 1940s.[170]

At least parents in Blairmore *had* access to a high school. Those in a rural school division not too far away had none, as this letter, mailed prayerfully to Premier Aberhart himself, attests:

I am writing this letter as an appeal to you for aid and the backing of the department in obtaining permission for the teaching of the high school grades in our school. I live in Utopia S.D. #840, where there are at least 5 or 6 high school pupils ready for x, xi and xii grades. Also I believe there are other pupils in adjacent districts who wish to attend some of these grades. The parents of these children cannot afford to send them to the nearest high school (i.e. Pincher Creek) for instruction, meaning board at $25.00 or $30.00 per month besides other extra expenses.

Could we not get a small addition built to the present school building for a high school room and obtain another teacher. Actual work on the building would be contributed by people of district – if material is supplied by large S.D. Division – also parents of high school pupils would pay *part* of teacher's salary privately.

   Kindly advise me what can be done to help us in this very important problem.

The reply, from Alberta's chief inspector, wasn't a flat no – he was willing to leave the final decision to the divisional authorities – but he warned that the total average attendance was under twenty and that was too small to warrant a two-classroom school even with the addition of five or six high school pupils.[171]

When teachers in one-room schools couldn't cope with high school instruction, it was the various department of education Correspondence Divisions, established in nearly every province during the interwar years, that came to the rescue. Initially intended to serve special cases of pupils who, because of sheer isolation or for any other reason, couldn't attend a local school, these divisions increasingly found themselves engaged in guiding high school pupils through all or part of the high school curriculum. In Saskatchewan in the early 1930s, some 750 students were doing correspondence courses because they were unable to attend any school, but "over 4,000 students enrolled in Grade IX in one-room schools are receiving regularly the outline of work to supplement the instructions of their teachers."[172] By the late 1930s the number was over 7,000.[173] In Manitoba in 1935–36, 784 pupils were doing some of their core grade IX and X subjects by correspondence; an additional 309 were trying to master French and Latin that way in grades IX, X, or XI.[174] By the mid-thirties the Nova Scotia Department of Education was providing correspondence courses for grade XI pupils where local trustees and teachers had agreed not to offer instruction in that grade. Such courses "are now extensively used for this purpose, each pupil receiving instruction in not fewer than 6 subjects on the Grade XI programme of studies. Since six subjects are required for an examination pass, the rural pupil is not deterred or precluded from writing the [matriculation] examination, if he so wishes."[175] British Columbia did things differently. On the one hand, it discouraged pupils from taking high school subjects in elementary schools; on the other, significant numbers of them were out of range of a high school, so correspondence courses were carried on at home or in some similar setting. In 1936–37 some 2,000 young people were pursuing their high school program in this manner, 44% of whom lived between three and ten miles from the nearest high school and the rest further away than that.[176]

While access to some form of secondary schooling was widespread in rural Canada, it is impossible to estimate foregone demand. We do not know how many children went without because it wasn't available. We do know that there were places – Kipp School District is one good example – where trustees were reluctant to offer it, where ratepayers or trustees flatly refused to invest in the advanced schooling of one or two children a year, or where the inspectorate refused to authorize such instruction either because the teacher was unequipped for the job or because it would unduly interfere with the work of the lower grades. In the late 1930s an Ontario commission did a thorough canvass of public opinion on the arrangements for secondary education, and access was not one of the issues raised; but that may have been because of the relatively dense network of continuation and village high schools, in southern Ontario at least.[177] Access to *graded* secondary education in Manitoba, D.S. Woods found, was unequally distributed: "In general, the larger graded schools with more highly departmental secondary school levels are located in the better rural areas; while the one-room high schools and schools conducting work to grade XI, with several elementary and high school grades under one teacher, are distributed throughout the province. They are typical of secondary schools of the poorer lands and areas."[178] And while many one-room elementary schools did offer some form of high school instruction, many did not.[179] All we can be sure of is that some rural children who may have wanted it, or wanted something better than the one-room school could offer, went without. As W.F. Dyde would write at the end of the 1920s, in any case, there were "great differences in the conditions under which high school pupils are working and the varieties of opportunities open to them. The sharpest difference will be found to exist between urban and rural conditions. In all but the prescribed syllabus and textbooks the country pupil is often receiving his secondary education under conditions which are far removed from those enjoyed by the city child. The discrepancy between urban and rural secondary education presents one of the most pressing problems which the country as a whole is facing."[180]

Which brings us back to where we started – two distinct kinds of provision, one urban, one rural, for Canadian schoolchildren, elementary and secondary alike; or perhaps better put at the end of this chapter, a remarkably wide range of provision in terms of access and quality, stretching from Winnipeg or Fredericton to Blairmore and Saskatchewan's Kipp School District No. 1589.

5

Teachers

What of the teachers who staffed the schools of English Canada during the first four or five decades of the twentieth century? We begin with a brief overview of their numbers, then turn to a much more intensive analysis of the occupational characteristics of the workforce: the formal qualifications required for entry to teaching, the level of academic and professional qualifications teachers actually acquired, the amount of experience they brought to the job, and the ethnic and social composition of the occupation. Since teaching engaged both men and women, we will also explore how qualifications, experience, and some other pertinent characteristics differed by gender.

I

In 1900 Canadian public school systems employed some 19,000 teachers. By 1920 the figure stood at 40,600, and another 9,000 were added by 1930. This represented a 45% rate of increase across the first decade of the century, 47% in the next decade, and about 21% between 1920 and 1930. These growth rates were usually well above those for pupil enrolments (see Table 2.1).[1] This may have been due in part to modest reductions in class size in graded schools, especially after 1920, but in the main it was the result of the rapid expansion of settlement. Each of the multiplying number of rural one-room schools required a teacher no matter how small the enrolment. Since high school enrolments were growing faster than elementary enrolments, one might expect that the number of secondary school teachers was increasing much faster than that of elementary school teachers. If the Ontario figures are indicative, that was indeed the case. Between 1920 and 1930 the rate of increase for Ontario's elementary school teachers was 23%; for teachers in the academic high schools alone it was 75%. While the rate of growth for high school teachers was substantial, it started from a very small base, and the overwhelming majority of the teaching workforce – in

Ontario in 1930, for example, some 84% – were elementary school teachers.[2] Thus, while we will give some attention in this chapter to secondary school teachers as a distinct group, our emphasis falls mostly on that large majority who taught in English Canada's elementary schools.

From the time Canadian public school systems were first organized, anyone wishing to teach in the system required a licence issued under the authority of a provincial education act. The licence, however, was accompanied (and usually took the form of) a certificate that attested to the qualification the particular individual held. Certificates were ranked according to the level of qualification obtained so that public authorities could adequately assess an individual's competence to teach particular subjects or grades. School boards were required to hire only teachers who possessed a provincial licence on pain of forfeiting grants or other penalties. But certification systems tended to be more permissive. There might or might not be some restrictions, for example, about who could teach high school, but in the main, boards were free to pick and choose among levels of qualification according to their budgets and ambitions.

Those levels were assessed according to two criteria: academic education and professional training. Nowadays Canadians rather take it for granted that teachers will have a mix of academic and professional training acquired in a university setting. Indeed, a university degree is not only expected but required for both elementary and secondary teachers. But during the first half of the century, only high school teachers were likely to have a university degree; elementary school teachers were required to have only a high school education (and *not* a university education). An adequate general education was conventionally identified as the completion of "junior" or "senior matriculation."* Junior matriculation indicated the completion of that standard of high school education that allowed a student to enter first-year university. In the early twentieth century this normally required three years of high school study everywhere except in Ontario, where it was set at four years.[3] Senior matriculation required an additional high school grade and usually admitted the student to the second year of an undergraduate program. By the turn of the century there was quite often a parallel "teacher's course" in the high school program, in which students might not be required to have Latin, advanced math, or the same number of foreign languages required of the university matriculation course; but both required the same number of years of study in high school.

* Originally a term used exclusively by universities to identify the standards set for university entrance, "matriculation" had also come to mean the completion of the regular high school course of study. Even in those provinces that abandoned the term in their school systems, it was a conventional designation simply because the universities used it.

Most professional training took place entirely outside the ambit of the university, in "normal schools" funded, controlled, and staffed by provincial departments of education.[4] The length of the program varied by decade and level of certification but, for the higher-level elementary certificates, was usually set at one full academic year. The program of studies incorporated four broad areas: school management and law; "Principles of Education" (aims, learning theory, child development, curricular and pedagogical theories, and the like); the pedagogy appropriate to particular subjects and grade levels; and practice-teaching in local schools.

While no two provincial certification systems were exactly the same with respect to the number of categories employed, the labels attached to them, or even the levels of education they signified, for illustrative purposes a typical certification system might be organized in the following way. A distinctive top category, labelled perhaps "academic" or "collegiate," identified those who held a university degree and were considered best qualified to teach high school. At the turn of the twentieth century, secondary school teachers rarely were required to have any professional training, but as this was introduced in later decades, it was integrated into their certification requirements. Next in order was the first-class certificate, which would usually require senior matriculation and a full year of professional training. This was the highest elementary school certificate, but it might qualify an individual to teach at the secondary level as well. The second-class certificate commonly required junior matriculation plus a full year or some lesser amount of professional training. The third-class certificate, usually the lowest category, required something less than junior matriculation and a short period of professional training or none at all. Beyond that, there were "temporary certificates," "local licences," or "permits" for those who didn't meet the requirements for a regular certificate. In the main, these types of licences, which we will generally term "permits," were valid only in a particular locality and issued only when no qualified teacher was available.[5]

This description, however, is highly schematic and only loosely fits actual requirements at any point in the first four decades of the century or those in any particular province. When, for example, James Miller surveyed the country in 1913, he found that one could obtain a third-class New Brunswick certificate by completing grade VIII; a second-class certificate required grade IX. In Nova Scotia, grade IX was required for third class and grade X for second class. Professional training for third class varied from a five-month normal school course in New Brunswick to none at all in Nova Scotia.[6] In both provinces the highest elementary certificate required junior matriculation (grade XI) and a full year of professional training. The requirements in Protestant Quebec were about the same. West of Quebec, standards tended to be somewhat higher. A third-class certificate required grade x, and a second-class certificate, junior matriculation (or three years of high school). First-class certificates were reserved for those with senior matriculation. Professional training varied from three or four months to a full year, depending on the level of certificate. The age restrictions varied from province to province; most candidates for a certificate had to be at least 17 or 18.[7]

How many teachers held the various levels of certificates? In an important quantitative study that covers a century or more, Patrick Harrigan has demonstrated that teacher qualifications rose every decade from 1870 onwards.[8] But the percentage of teachers who had completed high school (let alone university) remained modest until after 1920. According to Miller's 1913 data (and excluding Quebec), 9.7% of Canadian teachers held first-class certificates. Forty-two per cent had second-class and 30% third-class certificates. Miller ranked another 18% "below third class," a category that included a large number of individuals teaching on permits.[9] Not all of this latter group, Miller pointed out, were ill-educated: there were university students flocking west to earn some money, or for sheer adventure, teaching in isolated schools that operated only during the summer months, and others who for one reason or another didn't meet the fine print of the requisites for a certificate.[10] But many permit teachers were clearly unqualified even by the standards of the time, and altogether third-class and permit teachers constituted 48% of all elementary teachers.

In Table 5.1 we offer an alternative measure based on years of education rather than certificates held; this is a different way of estimating qualifications and thus gives somewhat different results, but the trend is similar.[11] We estimate that in 1910 some 20% of Canadian elementary teachers had less than junior matriculation and 10% grade x or less. Just over 70% had attained junior matriculation level (three or four years of high school) and had some degree of professional training. Seven per cent had two or three years beyond junior matriculation, including one full year of professional training, a level that would qualify for a first-class certificate. The figures for 1920 are about the same. Whether one draws on Miller's figures or our own, it is clear that in early twentieth-century Canada there were large numbers of teachers whose qualifications were, by any modern standard, modest, to say the least.

During the interwar years, however, there were dramatic improvements. Between 1920 and 1940 those with less than full qualifications for a second-class certificate practically disappeared (Table 5.1, columns 1 to 3). More remarkably, there was a spectacular rise in the percentage of those with qualifications above junior matriculation and a concomitant shrinkage of those with second-class certificates (Table 5.1, columns 4 and 5). In 1920

Table 5.1
Educational qualifications, elementary school teachers, Canada (excluding Quebec),
1900–1958

	Grade X or less (1)	J minus (2)	J (3)	J + 1 (4)	J + 2 or 3 (5)	Total
1900*	290	5,274	5,596	2,934	947	15,041
	1.9%	35.1%	37.2%	19.5%	6.3%	
1910	2,342	2,558	7,877	9,119	1,731	23,627
	9.9%	10.8%	33.3%	38.6%	7.3%	
1920	3,161	4,313	9,957	15,827	2,893	36,151
	8.7%	11.9%	27.5%	43.8%	8.0%	
1930	785	548	2,246	28,355	13,217	45,151
	1.7%	1.2%	5.0%	62.8%	29.3%	
1940	52	77	883	14,477	28,647	44,136
	0.1%	0.2%	2.0%	32.8%	64.9%	
1950	3,984	–	681	10,401	30,334	45,400
	8.8%		1.5%	22.9%	66.8%	
1958	2,544	1	2,830	11,691	46,455	63,521
	4.0%		4.5%	18.4%	73.1%	

*No data for Saskatchewan, Alberta, and British Columbia.
Headings Legend
1. Grade x or less: no professional training, including those teaching on permits.
2. J minus: training and education below junior matriculation (JM) level; usually the professional training required was less than one year, sometimes as short as six weeks.
3. J: training and education up to JM level; includes at least some professional training (usually less than one year).
4. J + 1: JM plus one year of professional training.
5. J + 2 or 3: JM plus two or three years of further education, including at least one year of professional training.

Source: Urquhart and Buckley, *Historical Statistics,* 594–5.

almost half of Canadian teachers were below the standard necessary for a second-class certificate; by 1940 close to two-thirds met the standard for a first-class certificate.

These changes are relatively easy to explain. Then, as now, standards for entry into teaching were driven primarily by supply and demand. Between 1900 and 1920 increasing enrolments, new settlement, the annual migration of eastern teachers to the West, and the dislocation caused by the First World War created shortages of well-qualified teachers and made it impossible to exclude third-class and permit teachers.[12] Rising certification standards during the interwar years were associated with increasing numbers of young people completing high school and, in the 1920s, with rising salaries. Both factors pushed up the number of those entering teaching. During the Great Depression salaries were hit hard, especially in rural Canada, but lack of job opportunities kept even more young people in high school and flooded the normal schools with applicants. These circumstances allowed educational officials to raise entry standards and eliminate the least qualified; in nearly all provinces third-class certificates were gradually phased out and the number of permits reduced to near zero.[13] As well, prerequisites for entry to normal school were pushed up, especially for second-class certificates. The historian of Alberta's education system has described the 1930s as "the golden age" of the normal school, and that was equally true for the rest of Canada: "Never had their students been so well qualified academically; never before had they been required to meet so many other criteria of selection. Never had they spent longer in their professional preparation, or had that preparation been better adapted to their needs."[14] Not all of the improvement was due to changes in initial teacher training, however. From the early twentieth century onwards large numbers of teachers, especially those intent on making a career of it, invested in massive amounts of academic and professional upgrading through department of education and university summer schools. By 1939, in any case, several provinces were moving towards the abolition of the second-class certificate; teachers were required to upgrade their academic or professional qualifications, or were forced out of the job altogether. An occupation made up exclusively of those with first-class certificates – those who had completed senior matriculation, the equivalent of first-year university, and a full year of professional training – appeared to be just around the corner. And the leadership in Canadian education was beginning to whisper, among themselves at least, about the imminent arrival of a fully graduate profession.[15]

National figures, nonetheless, mask sharp differences among Canada's provinces and regions. Between 1900 and 1940, and more particularly during the interwar years, the qualifications of teachers in *all* provinces substantially improved.[16] But some started from a higher base, and some improved much more rapidly than others. For example, in James Miller's 1913 survey, about 27% of British Columbia's teachers held third-class certificates or permits; in Nova Scotia the figure was 73%. Forty-one per cent of Ontario's teachers fell into these two categories; in New Brunswick it was 74% and in Prince Edward Island 80%.[17] Between 1900 and 1920 the new provinces of Alberta and Saskatchewan, with their rapidly expanding agricultural settlements, had far more third-class and permit teachers than Ontario, but during the 1920s the difference disappeared entirely. The gap between the Maritime provinces and those west of Quebec, however, persisted across the period. By 1930 Ontario and the four western provinces had almost no teachers with less than junior matriculation but in Nova Scotia the figure was 27%. During the 1930s Nova Scotia pushed up its requirements for certification and eliminated most of its least-educated teachers. But in 1940 that province still lagged behind, with far more second-class teachers (and far fewer first-class) than Ontario and the West. While New Brunswick had reduced the number to a relatively small proportion, there were still some third-class teachers in the system and the standard for second-class certificates was substantially lower than that of Ontario or the western provinces.[18]

The other disparity was the gap between urban and rural teachers. Those with better qualifications went where salaries were higher than average and where living and working conditions were better – that is to say, they went to the graded schools of the cities, towns, and larger villages and then to the consolidated schools of the countryside located near urban centres. The least-attractive jobs were in the one-room schools. Even here there was a gradation: "Annual reports sent to the Department of Education by school inspectors," writes one historian of Prairie education, "reveal that, in general, the competency and qualifications of a teacher in any school seemed to vary with the distance of that particular school from the railroad; the closer it was, the better the qualifications ... Teachers preferred to teach in schools as near as possible to centres of civilization."[19]

This pattern was already well established in the first two decades of the twentieth century. James Miller's calculations in 1913 reveal startling figures for the three provinces where the pertinent data existed. In Alberta, Saskatchewan, and Ontario, well over 90% of the permit teachers and around 90% of the third-class certificate teachers were located in the rural schools.[20] The reason for this, said Miller, was simple: department officials had to choose between insisting on qualified teachers and keeping a school open at any cost. "In very many cases the authorities are reluctantly forced to grant 'permits' to those whom they consider quite unfit to do even fairly good work in rural schools. When faced with the plain issue – none at all or a makeshift teacher – the attempt is usually made to keep the local school open."[21] Urban school systems, on the other hand, had choices and exercised them. When W.L. Richardson surveyed the policies of fifty-nine Canadian city school boards in the late teens, he found that "elementary school assistants must almost invariably have at least a second-class certificate or its equivalent to secure employment to the teaching staff of a Canadian city."[22] Since the 1890s, Winnipeg had had the pick of Manitoba's best teachers, and all of them held first- or second-class permanent certificates.[23] In 1910 only three of Fredericton's fifteen elementary school teachers had second-class certificates; the rest had either first-class (four) or higher certificates (eight).[24] By the 1930s Saint John, Fredericton, and Moncton all required their elementary teachers to have at least a first-class licence and three years of experience.[25] New Brunswick's chief superintendent of schools, indeed, would remark in 1925 that "nearly all cities and towns, which at present pay the highest salaries, have a standing rule to employ none but first or higher classes of licensed teachers."[26] From the beginning of the century

London's staff consisted exclusively of teachers with first- or second-class certificates, the only exceptions being those with specialist certificates in areas like kindergarten, domestic science, or manual training; even its supply teachers had at least second-class certificates.[27] Other evidence confirms the pattern time and time again; in 1911 an Alberta inspector reported, typically: "Some very superior teachers are found of course in the country, but the tendency is for the best teachers to gravitate to the towns leaving the rural and especially the outlying and short-term schools in the hands of third class and permit teachers. These teachers are, as a rule, inferior in all that constitutes equipment for efficient work."[28]

Though the data are incomplete, figures for the interwar years suggest two trends. First, there was a persistent gap between levels of certification in urban and rural areas; but second, rural areas substantially closed that gap. The most dramatic changes, compared to Miller's 1913 figures, were, in the countryside, the near-elimination of permit and third-class teachers, the remarkable increase in those holding first-class certificates, and the concomitant decline in the number of second-class certificates (Table 5.2). By 1940, 67% of urban teachers held first-class or higher certificates but so did 64% of rural teachers. Both categories include communities and schools of various sizes, but even when we isolate the largest and the smallest, the difference is minimal: 66% of the teachers in Canada's city schools held first-class certificates, while in the one-room schools that figure stood at 64%, an enormous change from the situation two or three decades earlier.[29]

There are no national-level longitudinal data that identify the qualifications of those who taught secondary-school subjects. Some provinces didn't distinguish between elementary and secondary teachers, and when others did so, categorization was too idiosyncratic to allow much in the way of comparison.[30] For that reason we settle on Ontario as an exemplar, in large part because the data are consistent over the entire period and the *Annual Reports* clearly distinguish between the different kinds of schools offering secondary education (see Table 5.3). What is most important here is the sharp difference between the qualifications of teachers in urban and rural areas. Ontario's collegiate institutes and high schools, located in the cities, towns, and larger villages, were staffed in the main by university graduates, indeed largely by subject specialists (those holding honours degrees in particular subjects). Thus these urban schools had a corps of teachers well prepared to offer the high school curriculum. The continuation schools were far less well equipped for that. Before 1939–40 the majority of their teachers held first-class elementary certificates: that is, the majority had completed senior matriculation (five years of high school) but not university. Instruction in the fifth classes of the elementary schools was even more

Table 5.2
Rural/urban distribution of Canadian teachers by certificate, 1922, 1931, 1940

	1922		1931		1940	
	Rural %	Urban %	Rural %	Urban %	Rural %	Urban %
Class I[a]	8.2	19.6	26.9	41.7%	63.9	66.9
Class II	60.4	66.9	66.3	50.5	31.4	24.3
Class III	24.6	5.2	3.4	0.6	2.1	0.5
Temporary, permit, etc.[b]	6.5	2.5	2.8	0.1		
Special[c]	0.3	5.7	0.5	6.7	2.1	8.1
Unspecified	–	–	0.1	0.3	0.6	0.2

[a] In 1931 "academic," "grammar school," and "superior" are included. In 1940 the category is "Class I or higher."

[b] Includes temporary, district, provisional, permanent ungraded (a category used only for Roman Catholic separate school teachers in Ontario), permissive, permit. No such category in 1940.

[c] Includes special, specialist; in Ontario in 1922, kindergarten, kindergarten/primary, manual training, household science; and in 1931, kindergarten, primary, special subjects. In 1940, the category is "miscellaneous and special."

Notes:

1. Ontario figures in 1922, but not in 1931, include urban and rural Roman Catholic separate school teachers. Roman Catholic separate school teachers in Alberta in 1922 were listed but excluded here because no rural/urban distinctions were made. Ontario in 1922 and 1931 and British Columbia in 1930 include only elementary teachers. In 1940, elementary and secondary teachers in all provinces are included.

2. Rural versus urban: provincial categories differ in 1922 and 1931. When not labelled as urban or rural, they were grouped as follows:
   • 1922. Prince Edward Island: "primary" school teachers were assigned to the rural category, "graded" school teachers to urban. Alberta: town, village, and consolidated schools designated as urban. Ontario: city, town, and village schools designated as urban.
   • 1931. Nova Scotia, "city and town," urban; "rural and village," rural; New Brunswick: "grammar, superior, other graded," urban; "ungraded," rural; Ontario: city, town, and village schools designated as urban; Manitoba: "consolidated" and "other graded," urban; "rural ungraded," rural (542 out of 4,427 teachers are missing from the original data, and they were probably urban); British Columbia: "city municipalities" versus "rural municipalities" and "rural and assisted."
   • 1940. All provinces: the categories are "city," "town and village," "rural, more than one room," "one-room rural." The first two are combined in this table as urban, the last two as rural.

3. See additional commentary on the construction of this table in appendix B, section 4.

Sources:

1922: DBS, *Annual Report 1922*, 132–3 (Prince Edward Island, Saskatchewan, Alberta); DBS, *Annual Survey 1923*, 68–9 (Ontario, 1922).

1931: DBS, *Annual Survey 1930*, 69 (British Columbia, 1930: data not available for 1931); DBS, *Annual Survey 1931*, 75–6 (Nova Scotia, New Brunswick), 80–1 (Manitoba, Saskatchewan); DBS, *Annual Survey 1932*, 77 (Ontario, 1931).

1940: DBS, *Elementary and Secondary Education 1938–40*, 70–7 (Prince Edward Island, Nova Scotia, New Brunswick, Ontario, Manitoba, Saskatchewan, Alberta, British Columbia).

Table 5.3
Ontario secondary school teacher qualifications, 1915–1945

	Collegiate institute/high school		Vocational		Continuation school		5th class	
	% G	% S	% G	% S	% G	% S	1st-class certificate	2nd-class certificate
1915	71.0	59.0	–	–	–	–	29.7	69.3
1920	73.1	72.1	–	–	27.4	23.4	39.4*	59.6*
1925	82.5	72.3	57.4	47.6	12.1	16.4	38.3	61.1
1930	89.8	74.4	67.0	49.1	11.6	7.9	45.3	53.8
1935	94.7	78.4	69.1	57.1	44.2	19.3	–	–
1940	93.7	80.1	71.6	65.0	59.4	35.7	–	–
1945	91.6	68.8	73.9	61.1	56.9	19.8	–	–

*1921 data
G: university graduate
S: subject specialist
Note: Fifth-class teachers: In each year a very small number of those who hold first-class certificates also have BAs; an even smaller number have third-class certificates. The year 1930 is the last in which fifth-class teachers and their certificates appear in the *ARs*.
See additional commentary on the construction of this table in appendix B, section 5.

Sources: Ontario, AR *1915*, 218–23, 309; *AR 1920*, 346, 386; *AR 1921*, 282–7; *AR 1925*, 256–63; *AR 1930*, 424–41; Ontario, *Schools and Teachers in the Province of Ontario*, 1930, 673, 696; Ontario, *AR 1934*, 113; *AR 1940*, 121; *AR 1945*, 110.

problematic. Though the statistics are not complete, a majority of those teaching fifth classes had second-class certificates – that is, they taught high school subjects at a level only marginally below the grades they themselves had completed.

This hierarchy of secondary school qualifications, we suggest, applied everywhere in Canada where the one-room high school or the equivalent of Ontario's fifth classes had been allowed to develop. It was obviously true, for example, in Nova Scotia, with its well-educated urban high school teachers on the one hand and, on the other, students studying secondary subjects in the rural common schools, taught by teachers with, *at best*, second-class elementary certificates.[31] The pattern also held in British Columbia in the 1930s. There, most high school teachers, even in the small rural high schools, were university graduates.[32] In the "junior high schools," nearly all located in the larger urban areas and combining the senior elementary and junior secondary school grades, almost half the teachers had academic certificates by 1940. But in the rural "superior schools," far fewer teachers held such qualifications; the vast majority had only first- or even second-class certificates.[33]

In Alberta's cities, writes one historian, "practically all the members of the academic high school staffs held university degrees," but of those "who taught in one-room high schools in rural areas," only 25% had university degrees and the rest had first-class certificates.[34] By 1939–40, 80% of city high school teachers had degrees; in the non-urban high schools, 56%.[35] As for Alberta's rural elementary schools, where, by 1935, high school subjects were widely taught, only 47% of teachers held first-class certificates; that year the province's chief inspector of schools noted that "the inclusion of so much high school instruction in our one-room rural schools makes it imperative that a proportionately higher number of teachers hold First Class Certificates."[36] While it might have been true, in sum, that the qualifications of rural and urban elementary school teachers were converging in the interwar years, it is clearly not true of those responsible for teaching secondary school subjects.

II

Formal qualifications, in any case, tell only part of the story. One also has to take account of experience, which is at least as pertinent for teacher effectiveness as academic and professional training. Twenty years' experience is not necessarily twice as good as ten. But what is true for many other occupations is equally true for teaching: there are significant differences in the quality of work performed as practitioners pass from novice level, through competent and proficient levels, to expert status.[37] There are, however, two kinds of experience that matter. One is cumulative or total experience: how many years did an individual work as a teacher? The other is the degree of continuity in a particular school: an individual may have accumulated five years of teaching but teacher effectiveness will also depend on whether that teacher spent those five years in one school or in five different schools. There is no question that this latter form of experience – continuity in the classroom, or low rates of turnover term by term, year by year – was valued in the early twentieth century as indeed it is today. Higher rates of turnover, a Prince Edward Island commission argued in 1910, operate against the success of the school system in two ways: "[T]he ever-flitting teacher does not identify himself sufficiently with a district to gain for himself and the school system the intelligent and sympathetic support of the people of his district – [high turnover] also thwarts any plan or purpose that might be introduced into school work and school methods were there no change of teachers ... A paralyzing laissez-faire characterizes teacher and pupils: nothing is attempted but the most formal textbook work."[38] For Manitoba's Murray Commission, high rates of turnover meant "there can be no continuity of plan and no sustained interest. At the beginning of each school year, the most valuable assets of the teacher, an understanding of the interests, needs, aptitudes and abilities of her pupils and the confidence of the parents, have to be acquired anew and always with a loss of time."[39] Ruminating on the effect of high turnover rates in Nova Scotia, McGregor Dawson, at the time one of Canada's most distinguished academics, would comment in 1944 that "while a certain shifting about is stimulating for both the teacher and the school, instability on this scale throws many schools into a never ending confusion, and by breaking the continuity, largely destroys the effectiveness of teaching."[40]

What, then, do we know about total experience in teaching, on the one hand, and "experience at present school," on the other? Lacking good national-level data for cumulative experience in the first decade of the century, Miller used age as a surrogate and thought it a safe generalization that "the great majority of rural teachers in Canada are between 17 and 23 years of age. Youthfulness, with inadequate experience in life, learning, and professional work is one of the chief characteristics of rural teachers."[41] As for turnover rates, in the case of Alberta, where Miller had better data, he concluded that in the school year 1910 no fewer than 749 out of a total of 2,651 teachers changed their position *during* the year.[42] In 1915 Harold Foght prepared a careful statistical profile of rural teachers in Saskatchewan. Of 2,301 teachers reporting, 1,400 were 25 years old or less and 684 were between 17 and 20. Thirty per cent had only one year of teaching, 14% had one to two years, 23.2% had two to five years, and 24.6% had five years or more.[43] In 1916 one inspector in rural Manitoba reported that "of his 44 teachers, 3 have no experience, 8 have had one-half year's experience, 12 have had experience of from one to one-half years, 3 from 2 to 3 years and 8 over 3 years."[44] Between 1910 and 1920 nearly 70% of Nova Scotia's teachers had five years' experience or less and just over 40% had two years' or less.[45] In the rural districts of the same province, there was, according to one report, "a turnover of 50% of the teachers annually. This is probably correct, as about one-third of all teachers have but one year's experience."[46] Ontario also consistently collected data on total experience across several decades: in 1910 urban elementary teachers averaged about eleven and a half years and rural elementary teachers five years of experience; these figures hardly budged through to 1920.[47]

The greater experience of urban teachers was partly owing to individual preferences and better salaries, but also because urban school boards tended to hire only experienced teachers – experience that had to be acquired in rural schools. According to Richardson's survey of fifty-nine city boards in the second decade of the century, nearly all "required 2 or 3 years of experience."[48] Vancouver and Calgary, for example, demanded at least two years' experience.[49] Though somewhat more flexible when it came to those who had first-class certificates, Winnipeg's policy was that "teachers holding only second class Professional Certificates to be eligible for appointment, must present satisfactory evidence of having at least 3 years experience in teaching, subsequent to a recognized course of Normal Training."[50]

Compared to the first two decades of the century, we have suggested, qualifications improved dramatically during the interwar years. Did experience follow a similar trajectory? Trying to get a national approximation for the shifts taking place between 1913 and 1931, the Dominion Bureau of Statistics' (DBS's) education specialist estimated that "half the Maritime teachers of 1913 had taught less than 3½ years; those of 1931, more than 4½ years ... There was a corresponding change in Ontario, though not as great, for the Ontario teachers were more permanent in the earlier year. The Western provinces have not kept a record of teachers' experience since 1913. But the Education Branch of the Dominion Bureau of Statistics has compiled a record for Manitoba for about half of the period, and if it is a fair indication of what has been happening in these provinces, as there is good reason to believe, the increase in length of tenure has been even more pronounced than in the more easterly provinces."[51] Where a continuous record exists, however, it is clear that increases in experience took place in the postwar period and not before. Average experience in Ontario improved only marginally between 1910 and 1920 but by something like a full year during the 1920s, from 8.5 to 9.5 years.[52] In Nova Scotia, average experience declined between 1910 and 1920 and only began to improve after that.[53] During the 1920s, nevertheless, the gains were modest, and it was only in the 1930s that substantial change occurred. Between 1929–30 and 1936–37 alone, for example, average experience in Ontario increased by two full years, from 9.5 to 11.6 years; sharp increases also occurred across the decade of the 1930s in Nova Scotia, New Brunswick, and Manitoba.[54]

In 1938 the DBS managed to get seven provinces to submit data on total experience. By this point Canadian schools had acquired a workforce that was far more experienced than ever before. Close to 40% of teachers had ten or more years of experience, and another 20% had between six and nine years – that is, nearly 60% had six or more years, an arbitrary marker but one that indicates something substantially more than that of a novice practitioner.[55] During the interwar years, in other words, increases in experience initially lagged behind improved qualifications but in the 1930s both rose substantially.

Some DBS data were presented only as medians – that is, the point at which 50% of teachers were below it and 50% above. There were, as one might expect, differences between provinces, but even here our guestimate is that these narrowed during the 1930s. In 1941 the median experience for Canada (including Ontario and Quebec) was seven years and five months. While British Columbia, Manitoba, and Ontario were just above a ten-year median, Nova Scotia, at six and a half years, was close to the national median and not much different from Saskatchewan and Alberta. Compared to other provinces, on the other hand, Nova Scotia and Prince Edward Island (and probably New Brunswick) had an inordinately high percentage of teachers with one year's experience or less. Whereas the other provinces hovered just above or below 10%, Nova Scotia stood at 20% and Prince Edward Island at 25%.[56]

Levels of total experience for both urban and rural teachers appear to have improved during the interwar years, but there was no diminution in the gap between them.[57] In a British Columbia study based on data from the early 1920s, the median total experience for city elementary school teachers was 7.4 years and for rural school teachers 3.2.[58] By 1936 the gap had widened to between 10 and 15 years in the city, but only 4 years in rural one-room schools.[59] During the 1920s in Ontario the average experience of rural teachers was 4 or 5 years; in urban communities it was more like 12 or 13.[60] In the early 1930s, when the data begin to improve, the urban–rural gap is sharp in all reporting provinces.[61] In Nova Scotia the median total experience for city and town teachers was 7.8 years, and 40% had less than five years' experience. In the rural and village schools, the median was 1.9 years, and 77% had under five years' experience. In Ontario and Manitoba, the median experience of both urban and rural teachers was greater but the gap was just as wide. In Table 5.4 we present the equivalent data for 1938. This is especially useful because the data is broken down in a consistent way for all seven reporting provinces: "city," "town and village," "rural, more than one room," and "one-room rural." The table makes two things obvious: first, there is a rough hierarchy of places, with cities at the top and one-room schools at the bottom; and second, the difference in total experience, even at the end of the Depression, is wide indeed – very large numbers of city teachers had many years of experience but almost two-thirds of those in one-room rural schools had five years or less and a third two years or less.

Thus far we have been examining *total* teaching experience. What about that second category, "experience where teaching" (that is, years of continuous teaching in the same school)? Until the late 1930s there are no systematic national data over time but there is also no shortage of spot surveys or commentary. In Ontario at the turn of the century there were already near-annual complaints and the differences between town and country were well established. In 1904, for example, one informed estimate was that "about 40% of the public schools change teachers every year"; yet only a few years later London's school inspector could declare that "the public

Table 5.4
Total experience, elementary and secondary school teachers, Canada, 1938

	City		Town and village		Rural, more than one room		Rural, one room	
Up to 2 years	296	4.4%	451	8.7%	681	17.1%	4,080	33.3%
Up to 5 years	894	13.2%	1,320	25.8%	1,678	42.4%	7,707	63.2%
6+ years	901	86.3%	1,285	74.3%	1,000	57.4%	2,636	36.7%
10+ years	4,947	73.0%	2,516	49.2%	1,268	32.1%	1,837	15.1%

Notes:
1. Totals from which percentages were calculated include "unspecified."
2. Provinces included are Prince Edward Island, Nova Scotia, New Brunswick, Manitoba, Saskatchewan, Alberta, and British Columbia.
3. No data for Ontario or Quebec.
4. See additional commentary on the construction of this table in appendix B, section 6.

Source: DBS, *Elementary and Secondary Education 1936–38*, 60–7.

school staff in London is practically permanent, less than 5% being newly appointed each year."[62] Foght's Saskatchewan survey of 1915 revealed that 41% of rural teachers had one year or less in the same school, 20% had one to two years, and 16% had between two and five years. Thus the vast majority of rural school teachers had five years' or less experience in the same school, and a large minority had one year or less.[63] In the early 1920s in British Columbia, teaching experience "in present position" was far less than total experience but still much longer in urban than in rural schools: in city elementary schools, 3.37 years, and in the rural schools, 1.64 years.[64] At just about the same time, Manitoba's Murray Commission reported that "a study made of an extensive rural area, covering a period of five years, showed that 88% of teachers in the area, which was typical of rural Manitoba, remained only one year in a school."[65] Turnover in his district, one New Brunswick inspector noted, was a major problem for the ungraded schools: "Not less than 70% of these had a change of teachers at the end of the school year, June 1928, and 20% had a change at the end of the first term."[66] "The frequent changing of teachers," Saskatchewan's chief inspector reported in 1927, "still remains a serious problem. From one of the older areas, one inspector writes that only 10% of his 75 rural schools have teachers who have been with them 2 years or more."[67] In the mid-1930s more than 50% of Nova Scotia's rural and village teachers changed "from one section to another from year to year; thus many communities do not receive the benefit of long teaching tenure."[68] An Alberta study reported that "a second serious aspect of the teaching profession is the unfortunate and frequently wasteful shifting of teachers from school to school. In 1939

... 2,175 of the 5,963 teachers in the province were new to the positions which they filled for the year. In one-room schools the position was still more unstable; over half – 1,469 of the 2,757 teachers in one-room rural schools were new to their positions."[69] In British Columbia's one-room rural elementary schools, 33% of teachers in 1936 had six or more years' experience, but only 9% had chalked up six or more years at the same place; 78% had held the same job for three years or less.[70]

Beginning in 1938, "experience where teaching" was added to the data the DBS was trying to collect from all provinces, and thus for the first time there are good national figures for teacher turnover. Since the question referred to continuous experience within a school board and not at a particular school, we cannot compare urban and rural turnover rates; in the larger urban communities a teacher might serve the same board for long periods of time but not necessarily work at the same school. But it certainly tells us a lot about the situation in rural Canada, where most school boards operated only one school. While 37% of the teachers in one-room schools had six or more years of total experience, only 5% had held the same job for six or more years; a whopping 88% remained at the same school for three years or less![71]

III

Questions about the ethnic and social origins of teachers are as pertinent as they were, in chapter 2, for pupils, but the data are much more limited. The only published national-level source for the ethnic origin of teachers is in the census of 1931 and 1941.[72] This includes all teachers, not just those in the provincial school systems, but the tabulations offer us regional breakdowns, excluding Quebec, and a portrait of two different (though overlapping) generations – those teaching in 1931 or 1941 would include not just those who had recently entered the occupation but also those who had taught for a decade or more beforehand. In most of the country the two charter groups, British and French, together constituted over 90% of Canada's teachers; for 1931, in the Maritimes, Ontario, and British Columbia, the figures for the British alone are 80%, 85%, and 90% respectively, and they are only marginally different in 1941. Given the educational advantages that accrued to children of British origin as they progressed through the school system, it should come as no surprise that, in Ontario for example, teachers of British origin were, compared to the labour force as a whole, substantially over-represented in teaching.[73] The three Prairie provinces, however, constitute something of a special case. By 1931 the large influx of prewar European immigrants was just beginning to make itself felt. Their children, nearly all Canadian-born, constituted about 20%

of the workforce in teaching – 13.7% of German, Dutch, or Scandinavian origin and 6.5% from Eastern Europe. By 1941 the former group constituted some 15%, and the latter 12%, of Prairie teachers. Compared to their numbers in the labour force as a whole, they were still under-represented in teaching; the percentages, nevertheless, are substantial. That is to say, the interwar years saw the gradual penetration of significant numbers of newcomers into the occupation and provide a demonstration of the way in which first the schools and then teaching itself could be used as a means of social mobility by individuals from subaltern groups. And it is probably telling on this latter point that, in contrast to teachers of British or French origin, there was a substantially higher percentage of males of East European origin than of females.

Indeed, in the case of new teachers, the influx of those of non-British origin was in danger of becoming a flood, and because this was causing a good deal of unease among Prairie education officials, they were good enough to leave us a record. In 1930, for example, at the Regina and Saskatoon normal schools, 30% of the students were of non-British origin, and at Moose Jaw normal school in 1929 the figure was 39%. By 1937 the principal of the Saskatoon normal school was reporting that 45% of the students were of non-English origin.[74] A study that covered the years 1927–28 through 1935–36 concluded that 24% of Manitoba's normal school students were of non-"Anglo-Saxon" or non-"French" background.[75] An Alberta analysis done in 1943 of the ethnic origins of students at the Edmonton normal school found that 30% were of non-British origin in 1930–31, but by the late 1930s and early 1940s the figure was hovering around 50%; the percentages were only somewhat lower at the Calgary normal school.[76] Whatever was happening in the rest of the country during the interwar years, on the prairies the ethnic complexion of teaching was gradually undergoing a transformation that would provide a concomitant diversification of the experiences and values teachers brought to the classroom.

We know almost nothing about the social origins of twentieth-century teachers, and this will probably remain the case until historians have access to the household census returns – sources that have proved so productive in understanding many aspects of nineteenth-century Canadian education. Indeed, the only solid evidence we have comes from those sources and for a period just preceding the main focus of this chapter. In 1881, writes Eric Sager, the odds were that young women teachers in Ontario "came from a farm family or a working-class family." Some 46% of their fathers were farmers, another 15% were in manufacturing and construction, and only the rare father was in one of the professions (5%). Then, comparing the 1881 and 1901 censuses, Sager adds that "in both years almost half of [women] teachers' fathers were farmers and a similar proportion (15% or 16%) were in manufacturing or construction. But by 1901 many more were in the professions or government (12.5% compared to 5%), and more (10% versus 6% in 1881) were in other white-collar jobs (clerks, merchants, dealers, agents and the like)."[77] Aside from the occasional biographies of individuals, we have almost nothing else to help us except some returns from the Saskatoon normal schools during the interwar years, which reveal that a majority or near-majority came from farm families and many of the rest from small shopkeepers', skilled artisans', and even labourers' families. Take, for example, the Saskatoon normal school in 1930: 49% of its 383 students' fathers were listed as farmers, 11% as "skilled mechanic," 10% as "storekeepers," 9.4% as "executive," 6.5% as "unskilled labourer," 5% as "professional," and 6% as deceased.[78] How typical this would be of the rest of the country we do not know, though it's plausible to think that in, say, Ontario, we would find a smaller proportion of students from farm families and far more from urban occupations.[79] Since American parallels can sometimes be applied to Canada, we also have instructive studies from historians or contemporary observers, especially for the early twentieth century, where one major survey similarly found that farmers' children constituted a majority of teachers but that there were also substantial minorities from artisans' and labourers' families.[80]

All this is hardly more than suggestive, let alone conclusive, and thus the reader may well ask why we even bother to raise the matter. There are two reasons. First, we think it is an important question that needs to be flagged for further work. The study of social origins is a constituent part of social analysis, and the literature on twentieth-century teachers, especially women teachers, is now considerable; yet on this basic issue, Canadian scholarship is remarkably uninformed. Any future release of the twentieth-century household census may answer key questions here, and it may also be possible for someone to locate and exploit an alternative source that allows, at least, an illuminating micro-study.[81]

The second reason, though, is more in the form of a cautionary alert. In a penetrating study of women elementary school teachers in late nineteenth- and early twentieth-century London, England, Dina Copelman was able to trace the social origins of many of her teachers and found they were, in the main, from lower-middle and upper-working-class families that had distinctive constellations of values and experience. These were families where working women were ubiquitous, though often working within the home or in a family business; where young men and women were expected to find occupations for themselves; where, in any given family, those occupations might include jobs on both sides of the manual/non-manual divide; where family or individual economic circumstance might be precarious; and where, in any event, they were exposed to close and extended contact with others even less well off than themselves.[82] That is to say, the values Copelman's teachers may have brought to the job cannot simply be described as "middle class" and, in important respects, need to be distinguished from patterns of behaviour and belief common among those more highly placed in the social hierarchy. The little we know about Canadian teachers tells us that they were the children of farmers, artisans, small shopkeepers, clerks, and others who, overall, might certainly be described as "middling" but who were not from the upper echelons of the professional and entrepreneurial classes. Copelman's argument should encourage us, at least until we know far more than we now do, to avoid glib assertions about teachers' "middle-class" origins and "middle-class" values, or their role in transmitting purportedly "middle-class" values to those whom they taught.

IV

The feminization of teaching that had begun in the middle decades of the nineteenth century reached its apogee in the early twentieth century, when just over 80% of the teachers in English Canada's public school systems were women (see Table 5.5). Though the percentage of female teachers would remain high, there were modest changes in the pattern across the first four decades of the century. The percentage of men fell to its lowest figure, 15.5%, during the latter stages of the First World War, then gradually rose during the early 1920s.[83] By 1925 the proportion of males was about equal to that of 1914, about 20%. The most dramatic change, however, took place during the Depression, when the number of males increased by nearly 10%.[84] By the end of the 1930s, the proportion of women to men was, roughly, 7:3, and while the Second World War would bring a temporary reversal, 1930 marked the end of the long-term trend towards the feminization of teaching. The occupation would never again be as overwhelmingly female as it was in the first three decades of the twentieth century.[85]

There were, however, substantial regional variations. Between 1910 and 1930, Nova Scotia and New Brunswick had extremely high levels of feminization – 90% or higher – and there were only slight declines in the 1930s. Ontario and Manitoba sat on the national average, but across the entire four decades, Saskatchewan, Alberta, and especially British Columbia had much higher percentages of males. By 1940 the differences looked something like this: about 85% women in Nova Scotia and New Brunswick, just above 70% in Ontario and Manitoba, and as low as 62% in British Columbia.[86] The causes or consequences of these differences remain unexplored, but they certainly gave a different complexion, and perhaps a different image, to the occupation in different parts of the country. Once again, in any case, we have a distinct east-west pattern for the country as a whole.[87]

Table 5.5
Male and female school teachers, Canada, 1905–1970: percentage female and rates of growth

	Male		Female		% Female
	N	R	N	R	
1905	4,970		16,039		76.3
1910	6,063	22.0	21,523	34.2	80.8
1915	6,526	7.6	28,370	31.8	81.3
1920	6,969	6.8	33,608	18.5	82.8
1925	8,894	27.6	35,824	6.6	80.1
1930	10,504	18.1	38,770	8.2	78.7
1935	13,871	32.1	35,647	-8.1	72.0
1940	14,352	3.5	35,726	0.2	71.3
1945	11,774	-18.0	39,241	9.8	76.9
1950	18,521	57.3	44,510	13.4	70.6
1955	24,382	31.6	56,152	26.2	69.7
1960	34,975	43.4	72,371	28.9	67.4
1965	53,089	51.8	88,583	22.4	62.5
1970	73,312	38.1	111,167	25.5	60.3

R = rate of growth every 5 years
Notes: Excludes Quebec. Includes all elementary and secondary school teachers in public systems. Data for Saskatchewan and Alberta not given before 1905 in original table. After 1945, includes Newfoundland.

Source: Leacy, *Historical Statistics,* Series W150–191.

Leaving aside the issue of gender differentials both in salaries and managerial control, we still want to know what other types of differences existed between male and female teachers.* It might be supposed, for example, that men were more likely to be found in urban, and women in rural, areas. The data available to address this issue are limited, but they indicate that there were no significant differences: men were as likely as women to teach in rural areas and women as likely as men to teach in urban areas.[88] We think there are at least two plausible explanations for this: whether they stayed in teaching or not, young men, like young women, usually had to begin in rural rather than urban schools, since urban boards preferred experienced personnel; and in rural schools with two or three teachers, men could often (but not always) be found as senior teachers or principals. Be that as it may, it seems worthwhile to note that the rural school was not the exclusive preserve of women teachers.

In the attempt to distinguish qualifications by gender, the only data at our disposal are compilations of provincial certificates, and even then

* We tackle managerial control in chapter 12. We have explored salary differentials at some length elsewhere; see Gidney and Millar, "Salaries of Teachers in English Canada," 13–18.

there are no adequate national-level data before 1920.[89] On the other hand, there are three tolerably good data points for the interwar years: 1922, 1931, and 1938. During the interwar years both men and women improved their qualifications at roughly equivalent rates; that is, the rising qualifications characteristic of these two decades were not the result of some unexpected surge by either sex. But men tended to be somewhat better qualified than women, and this male advantage persisted throughout the 1920s and 1930s.[90]

National or provincial totals, however, minimize the gender gap in qualifications because they fail to take account of urban/rural differences. Except in the Maritimes, where even in one-room schools women were substantially less qualified than men, women and men were roughly equally qualified in the ungraded schools; men held an edge but we don't think it is very significant. This, it seems to us, simply reflects the fact that these were the schools of the inexperienced and of those most likely to hold second-class certificates. But in all other categories of school – "two or more rooms rural," "town and village," and "city," men were substantially better qualified, and by margins of 20% or more. By 1938, in British Columbia's cities, for example, 81% of men held first-class certificates compared to 63% of women, and the gap in the rural schools with two or more rooms was even greater. In Nova Scotia's cities, 95% of men held first-class certificates but only 63% of women; in its "town and village" schools the figures were 89% and 41% respectively, and in every category women were far more likely to hold third-class certificates (a level virtually non-existent beyond the Maritimes).[91] Again, we can only speculate on the reason for the gap that, to one extent or another, existed right across the country, but our guess is that if males intended to make a career of teaching, then even though they might begin with second-class certificates, they tended to upgrade to first-class early on in order to get the better salaries and better posts that first-class certificates helped secure. Plenty of women must have done this too; after all, Canada-wide, by 1938 an absolute majority of women – and an absolute majority in each category of school – held first-class certificates. But the difference may be that a much larger percentage of women left the occupation to get married or for other reasons, and thus, not expecting to treat it as a career, they diluted the proportion who sought first-class certificates.[92]

There are no national data for experience by gender until 1938, and these figures probably reflect the cumulative pressures of the Depression. But at that point, 62% of the men and 57% of the women had six or more years' teaching experience; 42% of the men and 36% of the women had ten years or more. While men tended to have somewhat more experience, in other words, the difference was relatively modest and in some provinces it was marginal. Moreover, while levels of experience in urban and rural schools varied sharply for both men and women, there was no great difference within each category of school. In the cities, for example, 72% of men and 74% of women had taught for ten or more years, whereas only 21% of rural men and 13% of rural women had that level of experience. Taking the cities, towns, and villages together, women had just as much experience as men, and these urban women had more experience than men in rural schools, graded or ungraded.[93]

While the 1938 national data offer us no help with change over time, there is a run of Ontario statistics extending from 1912 through 1936–37 covering public elementary school teachers only. In 1912 the average experience for males was 11.8 years and for females, 7.4. But over the next two decades that gap closed steadily until, in 1932, it was, for both sexes, just under 10 years. Women then pulled ahead, and by 1937 the average experience for women was 12.6 years and for men 9.8.[94] We assume that the shift was due to the flood of young men into teaching during the Depression and a concomitant tendency for women to hold on to their jobs during hard times. For certain years we can also distinguish between categories of Ontario communities, and clearly both place and gender played a role in determining levels of experience. Both men and women teachers in city schools had more experience than their counterparts in rural schools, and indeed in smaller urban centres. But in the 1920s men were generally more experienced than women in each location, *except* in city schools, where over the entire period women teachers had more experience than men. In other places the gap between the career length of men and women teachers lessened into the 1930s; the only really sharp differences then for either sex were along the urban/rural hierarchy, though there was a tendency for women to have slightly greater experience than men in most geographical locations by 1932.[95]

Over the first four decades of the twentieth century, in any case, levels of experience for all teachers rose, moderately in the larger cities and towns, where they were always relatively high, and substantially in rural areas, where by 1941, 60% of teachers had six years or more experience and nearly 40% had ten or more. But the most dramatic changes occurred among women teachers. By 1941, the median for city women in Ontario was nearly seventeen years, two years longer than for men; in towns and villages it was twelve years, a year longer than for men. The gap between town and country was still larger; the 1941 median in rural schools was six and one-half years for both men and women. But this meant that half the women teachers – who formed the large majority of rural teachers – had more than six years' experience. While by 1941, right across Canada, rural pupils were less likely to encounter experienced teachers than their urban counterparts, they were far more likely than two or three decades earlier to have a teacher who had already learned her job.[96]

Not only did experience increase over the first four decades of the twentieth century, but the workforce grew older. That may strike the reader as tautological, which it is; but there are implications nonetheless. According to the census of 1921, nearly 30% of male teachers and 50% of females were under age 25 and another 30% of both sexes were between 25 and 34 – that is, about 60% of males and 80% of females were under 35. Between 1910 and 1920, in other words, we are dealing with a workforce that is very young. The 1941 census, measuring those who were teaching in the interwar years, recorded a much different picture. Eighty-five per cent of men and 73% of women were 25 years or older.[97] The percentage of women who were under 25 had dropped from 50% in 1921 to 27% in 1941, a change that narrowed the gap between men and women and thus reduced some of the psychological imbalances encouraged by the earlier disproportions between young women and older men. But perhaps the most important consequence for the classroom was simply the increasing maturity of the workforce. By itself, greater maturity is hardly a substitute for experience (or common sense), but it does contribute to establishing and maintaining the pedagogical authority necessary for effective instruction.

Because of the lack of data, we cannot identify, at the national level, any distinctive gender patterns among high school teachers. All we can do, once again, is to rely on the relatively rich Ontario data (along with some more limited figures from British Columbia) and hope that they approximate patterns in the rest of the country.[98] For most of the nineteenth century, teaching in Canadian secondary schools was a man's job. Even in 1900 less than 20% of Ontario's collegiate and high school teachers were female. Rising high school enrolments, however, expanded job opportunities for the growing number of women with university degrees, and the First World War drained men out of high school classrooms. By 1920 half of Ontario's secondary school staffs were women, and by 1930 the figure stood at 55%. The collegiate institutes were more resistant to the trend than the small-town high schools, but by 1930, 46% of even their teachers were women. From their inception, moreover, the continuation schools were dominated by women teachers – 53% in 1910 and 64% in 1930. As in the elementary schools, the 1930s witnessed a return of male teachers and modest declines in the percentage of female teachers in the collegiate institutes, high schools, and continuation schools alike.[99] Nonetheless, over the course of four decades, secondary school teaching in Ontario had ceased to be a male preserve. The same pattern apparently holds for British Columbia. Though there is no breakdown by gender before 1922, at that point 40%

of that province's high school teachers were women, the percentage of women throughout the period tended to be higher in rural than in urban high schools, and there is the same modest decline in the proportion of women teachers during the 1930s.

The data on experience are extremely limited, coming from the same two provinces and for a few years in the 1930s only. In both Ontario and British Columbia, male high school teachers tended to have somewhat more experience than females, though this may be nothing more than a surrogate for their earlier disproportionate access to the job. Though hardly novel in light of all the other conclusions in this chapter, urban high school teachers, male and female alike, tended to have more experience than those in rural areas, which also meant a hierarchy of experience according to the type of school; in Ontario, for example, continuation school teachers had less experience than teachers in urban high schools.[100] Perhaps the only surprise here is the comparison of high school teachers and city elementary school teachers. Women elementary school teachers in the cities of both Ontario and British Columbia were the most experienced teachers in their respective provinces – not, as one might expect, their better-paid, better-educated counterparts, male or female, in the secondary schools.

Before the turn of the century, in Ontario at least, those women who did teach high school were less likely than men to have a university degree – having instead a first-class elementary certificate – and thus more likely to be consigned to teaching the lower high school grades. In each decade after 1890, however, this gap narrowed: by 1920, 81% of male high school teachers had university degrees but so did 67% of women; by 1930, nearly all women in Ontario's academic secondary schools had degrees but only 78% of the men did.[101] This too had consequences. Traditionally, teaching had been dichotomized by gender distinctions aligned with social status. The male secondary school teacher held a much higher social status than his female elementary counterpart by virtue of his university degree and his distinctive role in preparing an academic elite for social leadership. By 1940 the social distinction between secondary and elementary teachers held fast: the degree was not just an academic or occupational denominator but a social one as well.[102] But the link between occupational status and gender had been largely shorn. Women were as likely to teach secondary school as men, to do so with the same qualifications, and to share the social prestige that, together, both circumstances conferred.

Over the past several decades much attention has been lavished on the comparatively small number of professional women – secondary school teachers among others – who first succeeded in gaining access to Canadian universities. In large part this is due to an understandable but persistent presentist bias that equates high levels of educational achievement and equality of opportunity with the possession of an undergraduate arts degree and access to post-graduate professional training. A plausible interpretive stance for the last half of the twentieth century, it fails, before that, to take adequate account of the critical importance of the selective secondary school and more particularly of the senior high school grades rather than the under-graduate degree as the gatekeeper for professional careers. The result is a tendency to underestimate or overlook the educational achievements of those who taught elementary school in an era before the credentials spiral had entirely transformed both the high school and the university. During the first four decades of the twentieth century, teachers' academic education and professional training improved, and in the interwar years, improved dramatically. Permits and third-class certificates virtually disappeared; a full year of professional training became the norm; nearly all teachers had completed high school; and a large number held senior matriculation certificates, the equivalent of completing first-year university. While these achievements may seem modest by today's standards, they need to be put firmly in their historical context. Those who completed grade IX or X (the requirement for a third-class certificate in 1910 or 1920) achieved a higher level of education than most of their peers. A junior matriculation certifi-cate (grade XI or XII), let alone a senior matriculation certificate (grade XII or XIII), was far above the average education young people attained in the first four decades of the century. Even among the "well educated" it was a substantial achievement at a time when a high school and not an undergraduate education admitted students directly to law, medicine, or engineering schools, and when the only occupations that required (or at least preferred) an arts degree were those of high school and university teachers and clergymen of the mainstream Protestant churches.[103] In the decades immediately around mid-century, as the secondary school began its transition to a mass-enrolment institution and as academic requirements for white-collar occupations (professional, managerial, clerical, and public service alike) became more demanding, qualifications to enter elementary school teaching began to look less impressive. But even in the 1930s or 1940s, let alone before that, young women who held junior – and especially senior – matriculation certificates plus a full year of professional training were among the best-educated members of their generation. From the turn of the century onwards, moreover, the creation of university extension pro-grams meant that even when they did not live close by, an undergraduate degree was within easy reach. For many career teachers, their education didn't end when they completed high school.

That was, of course, equally true of young men, and as we have tried to suggest, it is misleading when discussing teaching as an occupation to focus exclusively or primarily on women. Even in Canada's elementary class-rooms, men were always present as teachers, not just as managers, and after 1920 their numbers were hardly negligible, rising to 30% of the teaching workforce by the late 1930s and in some provinces to a higher percentage than that. It is obviously important to recognize the changing gender balance in the secondary schools but equally to acknowledge the reversal, during the interwar years, of the long-term trend towards the feminization of elementary school teaching. Indeed, we cannot even ken what constitutes the distinctive experience of women teachers until we identify how and why it differed from the experience of their male counterparts. And whatever the differences, we also need to take account of the common elements in any profile of the occupation. Like women, men could be either career teachers or "birds of passage"; they were as likely as women to work in the rural schools; and they too were responsible for the trend towards better qualifications and greater experience. These were occupational characteristics rather than the particular attributes of women teachers.

Women, nonetheless, were critical to the occupation, and for many women, the occupation was critical for them. No matter what the exact numerical balance, most elementary school teachers were women, and the changing occupational profile was due more to the rising qualifications and levels of experience among women than among men. We are not certain that an increasing number of women were becoming "career teachers" in the sense of a lifelong job, but a median of seventeen years of experience for women in Ontario's cities means that *half* were teaching seventeen years or *more*. On the other hand, if a woman began teaching at age 17 or 18, she could accumulate ten or fifteen years' experience and still be just under or over age 30, at which point she might abandon teaching for marriage or some other occupation. Our own use of a marker like "6 years or more experience," moreover, is not intended to identify career teachers but simply to direct attention to experience as a component of pedagogical efficacy. And it is obvious that large numbers of young women left teaching with five years' experience or less; as late as 1938, some 30% left with no more than three years' experience, and this was particularly characteristic of rural Canada.

Whether as a career or a way station to somewhere else, in any case, teaching played an important role in the lives of many Canadian women. Taken together, male and female teachers constituted a minor proportion of the paid labour force between 1900 and 1940 – never more than 2%. But teachers represented 8%–10% of the female labour force – that is, one out of every eight to ten women who worked outside the home was a teacher.[104] Even more significant, perhaps, teaching accounted for a very high percentage – 50% or more – of women in those female occupations that required a substantial amount of education.[105] That is to say, for the growing number of young women who stayed in school longer than their peers, completed high school, or went beyond that, teaching was a critical occupational opportunity at a time when there were few other outlets for their education and skills.

Just because so many young women taught for relatively brief periods, moreover, very large numbers had to be recruited to staff the schools. Thus the number touched by teaching was far greater than the number of jobs available. Even in 1930, for example, Saskatchewan had only 6,800 teaching jobs, and far fewer than that twenty or thirty years earlier; yet cumulatively, between 1906 and 1930, the province trained some 24,000 elementary school teachers, over 18,000 of them women.[106] In 1940 Ontario had nearly 22,000 teaching jobs, though somewhat fewer than in earlier decades; yet between 1908 and 1940 it issued 56,142 teaching certificates. Not all of these were awarded to women but most were.[107] Nor was this sort of over-production peculiar to these two provinces. Summing up his own estimates, Patrick Harrigan writes that "if we calculate from a base of 32,000 women teaching in 1910, add to that expansion of the teaching corps, and replacement rates until 1930, we find that, in Canada, approximately one woman in six between the ages of 20 and 40, exclusive of recent immigrants, had taught in a public school at some point in her life. Similarly, one in six women would become a teacher at about the age of 20 in ... the interwar period."[108] At some point in their lives, in other words, a great many women taught school, and among educated women the percentage was larger still. Aside from the fact that teaching was an integral part of their own life experience, one can only speculate on the implications that their participation would have had for their families *and* for the larger society around them.[109] In the making of twentieth-century Canadian society, in any case, their sheer numbers, as well as the particular values they held and disseminated, deserve more sustained attention from historians and other students of Canadian society than they have received thus far.

6

Money

Does money matter? Obviously so. If children are to be educated, schools have to be built, equipped, and maintained, and teachers have to be hired and paid. Ultimately, the edifice of public education rests on dollars and cents, contributed, willingly or not, by the nation's taxpayers. But more than that, financial resources are the final arbiter of the quantity and quality of schooling. Money underpins the ability to attract and hold good teachers, the breadth of the curricula and the other educational services schools offer, the pupil-teacher ratios in individual classrooms, the quality of the physical plant, the accessibility of secondary and post-secondary education, and the promise of equal educational opportunity regardless of where children live. Whether past or present, moreover, the sources of funding and the power to raise and direct funds can usually tell us more about who is in charge, and where initiatives come from, than all the abounding rhetoric of any era. As one American historian has put it, "beneath educational claims ... lie questions about meaningful priority and how much, and for what purposes, public money is spent ... educational funding tells historians in powerful relative terms some of what communities wanted, could not afford, or did not care about. For good or ill, funding reveals social vision, intention and planning, and it can belie educational rhetoric as mere hyperbole ... Limiting the story to educational intentions, without examining the amounts and sources of allocated funding and how the money was spent, leaves the analysis afloat."[1] We would go further: not "afloat" but sinking. There is hardly an issue raised in previous chapters, or in those to come, that doesn't hinge on money. So we invite the reader to follow the money trail and read on.

Much of the system of educational funding in place a century ago was fundamentally different than it is today. It was mainly the product of the mid-nineteenth century, created as part of the founding architecture of Canadian public education, and it would survive largely unmodified until the 1940s. Because the system was so different, and because it is so important in understanding the contours of both provision and policy, it needs to be explained clearly and with some attention to detail.

We begin with a description of how local schools were funded and the kind of economic and political issues this presented for the communities that raised the money to pay for them. In the process, we introduce some key concepts common in the study of educational finance and some elementary formulas used to raise tax revenues. The basic rules governing local finance were set out in various pieces of legislation, some of which applied to municipal taxation generally, but the most important were the provincial school acts and their associated regulations. Together, these rules established what we will refer to as the structure of local school finance.

In the second part of the chapter we turn our attention to a larger stage: patterns of funding at the provincial and national levels from the beginning of the century until 1929. Here we link educational finance to the variable fortunes of the Canadian economy. These were mostly years of prosperity, but they also encompass the dislocation of the Great War and two sharp downturns in the economy; even in the best of times, moreover, particular communities and their schools did not always share in the prosperity around them.

The fiscal collapse of the 1930s demands its own distinctive place in any discussion of educational finance. During the Great Depression, Canadian public education confronted the worst crisis in its history, with ramifications that touched nearly every aspect of the school system. We take up that part of the story in the next chapter.

I

First, then, the structure of local school finance. In 1934 the dominion statistician offered an illuminating calculation that provides a good place to start. There were, he estimated, some 23,000 local school authorities in Canada, responsible for raising 80% of the funds needed to finance the schools. These units could be divided into two categories. On the one hand, there were the urban boards, presiding over school districts contiguous with the municipality itself. That is to say, city hall and the board of education occupied the same territory. These boards constituted about 2,000 of the 23,000 school districts. On the other hand, there were units where the municipality (township, rural municipality, or some other nomenclature) was divided into several school districts, most small enough that children could walk to the schoolhouse. While the municipal government might perform important subsidiary functions, such as establishing districts in the first place, assessing property values, collecting school taxes, and in some places raising a portion of those taxes, the school district trustees were primarily responsible for the school. There were some 21,000 of these school districts, serving about 5 million people, a little less than half of Canada's population. This amounted to an average population in each school district of fewer than 250 persons.[2]

Just to make the arithmetic that follows easy, suppose that these 250 people constituted family units of five members and that each family unit owned one piece of property in the school district. The legal owner, known as a "ratepayer," was responsible for paying the taxes assessed against the property. So that gives us fifty ratepayers. Assume, for the moment, that these fifty ratepayers were, near-exclusively, responsible for financing the school and that the only supplement was a modest government grant amounting to something like 15% of the total bill.[3]

How, then, did these fifty families go about paying the cost of their children's education? The three trustees of the school district, elected by the ratepayers at their annual meeting in January, began by estimating *operating* expenditure: the teacher's salary, maintenance and repair costs, janitorial services, the honorarium due to the trustee who acted as secretary-treasurer, the cost of fuel, and the like. They would then deduct the amount they expected to receive from the government grant. These calculations gave them a figure that would cover the annual running costs. But the school district might also be carrying debt incurred for *capital* expenditure – money spent in a previous year to erect a new building or some other expensive investment in school facilities. This money was commonly raised by the sale of *debentures* (a type of bond). Annual payments had to be made to cover the interest on the debenture, and an additional amount accumulated in a "sinking fund" to pay off the lender when the debenture came due. Added together, the sums for operating costs and the annual levies for capital expenditure gave the trustees a dollar amount that our fifty families had to raise to finance the school in the following year.

A municipal employee would already have assessed the value of each ratepayer's property, since taxes on that property also had to support municipal services such as local roads. All the trustees had to do was to divide up the cost of the school among the fifty families whose property lay within the school district. This was done by setting a tax rate, expressed as a "mill rate," which simply means 1/1000 of each dollar a property might be worth. Thus, if a piece of property was assessed at $10,000 and the mill rate was set at 10, its owner would pay $100 ($10,000 multiplied by 1/1000 multiplied by 10 equals $100).[4]

The mill rate is a mechanism for equalizing the burden of taxation among ratepayers whose properties will vary in value. Among our fifty families, some will own more land, or better land, or have more acreage cleared and productive, and so on. Some will have better homes and outbuildings than others. Because their property is worth more, they will pay more cash than others in the school district. But each will pay the same *rate* of taxation – that is, pay the same mill rate or proportionate amount on the value of their property. Each taxpayer, in other words, will put forth *an equal tax effort*, a principle that has long governed fair and equitable taxation.

Now consider how this system might operate in four imaginary school districts at, say, some indeterminate date in the prosperous years of the middle or late 1920s. School District No. 1 is a relatively well-off farming community whose members are eager to ensure that their daughters and their younger sons (who will not inherit the farm) will achieve some independence in life through schooling. They have a relatively new and substantial brick schoolhouse and will have to raise money to pay interest and put away a sum to retire the debenture. They are willing to offer a competitive salary to obtain a teacher with a first-class certificate who can prepare their youngsters for the high school entrance examination and, when required, teach some of the initial high school subjects to the handful of girls studying for their second-class teacher's certificate. That teacher is going to cost them $1,200 next year, but they also want to raise an additional amount for new blackboards, some new maps and readers, and to dig the school's first water well. Total expenses will amount to $2,000 next year – a budget somewhat larger than that of most other rural communities.[5] Since the total assessed value of the section is $200,000, the trustees set the mill rate at 10, which requires each of their fifty families to pay an average amount of $40 ($200,000 multiplied by 1/1000 equals $200; multiplied by 10 mills, equals $2,000; divided by 50 families, equals $40). The money is collected from each ratepayer by the municipal tax collector and deposited in the school district's bank account. (The trustees will have to borrow money from the bank to tide them through a part of the school year until they have received all the money due them from the municipality, but these are short-term loans, normally paid back within the school year.)

Next door, in School District No. 2, there are another fifty families, some of whom eke out a living on poorly drained soils near the local swamp and others whose lands, though promising, are only half cleared. They owe nothing on the schoolhouse, a cramped frame room with old-fashioned double desks and painted pine blackboards, built twenty years ago by the voluntary labour of the parents themselves. But they aspire to the same educational opportunities for their own children as their neighbours do in sd No. 1. They too would like to raise $2,000 next year. But their total assessment is only $100,000. If they want to raise $2,000, they will need to set their mill rate at 20 mills – twice as high as their neighbours'; an equal mill rate of 10 mills would only raise $1,000. They would, in other words, have to make a much greater "tax effort" to raise the same amount of $2,000. In the best of all possible worlds, they might be willing to make this extra tax effort; even then, it would violate a basic rule of tax fairness – equal resources for equal effort. But the community is not only "assessment poor," it is cash poor. An average $40 per family is beyond their ability to pay even if they were willing to make twice the tax effort of their neighbours. That is, their *tax capacity* is much less than that of SD No. 1. Thus the trustees are forced to set a mill rate in line with what the community can actually afford, say, 5 mills. But this only raises $500, and the best teacher they can afford is an inexperienced young woman who holds a third-class certificate and can do little better than manage the 3 Rs.

Up the road, in School District No. 3, two-thirds of the fifty families are farmers; the rest live in an unincorporated hamlet and include two grocers, a blacksmith, a doctor, two ministers, and an automotive mechanic who owns a brand-new garage that sells gasoline and services the cars and tractors of the more prosperous in the municipality. There are also several heads of households employed in these enterprises and one war widow in receipt of a small pension from the federal government. Most of the villagers own small lots and make their living selling goods or services for cash. But only their property, not their income, is taxed for municipal services, including the school (the post office and the two church properties are not taxed at all). While the most prosperous among the villagers may have assessed property equal to that of the farmers, in the main they do not. SD No. 3 can afford as good a school as SD No. 1, but the costs fall almost entirely on the land. Or as the farmers like to grumble among themselves, the village provides most of the children and the farms most of the money.

Not too far from these three school districts is the urban community of Agricola. A market town where the economy depends primarily on servicing several rural municipalities, it is a thriving sort of place with a population of 2,000. It offers a choice of several sizable establishments specializing in groceries, hardware, and dry goods, and some smaller businesses such as ladies' corsetry, millinery, books and music, and footwear. It has a feed mill, a brickworks, three banks, and a wide range of personal services. The town has its own school board and possesses a two-storey, four-room schoolhouse that includes one room devoted to high school work. Town children, of course, attend free, but if rural children want to make use of the high school class, they have to pay a non-resident fee and, if from any distance, board in town during the school week. Like School District No. 1, the Agricola board of education sets a mill rate of 10 mills, but the residential property rate is set at 5 mills and the commercial/industrial rate at 12 mills. The larger business properties in town generate substantially more revenue for the board than its residents, but altogether, 10 mills produces enough money to sustain a well-equipped, graded elementary school, even if the high school facilities are primitive compared to those in the big cities. Each of the three elementary school teachers is paid $1,200 a year, and the male high school teacher and principal, $1,500. Now in fact $1,200 a year is no more than the trustees in SD No. 1 pay their teacher. But the fifty families of SD No. 1, despite their relative prosperity, can afford only one teacher for all the grades, and even she struggles to cope with the three or four students attempting the first year or two of high school subjects. To boot, there are always some parents in SD No. 1 who complain bitterly to the trustees that the teacher showers far more attention on a handful of high school students than she does on the majority of children just learning to read and write, a complaint that never arises in the graded school in town. Its students, moreover, are far more likely to pass the high school entrance exam, enter the high school class, and finish enough education to open doors of opportunity lost to most of the children in the other three school districts. Perhaps no less important, while the school has not yet acquired manual training or domestic science rooms, one of the trustees, just back from the provincial education association's annual meeting, is excited about the idea, eager to prove that his town, too, is somewhere near the vanguard of progress; one of the local doctors earns a modest but welcome honorarium providing semi-annual medical and dental checkups for all the pupils; and the one new teacher, just learning the ropes, has experienced colleagues to turn to when she encounters problems with pedagogy or discipline.

Now this sketch of the provisions for financing Canadian schools, with its implications for the quantity or quality of education, is, for any point in the first half of the twentieth century, simple-minded to the point of caricature. Nowhere on the ground did it actually operate exactly like this.[6] It does, nonetheless, point to the central features of school finance. Financing schools was primarily a local responsibility: provincial governments contributed to the total cost of local schools, but most of the burden fell upon local ratepayers. The fiscal weight of sustaining the school often fell upon a small number of families located in a multitude of geographically small school districts. Property bore the lion's share of the costs; while income and property might bear some relationship to each other, income was not taxed for municipal purposes, only the value of the property individuals owned.[7] Within school districts, different kinds of property could bear different burdens. Taxpayers in different districts had different abilities – or tax capacities – to pay. Assessment-rich districts, even with mill rates set at the same or less than the same value as those of assessment-poor districts, could raise far greater amounts. As a consequence, the quantity and quality of education available to Canadian children depended, in fundamental ways, upon where they lived.

On the face of it, this might seem to apply mainly to urban/rural differences. "Agricola," after all, was far better provided for than any of its neighbouring school districts. But in large measure it applied to town and country alike. Among Canada's 23,000 school districts, a couple of thousand were classified as "urban." But these included everything from Canada's largest cities and towns to villages of 500 or 1,000 people, from communities that could afford comparatively lavish educational establishments to those distinguished from nearby rural districts only by their ability to maintain a two-teacher elementary school or perhaps a three-teacher school that included a room set aside for high school instruction. Urban communities were as dependent on property taxation as the countryside, and their assessment base varied as much. The cities and larger towns had as a tax base a rich mix of residential, commercial, and industrial property; not only could they raise comparatively enormous sums of money because of that, but they could also shift substantial portions of the tax base off the shoulders of residential property. Smaller urban communities had fewer resources, fewer alternatives, and made do with less.[8] The difference in buildings, teachers, other facilities, and services between Winnipeg, Fredericton, and Blairmore, in other words, arose fundamentally from differences in the fiscal resources available to each community.

Still, even villages with 500 or 1,000 people could marshal greater resources per pupil than the residents of Kipp SD in Saskatchewan or the hypothetical fifty families in our rural school districts. But the disparities among rural communities could be vast as well. In British Columbia in the early 1920s, mill rates in the rural districts ranged from 1 to 36.6 mills, and total assessments from $59,140 to $3,958,340.[9] In New Brunswick in the early 1930s, the average mill rate for the province was 28.99 mills, but in order to raise scarcely more than enough to keep their schools open, desperately poor areas like Restigouche and Gloucester counties averaged 33.9 and 45 mills respectively, which indicated, as the provincial director of educational services remarked, "the very high rate which is being paid even for the poor schools which we have, comparatively speaking, and also the wide variation or inequality of the tax burden."[10] Canvassing public opinion in the late 1930s, Ontario's Committee on the Costs of Education found that the most frequent complaint "was the gross inequality in the assessment of school sections. Several instances were reported in which the assessment of the wealthiest school section within a single inspectoral district was ten times as large as the assessment of the poorest school section in the same district. Several rural sections were reported as having an assessment of more than $700,000, while other rural sections throughout the province were assessed for less than $1,500."[11] Since the small school district was by far the most common arrangement for financing education, these "gross inequalities" existed almost everywhere in Canada.[12]

There were exceptions. In a few parts of the country larger units of governance had been introduced, either in the nineteenth or early twentieth century, as ways of mitigating the inequities endemic to the school district. In British Columbia's lower mainland (though not beyond that), the rural schools were organized in the same fashion as the urban schools – administered and financed by a municipality-wide board. Thus assessment was *equalized* across the municipality so that all schools within the unit had roughly the same resources.[13] In Manitoba the rural municipality provided something like 60% of funding to the school districts, so that here too assessment was substantially equalized. But municipal-level organization was at best only a partial solution because municipalities themselves varied in population and wealth. "Compare the municipalities of Ethelbert and Wallace," one Manitoban noted in 1929: "Ethelbert had 19 teachers, an assessment of $51,000 per teacher, a rate of 30 mills and an average of 43 scholars for each teacher. Wallace had 19 teachers also, an assessment of $290,000 per teacher, a rate of 6 mills, and an average of 22 scholars for each teacher. The disparity of treatment shows the unfairness to the taxpayer who pays a greater rate because his district is poor, and to the child, who gets less teacher attention, though his parents pay a higher rate."[14]

Thus two different things follow from our discussion here. First, the central structural problems of school finance bore upon all kinds of communities, rural and urban alike. They defined the resources available to villages versus rural school districts but also to villages and small towns versus larger towns or cities, determining the quantity and quality of schooling everywhere. Second, the system incorporated two kinds of inequalities. One of these related to tax fairness. In 1939 a Nova Scotia commission could point out that "the assessed valuation per classroom ranged from $700 in a poor fishing village to $166,667 in a wealthy village with an industrial plant," and it might have gone on to compare the latter with the more diverse industrial base of a town like Dartmouth, or all three with the city of Halifax. But the commission's conclusion held regardless: "It is the antithesis of democracy for some sections to put forth from 2 to 40 times as much [tax] effort as other more favoured sections, and still be able to provide [only] the most elementary educational services."[15] A decade earlier, according to a Saskatchewan report, "an average mill rate of about 10 mills would have been necessary to meet the operating cost of the rural and village schools ... and 13½ mills for city schools. Can the city dweller pay a school tax of 13½ mills or $33.75 on his dwelling assessed for $2,500 more easily than a farmer can pay 10 mills or $60.00 on his half-section of land assessed at $6,000?" People might disagree on the answer to that question, but "notwithstanding the fact that the urban dweller pays a higher mill rate for school purposes than does the farmer, it cannot be safely said that he is taxed higher for school purposes, and when the efficacy of the school is considered there can be little doubt but that at present the rural taxpayer does not receive the same educational return for the money paid in school taxes as does the city dweller."[16]

That conclusion, in turn, identifies the second form of inequality – the gaps in the quantity and quality of educational services available to children. Large numbers of school districts were so assessment-poor that they would have no school without outside help and even then in many cases would be unable to keep a school open for a full school year.[17] Larger numbers of school districts would be forced to hire, year in, year out, the cheapest, least-qualified, least-experienced teacher available.[18] Many young people would have no access to a high school unless they could afford to board in town. Others would be taught in one- or two-teacher schools, lacking even the most elementary facilities taken for granted in larger communities. Yet others would attend a one-room school crowded with pupils because the school district could not afford the luxury of a second teacher, and would, as a consequence, fall measurably behind the progress being made by their peers in rural classrooms with fewer numbers.[19]

Not all the inequalities can be explained by differing assessment values. Within any given school district, determining how much money was to be spent on the schools was a political process. In urban Canada that decision was usually made by the elected school board alone; the influence of the ratepayer was limited to the choice made at election time. But in most of rural Canada the ratepayers not only elected their trustees, they also voted on the mill rate at the annual meeting. And no rural school district consisted of our hypothetical fifty families, all with children to educate and all of one accord when approving the mill rate. More likely, the district would include bachelors, childless couples, those with children beyond school age, and others with no direct stake in the school. Even those with children might differ about just how much should be spent on the teacher's salary, the need for a new schoolhouse, or other investments in schooling. Moreover, there was, as the saying goes, only one taxpayer: the money for schools had to be weighed against other municipal needs, such as improved roads or snowploughs, and the same ratepayers had to pick up their share of these costs. That is to say, people had choices about how much to spend and on what. While it was hardly his intent in what was a memoir and not an exposition on economics, John Kenneth Galbraith explains the politics of tax effort with inimitable clarity. "Two educational philosophies contended, although on the whole peacefully, for control of the school," he writes of the southwestern Ontario school district where he received his elementary education. There were "those who believed that education had independent utility for improving a man's position in the community or preparing him for a profession" and were thus "anxious to have a well-paid teacher. And they tended to look with favour on improvements, even those such as better heating, which added to the comfort of the children." Those, on the other hand,

> who viewed education in minimal terms kept their older boys at home in the autumn until the field work was finished. And they withdrew them from school when work became heavy in the spring. Since it did little for them, they wished to have the school run at minimal expense. They resisted increases in the teacher's salary and did not hesitate to point out that she worked only from nine to four, had Saturdays and Sundays off and enjoyed generous holidays in a community where holidays were almost unknown. They opposed improvements to the school, especially those that added to the convenience or comfort of the children. These they felt contributed to the debilitating effects of education.
>
> As always, the issue was compromised. The $500 to $600 annual salary of those days struck a balance between the two extremes. When the educationally inclined were dominant, fifty or seventy-five dollars would be spent for school desks or a better blackboard. These would tide over leaner years when the forces of economy were in power.[20]

The odds are that every small community had its "minimalists" and its "maximalists"; the proportions between them influenced expenditure levels. But the same preferences could also account for differences between school districts. Writing about a frontier region in British Columbia's interior during the 1920s, Paul Stortz and J. Donald Wilson note that school buildings and equipment in many poor school districts were wretched. But "other communities provided fine school buildings, sometimes, significantly, in extremely impoverished areas." Uncha Valley, for example, "was a struggling farming and trapping community, but one which [had] a large, clean and well-lit school, equipped to the hilt, with a library which in 1929 contained over 200 volumes."[21] Internal discord could arise over petty issues and important ones: "Farmers send their pupils to schools 2½ or 3 miles distant from home only under protest," wrote one Ontario observer in 1912, but agitation that resulted in the creation of a new school district was most likely to impoverish both.[22] And the politics of the small school district could be as brutal as any other form. Up on the Peace River, one settler owned "two quarters of land. One quarter was in one rural school district with a tax rate of 18 mills; the other quarter was in the adjoining school district with a tax rate of 7.5 mills. It happened that the settler had

six children of school age, and the attendance of these children was necessary to keep [the school] open. This man told members of the school board
that, if he didn't get the contracts for wood and ice, he would move over
to his adjacent quarter and thus force the school to close down. The settler
eventually did this, and the school was closed."[23] Levels of school expenditure, then, depended on the micro-politics within each school district – on
differences in the value placed on schooling per se, on differences over the
relative value of investing in schools versus other municipal improvements,
and on the relative willingness of ratepayers to dig more or less deeply into
their own pockets to pay any taxes at all.[24]

Yet ultimately the local school district was fortune's hostage: choice was
constrained within a range limited by economic circumstance. The rapid
expansion of prairie agriculture after 1900 added an enormous number
of new school districts, some of them with adequate tax bases and others
where settlement was thin, land marginal, or much of the acreage as yet
uncultivated, and thus lacking the resources to maintain anything but short-
term summer schools. In the mid-1920s, for example, there were many new
settlements in northern Alberta's Grande Prairie and Peace River districts

> where total assessment is not higher than $40,000. A tax of 10 mills on
> $40,000 raises $400. It requires at least $1,200 per annum ... to finance
> a one-room school ... This means [for] the school district that desires to
> provide the citizens with a minimum standard of educational facilities
> by law for their children, 30 mills must be the set rate. A mill rate of 30
> mills is not set for the simple reason that even if it were set the heavy
> tax could not be collected. The rate is set at about 10 mills and the
> school is operated just as long as the proceeds of the tax collections will
> carry them. If the school board decides to overstep the limits of their
> resources and carry on for six months, then the teacher must "scratch"
> for her salary.[25]

In that part of Alberta, conventional school districts could at least be established with some hope that they would eventually produce sufficient revenue to sustain a school, but in much of the country, beyond the agricultural
frontier, geography and economics combined to defy even that promise.
In "new Ontario," wrote one northern inspector, "[t]he farmers ... settle
promiscuously, often in secluded spots where a promising pocket of land
offers a hope. The small mill owner plants his portable mill and group of
workmen on some vantage point or lake or stream accessible to timber and
transportation. The railway road gang settle with their families every six
miles or so, and way station operators at other intervals over our 4,000 miles

of rail ... the fisherman, hunter, trapper ... locate where nature invites."[26] No system of educational finance primarily dependent on local resources was going to prove effective in circumstances such as these.

Economic and demographic change could also undermine the finances of long-established, successful school districts. The decline of the East Coast fishery after the First World War reduced the tax base of communities dependent upon it. "West Green Harbour, a very populous section in Shelburne County whose schoolroom is much too small to accommodate the children of school age, is one of our hard problems," wrote a Nova Scotia inspector in 1931: "The men of the section are nearly all fishermen, and under conditions now existing in the fishing industry it is quite impossible for them to enlarge their building."[27] Migration westward and into the burgeoning towns and cities created pockets of rural depopulation in many parts of eastern Canada. "During the last thirty years," one Ontario report noted in 1938, "extensive and clearly defined changes have occurred in the distribution of population in many parts of rural Ontario. Migration ... has created vacancies in rural districts which have not been filled. Rural schools, which a generation ago were attended by 30 pupils or more, today have an attendance of 6 or 7."[28] Nor did school districts in the West escape unscathed. During the 1920s, hard times in Manitoba's Interlake district led to "considerable shifting of population and desertion of land, so that the burden of maintaining school and municipal services has continued to fall upon a reducing population and dwindling sources of revenue."[29] The drylands disaster that struck southeastern Alberta and southwestern Saskatchewan devastated whole communities. During the first half of the 1920s, writes David Jones, "between a fifth and a quarter of all the townships in south-eastern Alberta – a whopping 138 of them covering 3.2 million acres – would lose at least 55% of their population. These and the farm abandonment figures even the Great Depression never equalled."[30] We began this chapter with a Dominion Bureau of Statistics (DBS) figure – an average population for each rural district of about 250 residents. As farms were enlarged owing to mechanization or abandoned for other reasons, the number of ratepayers declined, as did the number of children to be schooled. By the 1940s the *average* school district in Nova Scotia had 185 people; in Saskatchewan the figure was 120; in parts of rural Ontario by that point the typical school district was sustained by no more than twenty or thirty families living on an equivalent number of farms.[31] All the reader has to do to grasp the consequences is take the figures and formula we used for our hypothetical fifty families and apply them to real school districts where once-viable communities withered through loss of population or where taxes reached an intolerable maximum for the few families left to support schools and other municipal services.[32]

The wealth generated in communities growing up around newly opened mines or pulp and paper mills might ensure the maintenance of good schools. But mineral resources might eventually be exhausted, or the plant shut down in a one-industry town, or workers might leave or find themselves unemployed, so that "the burden of taxation for the maintenance of schools becomes unduly heavy on the relatively small portion of the community which is able to continue to pay taxes."[33] Nor did newly generated wealth necessarily guarantee prosperity. Eager to see International Paper Limited of New York establish a new pulp mill in their town, in 1927 the town council of Dalhousie, New Brunswick, gave the company not only generous long-term financing but a fixed property evaluation for the next fifty years. "Who," writes Richard Wilbur, "made up the difference? Dalhousie's other property owners. Individual families were assessed about 70 per cent of the value of their homes, while IP paid as little as 5 per cent. Small wonder that Dalhousie's schools, hospitals, waterworks, streets and firefighting facilities were starved for money." As Wilbur points out, this was not unusual in other northern New Brunswick communities or, one might add, in other parts of Canada.[34]

In Canada's cities and towns, rapid population growth meant sharp and sometimes explosive growth in enrolments during the postwar decade, creating its own stresses for school finance. But if there was an emerging urban crisis in the 1920s, it lay mainly in areas where city populations were spilling over into adjacent rural communities, turning farmland into suburbs or nearby villages into "satellite towns." On the borders of Toronto, one local trustee pointed out in 1925, the townships of York and East York were still divided into school sections even though each section "now has the population of an urban community," greater indeed "than towns like Goderich or Cobourg." But the population, he continued,

is out of proportion to the assessment because these are purely residential districts whose breadwinners are employed in Toronto. There are no industries or commercial concerns to be taxed for school purposes as there are in the usual urban community. Hence, these school sections have large school populations and limited resources from which to provide school facilities.

Take York Township, for instance. It has a total assessment of over twenty-one millions, about equal to that of St Catharines. But York's business assessment is less than $300,000, while that of St Catharines is over $2,000,000. York Township's population is 47,000 while St Catharines' is half that. Our population is out of proportion to the assessment. These conditions apply in the Township of East York also. These conditions exist on the border of not only Toronto, but

Hamilton, Ottawa, Brantford, Windsor, and other such centres. Wherever you have cities you have on the borders satellite communities whose school problems are similar to ours.[35]

A decade later, Maxwell Cameron would note that the greater Toronto region consisted of thirty-four school authorities, including four towns, three villages, five townships (three of which were partly rural), plus the City of Toronto itself. Assessments ranged from $2,313 to $28,107 per pupil, and expenditure per pupil from $41.05 to $105.24. Teachers' average salaries ranged from $958 to $1,906. Pupil-teacher ratios ranged from 24 or 25 to 1, to 41 or 42 to 1.[36] To one extent or another the problem existed from Vancouver to Halifax.[37] In the late 1920s, Winnipeg raised about 43% of its school taxes from "buildings which house industry, commercial, professional and departmental businesses," wrote one disenchanted suburbanite. "Only 57% of the taxes have to be levied on Winnipeg residential property. In the suburbs there are very few industries, therefore 95% of the school taxes must be levied on residential property. This makes school taxes very heavy in the suburbs and causes the children's educational opportunities to be curtailed. For example, the school mill rate in Brooklands is more than 3½ times the school mill rate of Winnipeg."[38]

II

In the second part of this chapter, we shift the focus, from the structure of local finance and the consequences that entailed, to the actual levels of school funding. Just how much money did school boards have to build and operate their schools, and how did that change over the first four decades of the century? What were the expenditure patterns for the nation as a whole and in different parts of the country? And what was the interplay between the little world of the school district and the larger economic forces at work that ultimately determined how much revenue was available to spend on education? We begin here with a survey of the period from 1900 through 1930, focusing initially on a national-level portrait – the combined effects of spending in all provinces together – and then turn to the ways in which various provinces diverged from the national pattern. Following this, we attempt to explain the expenditure patterns that emerged during the first thirty years of the century.

Exploring these patterns of educational finance necessarily involves some resort to quantifiable data. While we draw on a variety of sources for this part of the chapter, of particular importance are the tables we have constructed from several data series: total expenditure (Table 6.1); the relative

Table 6.1

Total school board expenditure[a] (including provincial grants), Canada,[b] 1914–1941 (selected years)

	Total expenditure $
1914	36,483,125
1915	34,854,273
1916	34,574,381
1917	36,643,056
1918	40,880,382
1919	46,437,828
1920	58,875,791
1921	69,114,323
1922	74,843,225
1923	78,517,719
1924	80,539,015
1925	82,515,481
1928	90,315,656
1930	96,998,598
1931	96,282,070
1933	82,633,016
1934	81,142,140
1935	79,064,305
1936	81,616,065
1937	84,216,451
1939	94,182,246
1941	96,238,124

[a] That is, revenues: see appendix C.
[b] Excludes Quebec.

Sources:
1914–28: DBS, *Annual Survey 1935*, 56ff.
1929–41: DBS, *Elementary and Secondary Education 1942–44*, 73ff.

percentage of costs borne by local and provincial authorities (Table 6.2); per capita expenditure (Table 6.3); and per-pupil expenditure (Table 6.4). These tables are national-level only; for those interested, we offer additional provincial-level tables in appendix C.*

As we begin to introduce our numbers, there are two points to be kept in mind. First, in this and other chapters we make extensive use of per capita and per-pupil expenditure. Both were conventional measures routinely

* Like all our other quantitative data thus far, there are associated technical problems. Explanations about the data themselves and how we have used them are also provided in that appendix. In order to limit the amount of documentation included in the text, we will not provide references when we draw upon data from these tables. Our own national-level tables exclude Quebec, but that is often not possible when using other data sources. Wherever necessary, we note the inclusion or exclusion of that province.

Table 6.2
Government grants as percentage of total school board expenditure,[a] by province,
1914–1950

	PEI	NS	NB	ON	MB	SK	AB	BC
1914	66.9	18.3	20.5	6.3	12.7	16.7	14.4	38.1
1915	61.1	18.1	19.9	7.2	13.3	20.3	12.6	38.0
1916	67.5	19.0	18.9	7.4	13.3	17.8	12.8	46.0
1917	67.5	17.8	18.9	7.4	13.2	18.9	21.2	46.1
1918	63.4	16.3	17.4	7.7	14.2	17.8	10.8	43.8
1919	60.9	14.0	14.3	9.0	12.3	15.3	11.3	38.8
1920	57.8	11.0	12.4	9.5	12.3	12.8	11.3	34.5
1921	57.5	10.0	12.6	11.9	10.6	13.0	13.3	33.7
1922	59.9	9.9	11.6	12.5	13.1	15.8	14.2	32.8
1923	56.0	11.0	12.3	12.7	11.0	14.9	11.8	34.1
1924	58.7	10.6	12.7	12.7	12.8	16.6	11.1	31.5
1925	59.3	10.6	12.4	12.7	13.3	16.9	11.6	31.7
1926	58.5	11.2	17.1	12.7	13.0	17.3	12.0	31.8
1927	58.3	11.2	16.4	12.6	13.1	17.4	11.9	30.8
1928	57.8	12.3	14.5	12.2	13.6	17.2	12.3	32.0
1929	56.7	12.5	14.6	12.2	13.7	19.4	12.4	28.4
1930	56.8	12.8	14.7	11.7	14.1	20.2	15.0	30.3
1931	57.8	13.9	14.6	12.7	14.6	24.5	14.3	31.4
1932	54.6	14.6	14.2	13.2	16.0	21.5	16.4	35.1
1933	59.1	15.5	14.3	12.1	16.7	20.7	18.1	27.4
1934	61.3	16.4	16.6	11.6	17.0	21.1	15.1	26.8
1935	54.2	17.0	17.1	11.7	14.8	20.6	15.8	27.9
1936	57.2	17.6	17.4	11.3	14.9	20.2	15.3	28.1
1937	59.8	17.8	18.0	12.5	13.8	25.2	16.3	28.0
1938	61.5	18.0	–	14.1	12.5	29.4	16.6	28.2
1939	61.0	18.2	16.8	14.4	14.6	23.7	17.5	28.0
1940	60.4	18.6	17.2	14.2	14.9	25.2	17.5	27.5
1941	59.3	18.1	17.5	15.2	15.7	23.3	18.9	30.0
1942	57.6	20.6	17.4	15.2	15.1	22.0	18.7	30.0
1943	57.2	21.1	17.4	15.6	16.0	17.6	17.9	28.2
1944	59.4	26.8	17.6	16.3	16.6	16.7	20.5	28.4
1945	–	–	–	–	–	–	–	–
1946	54.4	37.7	25.6	42.5	14.1	24.4	21.2	30.3
1947	52.0	42.1	27.6	38.7	21.3	27.7	27.8	39.2
1948	57.1	45.6	34.4	36.1	25.2	28.9	29.0	41.8
1949	52.7	47.6	43.3	36*	25.9	26.6	26.1	45.5
1950	50.9	48.6	42.2	36*	23.6	29.2	27.9	45.7

[a] That is, revenues: see Appendix C.
* Approximate
– Data not available

Sources:

1914–28: DBS, *Annual Survey 1935*, 56ff.
1929–44: DBS, *Elementary and Secondary Education 1942–44*, 73ff.
1946–50: DBS, *Elementary and Secondary Education 1948–50*, 80ff.

Table 6.3
Per capita school board expenditure,[a] Canada,[b] 1914–1946 (selected years)

	Education expenditure $ per capita
1914	6.38
1915	6.01
1916	5.93
1917	6.23
1918	6.88
1919	7.66
1920	9.43
1921	10.77
1922	11.52
1923	11.98
1924	12.14
1925	12.26
1928	12.71
1930	13.16
1931	12.86
1933	10.81
1934	10.44
1935	10.17
1936	10.42
1937	10.68
1939	11.74
1941	11.80
1946	10[c]

[a] That is, revenues: see appendix C
[b] Excludes Quebec before 1946; includes Quebec in 1946.
[c] Number is rounded in source.

Sources:

Expenditure: 1914–28: DBS, *Annual Survey 1935*, 56ff.; 1929–41: DBS, *Elementary and Secondary Education 1942–44*, 73ff.; 1946: DBS, *Elementary and Secondary Education 1948–50*, 8off.

Population: 1914–30: Estimates of Population, *Canada Year Book, 1946*, 127; 1931–46: Estimates of Population, *Canada Year Book, 1952–53*, 143.

used by departments of education in their annual reports and by many studies of educational finance. They are useful in directing attention to money actually spent, but by themselves they tell us nothing about capacity to pay or about relative levels of commitment to the educational enterprise. To interpret them, one has to use them in conjunction with other kinds of data that render them intelligible and place them in their larger economic and historical context.[39]

Table 6.4
Per-pupil school board expenditure[a] by average daily attendance, Canada,[b] 1914–1946 (selected years)

	Education expenditure $ by ADA
1914	51.58
1915	46.36
1916	46.42
1917	47.26
1918	57.58
1919	56.88
1920	68.88
1921	72.94
1922	74.14
1923	75.37
1924	75.05
1925	75.24
1928	77.06
1929	77.54
1930	76.51
1931	74.12
1933	62.05
1934	60.94
1935	60.00
1936	63.14
1937	64.57
1939	71.87
1941	77.21
1946	102[c]

[a] That is, revenues: see appendix C.
[b] Excludes Quebec before 1946; includes Quebec in 1946.
[c] Number is rounded in source.

Sources:
Expenditure – 1914–28: DBS, *Annual Survey 1935*, 56ff.; 1929–44: DBS, *Elementary and Secondary Education 1942–44*, 73ff.; 1946: DBS, *Elementary and Secondary Education 1948–50*, 8off.
Average daily attendance: DBS, *Elementary and Secondary Education 1948–50*, 28.

Second, a major drawback in all our tables is that the data do not distinguish between elementary and secondary education. For our purposes, that is unfortunate: if the two could be disentangled, per-pupil costs (or per capita costs or almost any other indicator) would show *much lower* levels of funding for elementary than for secondary schools.[40] Canadian secondary schools were generally privileged by far richer provincial grants, by customs and regulations that led to substantially higher salaries for teachers and funding for equipment, and by the fact that high schools were located in urban communities with rich assessment bases. As commercial and technical departments began to be added, per-pupil expenditure rose sharply (a roomful of typewriters is a lot more expensive than a roomful of Latin texts; a roomful of typewriters is still a lot cheaper than a shop full of lathes). In what follows, in other words, the reader needs to keep in mind that our expenditure figures are for elementary and secondary education *combined.* Financially, the elementary schools were poor cousins to the secondary schools even though it was the elementary schools that carried the main burden of universal education throughout the decades before mid-century.

Between 1900 and 1930 there was an impressive increase in the cost of financing Canadian schools. In just three decades operating expenditure rose from $8.5 million to over $100 million. In the first decade it more than doubled, in the second more than tripled, and though the rate of increase slowed, in the 1920s it still grew by some 40%. Capital costs increased from $1.7 million to nearly $12 million between 1900 and 1915, and to $24.6 million by 1930.[41] Between 1914 and 1930, hardly more than fifteen years, per capita spending rose from $6.38 to $13.16, and per-pupil expenditure from $51.58 to $76.51. Good times encouraged investment. During Canada's great wheat boom before 1913 or the prosperity of the later 1920s, there were large increases in spending. But more surprisingly, adverse economic circumstances imposed few restraints. Total expenditure decreased modestly in 1915–16, due more to the depression that began in 1913 than to the diversion of resources caused by the First World War.[42] Spending started to rise again in 1917 and continued to do so more rapidly each year through 1920. Per capita spending stood at $6.38 in 1914, dropped to a low of $5.93 in 1916, began to recover in 1917, by 1918 exceeded that for 1914, and by 1920 stood at $9.43. Despite the postwar depression that settled over the country in 1921, short and sharp in some regions, more prolonged in others, spending on education increased rapidly between 1921 and 1924; total expenditures rose from just under $59 million in 1920 to $80.5 million in 1924, and per capita from $9.43 to $12.14 in the same five-year period. In the mid-1920s there was a sharp decline in the *rate* of increased spending, belatedly reflecting the impact of hard times and unease about the size of the annual increases in preceding years. From 1926–27 spending resumed its upward momentum, with a major growth spurt from 1928 through 1930.[43]

Rising expenditure in the first three decades of the century invites an obvious question: was there anything distinctive about the period or was it simply a continuation of long-term trends? There are no national-level statistics to help here, but provincial data are suggestive. In Ontario between 1875 and 1900, total expenditure increased by 58.3%, though in the 1890s by only 9.8%. Between 1901 and 1911, however, expenditure rose by 107%, and in the next decade by 194%. Between 1920 and 1930 the growth rate declined but was still a substantial 61%.[44] In Nova Scotia the changes were more modest but the pattern is the same: between 1875 and 1900 spending increased by 45%; between 1900 and 1911 alone, by 50%; over the next decade, by 103%; and in the 1920s, by 47%.[45] Compared to the late nineteenth century, in other words, there were sharp increases in Canada's older provinces, especially during the first two decades of the century. In the West it was somewhat different. Noting in 1918 the much higher per-pupil costs of schooling in Saskatchewan compared to those in older American states, Harold Foght remarked that building new school systems was always more expensive than maintaining existing ones.[46] In the two decades before 1900, British Columbia's expenditures increased by 135% and 146% respectively – enormous increases compared to those in nineteenth-century Ontario or Nova Scotia. Still, British Columbia's expenditure jumped by 260% between 1900 and 1910, by another 107% between 1910 and 1920, followed in the next decade by a more modest but not inconsiderable 40%.[47]

All our figures thus far are based on "current dollars" – annual dollar amounts that take no account of inflation or other changes in purchasing power. But this was a period when there were substantial shifts in the dollar's value – downwards, during the First World War, and upwards, in the 1920s.[48] What do the increases in expenditure look like when reduced to what is often termed "constant dollars" or "real expenditure"? In the early 1930s the Dominion Bureau of Statistics attempted to answer that question using Department of Labour estimates that began in 1913. This unfortunately takes no account of the earliest years of the century but does indicate that between 1913 and 1931, while gross expenditure appeared to have increased by 160%, in constant dollars the increase was actually 91%.[49] A more recent estimate by the political scientist Ronald Manzer has the advantage of incorporating data from the first decade of the century; calculated in 1986 dollars, average real expenditure per pupil in 1900 was $160, in 1915, $314, and in 1925, $394, an increase over these twenty-five years of 146%.[50] The estimates by the DBS and by Manzer are not comparable; they begin from different bases and measure different things over different time periods. But what both point to is that growing expenditure was not simply an artifact of changes in the value of the dollar; rather, it was real and substantial.

How different do expenditure patterns look when the national data are disaggregated by province? Whatever measure one uses – per capita or per pupil, total current expenditure, local or provincial government expenditure – all provinces invested more money at the end of the period than at the beginning.[51] While the trends roughly parallel the national figures, the provincial patterns vary modestly. In some provinces, for example, the prewar recession and then the First World War had a larger impact than in others, and recovery to 1914 levels was slower. In large part because spending in Ontario increased annually during the 1920s, the impact of the postwar depression is washed out in the national-level figures. Other provinces experienced at least one year, and in some cases two, of declining expenditures that were almost certainly depression related. In 1923 or 1924 Nova Scotia, Manitoba, Saskatchewan, Alberta, British Columbia, and Prince Edward Island all saw a dip in total spending, and seven out of eight provinces had at least a one-year decline in per-pupil expenditure. Per capita decline in the same years hit every province but Ontario and New Brunswick. Peak years of spending varied but nearly everywhere came at the end of the period: in British Columbia, Alberta, and Saskatchewan in 1929; in Ontario, Quebec, and New Brunswick, 1931; and in Nova Scotia and Prince Edward Island, 1932. Manitoba was something of an exception. After years of annual increases, its spending peaked in 1923. A sharp dip occurred in the following year, and while modest increases occurred in the late 1920s, the province was still spending less in 1930 than in 1923, the result of tight expenditure controls imposed by the Bracken government that restrained education costs even in the relatively prosperous years of the late 1920s.[52]

It is also important to distinguish between the contributions made by provincial governments on the one hand and local school boards on the other.[53] Provincial grants rose across the period but at different rates of increase. Between 1921 and 1929, for example, the rate of increase for Saskatchewan was far higher than the national average, while Ontario was close to the latter figure and Alberta and British Columbia well below it.[54] Such indicators, however, only partially reflect levels of commitment in the 1920s; if one measures rates of increase between 1913 and 1929, one gets a different ranking, with some provincial governments expanding their spending more rapidly in the first decade, then pulling in their horns during the second. But overall, and after 1920 especially, provincial government spending increased at a higher rate than that of school districts or municipalities. To keep pace with local spending, a DBS survey explained, provincial expenditure would have had to increase by a third, but it actually increased by close to half, and "if the improved dollar is taken into account, the increased purchasing power devoted by the provinces to education [was] more than two-thirds, 68.41%."[55] This doesn't mean that education necessarily absorbed a growing share of total provincial budgets. As the provinces assumed new or expanded responsibilities for welfare and public works, the share allocated to education remained roughly stable and in some provinces declined modestly. "Expenditure on education increased from before the war, indeed from the beginning of the century," the Rowell-Sirois Commission remarked, "in almost the same ratio as all government expenditure until the 1930s."[56]

Among the most striking features of the period, however, and particularly when compared to the early twenty-first century, is the relative contribution of provincial governments on the one hand and of local ratepayers on the other (Table 6.2). Prince Edward Island is a special case: the provincial government had always contributed a majority of school funding – between 1914 and 1930, roughly 60%. Elsewhere, it was different. In 1914, in six of seven other provinces, local sources accounted for 80% or more of total revenue – in four provinces, it was 85% or more. In 1930 it was much the same: local contributions were still 80% or more in six of the seven provinces, and in five the figure stood at 85% or more. The seventh province was British Columbia, where the percentage in 1914 was 62% and during the 1920s about 68%.[57] Across the entire period, in other words, and with the sole exception of Prince Edward Island, the main burden of sustaining the schools fell upon local people. As in the nineteenth century, so in the early twentieth, the provision of schooling remained the responsibility of families and local communities. The state might impose minimum standards, routinely provide a modicum of financial support, or offer incentives for this or that innovation, but it was local people who paid most of the bills and, within the limits of their resources, decided what kind or amount of schooling they were willing to pay for.

There were a variety of reasons for the expenditure patterns that marked the first three decades of the century. Enrolment growth was certainly one of these, though not the only one. Between 1900 and 1925 Canadian enrolments very nearly doubled. Year by year there were more children to be schooled, more of them attended regularly, and more stayed in school longer. Aside from anything else, increasing numbers meant more money had to be raised to pay the bills.

The progress of urbanization and the attendant enrolment explosion put enormous pressure on most town and city boards. Analysing school expenditure between 1911 and 1917 alone, W.L. Richardson recorded increases of 40% in Saint John, 80% in Toronto and Vancouver, 122% in Winnipeg, 156% in Calgary, and 230% in Edmonton.[58] And this misses some of the biggest spending years immediately after the First World War. But it was not simply an urban phenomenon. The expansion of agricultural settlement in the prairie West meant thousands of new schools and teachers to staff them. More modest expansion took place elsewhere in rural Canada. Nor did the decline of rural population in some parts of central and eastern Canada reduce expenditure; whether a local school district contained forty or ten children, a teacher still had to be hired and paid. Secondary education contributed a disproportionate share to rising costs. According to one DBS estimate, while elementary enrolments increased about 50% between 1913 and 1931, "there was an increase of more than 200% in the secondary grades, and pupils in the latter category are just about twice as expensive as in the former."[59]

Capital costs posed particular challenges.[60] Prosperity in the early years of the century and rising land values, especially in the West, brought growing assessment revenues and encouraged generous expenditure on schools, as on other public institutions and utilities. Amidst unprecedented optimism, fed in part by civic boosterism, school boards and municipalities issued bonds and debentures, borrowing against the future to cover the construction costs of new elementary and high schools. In 1913, according to a later DBS study, current revenue in the three Prairie provinces combined covered only 56% of expenditure on education; in Alberta it was just 47%. The rest was deferred by assuming long-term debt. The depression that began in 1913 brought a stunning collapse in land values and thus assessment revenues, putting a stop to new construction, cutting deeply into operating revenues in many municipalities, and making it difficult even to service payments on previously acquired debts.[61] By 1917 or 1918 the war had brought some degree of recovery, but its demands put a further damper on school construction. Meanwhile inflation began to bite into the value of every dollar school boards could raise. In Ontario, expenditure during the war years on rent, repairs, and fuel rose by 66%; the only substantial decline in dollars spent, by some 73%, was on sites and buildings. In Manitoba, expenditure on fuel alone rose 35%, while that on school building and repairs dropped 69%.[62]

The short-lived postwar boom of 1919–20 relieved some of the pressure on municipal finances, and even during the depression that followed, resources were less scarce than they had been after 1913. But the cessation of construction during the war meant that boards now faced an enormous backlog of demand, as well as higher costs to meet it.[63] Once school building resumed, moreover, it had to be financed by additional debentures, with payments scheduled to come due during the decades ahead. And like operating costs, interest on the debt and provision for eventual repayment of the capital amounts (through reserve or sinking funds) had to be included in the annual school levy charged to ratepayers.

But whether driven by capital or operating costs, expenditure rose a good deal faster than enrolments. In its annual report for 1929, for example, the DBS pointed out that across the preceding decade expenditure in current dollars had risen at about double the rate of increase in enrolment: "When allowance is made for the increasing purchasing power of the dollar since 1921, the real increase ... has averaged ... about 3 times the increase in enrolments."[64] In the cities it might be even greater than that. Writing in 1930, the Calgary board's secretary-treasurer remarked that "while our attendance increased approximately 4 times, our expenditure has increased 8 times in the last twenty years."[65] Some of that difference can be accounted for by the program and construction innovations so widespread in the cities and larger towns. Buildings acquired not just regular classrooms but special-purpose manual training, domestic science, and kindergarten rooms, science laboratories, libraries, gymnasiums, and auditoriums. Heating systems grew more efficient but also more expensive. Water fountains in the hallways replaced common drinking cups in the washrooms. High schools added commercial and vocational departments or even entire vocational schools. In Ontario, where vocational education had spread fastest, the per-pupil cost of the academic high school in 1921–22 was $108.91; for the vocational school it was $210.37.[66] In 1920 Winnipeg spent nearly $54,000 on manual training and domestic science instructors, $33,000 on school medical and dental services, $10,000 for the attendance department, and nearly $52,000 for the evening school program. Its handful of specialist subject supervisors cost another $20,650. And these costs would grow steadily through the 1920s.[67]

There were also growing amounts devoted to teachers' salaries.[68] Aside from anything else, more pupils in more classrooms meant more teachers. Between 1900 and 1930 their numbers grew from 19,000 to over 49,000, and they all had to be paid. But across the same decades the salaries of most teachers improved considerably. We have explored this matter at length elsewhere and will not reiterate our discussion here.[69] Our conclusion, however, is pertinent: while much qualification is necessary to account for variations in time and place, between 1910 and 1929, nationally and in constant dollars, average salaries rose by about 40%. While it is more difficult to verify because of the nature of the sources, we think that salaries were rising during the first decade of the century as well. Thus it was not only the demand for more teachers but also the need to pay them more that contributed to increasing educational expenditure across the period. Whatever the exact balance between these two causes, in any case, in Ontario the total salary bill rose – from 1901 to 1913 by 118%, 1914 to 1918 by 25%, and 1919 to 1925 by 83%. Alberta experienced a staggering increase between 1907 and 1913 of 236%, during the war years a further increase of 39%, and another 54% from 1919 to 1925. The pattern and the percentages in Saskatchewan were about the same as in Alberta.[70] In 1914 Prince Edward Island's government grant (covering 60% of salary costs) was about $150,000; by 1928 it had risen to over $245,000.[71] During the 1920s alone, according to the DBS, "in five of the provinces where expenditure on teachers' salaries has been recorded ... and in which two-thirds of all [Canadian] expenditure on education occurs, the increase in the outlay for salaries was about 34%."[72]

In some respects there was nothing distinctive about the patterns of expenditure in the Maritimes. Spending, both local and provincial, rose, as it did elsewhere. Resources in urban areas allowed for the construction of new high schools, the introduction of programs such as manual training and domestic science, medical inspection, regular day classes in new vocational schools in places like Saint John, or the extension of evening vocational instruction in urban Nova Scotia. As in other provinces, teachers' salaries improved as well. But when one compares educational expenditure in the Maritimes and in those provinces west of Quebec, the disparities are nothing short of shocking.

While teachers' salaries in the Maritimes did indeed rise over the period, they were universally dismal compared to those in other provinces. To cite but one example, in 1910 British Columbia's teachers, at the time the best paid in the country, earned on average three times as much as those in Nova Scotia; by 1929 improved salaries in Nova Scotia meant that British Columbia teachers earned "only" twice as much.[73] The same gap existed for other key indicators. In 1926 Saskatchewan was spending 30% of its provincial budget on education and in 1929, 24%. Ontario, closer to the national average, allocated 24% in 1926 and 22% in 1929. Nova Scotia and New Brunswick, on the other hand, were well below the national figure, at about 13%.[74] And it was equally true of total expenditure judged by either per capita or per-pupil expenditure. In 1914 the national average per capita spending stood at $6.38 and the per-pupil expenditure at $51.58. Nova Scotia spent $2.76 per capita and $21.22 per pupil. Or consider one of the peak spending years. In 1928 the national average for per capita spending on education was $12.71. Alberta spent $16.30, Saskatchewan $16.22, British Columbia $13.14, and Ontario $12.69; New Brunswick spent $7.44, Nova Scotia $6.64, and Prince Edward Island $4.82. The national per-pupil expenditure was $77.06. Alberta spent $92.28, British Columbia $91.77, and Ontario $77.68; New Brunswick spent $47.65, Nova Scotia $41.42, and PEI $35.01.

Once as thriving as most other parts of the country, the Maritime provinces had undergone a long period of economic decline, and in the immediate postwar years especially were battered by economic forces beyond their control – by international competition in primary industries that were staples of their economies, and by national policies that concentrated more and more of the country's industry and commerce in central Canada. Throughout the 1920s, the three provinces ranked at the bottom of provincial per capita income and most other indices of personal or social welfare.[75] Resources for schooling were no less constrained. Nova Scotia and New Brunswick were more reliant than other provinces on property taxes – property that had less assessable value – and like Prince Edward Island, were less urbanized, with a concomitant lack of industrial and commercial wealth.[76] But that is only a partial explanation for the gap. Another factor involved the revenues available from the sale of school lands set aside early in the history of Quebec, Ontario, Manitoba, Saskatchewan, and Alberta. In all five provinces this amounted to substantial sums each year, which meant in turn that these provinces had considerable revenues for the support of schools additional to those raised from taxation.[77] The three Maritime provinces – the poorest in the country – had no such resource.

The inequalities in school spending added to the sense of grievance animating the Maritimes throughout the 1920s. Departmental reports and commissions of inquiry drew attention to both, including the role of the school lands funds in other provinces. Under the subheading "Federal Aid," Nova Scotia's superintendent of education remarked in 1929 that "an appreciable part of the school revenues in the Western provinces is derived from public lands specially set aside for the purpose. The school system of Ontario also benefits from funds accruing from the Clergy Reserves. From time to time, the claim is made that the Maritime Provinces are entitled to a share of these western school funds, on the ground that they contributed to their purchase. Such claim would probably be found not to be well-based in a legal sense. Much, however, may be said in its support by way of equity."[78] Nor was he alone in this opinion. In 1930 Prince Edward Island's Royal Commission on Education drew attention to the same source of inequity.[79]

Expenditure on education does not translate in any simple way into value received. Long-established school systems tend to be less expensive than those in the process of creation. Close concentrations in thickly settled countryside may cost less than a more scattered population. Fewer children to be served in a school district will raise per-pupil costs. Teachers' salaries don't necessarily guarantee anything about the quality of instruction. Because of enormous salary differentials, nonetheless, teachers from the Maritimes – often the best qualified among them – continued to flock westwards as they had since before the turn of the century. And simply to maintain existing schools, provincial governments in the Maritimes, as well as their local ratepayers, had to make a greater tax effort than those in other provinces. "Far from school support in Canada being on a democratic basis of equality," Nova Scotia's superintendent of education once wrote, "the contrary prevails – inequality as between provinces, inequality between municipalities, and gross inequalities as between [school] sections."[80] The latter two, we have suggested, were structural features embedded in the school law of each province. The first had nothing to do with school legislation but was embedded in the structure of the Canadian economy itself. Thus Canadian education incorporated not two but three sources of inequality – unequal tax effort and tax capacity among ratepayers within a province; unequal educational opportunities between school districts within a province; and both forms of inequality between provinces belonging to a single nation-state.

Yet despite the egregious regional disparities, one can still ask, was Canada spending a little or a lot on its schools? In large part, any answer to that question is a subjective one, depending on where investment in education stands on one's list of priorities and on what one considers good versus wasteful or unnecessary expenditure on education itself. But there are at least two indicators that offer international comparisons. Both tell us something useful, though they point in different directions. While the figures are based on different calculations than our own and are therefore not consistent with the per capita spending we cite elsewhere in this chapter, one indicator is a comparison of spending by American states in 1930 and Canadian provinces in 1931.[81] Since the Depression's bite on educational spending was still limited in 1930–31, we think this represents the peak spending years of the 1920s more than the Depression lows to come. According to the comparative data, Ontario and Manitoba, at this point the two highest-ranking provinces, were spending $16.73 per capita on elementary and secondary schooling; this put them below twenty-eight of the forty-eight American states. Inserted into the American list, British Columbia would have ranked thirty-sixth. Nova Scotia and New Brunswick would have fallen near the bottom, above only Arkansas and Georgia, with Prince Edward Island lower than all of them. It is perhaps more telling to compare contiguous states and provinces. Maine spent $14.03 per capita, New Brunswick $7.80; New York $28.72, Michigan $24.67, Ontario $16.73; North Dakota $24.37, Manitoba $16.73; Montana $25.44, Alberta $16.56; Washington $21.50, British Columbia $13.71. Judged on per capita spending, in other words, Canadian spending fell far below American levels. On the other hand, the United States was a far wealthier nation. Recent work by Ronald Manzer offers a helpful comparison of five countries: Australia, Canada, New Zealand, the United Kingdom, and the United States. He uses (among other measures) "government expenditures on public elementary and secondary education as a percentage of gross domestic product." According to Manzer's calculations, over the period 1905 through 1930, not only did spending in Canada as a percentage of gross domestic product

(GDP) rise sharply, but it was consistently higher than that of the United States, the United Kingdom, or Australia, and only marginally below that of New Zealand. In 1925 the figure for Canada and New Zealand was 2.3% of GDP; for the United States 2.1%, for the United Kingdom 1.9%, and for Australia 1.2%.[82] Two points follow. Over the first three decades of the twentieth century, Canada was investing a rising percentage of its national wealth in elementary and secondary education and, though less wealthy than the United States or the United Kingdom, was investing a greater percentage of its GDP in education than either of those countries – or, perhaps put in a different way, though Canada's tax capacity was less, it was making a greater tax effort.

Yet the Canadian economy was also peculiarly vulnerable because of its dependence on export staples. Writing a decade later, the Rowell-Sirois commissioners would pen a kind of epitaph for the vibrant growth that characterized the later 1920s in most parts of the country: "Large areas of the country, where it was either wheat or nothing, pulp and paper or nothing, lumber or nothing, non-ferrous metals or nothing, became dependent upon the exportation of a single or a very few commodities. If the foreign prices of these fell to unprofitable levels there would be no alternative occupations. On the Pre-Cambrian Shield and over a large part of the prairies, self-sufficiency even for a bare subsistence would be impossible."[83] And, the commissioners might have added, for those reliant on them, from the stevedores at the Port of Vancouver, which shipped the wheat or lumber, to the railway workers who moved Canada's staples across the country, to the managers and employees in Brantford who made the tractors and combines for the agricultural producers, to the teachers and children who depended on all of them for the revenues to keep the schools open.

7

The Crisis in Educational Finance:
1930–1939

The Great Depression began with no more than modest cuts in spending, and the national totals obscure even these, since the first reductions in the three most westerly provinces were countered by increasing expenditure everywhere else through 1930 or 1931.[1] There was, in other words, no sudden catastrophic reversal of fortune, and the full impact was slow to make itself felt. By 1933 or 1934, however, the damage was obvious everywhere. In 1930 total provincial revenues for education peaked at close to $97 million; by 1935 they had fallen to $79 million.[2] Per capita spending on the schools dropped from its 1930 national peak of $13.16 to $10.17 in 1935; per-pupil costs from $76.51 to $60.00 over the same years. In 1929 education was allocated 19.1% of provincial budgets; by 1935 the figure stood at 11.5%. Looking back at the debacle from 1940, the Rowell-Sirois Commission would remark that education "bore the brunt of depression retrenchment and total budgets were cut by a sixth. There has been some expansion since 1936, but total expenditure is still (1939 estimates) some $10 million below the 1930 peak."[3]

During the worst of the Depression, every province experienced at least one year of falling revenues and some recorded declines for several years in a row.[4] But the impact was uneven. Nova Scotia had only a single year of decline (1933) and in 1934 was spending more than it did in 1929; per capita spending was higher in 1933 than in 1930; and per-pupil expenditure dropped by over two dollars between 1932 and 1933 but was nearly as high in 1935 as it was in the peak year of 1931. Total expenditure on education in Prince Edward Island actually went up between 1929 and 1932, and by 1937 was more than $100,000 above the 1930 figure. In the Maritimes, comparatively poor even in the most prosperous years of the previous decade, the difference between expenditure levels in the late 1920s and the mid-1930s was marginal; indeed in Prince Edward Island and Nova Scotia things got better, not worse, at least if one looks at provincial-level tallies alone.

At the other extreme was Saskatchewan, which suffered a reversal nothing short of stunning. In 1928 per-pupil expenditure was $88.92, only marginally less than that of the front-runners, British Columbia and Alberta, and well above the national average of $77.06. In 1929 the province spent more per capita on education, $16.53 a head, than anywhere else in Canada. Then the international price of wheat collapsed: a bushel of No. 1 Northern that was worth $1.03 in 1928 earned the farmer 29 cents in 1932.[5] In a one-crop economy, that was disaster enough; drought, especially in southern Saskatchewan, did the rest. By 1934, per-pupil expenditure had plummeted to $43.07, per capita spending to $8.14. Between 1930 and 1937 total expenditure on the schools dropped by 40% and rural municipal expenditures were cut by two-thirds.[6] Manitoba was not very far behind, and education in other provinces suffered as well, but nothing quite matched what happened in Saskatchewan, in education as in other things.

Generally speaking, recovery began in the mid-1930s, though it too was uneven. By 1937 all provinces except Saskatchewan had exceeded their Depression lows on per-pupil expenditure and all provinces except Nova Scotia, Saskatchewan, and Alberta were spending more per capita. By 1939 all provinces had exceeded their 1934 figures on both indicators. However, no province except Nova Scotia was spending as much in 1939 as it did in its peak year after 1930.

The impact of the Depression was uneven in other ways. In most parts of the country, urban areas appear to have suffered less than rural school districts. While Ontario's cities collectively experienced sharp expenditure reductions between 1931 and 1936, by the latter date they were spending more on education than they had a decade earlier. In rural areas the reverse was the case: far less spending in 1936 than in either 1926 or 1931.[7] Across the country there were enormous differences in per capita expenditure between the cities and the province where they were located. In Halifax in 1936, it was $12.33, in Nova Scotia $6.80; in Saint John versus New Brunswick, $15.79 and $6.12; in Edmonton versus Alberta, $17.26 and $11.73; in Vancouver versus British Columbia, $13.18 and $10.84.[8] In the late 1930s, a Manitoba study had this to say about urban/rural differences:

> In the terms of actual cash, rural Manitoba has decreased its cash contribution to education from $4,747,164 to $2,951,733, a reduction of $1,795,431, whereas in the same period a broader and firmer basis of taxation in the city of Winnipeg has permitted an increase of local support from $2,175,700 to $2,683,740. Possibly no other example could more definitely illustrate the very great difference in ability to pay than this fact, namely, that in the period of depression rural Manitoba was forced to reduce its contribution from local taxes by approximately

$1,800,000, while Winnipeg was enabled to increase its contribution by over one-half million. It cannot be argued that there was a greater desire to pay in the city of Winnipeg, because as a matter of fact the rural areas taxed themselves far beyond the limit of their ability to pay.[9]

The cities, of course, had more expensive facilities, secondary schools with teachers' salaries higher than those for teachers employed in the elementary schools, rising enrolments, much higher levels of school-related debt, and other costs to meet that rural schools did not. The gaps, nonetheless, are telling. When Carl Goldenberg pulled together the data for the Rowell-Sirois Commission, he found that "rural areas everywhere were more seriously affected than urban districts, and have shown the least recovery."[10] On the other hand, this doesn't mean the cities got off scot-free. Winnipeg may have looked rich to rural Manitoba, but between 1929 and 1933 it reduced school expenditures by 25%, the largest cut of any of Canada's big cities, though Vancouver was not far behind with a reduction of 20%. Out of fifteen urban communities, seven, ranging from Sydney and Peterborough to Saskatoon and Victoria, saw expenditure drop between 1929 and 1933. What is perhaps more remarkable is that eight cities actually *increased* expenditure between 1929 and 1933: Halifax, Saint John, Quebec City, Toronto, Hamilton, Ottawa, London, and Edmonton. By 1936 the list of cities that were still below 1929 expenditures was almost exclusively western: Vancouver, Victoria, Winnipeg, Saskatoon, and Calgary.[11]

For many of Canada's suburbs and satellite towns, it was a different story. The relative handful of suburban communities that were primarily upper-middle-class enclaves weathered the storm without great difficulty – or at least didn't go bankrupt. But in those mainly dormitory suburbs where the lower-middle and working classes had flocked to find cheap land and housing, where industrial or commercial properties were few, where municipal tax bases had been strained near the breaking point even in the prosperous 1920s to provide basic services like sewers, roads, and schools, the results were disastrous. By the late 1930s, St James, a Winnipeg suburb, found itself "with a bonded debt of $4,204,622.00, totally unsupported by adequate assets ... This amount is being increased yearly by an annual operating deficit of approximately $250,000.00," this despite the fact that St James "had the highest taxation per $1,000 in the province."[12] Though not the only cause of its deficits, the large number of residents unable to pay their taxes played a significant role. As the local newspaper put it in 1934, "approximately 15% of the taxpayers are on relief; tax collections are estimated to be below 50% – so another 35% are in such straitened circumstances as to be unable to meet their community obligations."[13] The Ontario Committee on the Costs of Education summed up the problem this way:

Because the population belongs largely to the wage-earning class, its
ability to pay taxes is dependent on conditions of employment within
the city. This type of district, as is illustrated in the cases of the suburban
areas edging the cities of Toronto and Windsor, was among the first
to suffer from the decline in employment in the late 1920s. Here the
burden of unemployment relief became greatest, at a time when the
necessity for providing facilities for education became most acute and
the ability to pay taxes had reached a minimum ... Where these conditions prevail the township and the school section have been required
to assume a burden beyond the capacity of their resources. It was represented to the committee most effectively that the children of parents
living in these suburban areas were placed under a severe handicap in
their efforts to obtain an education.[14]

Finally, what effect did the Depression have on regional inequalities?
As per capita and per-pupil expenditure declined in other provinces, the
gap, compared at least to the late 1920s, became narrower. In 1930 all but
the Maritime provinces were spending more per capita than the national
average; by 1934 only three provinces were: British Columbia, Alberta, and
Ontario. Manitoba and Saskatchewan in particular began to approach the
figures for Nova Scotia and New Brunswick. Nevertheless, the gulf between
rich and poor remained large. Between 1930 and 1934 British Columbia's
per-pupil expenditure dropped from $93.39 to $74.03, but in the latter
year Nova Scotia's was $40.04 and New Brunswick's $35.62. Even devastated
Saskatchewan spent more than that – $43.07. And while the cities did bet-
ter than the countryside everywhere, the East-West differentials appeared
there as well. Halifax's per capita spending in 1936 was $12.33, higher than
Montreal's ($10.09) but below that of fourteen other large Canadian com-
munities. Saint John ranked better at $15.79, above Vancouver, Winnipeg,
Ottawa, and several other cities, but well below Toronto ($18.76), Saskatoon
($22.73), or Regina ($18.90).[15] As for the larger meaning of the provincial
differences, New Brunswick's superintendent of education had this to say
to the Rowell-Sirois commissioners near the end of the decade: "Ontario
spends $83.33 per pupil in the public schools per year ... New Brunswick
spends less than half of that, which would mean that in order to give New
Brunswick a service like they have in Ontario, as costly as Ontario, we would
have to add ... $3,600,000. It is an astounding thing, it is a thing to set us
thinking in the smaller provinces of Canada, that we have Ontario, closely
followed by two or three other provinces, spending twice as much per child
on elementary and secondary schooling. It seems most significant. It makes
us wonder about our future."[16]

Why was it that, as the Rowell-Sirois Report put it, education "bore the brunt of the depression retrenchment"? This brings us back to the interplay between the structure of educational finance and the economic circumstances of the times. When workers are unemployed, they can't pay taxes. When primary producers can't sell their produce, they may well survive by reverting to a subsistence economy but cash disappears and so do tax payments. When the incomes of entrepreneurs or white-collar workers fall, they pay less income and consumption taxes. In a depressed economy, real estate values fall, and with that, assessable values decline. Accordingly, both provincial governments, dependent on income and consumption taxes, and municipal governments and school districts, dependent on property taxes, see their revenues fall.

At the extreme, pushed to the wall, ratepayers simply walk away from homes, farms, or business properties, abandoning them to the municipality or the banks that hold their mortgages. More commonly, people hold on as best they can, paying what they can, falling into arrears, sometimes for years at a time. In turn, municipalities see their debts mount and, when not forced into bankruptcy, can only hold the line through rigid economy. They raise property taxes where and when they can, but this invokes the law of diminishing returns – as taxes go up, fewer people can pay them – so this is an option of limited value.[17]

Not all industrial and commercial activities were hit equally hard, so not all communities suffered equally. Public servants and many other workers might see salaries and wages cut but they remained employed, and since the cost of living – prices for food, rent, and other necessities of life – fell faster than wages, those who were employed might find themselves no worse off, in some cases actually better off, and able to pay provincial or municipal taxes even when rates were raised.[18] In the worst year of the Depression, 1933, some 27% of the non-agricultural labour force were unemployed; still, that left over 60% earning some sort of income.[19] Where provinces or municipalities included large numbers of those who could pay their taxes, the damage inflicted by the Depression was limited; a richer and more mixed tax base offset hard times, to some extent at least. But any community consisting of primary producers dependent on international markets was at extreme risk. And the smallest unit of government, the rural school district, was even more likely to be dependent on a workforce engaged in a single enterprise.

As the number of unemployed multiplied, expenditure on relief payments exploded. Canada-wide, the provinces spent just under a million dollars on relief in 1929; by 1934, the figure stood at $55.5 million; in 1937, nearly $43 million.[20] Although some of this money came from the federal

government, the lion's share was borne by the provinces and the municipalities. Thus economies in other public spending had to be found. The
alternatives were limited. Both provinces and local governments had fixed
costs to meet; they could not simply shut off the water supply, abandon the
administration of justice, shut down police and fire services, or close down
the schools for a year or two (though this option was actually canvassed by
one provincial cabinet).[21] Yet where expenditure could be reduced, it was.
While the total expenditure on relief by all provincial governments rose
21% and interest charges rose 5.4% between 1929 and 1935, every other
major expenditure category was reduced. However, reductions were 2.6%
or less in all categories but two. "Highways, Bridges, etc.," which included
both building and maintenance, fell 7.1%; education fell 7.6%. These two
budget lines were inevitably targets for cuts because, after the provincial
debt, they constituted, in 1931, the two largest expenditure categories in
provincial budgets.[22] But they were also vulnerable because they promised
substantial and relatively easy cuts; investment in roads could be put off
till better times and education costs could be shuffled off to local school
districts, leaving them to decide whether to raise taxes or make their own
reductions in capital expenditures, operating costs, or both. Thus, for
example, in 1934 the Ontario government's regular grants to public schools
were reduced by 10% and in 1935 by another 15%, while in 1936 the grant
to vocational schools was reduced by 20%.[23] Among other retrenchments,
British Columbia cut 50% of its grant money to school libraries for the purchase of new books.[24] The schools did not have to absorb all the reductions:
in several provinces, provincial support for post-secondary education was
hit harder, as was department of education spending on things like inspection, examinations, and administration. But Canada-wide, total provincial
government grants to schools fell from their 1931 peak of $18,468,000 to
a low of $14,233,000 in 1933.

   Mainly dependent on local property taxes, school districts and municipalities were hardly in a position to compensate for declining government
grants. As the Depression deepened, much of rural Canada reverted to
a subsistence economy: "in some places money virtually disappeared as a
medium of exchange."[25] Families survived by cultivating their own vege-
table gardens, remodelling outgrown clothing, bartering goods and services with their neighbours, or "making do" in a variety of other ways when
sources of cash income evaporated. But money was never entirely dispensable, even for individuals and families, and for the schools it was crucial.
Fuel had to be purchased, debenture debt to be met, and teachers paid.
Property taxes could only be paid in cash. As incomes declined and sources
of money dried up, school board revenues plunged in every province, and
with their limited, inflexible tax base, rural boards in particular suffered

catastrophic losses.[26] School tax arrears soared. Long before the disaster in Saskatchewan reached its nadir, the province's Committee on School Finance would report that "the present economic situation with depressed prices for all agricultural products, resulting as it has in arrears of taxes municipally levied of almost $31,000,000 as at Dec. 31, 1930, raises the question of the wisdom of placing such a heavy part of the tax burden upon real estate and particularly on farm lands. Unpaid taxes, with which taxing bodies are blessed even in good years, are at the bottom of many of our present troubles."[27] By 1933, in rural Saskatchewan, amounts "due from taxation" were roughly twice the "receipts from taxation"; the ratio was only slightly better in the province's villages and towns.[28] By 1934 tax arrears in Manitoba had risen to about $5.5 million, in Alberta to over $8 million.[29] When school boards raised mill rates to compensate for lower revenues, they only increased the number unable or unwilling to pay their tax bills. Disaster rippled outwards to the banks and other lenders as boards, year after year, failed to make debenture payments.[30]

But banks also contributed to the crisis in school finance. As an Ontario Educational Association brief to the Royal Commission on Banking explained in 1933, school boards had to borrow "considerable sums" to meet immediate costs, since the majority of municipalities didn't operate on a "pay-as-you-go" principle for education. "This has led to action by the banks ... which has seemed not only coercive but unintelligent" and affected "a large number of municipalities." The brief offered one example of "a populous county" near Toronto: "Last winter a supervisor from one of the banks met representatives from all the High School Boards in the county, and told them that each of these Boards must cut its educational budget to 80% of the previous year's figures, or no money whatever would be forthcoming from the banks. This decree was absolute; it made no difference that in some schools the attendance had increased by as much as 20% and that additional teachers were urgently needed, even if extra school accommodation were not provided." No board, the brief protested, could afford anything like a 20% budget cut without substantial damage wreaked upon its programs and staff.[31]

In many parts of rural Canada, revenues fell to the point where schools faced outright closure. Towards the end of the decade 30% of New Brunswick's rural school districts were receiving some form of "poor aid" from the provincial government.[32] In Nova Scotia the figure was somewhere between a quarter and a third.[33] "In the entire drought area of Alberta, comprising 50% of the more than 5,000 school districts," the Rowell-Sirois Commission was told, "the only financial resources available to the boards of trustees are the meagre government grants."[34] In one of the worst-hit areas, the secretary of the local school trustees' association informed the

Alberta Department of Education that "owing to the present conditions, this Association go on record of closing the schools for one year, as the crops are far beyond recovery regardless of the amount of moisture we may get, few taxes were paid last year and none will be paid this year, besides feed and relief and seed will be required in the district during the winter and spring. As you can see our position is hopeless."[35] Governments responded in various ways, attempting to enforce tax recovery measures, allowing tax write-offs to limit indebtedness, or boosting the special funding for poor school districts.[36] Several provinces were able to offset declining local revenues through increased grants to all school districts. Singularly, Nova Scotia's grants rose every year throughout the Depression. Beginning in the mid-1930s, grants in other provinces crept upwards from their Depression lows. Since local revenues continued to provide most of the funding, this was no cure-all but it helped to prevent the situation getting any worse. In some cases, on the other hand, grant formulas were also rejigged disproportionately in favour of rural schools, provoking predictable squawks from urban boards, which saw their own grants reduced accordingly.[37]

There is no easy way to describe the impact of reduced funding on school facilities and programs, as it varied from community to community and province to province, depending on how hard each was hit by the Depression and the variable timing of recovery. Here and there, new schools were being built even in the worst years of the Depression; this appears to have been mostly an urban phenomenon, but not always. In 1935 rural Albertans built or renovated fifty schools by voluntary effort alone, thus avoiding debenture commitments, the department of education assisting with small grants "to enable the school board to purchase such finishing material as window frames, doors and hardware which could not be procured locally."[38] In the main, costly programs in areas like special education and health services seem to have been maintained, even if some trimming took place, and occasionally new auxiliary programs were added.[39] Some reductions were relatively benign; falling birthrates in the 1920s, for example, reduced enrolments in the elementary grades, allowing classrooms or entire schools to be closed, though this may have merely enabled boards to move funds to overcrowded high schools.[40]

More generally, however, funding reductions put an end to new construction, renovations, and all new investment in school equipment and libraries. Comparing the figures for 1930 and 1932, the Saskatchewan Department of Education reported a decrease in expenditure of 88% for grounds and buildings, 77% for furniture and equipment, and 63% for libraries.[41] Raising pupil-teacher ratios was another expedient. "Since 1929, in their effort to reduce expenditure," one Ontario report noted a decade later, "school boards have increased the enrolment per classroom to a degree which is not consistent with maintaining satisfactory standards of instruction."[42] Indeed, Ontario's minister of education admitted in 1937 that "it has been necessary in many cases throughout the entire province to permit classes to rise to 50 and in some cases to over 60 pupils."[43] From New Brunswick: "Another evidence of poverty is the number of one-room rural schools with enrolments over 50 ... unable to employ another teacher or to make the necessary addition to the school building if the teacher could be employed."[44] Despite the financial exigencies in rural Canada, outright school closures on that account appear to have been rare,[45] though the school year was shortened by a month or two in many communities, and summer holidays shifted to January and February to save money on coal and to maintain attendance for children whose parents couldn't afford winter boots and clothing.[46] In urban Ontario, boards invented ingenious schemes for double shifts in overcrowded high schools ("staggered classes"), which meant no capital expenditure for additional classrooms and more teaching time with the same number of staff; in other places manual training, domestic science, small-enrolment subjects, and vocational classes were reduced or eliminated.[47] G.A. Wheable, London's director of education, summed up in the following list the measures being taken by school boards everywhere: "Eliminating from the school system services which were formerly provided; shortening the school term; reducing the amount expended for equipment and supplies; decreasing the salaries paid; postponing the capital expenditures; enlarging classes and reducing the number of persons employed."[48]

There was also a sharp increase in secondary-level instruction in the elementary schools. In rural areas this was mainly a response to parental demand – to the pressure to provide some form of advanced schooling close to home and less expensive than sending a child to an urban high school.[49] But it was also an urban phenomenon. In Ontario, for example, it was the big-city boards, surprisingly enough, that were at the forefront of the movement to expand their "fifth classes." Falling fertility rates in the 1920s had led to declining elementary school enrolments in the 1930s, which meant that there was excess space in the elementary schools at the very moment when adolescents were crowding into the secondary schools. And placing the first two years of high school in an elementary school setting meant reduced costs in operating budgets and especially in teachers' salaries. In Toronto, for instance, the board estimated that the per capita cost of a fifth-form class was one dollar compared to $261 for the collegiate institutes; by 1933 Toronto had thirty-one of these classes with an enrolment of 1,131 pupils.[50]

Though harder hit than most major Canadian cities, Winnipeg was probably typical in its response to the Depression. Between 1930 and 1933 the board cut its budget lines for "Instructional Supplies" from nearly $79,000 to just over $35,000, and for "Repairs and Replacements" from $109,000 to $71,400. While both budget lines increased each year after that, they were still well below the 1930 figure in 1937.[51] But overall, programs were trimmed rather than eviscerated. Manual training and domestic science were deferred by one grade, and vocational education for high school students was modestly reduced. Because it was an optional year, instruction in grade XII was eliminated, and clamps were put on grade XI repeaters. "Economical staffing" sent "supervising principals" back to the classroom part-time, the number of specialist supervisors at central office was reduced, and there were some staff cuts in the medical and dental departments. Special education programs were preserved, though at the cost of raising pupil-teacher ratios in regular classrooms. And not all the changes were reductions: in 1937 the board introduced a new program for identifying and assisting children who were hard of hearing; and by 1939 more schools were being equipped with movie projectors.[52]

Buildings could be allowed to run down, library books might fall into tatters and not be replaced, program "frills" might be reduced or eliminated, but schools had to remain open because children had to be taught – that much was not only a matter of law but the custom of the country. Where special education programs or health services had been established, trustees, like others, were loath to simply cut children adrift.[53] Keep the elementary schools open but close the high schools, where attendance was mostly voluntary and provision more expensive? This was hardly an option when pressure not just to maintain but to extend access to secondary education was intense in both urban and rural Canada. There was, in other words, only so much that could be done by way of reducing expenditure through cuts in facilities and programs. Salaries, on the other hand, constituted by far the largest bulk of school board annual budgets. And teachers' salaries were a peculiarly vulnerable target during the Great Depression.

Simply put, salaries were vulnerable because of oversupply. Experience levels rose sharply during the 1930s – teachers who had jobs clung to them as never before. But as alternative employment opportunities for young people declined and as other forms of post-secondary education that required large investments became unaffordable, successive crops of high school graduates crowded into the normal schools. Although numbers would gradually shrink in later years, normal school enrolments in Ontario stood at just over 2,000 in both 1932 and 1933, in the following year 1,600, and 1,000 the year after that.[54] Alberta issued nearly 1,100 new teaching certificates in 1931 and 800 in each of the next two years, while Saskatchewan expected 1,200 new graduates in 1931 alone.[55] Authorities in Nova Scotia noted, with a certain satisfaction, the increase in enrolments among young men: "With so many industrial doors closed to them, they are turning to the schools."[56] A less sanguine interpretation was offered by one woman writing to a Prairie newspaper: men, who had avoided teaching before the Depression because the salaries were too low, were now "trying to put women out of their traditional jobs."[57] Beyond that, there were thousands of men and women who already held valid teaching certificates; as times grew tough, they too turned to the schools. Worried federation leaders took note of the number of "re-entrants" – "persons who had left the profession in better times for more remunerative occupations" but had since lost their jobs or failed in business.[58] "During the past few years," Ontario's minister of education remarked in 1937, "the teaching profession has received quite a substantial number of recruits from other professions – from engineering in particular, even in certain cases from the church, from law, and from medicine. These men abandoned their original professions and started teaching by reason of the security which the teaching profession offered in the times of stress."[59] In parts of rural Canada there was a marked increase in married women applying for schools, in many cases wives attempting to compensate for the collapse of family farm incomes.[60] Altogether a large surplus of qualified teachers developed, desperate to obtain jobs in the schools and often willing to underbid those who already held them. And that, given the state of municipal finance, was a certain recipe for salary cuts.

These cuts were of two kinds: in the countryside, ad hoc adjustments downwards, district by school district, as local revenues dried up and applicants multiplied; and in urban communities, across-the-board reductions in salary schedules. But one way or another, in current dollars at least, salaries declined everywhere. It is not easy to ascertain the extent of the reduction in urban areas: in most cases they were cumulative over several years, in some communities they were restored or partially restored by the mid-1930s, and they often differed for elementary and secondary teachers or at different points in the salary grid. Yet over the period 1929 to 1933, cuts of 20% or 30% appear to have been common. In Calgary they ranged from 20% to over 33%; in Vancouver, 23% to 31%; in Winnipeg, 15% to 25%; and in Saint John, 23%. A series of reductions between 1930 and 1933 in Prince Albert's seven public schools amounted to 40%, the board saving $16,000 in expenditure with no dismissals as a trade-off.[61] That tended to be a general rule in urban Canada – salary reductions and in many cases heavier workloads, but few teachers actually losing their jobs through staff reductions.

While school boards had to bite the bullet everywhere, the pressures were most severe in the countryside. As the Alberta brief to the Rowell-Sirois Commission put it, "The size of the small unit had the effect of making the Board of Trustees very susceptible to the demands of the ratepayers in the district. It is probably true that the extremely low prices prevailing, especially during 1931, 1932, and 1933, had a moral effect upon the people even beyond what the income from the farms may have warranted, in the attitude toward the payment of taxes. Undoubtedly the trustees met a widespread demand for the reduction of school costs to the absolute minimum. Unfortunately this had its effect upon the salaries which these boards were prepared to pay its teachers. While teachers' salaries in the Province did not sink to the low levels reached in other Provinces, nevertheless they did reach low levels."[62] Manitoba's provincial treasurer made the same point: "The first effect of the depression is met in a school district by the trustees pulling in their horns and economizing ... the first cushion of the depression is the expenses of the school district and the teachers' salaries, which is usually the largest single item."[63] Measuring pre-Depression highs against Depression lows, the Dominion Bureau of Statistics calculated that in British Columbia urban salaries had declined by about 12% and rural salaries about 16%; in Alberta, 9% and 28%; in Manitoba, 17% and 37%; in Ontario, 7% and 28%; in New Brunswick, 3% and 20%; and in Nova Scotia, 1% and 4%.[64] The low levels of rural salaries, even in 1930, and the extraordinary reductions since then, Carl Goldenberg would remark, "constitute a severe indictment of present methods of school support."[65]

With one or two exceptions, the Depression did little to alter salary differentials among the provinces. British Columbia and Ontario remained at the top of the heap, and while the rich got a little poorer, the gaps were little short of astonishing. In 1933 teachers in British Columbia earned, on average, $1,416; in New Brunswick, $628; in Prince Edward Island, $551; and in Nova Scotia, $741.[66] And though teachers in rural Manitoba and parts of Alberta were also hit hard, Saskatchewan was a story of its own. In 1930 total teachers' salaries in the province stood at $8 million; by 1934 that figure had fallen to less than $4 million. The amount paid to rural teachers declined in the same period from $4,537,000 to $1,939,000 – a decrease of about 68%.[67] Saskatchewan, which had paid its teachers relatively well in the 1920s, fell to Maritime levels in the 1930s. Or consider, again, Saskatchewan's Kipp School District No. 1589. In this hitherto modestly prosperous kind of place, the Kipp trustees had paid their teacher $1,100 per annum in the late 1920s. In 1931 they were paying $600; in 1932, $500; in 1933, at least $200, the amount of the government grant, which was the only portion they would guarantee. In 1936 they offered $350 "plus increase if funds can be collected from municipality." Yet that year "there were 45 applications for the school." By 1939 the trustees felt able to pay $500 – less than half the amount a decade earlier. And with but a single exception, every one of the Kipp teachers, from 1929 through

1939, held first-class certificates.[68] In 1930–31 the average salary for teachers in Manitoba's one-room rural schools was $856. Salaries fell by 15% in each of the next two years, by 21% in 1933–34, and by 3% in 1934–35, by which point the average salary was $478.[69] It was not much different in small-town Manitoba; yet when, in 1931, the Cartwright school board advertised a new appointment for its six-teacher school, it received "upwards of 450 applications."[70]

At various points earlier in the century, most provinces had introduced minimum salary requirements in order to deal with teacher shortages and secure for rural teachers a set amount that even the poorest school board was supposed to meet.[71] But provincial authorities were unable (or unwilling) to hold the line in the 1930s. In 1933 New Brunswick suspended its minimum requirement. Although the province renewed the law in 1934, minimums were set at a lower level and inspectors could still make exceptions, with the depressing proviso that "in no case shall the salary from all sources be less than $300."[72] Alberta managed to maintain its minimum of $840 until 1932, though only by allowing a growing number of exceptions;[73] but the law was suspended in the spring of 1933. By 1938 some 32% of the province's teachers were earning less than $800 (though no salaries were under $500, in contrast to the situation in Saskatchewan, where 32% of teachers earned $500 or less and another 28% between $500 and $600).[74]

There were, in any case, ways around the law. One federation official complained to the Alberta Department of Education that in her region "a school district has engaged their teacher at $840, but the teacher gave a note for $190 to the school board, this to be deducted from her salary. This will give the teacher $650, which they claim, is a great help to the school district."[75] Although there were decreases in rural salaries in the Annapolis/Digby District, one Nova Scotia inspector wrote in 1932, they were still mostly above the minimum, but "when the new regulation became known, enabling trustees to discharge a teacher by giving a month's notice, a number of boards of trustees, knowing there was a surplus of teachers, gave the month's notice, and then re-engaged the teacher at the minimum salary."[76]

In some parts of rural Canada, teachers were lucky to get paid at all. In Nova Scotia, according to one report, "arrears in teachers' salaries reached their maximum of $187,000 in 1936."[77] The same year, in Alberta, they amounted to $304,000.[78] Predictably, it was even worse in Saskatchewan: by 1935 arrears exceeded $850,000, and by 1937 they were just over $1,207,000.[79] In a survey of representative school districts carried out near the end of the decade, two inspectors reported that half the teachers in their areas were in arrears of salary. When, in 1938, eighty-nine teachers assembled at Weyburn to report on their situation, "there were 13 with arrears of salary accumulated prior to January 1, 1935, 34 received no salary for the term from January to June 1938 until the month of June, and 22 received less than $50. On June 30, 15 had received less than $100 and 20 less than $200." Forty of the eighty-nine teachers were under contract for less than $500, and one for less than $400.[80]

All of this is but to say that teachers bore their share of human misery wrought by the Depression. There were young women with first-class certificates eager to try their hand at a challenging job who never got the chance. There were those who joined the ranks of the unemployed because others were willing to do the work for less. There were even more – and far more women than men – who had good salaries slashed without regard to their responsibilities for unemployed spouses, children, or aged parents. There were those who taught, term after term, and didn't get paid at all or received only a miserable pittance of what they were owed.

But then they were hardly alone. The record is rife with accounts of children unable to attend school for lack of winter boots, who arrived in classrooms without shoes or adequate clothing, who were "forced to stay out of school because of not having text-books and supplies," who were so ill-nourished they lacked the capacity to learn.[81] And stories of thwarted aspirations were a dime a dozen, as common among the young as among adults – youngsters forced to drop out of school, denied opportunities for post-secondary education, or abandoning their university studies, for lack of funds. Let one short memoir, told to Barry Broadfoot in his oral history of the Depression years, suffice: "I grew up on a stump farm about 12 miles from Carrot River. In Saskatchewan. I remember not going to school my fifth grade, about 12 years old, because I didn't have shoes. My sister Helen went, though, because she could use the ones I grew out of. My mother was a widow and she asked the relief people for two dollars for shoes for me but they said no, there were folks who needed things worse than me. I got around, doing chores and that, by making sort of moccasins out of deer skin, rubber from an inner tube and binder twine and staples but my mother wouldn't let me go to school that way. Foolish pride. I missed that year and I never went back. I missed a lot by her pride. I would have gone in them moccasins."[82] Parents might be forced to make their own hard choices. Again, from Barry Broadfoot: "The school at Chilanko Forks had to close down, and we had four kids. They needed an education so we had to get closer to a school. The nearest one was many miles away, far too far for children to ride to. We tried to sell our ranch, and it was a good one, but nobody would buy it. Who would in those days when cows were selling for about six dollars each? For a first class bull you wouldn't get more than $75. Finally the time came when those children just had to get to a school, so we just loaded up the wagon and drove away from it. We just left the ranch. Nobody wanted it, and we never went back."[83]

While school boards played an important role in identifying needy children when food and clothing were at issue, they generally referred cases of indigence to municipal or charitable relief agencies. But supplying textbooks to those who couldn't afford them was more directly the responsibility of provincial and local educational authorities. Some provincial departments increased textbook subsidies or continued pre-Depression policies of supplying free texts to pupils, but not in every case. In 1933 the New Brunswick government suspended the purchase and distribution of free texts except, on the recommendation of local boards, in cases of indigence (the suspension was partially lifted in 1936).[84] Among other measures, the Saskatchewan department mounted a campaign to collect used texts and distribute them to needy districts.[85] Despite its fiscal constraints, the Winnipeg board continued its policy of supplying free textbooks; at least for the elementary grades, asking only that parents who could afford it purchase their own (which some 20% agreed to do); even desperately poor Blairmore managed to find the textbook money for the children of those on relief.[86]

Many rural school districts had no equivalent resources. Across the country, voluntary agencies stepped in to help, among them the Imperial Order of the Daughters of the Empire (IODE). A remarkable file of correspondence between the Alberta branch of the IODE and the provincial department of education contains dozens of pleas for help with textbooks and school supplies such as scribblers, pencils, and pens. With model elementary school penmanship, "Miss Bernice LeMay," from Rich Lake, Alberta, wrote directly to Premier Aberhart: "I am a girl in Grade v. Will it be asking too much from you a Geography and a Arithmetic book No. 1 as I have no money to by [sic] one and as I need them." From the secretary of the Meridian SD No. 3823: "We the board of trustees ... are having great difficulty in operating the school owing to lack of finances. In fact, we can scarcely supply the present teacher with the bare necessities of life owing to there being so many sharing the grant and no taxes coming in – this being a homestead area. Now, we require the enclosed lot of text-books or we might as well shut down the school. I am instructed to enquire whether there is any source – charitable or otherwise – from which we might obtain them."[87]

Sometimes in the inspectors' reports or other contemporary comments, and occasionally in the work of historians, one finds a tendency to treat rural trustees and ratepayers as mean-spirited skinflints willing to pinch pennies at the expense of the easiest target they could find, the young women they hired as teachers. There were undoubtedly such instances: taxes are rarely cheerfully paid, school taxes less cheerfully paid by those with no direct stake in them, and the Depression offered a better excuse than almost anything for trying to reduce or avoid them.[88] But caricatures hardly do justice to the plight of rural Canada, or the hard realities of local finance, during the Depression. A study of local taxation in southern Ontario by S.C. Hudson, an employee of the federal Department of Agriculture, is telling on this score.[89] Hudson conducted an intensive study of selected townships and also examined a sample of individual farms. Municipal taxes in his townships fell during the Depression, but farm prices fell far more rapidly and the decline was much more severe. Thus farm incomes shrank far more than the decline in taxes. By far the largest group of farmers had incomes of $1,000 or less; by 1931–32 they were being asked to pay 30% of their income in municipal taxes; for apple farmers the figure was over 40%. During the 1920s, moreover, Hudson's townships had borrowed money to meet the demand for rising levels of services, so that total debenture debt rose very rapidly in the late 1920s. There was reluctance to cut services in the early 1930s, and municipal debt didn't peak until 1932; interest rates, along with other fixed costs, made it difficult to reduce tax rates after that. Even though spending on education dropped substantially, it was still the single biggest item in township budgets, at something like 36%. In Manitoba, one survey reported, "the *total* revenue from local taxation in many municipalities sank below that necessary for schools alone." Yet what individual ratepayers were asked to pay might well go up because "in difficult economic periods the council usually finds it necessary to levy an additional 10 to 20% in lieu of tax arrears."[90] Given these kinds of circumstances, it's hardly surprising that the pressure on trustees to reduce the cost of education was intense.

"At the bottom of the depression," the Rowell-Sirois Commission noted, "the average price of Canadian fish was cut in half; the price of dried cod was down nearly 70%."[91] In the Maritimes, "while total farm income, including income in kind, fell by half from 1928–32, net cash income fell by four-fifths."[92] "Unless times change for the better," wrote Nova Scotia's school inspector for Cape Breton East in 1933, "not only free books but free clothing will become an absolute necessity in cases where parents, through no fault of their own, have long been without any remunerative work." His inspectorate, he continued, "consisting to a large extent of fishing and mining communities, has felt the depression perhaps more than many other parts of Nova Scotia. Fishermen in my district, for instance, have frequently excused the backwardness of their school finances by stating that they had been unable to market their fish. Naturally I could not show them how. Likewise the market for coal during the past school year has been an exceedingly poor one. And if the towns and villages throughout the inspectorate cannot sell they cannot purchase and further they automatically pass both disabilities on to the surrounding farmers of the rural sections."[93]

On the prairies, Rowell-Sirois noted, total income "fell almost by half, and income from agriculture by almost four-fifths, from the 1926–28 average to the 1930–37 average." Then, in a rare departure from its normally dispassionate prose, the commission added, "These basic statistics, however, cannot convey the full measure of the Western debâcle with its shattering blows to living standards, to adequate nutrition, to health services, to educational standards, to community equipment such as highways, and to individual hopes and dreams and ambitions."[94] The historian of the Canadian prairies, Gerald Friesen, writes that "the crisis was worst in the wheat belt of Saskatchewan where, by the end of the terrible crop failure of 1937, it was estimated that two in three members of the farm population were destitute."[95]

Viewed from this perspective, just how badly were teachers served during the Depression? Again, Rowell-Sirois: "On average, employed wage earners and persons receiving salaries suffered no reduction in real income. Most of the workers in the skilled trades, the professions and white-collar occupations who retained their jobs actually enjoyed a considerable improvement in their real position. The losses were completely borne by the 500,000 to 600,000 unemployed ... by the farm and other primary producers, and by [those] ... who received the profits from industry and trade."[96] Unlike in many other occupations, there was no significant reduction in the total number of teaching jobs available.[97] Salary reductions were common among all those who worked for public authorities, not just teachers. And those teachers who remained employed benefited from the massive price deflation occasioned by the Depression.[98] Between 1929 and 1933, in constant dollars, average salaries – and it is important to emphasize we are referring to *averages* here – went up, not down: that is, in terms of purchasing power, teachers, on average, were better off in 1933 than in 1929, in some provinces substantially better off; only in Saskatchewan did constant-dollar averages decline across these years. Nationally, and again, on average and in constant dollars, teachers' earnings rose from $1,400 in 1929 to $1,675 in 1933, though as the economy revived, the figure began to slip back – to $1,474 in 1938, for example.[99] The 1957 study by the Canadian Teachers' Federation includes a national overview showing that, from 1929 until about 1939, teachers' salaries remained well above the average for "all persons in the Labour Force receiving income."[100] And while, in current dollars, teachers' average salaries fell between 1929 and 1933 from $1,061 to $985, wage earners saw a decline from $1,073 to $777; among the self-employed, farmers experienced a drop from $599 to $158.[101] When rural folk grumbled about the salaries young women teachers earned, or cut their wages to the bone, they had, according to their own lights, some good reasons. In a fine article recounting her mother's experience as a young teacher in rural Nova Scotia during the 1930s, Dianne Hallman writes that out of a typically meagre salary in rural Nova Scotia, "my mother paid three to five dollars a week for board ($120 to $200 a year for a 40-week school year). She generally spent summers at the home of her parents. Being a single woman with no dependents, she was able to save enough in three years to buy a car, and from then on, often travelled to her parents' home for weekends. She found the pay low, but reasoned that 'men in their thirties (labourers) with families worked at any kind of work they could get for *$1.00 a day*, often walking several miles to and from jobs.' Like [other women] she was 'grateful to be working.'"[102]

The Great Depression could be hard on people everywhere – ratepayers, teachers, parents, and children alike – and hard as well on the physical infrastructure of the schools. Still, the Depression was not the sole cause of breakdown. It was not only a matter of drought, or the collapse of wheat and fish prices, or the closure of the local mill, or the numbers of unemployed in a working-class suburb that created the plight they found themselves in. It was also due, in fundamental ways, to the combined effects of the decentralization of decision making and the limited tax base. Unable to lay hands on sources of revenue other than the local property tax, burdened with the customary assumption that education was ultimately a local responsibility, all were trapped by the Depression within an iron cage.

8

The Organization of Instruction

How did teachers know what to teach? How did they know if their pupils were learning what was taught? How indeed did they know *how* to teach or what constituted exemplary pedagogy? How did anyone else know if the teachers were earning their keep by providing effective instruction? In the early twentieth century or at any other time, these questions went to the heart of the educational enterprise: What is it that children are to be taught? How are they to be taught? How is their progress to be assessed? How is public accountability to be achieved? And it is these questions that provide the focus for this chapter and the next. We begin with the basic structures around which the curriculum was organized. Following that, we examine the elementary and then the secondary curriculum. In chapter 9 we turn to assessment and accountability – the methods used to measure achievement, the policies and procedures governing promotion from grade to grade, and the controversies that emerged during the interwar years over two competing models of assessment.

I

How, then, did teachers know what to teach? In Canada's highly centralized provincial school systems, the answer to that question was left to neither teachers nor local school boards. The content of the curriculum was determined by each provincial department of education through its *Programme of Studies*, the keystone document that specified what was to be taught and when in all grant-aided schools. Nor was this a "guideline" that teachers or others might modify at will. While there were always areas for the exercise of some discretion, all of the important decisions about the organization of instruction were made by provincial governments acting through their departments of education. As the Alberta school regulations explained in 1910, "The course of studies prescribed by the Department of Education shall form the basis of the teacher's work. It represents the minimum

requirements for each standard and should be followed as a guide in classifying pupils. It may be modified to meet the needs of special schools but
not without the written consent of an inspector who shall forthwith report
the fact to the department."[1]

Compared to its modern counterpart, the official program of studies
was, in the early twentieth century, a remarkably terse document. It rarely
spelled out course content in any detail; rather it simply referred teachers to a textbook or some portion of it. The content of the curriculum
was contained within the covers of textbooks authorized by the department
of education, usually one text per subject for each grade. In 1901 Nova
Scotia could outline its entire program, grades I through XII, including
its "General Prescriptions," in sixteen or seventeen pages; Ontario did
the same for its elementary program in only four.[2] A decade later, British
Columbia's course of studies for elementary schools could be encompassed
in three pages of laconic text; in the senior classes, for example, students
were to be taught "*History*. British and Canadian as in the prescribed texts"
and "*Arithmetic* – Milne's *Arithmetic*, Book II, Part II and Book III (except pp.
116–34, 268–97 and pp. 319–30)."[3] The 1921 Nova Scotia program gave
this minimal directive for grade III reading: "Reader No. III. Occasional
phonic practice as in Grade I. Increasing attention to expression in reading
and reciting." Grade III arithmetic received a scant three and a half lines;
the entire grade VIII program of studies took less than a page.[4] Manitoba,
Ken Osborne notes, could define the entire grade XII history course in
two sentences.[5]

In the reorganization of instruction that accompanied the creation of
public school systems in the last half of the nineteenth century, the program of studies was increasingly divided into two distinct sequential levels,
elementary and secondary.[6] By the early twentieth century this was a conventional arrangement, the former usually occupying a space of seven or
eight years and the latter anywhere from three to six years, depending on
the date and the province. These two broad levels of instruction, elementary and secondary, were in turn routinely broken down into smaller units.
In some provinces these had long been designated as "grades," each grade
indicating the equivalent of one year's work. This was the case, for example,
in the program of studies for Manitoba and Nova Scotia.[7] But the term was
not yet in universal use. Alberta and Saskatchewan inherited from the territorial period the term "standard." The completion of a standard was spread
over one and a half to two years, the first five standards approximating
grades I through VIII, with standards VI to VIII covering the secondary curriculum. Both provinces converted to "grade" early in the century, Alberta,
for example, in 1912.[8] During the first two decades of the century British
Columbia used "grades," but there were just three of them – junior, inter-

mediate, and senior – to cover the entire span of the elementary school curriculum; the more conventional organization of eight grades was adopted only in 1923.[9] For its elementary schools, Ontario used the term "form" until the late 1930s. The four forms, of roughly two years each, were subdivided into "junior" and "senior" sections; the common terminology, for example, was "junior third" or "senior fourth." Likewise, Ontario's secondary levels were, from 1913, labelled "Lower School" (two years), "Middle School" (two years), and "Upper School" (two years, later one). While Nova Scotia's program of studies had always been divided into "grades," for the one-room rural schools, where children had to be grouped for ease of instruction, the term "forms" was used, indicating pupils taught together for two years. New Brunswick used "grades" in its urban schools but "standards" of approximately one and a half to two years each in its rural schools, for much the same reason.[10] The weight of American precedent, however, and the increasing standardization of terminology across Canada gradually transformed usage into grades everywhere.

Just where elementary education ended was fuzzy. The various programs of studies conventionally included grade VIII (or its equivalent – in Ontario, for example, "senior fourth form") as an elementary grade. But in most of the country, grade VIII was primarily devoted to preparation for high school. Equally, in some provinces – Prince Edward Island, New Brunswick, and Nova Scotia are examples – pupils could begin high school subjects like Latin, French, or algebra in grade VIII, while in Saskatchewan grade VIII work could be offered in the collegiate institutes, and in Alberta high school grants began with grade VIII. There is, in other words, good reason to think that before 1920, at least, "a good common school education," as the phrase had it, included grades I to VII and that grade VIII was a kind of intermediate or preparatory year before students proceeded to high school.[11] During the interwar years, however, as more and more children stayed in school for longer periods of time, grade VIII or even IX became the standard measure for the completion of elementary education.

II

Since the elementary school was the exclusive vehicle for universal education, its program of studies was intended to serve two overlapping academic purposes: to provide the necessary core of knowledge all children should have acquired before they left school and to erect the scholastic scaffolding for that minority who would continue beyond the elementary school. As James Miller put it in 1913, "the fundamental idea" behind the elementary school curriculum "is that it should represent what is considered to be the minimum body of common knowledge, appreciation and abilities which every child should possess regardless of his station in life or the location of his home."[12] And when he surveyed the various provincial curriculum documents, he found a group of subjects obligatory across English Canada: reading, spelling, grammar, composition, writing, arithmetic, geography, Canadian and English (or British) history, hygiene with physiology or temperance, drawing, and nature study (or elementary science). Physical education, music, manual training, household arts, "while usually on the optional list, are encouraged." Subjects like grammar, geography, and history usually started in grades IV to VI, but most subjects were taught in all grades.[13] The differences among the provinces largely hinged on Miller's "optional list." During the first two decades of the century, for example, physical education might or might not be required, depending on the province. It was the same with music; in Alberta it was not obligatory whereas Nova Scotia's program of studies warned that "inspectors should accept no excuse for the absence of singing in a school." If the teacher could not sing at all, then "one of the older students may be made use of."[14]

There were also minimalist and maximalist programs of studies. In its early documents Manitoba listed only those subjects that had to be taught in all schools, despite the fact that subjects like domestic science and manual training were compulsory parts of the curriculum in Winnipeg and a few other urban centres in the first decade of the century. Other programs provided a compulsory core and then a list of subjects that could be taught if the local board chose to do so.[15] Agriculture, domestic science, and manual training are examples. These, it's perhaps worth adding, were optional only for school boards, not pupils; if offered by a board, they became part of the obligatory curriculum.

There was, however, a clear hierarchy of school knowledge, even within the obligatory core. The first job of the school was to teach what were commonly known as the "tool" or "instrumental" subjects – those necessary to further learning. This meant, above all, the various branches of English (reading, writing, spelling, composition, grammar, and literature) and arithmetic. Other subjects, whatever their importance, took second or third place. These priorities revealed themselves in several ways, one being what counted for promotion. In Alberta's revised program of 1922, for example, "the following subjects are considered as fundamental: English (including Reading, Literature, Composition, Spelling and Grammar); Arithmetic; Elementary Science (including Nature Study, Geography, Hygiene, and Agriculture); Writing; and Citizenship (including History, Civics, and Ethics). Promotion examinations are to be based on these subjects. The secondary group includes the following subjects: Music, Physical Education, and Industrial Arts (Art, Manual Arts and Household Economics)."[16] Another indicator can be seen in Nova Scotia's scheme for instruction in its one-room schools; while all subjects had to be taught, music, nature study, and drawing could be taught to all grades simultaneously (i.e., to the whole school), whereas the tool subjects were to be taught separately to each grade.[17] Most obvious were the prescriptive or suggested time allotments for each subject, sometimes given in minutes per week, though more often in percentage terms. According to the Ontario normal school manual of 1915, for example, English was to be awarded 34% of a pupil's time, arithmetic another 12%, geography, history, nature study, and art 6% each, physical culture 5%, and vocal music and hygiene 3%.[18] Usually such guidelines were also broken down by grade, so that in grades I and II the overwhelming time allocation went to reading, spelling, and writing; while English remained dominant in the other grades, an increasing amount of time was indicated for the other core subjects. Even in the late 1930s, when program revisions introduced an optional element in the senior grades, the priorities remain evident. British Columbia's 1936 program for the "junior high school" (grades VII through IX) allocated thirty-five periods a week to the "constants" (the obligatory core) with only four or five left over for the options. And among the constants, English, social studies, and mathematics were to be given fifteen periods a week, while science, music, and art got two each.[19] Across the four decades, provincial programs of studies relentlessly reminded teachers that all subjects were of equal educational value; the fine print made it clear that some were more equal than others.

The programs of studies that emerged during the interwar years were quite different from their predecessors in both style and content and would establish precedents familiar to later generations. Most obviously they were far more verbose. Between 1912 and 1920, for example, Manitoba's program for grades I through VIII took 26 pages; a revised version of 1928 covering *only* grades I to VI ran to 350 pages.[20] There were some practical reasons for this, such as an inexperienced workforce that officials had come to believe needed far more assistance in organizing their work than earlier programs provided.[21] Thus subject content was fleshed out topic by topic, often with a running commentary offering even finer detail. Given the number of subjects involved, this in itself necessitated substantial expansion. But the documents also gushed with advice about new pedagogical techniques, justifications for inclusion in the curriculum of the various subjects, and general discussions of the aims of education. Increasingly the programs became not merely directives about what to teach but vehicles for selling fashionable theories and teaching methods to teachers.

It became common, moreover, to organize the program of studies in tripartite fashion: six years of primary work, two or three years of "intermediate" or "junior high school" studies, and two to four years of senior high school. By the mid-1930s Nova Scotia, Ontario, Manitoba, Alberta, and British Columbia had all adopted this pattern.[22] For most teachers and pupils, nonetheless, the real dividing line remained at grade VIII/IX, except in that handful of large urban areas where the critical mass of pupils – and the money for new buildings – allowed reorganization along the lines the latest program decreed.[23]

Within the academic core of the elementary programs of studies, there was some rejigging of labels and regrouping of subjects. "Hygiene with physiology or temperance" was gradually transmuted into "health," and the subject itself gained a far more prominent place in the curriculum than hitherto. In some provinces, history and geography became "social studies." "Nature study" tended to be relabelled "general science." The various academic subjects also underwent some significant changes in emphasis and content. However, especially before the late 1930s, when a new and more radical round of curricular and pedagogical innovation began, the rate of change in either program or practice should not be exaggerated. In the elementary schools, where so much of the program of studies was prescribed for all children and in all grades, there was a close match between prescription and what was actually taught in classrooms, a high degree of stability over time, and a high degree of uniformity in different parts of the country and between urban and rural schools. The elements of literacy and numeracy were not only universal staples in the primary grades but, relabelled "spelling," "composition," "literature," and "arithmetic," they were taught in every grade thereafter. So indeed were nature study, physiology and hygiene, and, in one form or another depending on available facilities, physical training. Geography was added at some point in the middle grades, grammar and British and Canadian history in the senior grades. Art was generally taught, though music, optional in some provinces, might or might not be included. Agriculture was widely taught, sometimes as a separate subject in the senior grades but more commonly integrated into nature study. By the 1920s manual training and domestic science were increasingly common, at least in the larger cities and towns. Overall then, there were areas of change over time, but in terms of priorities and time allocations, the elementary school curriculum of 1930 or 1935 was only marginally different than that described by Miller in 1913, or even than what one might have expected to find in Canadian schools in the 1880s.[24]

The rationale for the curriculum, as well as the pedagogical principles intended to guide practice in Canada's elementary classrooms, can be illustrated through the prescriptions included in teacher-training manuals, in the professional press, and in the programs of studies themselves. Attention to these prescriptions, moreover, will serve as a reminder that the common run of practices and routines that teachers adopted was not merely the result of inadequate training, the suffocating effects of large classes, or other contingent circumstances, but also part of the exemplary pedagogy recommended by provincial authorities or other influential and mainstream voices with a say in such matters.[25]

By the early twentieth century and especially by the interwar years, the doctrines of mental discipline and pedagogical formalism, always more influential in justifying the secondary than the elementary curriculum in any case, were being supplanted by a rationale grounded in utility.[26] Increasingly, the first duty of the elementary school was to offer a *practical* or *useful* education. This new emphasis incorporated two components: on the one hand, there were the tool subjects, comprising the elements of literacy and numeracy, essential for the demands of everyday life and requisite for all further learning; on the other, there were the subjects related to acculturation, such as literature, history, geography, or science, which promised to enrich experience and make it more comprehensible, connect children to the cultural heritage, and introduce them to the nature of social relations and their relationship with the physical world.

"Usefulness" most obviously resided in the tool subjects. In Ontario's 1934 program of studies, arithmetic "shall be directed towards giving the pupil power to use numbers rapidly and accurately in the calculations required in practical life."[27] According to the 1929 program for Saskatchewan, "as far as possible, [arithmetic] should be related to ordinary business transactions within the experience and understanding of the pupils."[28] In the 1916 Ontario Teachers' Manual for *Composition and Spelling*, teachers were warned to avoid meaningless lists of unusually difficult or esoteric words, and told that children should learn to spell correctly those words they used in their own expanding vocabulary: "In and for itself, spelling has no value; its chief use is as a handmaid to composition, in making records, or in communicating with others by means of writing."[29] "Written composition," Nova Scotia's 1921 program advised, "attains its chief ends in the common school when the pupil is able to write ordinary business, private and social letters correctly and with the customary forms of courtesy."[30] "The most important of the tool subjects is reading," wrote one Ontario school administrator in 1918, silent reading above all, "since most of the reading of the great majority of people in afterlife will be of the silent variety. Silent reading will always be one of the chief instruments for gathering information and continuing the education begun at school. The public school can render few greater services to the child than to teach him this useful art."[31] But reading served other ends as well. "The emotional and literary element in the prescribed readers increases with each grade," the Nova Scotia program explained. "This is of purpose. The reading class is a literature class, and is intended to provide a medium for emotional expression. In this connection, the careful study and memorizing of choice passages suitable to each grade is important. These, through study, contemplation, and recitation, will not only give pleasure and afford training to the learner, but will serve later as touchstones of literary merit."[32] Similarly, the 1929 Saskatchewan program: "Committing to memory of choice passages in prose and poetry should also be required. Those chosen ... above all should possess literary beauty and charm ... To develop a taste for good literature is an aim every teacher should always keep in view."[33]

Aside from the teacher, the chief vehicle to promote this end was the "reader," which incorporated models of what constituted "touchstones of literary merit." To take but one example, the *Ontario Readers, Third Book* [grades v and vi] included poetry and prose selections by such international luminaries as Carlyle, Tennyson, Longfellow, Parkman, and Dickens, along with Canadians like Bliss Carman, Charles G.D. Roberts, and John McCrae. The *Readers* were not intended simply to further reading skills but to teach aesthetic values.[34]

To be useful to the individual, however, large portions of what was learned had to become matters of habit. According to Ontario's *Principles of Method* (1930), "reading, spelling, writing, language, which form the basic materials of the curriculum, are predominantly habit subjects; a large part of arithmetic, certain aspects of history and geography, such as the association of important events with their dates and place names with locations, and many phases of art, manual training and household science, are matters of habit ... It is essential, therefore, that each teacher should understand clearly the application of the principles underlying habit formation, in order that desirable habits may be established in his pupils in the most efficient and economical way."[35] The two key principles involved were "(1) a clear understanding" by the child "of the idea, process, or activity to be mechanized, and (2) repetition with attention and self-criticism until the habit is firmly established." The first principle represented "the learning phase" and was substantially the responsibility of the teacher; the second was "the practice phase," with which "the pupil is almost exclusively concerned."[36]

"The period from eight to 12 or 13 years of age," an earlier Ontario Teachers' Manual declared, "is recognised as the best in which to form habits. Neglect ... will necessarily interfere with efficient work in the years that follow" – thus the importance of "the cultivation of good habits of reading, writing, accuracy in arithmetic, and in all other activities, during the most favourable habit-forming period." It followed that the teacher must "seize every opportunity for the practice of the habit, and to allow no exceptions to occur until the habit is established."[37]

The emphasis on habit formation led, more or less logically, to two characteristic elements in elementary school pedagogical routines. One was an insistence on precision or accuracy. In all the programs of study, for example, great stress was placed on correct usage of the spoken language prior to and then concurrent with written composition. In what was commonly called "oral composition," children were to be taught by precept, example, and constant correction to express themselves clearly and correctly. Between 1912 and 1920, indeed, Manitoba's program of studies opened with this salvo: "In issuing the following syllabus of work for the grades below the high school, the Department of Education desires to emphasize strongly the importance of training pupils to express themselves clearly and accurately. With this object in view, the opportunities offered for correction of common errors of speech, such as incorrect and unauthorized forms, indistinct articulation, faulty enunciation, and wrong pronunciation, should be made use of, while correct construction and logical succession of sentences should be one of the chief aims of every recitation. It is only through constant practice in careful expression that the child acquires that habit of orderly and exact statement which is the evidence of orderly and exact thinking. Every lesson should be a language lesson." And just in case anyone failed to take the injunction seriously, the department added, in italics, "*The public school inspectors have been asked to report particularly as to the carrying out of this suggestion.*"[38] Saskatchewan's teachers were told that "accurate spelling should be insisted upon in all written exercises ... Pupils should be required to make lists of familiar words commonly misspelled, and frequent tests should be given on words in common use."[39] Reviewing the Ottawa school system in 1918, C.E. Mark concluded that less time should be spent on spelling in the higher grades: "In order to accomplish this, a strict insistence [in the junior grades] on the correct spelling of words in all written work will be necessary. The requirement that all exercises containing careless spelling shall be re-written will soon reduce mistakes to a minimum."[40] According to Nova Scotia's "General Prescriptions" for the elementary program, "No *written* exercise should be accepted from any pupil unless the evidence is clear that a serious and more or less successful attempt has been made to have the writing carefully neat, with due attention to good form in every detail – margins, paragraphs, indentations, punctuation, spelling and grammar, etc. Otherwise a possibly brilliant pupil may be accidentally developed into a bungler."[41]

In an age long before the hand-held electronic calculator was even dreamt of, there was an enormous emphasis on "mental arithmetic." Again, among Nova Scotia's General Prescriptions: "*Arithmetic:* The first essential is accuracy in the fundamental processes; the second, rapidity in applying them;

the third, clearness in expression. Absolute accuracy must be insisted on from the outset. 'Mental' Arithmetic is the primary process, and it should be practised in every grade and with every sort of problem and operation."[42] Similar sentiments were expressed everywhere. Writing in 1935, Stanley A. Watson, most commonly associated with the first "progressive" revision of Ontario's elementary curriculum, insisted that since mistakes would not be tolerated by employers once a young person went to work, "our required standard of accuracy should be 100% in all the processes for the mastery of which pupils have reached the necessary mental age." Watson went on to suggest how this was to be achieved: "There must be a thorough mastery of the facts of addition, subtraction, multiplication and division; the pupil must attain skill in the four fundamental processes with integers, fractions, and decimals; he must be able to apply these to the most common unit of measure ... [and] the habit of checking all operations as soon as performed must be developed."[43]

But how to achieve precision and accuracy? That brings us to a second characteristic element in classroom routines, the prevalence of drill. "I would like to impress upon all teachers," New Brunswick's chief superintendent wrote in 1916, "the importance and necessity of thorough drill upon the fundamental rules of arithmetic in the early grades"; referring to spelling, he added that "blackboard work, frequent drill and review are indispensable."[44] In Saskatchewan the 1929 program advised as follows: "*Reading.* Frequent drills to secure rapid recognition of words and groups of words ... *Arithmetic.* Speed and accuracy may be secured by repetition and use, and facts can be fixed in the mind through review."[45] In 1930 Ontario's *Principles of Method* introduced its chapter on "The Drill Assignment" with the following: "As a feature of schoolwork, drill requires that certain responses which we wish to establish as habits in the pupil should be repeated in an efficient and economical way until mechanized. The number of such responses in the field of school subjects is practically unlimited." To illustrate, the manual gave as examples "the learning of number combinations in arithmetic, the memorization of a poem, the use of past tenses and past participles, ... the mastery of the button-hole in sewing, etc." Indeed, it added, just for extra emphasis, "the places for drill assignments for the purpose of improving skill are legion."[46]

A variant upon drill was the advice offered for teaching composition. Beginning in grade II or III, the pupil would be ready "for writing exercises in which he expresses his own thoughts or reproduces in his own language the contents of stories which he has read or heard." Language exercises should "be frequent rather than long. The aim is to form habits, not give knowledge." Even if only a paragraph or two, a written exercise should be given daily to all grades. "The simplest exercise," the composition manual continued, was "transcription" – that is, simply copying out some passage from a book or other source. While some teachers condemned transcription as a waste of time and others abused it by treating it as busywork, when rightly employed and for well-defined purposes, "it trains in the mechanics of composition, promotes accuracy, enlarges the vocabulary, strengthens the memory, and it may even develop literary taste." When selecting passages to be copied, the manual suggested, it was important to have "some desirable end in view. This may be to impress some noble thought or beautiful expression, since slow, thoughtful copying results commonly in fixing attention both on ideas and their mode of expression. It may be to reinforce some lesson on form – not merely such matters as quotation marks, but also letter and business forms. Such social and conventional requirements as notes of invitation, bills, notes, receipts, etc., are all better understood when correct examples are given to be faithfully copied. Nor should suitable poems be overlooked. Usually the pupil's interest should first be aroused in the selection to be transcribed, so that the exercise is not purely mechanical, and then he should be held accountable for a perfect reproduction."[47] Thus, once again, habit formation was the end in view but it could only be achieved by demanding precision and accuracy: the pupil must "be held accountable for a perfect reproduction."

A practical education, however, involved not just the mastery of skills but the acquisition of a large body of factual knowledge. "A great part of the pupil's time up to the age of ten," one Ontario manual asserted in 1915, "should be spent on learning facts, both from books and from actual experience." The accumulation of factual knowledge was not only an end in itself; it provided a basis for training in reasoning, the means by which a teacher could lead pupils, by deduction, from the known to the unknown. And as pupils matured, they could increasingly apply the same process themselves, deducing principles and generalizations from bodies of fact. But, the manual warned, "some things cannot be developed by any process of reasoning; they must be told by the teacher, or learned from books. To develop from any previous knowledge the terms used in grammar, the facts of history, or the names given to the elements or to natural forces, would be tantamount to making bricks ... without either straw or clay."[48]

Writing about the Alberta history curriculum, Amy von Heyking offers a nice example of contemporary views on the role of facts, and one we think applies equally well to any other subject or any other part of the country: "Many educators defended the emphasis on the memorization of historical facts. The author of one teaching methods text used in Normal Schools stressed that 'So much is said to-day about the uselessness of teaching facts that it is well to remind teachers that there can be no lessons drawn from history without a knowledge of the facts upon which these are based ... for

beginners history must necessarily be largely a study of facts.' Educators
stressed that history developed imagination and taught critical judgment
but it must first be grounded in the memory. Others argued that a familiarity with historical facts was simply essential for anyone who claimed
to be educated." Yet others, she adds, insisted that "historical literacy,
familiarity with the basic facts of history, was important for the citizen 'of
good character.'"[49]

Thus "facts" – a historical date or the significance of a historical figure,
the definition and proper use of a noun or adjective, geographical features
or scientific terminology, and a great many other sorts of factual knowledge
– formed, along with skills, a constituent part of the early twentieth-century
elementary curriculum. And in the main, facts were to be learned from
textbooks. According to *Principles of Method*, "A school textbook in any subject contains the material necessary to be learned by a pupil ... It is desirable that the pupil should read and understand the textbooks, not merely
because this will enable him to learn the necessary material, but because it
will lay the foundation for a habit of reading." Merely to assign "so many
pages" of a textbook or require verbatim memorization was, unequivocally,
bad pedagogy; but with proper preparation and intelligent explanation,
the textbook provided the fund of facts around which assignments could be
framed for seat-work or homework.[50]

The pedagogy recommended by provincial authorities was not, by any
means, merely mechanical or limited to the methods we have been discussing in the last few pages. The nineteenth-century "recitation," where the
teacher simply heard pupils repeat paragraphs or pages they had memo-
rized from textbooks, was to be replaced by the "lesson," where teachers
explained an idea, a principle, or a task and tried to do so in an interesting
way. Motivation was advocated as an important tool in learning. Arithmetic
consisted of far more than drill, as children also confronted reams of problems intended to hone their reasoning skills. Assignments were not limited
to drill or mechanically transcribing passages of prose. Indeed, in *Principles
of Method*, drill was only one type of assignment; the manual gave equal or
more weight to the project method, to well-organized and original "problem assignments," and to the "review assignment," which was an exercise
that taught pupils how to organize large units of work and to order and
impose coherence on a mass of disparate material. Nor was the textbook
the only source of information. Children were expected to learn to use
dictionaries and encyclopaedias, with substantial amounts of other supplementary reading routinely encouraged. Facts were to be learned not only
from books but by observation and experience – of local geography, for

example, and "nature study."[51] Drill could incorporate games and other imaginative activities. And in the hands of good teachers, all but the most tedious of classroom routines could achieve a lively purpose. Yet we have been at some pains to explain the thinking behind particular pedagogical practices not only because drill, the memorization of facts, and vast tracts of bookwork feature so commonly in contemporary and historical portraits of early twentieth-century classrooms, but because explicating rationales may reduce the tendency to dismiss such practices as mindless busywork or merely rote-learning. Whatever later generations might think, it should at least be clear that contemporaries had well-considered reasons for believing in its pedagogical efficacy.

At bottom, then, the elementary curriculum turned on two things: first, learning a particular set of skills, primarily those related to literacy and numeracy, that incorporated both mechanical and reasoning skills; second, learning particular areas of human knowledge, mainly from books, and committing large portions of that knowledge to memory. At the very least it was, undeniably, a "bookish" curriculum delivered by means of a "bookish" pedagogy, and there was no question that the job of the teacher was to direct instruction, to determine the what and how of learning. It was also a rigorous course of instruction that left many behind. The official programs themselves give a fair indication of the demands made on children, as do the formal examinations, a matter we will return to. But there are also other sorts of evidence that do it even better. Unfortunately there is no easy way to summarize them, and all one can do is refer the reader to the sources themselves. There are, for example, published outlines of the daily or near-daily work used by individual teachers, or outlines published by urban school boards in order to standardize instruction beyond the less detailed guidelines in the provincial programs.[52] An even more indicative source is to be found in an influential professional magazine, *The School.* Year after year it published, monthly or quarterly, articles entitled "Proficiency Tests for the Grades." As the title suggests, these consisted of questions and problems, covering all grades and subjects, suitable as test items for assessing progress during the year and qualification for promotion at the end of it. Drafted by experienced teachers, the proficiency tests are singularly useful in indicating not just what the official programs prescribed but also the knowledge and skills pupils might reasonably be expected to master.[53]

Success in a rigorous course required effort. "Without persistent effort on the part of the child," said Ontario's manual on *School Management,* "the teacher's admonition and aid, however wisely directed, will prove unavailing ... There is no royal road to learning." Difficulties must be confronted and overcome: "The teacher's aim should be, not to make a difficult subject

easy, but to arouse such an intense desire for knowledge that the pupil
will bring to bear on it all his powers of intellect, until he wins the victory.
Too often, the teacher destroys, rather than creates, interest and effort, by
smoothing away all difficulties."[54] Concomitantly, pupils were to learn to
work on their own, to develop a capacity for independent work. This was no
problem in the rural school, where pupils learned early to apply themselves
at their seats while the teacher worked with other classes. But in the urban
schools, where a teacher was responsible for a single class, pupils tended
to be exposed to too much instruction "with little or no intermission for
attacking and trying to solve for themselves the difficulties that confronted
them," and thus "they are apt to lose the power to think for themselves."
It was, the manual suggested, actually preferable to have two classes in one
room, "one engaged in seat work, while the other is having class work."[55]
A few years later, the Ontario department imposed a regulation requiring
a teacher's timetable to show one and a half hours each day for seat-work
"including independent work" because "one of the charges brought against
the [graded] elementary school was that the pupil was not trained to study
independently or to work things out for himself."[56]

Schooling was not, and not intended to be, about academic learning alone.
Nor was the moral content of the curriculum "hidden." Since *all* children
would attend the elementary school for at least a few years of their lives, it
was the school's explicit job to build upon the values of the church and the
good family and to counteract what were perceived to be evil influences
from whatever source they might come. The pedagogy of habit formation,
in other words, applied just as forcefully to moral as to mental training. In
Nova Scotia as in Ontario, teachers were by law required "to inculcate by
precept and example, a respect for religion and the principles of Christian
morality, and for truth, justice, love of country, loyalty, humanity, benevo-
lence, sobriety, industry, frugality, chastity, temperance, and all other virtues."[57] In New Brunswick the phraseology was only slightly different.[58] In
the West, the specific reference to "Christian" morality tended to be excised
but otherwise the directives were similar.[59] In the provincial programs of
studies, instruction in manners and morals was mostly to be found under
"General Prescriptions" – special sections covering instruction to be pursued in all grades and expected to permeate pedagogy throughout the
school year. But that was not always the case. Along with its subject prescriptions for each grade, Prince Edward Island specified the content to be
covered each year under "Manners and Morals" as well as the time allocation – "two or three times a week."[60] Uniquely, in Manitoba, facing pages in
the early programs of studies listed on one side the academic content for a
grade and on the other the moral instruction appropriate to that grade (see

Figure 8.1). One way or another, morals and manners were an integral part of the programs of studies for Canadian elementary schools.*

This kind of moral instruction mostly fell under the rubric of "character training" – the inculcation of good habits and appropriate forms of behaviour. It was not, as some historians would have it, merely training for the new industrial order, nor did it discount the value of academic learning in favour of moral training. In most human realms (even in academic life), character counts for more than learning does, and though conceptions of what exactly constitutes a life well lived may vary over time or by class and culture, the sober virtues that teachers were expected to inculcate are rarely deprecated.[61] When compared with the role of families and churches, the particular task of the school was systematic instruction in a set of intellectual skills and knowledge. But as one key agent in the socialization of the young, the school was expected to play a major role in the moral growth of the child; character formation was an indispensable part of its mandate, then as now. "Good Manners," the Nova Scotia program of studies insisted,

> are one of the most conspicuous evidences of education. In only the smallest sense are they merely conventional and arbitrary. They are, in reality, founded upon an intelligent conception of our moral and social order. The power of self-effacement at the proper time; of physical control; of putting others at their ease and on good terms with us; of comporting oneself fittingly in public and towards age, youth and rank; of giving precedence to women; of applauding merit no matter where found; of presenting a cautious attitude toward gossip and disparagement – these good manners, wherever displayed, are evidences of moral insight and control, and are worthy of unremitting effort and study. It is intolerable that a teacher should disregard the importance of example and instruction in respect to his pupils' conduct in these matters.[62]

While Amy von Heyking, in *Creating Citizens*, is referring more particularly to Alberta in the early twentieth century, she could just as well be commenting

---

* In the section that follows, the reader needs to keep in mind that we are describing precepts, not practice – what was supposed to be, not what actually was, taught or learned. Teachers, as we point out in another chapter, were *very* busy people, and they were pressed by priorities other than imparting little moral tales. Manners, morals, patriotism, and so on were not on any examination list, and even if they were taught, we have no idea what lessons children actually took away with them (if any). We can gauge fairly well what was taught subject by subject; as previous paragraphs suggest, we know for example that English or arithmetic was systematically taught in nearly all schools and in at least a rough way we can judge the match between program prescription and actual teaching and learning by examination results. But no such measures for "values education" exist, which may also help account for the insistent and reiterated emphasis on the topic in the programs of studies.

Grade 2.

READING

*The Manitoba Readers, book II. Retail price, 20 cents.
Authorized Supplementary Reading.*

To create a desire for reading, stories should be read or told to the pupils in the primary grades. These stories should be re-told by the pupils to secure easy and natural expression. The following material will be found suitable—

Fairy Tale, Fable and Myth; stories of primitive life; stories from the Old Testament; stories of occupation and industrial processes; stories of animals and pets.

SPELLING

Rice's Speller, first year. Dictation from Speller, and easy extracts from Reader, with careful attention to punctuation and use of capitals.

WRITING

Continuation and extension of the exercises of Grade I, with the same aim in view; correct form of letters, and the formation of correct habits of position, pen and pencil holding, and free movement. Careful supervision of all written work.

ARITHMETIC

Study of numbers to 50. Drill to secure quickness and accuracy in the use of the addition and multiplication tables. Simple measurements continued.

MUSIC

Rote singing.

DRAWING AND COLOR

Same as in grade I. Applied Art Drawing Books, No. 32, Educational Book Co., *price 15 cents.*

HYGIENE

Simple rules in personal Hygiene.

NATURE STUDY AND SCHOOL GARDENING

(See under grade IV.)

PHYSICAL EXERCISES AND GAMES

The syllabus of physical exercises for public elementary schools, Canadian edition. *This manual must be followed and instruction given daily.*

Grade 2.

MANNERS AND MORALS

1. *Cleanliness—*

   Use and care of parts of the body—e.g., hair, eyes, ears, nose. lips, teeth, hands and feet.

2. *Manners—*

   (a) In eating and drinking—moderation;
   (b) In question and answer—politeness;
   (c) In bearing—quietness, unobtrusiveness, patience in waiting;
   (d) Punctuality in the home and in the school.

3. *Kindness—*

   (a) To companions at play;
   (b) To pet animals—e.g., rabbits.

4. *Gratitude—*

   To parents and teachers.

5. *Fairness—*

   Ungrudging disposition, especially when favors are distributed.

6. *Truthfulness—*

   (a) In speech—the importance of exactness; the avoidance of exaggeration;
   (b) In manner—the importance of simplicity; the avoidance of affectation.

7. *Courage—*

   (a) Cheerful endurance of little pains and discomforts; manliness;
   (b) Tale-bearing—when justifiable;
   (c) In relation to creatures inspiring instinctive fear in children—e.g., mice, frogs, spiders and beetles.

Fig. 8.1   Program of studies, grade II, Manitoba, 1912

on any Canadian province, for the schools were quite explicitly intended to deliver "powerful messages about order and self-discipline."[63]

Though attenuated, compared at least to the nineteenth century, morality remained inextricably linked to Christianity. Formal religious instruction of a denominational sort during school hours was discountenanced in most provinces – restricted by law or regulation, offered after school on a voluntary basis and then only with the consent of trustees or by petition of a specified number of parents. It formed an obligatory part of the curriculum only in the legally constituted, grant-aided separate schools of Ontario, Saskatchewan, and Alberta, although it could also be offered in the Maritimes if a consensus existed within the school community.[64] But "religious exercises" at the beginning or end of the school day were a different matter. In Ontario the law required that schools "shall be opened with the Lord's Prayer and closed with the reading of the Scriptures and Lord's Prayer or the prayer authorized by the Department of Education."[65] Virtually everywhere else religious exercises were left to the discretion of local school trustees, who in most cases insisted on it. "Nearly every school," wrote Alberta's deputy minister of education in 1922, "is opened by the repeating of the Lord's Prayer, the singing of a hymn or some other method which is of a religious character."[66] But religious lessons permeated the curriculum in less obvious ways. "Music" included the singing of familiar hymns, and Bible verses or stories were to be found in the readers every child ploughed through.[67] Memory work might routinely include Bible passages.[68] Christmas concerts and pageants, the very stuff of school life in December, were imbued with the gospel message.

The schools also had a duty to contribute to the creation of a national identity, to teach "citizenship." That word was not always used, especially before 1920; more commonly it was subsumed under "character" or, as in the case of Nova Scotia, under "moral and patriotic duties." But whatever the exact terminology, when schoolmen used words like "citizenship," as Ken Osborne remarks, "they had four things in mind. For them citizenship was an amalgam of national identity and patriotism; political literacy; a balanced awareness of rights; and the fulfilment of duties."[69] Even that nice definition, perhaps as suitable in the opening decades of the twenty-first century as it was a century before, needs a good deal of fleshing out. It is not surprising that a generation of schoolmen born and bred in the post-Confederation decades would be especially sensitive to the need to create a common Canadianism. But patriotism, citizenship, and nation building had their own distinctive resonance by 1910. In English Canada they meant one language and one cultural style. National identity could not be built from a babble of tongues and competing identities, and it was one core job of the schools to Canadianize those children not already so blessed.

Moreover, central to English-Canadian understanding of citizenship was Canada's place as a senior member in a British Empire that bestrode the world, bringing freedom, justice, and enlightenment to millions of its subjects, "black and yellow, red and white," as the Sunday school song put it. In Tim Stanley's words, the British Empire was a "moral enterprise," an idea that schoolchildren were expected to grasp and share.[70] "When I speak of our country," said one of the nation's most distinguished educators in 1908, "I mean our Empire, the whole Empire, and not just Canada."[71] The solid virtues of citizenship, in other words, were to be taught within a framework of loyalty to the imperial idea, to the British monarchy, to the Union Jack as its symbol, and to the idea that patriotism meant being prepared to fight side by side with Britain in its defence of freedom.

In most provinces there were regulations requiring the flag to be flown on the school's flagpole or hung on classroom walls.[72] From small beginnings in turn-of-the-century Ontario, Empire Day celebrations had spread to most of the country's schools.[73] The Alberta school regulations of 1906 declared Victoria Day a school holiday "to commemorate the anniversary of the birthday of Queen Victoria, to familiarize pupils with the growth and development of the Empire, and to encourage and foster patriotic and imperial sentiments." To that end, special exercises on 23 May "should include short addresses, suitable recitations, the singing of patriotic songs, and the raising of the national flag."[74] The school cadet movement was popular everywhere in English Canada, and history and geography textbooks were permeated by the imperial idea and by stories of empire building.[75] Canadian history itself was cast in that mould. The ubiquitous Mercator wall map reminded pupils daily that Canada was but one blotch of red in a sequence that girdled the globe.

The First World War did not create these values – they were pervasive in English Canada beforehand – but it gave momentum to them. Children were taught the righteousness of the Allied cause in special lessons and in history classes. Pamphlets on the causes of the war and its ongoing events flooded classrooms. Teachers and children were mobilized to raise money, grow food in school gardens and at home, conserve food and other material valuable in the war effort. In all of these activities, girls had as vital a role as boys; indeed, as Nancy Sheehan notes, one wartime pamphlet was directed at them specifically, indicating the crucial part they had in encouraging enlistment and filling in for the fighting men.[76]

The solid virtues of citizenship that informed the moral content of the curriculum were enmeshed, as they always are, in the particularities of a historical moment. Patriotism and love of country too easily shaded into jingoism and militarism. The imperial version of Canadian identity was laden with racism, as Tim Stanley's careful survey of school texts and other materials demonstrates.[77] "Political literacy" included the notion of a fluid but hierarchical social order. "Religion" in all public schools was synonymous with "Christian" and, outside the Catholic systems, meant the muted evangelicalism of the three mainline Protestant churches of English Canada. The imposition of unilingual schools, as well as the superiority of "British values" (in reality an invention of eastern Canadian loyalism),[78] went hand in hand with the creation of a national identity. These values were not invented by those who drafted the programs of studies or wrote the textbooks; rather, they were products of the larger society of white, English-speaking Canadians. But the schools were as complicit as other institutions in cultivating them.

Finally, here, one other point deserves attention. The program of studies, along with its accompanying pedagogical prescriptions, assumed the presence of a set of activities that extended beyond the academic content of the curriculum. These activities were conventionally known as the "extra-curriculum," in some respects a misleading term, since it implies something apart from the curriculum proper. But whatever actual practice might have been in any given school, these activities were not intended as dispensable add-ons. Deliberately organized under the aegis of the school, they were intended to serve as essential tools for both intellectual and moral training. Some were promoted and subsidized, through special grants, directly by provincial departments of education – the school garden movement, for example, or the school fair, both of which involved individual and co-operative efforts throughout parts of the school year.[79] There were arbour days, field days, and the special exercises, school parades, and other pursuits associated with various patriotic holidays. There were choirs and organized sports. These were activities, writes Ken Osborne, "where students learned both to compete and co-operate, to deal graciously with victory and defeat, to set and surpass personal goals, to put aside personal gain for a common cause."[80] Put another way, these were opportunities to practise the precepts taught about manners, morals, and patriotism. They were also an integral part (though only one part) of Neil Sutherland's "culture of childhood," where children "learned to behave toward each other," absorbing "the knowledge, customs, expectations, beliefs, norms, and social roles that governed relationships between them."[81]

During the 1920s and 1930s there were changes in emphasis. In the provincial programs of studies, training in citizenship tended to replace patriotism. Phraseology like "morals and manners," "character training," or "Christian morality" tended to give way to the language of "social education." Some turn-of-the-century moral virtues were scienticized and transmuted into "health" or "hygiene": cleanliness, for example, good health habits, or temperance. But this didn't mean that these studies were to receive any less emphasis. In 1931, under the subject of "Hygiene," Nova Scotia's program of studies directed that "[t]eachers shall supplement *Canadian Health Book* by instruction from *The Canadian Lesson Book on Temperance and Life* ... This book must be on each teacher's desk and instruction shall be given from it by the teacher to Grades VI, VII and VIII."[82] During the 1920s Manitoba's program of studies underwent a major revision, and by 1928 the matching pages covering both academic subjects and morals and manners were gone; instead, "The whole self is employed in moral matters. There is no special education to be termed moral. Everything has moral significance." One key to success was instilling "the spirit of co-operation and goodwill." But that didn't prevent the new program from spelling out "Behaviour Necessary to Preserve Social Relations," which included the same old list of virtues, to be taught by "formal talks on virtues and manners," "incidental talks" when an appropriate teachable moment arose, "readings from history and literature," memorizing "memory gems," and "Bible stories," which were "the birthright of every child."[83] Convinced that the home was failing to teach "manners, general behaviour and deportment," the London Board of Education introduced a syllabus in "good manners as part of the regular school curriculum," intended to "inculcate politeness," including the use of "please" and "thank-you," "the proper manner of raising the hat when meeting a lady, and the proper manner of greeting a visitor in the classroom," standing at attention with head uncovered during the playing of the national anthem, the use of "good morning" or "good afternoon" instead of "hello," and, generally, behaviour "respectful to their seniors and those in authority."[84] And a major revision of the British Columbia curriculum, much influenced by the doctrines of progressivism, could still assert in 1936 that "character is the main objective in education. Learning should result in knowledge, correct habits, certain skills, interest in an appreciation of a number of definite things of value in life, right attitudes, high ideals."[85]

The patriotic enthusiasms generated by the Great War, the bravery of Canadian troops overseas, and the battles won by Canadians began, ironically, a long, slow undermining of the imperial idea and a reorientation of subjects like history towards a more distinctive Canadianism. Imperialism itself ceased, more or less, to be a moral enterprise and acquired a more ambiguous reputation. In many parts of the country, Goodwill Day became a fashionable school event, celebrating the cause of the League of Nations and promoting international understanding.[86] Perhaps the most significant addition to the list of extracurricular activities formally encouraged by provincial departments was the Junior Red Cross movement, which combined citizenship training through pupil-organized activities and fund-raising for worthy causes with a heavy emphasis on teaching good health habits.[87] But nothing supplanted Empire Day, and for teachers and schoolchildren, like the rest of the country, the coronation ceremonies of 1937 were an apotheosis of the imperial tie, surpassed only by the royal visit two years later.[88]

Over the long haul, subtle changes in language and practice matter, but emphases are just that. Between the turn of the century and the mid-1930s, the academic content prescribed in the provincial programs of studies changed somewhat, and broadened somewhat for some children. But the changes were modest, and so indeed were the shifts in values to be instilled in Canadian children.[89]

III

Today, Canadians pretty much take it for granted that a complete high school education takes four years, that most young people will complete those four years, and that there will be diversified programs of studies catering to a wide range of interests and abilities. None of this was true at the beginning of the twentieth century. In 1900 or 1920 only a minority attended high school and a much smaller minority completed it. Program choices and subject options were very limited. And with the exception of Ontario, where it had long been a four-year program, the Canadian high school consisted of only three years of study, grades IX through XI. Formally speaking, all provinces had a grade XII (or, in Ontario, an Upper School, which in the 1930s became grade XIII). But this last year of high school was a "post-graduate" year. Entry (or "matriculation") to the universities, to professional training (not yet fully integrated into the universities), or to the normal schools required the completion of grade XI. Though technically it referred only to meeting the requirements for university entrance, the completion of grade XI was commonly referred to as achieving "junior matriculation." Grade XII (or the "senior matriculation" year) was equivalent to first-year university, and its successful completion allowed a student to enter second-year university or qualify for a first-class teacher's certificate. Even in those provinces that had introduced a four-year high school program during the interwar years, it remained possible to complete matriculation or enter the normal school at the end of grade XI.[90] During the interwar years, grade XII (or XIII) enrolments steadily increased. But until at least the late 1930s, most high school students intent on further study proceeded only as far as grade XI (or in Ontario, grade XII). And as we've suggested in other chapters, many small schools didn't even offer the final year of the formal program of studies or simply abandoned it in the hard years of the Depression.

During the first two decades of the century, provincial programs of studies for the secondary schools were built around a pattern of "core plus options," which usually involved a substantial core providing the common subjects necessary for entrance to the normal schools, universities, or any form of white-collar work and a set of options that were prerequisites for further study. Either formally or informally, this amounted to two packages of courses, one leading to the university (commonly labelled the classical or matriculation course) and requiring Latin, French, and advanced mathematics, and an "English" or "teacher's" course leading to normal school entrance. The 1902 program of studies for the North West Territories (the future provinces of Saskatchewan and Alberta) is pretty typical. In standard VI, roughly equivalent to grades IX–X, eleven subjects were compulsory: four were various branches of English; three comprised arithmetic and mathematics; history and geography added two more; and to these were added botany and drawing. The optional subjects consisted of bookkeeping, agriculture, physics, Latin, French, and German. In standard VII (roughly equivalent to grades X–XI), there were slightly fewer obligatory subjects, some new additions (chemistry, for example), and a few optionalized subjects (such as drawing), as the program became more narrowly focused on preparation for matriculation or normal school entrance.[91] In principle, pupils could take a general course that led to neither – only the obligatory courses along with some self-selected options – but few did. There might also be a distinct commercial program requiring two or three years of study, as was the case in Ontario, Manitoba, and British Columbia; such courses also existed in a handful of large cities even when they were not listed in the provincial documents.[92] Similarly, subjects like manual training, domestic science, or agriculture might or might not be listed in provincial programs of studies even though they were being offered in some secondary schools.

Beginning in the second decade of the century but most frequently during the interwar years, nearly every province rewrote its secondary school program, introducing a broader range of programs, usually in the form of packages of courses, and a wider variety of options, conventionally including domestic science, commercial subjects, and shop work, which might be simply an extension of elementary school manual training (general shops) or more specific training in wood- or metalwork, electricity, and automotive mechanics.[93] The number of packages and range of subjects varied from province to province, but British Columbia is perhaps representative. In its first major revision of the secondary school program, carried out in 1929–30, the province introduced five courses: matriculation, normal school entrance, general, commercial, and technical. In all five packages there was a core of compulsory subjects: English, social studies, health, and physical education. Then followed a set of "group requisites," "group electives," and free electives "representing subjects ordinarily essential in certain lines of activity." So, for example, in the matriculation course a student would take three core subjects; group requisites such as mathematics, Latin or

French, and science; and an additional one or two from a long list of electives that included agriculture, home economics, and industrial arts. In the general course, the only requisites were the three core subjects; the rest of the program would consist of free electives. Successful completion of the general course earned a high school graduation diploma but not the qualifications for university or normal school; nor did it provide the kinds of skills required for completion of the commercial or technical programs.[94]

By the interwar years it was both possible and, in the larger urban centres, increasingly common for students to take a vocational subject option along with their academic subjects. Students might well enrol, for example, in one or two courses in typing, business practice, shop, or home economics to complement or enrich their academic education or to avoid a difficult second foreign language or advanced math. But this practice has to be distinguished from full-fledged vocational programs, which were much more intensively and sharply focused on technical training. As one sector within the public education system, the vocational schools were not, it is perhaps worth emphasizing, mere "trade schools" narrowly conceived; they were in the business of completing the general education of adolescents, and the provincial programs prescribed for the vocational schools always included a substantial academic component, with standards and course content similar to those in the academic program. But the vocational programs were also specifically tailored to produce technical know-how and craft skills.

The proportion of time devoted to vocational subjects was fairly uniform across the country owing to the influence of federal funding for technical education and related federal-provincial agreements that set the time in regular full-day programs at roughly 50% for vocational courses and 50% for general education.[95] This did not necessarily mean 50% in every grade; a program might require a heavier academic weight in grade IX, while vocational subjects were allocated more time in each successive grade. But whatever the exact arrangement, what marked the vocational school off from the academic high school was a large component of practical work and a much more limited range of academic subjects.[96]

By the 1920s Ontario had the most extensive provision for vocational education, and for that reason alone its program of studies may be atypical, but it is at least illustrative of the way provincial authorities thought vocational instruction should be organized. The program was to extend over at least three years and preferably four. The compulsory academic core for all students included "physical training and hygiene"; "English literature and oral and written composition (including the essentials of grammar)"; "history, civics, and economics"; and "arithmetic, geography, and elementary physics." Only English and physical training were to be taken in all years of the program. Six different vocational packages could be offered: industrial, homemaking, art, technical, commercial, and agriculture. Within each, general directives were spelled out but no detailed course outlines provided. In part this was because vocational programs were new and still experimental, but also because each school was supposed to be responsive to local industrial circumstances and labour demands. Yet the industrial program, for example, was expected to begin with an introduction to general industrial processes and then lead on to specific craft training. The technical course was intended as "preparation for junior executive or technical positions in trade, industry," or entry into "engineering colleges," and included the requisite mathematics and science courses along with an introduction to surveying, architecture, mechanical engineering, metallurgy, and so forth.[97]

What the vocational schools actually offered varied enormously. In some of Ontario's largest communities, high-enrolment, stand-alone schools might offer a rich array of sophisticated courses, including programs in "architecture, machine drawing and design"; "art and design"; "chemistry and geology"; "commercial work"; "industrial shop work" specializing in a variety of skilled trades (pattern making, auto mechanics, electrical wiring, carpentry and construction); "domestic science" (cooking, foods, hygiene, dietetics); "domestic art" (dressmaking, millinery, textiles, history of costumes), and "printing and bookbinding." Three schools offered a comprehensive course in agriculture.[98] In Ontario and other parts of Canada, on the other hand, smaller communities offered a much more restrictive set of options. Though far from universal, commercial programs were widely available in Canada's larger urban communities, but technical programs might be limited to a handful of craft skills, such as carpentry or auto mechanics, and domestic science to sewing and cookery.[99]

While there were important differences between the academic and vocational schools in program emphases, one constant was the presence of extracurricular activities. Cynthia Comacchio has offered a fine extended exposition of the purposes and practices these secondary school activities were intended to encompass, and there is no need to reiterate her analysis here.[100] Suffice it to say that, as was the case in the elementary schools, extracurricular activities were considered to be an integral part of the program of studies, encouraged by provincial authorities, school boards, and local administrators, and intended to help students become the kind of adults who embodied the dominant intellectual standards and moral values of the times. There were, at least in many of the schools in the larger towns and cities, debating and literary societies, school magazines and annual yearbooks, choirs and orchestras, inter- and intramural sports, and a variety of others clubs besides. None of this was new in the interwar years

– the same range of activities could be found in the last quarter of the nineteenth century or the first two decades of the twentieth[101] – but as high school enrolments increased, the extracurriculum probably touched more young people than ever before. Just how many is another matter, one we will return to in chapter 10.

During the interwar years there was a significant change in the length of the high school program. A four- or five-year, rather than a three-year, course became increasingly common for many high school students. In part this was a consequence of choices students themselves made. Attempting to combine both matriculation and normal school entrance requirements, and to complete them in three years, created impossible workloads and high failure rates on departmental examinations, with the result that more and more students spread (and were encouraged to spread) their courses over four years.[102] Much to the satisfaction of departmental authorities, this also had the effect of opening up opportunities for some modest additions of optional subjects. A similar kind of pressure in small high schools added to the phenomenon. One or two teachers could only timetable so many subjects in any given year, so there was considerable incentive to spread the curriculum over four years by offering, for example, some grade XI subjects one year and others the next. The other important factor was a consequence of rising standards for entry to the universities and normal schools (and, one might add, to the more prestigious hospital nursing schools). As we noted in chapter 5, the flood of students passing through the high schools during the 1930s enabled departments of education across the country to jack up entry standards to the normal schools from junior to senior matriculation. For a similar reason, the universities were doing the same thing.[103] The result was that more students had to complete grade XII or, in Ontario, grade XIII. And even before the full impact of the Depression was felt, students and parents were tempted by the cheaper costs of living at home. According to a Dominion Bureau of Statistics (DBS) report of 1932, "Three out of four students now admitted to the University of Saskatchewan have completed the first year on entry. The proportion is similar in Alberta, but much lower in Manitoba, no doubt because the University of Manitoba is located in a large city from which it draws the majority of its students and where it is as convenient for students to take their first year, or senior matriculation, at the university as at a collegiate."[104] This also helps to explain the intense local pressures to maintain or establish grade XII classes that we noted in chapter 4.

There was, it must be said, a lot of opposition to stretching out junior matriculation to four years because of the additional out-of-pocket expenses and opportunity costs this entailed for parents and students, as well as the increased taxation for ratepayers.[105] So in most provinces four years were encouraged but not mandated. Well after the 1930s one could still do junior matriculation in three years in Alberta if one chose to, and in Manitoba and the Maritimes it remained the norm.[106] But by the end of that decade British Columbia had fixed its junior matriculation course at four years.[107] In Ontario most of the universities continued to demand only junior matriculation (four years), but in 1931 the University of Toronto had begun to demand senior matriculation (grade XIII) – a harbinger of things to come.[108] Thus, during the interwar years, "the high school experience" was gradually being extended to encompass not only more and more Canadian young people, but more of their young lives.

9

The Examination System and Its Fate

At the beginning of the twentieth century, indeed well before that, instruction in Canadian schools was organized not only through a graded program of studies, but also by a set of rules and conventions governing the adjudication of pupil progress through the grades and teacher accountability for efficient instruction. These formal and informal rules established the criteria for promotion from grade to grade, the approved tools for assessing achievement, the guidelines for rates of promotion, and the prerequisites for the award of provincial certificates testifying to the completion of particular grades or programs.

Unlike the prescribed curriculum, tidily laid out in a single document, the rules governing assessment and accountability tended to be scattered in a variety of publications, including departmental bulletins, memoranda, normal school manuals, and the like. But the most important of them were nearly always set out either in the education acts and the accompanying regulations or in the pertinent program of studies. And like the program of studies, the policies and procedures were *prescribed*, mandated by the provincial departments and obligatory for teachers and pupils alike.

From grades I through VII, promotion decisions were, most immediately, in the hands of teachers (or teachers and principals). In these grades, pupils' progress was gauged by a mix of assessment tools – by the quality of their daily work in class, of their homework and other assignments, and through regular spot testing. But teachers also made use of, and were expected to use, formal examinations, even with very young children. Describing best practice in 1915, Ontario's manual on school management had this to say: "From Primary Grade to Senior First [grades I and II] there should be no examination; the teacher's judgment of term work is quite sufficient. No child of this age should be subjected to the strain of a written examination." For all other grades, "those pupils receiving a term standing of 75% should be promoted without examination" – there was little point in imposing a final examination on those who had unequivocally proved their mastery of the work during the school year. But below that cut-off point, pupils should be required, in addition to their term work, to prove their "fitness for higher work" through formal examinations at the end of each school year.[1] Surveying practices across the country in 1921, the DBS reported that promotions were "usually done after the first or second grade by means of written examinations; these examinations are supplemented by the teacher's impressions based on personal knowledge of the work, attainments, and capacity of the child."[2] In Winnipeg in the mid-1920s, the schools held "a complete set of examinations before Christmas, before Easter, and again in June, and these are additional to the regular monthly examinations on which reports on the pupils' work are prepared."[3] At about the same time in Moncton, promotions from grades I through VII were based on "monthly examinations and a full set of final examinations in every school subject in June." The two sets of examinations were averaged: "for example, if John Doe made an average of 76.3% on all the monthly examinations ... and 64.7% on the final examinations in June his grading average would be 70.5%. The grading average necessary for promotion is 65% or more."[4] Thus, while the formal examination was not the only method of assessing progress in the elementary grades, it was assumed to be an essential element in any sound promotion policy, and was usually treated as decisive whenever the outcome might be in doubt.

The decisions made by the local school, however, were never autonomous. Final authority rested with each provincial department of education, and it was one key job of the inspectorate to patrol the promotion practices of teachers and schools.[5] This could be done by spot tests during an inspector's visit or by requiring teachers to keep examples of pupils' assignments or tests that he could review. But it was also common for inspectors to hold their own local promotion examinations. These might be drafted by the inspector himself, by the inspector and a team of his teachers, or provided to the inspector by the department. Nearly always they would be marked by the teachers in each school, with the answer papers preserved for his perusal.[6] In the larger urban areas, provincial supervisory powers were usually delegated to the superintendent's office. "At least once during the year a general examination of all students is given under the direction of the Superintendent," the Winnipeg School Board explained in its annual report for 1934: "Papers for this examination are prepared and sent out from the Superintendent's office. They serve the triple purpose of a corrective to the estimates of the individual school, a directive to teachers as to emphasis in instruction, and a general equalization of standards throughout the entire system."[7] In London a committee of principals and teachers "set the promotion papers from Grades IV to VII inclusive," a process organized and overseen by the city inspector.[8] Thus there evolved a common pattern in urban and rural schools alike: as a matter of custom and practicality, initial promotion decisions were made by teachers and principals; in the vast majority of cases they probably had the final say. But there were always checks and balances built into the system, and their decisions were, as the law in every province had it, "subject to the approval of the inspector."

Beginning in grade VIII, the rules and procedures changed dramatically. For the first time, pupils confronted a province-wide qualifying examination that determined whether or not they would be admitted to high school. Results were assessed by independent examiners without regard to the quality of daily work in grade VIII, regardless, indeed, of the cumulative success pupils might have experienced throughout their prior school careers. Those pupils who were successful faced similar high-stakes examinations at the end of each high school year. If we seem to give undue attention to the high school entrance examination (HSEE) in the paragraphs that follow, it is partly because the procedures for this first province-wide examination were the same for those that followed, but also because the HSEE reveals a fundamental cleavage in the organization of public education that is wholly unfamiliar today.

Writing in 1918 about the Saskatchewan school system, Harold Foght, an American observer, remarked that "the examination bar placed at the end of the eighth grade emphasizes ... that the Province does not yet view the high school as an integral part of the public school system."[9] This is, at best, a half-truth reflecting American preconceptions about the purpose of secondary education and the differences that existed between American and Canadian schools. The high school was indubitably a part of Canadian public education, fully integrated in terms of public control, finance, and curriculum, linked to the elementary school through the HSEE, embodying the principle of an "education ladder" stretching from the elementary school, through the high school, to more advanced studies. A product of one strand of nineteenth-century liberalism, the HSEE was the institutional vessel for widely shared values about the importance of "a career open to talent" and the promotion of merit regardless of social circumstance.[10] But these values neither incorporated nor implied the principle of "secondary education for all." Rather like the prevailing view in Britain or Australia, the elementary school was thought to be the appropriate vehicle for universal education, delivering, as James Miller put it, that "minimum body of common knowledge, appreciation and abilities which every child should possess." Until at least the third or fourth decade of the century, on the other hand, the Canadian high school was a special-purpose, severely selective institution, and the role of the HSEE was to select that minority of pupils best equipped to benefit from its intensively academic curriculum.

At the turn of the century, all provinces held such an examination, almost invariably at the end of grade VIII.[11] But not all pupils wrote the HSEE. Uniquely, in Nova Scotia it was only required if pupils wanted to attend a county academy or to obtain the provincially recognized certificate indicating they had completed grade VIII; otherwise local authorities could promote pupils into the high school grades as they saw fit.[12] Elsewhere pupils judged too ill-prepared or not capable of standing for examination might not be allowed to write the HSEE; in several provinces it was not an automatic right, with pupils requiring a principal's certificate to be admitted as a candidate.[13] In order to recover some of the substantial administrative costs involved, most provincial departments of education charged fees to write the HSEE, as indeed they did for the external high school examinations. Depending on the province and the decade, these could range as high as five dollars, though by the interwar years one or two dollars was more common. Such fees almost certainly discouraged some potential candidates from families in precarious economic circumstances.[14] Rural folk might have to pay not only the examination fees but transportation or boarding costs to maintain their children for a few days at the nearest urban examination centre.[15] Other parents took it for granted that grade VIII was the final year of their child's school career, and even larger numbers of pupils never reached grade VIII in any case. Thus those who were allowed, or chose, to attempt the HSEE were a select group among all those enrolled in Canadian elementary schools.[16]

The mechanics of administering the HSEE varied somewhat from province to province. Universally, papers were drafted by committees of inspectors, teachers, and others appointed by the department of education or by semi-independent examining boards operating on its behalf. In some provinces – Saskatchewan and Alberta are examples – the marking of answer papers was also centralized, carried out by teams of teachers, hired and paid by the department, working in the early weeks of each summer.[17] In Nova Scotia, marking was under the control of the individual county academy, though the answer papers were to be preserved for a year and the inspector required to recheck them at the time of his next visit.[18] In Ontario the examination papers were distributed in each school district to the "local high school examining boards," which consisted of a public school inspector, the principal of the high school, and a member appointed by the public and separate school boards situated in the high school district. This board conducted the examination and evaluated the papers, but its work was subject to departmental review and high school inspectors were expected to keep tabs on its decisions by spot-checking, in the following year, the attainments of the grade IX pupils it had promoted.[19]

John Charyk, who knew whereof he spoke, having prepared his own pupils for Alberta's HSEE, offers the best short description of the workload the examination entailed for that province's department of education:

> Consider all the organization and work that had to be done, much of it confidentially for obvious reasons: setting the examination papers; printing them; sealing them in special brown envelopes, subject by subject, with the required number for each rural school in the province having grade eight candidates; sending these papers to such centers ... by registered mail or express; compiling a set of regulations for conducting the examinations and enforcing them strictly; receiving and organizing the written answer papers at the examination center; assuring the anonymity of each student's paper by a suitable code system; supervising the marking of the answer papers; recording the results not only for the records of the Department of Education, but also for release in the province's daily newspapers; furnishing unsuccessful candidates with a statement of the marks they had obtained in each subject; and sending a grade eight school-leaving diploma, signed by the minister of education, to every successful student.[20]

And that, Charyk goes on to say, was only the departmental role. Arrangements were nearly as complex at the local level, with the entire enterprise embedded in a lengthy and rigorous set of rules to be followed by trustees, presiding examiners, and pupils.[21] With only modest changes, the same procedures were followed in each of the high school examinations. And since all of these examinations from the HSEE on up were packages of separate subject test papers, the marking load was enormous. To take but one example, in 1926 Saskatchewan's department was responsible for organizing the marking of 80,000 HSEE papers, at a cost, in sub-examiners' fees alone, of $21,000.[22] And that doesn't include the tens of thousands of high school examination papers that had to be marked at the same time.

Like the subsequent high school examinations, the HSEE was demanding in terms of the concentrated effort it required of pupils, and searching about their mastery of a broad range of content and skills. At the turn of the century, for example, Nova Scotia's HSEE consisted of five hour-long papers, written over two days in early July: English; mathematics; drawing, writing, and simple accounts; geography and history; and "general knowledge."[23] At the same point in time Ontario pupils wrote eleven specific subject papers over the span of a week.[24] Manitoba's 1913 schedule called for thirteen papers to be written over four days in June: tests in spelling, writing, and arithmetic took half an hour each; history, English composition, and written arithmetic each took an hour and a half.[25] In 1910 British Columbia pupils wrote eleven papers in three days, the total taking about five hours, split between morning and afternoon each day; by 1926 they wrote "only" five papers, ranging from three hours for mental and written arithmetic to two and one-quarter hours each for geography and grammar and composition.[26]

As to the challenge of the examinations, all we can do here is to provide a handful of representative examples (though it must be said that to gauge the full range of demands there is no substitute for sets of these examinations seen whole).[27] Consider the Saskatchewan HSEE in 1910. Pupils were asked to spell, among an extensive list of other words dictated to candidates by the presiding examiners, "embroidered," "penitence," "pernicious," "parliamentary," "whimsical," "perjured," "phantom," and "fantastically." In history: "Explain the meaning of Representation by Population and show clearly how it was secured." "What is meant by a *Reciprocity Treaty*? Name the principal provisions of the Reciprocity Treaty (1854). How is commerce between Canada and the United States regulated at present?" In literature: "Quote three consecutive stanzas, either from Wordsworth's *To the Cuckoo* or from Tennyson's *Song of the Book*." "Tell the story of the Ancient Mariner's voyage up to the time of reaching the tropic calm." In grammar: "Construct sentences that illustrate (a) future perfect tense, (b) gerund, (c) interrogative pronoun, (d) indirect objective, (e) imperfect participle."[28] In British Columbia, two typical mental arithmetic questions: "Find the cubic contents of a brick 9 inches long, 5 inches wide and 4 inches thick," and "What simple fraction is equal to 7/10¾?" Written problems included "The owner of a square field containing 40 acres put a 3-strand wire fence around it. What did the wire cost at 4½ c. a foot?" In geography: "Describe briefly either Siberia or China under the following headings: – a) surface drainage; b) climate; c) principal products and exports; d) cities."[29] In Manitoba, in 1922, candidates writing the history paper were asked to "Give the names of eight prominent Canadian writers, three of them to be poets," and to "Explain what is meant by a) The Tariff, b) The Budget, c) The Dissolution of Parliament, d) The Cabinet."[30] The instructions for Ontario's oral reading test in 1901 were as follows:

The examiners will use one or more of the following passages, paying special attention to Pronunciation, Emphasis, Inflection and Pause. They will also satisfy themselves by an examination on the meaning of the reading selection that the candidate reads intelligently as well as intelligibly. Twenty lines, at least, should be read by the candidate. Selections, *Ontario Readers*:

Discovery of the Albert Nyanza

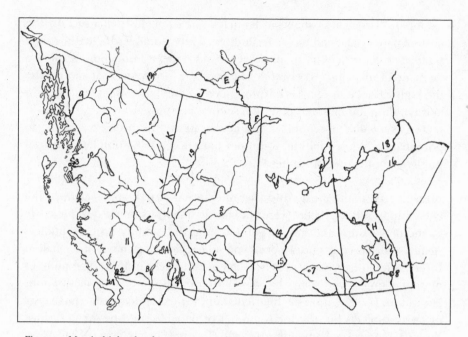

Fig. 9.1   Map in high school entrance examination, geography, British Columbia, 1929

Lochinvar
The Two Breaths
The Ocean.[31]

Given the endurance required and the range of subject matter and skills demanded, one cannot help but wonder how many of today's adults, including those educated in our universities (let alone our high school students), would receive a passing grade on the battery of tests that comprised the early twentieth-century HSEE, written by grade VIII pupils aged anywhere from 11 or 12 to 15 or 16. An attempt to answer any of the above questions should prove of heuristic value; or the reader might consider the accompanying map of Canada (Figure 9.1) and attempt to list, as required on British Columbia's 1929 HSEE in geography, eight cities and ten rivers (identified as numerals), plus the eight lakes and three parallels of latitude (identified alphabetically).[32]

A pass on the HSEE commonly required a certain minimum percentage on each paper and an aggregate total above that on all the papers combined.[33] The numerical values for each question were usually indicated on the paper itself, placed opposite each question, and a common marking scheme told the examiners how to assess papers and award marks.[34] Most marks were awarded for content but not exclusively. In Ontario, for

example, "Two marks shall be deducted for each misspelt word on the
answer papers in Spelling ... In addition ... reasonable deductions shall
be made for misspelling in all other answer papers. Deductions shall also
be made in the subjects for lack of neatness."[35] The reward for success was
the high school entrance certificate, issued by the department of education
and entitling a pupil to attend high school. For those who didn't go on, it
served as a valuable school-leaving certificate useful in demonstrating to
potential employers that the youngster had successfully completed the full
public school course of studies.[36]

After the HSEE, the most critical set of external examinations came at the
end of high school. These were the matriculation examinations for entry
to the universities, the normal schools, and the better nursing schools.[37]
Again, students confronted a gruelling set of papers, each two and a half to
three hours long, written over ten days or two weeks in June. The number
of papers might vary somewhat depending on the pupil's subject options
and future plans. University matriculation, for example, might require six
or seven subjects but the total number of papers would be greater, since
English, French, or Latin conventionally involved two papers each, one on
composition and the other on literature or translation. If one was fortunate, examination schedules might allow modest breaks between papers,
but just as likely, one might find oneself writing, say, Latin composition on
a Wednesday morning, Latin authors in the afternoon, and, sharp at 9:00
am on Thursday, yet another three-hour examination on history or chemistry.[38] Once the examinations were over, teams of high school teachers and
university professors, hired and paid by the provincial department of education, assembled at headquarters to mark the tens of thousands of papers
– or more. Referring only to the junior and senior matriculation examinations, the president of the Ontario Educational Association complained in
1929 that "there are upwards of 200,000 papers to be examined in Toronto
during the midsummer vacation, and it is nearly the end of August before
the results can be announced; the consequence is that the whole province
is kept in a state of nervous uncertainty long past the time when decisions
for the future should be made."[39] When the job was finally finished, the
department collated and released the results, students most likely discover-
ing their fate – marks and all, subject by subject – through the very public
forum of the local newspaper.

Today we rather take it for granted that the number of children promoted
will roughly match the number in each grade and that there will be a tight
linkage between age and grade. Though exceptions are made for a variety
of reasons, we are generally reluctant to see children fall much behind,

or get much ahead of, their age cohort – a policy sometimes described as "social promotion." In the early twentieth century this was not an operative principle. Any elementary grade included a much wider spread of ages than we would now find acceptable, many pupils were "grade retarded," and a steadily diminishing number entered the senior grades of the elementary school or continued through high school. There were, as we suggested in chapter 3, potent socio-economic reasons for this pattern that had little to do with the internal organization of the school system. But just as assuredly it was also "school-caused"; the expectation that some children would fail one or more years was an essential element in the promotion policies of all Canadian school systems. The program of studies set a single standard of achievement for each grade, the criterion for promotion was the ability to meet that standard, and formal examinations were the ultimate guarantee that pupils met it. It was this policy, for example, that helped to account for the high level of retardation in grade 1: children either learned the elements of manipulating language and numbers demanded by the grade 1 program, or they did not and were consequently held back until they did – and so on, through the grades.[40]

Since promotions were linked less to age than to satisfactory completion of the specific program prescriptions, there was a good deal of flexibility in the grading of pupils. A significant minority were "accelerants." Having completed the work of a particular grade faster than their peers, they were promoted more frequently than once a year. Two precocious schoolboys, Woodrow Lloyd and John Kenneth Galbraith, as we have already noted, completed grade VIII and started high school at age 11. One rural Alberta woman who started school in 1928 reminisced, "We were allowed to skip grades in those days, if the teacher thought us capable of better work. So I attended school five years, to be exact, in which time I completed my eighth grade with an 87.12% average."[41] Literally skipping an entire year's work tended to be discountenanced.[42] More likely, this pupil, like many others, moved through the work of two grades during a single year, or through three grades in two years.[43] Contemporaries assumed this to be a common practice in the rural schools, where individual children could easily be moved from one grade to another at any point in the year, but it was also common in big-city classrooms as well, though usually at the end of a term.[44] This also meant that children could start school at age 7 or 8 (or occasionally even later) and still hope to complete the elementary grades by the time they were 13 or 14. When 14-year-old Edith Van Kleek arrived in Alberta from South Dakota in 1916, she had completed only grade IV. Desperate to continue her education, she entered the local one-room school and completed grades V through VIII and passed her HSEE in only two years.[45] Nor are we simply citing in this paragraph a handful of unusual exceptions. A 1914 analysis of students at the Ottawa normal school, for example, found that they had completed grades I through VIII, on average, in 6.3 years.[46]

Conversely, the criterion of mastery also meant that substantial numbers were expected to repeat grades – "held back," as the common phrase had it, until they had either attained the set standard or left school altogether. The rule of thumb recommended in Ontario's normal school manual on school management (1915) was that failure rates in each of the grades would range from 10% to 20%.[47] As one Nova Scotia study revealed, that might mean that anywhere up to 30% or 40% repeated one or more grades at some point in their school careers.[48] But a failure rate of 10% or 20% a year was modest compared to the slaughter of the innocents when grade VIII pupils confronted the HSEE. Despite the fact that the candidates for this first external examination were already a pre-selected group, failure rates were astonishingly high. In the first two decades of the century, 30% or more was common. In Ontario in 1912, for example, the failure rate was 38%; in Manitoba in 1910 and 1915, 33%; in British Columbia in 1915, 29%; in Nova Scotia's county academies in 1920, anywhere up to 50%.[49]

It was no different at the annual external examinations in high school. In 1912 in Alberta the failure rate in the grade IX, X, and XI examinations was about 40%, and higher than that for grade XII.[50] W.F. Dyde, collating the data for the early 1920s, found that "in five provinces over a period of two years 26 per cent of the pupils failed to secure a passing mark. In three of these provinces the percentage of failure at the close of grade X was 37. At the grade XI and XII examinations in the same provinces failures of 30%–50% were the rule rather than the exception. In Ontario at the Middle School examinations 50% of the papers over a period of years resulted in failure percentages of 24 or more. Although the great majority of pupils have been admitted to high school through success at a provincial examination, they fail in their high school work in ever-increasing numbers through the succeeding grades."[51] There were, as Dyde pointed out, proximate causes for these high failure rates. One factor was "the large number of pupils in rural areas taught in small groups, often by ill-qualified teachers." Another was the three-year high school course in most provinces, which was too short to cover the content demanded by the program of studies and matriculation requirements. But he also recognized that high failure rates were inevitable as long as mastery of a single academic standard remained the chief criterion for progress through the grades.[52] As two American observers put it in a review of education in the Maritimes that could just as well be applied to all of English Canada, "Examinations are everywhere, they play a leading part in education, and the selection is ruthless."[53]

Beginning very tentatively in the second decade of the century, but gaining momentum after that, provincial departments of education began canvassing for alternatives to the external examinations that had dominated Canadian education for two generations. There had always been those who believed that the best means of assessing progress was daily evaluation and regular testing carried out by the pupil's own teacher.[54] Increasingly, there were doubts about the validity or reliability of the departmental examinations.[55] Broadening the high school program of studies made little sense, moreover, if the HSEE eliminated most of the clientele for the new courses. And there were also rising costs and administrative burdens as more and more pupils completed grade VIII and began to move into the high school.[56] Much of this investment, indeed, was condemned as wholly redundant: "There is a great waste of effort in at least half the examining," the president of the Ontario Educational Association pointed out in 1929, "for many candidates are certain of passing. To read the papers of such candidates is needless, for the teacher could certify to their excellence."[57] These kinds of arguments encouraged nearly every province to introduce some form of the "recommendation system" – a shift in policy that allowed teachers and principals a much greater degree of latitude in promotion decisions.

Recommendations were most easily introduced in the lower grades of the high school, where teachers already worked with a pre-selected group of students and where, it was assumed at least, the looming matriculation examinations would encourage the maintenance of high standards without the need for externally imposed tests. By the mid-twenties, Nova Scotia, New Brunswick, Ontario, Manitoba, Saskatchewan, and British Columbia had all delegated most promotions in the pre-matriculation years to local authorities.[58] That doesn't mean that departments ceased to set examinations. In some jurisdictions, students who failed to maintain a certain average had to write the examination, and there were various other reasons why external examinations were necessary.[59] But it did mean that provincial departments no longer had to organize and pay for the marking of most examinations in the lower high school grades. Nor was it the end of formal examinations for high school pupils. Most local schools continued to hold their own finals but used them as only one part of a more broad-based assessment system. Term examinations and daily work might even be used to recommend the best students without requiring them to write a final examination.

When it came to the HSEE, however, the provinces proceeded more cautiously and the process of devolution was more circuitous.[60] Initially the general rule was to allow recommendations only in the larger urban areas, where appropriate controls were already in place – where a high school was established, where the elementary schools were fully graded, where the workforce was well qualified and experienced.[61] In Ontario the decision was delegated to the local high school examining boards, which could declare some of their feeder schools eligible to recommend, or none at all. Everywhere, those pupils not recommended continued to write the HSEE, and all pupils in smaller communities had to write as well. As W.F. Dyde summed it up, "The limitations upon the size of schools which may recommend pupils obviously exclude from the privilege the great body of small rural and village schools. On these schools the incidence of examination will weigh most heavily."[62]

From the mid- or late 1920s onwards, the rules tended to be liberalized – extended to most graded schools and, in some provinces, to the rural schools as well.[63] But this did not mean the end of departmental oversight. In Manitoba, for example, the decision to recommend promotion lay with "the public school inspector or Superintendent in consultation with the principal of the high school and the teacher of Grade VIII."[64] In Ontario it was the responsibility of the inspector to vet each school and report his views before the local examining board even considered the expediency of adopting the recommendation system for that school.[65] In British Columbia, recommendations were made "by a committee, composed of the Principal of the school, the Principal of the High School or of the Superior School, and the Inspector of Schools ... having jurisdiction in the district." The power to recommend, moreover, was limited to elementary schools located in a district where a high school or superior school was in operation.[66] In the early 1930s, with some fanfare, both Manitoba and Saskatchewan announced that they were abandoning the HSEE altogether, but this meant only that the two departments got out of the business of marking papers. They continued to set and distribute papers, and made their use *compulsory*, leaving the marking to local teachers with the oversight of the inspectorate.[67] Still, this brought a significant degree of devolution. All schools became eligible to recommend, and examination results were to constitute only one portion of a more broadly based assessment for promotion to high school.

Big urban boards were quick to adjust their promotion policies to the recommendation system. By 1914, almost as soon as it was permitted in Ontario, Ottawa had begun relying on principals' recommendations near-exclusively, requiring only non-resident pupils to write the HSEE, while Toronto and Hamilton allowed recommendations for the vast majority of their pupils.[68] London followed suit in 1918.[69] By 1930, one observer noted, Toronto had used the system "for 16 years and it has been considered quite as satisfactory as the previous plan of making all candidates write." In 1929, for example, 79% of the city's grade VIII pupils were promoted by recommendation; only 21% had to write the HSEE (of these, 72% failed).[70] When the Saskatchewan Department of Education authorized recommendations, in 1917, Saskatoon immediately introduced the practice; that year, out of 252 grade VIII students, 204 were promoted while of the 48 required to write the examination, only 20 passed.[71] Vancouver first adopted the scheme in 1926, with much the same result: "Of the total Grade VIII enrolment of 1788, 1339 pupils were promoted to high school on recommendation. Of the remaining 449 who were allowed to write the entrance examination, only 69 were successful."[72] In the big urban school systems, in other words, teachers' recommendations quickly became the crucial determinant for most pupils, with the written examination serving to sort out the marginal cases. And teachers became pretty good at predicting those marginal cases.

At the provincial level, however, the recommendation system spread much more slowly. Dyde's estimate for five provinces in 1923–24 was that only 22% of all candidates were recommended – and he was including the early adopters in the urban centres.[73] The caution with which Ontario's local examining boards approached the issue is nicely illustrated by a set of 1926 statistics. Even in those urban areas where the feeder schools were entirely or predominantly within the jurisdiction of a collegiate institute, only twenty-five of forty-three examining boards had adopted the recommendation system; most of those that did not were in smaller communities where the clientele would have been drawn from other elementary schools. And in the case of the high schools – almost all located in smaller towns and villages – examining boards proved obdurate: only 10 of 133 high schools worked on the recommendation system. Overall, 60% of the candidates for entry to the collegiate institutes were recommended; for the high schools, the figure was 5%.[74] Clearly, the examining boards had reservations about variable standards in the rural elementary schools and probably in the two- or three-teacher schools of the province's hamlets and villages as well.

From the early 1920s through 1934 the DBS tried to compile national data for grade VIII pupils, and while the series covers only four or five provinces and some of the data are non-comparable between provinces, it indicates how Canadian schools at that time disposed of their senior elementary pupils. First, it demonstrates that during these years, as was the case in the previous two decades, large numbers were not even candidates for promotion. In 1921, for example, in Saskatchewan, only 34% of grade VIII pupils were candidates; in Ontario in 1923, 64%; in Alberta in 1925, 74%. Many pupils, in other words, left elementary school without attempting (or being allowed to attempt) the credential the HSEE promotion certificate represented.[75] Second, the numbers promoted, by either recommendation or written examination, ranged between 50% and 60% of the total grade VIII enrolment, and vice versa, somewhere between 40% and 50% either failed the examination or were not candidates. Third, candidates who were recommended remained a minority across the decade in Ontario, Saskatchewan, and Alberta, though by 1930 in British Columbia they constituted a majority (78%) of all candidates; failure rates on the written examination, however, remained high – in Ontario hovering around 30%, though declining somewhat in Saskatchewan and Alberta.[76] In sheer numbers, more children were enrolled in school than ever before, more were crowding into the high school, and more were reaching its senior grades. But in percentage terms, there were still a great many who never reached beyond grade VIII and large numbers who tried and failed the HSEE and the other external examinations that lay beyond it.

What was it that gave the external exam its hold on Canadian school systems? What was wrong with the devolution of promotion decisions to local schools – or why, at least, was it approached so gingerly? The answer is that for many of those engaged in the enterprise, and for large segments of the public generally, the departmental examinations underwrote the credibility of the school system itself, offering a universal, transparent standard by which its efficacy could be judged. The job of any assessment system was, said one senior Alberta official in 1922, to assure "teachers, pupils and parents as well as the Department ... that courses were being covered, standards being met, and promotions ... warranted."[77] The external examination appeared to do this in spades. All pupils were tested by the same questions on the same material; papers were ostensibly marked to the same standard by independent examiners; and thus results were comparable between schools and between different localities in the same province. Results were public knowledge, available to teachers, principals, trustees, parents, and other ratepayers because they were widely disseminated through the newspapers as well as in official local and provincial reports. The external examination, in other words, appeared to provide an objective standard for judging the progress of pupils and assessing the effectiveness of local schools in a fair and open manner. Even the editorial board of *The School*, sceptical at best about the principles and practices embedded in the departmental examinations, had to admit in 1928 that "the public generally values the external examination as setting a standard that has for them a fairly definite and assured value. Its development is felt to have been the result of experience, the answer to felt needs. In practice, it has been found to work and there will naturally be a good deal of hesitation about discarding it until some better and practicable substitute is found. A definite standard to be reached is an aid to both pupil and teacher."[78]

In reality, the departmentals were no more than the public face of accountability. The provincial department of education established what was to be taught and published the programs of studies that all teachers had to follow. It trained the teachers who would deliver the requisite instruction. It sent out inspectors to ensure, grade by grade, year in, year out, that the program of studies was being taught well enough to meet at least minimal levels of competence. But it was the external examination results that were most visible to those outside the system itself and that provided the proof that it was working effectively and efficiently.

Thus the devolution of promotion decisions to local schools was commonly viewed with reservation, and by some with suspicion. The recommendation system was not only new and experimental but vulnerable to high levels of variability, allowing strict or lax modes of evaluation depending on the idiosyncratic assessment of individual teachers. Potentially, this was both unfair and a threat to academic standards. Before the advent of the recommendation system, this was mainly seen as a rural school problem – as a problem peculiar to those schools where teachers worked alone, were largely inexperienced, and were uncertain about just what the program of studies demanded of them or their pupils. Below grade VIII, wrote Saskatchewan's chief inspector in 1924, teachers normally made promotions at such times as they saw fit, subject only to review by the inspector on his visit: "Where schools are under the care of experienced teachers who remain for some considerable time in charge of the same school no great problem occurs; but in schools where teachers have inadequate standards, and especially in schools where there are frequent changes of teachers, much is to be desired in the matter of promotions, and the grading in different schools is far from uniform."[79] It was to overcome this problem of variability that inspectors so frequently resorted to their own system of local examinations in the lower grades of the elementary schools. It guaranteed a common standard and provided teachers with guidance about just what that standard was supposed to be.[80]

Once the recommendation system was allowed to replace the HSEE or the annual high school examinations, however, it became clear that the problems were not peculiar to the rural schools. Up until 1922, Ontario's first set of high school examinations, held at the end of Lower School, had always resulted in high failure rates. Beginning the following year, the province introduced the recommendation system for all students. In both 1923 and 1924, as W.F. Dyde noted, "in every subject the percentage of successes has risen perceptibly."[81] "Perceptibly" was something of an understatement. In 1921 the Lower School failure rate was about 46%; in 1925 the vast majority of pupils were promoted on recommendation and the pass rate was around 90% in all subjects.[82] In 1918 British Columbia introduced a limited recommendation system for high school entry; only a few years later it was forced to tighten even these rules due to widespread complaints that too many recommended pupils were unprepared for high school work.[83]

In 1920 Alberta provided a relatively restrictive set of rules allowing recommendations for entry to high school and for the first two high school
years; by the mid-1920s it had restored compulsory examinations for each
of these grades. The reason was rising failure rates in the senior high school
examinations. Promotions without examination, as Alberta's high school
inspector explained, "allowed a great many students to pass from grade to
grade without having the required foundation work to satisfactorily attack
the work of the next higher grade ... When students reached Grade XI
they were looked upon as students preparing for entrance to the Normal
Schools and the University. They were suddenly faced, and justly so, with
high standards and exacting examination requirements that they could
not meet."[84] In 1932 the Maritimes Common Examining Board reached
a similar conclusion: "Again, this year's examinations felt the effect of the
individual schools passing the students in Grade IX and X. Under this system there is a tendency to let standards slip in these two grades. It also
means that students come to Grade XI without experience in writing Board
examinations. While this policy of grading is a move in the right direction,
it cannot succeed unless the individual schools maintain a uniformly high
standard of admittance into Grade IX, and again into Grade X."[85]

In 1935, years after Manitoba had abandoned external examinations in
grades IX and X and had more recently introduced recommendations for
high school entry, Ivan Hamilton carried out a study of promotion rates in
a sample of rural elementary and high schools in the western part of the
province. Almost all children – around 95% – were being passed through
each successive elementary grade and then into grade IX.[86] In the first two
years of high school, failure rates were somewhat higher, but when, for the
first time, pupils confronted the external examinations in grade XI, failure
rates shot up to 43%. Teachers, he wrote, "who have just completed their
normal school course are usually placed in one-room schools where the
need of supervision is greatest and the least is given. Due to their inexperience they are usually much more optimistic as to the effect of their lessons
and the soundness of their promotions than the teachers who have had
experience." Because teacher turnover was high, "each new teacher apparently carries on in the manner of her predecessor and the pupils advance
at more than the normal rate. Since practically all the pupils drop out when
past the age of compulsory attendance, the process goes on and the day
of reckoning never appears, with the net result that everyone concerned
is pleased with the progress made." Those who did continue on, however, paid the price. Failure rates rose sharply in grade IX because of "the
tendency in the intermediate grades toward promoting all pupils except
those who exhibit glaring deficiencies." The result was too many "poorly
grounded students reaching the high school. There appears to be some

foundation to the frequent complaints of high school teachers that pupils are promoted too rapidly in the elementary schools." But the high school teachers themselves were adopting similar policies, "that is, postponing an inevitable failure to the latest possible grade." Much of this was done with the best of intentions – for example, "pupils known to lack opportunity for higher education" were deliberately promoted "upon the assumption that they will benefit to some extent from the advanced work." But all that accomplished was to pass the buck upwards with the result that excessively high failure rates were experienced on the grade XI departmentals.[87]

Without either the HSEE or the annual high school examinations, the responsibility for patrolling promotion policy, especially in the one-room rural schools, fell almost entirely on the inspectorate. But as Hamilton pointed out, there was "no definite check upon promotions other than the infrequent visits of the inspector" and "the present inspectoral staff is too small for the territory covered."[88] Given the burden of other duties, they could hardly be expected to keep a close eye on promotions, grade by grade, school by school, across their territory. Nor could they be expected to walk in and revoke promotions seriatim, provoking the wrath of teachers, parents, and trustees and consequent censorious rumblings from senior officials at central office.

We are not maintaining that the external examination was, definitionally, a better method of determining promotions than teachers' recommendations. What we are trying to do is illuminate the resulting dilemma. As a 1930 editorial in the ATA *Magazine* put it succinctly, "The problem, of course, is how to vest final authority for examinations in teachers and at the same time maintain a uniformly high standard."[89] In the nation's larger urban school systems, where teachers were experienced and well qualified, where schools were finely graded, and where there were principals and system-wide supervision, the dilemma hardly seemed to exist. The London Board of Education, for example, adopted the recommendation system in 1918. Annual records from early in the century through 1940 show no important differences in promotion rates. Until 1918, 10%–15% of pupils failed to gain entry to high school through the only gateway, the HSEE, but the percentage was just about the same under the recommendation system.[90] Outside the larger urban areas, however, the issue was less easily resolved, and departmental officials, the inspectorate, and other observers were converted only gradually, and in many cases only very tentatively, to the view that the recommendation system could be applied fairly and uniformly, in the nation's one-room schools especially.

We also want to suggest that the liberalization and extension of the recommendation system, in the 1930s particularly, *help* account for declining retardation rates in the elementary schools and in the junior high school grades. By 1937, 87% of British Columbia's pupils were entering high school on recommendation.[91] By 1940, in Ontario's cities, towns, and suburban areas, 85%–90% of pupils were passing each grade and, more telling, very nearly the same percentages were completing each grade in a single year.[92] One can argue quite legitimately that much of this could be explained by the substantial gains made during the 1930s in teacher quali-fications and experience. Better teaching meant more children were suc-cessful in negotiating the passage through school. But if that were the only explanation, one might equally expect declining failure rates on the senior high school departmental examinations, and that was not what happened. Whatever the virtues of the recommendation system, it did not result in better-prepared students when they had to face the challenges of what was, by the late 1930s, the last set of uniform, externally marked, and publicly reported departmental examinations left in Canadian school systems.[93]

Teachers, in any case, couldn't win under either regime. By the early twen-tieth century the external examination was firmly established as a test, not only of pupils, but of the efficiency of the teacher. Since results were a part of the public record, it was easy for parents, ratepayers, trustees, inspectors, and any other interested parties to compare how successful a teacher was in preparing pupils for the examinations. As the editors of *The School* put it in 1913, "Despite all the Department of Education may hope to the contrary, State examinations are still a chief test of efficiency as between teachers and as between schools. And more or less remotely, appointments, promotions and increases in salary still depend on the results of examinations."[94] In the village of Blairmore, Alberta, the school trustees wanted no truck with merely locally determined standards. In 1926 they passed a resolution that pupils in grade VIII were to write the HSEE "and no pupil [was] to be passed by the teacher."[95] They routinely recorded examination results in the board minutes, reported on them at the annual public meeting, demanded expla-nations when discrepancies appeared between the annual examinations and the "periodical" tests held by their own teachers, and delayed rehiring their staff until after they had received the examination results.[96] Nor was there anything atypical about Blairmore – complaints that teachers were abruptly fired for poor examination results were common in the teachers' journals right across the country. "We would agree," wrote the editor of the *Manitoba Teacher* on one occasion, "that if a teacher consistently over a period of years fails to secure a reasonable success for his pupils at the annual examinations, there would be probably, though not necessarily, adequate grounds for dismissal. But to make a teacher's re-engagement for a second year conditional upon satisfactory examination results in the first year (the modern variety of payment by results) is ridiculous nonsense, for failure in examinations may be due to a variety of causes over which the teacher has absolutely no control."[97]

But if that was Scylla, what of Charybdis? One might expect that the gradual spread of the recommendation system would release teachers from the thrall of examination results. Yet it also placed the onus for promotion squarely on them. As one senior Manitoba official put it, in the absence of the HSEE, "[o]ne of the chief difficulties connected with the present system of promotions is that of local pressure. There is often a conflict between the wishes of ambitious but uninformed parents and the teacher's requirements for promotion."[98] One of the reasons for "premature promotions" in rural Manitoba, Ivan Hamilton noted, was "the knowledge of the teacher, especially in one-room districts, that her success will be judged to a considerable extent by the promotions she makes."[99] When Alberta was preparing to abandon its external examination system in 1931, the editor of the *ATA Magazine,* John Barnett, who always had a way with words, especially when in high dudgeon, penned a scathing editorial entitled "Alone in No Man's Land." It was simply wrong, he argued, "to throw the entire responsibility on the teacher to make promotions in Grade VIII and Grade IX." In the larger schools "with considerable staff," the decision would be the joint responsibility of the principal and his teachers. "Then when John Taxpayer comes to the school with 'red in his eye' and demands to know why his much-admired offspring has not measured up ... he is met with the considered judgement of a group of people" and he was likely to be "four times as decent in dealing with, say, four people as when bludgeoning one." But "the lone teacher in the rural, village or small town school is pushed out in front to meet the whole attack alone. Not one word of protection from the law of the land." The central problem, Barnett continued, was "security of tenure for the teacher and we can declare unhesitatingly that teachers are now placed in an impossible predicament. If they insist on honesty in promotions ... they are in for an abundance of trouble," including the outright loss of their jobs. "If worst comes to worst," on the other hand, "and any significant number of teachers not possessing such vast stores of courage, prove dishonest, the promotions will be in danger of developing into a farce or a falsehood." In the meantime, a teacher could count on "a series of delightful homilies, ... reminded by all and sundry that he will lose reputation and caste if he promotes too freely. 'Rather lose your job than lose caste.'"[100] When the *ATA Magazine* polled its high school teachers for their opinion on the elimination of the exams in grades VIII through X, one city teacher summed up widespread opinion bluntly: "The new scheme would result in – 1. Indiscriminate promotion after a few years. 2. Unceasing solicitation by parents. 3. Unjust dismissal of conscientious teachers. 4. Laxity on the part of teachers but more especially of students."[101]

Not surprisingly, then, at the very time when departments were anxious to dispense with the entire apparatus of departmental examinations, it was, above all, rural teachers who most commonly called for the retention or restoration of some form of external examinations. In the words of one Saskatchewan inspector, writing in 1934, "many teachers have expressed a desire for the retention of departmental grade VIII examinations or some system where the responsibility of promoting pupils from grade VIII to grade IX will not be left to the individual teacher."[102] Having been abandoned by the Nova Scotia department in the 1920s, the teachers in one Nova Scotia inspectorate set up, with the inspector's help, their own system of common examinations for grades VIII, IX, and X. "In spite of the weaknesses of the system," he reported, "the teachers feel it relieves them of part of the responsibility of a delicate task."[103]

By the end of the 1930s both promotion policies and promotion rates were far different than they had been in 1900 or 1920. During the interwar years the external examination had dwindled in significance and more and more pupils were being promoted by their own teachers and principals. The external examinations in the junior high school grades had largely disappeared all across the country, and the HSEE was either being abandoned outright or replaced by a combination of recommendations and externally set but locally marked papers. But the devolution of control over promotion decisions was still far from complete – and still controversial.[104] Moreover, the system remained crowned by the matriculation examinations, an essential prerequisite for all those wishing to go on to some form of post-secondary education, a valued credential to present to employers, and a potent force in shaping enrolment patterns, subject choices, and academic standards, not only in the senior grades of the high school but much farther down the educational ladder as well. It would take both a different kind of school and a different way of thinking about evaluation before the authority of the external examination would be wholly undermined and its last vestiges swept away.

And what of the quality control and public accountability the external examination had represented? The introduction of the recommendation system didn't necessarily or inevitably reduce the amount of quality control within the system. The prescribed curriculum and the inspectorate were still in place, formal examinations open to supervisory scrutiny remained a staple of promotion policy, and a variety of standardized achievement tests were increasingly used to monitor individual and system-wide progress. But recommendations did internalize the locus of accountability, increasing the opacity of the system to outsiders and elevating the judgments of professionals over parents, trustees, and ratepayers. It contributed, in other words, to a process of excluding, or at least substantially reducing, the role of the laity in judging competent teaching or successful learning. The external exam may have been inadequate and unfair, as its critics claimed, and the search for better methods of evaluating teaching and learning a justified quest. Abandoning most of the departmental examinations, however, didn't make the central issues go away. How much testing should be done, by whom, when, and with what kind of assessment devices? Was its central purpose limited to its use as a diagnostic tool by classroom teachers and system administrators, or should it be used as a public, comparative measure of individual, school, and system-wide achievement? To what extent should the laity have access to, or be excluded from, the process of evaluation? Or put another way, to what extent should the public have the right to assess the state of *public* education? Successive attempts to answer these questions have produced no end of conflicting opinion, and the ensuing debates they generated – indeed the recurring open warfare over them – have persisted to this day.[105]

The Secondary School Program
at Work

In the elementary schools there was a high degree of congruence between the prescribed program of studies and what was actually taught. The nature of the elementary curriculum made it the common base for all subsequent learning, so that, within the core subjects at least, schools large or small, urban or rural, and those in different provinces all taught pretty much the same thing. Was this equally true of the secondary school? Especially after 1920 provincial programs were broadened through the creation of new course packages and subject options. But just how widely were such innovations introduced? And even when introduced, to what extent did they change traditional enrolment patterns? Who enrolled in which courses, and why? To what extent were students exposed to a variety of extracurricular activities? In this chapter we probe the matrix of influences, including local board policies, the grip of cultural tradition, the impact of small units of instruction, social class, and gender, that determined what students actually experienced of the offerings available in English-Canadian high schools.

I

In their enthusiasm to promote the new and revised secondary school courses of study, Canadian schoolmen were occasionally wont to convert paper programs into real schools. Writing in 1928, for example, Fred McNally, one of Alberta's senior education officials, described "four types of secondary school *experience*" available to Alberta students: "the usual high school leading to normal entrance and junior matriculation; the commercial high school, offering a three-year course with a thorough training in English in addition to the purely vocational studies; the agricultural high school with a fully stocked and equipped farm attached ... ; and the technical high school with a central course comparable to that given in other schools but with special opportunities in short courses for students who wish to equip themselves for some specific task in a minimum of time."[1]

This was, to put the best face on it, the normally sober-sided McNally's version of "virtual reality." Attending secondary school for most Albertans – and most Canadians – was quite different.

According to W.F. Dyde, "the backbone of the secondary curriculum in Canada is made up of five branches: English; mathematics including arithmetic, algebra, and geometry; foreign languages, almost exclusively French and Latin; the social studies, history and geography; and science, embracing physics, chemistry, physiology, botany, zoology, and the composite of two or more of these called elementary or general science. Art, too, holds a high place mainly because in many provinces it is a required subject for prospective elementary school teachers." This curriculum, Dyde went on, was driven by three things: the subjects mandated by departments of education, the requirements for normal school entrance, and entrance qualifications for the universities. "Subjects which fall outside this list are studied by very small percentages," and "the smaller the school the more strictly do the requirements govern the curriculum." Despite the variety of programs and additional subjects in the new programs of studies, in other words, most students were enrolled in a narrow range of academic studies. This was true, Dyde pointed out, even in Ontario, where there were more large schools and more vocational programs in place than in other provinces. Thus, he concluded, his analysis of the actual curriculum "may, without fear of error, be extended to the country as a whole."[2]

As the full impact of program revisions was registered across the interwar years, there was unquestionably a considerable expansion in the range of subjects available to high school students. In 1918 twenty-five subjects were taught in British Columbia, but in terms of enrolments the top ten were entirely academic; the various branches of English headed the list, along with three mathematics, Latin and French, physics, drawing, and botany. Two decades later, forty subjects were listed. Art had dropped to fifteenth place, Latin to sixteenth. Typewriting had risen from fourteenth to ninth, and home economics had crept up from eleventh to tenth. General science had replaced physics within the top ten, and health and physical education now stood in fourth place. But English literature and composition, social studies, and French were among the other subjects that registered heavy enrolments. And, except for typing, no commercial or industrial shop subjects made the top ten. In fact Latin enrolments still outnumbered nearly all of the more specialized commercial and technical subjects.[3] While subject enrolments had become somewhat more diversified, even in urbanized British Columbia the conventional high school curriculum remained solidly academic.

In 1930 the Dominion Bureau of Statistics (DBS) put together the subject enrolment statistics for six provinces, incorporating the vast majority of high school students in English Canada. Nearly all of them, not surprisingly, were enrolled in English (92%), since it was taken for granted that intensive immersion in English composition and literature was essential for every high school student. But the two "foreign languages" (one not foreign and the other spoken by no foreigner) ranked second and third: 70% of students took French; 50% took Latin. The various branches of mathematics and science were next. Manual training enrolled 10%, typewriting 16%, and stenography 16%. In New Brunswick, Ontario, and Saskatchewan, Latin enrolments were over 50%, peaking at 75% in New Brunswick; even in Alberta and British Columbia, where two foreign languages had ceased to be a prerequisite for university entrance, Latin absorbed about a third of enrolments and French remained popular just because one foreign language continued to be required.[4] In 1942 the Ontario Department of Education displayed, in graphic form, the decline of Latin enrolments in that province's secondary schools – from about 80% in 1910 to 50% in 1930, then dipping just below 40% in the late 1930s.[5] Still, even 40% meant thousands upon thousands of Latin students – nearly 42,000, spread across grades IX through XIII. French, on the other hand, stood its ground at 70% or 80% over the entire period. In 1935, more Alberta students enrolled in physics (just over 4,000), and as many in trigonometry (just under 2,000), as in stenography and typing, the two largest enrolments in commercial subjects. Latin enrolled 3,088, art 1,301, "drawing, design, and woodwork" 453, domestic science 281, music 120.[6] Of the 9,645 high school pupils in Saskatchewan that same year, 3,457 took Latin, 1,189 domestic science, and 577 agriculture.[7]

In the main, the figures in the preceding paragraphs reflect subject enrolments in the academic high schools. But in some parts of the country vocational programs were increasingly a significant component of the secondary school sector. Comparatively speaking, just how many Canadian students were enrolled in full-time day vocational programs? If one excludes commercial subjects (which were often found in the nineteenth-century high school curriculum), the figure would be virtually nil in 1900. By 1925 just over 24,000 students were enrolled in the technical, industrial, domestic science, or commercial courses included in Canadian vocational programs.[8] To that point, most of the growth had taken place in Ontario, and vocational programs everywhere tended to be concentrated in the cities and larger towns. But as a percentage of total secondary enrolments, growth was rapid across the interwar years. By the 1930s Vancouver's vocational enrolments stood at 27% or 28%.[9] In Winnipeg they rose from about 30% in the mid-1920s to something closer to 40% in 1933.[10] By 1930 the figure for Toronto was 44%.[11]

Obviously there is nothing trivial about such figures. Across the inter-war years there were an increasing number of communities where young people did indeed have access to alternative programs of studies, and annually it was more young people rather than fewer. Yet even where such alternatives existed, a majority opted for an academic program of study. In 1926, despite Winnipeg's well-established technical and commercial pro-grams, and with a new general program to boot, 70.7% of its students were enrolled in only three courses: the matriculation, teachers', or "combined" program, the latter preparing for entrance to either the university or nor-mal school.[12] In 1931, when Calgary had both a technical and commercial high school, 79.4% of its grade VIII graduates entered an academic high school.[13] The same kind of proportions were found in Edmonton in the 1920s or Vancouver in the 1930s.[14] Once we move to province-wide figures, the percentages rise higher. In 1930 close to 8,000 students were enrolled in schools established under Saskatchewan's Secondary Education Act; only 990 were enrolled in full-time vocational classes.[15] Nearly fifteen years after Alberta had introduced its revised and broadened program of studies, the graduating class of 1935 included "1,533 students qualified for the normal school entrance diploma, 745 for the matriculation diploma, 117 for the commercial diploma, 57 for the general diploma, and 7 for the technical diploma."[16] In Ontario the same year, despite the massive growth in voca-tional enrolments that had taken place since 1920, two-thirds of the prov-ince's secondary students were enrolled in academic programs.[17]

One might very well respond that province-wide figures are fundamen-tally misleading here – in most Canadian communities there were no voca-tional programs, so no alternatives were available. Even in Ontario there were only 64 vocational schools or departments by 1939–40 compared to a total of 228 collegiate institutes and high schools and another 202 continuation schools.[18] Conveniently, however, the Ontario Department of Education kept distinct enrolment records for the academic and voca-tional programs; thus it is relatively easy to distinguish where full-dress voca-tional programs were offered and, comparatively, how many students were enrolled in each. In 1922, about a decade after the enabling legislation was passed, Ontario had eleven cities with vocational programs (housed either in stand-alone institutions or as departments within composite schools), and enrolment was already 32% of total secondary enrolment in those com-munities. By 1930 there were thirty-eight places with nearly 43% of enrol-ment, and by 1935 forty-nine places with nearly 44%. In those forty-nine communities the actual percentages varied enormously, from lows of less than 20% to highs of over 50%. In thirty-one of the forty-nine communi-ties it was less than 40%, and in the seven with a majority in vocational enrolments six were very close to the 50% mark.[19] While we believe these figures are somewhat inflated, it is also clear that wherever alternatives existed in Ontario, very large numbers of students were enrolled in vocational programs.[20]

But does that mean that very large numbers were *choosing* vocational in preference to academic programs of studies? Our own answer is that some did, but most did not. From 1921, youngsters in urban Ontario had to remain in school until their sixteenth birthday, and most vocational schools admitted both those who did and those who didn't have a high school entrance certificate.[21] Those who had obtained that certificate, either by writing the high school entrance examination or by principal's recommendation, had a choice of programs; for those who lacked the certificate the only alternatives were to stay in the elementary grades or attend a vocational school. In the mid-1920s, for example, the London Technical School (later, Beal Technical) attracted just over 40% of all students in the city who held the entrance certificate; that is, some 40% of students who had a choice opted for the technical school – a not inconsiderable figure. But the London school, like a relative handful of other big-city technical schools, offered an unusually extensive array of vocational programs and also provided the only commercial program available in the city secondary schools – a combination that attracted a great many students. Even then, nearly 60% of those who had a choice opted for an academic high school.[22] At the same time, those lacking the entrance certificate constituted an increasing proportion of technical school students – some 20% in 1927 and 45% by 1931.[23] Thus the two types of school, academic and vocational, were drawing from an overlapping but not identical pool, and choice was a factor for only some London adolescents. Similarly, in Vancouver, to take but one other example: until 1929 only those who had a choice were admitted to the city's technical classes; after that, rising enrolments in those classes were at least partly accounted for by the admission of those ineligible for the academic program. As Vancouver's municipal inspector of schools explained in 1928, "Hitherto only students of high school entrance standing have been admitted to our technical classes – there was no room for others. But now, with increased accommodation, we are planning to provide in technical classes for many overage pupils taken from the senior grades of the elementary schools."[24]

The other telling figure is the comparative retention rate. If a large percentage of pupils who enrolled in the vocational program were there by choice, one would expect to see some rough similarity in retention beyond the age of compulsion. But for Ontario at least that is not the case. Once vocational students reached the age of 16, they left in droves, abandoning the industrial program especially. One needs, of course, to keep the figures in perspective. This was, after all, an era when the majority of young people left school before they completed grade XII regardless of the program they enrolled in. But over the decade of the 1920s, retention rates to grade XII were far higher in academic than in vocational programs, a gap, as Robert Stamp puts it, "widening from 16% in 1925 to 31% in 1929." During the 1930s, indeed, the differences were "dramatic ... The academic student of the early 1930s was almost 4 times as likely to reach the 4th year of high school as his or her vocational counterpart; at the end of the decade he or she was still 2½ times as likely to progress that far."[25]

Taken together, what the two data sets suggest is that surging vocational enrolments were the result, in the main, of the extension of compulsory attendance to age 15, or in urban Ontario to age 16. Clearly some students had real choice between either an academic or a vocational program, though many did not. Nor did the majority of students select the practical subject options offered within the academic program or the "general" programs increasingly promoted in the provincial programs of studies. Rather, they enrolled in the matriculation or normal school programs, or some combination of the two.

The question is, why? Why the gap between the revised and broadened provincial programs of studies and actual enrolment patterns? Why indeed the enormous enrolments in the "foreign languages," or in algebra, compared to more practical subjects? Why the dominance, right across Canada and not only before but during the interwar years, of the academic curriculum?

The first answer is that while the provincial programs of studies for secondary schools listed a large number of subjects that might be offered, only a much more limited number were mandated. Increasingly, senior education officials did their best to encourage the introduction of a wider variety of subject options and program alternatives to meet what they believed to be a more diverse clientele and the need for a more relevant curriculum. But given the financial circumstances of the schools and the variation in school size, they were not prepared to impose these innovations; it would have been impossible to do that and they well knew it. So implementation remained optional for local boards. A condition of the high school grant was a level of instruction beyond elementary school in a group of core subjects. But nothing required a board to buy typewriters, open a general shop, or equip a classroom kitchen, let alone add entire new programs of studies. It was not until the late 1930s or early 1940s, and only in some provinces, that department officials began to mandate a broader curriculum, and even then only for the intermediate years, grades VII to IX.

A second answer applies more specifically to the introduction of vocational programs. We know of only one systematic record of the relative cost of academic and vocational programs, that for Ontario, year by year, beginning in the early 1920s. This does not include capital costs – the price of a new building or the cost of adding a new wing to an existing school. But in 1921–22, the *per-pupil operating cost* for Ontario's continuation schools was $87.55; for its high schools and collegiate institutes, $108.91; and for its vocational schools, $210.37. In 1936–37, simply to cite another example, the costs were $95.07, $119.60, and $169.44 respectively.[26] That is to say, vocational programs were *very* expensive, so expensive indeed that during the 1920s whole provinces failed to take up their share of the funds for vocational programs available from the federal government under the Technical Training Act of 1919 because they could not (or chose not to) provide the matching grants the act required without plundering other essential services.[27] During the Depression, not surprisingly, even Ontario added only ten new vocational programs to the fifty-four it had established in the first three decades of the century.[28] Vocational schools remained the preserve of high-enrolment, assessment-rich school boards. Analysing the statistics from the Ontario *Annual Report* for 1934, one advocate of vocational education took note of the fact that the province had 426 academic secondary schools, 321 of which had fewer than 200 students: "These schools have approximately 25,000 students. A further examination of the same report reveals the astonishing information that not more than four of these schools are making any attempt whatever to offer opportunities for vocational training to their pupils."[29]

But it was not just a matter of full-fledged programs of studies. *Any* additional subject option beyond the minimal core could present problems for Canada's smaller school boards. Enrolments in domestic science classes, for example, were far lower in Ontario's high schools than in its collegiate institutes, either for reasons of cost or the unavailability of specialist teachers; in Ontario's continuation schools, manual training or domestic science classes were virtually unknown.[30] By 1930 in that same province, nearly half the collegiate institutes offered commercial subjects but only 44 of 128 high schools did, and almost none of the continuation schools.[31] In the mid-1920s none of British Columbia's rural high schools offered any commercial or technical subjects, nor did they provide instruction in manual training, domestic science, or even agriculture.[32] In Manitoba in 1939, 46% of grade ix urban boys took "Practical Arts" (i.e., manual training); in rural Manitoba the figure was 1.6%. Nor was the gap in available options limited to the so-called practical subjects: grade ix Latin enrolments in urban centres stood at 28.6%, and in rural areas, at 7.5%.[33] Some of the difference might be explained by lack of demand, but more likely it was due to the lack of a qualified teacher or to the fact that the only qualified teacher was investing all her time in French instruction – or that the high school only had one or two teachers to cover the entire curriculum. If Latin was wanted in Calgary or Lethbridge, one took it for granted that it would be available. But not in the Crowsnest Pass. Latin wasn't taught in Blairmore until 1933, at which point the board was presented with a parental petition demanding it. There were, the petition claimed, about "twenty pupils who wished to start. That pupils studying for any of the Professions were handicapped on entering University by not having a knowledge of Latin." The board debated and the principal noted that there was also a demand for physics and art, but none of the three could be taught with the existing staff unless other subjects were sacrificed. So in the midst of the Depression the board, no doubt with great reluctance, hired an additional teacher and ordered that "Latin, Physics 2 and Art 1 be added to the curriculum."[34]

The simple fact of the matter was that the country was littered with small-enrolment high schools where one, two, or three teachers tried to teach all the subjects required by the program of studies along with those the majority of their students might need for their different career plans. "The chief defect of the small high school," wrote one experienced observer from British Columbia, "is the inelasticity of its program of studies. With a small staff and limited equipment, it can offer only a few, if any, electives or optional courses. Even if it makes use of as many as possible of the devices for conserving teacher time, its electives are usually 'more of the same thing': often they cannot include the so-called 'practical' subjects, which are bulking ever larger in the modern secondary school."[35] In its own survey of rural education, an Alberta legislative committee summed up the issues succinctly in 1935:

This general failure of school boards to provide a more diversified course is quite understandable. Until comparatively recent years there was no great demand for training other than of the traditional academic type. Since the demand became urgent money has been hard to get, and, to diversify, costs more. The great majority of our high schools are small, and it has been beyond the ability of the small school to diversify its programme. To provide technical courses requires extra room and equipment. Not being able to provide both the academic course and technical and commercial training as well, school boards have invariably chosen to meet the needs of the few who wish to prepare for the Normal school or the University, and this notwithstanding the fact that the teaching of technical and commercial subjects has been encouraged by extra grants.[36]

But the problem was not just small schools and limited fiscal capacities. There was also the sheer familiarity and prestige of the matriculation certificate, based as it was on external examinations. During the interwar years, departmental officials had done their best to give the high school curriculum a legitimacy independent of the matriculation certificate. In nearly every province the attempt to broaden the program of studies was accompanied by the creation of high school "leaving" or "graduation" diplomas, awarded to pupils who completed a full high school course regardless of the particular subjects or course packages they had chosen to pursue. And in most jurisdictions the diploma was detached from the external examination system by making it dependent on the principal's recommendation alone.[37] The aim was to provide public recognition for courses and programs other than the matriculation program and to encourage students to diversify their course selections. Yet students still poured into the matriculation program.

One explanation was that as high school enrolments rose, employers increasingly used the matriculation certificate as a winnowing device in their hiring policies for white-collar jobs. Despite the fact that Manitoba had a "School Leaving Certificate" that allowed a general education based on a wide variety of options, half of Winnipeg's grade x and xi pupils selected the matriculation subjects. "This does not mean that a university course is the objective of all these pupils," the board noted in 1937. "Matriculation standing is better known as a standard of achievement to employers and to the general public than is the High School Leaving."[38] Despite repeated attempts to broaden the program of studies through the introduction of general and vocational courses, one Saskatchewan educator complained in 1944, "the public has accepted the academic course as superior to any other high school course, and consequently, a large majority of students who do not plan to attend either the University or the Normal School still insist on taking the full academic course."[39] By 1931 Moncton's high school commercial program had been in place for nearly a decade, but the school board's annual report of that year asserted that "this course has never been as popular as its merits would seem to warrant. It is admirably suited to the requirements of many pupils who will not be going to Normal School or college. A large part of those pupils however continue to take the matriculation course."[40] "Most boys and girls beginning a collegiate institute course hope to obtain a matriculation certificate," one senior Toronto schoolman explained. "One of the chief reasons is that businessmen frequently demand a matriculation standard of prospective employees."[41] This common complaint among those who sought to broaden the high school curriculum throughout the interwar years was occasionally even echoed in the popular press. Writing in the *Globe* in 1929, the headmaster of St Andrew's College, Aurora, and vice-chairman of the University of Toronto's board of governors, a man who could hardly be accused of anti-intellectualism, remarked that "the public place far too much stress on the importance of matriculation. Businessmen, insurance companies, wholesale houses, even manufacturers have only one question to ask a boy who applies for a position: 'Where is your matriculation certificate?'"[42] A *Maclean's* editorial in 1934 ruminated upon the "fetish of matriculation." Employers "won't employ a youth to nail up packing cases or tend an electric switch unless he can produce at least a junior matriculation certificate. What necessary connection is there between a qualification for entrance into a university and for entrance into occupational life?"[43]

The universities had to bear their share of opprobrium. The "Latin bar" in Ontario was still firmly in place until well into the 1930s, accounting, according to the minister of education, for the fact that "84% of students enrolled in Lower School take Latin because of it."[44] In the West, the universities had gradually abandoned requirements for two foreign languages, so that Latin became far less of an obstacle (though that also explains the continuing reign of French).[45] That only encouraged the complaint to switch focus. "Even in the larger centres where alternative curricula are offered," sniffed one reform-minded group of Calgary schoolmen, "most of the students insist on taking the subjects leading to matriculation, regardless of any question of aptitude or suitability, owing to the glamour of university 'culture' which has been thrown around these courses."[46]

More generally, blame was laid on "the paralyzing hold of tradition on public opinion."[47] This was a familiar lament even early in the century. As John Seath once put it in an influential 1911 report, the hold of the academic program arose from "the general desire for an occupation that allows 'clean hands and good clothes.'"[48] A decade later James Bingay described Nova Scotia's departmental examinations as "a curse to education." No matter how often senior officials insisted that they were only suitable for candidates preparing for matriculation or teaching, "shoals of students who have not the remotest intention of teaching go up for them every year. Conditional admittance to colleges on a government certificate, and the premium placed on such a certificate by the public at large, is too powerful an incentive for any but well-staffed high schools to withstand. Even some of these, particularly county academies, are often ill-advised enough to advertise the 'success' of their students at these examinations ... The result is that the general public has almost lost sight of the object of high schools, conceive of them as cramming institutions for examination purposes, set before their children the passing of an examination as their goal, and demand that the subjects selected by them be such as will be most likely to assist in obtaining that object."[49] Commenting on a ministerial proposal to introduce practical agriculture courses in Ontario's schools in 1930, one prominent trustee told an Ontario Educational Association audience that there was no demand for such courses: "The general idea is that the academic course leads to the university, and is the road that must be travelled by all who wish 'to get on in the world.' It is also frankly said by many rural people that they do not want their children to have to work as hard as their parents have had to work, and academic education is looked upon as the way out."[50]

The virtues of vocational training, moreover, were often less obvious than its advocates claimed. In his study of business education in British Columbia, Graham Bruce observed that "less than 8% of female workers in the mercantile industry and less than 1½% of the female workers in office occupations are under 18 years of age." Yet most girls left school in grade IX or X, and a year or two of typing or shorthand followed by a long period of disuse "almost nullifies the value of early training." Benefits were only realized, he added, by completing a full course of commercial training.[51] But even then, wrote Harold Weeks, in yet another study, "[i]n the past business men have complained about the lack of general knowledge exhibited by most commercial graduates. They have in many instances preferred to employ academic graduates who have had a good grounding in the academic subjects and in so doing are perfectly willing to bear the expense of business training in their own offices. They feel justified in doing this because they claim they secure a product that is more likely to progress to advanced positions. If their claim is true they possess damning evidence against the efficacy of the commercial program."[52] There were also limits to the usefulness of other types of vocational education. In most places, wrote F.H. Sexton, a Nova Scotian and noted authority on technical training, instruction was limited to a relatively narrow range of occupations such as printing or automotive repair. While these trades were common in most communities, equipping school shops was very expensive "and it was manifestly impossible to give instruction for the wide range of trades that are found in every town and city where a vocational school might be justified." Large communities did better than smaller ones in this respect, "but there is still reason for just criticism that the day courses train too many people for a very few occupations and neglect to provide facilities for preparing young people to enter the great majority of gainful vocations."[53]

In all probability, any or all of these considerations played a role in weighting curricular biases towards the academic program. Undoubtedly there was the sheer, uncontested prestige (its enemies would have said tyranny) of the academic program among parents, students, and teachers alike. Intimately associated with the idea of a "liberal education," the gateway to the universities and the learned professions, the usual requisite for white-collar rather than blue-collar work, the academic program was sanctified by

tradition and exercised a palpable grip on the organization of the occupational and social hierarchy. But paradoxically perhaps, the academic program was also pre-eminently *practical*, in the sense that it led to good jobs. In
that respect, there was nothing more practical than Latin or algebra.[54] The
academic high school *was*, in its own way, a vocational school – or perhaps
better put, the pre-vocational program for the higher echelons of white-
collar work. The growing minority of pupils who stayed to complete grade
XI or XII were there to obtain qualifications – for the universities, the normal schools, the nursing schools, the one-year "special commercial" courses
that led on to many preferred and better-paying types of office work, and
other opportunities accessible only through the schoolhouse door. They
either knew where they were going or they had yet to make up their minds.
In the latter case, parents, teachers, and students alike colluded to select a
program that kept all their options open.

Even in urban communities where real program choices did exist,
Alberta's Committee on Rural Education noted, students still flocked to
the matriculation course: "Apparently parents and teachers, being uncertain when the pupil enters high school what aptitudes he may develop, are
reluctant to direct him into the Commercial, Technical, or General Course
lest he should afterwards wish to go to the Normal School or the University,
and find himself on the wrong road."[55] In a 1937 memorandum addressed
to "the Students of Grade VIII," Vancouver's head of educational guidance
judiciously explained each of the programs offered in the city's schools.
Students could pick, he pointed out, from any of the four – junior matriculation, normal school entrance, commercial studies, and technical – and
each offered advantages. But in a telling concluding paragraph he added,
"If you have not yet made any decision concerning your vocation, and if
there is no immediate necessity for doing so, your best plan may be to attend
a high school offering courses which will be accepted for both university
matriculation and [the] High School Graduation [diploma]."[56] Some years
earlier the Winnipeg school board had taken note of the fact that "even
in the Commercial Course, which is primarily intended for those who will
leave school on the completion of Grade X, many students elect one foreign language in order that they may either immediately upon completion
of Grade X, or at some later time proceed to a course in Grade XI leading to Matriculation."[57] Or as the Vancouver guidance memo pointed out,
while commercial studies were available in most of the city's high schools,
if students wanted to enter the University of British Columbia's BCOMM
program, they "must take university matriculation" – and even pharmacists
"must matriculate with Latin."[58]

Assessing the impact of Alberta's revised program of studies of 1922,
Lethbridge's superintendent of schools noted that it provided for six

different programs: "Of these we do not offer the Technical course, not through lack of desire but through lack of equipment and finances. We do not offer the Agricultural course for two reasons: in the first place we find little demand on the part of students ... and, in the second place those students who select [it] find themselves up against a real barrier to further progress, especially those wishing to obtain Junior Matriculation or enter Grade XII ... As for the General Course, only an occasional student selects it." Lethbridge, he continued, did offer the commercial course and had substantial enrolments in it. But the majority opted for an academic program. That meant either the normal entrance course, which had a fair variety of options, or the matriculation course, which had nearly none. "So, of these two academic courses, one says 'Choose' and the other says 'I dare you to choose.'" And since the majority of grade IX or X students didn't know which they wanted – and could hardly be expected to at that age – they opted for those subjects that would qualify them for both.[59]

II

The common academic curriculum, we have suggested, existed in large part because of a combination of financial exigency and the crippling effects of delivering so much secondary education in such small units of instruction. The same circumstances radically reduced the opportunity to offer extracurricular activities. Most schools in the cities and larger towns might have such facilities as gymnasiums, auditoriums, and outdoor playing fields, as well as support for student activities such as sports, clubs, dramatics, orchestras, and student councils. But high schools in smaller places mostly lacked such amenities. The chief inspector of schools for Nova Scotia noted in 1929 that "in the larger schools and *a few* of those of smaller enrolments, athletics flourish under the teacher"; the majority of schools evidently had little beyond athletics.[60] Writing in 1936 about provision on the other side of the country, a teacher in British Columbia remarked that except for some sports activities, the extracurriculum in the one-room high school was minimal or non-existent, citing "the lack of gymnasium equipment ... Clubs, etc. ... must be ruthlessly subordinated to the curricular subjects ... the small attendance in rural high schools also helps curtail such extra-activities."[61] Even where extracurricular activities were well established, moreover, we still need to know the extent to which they engaged substantial portions of the adolescent population. We have, after all, pointed out in chapter 2 that only a minority of those aged 14 through 17 attended high school, and only a minority of that minority persisted beyond grade IX or X; or to put it another way, the majority never experienced high school, and for the majority of those who did, the experience was fleeting. Was the experience of the extracurriculum equally limited?

We have been able to locate only three systematic, province-wide surveys on the subject, all made during the 1930s. One study reported in 1939 on student activities in differing sorts of Saskatchewan high schools. The "city high school," with more than four rooms and large enrolments, usually had a gymnasium and auditorium, though limited playground space, and a range of teacher-supervised student activities. Then there was the four-room high school, in smaller towns, which usually had adequate playgrounds and might have an auditorium and gym; extracurricular activities *might* be supervised by staff. A third type was the "characteristic small-town high school," with two rooms, drawing pupils both from the town and the surrounding countryside; its outdoor facilities might be adequate but its indoor ones were often not, and "the extra-curricular program being entirely or largely under the direction of two teachers, already overloaded with curricular work, will likely be limited." Finally, the "small village high school," with a higher proportion of rural youngsters, had an extracurriculum that was probably "under the direction of the principal, who will find himself even more overloaded with curricular work than his brother in the small-town school."[62] These last two categories included 90% of the schools and enrolled over 40% of the student population.[63]

In all Saskatchewan schools, whatever their size, sports were by far the most popular and common student pastime. But the extent and variety depended on available facilities and equipment and might be very restricted. According to the author of the 1939 study, "During the depression years, softball, requiring a minimum of playground space and equipment, became the high school sport most played by boys and girls." Participation in other sports was modest or minimal. And the larger the school, the smaller the proportion of either boys or girls taking part in extracurricular sports, both because in the smaller schools almost everyone participated and because pupils in the larger schools, intent on academic success in preparation for careers, tended to abandon extracurricular activities in their senior years of high school. Non-athletic activities involved many fewer students. About 30% of girls and 16% of boys took part in "literary societies"; the next five most popular activities – debating, dramatics, "civic organization" (i.e., class executive or student council), choir, and school paper – had far lower participation rates for both boys and girls. The author concluded that "a large percentage of the pupils are not being reached" by extracurricular activities and that "many may complete their high school courses practically immune to the important socializing influences ascribed to participation in the extra-curricular program ... About 80 percent of the Saskatchewan high school enrolment participates in one or more sports ... [but] about one third of the entire high school population does not participate in any non-athletic activities." No less indicative was the response of "70 out of 79 of the school principals" that the chief problems in mounting an extra-curricular program were "unsatisfactory facilities" and "financial support ... limited, mainly, to the efforts of the pupils, school boards donating only 25.3 per cent of all such costs." None of the one-room high schools sampled had an auditorium, a gymnasium, "adequate gym equipment," or "adequate outdoor equipment." Facilities in two-room schools were nearly as poor, with only 5% having auditoriums, 14% outdoor provision, and none rated as adequate for equipment indoor or out. Less than one-quarter of even the three-room schools had auditoriums, and barely 20% had good outdoor grounds.[64]

A second survey reported in 1938 on the extracurriculum in Alberta high schools.[65] In schools large and small, the author concluded, the major-ity of students took part only in athletics (softball, with its limited demands on equipment, ranked highest, as in Saskatchewan). "On the average, the time spent by students on work connected with [school] organizations is comparatively little. In many cases no time is devoted to this work," and the average student spent no more than one hour a week on non-athletic activi-ties outside class. The two main reasons for this were that many schools lacked any extracurricular clubs and, where established, they tended to be "dominated by cliques ... little attempt is made to attract other students."[66] In addition, it was clear that rural and small-town schools in particular had low participation rates in almost everything other than sports. Although in schools in the larger urban areas a minority of students were accused of engaging in a frenetic round of extracurricular activities, to the detriment, as teachers and principals often noted, of their academic work, many other students in those schools bemoaned the pressure of schoolwork that pre-vented much or any participation in the extracurriculum.[67]

A third study, this time of British Columbia high schools at the begin-ning of the 1930s, had anticipated many of these conclusions. Though athletics were, again, the most popular activity, the physical plant was inadequate. "[N]early 80% of the high schools are without gymnasia of any kind," and while most had playing fields, the quality of the fields in three-quarters of small schools was rated as only middling or worse.[68] Non-athletic activities tended to be very circumscribed in the small high school. Even in large ones, fewer than half had student self-government; just over half, dramatics; and much less than that number had other extracurricu-lar activities. The author blamed the heavy teaching load in small schools for the restriction on activities outside class time, as well as "the fact that many students attending small schools live a considerable distance away, and the necessity for a large number of rural children to work at home means that often if extra-curricular activities are to be engaged in, time must be taken out of the school day," which was already crammed full with the academic curriculum.[69]

More limited studies, in this case of Canada's larger urban areas alone, point in similar directions. A 1938 survey of schools in the greater Victoria area revealed, among other things, that long-established Victoria High School had a "large gymnasium ... admirably suited" for the physical education program but "the smaller room which has to be used frequently is quite inadequate" and "more recreational activities are desirable."[70] Student government was "too limited" and the few student clubs that operated "embrace a very small percentage of the student body." Oak Bay, in a prosperous suburb of Victoria, received a glowing report for facilities and the athletic program; but it too lacked participation in student government, and it had only two clubs. Elsewhere the situation was worse. Esquimalt High School had limited playing grounds and a gym "too far away to be convenient for effective use"; it had three clubs, but no student government. The three Saanich high schools were modern, and each had an auditorium that could be used as a gym; but one of them had no gym equipment and "the new playing field was not in shape for use at any time during the survey owing to the lack of drainage," although "a good programme of sports" was carried out. In the smallest school there was little equipment for physical activity, no student council, and clubs consisted of a weekly choir meeting and a Friday-afternoon literary society. In all the high schools "music was hardly functioning at all." It was not taught as part of the program except in Victoria High School and "to a slight extent" in Oak Bay. Most schools had only a girls' choir, and only Victoria had both a girls' choir and a student orchestra.[71]

Perhaps most revealing is the survey on the state of the extracurriculum in Toronto schools in 1935.[72] Here, if anywhere, we should expect to encounter a full range of activities engaging a substantial proportion of the student body. Yet in this large urban system, with its nine collegiate institutes and six vocational schools enrolling some 22,500 students, specific activities, apart from, as usual, intramural sports, involved quite small numbers.[73] In the most popular intramural sport, basketball, boys numbered about 4,500 and girls something just over 2,000. Softball, swimming, track and field, and volleyball had similar participation rates. In other sports the numbers were much smaller. Far fewer students were on inter-school teams: approximately 390 boys in senior rugby, 120 to 135 in soccer, and the largest group, 780, in track and field events. Then there were the non-athletic activities, with generally fewer participants again. Popular annual events like school bazaars involved perhaps a quarter of the students. But school choirs attracted only some 220 boys and 620 girls in all; school orchestras, about 200 boys and 120 girls; camera clubs, about 190 boys and 100 girls; dramatics, some 600 boys and 750 girls; school magazines, about 500 boys and 430 girls; literary societies, about 1,300 boys and 1,900 girls; and student councils, some 656 boys and 243 girls in vocational schools (there were none listed for the collegiate institutes). No doubt many of these separate activities involved the same students, and thus the number of students who did *not* participate in the extracurriculum may have been larger than even these figures suggest. Overall, we think it probable that many students in this metropolitan school system had nothing much to do with school activities outside of class.

The large urban high school, in sum, was only one, relatively modest, component in a pattern of educational provision marked by great diversity and dominated by small-enrolment high schools. The secondary school grades were offered in a bewildering variety of institutional settings, including many one-, two-, and three-room high schools, commonly enough even in one-room elementary schools, and by teachers whose qualifications for offering secondary-level instruction varied wildly. The high school, moreover, could not yet be described as "the central institution of modern adolescence," nor had the extracurriculum become the "normative culture" for youth. Until at least mid-century the majority of adolescents still did not attend high school, and for those who did, their experience, apart from the narrow core of academic subjects, had few common elements.[74] They were exposed to radically different learning environments and opportunities to participate in extracurricular activities. And this pattern of educational provision would persist until, in the two decades after mid-century, Canadian secondary education was transformed by growing prosperity, increasing urbanization, better roads and the school bus, and, in particular, spiralling participation rates, all of which gradually converted the high school into an indisputable centre for a universally shared adolescent experience and a powerful agent in generating a distinct and coherent youth culture.

III

In much of the literature on program or subject enrolment patterns, two factors are usually assigned an influential role in program choice or placement: social class and gender.* To take but one recent example, Scott

---

* Some readers may be puzzled by what they take to be repetition of points already made in chapter 3 about adolescent school attendance and social mobility. In that chapter we focused on total numbers by age; here we are investigating a different question: the distribution of students by programs of studies or curricular options.

Davies and Neil Guppy offer this sweeping generalization encompassing both gender and social class: before mid-century, boys and girls "were often segregated at older ages, with girls steered towards 'domestic science' and most boys towards trades, though a few boys were selected for advanced studies."[75] To what extent are claims such as these justified?

It is not easy to answer that question because the data are inadequate to the task. In the case of social origins, provincial-level data are available for Ontario only and one cannot simply assume they apply elsewhere. Even for Ontario, we can compare only academic versus vocational enrolments, and not matriculation, normal school, or other tracks within the high school.[76] Program comparisons, moreover, are possible for just a decade, from the early 1920s to the early 1930s. And the data that do exist are flawed. The salience of social class in patterns of program enrolment is, nonetheless, a central part of the literature on "streaming" or "tracking" in the schools; that literature, in turn, raises some fundamental questions about degrees of equality of educational opportunity and the extent to which the schools are complicit in the reproduction of social class. Thus the issues are too important to be ducked whatever the inadequacies of the data. Since this is all we have, we will make what use of it we can, with the caveat that conclusions should be treated with caution. They may be indicative but hardly more than that, and they may turn out to be wrong.

The Ontario Department of Education collected data on the occupations of the parents of high school students in each individual school, grouping occupations into categories such as the professions, "commerce," "trades," "labouring occupations," and a few others.[77] Historians have classified the former two categories (along with "agriculture") as white-collar, middle-class, or non-manual occupations, and the latter two as blue-collar, working-class, or skilled and unskilled manual occupations. Since there was only modest change during the decade when comparisons are possible, we will use a single year, 1929–30, to illustrate the results.[78]

In the academic programs in Ontario's collegiate institutes and high schools, 33% of enrolments were drawn from the manual categories ("trades" and "labouring"), with by far the largest proportion from trades. In the vocational programs, non-manual enrolments amounted to 24%. That is to say, neither program drew exclusively from a particular segment of the social hierarchy and one cannot adequately describe the vocational programs as near-exclusive enclaves for the working class.[79] There was, nevertheless, a clear bias in enrolments. In the academic program about 50% of students were from non-manual occupations, about 33% from trades and labour, with about 17% "other" or "without occupation." In the vocational programs about 24% were of non-manual origin, 51% manual, and 25% "other" or none. If we compare the 1929–30 enrolment figures with the distribution of the Ontario labour force in 1931, we find that in the academic program those from commercial backgrounds were over-represented by about 5%, professionals' sons and daughters roughly matched the percentage of fathers in the labour force, and trades and labour were under-represented by about 10%. In the vocational programs the professions were substantially under-represented, commerce matched its proportion of the labour force, and trades and labour were over-represented by somewhere between 5% and 10% (though this would be a much higher figure for the labouring category alone).[80]

Two local studies are also helpful.[81] In an essay on the Toronto Technical High School, Ruby Heap concludes that from 1905 to 1920 "students came mainly from the working class, although those heads of families who were engaged in commerce formed an important group" during these years.[82] The "mechanical occupations/trades" (or skilled manual workers) constituted a far larger proportion of enrolment than did unskilled labour, but overall, working-class representation in the Toronto Technical School was substantially greater than in Toronto's academic high schools during the same period.[83] Craig Heron's study of Hamilton offers a comparison of academic and vocational enrolments in that city. During the late 1920s and early 1930s, he finds, "the percentage of high school students whose father worked in a trade or labouring occupation increased in the academic schools to between 30 and 40 percent"; in the same period, students from blue-collar families increased from a half to two-thirds of vocational enrolments.[84] The vocational figure for Hamilton is somewhat higher than it is for the whole province, but the percentages inevitably varied from town to town depending on the relative proportion of the various social strata and the size and sophistication of the vocational programs.[85] The figures also vary because in the high schools (as opposed to the collegiate institutes and vocational schools) students from an agricultural background were an important component of enrolment. Finally, we noted that vocational enrolments included a substantial minority from non-manual backgrounds. We think much of this was due to the commercial course in the vocational schools and departments; certainly that was the case in both Hamilton and London, where, in 1930–31, students from non-manual backgrounds constituted a higher percentage in commercial (something like 30% entering the commercial course in London and 28% for all commercial enrolments in Hamilton) than in the technical courses (in London about 21% and in Hamilton 14%).[86]

To reiterate: the only large-scale database available to explore the social origins of English Canadian high school students in the interwar years – the data collected, organized, and published by the Ontario Department of Education in its *Annual Reports* – is flawed. And there appear to be few local

studies, either by contemporaries or historians, that can illuminate the matter beyond Ontario's borders.[87] We hope future research on this important question will improve on our efforts here. But to the extent that the
data can be relied upon, a summary might go something like this. Students
from both manual and non-manual backgrounds were to be found in
both Ontario's academic and vocational secondary programs – substantial
minorities of blue-collar students in the academic program (though far
more in the skilled than the labouring category) and substantial minorities
of non-manual students in the vocational schools (though more in the commercial than the technical courses). It is, in other words, more than a little
misleading to portray the Ontario secondary school as one where working-
class boys and girls were, willy-nilly, funnelled into vocational programs or
excluded from the academic high school. To put it bluntly, it just ain't true.
Indeed, in raw numbers, there were nearly twice as many Ontario students
from labouring families in academic as in vocational programs; similarly,
far more children from families in "The Trades" were in academic than in
vocational schools.[88]

But clear biases existed as well. By 1930 at least, higher percentages of
students from blue-collar families were to be found in vocational than in
academic programs, and for those from non-manual backgrounds, the
reverse was the case. Not all students had a choice in the matter, but for
those who held the high school entrance certificate, social origins played
one part in the matrix of factors that led them to select one type of program
over the other.

Where it existed, then, program differentiation within the secondary sector could serve as one site for both social mobility and class reproduction.
But Canada-wide the extent of program differentiation was limited before
mid-century by all the circumstances we have outlined in this and previous chapters. As we've tried to suggest in chapter 3, moreover, there were
far more powerful factors at work in determining career outcomes than
whether high school students found themselves taking Latin or woodworking, algebra or stenography.

To what extent can we say that the high school curriculum was gendered?
There were, obviously, some areas where boys and girls were educated
apart. Where physical education was taught, it was generally segregated by
sex, and that was probably true of health instruction for adolescents once
it started to include sex education of even the most tepid sort.[89] Two other
segregated subject areas were domestic science for girls and manual training or technical shops for boys. But just how many students were enrolled
in these two subjects? While the focus of this chapter is on the secondary school, we think that any fair assessment of the extent to which pupils

actually experienced gender segregation needs to extend across their entire school careers. Thus we propose to begin our analysis with the senior grades of the elementary school and then turn back to enrolments in the secondary schools.

By 1920 both manual training and domestic science were widely (though not universally) available in Canada's largest cities and towns.[90] A decade later, it was claimed that in Vancouver "every boy graduated from the elementary school has two or three years of [manual training]."[91] In British Columbia as a whole, manual training was "given in 15 cities, 12 rural municipalities, and several districts. Classes were conducted at 83 centres by 75 instructors with an enrolment of 12,250 elementary school pupils ... Home Economics was taught at 55 centres, to 9,250 elementary school pupils."[92] By 1927 Regina, Saskatoon, and Moose Jaw had between them four specialist teachers in elementary school home economics.[93] A couple of years later the Calgary school board could report that "manual training and domestic instruction are given for one-half day each week to all Grades VII and VIII pupils and overage pupils in Grades V and VI."[94] In Moncton by the 1930s, manual training for boys and domestic science for girls were taught in grades VI through VIII for one three-hour period a week.[95] By 1925–26, 71% of girls in Ontario's cities were enrolled in domestic science classes, and an even larger percentage of boys had access to manual training.[96]

But when it comes to province-wide figures, one has to draw a distinction between urban and rural enrolments, between larger and smaller urban centres, and, most probably, between urbanized Ontario or British Columbia and the other provinces. We say "probably" because hard figures are not easy to come by. As the education specialist at the Dominion Bureau of Statistics lamented in 1930, "Though most of the provinces made an effort to record the numbers studying each subject of the curriculum in secondary schools, data are seldom compiled on this subject for the elementary schools."[97] A co-operative effort to this effect between the DBS and the Saskatchewan Department of Education, however, was telling. In 1929–30, 24% of urban girls in grade VII but only 1% of rural girls were taught home economics, and 25% of urban grade VII boys received some instruction in manual training but only 2% of rural boys.[98] While a substantial majority of city girls in Ontario were enrolled in domestic science in 1925–26, the figure for town and village schools was only 6% or 7%.[99] Rural enrolments, at 11%, appear to have been somewhat higher, but that figure, we suggest, is misleading. In rural schools the subject was carried on by teachers with no specialist training and consisted, at best, of some sewing and general prescriptions about cooking and cleanliness. Hot lunches made on the school's wood stove might count as well, but needless to say, Ontario's one-room schools did not have kitchen classrooms.[100] A survey conducted by the Canadian Teachers' Federation found that in 1935–36 some 37% of urban boys in Nova Scotia took manual training, but in the rural schools only 75 of nearly 6,000 pupils were so enrolled. The figures were similar for domestic science. In Manitoba, that same year, all of the cities offered manual training and domestic science in grades VII and VIII, but only 2 out of 350 town schools did so, and none of the rural schools.[101]

This seems to have been the common pattern across the country: steady, if uneven, expansion in the cities and larger towns, much more limited provision in smaller urban centres, and little or none in the countryside; specialist teachers along with well-equipped shops and classrooms in the largest centres, much more makeshift expedients as one moved down the urban hierarchy.[102] That, of course, is not very surprising. Good intentions on the part of provincial authorities notwithstanding, the limited property tax assessment base of most rural school boards (and many small urban boards), an inexperienced corps of teachers, a crowded curriculum, and a heavy emphasis in the senior elementary grades on high school entrance examinations were hardly conducive to the encouragement of subjects that required considerable investment, specially qualified teachers, and some attention to that part of the curriculum that was not on department examination schedules. And all that is setting aside the doubts many local people had about the intrinsic worth or relative value of these two subjects.[103] For any or all of these reasons, manual training and domestic science remained optional subjects in the provincial programs of studies. Even when they were mandated as a symbol of progressive intent by provincial authorities – for example, in British Columbia's junior high program of 1936 – these two subjects were made compulsory only "in elementary schools in cities of the first and second classes" – the very places where such programs were already most likely to exist.[104] By the 1920s and 1930s, there were expedients that made manual training or home economics somewhat more available in rural areas than they might otherwise have been. Some manual training teachers, for example, worked a circuit that took them to several schools each week; perhaps the cleverest innovation was Nova Scotia's "shopmobiles" – buses converted into travelling manual training shops.[105] But effectively, manual training or home economics for many children would remain unavailable until after the Second World War.

During the interwar years, then, domestic science and manual training were widely taught in grades VII and VIII in the larger towns and cities, but more rarely in smaller urban centres or in rural areas. That is to say, large numbers of youngsters were never exposed to either domestic science or manual training in elementary school. It is also important to keep time allocations in perspective. An hour or an hour and a half a week, or even half a day, restricted to a couple of senior elementary grades, does not a gendered curriculum make when everything else is taught in common.

At the secondary level, in any case, these subjects had an even more limited reach.[106] When W.F. Dyde collected the 1923 statistics for enrolment by subject in six provinces, 7,759 students were taking manual training and 6,727 household science – this out of a total student population enrolled in English of 86,229. When he ranked the top sixteen subjects by enrolment, it was only in British Columbia that manual training and domestic science even appeared on the list and then in twelfth and fourteenth place respectively.[107] In the early 1920s, obviously, very few Canadian high school students took either subject. Across the period there were provinces where they were not taught at all – in Nova Scotia neither appeared before the 1930s, for example.[108] Until the late 1930s at least, Alberta's enrolments in either subject were negligible.[109] In Ontario, domestic science enrolments stood, in 1929–30, at 11% of the total number of girls in its collegiate institutes and 1.2% in its high schools. Only 4 of 143 high schools even offered domestic science, and only 1 of 217 continuation schools. Taking all Ontario's secondary schools into account – collegiate institutes, high schools, continuation, and vocational schools – something like 8%–12% of all girls enrolled in secondary education took some domestic science subjects.[110] In Saskatchewan's collegiate institutes and high schools in 1925, 29% of girls and 31% of boys were enrolled in either domestic science or shops.[111]

Enrolment figures such as these do not tell us how many girls or boys were actually exposed to either of these subjects. A total enrolment of, say, 33% might mean that all girls took domestic science for one year or that only 33% chose to take it at any time in their school careers. When in the mid-1930s domestic science was introduced in Nova Scotia, for example, it was taught in grade IX only and 33% of those in the urban high schools were exposed to it, almost all of them in Halifax and in the Sydney area. It simply wasn't taught elsewhere. If one takes into account all of the high schools in Nova Scotia – urban, village, and rural alike – only 18% of Nova Scotia girls had access to domestic science and only 19% of boys took "mechanic science" (the Nova Scotia term for manual training). And this is true only for the girls and boys enrolled in high school in the last decade of the period.[112] In Saskatchewan, on the other hand, 36% of the girls in the collegiate institutes and high schools in 1925 took domestic science in grade IX and 38% in grade X, but only 10% in grade XI (and just 1% in grade XII).[113] In British Columbia we have only total enrolments and not the distribution by grades, but as in Nova Scotia we can distinguish by geography: in 1929–30 some 33% of the girls enrolled in British Columbia's city high schools took domestic science; in the district municipality high schools the figure was 11%, and in the rural district high schools, 5%. Enrolments in woodworking, the most commonly available shop for boys, followed a similar pattern.[114]

While some domestic science courses might be available in regular academic high schools, the most vocationally oriented programs tended to be offered in the technical high schools. Here girls could obtain intensive job training, extending over two or three years, in either a commercial program or in domestic science and household arts. One track led to white-collar office work and the other to jobs with lesser or at least more ambiguous status (dressmaking, millinery, hygiene and dietetics, cooking, domestic service, etc.). Across the interwar years, two-thirds or more of those girls enrolled in Ontario's vocational schools were in the commercial program rather than domestic science.[115] The same appears to have been true in Saskatchewan and British Columbia.[116]

During the first three or four decades of the twentieth century, in other words, manual training and domestic science reached only a minority of Canadian high school students. A small number of girls were immersed in domestic science through their vocational school program. Many appear to have been exposed to it through one or sometimes two courses, taken in conjunction with a much larger number of academic courses taught in common to both boys and girls. And large numbers appear never to have taken it at all. The same holds true for boys' shops. In some provinces these subjects were options that students could select *if* their school offered them; many schools did not because local people were not willing to invest in the facilities they required. In other provinces they were not even part of the high school curriculum. Thus, at the very least, we need to exercise large dollops of scepticism when confronted by claims that a great many boys took manual training or that most high school girls were exposed to domestic science, to the particular values associated with it, or to the gender segregation it implied.[117]

A second area sometimes described as gender segregated is commercial studies. During the first three or four decades of the twentieth century the gender balance in office work was in transition, moving from an overwhelmingly male- to a female-dominated occupation, a transformation accompanied by a similar shift in the constituency for commercial courses in secondary education. What had begun in the nineteenth century as a business education exclusively for boys was on its way to becoming a near-exclusive preserve of girls. But either as options or as full-fledged programs, commercial subjects were still populated by males as well as females. In 1926–27, for example, typing and shorthand classes in British Columbia high schools were about 24% male.[118] In 1929 Saskatchewan's commercial enrolments in both its vocational and academic high schools averaged more than 30% boys.[119] From 1911 through to the Second World War, at Toronto's High School of Commerce, about a third of total enrolments were male, and in the interwar years the figure was only somewhat lower in Vancouver's High School of Commerce.[120] At the London Technical School, males represented about 20% of first-year commercial enrolments in the same period, and in 1930 about 24% of those attending Ontario's six stand-alone commercial high schools were male.[121] By 1939, in Manitoba's urban high schools, boys accounted for 25% of all those taking shorthand and fully 44% of those in typewriting.[122] Girls, in other words, were increasingly predominant in Canada's commercial classrooms, although boys continued to constitute a substantial minority of total enrolments and neither optional classes nor full-fledged programs could yet be described as a "pink ghetto." While the values taught in commercial classes might well equip students for subordinate roles in office work, moreover, we doubt they could be aimed exclusively at the girls when 20% or 30% of the classes were made up of boys.[123]

There is a more important question, however. While girls formed the majority of commercial students in the interwar years, just what *proportion* of all girls were enrolled in commercial? In Nova Scotia the answer is almost none up to 1939.[124] In Saskatchewan in 1925, 17% of high school girls were taking either a commercial program in one of the province's three vocational schools or typing, shorthand, and bookkeeping in a collegiate institute or high school.[125] In Alberta the figure was 14% in 1924 and 18% a decade later.[126] By 1926–27, 24% of the girls in British Columbia's city high schools were enrolled in typing, shorthand, and bookkeeping, about 20% in the district municipal high schools, and none in the rural district high schools. In 1929–30 the figures were slightly higher for city and municipal high schools but commercial subjects were still unavailable in the rural district high schools.[127] When, in 1929, commercial enrolment statistics first become available for the Hamilton school system, enrolments constituted 28% of that city's high school girls; by 1937 the figure stood at 33%.[128] For the entire province of Ontario, the proportion of girls taking commercial subjects out of all girls in secondary schools remained remarkably consistent in the interwar years, at around 27%.[129] Many of the larger Ontario secondary schools, moreover, offered both a "general commercial" stream begun in grade IX and a one-year "special commercial" course that required, for entry, all or most of a completed high school academic program. In London anywhere from 31% (1927) to 40% (1935) of girls enrolled in commercial were in fact taking special commercial, many of

them having graduated from high school and even a few who had graduated from university.[130]

Thus, not only did commercial classes absorb a substantial minority of
boys but most Canadian girls were *not* enrolled in commercial classes. Again
it must be said that this was not always a matter of choice. While commercial subjects were widely available in the larger urban centres, small high
schools often lacked either the staff or the facilities to offer them.[131] But
even where choice existed, a majority of girls were in academic, not commercial, programs.

Finally, here, is there any evidence of patterning by gender within the academic subjects themselves? Did girls, for example, tend to take Latin and
French, or boys math and science, in disproportionate numbers? The statistics, such as they are, suggest two things. In most high schools, where
enrolments were modest and teachers few, there was no gender patterning
because only the most limited number of courses could be mounted. In
the two provinces where we can distinguish by size of community, this is
clearly the case. In many of the rural and village high schools (and in some
of the smaller urban high schools) of Nova Scotia, in 1925 and 1931, not
even Latin or French was available and all students, girls and boys alike,
shared a narrow common curriculum. The same is true in the latter half
of the 1920s for the rural district high schools and district municipal high
schools of British Columbia. Where, however, enough subjects were taught
to allow academic options, there does appear to have been a modest tendency towards differentiation – in Halifax and in other Nova Scotia high
schools located in the larger urban centres and in urban British Columbia.
In 1926–27, for example, the statistics for the cities in the latter province
show a substantial number of *both* boys and girls enrolled in Latin, French,
algebra, and chemistry; but a greater percentage of girls took Latin and
French, and enrolments were proportionately higher for boys in algebra,
chemistry, and physics.[132] Whether these differences are proof of a pattern,
however, is a moot point. The statistical base is so limited, in time and space,
and the differences so modest, that we are reluctant to make a judgment
call. Given the evidence from later decades, we think it's plausible to suggest
that wherever choice existed, there were likely to be some patterned gender
differences in academic subject enrolments; but for the first three or four
decades of the twentieth century the record is just too thin, and alternative
interpretations too plentiful, to encourage conviction either way.

In our discussion here, we want to emphasize, we are not challenging the
idea that there were powerful currents of opinion favouring a differentiated

curriculum for girls and boys, or one peculiarly suited to girls, that we would now consider constricting, even misogynous. There were, indeed, women as well as men who, in the early 1920s, were complaining that the common curriculum and the co-educational classroom were far too co-educational for the good of either girls or boys.[133] Nor do we question the presence of bias in textbooks, other curricular materials, teachers' attitudes, or other manifestations in the life of the school.[134] What we have been describing is a historically specific set of circumstances that shaped program enrolments and patterns. In contrast to patterns that would become more common later in the century, the purpose of and clientele for secondary education in the early twentieth century were still relatively narrow. Except in urban Ontario, children could leave school at 14 or 15, many never reached high school, and those who stayed on tended to be preparing for a limited range of high-status professional and commercial occupations for which traditional academic training was a preferred criterion. Economic conditions, moreover, commonly discouraged gender-segregated programs. Whatever the level of rhetoric, Canadian schools were often too small and too poor to sustain the ambitions of educational missionaries intent on imposing domestic science on Canadian girlhood or turning them into well-trained and submissive secretaries. And even where the option existed, a majority of girls enrolled in academic, not commercial or domestic science, programs, testifying to the ability of students themselves, their parents, and probably a lot of their teachers to resist the dominant messages of the day. The result, in any case, was the common curriculum and the co-educational classroom that, with only comparatively modest exceptions, characterized early twentieth-century schooling.

The Teacher's Work

If the organization of instruction was largely directed by the provincial departments of education, it was teachers who translated regulations, policies, and programs of studies into classroom practice. In this chapter we turn to the teacher's pedagogical work. The weight of the chapter, however, falls upon the work of the rural teacher. While we devote some attention to the urban classroom, it is mainly to highlight the contrast between the urban, multi-grade school and its rural counterpart.[1] We begin, nonetheless, with the commonalities and more particularly the way in which law and custom determined the work routines that all teachers shared. We next turn to the work environment and then to the central pedagogical tasks teachers engaged in, describing what these were and how they were carried out. In the final part of the chapter we ask how well their professional training equipped them to do the tasks they were expected to perform.[2]

I

No matter what the setting, there was much that was generic in the teacher's work. In part this was because of requirements imposed on all teachers by the provincial education acts and their attendant regulations. Teachers everywhere, for example, had responsibilities for pupils' health and safety. "It shall be the duty of every teacher in the public schools," said the Nova Scotia Education Act, "to give assiduous attention to the health and comfort of the pupils, to the cleanliness, temperature and ventilation of the rooms, [and] to report promptly to the trustees the appearance of any infectious or contagious diseases in the school, or insanitary conditions of outhouses or surroundings."[3] These two injunctions were to be found in every school act. Teachers were not solely responsible for matters of health and safety; even more weight rested on the trustees, who were required to provide adequate accommodation, fenced schoolyards, a safe supply of drinking water, proper toilet facilities, and the like. But as the only adult in any Canadian classroom, the teacher bore a legal duty of care that demanded particular attention to anticipating, preventing or remediating, and reporting threats to the physical welfare of pupils both as individuals and as a group.

Similarly, all teachers had legal duties that went to the heart of the enterprise, the pedagogical task. In Ontario, for example, the section of the Education Act setting out the duties of the teacher began with this general statement: "to teach diligently and faithfully the subjects of the public school course of study, as prescribed by the Regulations; to maintain proper order and discipline in the school; to encourage pupils in the pursuit of learning." Subsequent clauses added specifics: teachers were to classify and promote pupils as directed by the program of studies, "to conduct the school according to a timetable accessible to pupils and visitors," and to hold public examinations at the end of term, "or at any other time the inspector might direct."[4] Clauses like this were to be found in every provincial school act, and the accompanying regulations often amplified them. A rather charming, though as a legal formulation unusually vague, British Columbia regulation required teachers "to furnish pupils with constant employment in their studies, and to endeavour by judicious and diversified modes, to render the exercises of the school pleasant as well as profitable."[5] In Alberta, on the other hand, there was the hard-edged injunction "to keep in a conspicuous place ... a timetable which shall show the classification of pupils, the subjects taught each day in the week, the length of each recitation period and the seat-work given; and to submit such timetable to the inspector for his approval and signature on the occasion of his visit to the school."[6] It was not, in other words, simply a matter of moral obligation or professional ethics to teach conscientiously, to do the best one could for each pupil, but a matter of law. In organizing instruction, teachers were told in no uncertain terms exactly what was expected of them, warned moreover that they could anticipate public scrutiny of their proceedings. The nature and extent of these prescriptions, and their similarity across the entire country, inevitably gave the teacher's work a degree of commonality regardless of particular settings.

Finally, the teacher's work also had a generic quality owing to what the American historians David Tyack and Larry Cuban term "the grammar of schooling." Everywhere, there were self-contained classrooms with one lone teacher in charge. All teachers taught lessons to groups of children; worked with them individually; prepared, supervised, and marked tests and seat-work assignments; oversaw playground activities; and kept the same kinds of records. Whether in urban or rural Canada, there were always rows of desks for the children and, at the front, a bigger desk for the teacher. There were blackboards, the compartmentalization of time around different subjects, and rules about raising one's hand to get the teacher's attention. By the early twentieth century these and other shared characteristics constituted "the cultural definition of a 'real school,'" a definition that most people – educators, children, parents, and other adults – took pretty much for granted.[7]

While law and custom created commonalities and gave teachers' work a certain homogeneity, settings nonetheless dictated differences. For one thing, in rural Canada teachers assumed a far wider range of work-related activities than did their urban counterparts. Preparing the building for the school day was one example. School boards in Winnipeg, Fredericton, or even Blairmore employed janitors to take responsibility for cleaning, heating, and building maintenance. When urban teachers arrived in the morning, they could expect warm classrooms, a supply of running water, clean floors and blackboards. While rural school boards usually contracted out major repairs or renovations and maintenance jobs such as painting the schoolhouse or providing a supply of coal or firewood, teachers, often with the assistance of their pupils, did much of the routine janitorial work. In rural British Columbia in the 1920s, for example, some 40% of teachers were wholly or partially responsible for cleaning the schoolhouse, lighting the fire each morning, hauling water for washing and drinking, even splitting the firewood.[8] Again, in the urban school, the teacher was part of a team looking after the welfare of children under their care. That meant shared duties for supervision before, between, and after classes, within the building and on the playground, and there was always help within reach in emergencies. As the only adult present, the rural teacher was singularly responsible, from the time children arrived in the morning till they departed in the afternoon. In an illuminating memoir of a career teaching in Alberta's one-room schools, Edith Van Kleek, recounting her experience with some unusually severe January weather, comments, almost in passing, "It was always necessary to show up at school; not to be there was unthinkable because no matter what the weather, surely some child would come."[9]

Rural teachers not only carried out the same daily health inspections as their urban counterparts, but when occasion demanded, they pulled out aching teeth or provided first aid in medical emergencies.[10] Again, Edith Van Kleek: "In one school where I went to teach I found many of the children had impetigo. No doctor or health nurse was available. The three-man school board ... was no help. Eaton's catalogue came to the rescue! Searching the index I found an item, 'Itch ointment for impetigo.' I sent for the biggest jar, which cost one dollar, postage paid. We used it according to directions on the jar. By the time the big jar was empty, all the impetigo in the school was cleaned up."[11] Rural teachers, indeed, might meet any exigency their skills or inclinations allowed. In compiling his several books about the one-room school, John Charyk left behind a remarkable archive of correspondence from ex-teachers across the country.[12] Reminiscing about teaching in rural Saskatchewan in the 1930s, one woman told him that she was also "the barber, having a pair of scissors and clippers. Any who did not have this equipment at home called on my services, and no one complained, even if the clippers did pull and they often did!"[13] After thirty years of teaching in Alberta's rural schools, Van Kleek would tell Charyk that her son "is presently working on new teaching methods in the very progressive city of Kitimat, BC. When I would tell him of the things I have done, like clean the long line of stove pipes after school or fish children's mitts from far below the toilet hole, he couldn't understand how any teacher could be fool enough to do such things."[14] Beyond all that, the rural teacher was exclusively responsible for relations with trustees and parents and for key parts of the community's social life. Teachers in urban schools, of course, had to do their part in the round of festivities that marked the school year, above all the Christmas concert, but they were part of a team. The rural teacher was on her own, and her reputation rested in part on the quality of the shows she could put on.[15]

In most urban schools the teacher's professional work centred on teaching a single grade filled with children approximately the same age. Their classrooms were directed by intellectual and behavioural norms appropriate to discrete stages of child development. In the main, teachers taught or supervised the class as a whole. They would normally prepare and conduct eight or ten different subject lessons a day, usually fifteen or twenty minutes long, and most lessons would be preceded or followed by seat-work and/or homework assigned to the entire class. (For an example of a timetable for the senior class in a graded classroom, see Figure 11.1.) The challenges of managing pedagogical routines and disciplinary requisites in a classroom of forty or more children could be demanding, and would be magnified if the teacher faced a "split class" of two grades with a wider range of ages and capacities. Urban teachers, nonetheless, worked in an environment with pre-established expectations, routines, and support systems. Timetables were mostly standardized, and subject content was often broken down into detailed, predetermined daily or weekly outlines of the work to be accomplished. While quantity and quality might vary, the odds favoured some tolerable level of equipment and supplies. When a neophyte stumbled or met unanticipated problems, advice and if necessary help were at hand. And at least in the larger urban boards, even experienced teachers could count on in-service professional development, routinely organized – year-in year-out – by the board's supervisory staff.[16]

TIME-TABLE FOR
ONE GRADE UNDER ONE TEACHER

Time	Mondays, Wednesdays, Fridays	Tuesdays, Thursdays
9.00- 9.07—	OPENING EXERCISES	
9.07- 9.12—Nature Study		Nature Study
9.12- 9.25—Spelling		Spelling
9.25-10.00—Arithmetic		Arithmetic
10.00-10.05—Physical Culture or Vocal Music		Physical Culture or Vocal Music
10.05-10.30—Grammar (Composition, Friday)		Grammar
10.30-10.45—	RECESS	
10.45-11.15—History		Composition
11.15-11.30—Writing		Writing, (or Book-keeping)
11.30-12.00—Reading		Supplementary Reading
12.00- 1.30—	NOON	
1.30- 2.00—Literature (Special Subject, Friday)		Literature
2.00- 2.15—Vocal Music and Physical Culture		Vocal Music and Physical Culture
2.15- 2.30—Nature Study		Nature Study
2.30- 2.45—	RECESS	
2.45- 3.15—Geography		Hygiene
3.15- 3.55—Manual Training, Household Science Agriculture (optional) (Special programme, Friday)		Art
3.55- 4.00—	CLOSING EXERCISES	

NOTE 1.—In this and the other time-tables in this Manual, the nature study of the first period in the forenoon consists of a discussion of the observations made by the pupils on their way to school. Such observations should be suggested by the teacher.

NOTE 2.—The teaching of Manners and Morals is to be provided for in connection with the lessons in Literature and Supplementary Reading. Further suggestions for conducting this Course will be found on page 187 of this Manual.

Fig. 11.1 A graded school timetable, Ontario, 1915

The experience of the rural teacher was fundamentally different. Once again, she was on her own, facing a group of pupils who might be of wildly varying ages, enrolled in several different grades, and to whom she had to teach all the prescribed subjects. The complexity of the task depended in part on the number of pupils in the school. Unlike urban classrooms, where a teacher could routinely expect forty or forty-five children (sometimes more but rarely fewer), numbers in the rural classroom were, on average, far fewer but also more variable.[17] Many schools might have twenty pupils or less, and fewer than eleven was not unusual. In her fine collective portrait of rural teachers in British Columbia's Okanagan Valley during the 1920s, Penelope Stephenson recounts an interview with one woman who "likened her position, ... where the numbers never rose above eight in the four years she taught at the school, to that of a 'governess job.'"[18] The metaphor is apt in another way: such schools were likely to consist of children from a handful of families. In rural Alberta in 1941, Pincher Creek School Division had thirty-five one-room schools and but a single two-room school. The average daily attendance per teacher was 11.48. Fourteen children from seven families attended Chipman Creek school; nine of them came from three families. At Dry Wood there were eight children from five families, *half* of whom came from one family; at Fir Grove, eleven of the twelve children came from three families.[19] One of Charyk's correspondents, schooled southwest of Medicine Hat, recalled that "we were the only family attending the school from 1932 to 1937, except for the first year when there were two other pupils. They moved away, which left our family the only ones attending the school."[20] Intimacy in the rural school arose not only from small numbers but from intricate family ties.

The number of grades and the number of pupils enrolled in each one mattered as well. In a rare piece of research from the 1940s, Norman High pursued these two issues in Haldimand County, Ontario. More than a quarter of the teachers in Haldimand's one-room schools (27%) had eight classes, 29% had seven classes, 30% had six classes, and about 12% had four or five. Sixty-two per cent of the classes had one to four pupils, and the most frequent number was three pupils per class; in a handful of cases, however, numbers per class rose to nine, ten, or eleven pupils.[21]

Teachers considered themselves lucky to have no more than five or six grades in any given year, and doubly so if there were no pupils to be prepared for the high school entrance exam (HSEE) and no pupils in a high school grade. But ten or twelve children could also be spread across all or nearly all the elementary grades, with quite possibly one or two above that. And the more grades, the heavier the workload. Then there were what one of Stephenson's interviewees labelled "teacher-killing" schools – those with thirty or more children enrolled in the full range of classes – schools where the workload of preparation, teaching, marking, supervising individual work, and maintaining discipline was so overwhelming that teachers left at the end of the first term or suffered mental or physical illness from the stress.[22] Complaining at mid-century about the number of low-enrolment schools with their high per-pupil cost, Manitoba's chief inspector noted that those schools "naturally are more successful in getting qualified teachers, with the result that heavy rural schools which need the best-trained and most experienced teachers are left to the beginners whose chances of success would be much greater in the low-enrolment schools."[23]

II

Like urban teachers, rural teachers had three central pedagogical tasks: teaching lessons, organizing the seat-work (or homework) intended to consolidate and extend the work of the lesson, and assessing pupil progress.* In rural schools, if there were enough children to warrant it, those in each grade would be seated together in rows or half-rows. Lessons might be taught where the children sat, but more commonly a group was brought together around the teacher's desk or at the blackboard for an explanation of new work, demonstrations of principles, practice exercises, or oral drill on previously assigned work.[24] Rural teachers, however, had to cover the subject matter of several grades and subjects. If taken literally this might mean, as one teacher titled an article, "36 Lessons in One Day."[25] Aside from imposing an impossible amount of preparation, this would have allowed "approximately nine minutes for each lesson" when anywhere from fifteen to thirty minutes was normally required. Thus priorities had to be set – and compromises made – that were unnecessary, or least avoidable, in the graded school. One result was a form of triage that put primary pupils and then senior pupils at the front of the line. Learning to read and write was the pre-eminent purpose of elementary education, so primary pupils got more than their share of the total time available. They also had short attention spans; as Nova Scotia's 1901 program of studies put it, primary pupils "may be necessarily made up of two or three if not more sub-classes, each of whom must be rapidly taken in turn – some in their letters, some in their primer, etc., but all must receive attention in these subjects three or four times a day, for they can do but little at a time."[26] Senior pupils came next because of the importance, to teacher and pupil alike, of preparing for and success at the HSEE.

A second kind of triage can be seen in the hierarchical ordering of subjects. Given the pressures of time and the fact that most children would receive only a comparatively few years of schooling, the emphasis in all grades fell upon the three Rs, often described as the "tool subjects" essential for all further learning. Other subjects were taught but received less time, and in some cases, such as music or art, were more akin to recreational breaks. This kind of subject ordering was more than just an ad hoc compromise; it was formally sanctioned. "It should be borne in mind by the teacher of the ungraded school in particular," noted an officially authorized Ontario normal school textbook, "that, with the inspector's approval, the content of the courses in Group II – hygiene, physical culture, art, nature study and vocal music – may be reduced, and that the subjects of Group III – bookkeeping, manual training, household science and agriculture – are

---

* Teachers' work extended beyond the strictly pedagogical, and we will review some of their other responsibilities in the next chapter. But our focus here is on that handful of key tasks that shaped classroom routines. By this means we hope to draw attention to aspects of the teachers' work that tend to be neglected or forgotten, and restore to the discussion the centrality of the pedagogical task. That, after all, is why teachers were hired in the first place.

110. A SUGGESTIVE TIME TABLE (Not prescribed).

(Miscellaneous "Common" School—40 pupils)

(a) = (Gr. VIII and VII), 7 pupils; (b) = (Gr. VI and V), 9 pupils; (c) = (G. IV and III), 11 pupils; (d) = (Gr. II and I), 13 pupils.

Time When.		Recitation in Class.		Seat Work.			
		Mondays Wednesdays Fridays	Tuesdays Thursdays	(a), (b), (c) and (d) as in Journal of Education.			
				(a)	(b)	(c)	(d)
9:00 to 9:10	10	Devotional Exercises........		......	......	......	......
9:10 " 9:15	5	Music........	Music........	......	......	......	......
9:15 " 9:30	15	(d) Readingetc	(d) Reading...	Arith.	Eng..	Eng....	......
9:30 " 9:50	20	(c) Reader etc.	(c) Reader etc.	Arith.	Eng..	......	Eng.
9:50 " 10:00	10	(b) Reader etc.	(b) Reader....	Arith.	......	Eng..	Eng.
10:00 " 10:15	15	(a) Reader....	(a) Hygiene...	......	Arith.	Arith.	Arith.
10:15 " 10:30	15	(a) Gram. etc.	(a) Comp.....	......	Arith.	Arith.	Arith.
10:30 " 10:45	15	Recess and a Song.					
10:45 " 10:55	10	(a) Arith......	(a) ArithorAlg	......	Arith.	Arith.	Slates
10:55 " 11:05	10	(b) Arith......	(b) Arith......	Arith.	......	Arith.	Slates
11:05 " 11:10	5	(c) Arith......	(c) Arith......	Arith.	Arith.	......	Slates
11:10 " 11:15	5	(d) Arith......	(d) Arith......	Arith.	Arith.	Arith.	......
11:15 " 11:30	15	(d) Reading...	(d) Reading...	Arith.	Arith.	Arith.	......
11:30 " 12:00	30	Writing.......	Drawing / Free or Math				
12:00 " 1:00	60	Noon Intermission.					
1:00 " 1:05	5	Music........	Music........	......	......	......	......
1:05 " 1:15	10	Geog. etc(oral)	His. etc. (oral)	G & H	......	......	......
1:15 " 1:30	15	(a) Geog......	(a) His........	......	Eng...	Eng...	Eng.
1:30 " 1:45	15	(b) Readeretc.	(b) Hygiene...	Arith.	......	Eng...	Eng.
1:45 " 2:00	15	(b) Gram. etc.	(b) Comp.....	or BK	......	Eng...	Slates
2:00 " 2:10	10	(c) Reader etc.	(c) Reader etc.	or Alg.	Arith.	......	Slates
2:10 " 2:30	20	(d) Reading...	(d) Reading...	Arith.	Arith.	Eng...	......
2:30 " 2:45	15	Recess and a Song.					
2:45 " 3:00	15	Nature Les.... (Botany, etc).	Nature Les.... (Physics, etc.)	......	......	......	......
3:00 " 3:05	5	(d) Arith.....	(d) Arith......	Arith.	Eng.	Eng.	......
3:05 " 3:10	5	(c) Arith.....	(c) Arith......	Arith.	Eng.	......	Arith.
3:10 " 3:20	10	(b) Arith.....	(b) Arith....	Arith.	......	Arith.	Slates
3:20 " 3:30	10	(a) Arith	(a)Arith orBK	......	Arith.	Arith.	Eng.
3:30 " 3:40	10	(c)Reading....	(c) Reading...	Arith.	Arith.	......	Eng.
3:40 " 3:55	15	(d) Reading..	(d) Reading...	Arith.	Arith.	Eng...	......
3:55 " 4:00	5	General Intimations........		......	......	......	......

Physical Exercises: When most convenient, preferably a little after the middle of each session for *two* minutes *three* or *four* times each day. Sometimes special time will have to be given to this subject, especially when the exercises are new.

Reading includes "Spelling," "Definition," "Grammatical" and other questions.

Geo. (oral) and *His.* (oral), includes "Geographical Nature Lessons," and 'M. and P. Duties."

Nature Lessons include Science generally from Gr. I to IX.

If there are IX pupils, they might aid by taking (d) classes sometimes, etc., and thus save time for Grade IX subjects.

Fig. 11.2   A one-room school timetable, Nova Scotia, 1921

at the option of school boards on the recommendation of the inspector."[27] Far up on the pioneer fringe, some fifty miles northeast of Edson, Alberta, in a small and desperately poor school division in the mid-1930s, the new teacher was told by her inspector "to forget History, Geography etc. and stress the three Rs as none of these children would ever have the opportunity of finishing school."[28]

There were other shortcuts. Nearly all the advice from officialdom, and from practising teachers, emphasized the necessity for groupings that cut across the grades. In the mid-1920s, for example, the editor of the *Western School Journal* suggested, as "Whole School Activities," penmanship, physical education, and school singing along with opening and closing exercises; "Junior and Senior Groups" for drawing, nature study, hygiene, and music; "In other subjects pupils will have to be treated as class groups."[29] Others suggested multi-grade groups for history, geography, civics, and science. The Nova Scotia timetable we reproduce here as Figure 11.2 offers another variation, effectively reducing eight grades to four, covering two years' work in all subjects. It was also common to send the primary children home in the early afternoon or for extended lunch breaks so that the teacher could give the older pupils some concentrated attention.[30] Yet another piece of advice was that "during the first couple of weeks of the school term considerable seat work may be given to Grades IV up to Grade VIII in way of review. This I found gave me some extra time for the little folks and an opportunity to 'break them in' and to teach them how to work on their own."[31]

Teachers generally were advised not to try to teach all the prescribed subjects every day, and extant timetables for both urban and rural classrooms indicate a conventional pattern in which the three Rs were taught daily and the other subjects on alternate days.[32] But this still left a very demanding workload. One Ontario guide suggested that "no teacher of an ungraded school should attempt more than 20 recitations a day" – which by urban (and one might add, modern) standards was a staggering amount of teaching.[33] Thus the routine in the ungraded school was round after round of rapid-fire lessons. As Nova Scotia's program of studies described it, "the pupils in such a school must be drafted to move without the loss of an instant of time, if the teacher is to be successful. There cannot be the leisure of a graded school."[34] Figure 11.2 gives some indication of just how demanding the rural teacher's day could be. Drawing up a timetable that fitted the circumstances of a particular school and, at the same time, giving at least a cursory nod to the full panoply of the prescribed curriculum was, wrote one Manitoba teacher, "almost like working out a Chinese puzzle."[35] Moreover, since timetables were, by regulation, public documents against which successful teaching might be judged by trustees and inspectors, they could become the stuff of nightmares. "Timetables – oh yes a living experience," one woman remembered decades later. "It was comparatively easy to draw up a timetable, but to adhere to it strictly was yet another matter. For years, I suffered a recurring dream, wherein the inspector on his arrival would find me teaching a subject contrary to what was designated on the posted timetable."[36]

The second pedagogical task was the provision of seat-work. While important in any classroom, this was a critical component of the ungraded school. A disciplined classroom absolutely depended on keeping most children quiet and busy while the teacher taught each succeeding group. And very large amounts of seat-work were essential because children spent so much time doing it. One Manitoba assessment from the mid-1920s estimated that "seat work represents about four-fifths of the school child's time"; another, that "the average student in the Rural School spends about 5 hours at seat work for one in classroom instruction."[37] In 1931 an Alberta inspector commented that "of the 4½ hours which a child spends daily on his school-work in school, he is engaged from 2½ to 3½ hours with the completion of exercises at his desk by himself. Much of his progress in school studies must depend on what he is doing this 65 or 75% of his time in school." For that very reason, the inspector added, "good educative assignments" were, in the rural school, "much more important than is the use of direct teaching through the lesson."[38] The teacher of only one grade also had to worry about seat-work, but it might amount to something like half the period or less for most subjects.[39] The rural teacher had to keep several classes busy for most of the day; each class or group required different assignments; and while teacher shoptalk tended to label much seat-work "busywork," it had, in the main, to be educative if a pupil's time was to be put to good use. Inspectors, indeed, expected to see the assignments specified in teachers' daybooks, and teachers were told, sometimes emphatically, that they must supervise seat-work: to maintain discipline and track pupils' progress, a teacher had to ensure that pupils were working at and completing assignments.[40]

The most serious seat-work problems arose with the younger children, who couldn't be expected to work on their own for long periods of time, were easily distracted, needed a variety of activities, and were best served by games and various handwork activities to keep them occupied.[41] But teachers also had to produce generous amounts of seat-work for all their pupils, and thus it's not surprising that the issue provoked endless articles in the professional press.[42] First-year teachers found the pressure to pro-duce adequate amounts of seat-work overwhelming. "There were two stu-dents in grade ix," Edith Van Kleek writes. "They had textbooks and could study by themselves, but the little ones nearly drove me crazy! I couldn't spend all my time with them and I couldn't find enough to keep them busy while I helped the older students." Over the years, however, she, like oth-ers, learned the tricks of the trade. Older pupils, for example, could learn geography by themselves from their texts without help from the teacher: "I discovered that drawing maps was very time-consuming, so I had them draw lots of maps ... I never taught a spelling lesson. They just wrote the words out umpteen times, which was delightfully time-consuming, giving me time to do something for the little ones."[43]

Such comments were not merely cavalier, or a cynical response by one teacher to a pedagogical problem. Rather they were *conventional* responses to a central structural feature of teaching in the one-room school. Another Alberta teacher, for example, bought sets of cards, covering nearly every subject and including instructions and exercises, that could be worked on at a pupil's desk and either self-marked or easily marked by the teacher. He taught in a "heavy ungraded school," an observer commented. "The cards do not enable him to teach without working, but they do relieve to an appreciable extent the pressing worry of keeping all the groups busy at once, and help out the poor blackboard space."[44] Or consider this advice from one teacher to another "for busywork for beginners": "Bring to school a bundle of magazines that have bright coloured pictures and advertisements. Give one to each beginner with a pair of scissors and you will find that they will sit quiet for half an hour. I have four beginners, and when thus occupied you would not know they were there." Another trick was to cut up postcards "into several pieces, put them into separate envelopes and number them." Each pupil received one envelope of these homemade jigsaw puzzles a day until he or she had completed the series. "Then, if the children can place the pieces together too rapidly, I cut each piece in half or thirds. I some-times cut a pretty card in eight pieces and before destroying the puzzle, of the eight pieces I have made as many as 15 or 16."[45] Productive seat-work, no doubt, often shaded into such pure busywork, especially for the junior pupils; but keeping children busy at all costs was a *sine qua non* of success-ful teaching in the one-room school, where time had to be allocated to instructing class after class, seriatim.

For teachers, the natural extension of seat-work was homework. It was used to clean up assignments left unfinished during school hours, to pre-pare students for the next day's lessons, for extra practice in new skills, and for other purposes besides. Though rarely banned outright, either by for-mal policy or by custom, homework below grade v or vi was discouraged; after that, however, it became a routine part of a pupil's life. But whereas classroom routines tended to be something of a closed shop, the business and sole prerogative of the teacher so long as she was judged competent and fair, homework was a different matter.

Even as the last century opened, the editor of the *Educational Review* would note that "there is considerable discussion in newspapers and else-where, of home study for pupils."[46] In 1934 Nova Scotia's superintendent of schools would label the issue "the perennial question of homework."[47] And he was certainly right. Over the entire period, homework provoked editorials and letters to the editor in both the daily and professional press, raised complaints directed at ministers of education, caused hand-wringing among their senior officials, and elicited petitions to or debates among local trustees.[48] Committees would study the matter and provincial departments issue policies attempting to establish appropriate guidelines, all without any apparent resolution.[49] There were few demands for outright abolition – the issue was not homework per se but how much was too much. And there was no simple split in opinion between teachers and parents; there were representatives of both on each side of the question. But generally speak-ing, it was a fruitful source of conflict. Parents objected to what they consid-ered excessive demands by teachers because they needed their children's labour after school, because they wanted time for family activities, because they objected to the supervision it entailed, because they thought it was the teacher's job, not theirs, to instruct their children.[50] Teachers, on the other hand, claimed that slow learners needed not only extra help at school but extra work at home if they were to keep up with the rest of the class. A crowded curriculum, and the limited teaching time available, provided incentives to leave as much as possible to seat-work and homework; and in the rural schools especially, the two most pressing priorities – teaching the beginners and preparing the grade VIII pupils for the HSEE – encouraged teachers to shuck off whole Middle School topics, expecting pupils to learn them on their own. Because promotion hinged so much on examination success in all grades, moreover, teachers were loath to leave preparation to chance; practice not only in school but at home was viewed as essential. It also mattered that a good showing on the examinations was important to a teacher's own future. So, however controversial, homework, like seat-work, was an integral part of the pedagogical task for teacher and pupil alike – assigning it, checking or marking it, and doing it up to whatever variable standard the pupil could bear and the teacher was willing to tolerate.

The third pedagogical task involved test construction, administration, marking, recording results, and reporting them. Because pencil-and-paper testing was assumed to be the most reliable means of evaluation, teachers were expected to do lots of it. Aside from the HSEE and the promotion exams organized by inspectors, regular class tests were a routine feature of classroom life. Primary pupils might well escape the more demanding formal examinations imposed on older children, but even they were not exempt from simple pencil-and-paper tests in things like spelling and arithmetic. Given contemporaries' faith in their efficacy, written tests would inevitably have consumed a significant portion of any teacher's time. But expectations about reporting to parents magnified the demands.

Either as a matter of formal government policy or by convention, elementary school teachers normally issued monthly or bimonthly report cards, with numerical marks or letter grades entered for each subject (usually along with an overall average mark, a ranking in the class, a grade for conduct, a record of punctuality and attendance, and some general remarks on the pupil's progress).[51] Monthly or bimonthly report cards, in turn, meant monthly or bimonthly testing. Music, art, or hygiene might or might not be evaluated this way, but each of the core academic subjects was. This imposed enough of a burden for the teacher in a graded classroom – to draft, administer, and mark a bevy of different subject tests, record the results, and then transfer these to individual report cards for, say, forty children. For the rural school teacher blessed with no more than a hand-

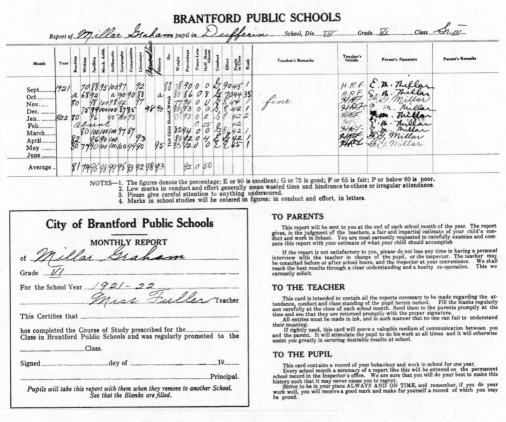

Fig. 11.3   Report card, urban school, 1921–1922

ful of children in only a few grades, it might have been less onerous; but if she had fifteen or twenty children spread across the grades, she needed to produce examinations in the several subjects for each grade. "Every two months," as one British Columbia teacher put it, "the rural school teacher had to prepare a test or examination of some kind for every subject and every grade. If there were eight grades in the school, some 56 tests had to be made, given and marked."[52] And all this, it should be added, takes no account of term and year-end report cards. Testing and reporting, then, constituted a third strand in the teacher's pedagogical work and were only somewhat less demanding than preparing daily lessons or generating, daily, the requisite amounts of seat-work. Trying to visualize the weeks when all three had to be done in tandem (not to mention the monthly tallies for the school registers), one can only shudder. For two examples of monthly report cards from the interwar years, one urban and one rural, see Figures 11.3 and 11.4.

MARKING

100% = Perfect = PP

Over 90% = E   Over 80% = VG

" 70% = G   " 60% = FG

" 50% = I   " 40% = P

Fail = F. 40 and Under

PARENTS and GUARDIANS

are cordially invited to co-operate with the teacher for the better advancement of the child.

Please examine this report carefully and note pupil's progress. This report should be properly signed and returned to the teacher.

....

Principal.

TEACHER'S REPORT

On .... *Helen*

Month .... *September* .... Grade .. *I. A.*

School .... *East Lynne*

Teacher .... *R. McStandal*

Subject	Possible Mark	Pupil's Mark	Subject	Possible Mark	Pupil's Mark
Reading		E	Writing		E
Literature			Drawing		
Composition			Handwork		
Grammar			Nat. Study & Agric		G
Spelling			Music		
Geography			Latin		
Hygiene		G	French		
Civics			Ancient History		
Can. History			Science		
Eng. History					
Arithmetic		E			
Geometry			Attendance		E
Algebra			Punctuality		P.P.
No. in Class		4	Total		
Rank in Class		1	Average		
Attitude to work		E	Times Late		0
Progress		E	Days School Open		21
Conduct		E	Half Days Absent		2

Teacher's Remarks: *Parents are invited to visit the school for a half day*

Mrs. ......

Parent's Signature

TEACHER'S REPORT

On .... *Helen*

Month .... *October* .... Grade .. *Im Bears*

School .... *East Lynne*

Teacher .... *R. McStandal*

Subject	Possible Mark	Pupil's Mark	Subject	Possible Mark	Pupil's Mark
Reading		E	Writing		96
Literature		E	Drawing		VG
Composition		VG	Handwork		VG
Grammar		—	Nat. Study & Agric		VG
Spelling		—	Music		
Geography	}	VG	Latin		
Hygiene	}		French		
Civics	}		Ancient History		
Can. History	}	E	Science		
Eng. History	}		M.W.		100
Arithmetic		E			
Geometry			Attendance		
Algebra			Punctuality		
No. in Class		6	Total		196
Rank in Class		1	Average		98
Attitude to work		E	Times Late		2
Progress		E	Days School Open		21
Conduct		E	Half Days Absent		0

Teacher's Remarks: ....

....

Parent's Signature

TEACHER'S REPORT

On .... *Helen*

Month .... *November* .... Grade .. *1. Bee*

School .... *East Lynne*

Teacher .... *R. McStandal*

Subject	Possible Mark	Pupil's Mark	Subject	Possible Mark	Pupil's Mark
Reading	86	E	Writing		84
Literature		E	Drawing		G
Composition		E	Handwork		—
Grammar		—	Nat. Study & Agric		VG
Spelling		—	Music		—
Geography	}	VG	Latin		—
Hygiene	}		French		
Civics	}		Ancient History		—
Can. History	}	VG	Science		
Eng. History	}		M.W.		100
Arithmetic		E			
Geometry			Attendance		
Algebra			Punctuality		
No. in Class		6	Total		270
Rank in Class		1	Average		90
Attitude to work		E	Times Late		0
Progress		E	Days School Open		20
Conduct		E	Half Days Absent		0

Teacher's Remarks: ....

....

Parent's Signature

Fig. 11.4   Report card, rural school, 1931–1932

To do their work, rural teachers had two traditional technologies at their command: the textbook and the blackboard. While a textbook could only be used effectively by older pupils, it provided basic information along with questions and exercises that enabled them to work on their own. If pupils lacked textbooks, as they did in some poor school districts, the teacher's work was multiplied because the material had then to be copied onto the board.[53] Blackboards, in any case, were indispensable. They were needed to provide opportunities for children, individually or in groups, to work arithmetic problems or other kinds of exercises at the board; to allow demonstrations and illustrations of new lessons by the teacher; to furnish tests and direct older pupils to their seat-work assignments; and to provide more detailed work for the primary grades or for subjects where no textbooks existed.[54] Lucky teachers had slate or slate-like "hyloplate" blackboards; unlucky teachers had to make do with homemade products such as lampblack mixed into plaster, coated cloth boards, or pine boards painted black (all cheap but lacking durability and/or difficult to write on or erase).[55] Even good blackboards had their drawbacks. One difficulty, writes John Charyk, "was that any time frost formed it was impossible to write on them with chalk. Since most country schools remained unheated during the weekends this was a usual problem every Monday morning throughout the winter months."[56] As well, lucky teachers not only had a blackboard that stretched across the entire front of the room but additional blackboard space along one side wall. The various departments of education recommended this arrangement not only for considerations of space but also because they wanted the room lit from only one side to provide proper lighting for young eyes. For aesthetic and social reasons, however, local people usually preferred windows on both sides of the schoolhouse, with the result that blackboard space was always at a premium.[57]

A third tool that many experienced teachers thought indispensable was the "hectograph."[58] Occasionally described as a "duplicating machine," it was actually a concoction of chemicals that, mixed together, formed a gelatinous pad, enabling a teacher to reproduce copies from a master sheet. Its nature and uses are nicely described in a passage from Elizabeth McLachlan's collection of reminiscences about teaching in the 1930s. Jessie Bissell, McLachlan writes, teaching not far from her home town of Athabasca, Alberta, between 1936 and 1939, had "49 students in nine grades." Desperate to provide seat-work for them all, and meagre though her pay cheque was,

Jessie drew on [it] for supplies to make a hectograph, yesteryear's precursor to the modern-day photocopier. A can of French gelatin, cookie sheet, and purple hectograph pencil were all she needed. She melted the gelatin to pouring consistency by placing the can in hot water. Then she poured it into the cookie sheet and allowed it to cool and solidify. With the purple hectograph pencil she wrote master copies of exams and seatwork. By wetting the surface of the gelatin in the cookie sheet with water, then laying her master copy face down upon it, she transferred her writing on to the gelatin. Then it was simply a matter of smoothing additional sheets of paper, one at a time, over the transfer to make extra copies of the same work. Although messy and time-consuming, the hectograph was state-of-the-art equipment in the thirties and saved Jessie copious amounts of writing.[59]

A good commercial hectograph pad, one teacher claimed, could make 80 to 100 copies, and a homemade pad, about 40.[60] Thus it was possible to supply a class with copies of any particular assignment, stockpile surplus copies for later use, or share copies between teachers.

The hectograph also had its drawbacks. As copies multiplied, they tended to become blurry and indistinct, with no remedy but to start over with a new master copy and a new batch of gelatin. Nor could several different assignments or tests be run in succession. "You couldn't copy a different test for another class on the same day," notes Van Kleek. "You had to wait a day or so for the purple to sink down far enough in the gelatin so you could copy a different test for another grade. For example, if you wanted to give all the middle grades their arithmetic test on the same day you were preparing for several days ahead."[61] And it was indubitably a messy and time-consuming way of copying exams and seat-work, "soaking the hands and everything else in wet purple ink."[62] There were, however, few alternatives. Duplicating machines, including the Gestetner and the Ditto, which would become near-daily tools for most teachers in the 1950s and 1960s, were being advertised in the educational press from the 1920s, but they were expensive and thus slow to penetrate even urban classrooms.[63] Photocopying, which began to replace both in the 1970s, had yet to be imagined. For Van Kleek and probably many other teachers with several small classes, carbon paper proved a preferable option. It was nearly as cheap and fast as the hectograph, and one could provide several different assignments for next day.[64] But carbon paper could produce only a very limited number of copies; for large classes there was no real substitute for the hectograph.

Though gradually becoming more common in urban schools, the hot new teaching technologies of the era – radio, slide projectors, and motion pictures – were unusual in rural schools, not just because of cost but because there was often no electricity.[65] Teachers could expect to find, or have to convince trustees to purchase, a few maps, charts showing birds, animals, or human physiology, printing blocks and plasticine for the primary pupils, and in many cases a piano or organ (bought as much for the Saturday night dances or Sunday church services as for the edification of the children). Flash cards home-made from inexpensive construction paper or cardboard were standard classroom items, used for drills in arithmetic, word recognition, and almost anything else with short answers.[66] Teachers also created sets of "counting sticks," bobbins, marbles, or almost any other type of small object that could be assembled easily to teach beginners their numbers. Picture books and primers might be available for initial word recognition, but Eaton's or Simpson's catalogues were used as well (when, that is, they were not already in use in the school's outdoor privies). In most photographs of classroom interiors, one sees borders running along the top of the blackboard, both decorative (colours and symbols for seasons and holidays for example) and instructional (the alphabet or numbers). These were conventionally made from commercially available stencils held against the blackboard and then coloured in with chalk or "dusted in" with a blackboard eraser.

A library of tolerable quality was a major asset, especially one with good reference works, since it allowed older pupils to find answers on their own, offered resources for projects in science or social studies, and provided silent and supplementary reading. By the 1920s all provinces, through often generous subsidies, were encouraging the creation of school libraries, but most of the financial costs still had to be borne by the locality. In the mid-1920s the number of books in Nova Scotia's rural libraries averaged only twenty-four per school.[67] Most other provinces were better supplied, though neither quantity nor quality should be overestimated. A study conducted about the same time found that "approximately one-fifth" of the 619 one-room schools in rural British Columbia were entirely without a library and many others "have a mere handful of books." Forty reported twenty-five books or fewer, another 104 schools had from twenty-five to a hundred, and only 13 had over two hundred volumes. "If, as reported in some cases and to be inferred in others, the totals submitted included the 54 pamphlets containing the Children's History of the War, it is necessary to discount still further the value of such libraries."[68]

It's not easy to get a good sense of the resources most teachers might have had at their command, and as we've tried to suggest here and in previous chapters, not all rural schools were alike. Some were well provided for, some were not. Yet it's also hard to avoid the conclusion that in many schools at least, resources were desperately thin, even in the relatively prosperous twenties, even in relatively prosperous provinces. In the Okanagan Valley in the 1920s, writes Penelope Stephenson, "virtually all the former teachers interviewed considered the paucity of apparatus, in terms of instructional resources and supplies, to be their major stumbling block to effective teaching. Even an essential item of equipment such as the blackboard was often small and of inferior quality. In many schools they were ... 'painted wall-board' and therefore 'unsatisfactory.'"[69] And everywhere, the situation deteriorated in the 1930s. However essential such items might have been considered by the mid-thirties, the teachers in Alberta's Camrose inspectorate were unlikely to have access to anything fancier than a blackboard, let alone a hectograph, to generate seat-work assignments and tests – and not much of anything else by way of libraries or classroom equipment.[70] In 1934 a sampling of Saskatchewan inspectors' reports concluded that no new library purchases had been made for years and the extant books and reference materials were falling into ruins; "there is difficulty in providing even the most necessary items such as chalk, erasers and blackboard surface."[71]

Resources for the classroom, however, were never restricted to what was available in the local school district. In the first place, the inspectoral unit or the district teachers' federation often became a site of co-operative activity where lesson plans, units of work, examinations, and a wide variety of other material could be produced and shared among teachers.[72] Beyond that, by the interwar years at least, there was a remarkable efflorescence of material on offer to teachers willing to dip into their own pockets or able to coax trustees to shell out a few extra dollars, or who paid dues to their provincial federation and thus had access to the advice columns and advertisements in its monthly magazine. Much of this material was intended to improve the level of pedagogical work and enrich the resources of the rural classroom, but perhaps most important, it promised to lighten the drudgery inevitably involved in teachers' daily routines and make their lives at least somewhat easier.

So long as the published program of studies simply directed them to so many pages of a textbook or provided only a scant topical outline for each subject, inexperienced teachers especially needed help in fleshing out course outlines into units of work scheduled over the year. By at least the 1920s (and probably earlier), such guidelines were in wide circulation. Typically, the ATA *Magazine* published a long-running series entitled "Our Teachers' Helps Department," which included, among other things, these kinds of outlines. During 1933–34, for example, it reproduced the Calgary elementary school curriculum guideline, which offered a year's work broken down into monthly and weekly units for each subject, included suggestions on how to teach topics and directions for related assignments, and even provided exemplary lesson plans – in February, a lesson for senior elementary school literature on the poems "The Highwayman" and "The Hanging of the Crane."[73] Another common device was a "Questions Box" where teachers could seek advice from other teachers on all manner of classroom challenges, from the conventional and routine problems of pedagogy or discipline to situations that spoke volumes about the unusual environments individuals could encounter. From up the British Columbia coast, for example, and not in 1890 or 1900 but in 1940, one young teacher would send this plea for help to the BC *Teacher*: "My school is on a raft – the playground is a log boom. How can I make the pupils understand about cities, towns, and ordinary people?"[74] While the exact format varied, all of the professional journals carried regular columns, mini-series, and occasional articles that together constituted a good deal of commonsense advice along with concrete material that could be reproduced on the board, turned into hectograph masters, or otherwise put to use in classroom teaching.[75] Additional resources were also to be found in the widely circulated *Canadian Junior Red Cross Magazine*, chock full of stories, history and science lessons, biographies, plays, and other materials that could be put to good use by teachers and pupils alike.

The federation journals or those like *The School* or New Brunswick's *Educational Review* covered a wide variety of subjects of professional interest and not just the nitty-gritty of classroom practice. But in terms of circulation, perhaps the most successful professional journal was the *Canadian Teacher*, a purely commercial venture that claimed a list of thousands of subscribers in large part because it was, resolutely and single-mindedly, a "Practical School Room Journal," providing reams of more or less immediately useful material. The journal, produced by the Educational Publishing Company of Toronto, dated back to the late nineteenth century and by 1918 was offering its subscribers sixteen issues, a total of 1,256 pages, at a cost of $1.25 a year.[76] By 1938 the price had risen to $2 per annum, but the publisher was promising that "*The Hectograph Section* has been ENLARGED to 48 pages an issue. A yearly subscription gives you 480 Pages of Hectograph Masters Seatwork all ready to reproduce for class use on any gelatin duplicator."[77]

The issue published on 13 June 1925 was typical, for the interwar years at least.[78] It contained a total of 63 pages, 47 of which were text and the rest advertising. There were several short articles intended to inform or enrich teachers' knowledge about nature, history, geography, English literature, and current events. There were guides for teaching particular topics with questions that could be dictated, put on the board, or turned into hectograph masters, and accompanying notes that provided teaching outlines. There were examinations and shorter tests with the answers provided. There were spelling lists and exercises in arithmetic, composition, literature, and grammar, again with accompanying answers. Not every subject was covered in every issue, but there was material for each grade – for grades III and IV in the 13 June issue, for example, a "reproduction story" (retell the story in your own words), spelling list, geography lesson, a poem and related exercise for literature, problems and drills in arithmetic, and language exercises that included "Answering a Letter" and "Starting a Diary." Towards the back there was an editorial section and a "mailbag," where correspondents could seek or give advice on classroom problems, and yet another section offering solutions to difficult arithmetic problems found in various authorized textbooks.

For a time at least there was a complementary publication for pupils that, month by month, contained all the exercises but none of the answers – in effect, a pupil workbook for which the teacher's copy of the journal provided a marking key. The same publisher also offered a plethora of stand-alone booklets that a teacher could purchase separately – complete courses for particular grades under titles like *A Year in Arithmetic, A Year in Literature,* or *Two Thousand Questions in Geography* (which promised, in 112 pages, an "entire course in Geography, Mathematical, Physical and Political" through "a set of analytical questions invaluable for review and examination"). One could purchase, from the same company, a complete timetable for an entire year; or ten different booklets containing "a complete Christmas programme of Songs, Recitations, Drills, and Dialogues"; or entire sets of the "Ontario Entrance Examination Papers for the past 22 years." Etc.[79]

Was the magazine put to good use? For at least one teacher, exhaustively and for years. Copies originally belonging to Mary Thompson, a teacher in a rural school near Exeter, Ontario, are now housed in the library at the University of Western Ontario. Successive issues contain her scribbled references to useful material, underlined items, and portions of a page carefully cut out (or entire pages removed). And with this collection there is a copy of a literature examination she gave two senior students in which a poem and attendant questions were taken in full from an old issue of the magazine.[80]

Producing useful teaching material, indeed, was big business. Supplementing their enormous, and enormously profitable, school textbook business, the major Canadian publishing houses had, by the 1920s, begun to sell "workbooks" for all the basic subjects and most grades. These were, in effect, professionally produced, "canned" seat-work fodder, relieving teachers of the need to create their own, often more amateurish, assignments and reducing the amount of work that had to be laboriously copied onto the blackboard or reproduced on the hectograph.[81] The big school supply houses got into the act as well. E.N. Moyer Company, for example, published an annual catalogue that, along with desks, blackboards, globes, maps, bells, stationery, record and report cards, and so on, advertised "Teacher Aids" that could be used for seat-work, including "Word Study in Grades 2 to 5," "Reading and Numbers Seat Work for Grades 1, 2 and 3," "New Pictures to Cut, Colour, Draw, Paste," "New Silent Reading Seat Work

for between Recitation Periods." "We have," said the ad, "many congratula-
tory letters from Teachers ... stating that our SEAT WORK and SILENT READ-
ING LINES have saved them considerable work and time."[82] Two fiercely
competitive international publishers of encyclopedias, *The World Book* and
The Book of Knowledge, eager to ensconce their wares in school libraries, were
among the most persistent advertisers in the educational press and offered,
as come-ons, sophisticated and attractive "Free Study Outlines," lesson
plans, and pre-prepared classroom projects.[83]

Beyond all that, there were government agencies, provincial and federal
alike, that published booklets, charts, maps, and bulletins on Canada's natural resources, industries, and services, freely available for classroom use
and which teachers could exploit as sources for essays and other seat-work
projects. Equally important were the commercial and industrial companies
that regularly advertised in the educational press, offering an array of teaching materials – dental hygiene kits from Colgate's, for example, containing
instructional charts, samples, and proficiency certificates; junior colouring
books and a wall chart, "The Story of Wheat," from the Shredded Wheat
Company; a package of material on the menstrual cycle from the manufacturers of Kotex; or, from Johns Manville, a booklet, complete with samples,
on "Asbestos – Canada's Magic Mineral." Distributed free upon written
request from teachers or trustees, all of this material was clearly branded,
designed to promote loyalty to a particular consumer product or, in a public relations exercise, to burnish the reputation of a firm or an entire industry. Undoubtedly the most famous of these branded teaching aids, however,
were the ubiquitous Neilson's "Chocolate Bar" maps of Canada and the
World, distributed free to thousands upon thousands of schools with only
one condition attached – that no-one mutilate or obscure the images of the
chocolate bars that prominently graced their four corners.[84]

In an age of big school boards with big budgets for supplies, it is easy
to be cynical about the invasion of such patently exploitive devices into
Canadian classrooms. But given the way in which schools were financed
in the first four decades of the twentieth century, and given the economic
circumstances of the interwar years especially, it is not difficult to understand why individual teachers, above all those in the often poverty-stricken
rural schools, would welcome any help on offer, especially a well-produced
teaching aid that couldn't help but enrich the pedagogical task and supplement the meagre resources of most rural classrooms. Among other examples, a series of lesson plans illustrates just how useful this material could
be. Published in 1927 in the *Educational Review* for class projects focusing
on salt, tea, health, cocoa, and cheese, each plan gave the address of a
commercial company (Lever Brothers, Kraft, etc.) that would provide pertinent teaching and assignment materials – resources that could be used

for everything from teaching primary language and arithmetical skills to lessons in geography, history, hygiene, or composition.[85]

Four basic points emerge from the preceding pages. First, the rural school teacher was, in effect, mistress of a four-ring circus, teaching a series of lessons for much of the school day to children of different ages and attainments; overseeing, at the same time, the progress of seat-work assignments for six, seven, or eight different classes; keeping beginners with short attention spans busy and interested; keeping older children focused and attentive to the tasks at hand; supervising the playground at recess while trying to get the next batch of assignments on the board; coping with unexpected emergencies while maintaining a modicum of orderly behaviour. "It is, indeed, a problem," as one woman put it, "to teach one class and still have one's eye on the rest of the room, but it is really necessary."[86] "Very often the teacher will have to do two things at once," echoed the editor of the *Western School Journal*. "She will teach a class and supervise seatwork. This is not easy but it is possible. When pupils in class are working on a problem [at the blackboard] the teacher may walk around the room noting penmanship, general appearance of work, application of pupils. In other words she will resemble the mother in the home who finds it necessary to do half a dozen things at once."[87]

Second, self-discipline was required of both teacher and pupils. Lessons had to proceed like clockwork, and pupils had to be able to get on with their own work quietly and efficiently without interrupting the lesson of another class. "It is not enough to construct a balanced, workable timetable," one British Columbia inspector insisted in 1934; "pupils – at least the older ones – must be made familiar with it, and must pass from the work of period to period with a minimum of directions from the teacher ... In the smoothly operating school, the pupil knows with little or no telling that his seat-work grows out of the teaching period, or that when he finishes his arithmetic he proceeds with a grammar exercise from his text, prepares his history by working at a completion test on the board, fills in details on an outline map, or reads a book from the table at the back of the room. Obviously these things do not happen by accident, but are the outgrowth of the most careful organization and preparation on the teacher's part."[88] Drawing on a deep fund of teaching experience in rural schools, Annie Ritchie, a "Rural Supervisor" in Queen's County, Nova Scotia, wrote that "the teacher must know *exactly* what is to be done each period of the day by each group. Above all, children should be taught respect for the time of others. When the teacher is working with a group, no child should interrupt. No teacher can work a timetable with any degree of success, and run a 'please-help-me' school. On the other hand, the child should know that his turn will come and that when he is being helped with his group, nobody will interrupt them. Children have to be taught to leave the question they cannot do and go on to the next one. All children need work to which they can turn when they have finished the assignment. (A book to read, a map to draw, an art project, will fill the bill.)" Ritchie went on to describe the pedagogical chaos that was sure to descend when the requisite discipline was missing:

9:15. The beginner's reading lesson is started. The teacher opens the manual, can't find the place and before she has found the page a grade 5 pupil asks, "Do we do what it says on the side board?" Another says, "We did that yesterday." Discussion follows and is settled by the teacher, who says she meant for them to finish the work – not do it all. Several explain that they started at the beginning. A grade 3 pupil asks to sharpen his pencil. The teacher has to do it as the sharpener works poorly, and before she finishes, the grade 9 boy asks for help, which she gives on the spot. She then returns to the beginners, finds the place in the manual, sees that this group is ready to work in the workbook, gets the workbook, finds the page and shows the pupils what to do. It is now 9.30, two more pupils are asking for help and nobody has been taught a thing. Will the time table work? *No.*[89]

While Richie's portrait here may be overwrought, there are plenty of other articles in the educational press that lay similar emphasis on the need for tightly disciplined classroom management.[90]

Third, there was the enormous burden of work. While there may have been a large volume of commercial and non-commercial teaching aids to help out, the limits of the available technologies, the pedagogical poverty of so many rural classrooms, and the sheer range of ages and grades to be managed and taught meant that nothing was accomplished easily without an imaginative ability to "make do" and, above all, without grinding effort. Both individual and collective memoirs record the long hours spent outside the school day preparing lessons, setting and marking assignments, arriving early to light the fires and put the morning's seat-work on the board. Again, Penelope Stephenson: "Timetabling and preparing individual lessons in every subject and for each grade, and then marking the assignments set, as well as keeping up to date with the compulsory school records such as monthly report cards for each pupil, was an administrative nightmare for rural teachers. Particularly for those with little experience, it demanded a seemingly inordinate amount of work. To Isobel Simard it seemed that 'every hour of the day practically I was preparing lessons.' Marianne Nelson expressed similar sentiments when she stated: 'I taught by one method, constant work, work, work, for me, that is.'"[91]

Fourth and finally, there was the sense of isolation and the concomitant weight of responsibility. This also appears prominently in many of the memoirs. The rural school teacher worked alone, without the advice and support of colleagues, without professional supervision beyond the annual or semi-annual visit of the provincial inspector, and as the only adult on the scene, solely accountable for the health and safety of those in her charge for five or six hours a day and, above all, for their entire education.

It is not very often we get a window that allows us to observe the routines used by particular individuals in the one-room school, but the following letter to the *Canadian Teacher*, written by "Rose" in 1926, reflects at least some of the practices and stresses we have been canvassing in the preceding pages. "I have taught for nearly six years in one rural school of 9 classes, during which time the highest number on the roll has been 56 and the lowest 38," she began. "I arrive at school at 8:30 a.m. and 'fill boards' till 9. I spend 20 minutes at least every noon hour at the same task. I never stay after 4 p.m ... [and] I give no homework to any but children in the 4th book and choose what will take very little marking ... I buy all the books of Arithmetic Exercises I can so save so much writing on the blackboard ... Since I have been here I have sent in 17 children for the Entrance Examination ... and have had only 1 failure."

Rose used cross-grade grouping extensively, teaching, for example, the children in the third and fourth books together for geography, history, and "new rules of Arithmetic." The writing lesson was taught once a week to the entire school. "I allot," she continued, "all the spelling at once, hear and correct the Fourths and they hear and correct the other classes, and they are as strict and careful as ever I should be." For the younger children there were "babyish" history and geography books; the children read these silently "and then are prepared to tell me the stories. This helps also in reading and composition."

Predictably, "the beginners are a problem. One year I had 22 of them. I endeavour to get them as soon as possible to do little addition sums, and to write from printing. That makes them independent a part of the day. I expect them in six months to be able to do much for themselves." However, she and the older pupils brought to school "pictures to colour, cut out, and put in the right order, or letters to cut out and form into words." This, she wrote, "helps wonderfully to visualize the words." Sometimes they were given an action sentence such as "'The wasp will sting you if you catch it,' which occupies time while they look through words and slowly read them to themselves and then draw and write. It takes only a glance to correct."

Finally, Rose noted, "we have dual desks, and each beginner sits beside an older pupil (brother or sister preferably), and they are supposed to keep an admonitory and helpful eye on them. They do it too," she added, though one can almost hear the unspoken corollary that she expected the older ones to set a good example, and saw to it, with a firm hand, that they did so.[92]

This, then, is the voice of one experienced teacher describing a pattern of work, capturing the complexity of the task, the discipline required of both teacher and pupils, and the investment of time spent beyond school hours in order to keep the momentum up during the school day. Now in her sixth year of teaching, Rose, obviously, had mastered the art of running a four-ring circus.

III

The fact remains, nonetheless, that large numbers of rural teachers were beginners. They didn't bring experience to the job, and many didn't stay long enough to acquire it. How well were they prepared to do the job that confronted them when they stepped into their first classroom? In an age when there were dramatic differences between town and country, that depended, in the first place, on the backgrounds of the teachers themselves. As June Corman has remarked, "Teachers who had grown up in the country had attended rural schools without electricity, running water or educational resources, and watched their teachers work without the help [of others]." Those from urban areas "were less comfortable with the lack of amenities in rural schools. These women confronted a sharp learning curve, making an adjustment from electric lights, running hot water and flush toilets to lanterns, heating water on pot-belly stoves, and outhouses in the yard." Nor did they have any first-hand familiarity with the mechanics and customs of a multi-grade schoolroom.[93] Reminiscing decades later in a letter to John Charyk, Katie Baker wrote: "[M]y teaching years began in 1925 … my first day of teaching remains clearly in my mind." Katie "had never at any time" lived away from home and had completed all her schooling, including normal school, in Calgary. Her first job was in eastern Alberta, seven long miles out of Hanna. "I arrived to find a group of wide-eyed children and a very little schoolhouse with locked door. At once I opened a window, and in short order we all were inside the school. This was my first introduction to the interior of a rural school. Everything was so very new and different to me. Down the centre of the room was a row of double seats, with a row of individual seats on either side. There was one small blackboard area, a course of study and a box of chalk. An improvised shelf had a half dozen more or less text books and the school boasted two windows."[94]

Katie's experience was not unusual. While many newly minted teachers had grown up in rural areas, many others had not. In 1914, for example, only 53% of the students at the Ottawa normal school had been born in a rural community; the rest came from villages, towns, and cities.[95] Writing a year later, the principal of the Camrose normal school, located in a small town deep in Alberta's countryside, would comment, "Of the 275 students leaving this school during the year, all but 20 began work in rural schools, some of them without ever having seen the inside of such a school before assuming charge of their own."[96] Fifteen years later the principal of the Saskatoon normal school estimated that "over 40% of the teachers-in-training had no experience of rural schools." He went on to point out, moreover, that of those who had attended rural schools, large numbers had received only a part of their schooling in ungraded classrooms and at ages where the experience would leave few impressions.[97] "A very large proportion of our students," wrote the principal of the New Brunswick normal school a few years later, "have been trained entirely in graded schools and therefore have no direct knowledge of the one-room Country School."[98]

Even those who had received all their elementary education in ungraded classrooms were not necessarily equipped to teach in one – the two are not the same kind of experience. But more troublesome, neither did their professional training equip them to do so. Those whose first job was in an urban classroom were probably well enough served by the programs offered in the normal schools. From city schools on down to those in the larger villages, new teachers could expect to find graded classrooms where their responsibilities were limited to instructing a single group of children all at roughly the same level of attainment, where lesson preparation was restricted to the subjects taught to that particular grade, and where they could expect help from more experienced colleagues and principals when they encountered difficulties. In this respect, normal school instruction and practice-teaching in urban graded schools might not finish the preparatory job, but they offered at least an initial induction into the demands of the craft.[99]

The vast majority of normal school graduates, however, did *not* begin teaching in urban schools. As one teacher put it in an article in 1927 in the *ATA Magazine*, "I think that any Normal graduate will agree that the course is admirably adapted to prepare one for a city school ... But how many take a city school? Ten per cent is a large estimate. What then is to become of the ninety per cent who teach in rural schools? From my correspondence with a good number of last year's graduates I have learned that for the first month they were totally at sea. The actual teaching is not difficult, they claim, but what seat work can they give to carry on from the lesson they have taught?" The author went on to call for "a course more suited to the needs of the rural teacher than the present one is."[100] And if the Ontario normal school manual on school management is any guide to what was actually taught, it illuminates the problem nicely. While it devoted several pages to detailing how pupils might be grouped and each subject handled in the ungraded classroom, the manual concluded that "it is difficult to prepare a time table for a rural school with one teacher that would show the exact working out of the fore-going plan." Beginners were left with this piece of bogus reassurance: "The plan presents difficulties to the inexperienced teacher, but these may be *gradually* overcome as he gains professional skill."[101] The italics are ours. Most of the rest of the volume was equally unhelpful to those confronting, for the first time, the realities of the rural school. It outlined, for example, the model physical plant, much of which could indeed be applied to the *model* ungraded school; but most teachers didn't inherit a model school, and it offered little or nothing to help teachers cope with the actual circumstances they would find themselves in.[102] Or consider its advice on pedagogy. After outlining various teaching techniques, it described "the most advanced form of teaching" – that is to say, the exemplary mode. This was "the deductive method," which invited the teacher to teach a general law or principle and then have pupils apply it to problems through reference "to some authority," which required library resources most rural schools didn't have.[103] The volume had some perfectly sensible advice on the quality of good seat-work but nothing on how to organize and produce it.[104]

The most serious criticism that could be mounted against the normal school program, however, was the lack of practice teaching in the rural schools. In the early twentieth century this seems to have been almost entirely absent, a situation that has led David Jones, one of the most perceptive students of the rural schools in western Canada, to remark that "Normal School training in the early twenties prepared trainees to teach on the moon better than in the typical one-room ... school."[105] Overstated perhaps, but only somewhat so. Penelope Stephenson found her Okanagan Valley teachers from the 1920s echoing Jones's sentiments: "The foremost block for new teachers was instructional: how to co-ordinate tuition in a multi-grade situation. The statements by former teachers indicate that in this regard they deemed their professional training to have been both impractical and irrelevant in the face of the actual circumstances they encountered in their rural classrooms."[106] A Manitoban writing about the problems of the rural schools remarked in 1923 that "for this type of school there is no special training whatever. The normal schools are in the cities, where the teachers-in-training observe the classroom with one grade and in it do some little practice teaching. The need for a special form of training for the teacher going to the rural school could hardly be more manifest."[107] Surveying the extent of the problem in New Brunswick, Allan McBeath concluded that the province's normal school graduates "spend one or two years at least learning to solve many of the situations which they should have met in normal school, and that further, all those schools which employ teachers with this amount of experience are really experimental schools" where teachers were left "to teach and learn for themselves many ways of doing things which may be very faulty."[108]

The consequences were predictable. While much teaching in the ungraded schools he visited was satisfactory, said one Alberta inspector in 1925, "some of the young and inexperienced teachers are hopelessly lost. They try to teach everything to every grade, and to give each subject equal prominence on the time-table. Of course it is possible by giving each subject in each grade about five minutes on the time-table to get them all in, but applying such a time-table to the actual class-room conditions is another question entirely. It does not and will not and cannot be made to work. It is just there that the inspector can do some very helpful work by showing the teacher whom he finds in this predicament, how to extricate herself from the bog in which she is being mired."[109] Teachers fresh from the normal schools, said another, more acerbically, "lack, in marked degree, the ability to combat the problems of the ungraded school, and in several cases seem mystified and baffled at the situation which confronts them. Their course in Normal has not warned them of the difficulties of teaching an ungraded school nor has it developed the ability to solve their problems."[110]

Neither department officials nor normal school principals and instructors were, it must be said, indifferent to the problem, and various expedients were tried to overcome it. For example, the normal schools in several provinces had model schools attached to them where attempts were made to have one classroom resemble conditions in an ungraded school.[111] Moreover, simply sending students out to rural schools had its own difficulties. As the principal of the Vancouver normal school (the only one located on the mainland) commented in 1938, "Unfortunately the simple expedient of sending a student to some ungraded school to practise for a week or two is, with us, scarcely possible and certainly undesirable. Consolidation, in whole or in part, has become so general in this area that there are now no ungraded schools within 30 miles of Vancouver, and the use of more remote districts presents rather serious problems of transportation and accommodation. Aside from this, experience in the usual rural school, taught by a novice, is not likely to prove of value to a student."[112] New Brunswick's normal school principal shared this latter reservation but added that even if sent to a "weak school," the student would at least "gain real first hand information regarding actual conditions under which he would have to work."[113]

Between the late 1920s and the early 1940s nearly all provinces introduced or extended the amount of rural practice teaching. Alberta, for example, began in 1928, requiring one week's experience; Manitoba and Saskatchewan, in 1929–30, two weeks; Ontario, in 1936–37, two weeks.[114] While universally students continued to receive more time observing and teaching in graded than in ungraded schools, by 1940 a minimum of at least two weeks was common nearly everywhere. Yet even two weeks was considered barely adequate. As one senior Alberta official privately acknowledged in 1940, "rural practice teaching is one of our unsolved problems."[115] When asked what they themselves thought, the students at the Edmonton normal school listed as their chief difficulties what were in fact the constituent characteristics of the ungraded school: "Seat work," "Limited time with each class," "Lack of library," and "Lack of equipment."[116]

None of this means the job was un-doable. Whatever its challenges, the rhythms of the rural classroom could be learned.[117] With increasing experience there was an expanding repertoire of skills, greater self-confidence, *and* a growing collection of pre-planned lessons, examinations, and seat-work assignments. Once the flash cards were made and the bobbins collected, it didn't have to be done again next year. And some intractable problems, such as recurring breakdowns in discipline or conflict with parents or trustees, could be solved by the simple expedient of moving on, writing mistakes off to experience, and making a fresh start elsewhere.[118] Rose, after all, was once a beginner, many other young women spent several years of their lives teaching ungraded schools, and some did it over the course of an entire career. Nor is it hard to find examples of teachers happy to say they loved the job.[119] But ill-prepared as they were for their initial encounter with the classroom, the difficulties overwhelmed some and at times must have appeared insurmountable even to the most resourceful and brave-hearted.

Supervisors and Their Work

To what extent was the work of the teacher supervised, how was it done, and by whom? These three questions provide the focus for this chapter. We title it "Supervisors ... " rather than "Inspectors" for two reasons. First, we are dealing not only with the provincial inspectorate but with other kinds of supervisors as well. More important, there is the dual connotation that supervision carries: on the one hand, the quasi-police or surveillance function implied by inspection; on the other, the notion of assistance, support, and the improvement of instruction. Across the period, and however subsidiary it might have turned out to be in practice, that latter meaning was always presented as the highest purpose of supervision.[1] Thus we want to pay attention to both functions of supervision – inspection and the promotion of exemplary practice. We also want to know, despite all the rhetoric about its importance, just how much effective supervision there actually was.

We begin with the provincial inspectorate. In most provinces the inspectorate was responsible for both urban and rural schools, but we will focus mainly on its work in rural areas. In parts two and three we turn to the urban schools, considering the role of principals and other local supervisory officers. In the fourth section we explore the gendered nature of supervision by asking how many of Canada's inspectors, principals, or other supervisory officers were women? Then, by way of conclusion, we turn to commentary on several interpretative and historiographical issues that our discussion raises.

I

Then as now, the legal authority to inspect the schools originated in provincial legislation that conferred upon the minister of education (or some equivalent body) the power to ensure that law and policy were being applied in all grant-aided schools.[2] By the end of the twentieth century these powers were largely delegated to officials in local school districts, but earlier in the century provincial governments right across the country appointed and paid a cadre of inspectors who acted at the behest and on behalf of each department of education.[3]

Depending on the province and the decade, there were usually several different types of inspectors. Nearly all provinces had one or more high school inspectors, and there might well have been other specialists. Ontario, with its large enrolments and variety of schools, was not necessarily typical, but in 1921, along with its staff of public school inspectors, it had three high school inspectors; two continuation school inspectors; an inspector for each of manual training, domestic science, agricultural education, and auxiliary classes; a small cadre of Roman Catholic and bilingual school inspectors; and a director of industrial and technical education who inspected the new vocational schools.[4] In what follows, however, we will focus almost entirely on elementary school inspectors, by far the most numerous in all provinces and those with the greatest influence over most teachers' work lives.[5]

Recruitment was through an old boys' network where candidates were identified by the inspectorate itself and recommended to senior officials at central office. But candidates were drawn from a pre-selected pool of individuals who had already proved themselves in a variety of classroom and administrative settings.[6] In most provinces they were required to have an undergraduate degree, and many had MAs as well. They were expected to hold the highest professional licences and have acquired several years' experience as teachers and principals. Before 1920 at least, nearly all inspectors had some experience teaching in one-room schools and most came from rural communities. The inspectorate, in other words, held high academic qualifications, possessed a broad range of classroom and administrative experience, and brought to the task substantial familiarity with social and economic conditions in town and country alike.[7]

When James Miller surveyed the country in 1913, he found the list of inspectoral duties "much the same in all provinces"; forty years later yet another national survey noted hardly any changes.[8] As servant of the department, the inspector was the key link between centre and locality in fostering "educational improvement," diffusing information about departmental policy, and encouraging its implementation – what Nova Scotia's superintendent of schools once described as the inspector's "important work of educational propaganda with school trustees and the public at large."[9] Within his inspectorate, however, he was also, as one Alberta official put it, "the eyes and ears of the department."[10] He was expected to know, in intimate detail, the state of the schools, the educational needs and aspirations of local people, and sources of unease or opposition to departmental procedures and policies. He was expected to explain their duties to teachers and trustees, to see that the law and regulations were being carried out, and when necessary to invoke police powers to enforce the law either directly or through the department or some other agency.[11] He also compiled and collated the mass of local records required by the department; nearly all the routine records were funnelled through or organized by him and then forwarded to central office. Above all, the inspector was responsible for ensuring that the standards demanded by the department were maintained in the schools. These standards were of two distinct kinds. One set consisted of what might be termed "standards of provision" – to ensure that trustees were meeting their obligations to provide at least the minimum facilities specified in the act, regulations, and policy documents, and through gentle (or occasionally not so gentle) arm-twisting, to encourage them to do better than that. The other set involved standards of teacher efficiency and pupil progress. To this end, as Miller described it, the task was one of both inspection and supervision – "to inspect the work of the teacher, to ascertain the standing of the pupils, demote or promote as he deems advisable, inspect register, time-tables, and written work of pupils. 'He shall also assist the teacher in selecting and planning the work; and by judicious criticism and advice and by teaching illustrative lessons he shall endeavour to improve the methods of instruction.'"[12]

The inspectorate engaged in prodigious amounts of clerical work. Along with record management, the inspector dealt with a constant stream of correspondence, answering basic questions about the law posed by inexperienced teachers and often unlettered trustees or ratepayers, arbitrating local disputes, or exchanging information with and submitting reports to his superiors at central office. Most of this was done without clerical assistance; he was his own typist, stenographer, secretary, usually working out of a makeshift office in his own home.[13]

The most vital part of the inspector's work, however, could only be done "on the road." The minimum number of visits to each school was usually stipulated by law or regulation – at least once a year in some provinces, twice in others. In some cases the minimum length of a visit was specified as well. The 1911 regulations in Ontario, for example, required at least one visit each half-year and set out the time requirements – one half-day for each rural school with one teacher, one day for a rural school with two or three teachers, one and one-half days for four or five teachers, and so on. "When the condition of the school renders it necessary, the length of the visit should be increased ... Teachers who need additional supervision from any cause, the Inspector should visit as often as circumstances may demand and his other official duties will permit."[14]

When the inspector stepped into the classroom, he was not there as a guest. Not only did he have the legal right to be there, and without any prior notice, but he was automatically in charge. The Manitoba regulation on this point was typical: "While officially visiting the school, he shall have supreme authority therein and shall have the right to direct the teachers and pupils in regard to any or all of the exercises of the school."[15] In 1906 John Dearness, already well on his way to becoming a distinguished London educator and community leader, provided this account of his usual procedure during a half-day rural school inspection. Arriving before the school day started, he began by surveying the grounds and exterior of the building, "never on any account omitting the latrines." On entering the schoolhouse, he requested teacher and pupils to proceed as usual. With teaching and seat-work underway, he moved around the room examining pupils' work and asking the occasional question. He then took a seat at the back of the room where he could observe both teacher and pupils and at the same time check the register and timetable and write up his report on the physical condition of the school. All of this occupied the first hour. Just before recess he assigned the pupils some simple exercises, and during recess he sent for the trustees, whom he hoped to meet at the noon break. After recess he examined the pupils' exercises and "tried to find time to teach at least one primary, one intermediate and one advanced class. With these were sandwiched opportunities to further test the teacher ... On the teaching side I selected lessons that were either in subjects that seemed in most need of improvement, or that the teacher had requested assistance in, and on the examination side in the subjects, if any, that seemed neglected." Over the course of the morning this "allows, on an average, about an hour's inspection, an hour's teaching, and an hour's examination. It need not be said here that when a man is teaching properly he is at the same time examining in the best way the mental habits of the class." At some point early in the day, Dearness also tried to find time to chat with the teacher about "any difficulties in method or management in respect to which I might be able to give advice or assistance." Still to be done was a brief word at noon with the teacher about his assessment of her teaching, which would appear in his official report on her work.[16]

Dearness liked to meet in person with the trustees, since "expenditures advised in a report are more likely to be made after *vive voce* explanations than without them." But that was not always possible, as inspectors might be trying to reach a second school on the same day or trustees were busy with their own affairs. Thus meetings might occur only when there were issues that could not otherwise be resolved.[17] In Nova Scotia, however, an annual meeting with each set of trustees was required by law; one inspector has left a record of a month of these meetings under the headings, "matters discussed," "improvements since last visit," and "recommendations." Under discussion in every school district was the state of school finances, improvements to the school plant, and policy issues ranging from obtaining building insurance to teaching grade XI in the one-room school. Specific local issues were addressed as well. Recommendations ranged from the mundane to the dramatic: from shingle the school roof, buy a pencil sharpener, or whitewash the toilets to "Trustees to proceed with erection of a modern two department school immediately" or "Move building to a better and larger site."[18]

The reports routinely arising from school visits were of two sorts. One was a general commentary on conditions in the inspectorate, including assessments of the physical plant in the district, the quality and effectiveness of instruction, the success of policy innovations, and the like. Without singling out specific schools or individuals, these reports usually provided quite detailed descriptions of local conditions, and they remain invaluable for historians.[19] Every province collected reports of this kind and, after suitable editing, published them verbatim or in summary form in the *Annual Reports*, constituting, inspectorate by inspectorate, a public record of the province's educational progress and the challenges still to be surmounted.

The second kind was a report on the individual teachers, usually completed in triplicate – one copy for the teacher, one for the trustees, and a third for the department (where, cumulatively, they formed a permanent record of a teacher's career). These reports were made on standardized forms that included grades taught; experience; certificates held; general comments on appearance, personality, and leadership abilities; recommendations to improve effectiveness; often detailed checklists based on the inspector's observations of the quality and methods of instruction, knowledge of the subject, and attitude to the job; and finally, a summative verdict, expressed as a numerical or letter grade – for example, "Excellent" or "7"; "Fair" or "3," etc.[20] Formats for these reports varied in detail by province and across the decades, but the Manitoba report form reproduced in Figure 12.1 is pretty representative of the genre.

An inspector's reports were serious business. They could result in the failure of a new teacher to obtain a permanent certificate from the department, they could limit the possibility of promotion or the chance of transferring from the one-room school to a better job in a graded system, or they could lead to the termination of a contract by the local board. In early January 1922, for example, Blairmore's board of school trustees ordered "that the Secretary write Miss Gray advising her that, according to the Inspector's report the progress of her class appears to be below standard and that the Board feel that she should seek the advice of the Principal in order to bring

New Inspectors' Report Form

In order that teachers may know what the new Inspectors' Reports are like, we are presenting a copy in this issue of the Journal.

PROVINCE OF MANITOBA

REPORT TO DEPARTMENT OF EDUCATION CONCERNING A TEACHER

.................................S.D. No..............Date of Visit..............................19......
....Sec.-Treas. ....Post Office

Grades	I	II	III	IV	V	VI	VII	VIII	IX	X	XI	XII
Enrolled												
Present												

Time spent with this teacher.......................a.m. to ....a.m.
                                                         p.m.   p.m.

Teacher .... Total teaching experience ....
                 (Name in full)   Service in this School ....

Address .... Conventions: M.E.A. ....
                 (in District)   Local ....

Certificates:
Teacher's ....Class. No...............
Principal's ....Kind. No........ Last Summer Session: Place ....
Valid to ....19...... Date.......................
Taught last term in ..........................S.D. Degree......................... University....................

GENERAL COMMENTS on appearance, personality, leadership in profession and community, and co-operation, whether favorable or otherwise:

IN CASE OF NEW TEACHERS: Is this teacher likely to become a definitely satisfactory teacher who might obtain later a permanent certificate? Yes............... No...............

IN CASE OF GRADED SCHOOLS: Does the Staff have regular meetings for discussion of school matters or study of educational questions? Yes............... No............... Give frequency of such meetings ....

RECOMMENDATIONS: To improve the effectiveness of this teacher's work, I recommend ....
....
....

I recommend that this teacher be granted (check): Permanent Certificate...............
Extension of Certificate...............

CLASS ROOM OBSERVATION:
Note: A check mark (x) in the appropriate column indicates the inspector's opinion concerning the item opposite which it is placed. When the grading of a teacher is not clear for any item at the time of the visit, the check mark should be placed on the dividing line between the two columns.

	Effective	Ineffective
I. Teacher's ability to:		
(a) Organize and plan his work		
(b) Follow his plan with due attention to flexibility		
(c) Discipline wisely		
(d) Use correct English		
(e) Speak distinctly		
(f) Present a problem clearly, logically and effectively, and guide pupils in its solution		
(g) Obtain well-distributed participation in work by all pupils		
(h) Adapt the instruction to varying abilities of pupils		
(i) Relate instruction to life interests of pupils and conditions and needs of community		
(j) Make definite and appropriate assignments		
(k) Organize and supervise play and extra-curricular activities		
II. Teacher's knowledge of:		
(a) Subject matter in the fields of the curriculum		
(b) Appropriate teaching procedures		
(c) Child psychology and laws of learning		
(d) Child guidance (educational, vocational)		
(e) System of records of pupil progress		
III. Teacher's attitude as shown by:		
(a) Industry and responsiveness of pupils		
(b) Preparation of his school work		
(c) Willingness to co-operate with Departmental program		
(d) Open-mindedness to suggestions		
(e) Interest in current educational developments		

Check the various methods you found this teacher using:
Socialized recitation ....Excursions, Surveys, etc...............Formal Drill...............
Activities: Individual ....Project Method ....Text Book Recitation...............
             Group..................Supervised Correspondence Instruction ....
Individualized Instruction...............

COMMENT on use or absence of supplementary materials and special aids in the schools: readers, radio, moving pictures, film slides, library, lectures.

GENERAL ESTIMATE of effectiveness of this teacher's work ....
           (Indicate as Excellent, Very Satisfactory, Good, Fair, Poor, Very Poor)
           ....
                                                         Inspector of Schools.

Fig. 12.1   Inspectors' report form, Manitoba, 1938

her class up to successful standing." His advice obviously didn't work, for
five weeks later she was notified that "her agreement expires March 31,
1922."[21] When, in 1926, a parent complained about Miss Hall's instruction in grade ix algebra, the board called in the high school inspector for
a special inspection; his recommendation was accepted and the teaching
of algebra was transferred from Miss Hall to the principal.[22] The board
also made salary increases dependant on good inspectors' reports, informing the entire staff on one occasion that they would not consider merit
increases because no inspector's report had been received "for the past
16 months" and they would consider increases only "upon receipt of the
Inspector's next report."[23]

Though true to some extent everywhere, particularly in the West, inspectorates tended to cover large geographical areas. According to Harold
Foght, writing in the mid-teens, in Saskatchewan "the smallest inspectorate embraces 1,548 square miles, or about 4½ municipalities; the largest
contains 6,372 square miles, or about 20 municipalities." In the larger
inspectorates, Foght continued, annual mileage ran as high as 7,000 miles.
"Inspectors in the newer parts of the province are obliged to endure considerable 'roughing it'; many of them carry their own camping outfits, including bed, cooking utensils, etc. These sections of the country require strong
men for the task."[24] J.B. McDougall was assigned his first inspectorate in
northern Ontario just before the turn of the century. It extended, he wrote
later, from "Nipissing District and East Algoma to White River, a territory
larger than all old Ontario measuring by continuous line throughout
almost 700 miles in length, or farther than from Toronto to Quebec City
... Over 14,700 miles was the distance made in one year's travel in the bare
work of inspection."[25] Alex Lord's first inspectorate, which included "only
44 schools and only 3 with more than one room," stretched from Prince
Rupert to the Alberta border and included "the British Columbia coast and
adjacent islands from Bella Coola to the Yukon and, in the northeast of the
province, the Peace River Block."[26] But piling up mileage was just in the
nature of the job; in 1935 Alberta's chief inspector reported that over the
past school year the inspectorate had travelled "on average, 9,091 miles."[27]
    Travel was accomplished by every imaginable means. Miller's basic cat-
egories when describing inspectoral workloads were boat, rail, horse, and
auto. But Alex Lord noted a long, hard ride by bicycle in rural British
Columbia.[28] "Taking a railway 'speeder' I 'pumped and pedalled' up an
eight mile grade to the nearest point by rail," J.B. McDougall records of one
trip; on other occasions he might be required "to travel 250 miles per week
by rail, to drive another 50 or tramp or canoe by land-trail or water route

Fig. 12.2   Inspector Everall crossing the Waterhen River, Manitoba, 1931

through unbroken solitudes, at intervals to toboggan behind the jogging dog-train, to camp where the trail ends and bunk where bunks may be."[29] By the second decade of the century, automobiles were beginning to take over from a team of horses but the transition was still far from complete. Making a pitch in 1915 for a travel subsidy given to some colleagues who had cars, one Alberta inspector proposed to sell his team on the grounds that an automobile immeasurably increased his efficiency. He was peremptorily slapped down by headquarters:

> I am of opinion that it will be impossible for you to do effective work, especially in the western part of your Inspectorate, unless you retain your team. Inspector McLean advises me that he was only able to use his auto for 4 weeks during the 6 months ending July 1st, and it is doubtful whether he will be able to use it for more than 9 or 10 weeks in the remainder of the year. He states it is absolutely necessary for him to have a team ... The Department therefore does not feel disposed to pay the extra grant.[30]

By the 1920s, nonetheless, improved roads and the telephone were gradually easing the workload in the more settled parts of the country.[31] And in June 1928 Manitoba claimed credit for the first school inspection made by airplane, north of Winnipeg in the Lake District. The inspector visited eight schools in a week, "completing what would otherwise have been six weeks undertaking. The schools are scattered and very difficult to reach except by boat. By the use of the airplane Inspector Dunlop was able to give these schools more than usual attention."[32]

Even under the best of circumstances, however, the "usual attention" was limited. While isolated schools and excessively large inspectoral districts always caused difficulties, the sheer number of schools tended to be a problem everywhere. There was, after all, a maximum of two hundred school days and in reality fewer than that due to severe weather conditions, the exigencies of other job responsibilities, personal health, and so on. "The total number of classrooms assigned to the men in 1922 was 5,730, several rural schools and most village schools having two or more classrooms in operation," wrote Saskatchewan's chief inspector; "the average number of classrooms assigned to each inspector was 133." Nearly all rural schools were visited once, he added, though a hundred did go uninspected; but on average only thirty-one second inspections were made during the year.[33] Throughout the rest of the 1920s the average load in Saskatchewan remained about 133 schools, leading the chief inspector to remark, at the end of the decade, that the work of the inspector "is greatly handicapped owing to the large number of schools under his jurisdiction."[34] With fiscal retrenchment during the Depression, the number of inspectors was reduced and thus inspectorates increased in size. "This had the natural result that the inspectors were not able to visit their schools as often as formerly. In fact in some of the areas it was difficult ... to make more than one visit to a school during the year."[35]

In 1910 Alberta had thirteen inspectors, and by 1920, with the aim of completing two annual visits to each school, the staff stood at thirty-eight.[36] Government budget cuts in 1923, however, brought that number down to twenty-five. "By this reduction," wrote the editor of the *ATA Magazine*, "the staff will be the same as in 1914 when the school population was little more than half as great as at the present time."[37] From 1923 until the later 1930s the inspectors averaged only slightly more than one visit per year.[38] But that average included many multiple visits and some schools not visited at all. In 1930, for example, 3,527 schoolrooms were visited once, 1,011 received two visits, 14 received three visits, and 249 rural schools "in which uncontrollable circumstances interfered" received no visit at all.[39] At that point inspectors were, on average, responsible for 131 school districts and 172 classrooms; in 1935 the average was still 170.[40] Nor was Alberta an extreme case. In 1926–27 Nova Scotia's superintendent of schools reported that nine of his fourteen inspectors had 200 schools or more.[41] The load was just as bad or worse in New Brunswick.[42]

School visits, in any case, represented only one part of the job. As early as 1913 James Miller's sample of inspectors were reporting, besides the large amount of time spent travelling, "the apparent equality or predominance of administrative duties over those of supervisor."[43] In the mid-1920s British Columbia's Putman-Weir Report estimated that only about a quarter of the inspector's time was spent in school visits; in Alberta in 1935 the estimate was no more than 40%.[44] Not every classroom, it must be said, required an annual, let alone semi-annual, visit. Some teachers were known quantities, considered competent and requiring no more than an occasional perfunctory appearance by the inspector.[45] But in many cases the bare minimum of visits required by law was all that inspectors accomplished, and in some provinces at some points of time, not even that.

In principle at least, the improvement of instruction through professional support, encouragement, direction, and advice about pedagogical methods or techniques of classroom management had always been one of the inspector's legally mandated responsibilities. And it gained increasing emphasis in each successive decade after 1900.[46] This role, commonly labelled "supervision," as distinct from inspection narrowly conceived, was particularly vital in the countryside, where the inspector was the only experienced professional the teacher in the one-room school had any contact with.[47] But this was one part of the job most inspectors were *not* doing, because, under existing circumstances, it couldn't be done. From one end of the country to the other, from the turn of the century to the 1940s, the lack of supervision was identified as one of the biggest impediments to the improvement of rural education. "At present," wrote Norman Black, a prominent British Columbia educator, "it is notorious that despite the best efforts of our public school inspectors, the country schools ... are all but unsupervised."[48] In 1930 Prince Edward Island's Royal Commission on Education met with "considerable complaint and criticism ... in almost all the places visited" that the inspectorate "spends an average of not more than two hours in the school twice a year, hears as many classes as possible, observes the teacher's methods, and leaves the district without having time to advise or help the teacher in her multifarious problems, or to suggest or demonstrate improved methods." Inspection was important, the commission suggested, but even more important, "it should also be directed to the improvement of existing conditions by all possible counsel and guidance; to the diagnosis of what is wrong in the school; to the prescribing of what he thinks the necessary remedy; not so much to test processes as to demonstrate better ways and means of instruction."[49] A decade earlier there had been this tirade from an experienced Ontario schoolman: "In Ontario, each inspector has over 100 teachers, who are in charge of between 2,500 and 3,000 pupils, distributed among 75 to 85 rural schools and a few urban schools; that is, an inspector has to reach his place of work on successive days in about 90 different centres, most of which are in the rural sections 1½ to 4 or 5 miles apart. One man might supervise 100 teachers if they were in the same building (even though that would be a gigantic task), but when these are scattered throughout the length and breadth of a county or inspectorate 20 miles square or more, in the most favourable case, the supervision becomes more or less superficial if not farcical."⁵⁰ In 1938 W.H. Swift, already an experienced Alberta inspector and a future deputy minister, pointed to the "factors operative to limit constructive work in the improvement of instruction, the press of administrative duties, the extent of the area to be covered, short and infrequent visits to schools, and the infeasibility of getting teachers together in groups." Alberta, he continued, "has no tradition of supervision. It has, rather, one of inspection. These two are very different." Inspection was about evaluation of teacher performance: "It serves to determine whether a teacher is earning his salary ... whether he should be continued in employment or dismissed ... It is not concerned with the improvement of instruction except by the indirect means of holding out rewards and punishments in terms of gradings on reports. Supervision, on the other hand, is concerned primarily with the improvement of the child's school experience by the more direct means of working with teachers, in the classrooms, in groups, by suggesting materials and methods – through a co-operative rather than an inquisitorial approach."⁵¹

Implicitly or explicitly, rural teachers drew the same distinction and reached similar conclusions. Based on her interviews with people who taught in the Okanagan Valley during the 1920s, Penelope Stephenson sums up their assessments about the efficacy of inspectoral visitations this way:

Just as teachers in rural schools were inadequately prepared for the tasks they encountered in the classroom, they also suffered from a professional support system that was sadly lacking and did little to mitigate the daily frustrations of one-room teaching. Teacher anecdotes about the nature of their relationships with the inspectors who supervised their work manifested an ambivalent attitude towards these men.
On the one hand teachers looked forward to visits from their inspector because they offered news of the "outside" and thus a welcome respite from the overwhelming feeling of isolation that was so common amongst those who taught in outlying rural districts. Often, as historian John Calam has pointed out, the inspector was the "sole educational professional in whom they could confide during an entire school year."

Generally, however, most teachers were not overly impressed with the quality of the service they received from their inspectors. In this context they cited a number of specific grievances related mainly to availability and utility.[52]

Stephenson goes on to discuss these grievances in some detail; they included minimal contact with the inspector, "few practical or constructive suggestions ... on how to improve their performance in the classroom," and a near-exclusive emphasis on inspection rather than support. The typical rural teacher, she concludes, "often felt very much alone as regards professional help and support. As Alice Gibson so succinctly stated: 'What do I remember about teaching in a rural school? That I was entirely on my own.' Marianne Nelson reiterated Alice's sentiments almost exactly: 'You were on your own. You were completely on your own.'"[53]

II

In Canada's graded schools, on the other hand, no teacher was ever "completely on her own." Aside from the presence of colleagues able to provide informal support and advice, there was the first, and most familiar, authority figure a teacher was likely to encounter in her professional career – the "headmaster" or "principal teacher."[54] If there were to be close or effective supervision of a teacher's work, it was most likely to originate from the principal's office.

Generally speaking, principals were well educated. At the high school level they were mostly university graduates, and in the elementary school they normally held first-class professional certificates. They were also highly experienced, having taught for lengthy periods in ungraded and graded schools. There was, however, little in the way of specialized training for the job anywhere in the country beyond the kind of informal apprenticeship garnered from watching others and learning on one's own. Through years of classroom teaching and absorbing the distinct but associated skills of building management, individuals acquired a store of tacit and rule-of-thumb knowledge that drew little or nothing from the theories of school administration just beginning to emerge in the period.[55]

Given the presence of a principal in the graded school, many of the duties and powers of the classroom teacher were transferred to the principal's office. As the Alberta act put it, more succinctly than most, "the Principal shall ... be responsible for the organization and discipline of the whole school."[56] Some provinces offered somewhat more direction than this, but in the main the specification of the principal's duties was left to the local board of trustees, who appointed the principal in the first place.

In British Columbia, for example, provincial regulations set out only a few general duties and powers that applied to all principals, in large and small school districts alike.[57] But by 1914 the Vancouver board's instructions to principals included a list of twenty-nine duties that took some eight pages to specify – and that on top of another thirty-seven that applied to them as classroom teachers.[58] By the 1930s Moncton had a set of nineteen rules governing the principal's job.[59]

Whether in Vancouver or elsewhere, much of the reporting and record-keeping tasks assigned to the teacher in the one-room school fell to the principal of the graded school, either through collating the returns of individual teachers or by generating his own. These included records relating to admissions, registration, attendance (of both pupils and teachers), truancy, marks, promotions, and anything else required by the trustees or the department of education. He was responsible for informing pupils of their duties, enforcing the rules, dealing with cases of discipline, issuing suspensions, ensuring adequate playground supervision, and exercising oversight for the physical and hygienic state of the building and grounds. He requisitioned and distributed supplies and conducted regular fire drills. He was expected to maintain uniform instructional and promotion standards among his teachers, assign them their subjects and other routine responsibilities, and prepare the school timetables. It was also his job to monitor the quality of instruction, a role that involved visiting classrooms, assisting with pedagogical problems, organizing regular staff meetings to discuss and improve instruction, and reporting to the trustees on the progress of pupils and success of the teachers.[60] What all this amounted to was an interlocking set of responsibilities that included clerical, managerial, and supervisory work – and, in many cases, janitor of last resort.

In his annual report for 1910 the chairman of the London board penned this effusive passage: "The duties of our Principals are manifold and important. Not only are they required to teach continuously a large class preparing for the Entrance examination, but they must also take charge of a large school plant; look after the admission of new pupils, consult with parents, receive and distribute the school supplies. There is another duty that calls for ability of a very high order – they must be able to furnish leadership, inspiration and criticism that will be helpful to their teachers, and assist them to do their best work with the least strain."[61] Just how principals were supposed to find the time, amidst all their other responsibilities, to provide "leadership, inspiration, and criticism" to assist their teachers "to do their best work" remained a puzzle throughout the period. In the first place, the principal, like the inspector, did his work without much clerical help. In his 1920 survey of Canadian city schools, W.L. Richardson found that "15 school boards provide their high school principals with a clerk full-time and in Vancouver and Calgary, high schools have a clerk for half time, but in 22 cities the principal of the high school receives no clerical assistance." Only four cities reported any clerical assistance for their elementary school principals, two of which provided only "a small amount."[62] Towards the end of the decade W.F. Dyde, writing about his nationwide sample of high school principals, found that only in the largest high schools was clerical assistance common. In other schools only a minority could count on it. "It may be said without fear of contradiction," he concluded, "that 60% of principals in schools of from 10 to 20 teachers are spending each week a considerable amount of time in routine clerical work which a secretary could do equally well or better – time, in fact, wasted so far as the important duties of the head of a high school are concerned."[63]

The other and far more pressing constraint was the fact that most Canadian principals remained, quite literally, head-*teachers*. Principals taught full-time or at least most of the time, fulfilling their other responsibilities on a catch-as-catch-can basis, much of it out of school hours. Most clerical and managerial tasks could be done this way, while regular staff meetings and fleeting individual encounters undoubtedly contributed to the principal's supervisory role. But above all, supervision of instruction required visiting classes *during* school hours, which could only be accomplished with release time from teaching; and it could only be done thoroughly with substantial release time. Even at the high school level, Richardson reported, most principals taught: in fourteen of fifty-seven cities they taught full-time, or 90% of a full load, and only in another fourteen were they entirely free of teaching regular classes. "For the majority of principals," Dyde added, "teaching absorbs more of their working time than all other school duties combined."[64] In the elementary schools a full teaching load was the rule, relief the exception. In 1920, according to Richardson, only in the large schools in Toronto and Winnipeg were principals relieved of teaching duties. In some schools in Ottawa "the principal teaches half time, and in Hamilton, Calgary and Vancouver, 4 principals teach almost full time. Elsewhere in Canadian cities the principal of elementary schools assumes the full amount of regular class work."[65] Even in the major cities, Richardson concluded, the principal's time for supervision was "deplorably meagre."[66] "In many of our schools," said the chairman of the Halifax School Board in 1931, "the Principals have little or no chance for supervision, which, in my opinion, is very necessary, especially in the larger schools."[67]

In the major urban centres, teaching relief became more common each decade, but even there it was mostly part-time. Describing the arrangements in Winnipeg in the early 1930s, the city's superintendent of schools wrote that there were twenty-nine large schools (twenty-four elementary and five high schools) with sixteen classes or more. Each had a "supervising principal" who was responsible "for general administration, is required to give detailed supervision to the work of the teachers, and whenever possible, takes the place of an absent teacher in order that a substitute may not be necessary"; but he still "spends a considerable portion of his time in actual teaching ... The remaining 27 principals of smaller schools are full-time teachers and are responsible for the work of the school as a whole, as well as for the class which they register."[68] In Toronto, in 1930, forty of the ninety elementary schools had a "principal's assistant" who taught half-time, thus relieving the principal for other work; another six or seven had some lesser amount of relief, but that still left half the city's elementary principals teaching full-time.[69] During the interwar years a few cities also began to convert ad hoc arrangements for relief time into the formal post of "vice-principal," who taught part-time but could also assist the principal in both administrative and supervisory tasks. In 1930, for example, London appointed vice-principals for each of its three collegiate institutes (though not for any of its elementary schools).[70] About the same time, Saskatoon began a similar process in its elementary schools.[71]

Beyond the larger towns and cities, however, a heavy teaching load was more or less taken for granted everywhere, principals doing most of their clerical and managerial work outside school hours. Blairmore was probably typical of small urban communities. Its principal taught full-time until 1925, when, after some undisclosed difficulties within the school, almost certainly discipline related, the trustees agreed to hire a substitute teacher "*one day in every two weeks* for the purpose of permitting the Principal to inspect the Public School."[72] In the mid-1930s Arthur Harris surveyed 109 graded schools in rural Manitoba, a sample of about 50%. Tabulating the results of his questionnaires, Harris concluded that "the supervising ... activities of the principal in relation to his staff is of a negative character. The great majority, 88 out of 109, do not visit classrooms, and only 3 of those that do visit classrooms really make the visits worthwhile." There were several reasons for this, he suggested, including a lack of training. But a major cause was "the heavy teaching load ... When a principal has from 1,200 to 1,385 minutes of teaching out of every 1,500 in an average week he has little or no time for direct supervision of teaching."[73] Another principal in a small Manitoban community asked rhetorically, "'How can a village Principal who has a full-time teaching job accomplish the work of supervision as it should be done?' My own answer to this question is that it is impossible unless his own classes are to be neglected, which no one has a right to do ... For a principal who is teaching the whole day very little can be done in supervising the work of individual teachers during school hours."[74] Supervision could prove problematic even in medium-sized towns. In Moncton all thirteen principals had some relief time but no clerical assistance. "The major function of a principal is supervision," wrote one observer, "yet the principals ... spend so much time teaching and attending to routine clerical tasks that they are not permitted to attend to their major function."[75]

By listing all teachers in British Columbia, school by school, and indicating those principals who did not teach, the British Columbia *Annual Reports* offer a rare data set that enables us to probe the matter systematically and over time. The data do not tell us explicitly if a principal had partial release time; many of those we count as teaching principals *may* have had some release time, though we are fairly certain many did not.[76] Before 1920 it was rare for *any* elementary school principals in British Columbia to have *any* release time. In Vancouver, however, 2 out of 27 principals were on full-time release in the school year 1920–21 (about 7%). The figure stood at 14% in 1923–24 (4 out of 29 principals) but then rose rapidly to 44% by 1928–29 (24 out of 54 principals). We also know from other sources that beginning in 1927, all Vancouver principals received some release time for supervising duties – full-time release in the larger schools, half-time in the rest.[77] Thus, in the latter half of the 1920s, many, perhaps most, Vancouver elementary schools did indeed have principals who could exercise close supervision. This changed dramatically during the Depression, however. Partial release time may or may not have survived,[78] but full-time did not: from 44% of principals in 1928–29, it declined to 15% in 1931–32 (8 out of 53 principals) and remained at that level for the rest of the decade – barely above the figure for 1920–21.

Outside of Vancouver in 1920–21 only three of sixty-two city elementary schools had a principal with full-time release. By 1928–29 the figure stood at seven out of sixty-seven schools; but during the Depression the number grew only marginally, and by 1938–39 several communities that, in the past, had provided release time for elementary principals had cut the position and given the high school principal supervisory responsibilities over the junior high and elementary schools as well. In the multi-teacher elementary schools of the province's rural municipalities, full-time release was very nearly unknown across the entire two decades. Even in suburban Burnaby, which had eighteen elementary schools by 1938–39, some of them very large, there were only two non-teaching principals that school year. What all this means is that, outside of Vancouver, only a few city elementary schools had principals with full-time supervisory roles; in the rural municipality schools, it was rare; in the few multi-teacher schools in the rural districts, it was unknown; and even in Vancouver the Depression cut deeply into the amount of supervision that principals could provide for their staffs.

High school principals in charge of large schools tended to be somewhat better off, though even here there was no simple pattern. In the larger schools included in Dyde's Canada-wide sample – "those with eleven to six-teen classrooms – some principals spend no time in classroom supervision, others spend as much as 2 hours a day."[79] In Nova Scotia, another study con-cluded, the principal of a high school or academy could rarely do proper supervision because "in nearly every instance his teaching load and other duties make it impossible to do any effective guiding of associate teachers except at staff meetings."[80] Visiting a succession of Ontario high schools in the mid-1920s, an experienced English school inspector was surprised to find that, except in the largest schools, "free periods are very much the exception and both Principal and staff alike often – nay usually – teach every period of the week. In such cases it is, of course, very difficult for the Principal to supervise the work of his colleagues and to exercise his full influence on the school as a whole."[81] A decade later, in a study of British Columbia's rural high schools, R.G. Gordon complained that "the lack of adequate supervision in small schools is a serious matter. In large urban centres we find the 'walking principal,' and in some semi-rural localities the principal with part-time supervising functions. However, when we come to discuss education in districts served by small rural high schools and supe-rior schools, supervision has practically disappeared, the whole time of the principal being absorbed in the everyday routine of teaching."[82] In sum, more principals received clerical assistance and relief from full teaching loads in 1940 than in 1900. But not all did, and most received both in limited amounts. Change came slowly under the best of circumstances, the Great Depression hardly encouraged expenditures on teaching relief or clerical assistance, and well into the decade of the 1940s most principals were as close or closer to the classroom as to the principal's office.

III

The principal might be head of a rural school with no more than one or two additional teachers or in charge of a large, multi-teacher central school in a village like Blairmore. So long as there was only one school in a school district, and thus one principal reporting to the board of school trustees, a principal could, within the constraints we have just outlined, oversee the school's activities and monitor pupil progress. Once there was more than one school, however, oversight became more complicated, if only because of the need to co-ordinate instructional practices and ensure a modicum of uniformity in issues ranging from promotion policies to the fair allocation of fiscal resources among the schools. Thus boards tended to centralize oversight by having one particular individual exercise, on their behalf, gen-eral authority over instruction. In a larger village or small town this might mean promoting the senior head-teacher to "supervising principal," making him the intermediary between trustees and each of the other schools even while he carried on as principal of his own. In a metropolitan centre, on the other hand, there was likely to be a distinct central office headed by a "superintendent of schools." These were not innovations peculiar to the early twentieth century; they had been gaining momentum for decades as urban growth created more and larger communities with several schools to administer. But one way or another, multiple buildings within a school district normally brought a shift in the locus of authority from school principal to some superordinate supervisory officer.*

Everywhere, provincial law provided for the appointment of these senior supervisors, and did so in much the same way as the law dealt with the principalship, either relegating this task to the residual powers of local trustees, or introducing clauses explicitly authorizing it. In some provinces only urban boards might be allowed to make such an appointment; in others, any board could do it. The duties of the supervisor might be specified or left to trustees; the appointment might be a local option or mandated. In Saskatchewan, for example, "the board of trustees of any town or city in which at least 15 teachers are regularly employed may ... appoint a superintendent of schools."[83] In Manitoba, "any board of school trustees shall have the power ... to appoint, with the consent of the Department, a superintendent."[84] In Ontario, every city had to appoint an "Inspector of Public Schools" and contribute to his salary. He was first and foremost the representative and servant of the department – the urban equivalent of the county school inspector; but it had long been a common practice for city boards to assign him additional managerial and supervisory duties.[85] In Nova Scotia, wherever there was more than one school in a district, "it shall be the duty of the school board to appoint one principal of all the schools of the section [i.e., school district], who shall be the advisory officer of the board with reference to the general management of the schools, and shall be responsible, together with the board and its secretary, for the harmonious co-ordination of the work of each school department ... When the schools are so numerous as to require the whole time of said principal ... in supervisory work instead of the regular teaching of a class, he may be known as the supervisor of the schools of the section."[86]

Except in Ontario and British Columbia, where city inspectors wore two hats, responsible as inspectors to the department and as local administrators to the trustees, the urban supervisory officer was not directly respon-

* While we will frequently refer to these senior supervisory officers as "superintendents," there was no common national nomenclature. Simply because of their numbers in Ontario (and to a lesser extent in British Columbia), the most frequent English-Canadian title was "inspector"; on the prairies, "superintendent" was common; and in the Maritimes, "supervisor." In small communities everywhere the title was likely to be "supervising principal."

sible to provincial authorities. But even where the appointment was of an entirely local character, the trustees were never free to choose just anyone who took their fancy. In all provinces the appointment had to be approved by the department or meet specified certification requirements. Senior supervisory officers, like principals, tended to be well educated. In 1920, for example, more than 80% were university graduates and a few had post-graduate degrees.[87] They also tended to have substantial experience as teachers and principals.

Unlike today's supervisory officer, however, there was no settled career trajectory leading to such appointments. Before 1940, few had professional training in educational administration, a specialty nearly unknown in Canadian universities, and not even extensive in-school experience was an essential prerequisite. When Calgary appointed its first superintendent of schools, it selected A.M. Scott, who served in that capacity from 1906 to 1930 and remained as part of a reorganized administration till 1935. His total teaching experience consisted of three years as a young man in rural Ontario. However, he held a PhD from a distinguished German university and was, at the time of his appointment, professor of chemistry at the University of New Brunswick.[88] Decades later, in the early 1940s, when the Saint John School Board went looking for a new superintendent of schools, it fell upon A.W. Trueman, who for a few years had taught both elementary and secondary school and went on to graduate from Mount Allison, then Oxford, after which he was appointed a professor of English at Mount Allison. Saint John hired him away from the university but held on to him for only three years before he went west to become president of the University of Manitoba.[89] What mattered in appointments like this was not trained expertise but a reputation for sound scholarship of a traditional sort and the aura of authority and respectability that clung to the nineteenth-century ideal of the professional gentleman.[90]

A second difference between then and now was that the superintendent was rarely the equivalent of a "chief executive officer" exclusively responsible to the trustees, to whom all other senior employees were subordinate. In the big cities, school administration was most commonly divided between a series of co-ordinate appointments, each responsible to the trustees for one major department – finance, physical plant, architecture and design, instruction, etc. As late as 1939, for example, the Winnipeg board had five heads of department, all of equal rank and responsible directly to the school board through standing committees that had control over them: a "secretary-treasurer (secretarial and financial)," a "commissioner of supplies," a "commissioner of buildings," a "chief operating engineer," and a "superintendent (educational)."[91] Toronto had a similar administrative structure.[92] In a series of gradual adjustments during the interwar years, London moved towards a unified organization where the "inspector-administrator" was chief executive officer, the model preferred by the leading educational theorists of the age.[93] But that was unusual. In the main the senior supervisor was not, strictly speaking, "superintendent of schools" but "superintendent of instruction," a much more limited kind of executive authority. That power, moreover, was always hedged in by the superior authority of departmental regulations and policies and the provincial inspectorate. Though much discretionary power rested with school boards and their senior officials and was sustained by big-city budgets that allowed many innovative initiatives, in Canada the province and not the locality determined the parameters of policy and practice.

Just as many of the duties of the teacher were, in graded schools, centralized in the hands of the principal, so the appointment of senior supervisory officers centralized much of the powers exercised by principals in single-building school districts. While the exact phraseology differed from board to board, the core directive for the "inspector-superintendent" in Stratford, Ontario, was typical: "He shall have a general supervision over and be responsible for the organization, discipline and teaching in the schools."[94] This involved at least three elements: advice to the board on all matters relating to instruction, broadly defined; inspection of teachers on behalf of both the department and the board of trustees; and "school leadership" – promoting good practice, monitoring pupil progress, and innovative policy-making. In carrying out these tasks, the superintendent prepared reports and recommendations for the board; dealt with correspondence from the provincial department, individual trustees, ratepayers, parents, and the press; recommended the hiring or firing of teachers; and established system-wide rules on matters great and small, from policies governing admissions, transfers, promotions, or corporal punishment, to "Occasional Day's Absence" of teachers and "Lates of Teachers and Pupils."[95] He also directed and co-ordinated the work of his principals, met with his teachers in individual schools and larger venues, and visited classrooms. "In the great majority of city systems," Richardson found, "the chief executive reports that he spends from one-half to nearly all of the school time each year observing the class teaching of his staff."[96]

In most of the cities Richardson investigated, the superintendency was a full-time job. Not always, however: he also noted that "the superintendent is engaged in teaching regular classes for one-half or more of his time in a few of the smaller cities, e.g. Fredericton, Fort William, Kitchener, Sault Ste Marie, and Lethbridge." In cities like these "the head of the school system definitely says that he has no time to observe other teachers at work because he is himself engaged in teaching almost full-time."[97] In yet smaller urban

communities this was the rule rather than the exception: though almost
certainly to have some release time from the classroom, he was unlikely
to escape teaching responsibilities entirely. A.S. Towell of Nanaimo was
perhaps typical. In 1933 he was supervising principal of that city's school
system, which consisted of a combined junior-senior high school and four
elementary schools. In the midst of a thoughtful article in the *BC Teacher* on
another subject entirely, he noted, almost in passing, that "the Principal
teaches 18 periods per week in the senior section besides undertaking a
share of study-room supervision. He is also responsible for the administration of the combined school and of four elementary schools, a total staff of
38."[98] This sort of arrangement was common. In Woodstock, Ontario, for
example, the principal of the central school was also supervising principal
for the town, responsible for thirty-three teachers in five schools.[99]

From early in the century and in some cases well before 1900, big-city
boards had begun adding additional supervisory staff at central office.
These were of two kinds: generalist assistant superintendents and supervisors of special subjects.[100] Examining the record in fourteen of English
Canada's larger urban centres, Richardson found that by 1920 eight had an
assistant superintendent, though only Toronto had more than one; seven
had a complement of between three and six special supervisors; and seven
of the fourteen had clerical assistance at central office. Toronto, with nearly
1,700 teachers, had by far the largest supervisory staff, with seven assistant
superintendents and twenty-three subject supervisors. Winnipeg, with 677
teachers, was second, with one assistant superintendent and ten supervisors.[101] Subject supervisors were most commonly hired for manual training,
domestic science, and physical education, more rarely for music and art.
In very large systems there might be two of each, working in the junior
and senior grades respectively. Three cities had supervisors for the primary
grades: three in Winnipeg and one each in Vancouver and Regina.

What did all these people do? The major task of the assistant superintendent was school supervision. "The Senior Inspector, with the weight of
important administration upon him," wrote Ottawa's assistant superintendent, "has very properly been relieved of much of the classroom inspection.
In 1917 he made 122 visits to schools while the Junior Inspector made 276
visits."[102] In 1920 Toronto's seven assistants, working under the authority
of the superintendent, each had responsibility for supervision in one district of the city.[103] A decade later, when Edmonton appointed its first assistant superintendent, he was given responsibility for the elementary schools
and, among other things, instructed to visit the schools regularly to inspect
and give advice to teachers, "direct the principals ... in the administration

of their respective schools and in their supervision of instruction," "submit to the superintendent an efficiency value on each teacher," and prepare the June test papers for, and supervise the grading of, the annual promotion exams.[104]

The job of the subject supervisors was to oversee and improve instruction in those areas of the curriculum that teachers were least well prepared to cope with. In 1922, for example, London's supervisor of art gave demonstration lessons "on technique, design and decoration, principles, mediums, ways and means ... to classes of from 40 to 70 teachers," as well as giving more advanced training to fifteen teachers "who, with special aptitude for drawing, and with the assistance and direction of the supervisor, are in charge of the work in two or more classes in those schools in which they are placed."[105] In 1914, explaining the value of employing a supervisor of primary work, Vancouver's municipal inspector also exposed the impetus by which central bureaucracies multiplied: "While we have many primary teachers who can do excellent teaching unaided, we find many who can be greatly helped by one who is an expert in the art of teaching a beginning class. The marked improvement in the primary work of our schools during the past two years under a supervisor naturally suggests the question, 'Why not have supervisors as well for the Intermediate and Senior grades?'"[106] Probably attempting to justify to his public the need for a bevy of central office supervisors in the midst of a depression, Winnipeg's school board chairman offered, in 1933, this helpful and unusually detailed explanation of their work:

> [The several subject supervisors] visit regularly the teachers over the whole system and give detailed direction to the work of their special subjects. They plan courses of study, assist the teachers and test the work of the pupils. The four general supervisors of elementary grades visit the teachers of the elementary schools in which the principals do full-time teaching and have no time to supervise in detail the work of other teachers in their schools. They also supplement the work of the supervising principals in the larger schools by assisting in the direction of the teaching in the primary grades. They maintain standards of achievement in all phases of the work ... They test pupils from time to time, advise principals in the matters of promotion and classification of pupils and generally stimulate the work of the teachers by keeping them in touch with the best methods of instruction and class management.[107]

It is the rarest of occasions when we get to see the urban superintendent or supervisor from the teacher's viewpoint, so we take the liberty of quoting

at length from an essay by Sybil Shack, who would go on to a distinguished
teaching career in Manitoba; here, she is reminiscing about her first year of
teaching in the mid-1930s.

> My second supervisor, Ms Maude Bradshaw, was quite different from
> my first. She had been hired in 1908, with a second-class certificate. By
> 1937 she looked like a caricature of an old maid schoolteacher, with her
> high necked dresses, her thin white hair in a tight knob on top of her
> head with a few stray wisps straggling from it. But Ms Bradshaw knew
> her business. She came into my room and said, "Ms Shack, if you are
> going to teach in the elementary school, you must know how to write
> properly." She was talking of penmanship, not composition. She then
> proceeded to spend an intensive half hour teaching me the relationship
> of the cursive letters to one another, how they should be spaced and
> joined, and what alternative forms of the capital letters were acceptable.
> What she taught me I have never forgotten. To this day I can choose
> between my two forms of handwriting, my natural and my school
> scripts.
>
> The visit of the supervisor was a source of anxiety. The first teacher
> or caretaker to note her arrival would send a messenger around with
> a certain book. On one occasion a note was included that read, "The
> old cow is here." It reached several of us before someone had the good
> judgement to take it out, tear it into small pieces and dispose of it. What
> if "the old cow" had stopped the messenger and read the note?
>
> All the primary supervisors were women, as were those of music,
> art, sewing and household arts. In my day in schools where there were
> teaching principals, the supervisors visited all the grades from one to
> six. In schools where there were full time principals, the supervisors
> were responsible only for the primary grades one to three. The super-
> visors had a great influence on the teachers entrusted to their tender
> mercies. Their recommendations were often the deciding factor in the
> matter of moves and promotions. Even more important was the effect
> they had on the mental health of those they supervised. A good super-
> visor helped a good teacher to become better. A miserable supervisor
> led to the departure from Manitoba or the profession of the same good
> teacher. Over the years we had examples of both kinds.[108]

Although the momentum was almost certainly slowed by the Great Depression, the general pattern in urban Canada during the interwar years was
continuing growth in the number of supervisory staff. By 1923 when J.H.
Putman and George Weir conducted their survey of the British Columbia
school system, Vancouver's school board had a superintendent and assistant

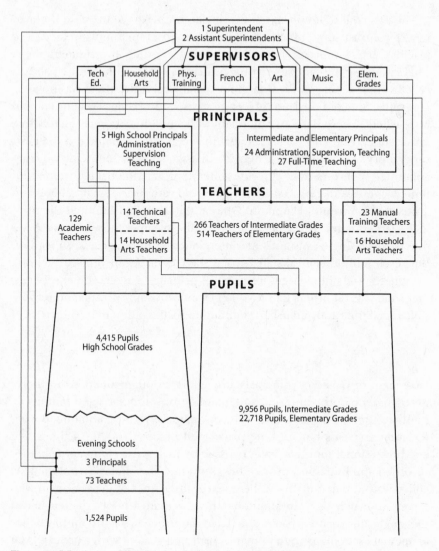

Fig. 12.3   Winnipeg public schools, administration and supervision, 1933

superintendent (both known as municipal inspectors of schools), a director of night schools, four supervisors of special subjects (manual training, drawing, sewing, and domestic science), one supervisor each for special classes and primary work, a psychologist, and a social worker (plus a large complement of medical doctors and nurses).[109] The substantial establishment for the supervision of instruction in Winnipeg is best illustrated in Figure 12.3 (the reader needs to keep in mind that this represents only one department of a much larger central administration in charge of the city's schools).[110]

This was typical, however, of only the largest urban centres. Consider by way of contrast some other examples. In 1940 Moncton, with about 150 teachers, had a superintendent and, at central office, two stenographers. There were two full-time supervising principals and the other principals had relief from teaching "for several hours each week." But there was no assistant superintendent and no subject supervisors. In Fredericton, with about 60 teachers, "there is a superintendent with a full-time secretary, a full-time music supervisor, and each principal in the city has a half-day a week for supervisory work with his teachers."[111] In 1930 some sixteen Ontario cities appointed their own inspector-superintendent, ranging from Toronto with ninety schools and 2,088 teachers to Welland with its five small schools and 49 teachers. Toronto, Hamilton, Ottawa, Windsor, and London, the province's largest cities, all had an extensive cadre of supervisory officers. A few others had a single assistant superintendent and one specialist supervisor. But seven had no central staff beyond the city inspector himself. Outside the cities, some of the larger towns had a principal's assistant or a supervising principal; yet others had no-one beyond the county inspector, responsible for all the rural and urban communities alike within his jurisdiction.[112]

IV

How many of Canada's principals, inspectors, or other supervisory officers were women? Both anecdotal and quantitative sources suggest that a substantial number of women served as principals, more commonly during the interwar years but in some places well before that. All of the teachers' professional journals, issue by issue or in regular summary columns, recorded appointments, promotions, retirements, obituaries, and the like; collectively and cumulatively, these reveal the names of many women who served as principals.[113] In Manitoba's intermediate schools, the teacher in the single high school room also acted as principal of the multi-teacher elementary school; in 1929 women constituted 30% of such teachers.[114] Of Calgary's forty elementary and junior high schools in the same year, fifteen were led by women.[115] The annual reports of the Winnipeg board always recorded appointments of women principals during the interwar years, and by the early 1940s, 80% of its elementary-level principals were women.[116] Of the eight schools in Fredericton in 1935–36, three had women principals.[117] In a study of two southwestern Ontario counties and the city of London, Carol Small found that, in 1917, 49% of the elementary principals were women, while in 1928 the figure was 41%.[118] During the school year 1929–30 there were, in two inspectoral districts at either end of Ontario, seven women elementary school principals versus six men in Huron West, and five women versus four men in Leeds-Grenville No. 1. In the same year,

55% of the principals in the whole province in the two-teacher continuation schools, and 33% in those with three or four teachers, were women.[119] A year earlier, in British Columbia, 37% of the principals in the city elementary schools outside Vancouver, 43% of those in the rural municipality schools, and 40% of those in the rural and assisted schools were women.[120] And Thomas Fleming has demonstrated that these provincial data are no fluke: in 1912, 58% of all British Columbia's principals were female, and in 1924, 49%, though falling to 38% in 1937.[121] In the years before the Second World War, in other words, despite a downward trend, plenty of women served as principals, and thus it was not unusual for many pupils and teachers to experience a school environment in which women rather than men exercised authority.

That point having been made, however, we can proceed to the qualifiers, which are substantial indeed. In the first place, women were largely excluded from the secondary sector. In W.F. Dyde's mid-twenties national sample of high schools and collegiate institutes, only 6.4% of the principals were women, with all but one confined to the smallest schools *within* his smallest category of schools by staff size.[122] In 1930, to take but one typical year, none of the 64 Ontario collegiate institutes had a woman principal, and only 7 of the 143 high schools. These 7 schools, moreover, with between two and four assistant teachers, were among the smallest high schools in the province.[123] While the number of women principals was far higher in Ontario's continuation schools, the larger the school the less likely were women to be in charge, and even in the two-teacher schools, where 55% were led by women, they were less likely to be principal if the other teacher was male.[124] In 1928–29, no British Columbia city had a woman high school principal; in the rural municipality high schools the figure was only 20% and they were to be found only in the smaller schools.[125] Similarly, in Manitoba: while 25% of the "intermediate schools" had women principals, the figure dropped to 16% of the high schools with more than one department and 10% of the collegiate institutes.[126] In Winnipeg by the early 1940s, women principals accounted for only 8% of the junior high school heads and were entirely absent in the senior high schools.[127]

At the elementary level the record is more variable. As we have already suggested, there were school boards, large and small, that over the years appointed a sizable number of women principals. But there were others where appointments were no more than token at best. During the inter-war years Vancouver had only a handful of women principals, mostly in charge of the smaller schools, and fewer still during the 1940s.[128] From 1909 through 1947 the Saskatoon School Board made ninety-four appointments; only four of these went to women.[129] In Toronto only seven of eighty-two elementary principals (8.5%) were women in 1930, and the percentage actually declined a decade later to less than 5%.[130]

Women were not always assigned to the smallest elementary schools. For a couple of decades in the early twentieth century, the unusually large central school in Trail, British Columbia, which by the early 1920s enrolled nearly 600 pupils, was led by a woman principal; in Moncton in 1928–29, where all the elementary schools were of approximately equal size, one woman was, like her male peers, in charge of an eight-teacher school; in Fredericton in the mid-1930s, one of the female principals led a school equal in size to those of her male peers; and in 1930 the largest elementary school in Calgary had a female principal.[131] There were small urban communities in Ontario where women were in charge of a substantial establishment as well.[132] But these appear to be exceptions. In the main, women headed the smallest Calgary elementary schools. In Vancouver and London, women were appointed "acting principals" of new, small schools, only to be replaced by men once the schools grew to normal size.[133] In those Ontario towns and villages willing to appoint women at all, they tended to be put in charge of the smaller annex and ward schools or those with substantially fewer teachers than the community's central school.[134] While women principals formed majorities in the multi-teacher schools of rural Ontario, the reverse tended to be the case in even small urban communities. Concomitantly, women were more likely to be principals of two- or three-teacher schools than men and to exercise authority over other women only.[135] And despite the substantial number of women elementary principals in communities outside Vancouver, they too were to be found mostly in the smaller schools of British Columbia.[136]

The other tendency apparent in Ontario and British Columbia was the declining percentage of women principals. In Small's work on southwestern Ontario, numbers peaked in the early 1920s, declined very modestly for the rest of the decade, and then fell more sharply during the 1930s.[137] In our analysis of British Columbia, similar declines occurred in the decade after 1928–29. The most dramatic took place in the rural municipality and rural district schools, which tended to be smaller than the city elementary schools.[138] This may or may not have been a national pattern – that issue deserves more research. But we suspect we are seeing the effects of the Depression we noted in an earlier chapter: an influx of men taking jobs they had been unwilling to take before.

All generalizations about the role of women principals, however, have to take account of the distinctive leadership characteristics of the grant-aided Catholic schools. Everywhere, these schools were mainly in the hands of women principals who were also members of religious orders. The only exceptions were single-sex boys' schools. Not only the relative handful of girls' schools but the overwhelming number of co-educational Catholic schools had women principals. And this was true not just in small rural schools but in the towns and cities as well.[139] Thus the entire pattern was different from that in the non-denominational public schools, and care must be taken not to conflate the two. Doing so can mislead in two ways: by inflating the overall number of women principals and, similarly, by inflating the number of those in charge of large urban schools. To take but one example, consider the gender distribution of principals in 1932–33 in Manitoba's secondary schools. In the intermediate schools (one high school room within a graded elementary school) nearly 26% of the principals were women, but once one deducts the religious the percentage drops to 21%; in the forty-three two-room high schools, there were only six women principals and two of them were teaching sisters; in the collegiate departments and institutes, the only two women principals were members of religious orders.[140] Thus, excluding the Catholic schools, where women's leadership was so overwhelming, further diminishes the extent to which women gained entry to principalships in the rest of English Canada's public schools.

Aside from the principalship, women were also to be found, at least in the larger cities, working as supervisors of special subjects. Primary and domestic science supervisors were, so far as we can tell, always women, as were most music, art, and special education supervisors. Other than that, they were almost entirely absent from the supervisory apparatus. Though political conflicts ended her administrative career after only two years, Margaret Strong, who served as municipal inspector of schools for the city of New Westminster, British Columbia, from 1913 to 1915, was probably the first female senior supervisory officer to be appointed in any local or provincial school system.[141] Aletta Marty was appointed as one of Toronto's school inspectors in 1920 and remained in that post until her untimely death in 1929.[142] After years as supervisor of French instruction in Winnipeg's secondary schools, Margery Brooker was promoted to a provincial inspectorate in Manitoba in 1941.[143] But these seem to be the only exceptions. During and long after the first four decades of the twentieth century, the senior administration of Canadian school systems consisted, in the most literal sense, of an old boys' club. Or at least, that is true of the public schools. In 1930, the Ontario Blue Book tells us, the Windsor separate schools had two senior supervisory officers, labelled "supervising principals," one of whom was a woman religious; London's lone "supervising principal" for its separate schools was also a woman.

Finally, here, it is perhaps worth drawing an international comparison. The early twentieth century has been described by American historians as a "golden age" for women school administrators generally, and especially for women principals. We are told for example that substantial numbers of local superintendents were women, that 62% of the nation's elementary principals in 1905 were women, and that in the early 1920s the percentage was 55%.[144] They were generally consigned to smaller communities and smaller schools than men, but even so, the figures are more impressive than any we have reviewed in the last several paragraphs: in contrast, Canadian women rarely served as senior supervisory officers and were less likely to attain the rank of principal. Still, things were about to get worse, not better. As the school consolidation movement gained momentum in the two decades around mid-century, it would with remarkable rapidity eliminate not only the small schools but most of their women principals. In Ontario, at least, there were far fewer woman principals in the 1950s than in the 1920s, and it would be another two or three decades before even an equivalent percentage prevailed.[145] Again, this is a matter that deserves more research, and on a national scale; but in the meantime we can perhaps declare the early decades of the century to be, if not a golden, at least a silver age for women principals in twentieth-century Canada.[146]

V

Assessing the quality or effectiveness of supervision in the early twentieth century is not an easy task. Compared to the relatively rich literature in the United States, for example, there is very little known about how local supervision actually operated in Canadian urban communities. As for the provincial inspectorate, it has received a mixed press from contemporaries and historians alike. There are clear examples where inspectors exercised their coercive powers, or tried to, and met stiff resistance. In several provinces, French-Canadian teachers and trustees, indeed entire communities, were at war with an inspectorate determined to impose English as a language of instruction or eliminate religious instruction from French Catholic schools.[147] Early in the century, the same was true for other ethnic minorities in the West.[148] There has also been no shortage of condemnation heaped on individual inspectors for acts of petty tyranny, stiff-necked arrogance, or inexcusably patronizing treatment of the teachers under their care.[149] On the other hand, it is not hard to find counter-examples where inspectors were judged admirable, kindly, or helpful, providing singular support at a critical moment, tolerating or encouraging imaginative pedagogy even when they had reservations about its orthodoxy, or, on a teacher's behalf, fending off overbearing trustees.[150] We think both appraisals speak some portion of the truth, but they also draw on particular cases that offer limited room for generalization.

Given what was at stake for beginners, it's not surprising that an impending visit from the inspector could make them quake in their boots or that a negative report would long remain a thorn in the flesh.[151] But beginners were not alone in this. An inspectoral visitation could usually provoke queasy premonitions even among the experienced. Thomas Fleming tells of one British Columbia principal who regularly informed his staff that an inspector was about to descend by passing around a note with this quotation from Tennyson: "The curse is come upon us / Said the Lady of Shallott."[152] Even in the best of circumstances, evaluation, especially external evaluation, tends to be unsettling, and it is all too human to interpret any form of criticism, however well-intentioned or well-grounded, as a personal affront and denigration of one's competence.

It was not the inspector's job, however, to raise corporate morale or individual self-esteem. He was there to ensure accountability – to assess and report on the ability of the teacher to offer effective instruction in return for the investment of public funds. This was not his only mandate, but it lay at the centre of his work. Exercising such power over others is always open to abuse, and personal style might lead to instances of rigid authoritarianism or insufferable paternalism. There were also occasions, on the other hand, when the firm slap of government was necessary regardless of how teachers or trustees might interpret it. Yet in the main, the job demanded a skill set that included much common-sense realism and the ability to be flexible in applying the letter of the law when circumstances demanded it. "Stories abound," writes Thomas Fleming, "of inspectors turning a blind eye to the fact that certain schools were not enrolling sufficient pupils to remain in operation. In some cases, inspectors were known to count infants, or even family pets, to arrive at a school population of 10 – the number required to keep a school open."[153] Similarly, inspectors were loath to close schools in new school districts when poverty threw up schoolhouses below departmental standards or demanded teachers with less than the requisite minimum certificates.[154] While the inspector's ultimate weapon was the power to cut off the grant to a school district, it appears that this was rarely, if ever, used. Everywhere, exhortation, negotiation, and the extraction of promises to do better counted far more than threats. Distinctions always had to be drawn between what must or should be done and what it was actually possible to do.

The politics of the job also has to be considered. While the inspectors' official comments in the *Annual Reports* are some of the most useful sources available to historians, they are not simply disinterested accounts of local conditions or practices. J.D. Wilson and Paul Stortz have noted the considerable gap between the tone of the Putman-Weir Report, a quasi-

independent assessment that presented a bleak portrait of the state of
British Columbia's rural schools, and the much more upbeat accounts
offered by the inspectorate.[155] The same gap can be found elsewhere.[156]
Inspectors were the department's "boys in the field," hand-picked for their
common outlook and common loyalties. They also had jobs and career
prospects to protect. Outright dissent from government policy was unlikely
for both reasons. Low ratings for too many teachers would draw protests
from the federations. Moreover, too much petty tyranny or harsh criticism
of local practices could raise a local ruckus and filter back to headquarters
with unpredictable and possibly untoward results. Thus negative assessments had to be tempered, had to be balanced with praise, or at least had
to take note of the progress made since the last inspection.

In recent decades the claim has been made that the inspectorate was part
of a distinctly male administrative culture that was inimical to the best interests of a predominantly female workforce and that was, in any case, inher-
ently discriminatory.[157] This is unquestionably true, though all it really tells
us is that, in public education as in most other social relations, patriarchy
ruled the day. Women were good, perhaps best, at teaching young children;
men were needed in the senior classes to ensure the proper development
of adolescent boys. Men were the appropriate choice for leadership roles
ranging from principal to superintendent and inspector. Women were not
unconditionally disqualified but were restricted, in the main, to principalships that men could not afford or were unwilling to take; as well, these and
other administrative roles they might assume involved only the supervision
of girls or other women. In the mid-1920s British Columbia's "progressive"
Putman-Weir Report would call for the appointment of women advisors
for high school girls; these advisors, it suggested, might be given the title
"associate principal," but with this caveat: "It would of course be distinctly
understood that the title of 'associate principal' carried with it no administrative power except in relation to female students and then only when
specifically approved by the principal and board of trustees."[158] Fully two
decades later, on the cusp of mid-century, in a study underwritten by the
Canadian Education Association (CEA), Selwyn Miller canvassed solutions
to the lack of supervision in the rural schools. One of these was to provide
inspectors with female assistants known as "helping teachers." But the drawback, Miller observed, was that they would have to limit their supervisory
visits "to the classrooms in the care of female teachers. It is all too likely that
a male teacher would suffer some loss of prestige if he were visited by a lady
supervisor offering him advice and assistance."[159] Women supervising men
constituted, by the very nature of things, a world turned upside down.

That having been said, nonetheless, to dwell on patriarchy alone, or to dismiss inspectoral judgments or values because of it, is to offer a truncated interpretation of the basis of authority for school inspection or supervision. Authority was exercised not simply by men over women, but by the mature over the young, the well-qualified over the less so, and the experienced over the inexperienced. These hierarchies were also part of the matrix that structured authority relations. Certainly they could breed pathologies of their own. But even in the best of all possible worlds, where irrelevant criteria are not a requisite for appointment, experience and expertise are essential prerequisites for the exercise of, and legitimate claim to, authority in any occupation resting on the practice of professional knowledge and skills.[160] The provincial inspector was uniquely qualified to assess the skills of his teachers and to pass judgment on the educational environment in which they worked; his voice deserves to be taken seriously, treated judiciously, and weighed in its full, not partial, context.

At the time, in any case, the critique of the inspectoral system took an entirely different direction. One thrust challenged the validity of the assessment process itself. There were, for example, reiterated complaints about the artificial atmosphere created by the inspector's visit – *pace* John Dearness, no class ever went back to its usual routines with the inspector in the room, and we doubt, as did some contemporaries, that any inspector actually witnessed a teacher's classroom (especially an inexperienced teacher's classroom) in its normal ebb and flow of activities. Teachers and pupils might freeze up and do themselves an injustice, but just as likely a teacher might whip out a lesson she knew pupils were familiar with in order to put on a good show.[161] Then there was the problem of high-stakes assessment dependent on a visit of two or three hours once or twice a year, a procedure too likely to produce facile or misguided judgments.[162] Moreover, inspectors, it was said, were prone to "faddism," insisting that there was only one best way to teach or run a classroom; they were also accused, after years on the job, of being out of touch with the feel or exigencies of real classrooms.[163] These were all familiar criticisms in the first half of the twentieth century that would, indeed, be repeated – and repeated, and repeated, ad infinitum – until the inspectorate was abolished in Canadian provincial school systems. Again, it must be said that there was a good deal of truth in these arguments. On the other hand, the tone of such criticism is reminiscent of recent attacks on standardized examinations, school rankings, or merit ratings – systems of teacher assessment that seem uniformly to provoke hostility among a substantial portion of those engaged in the enterprise. These devices are certainly not without their flaws. Teacher assessment, nonetheless, remains a Gordian knot without its Alexander. It is not beyond the realm of possibility that a provincial inspectorate may be the worst form of teacher evaluation except for all the rest.[164]

The other challenge arose from the conviction that the most important part of the inspector's job was, not merely to inspect, but to supervise – to work with teachers for the improvement of instruction. And here we return to the question posed at the beginning of this chapter – just how much effective supervision was there? Indeed, how much supervision at all? We have already pointed out that the provincial inspector was the only professional most rural teachers ever saw and that his visits were usually infrequent and brief. Across the entire period, moreover, there was at best only modest improvement in this state of affairs, and even that was erratic, subject to economic circumstance. In 1890, for example, Ontario had one inspector for about every 113 teachers; thirty years later the ratio had actually worsened, to one inspector for every 122 teachers; and by the early 1940s it stood at one for every 110, only fractionally better than in 1890.[165] If we use J.C. Miller's 1913 data as a baseline and compare them to 1940, the trend in most provinces shows modest improvement – only in Manitoba was provision worse – but progress was very uneven. In 1913, the ratio in Alberta was 129 teachers to each inspector; in 1930, 170; and in 1940, 100. Between 1913 and 1940 in Nova Scotia, the ratio dropped from 186:1 to 115:1; yet in 1926–27, out of fourteen inspectors, nine carried 200 or more schools.[166] In 1943 a blue-ribbon committee, appointed by the Canadian Education Association to carry out a national survey on the state of Canadian education, would echo four decades of cumulative complaint about the chief deficit of the inspectoral system: "There is a crying national need for improved school supervision in rural parts. According to a recent survey, over 16,000 of the more than 20,000 administrative units in Canada employ either one or two teachers each. These rural teachers are generally the least inexperienced and most poorly paid in the country. With few exceptions, all the supervision each teacher receives is given by one inspector who may have from 100 to 200 teachers under his charge, and these scattered over wide areas. Isolated and alone, the teachers face the manifold problems of conducting schools with from four to eight and sometimes ten grades in a single classroom. In the most difficult teaching positions the most inexperienced teachers receive the least supervisory help."[167] In contrast to some accounts that prefer to dwell upon the intrusive presence of the inspectors in the schools or treat inspectors as the shock troops of an oppressive bureaucracy, we might better conclude that these purported agents of hegemony were hardly ever there.[168]

In the cities and larger towns, however, the answer has to be a different one. Increasingly from the last quarter of the nineteenth century it became common practice for school trustees to appoint full-time administrators to oversee, co-ordinate, and standardize instructional policies and practices; to appoint assistant superintendents and supervisors of special subjects; and to provide at least some principals with release time from teaching. Each decade more communities reached thresholds of size and complexity that encouraged the multiplication of non-teaching staff.[169] By the early 1940s the CEA Survey Committee could declare that "the schools in urban areas are well supervised because local school authorities in cities and towns supply adequate supervisory services."[170] "Adequate," of course, has to be understood in context. Comparatively speaking, before mid-century, and especially before 1940, the provision of big-city supervisory officers was parsimonious. Hard times in the immediate aftermath of the Great War and during the extended depression of the 1930s put sharp limits on the expansion of non-teaching personnel, indeed often resulted in staff reductions at central office and the return of supervising principals to the classroom. Overall, the supervisory numbers were only somewhat larger in 1939 than in 1920, and nothing like the proliferating number of supervisory and support personnel that would typify the last forty years of the twentieth century. Compared with the situation in the rural schools, nonetheless, teachers in Canada's larger urban communities were not only inspected but supervised.

In drawing its contrast between urban and rural communities, however, the CEA committee offered a misleading comparison by pitting rural areas against provision in two cities with populations of 80,000 and 20,000 respectively. Even in 1940, let alone earlier, there were far more small urban communities than large ones, and while schools in the larger towns and cities were likely "well supervised," this was certainly not true in all urban schools.[171] In small towns and villages there might be nothing more than a harassed supervising principal carrying a part-time teaching load and struggling, at the same time, to meet the clerical, managerial, and supervising tasks his job demanded. Or, indeed, no supervision at all. As the editor of the ATA *Magazine* put it on one occasion, supervision might be effective in a large city school where the principal devoted 50% of his time to the task, but "teachers other than large city teachers will naturally ask, 'What about ourselves? We have no superintendent, and the school principal is teaching all day, and can give no time to supervision.'"[172]

The quality and extent of supervisory services depended, at bottom, on scale and resources. That is, a community had to have enrolments large enough to justify, and an assessment base rich enough to afford, non-teaching personnel. A small population might preclude that option altogether (though not necessarily: a compact community with one large central school might be able to manage release time for its principal but not the geographically extended town down the road with three smaller schools built to serve three different wards). A large population, on the other hand, didn't necessarily guarantee the requisite resources. Toronto and Vancouver had rich and diversified tax bases to underwrite a substantial cadre of supervisors. The burgeoning suburbs surrounding both cities had populations larger than many Canadian towns and, in some cases, schools as large as any in their respective cities; yet the suburbs were dependent on a mainly residential tax base made up of small property owners, and their provision for any supervising staff was meagre indeed.[173]

Universally, then, Canadian teachers were *inspected*. Provincial authorities made sure this was done in town and country alike. In each province a cadre of department of education officials spread out across the land to see that the law was being applied, that public money was being spent in the way intended, and that minimum standards were being met by teachers and trustees alike. The degree of success might be somewhat variable, but generally, year after year, inspection was accomplished competently and with that degree of efficiency circumstances allowed. *Supervision*, on the other hand, was at best a patchwork quilt. There was little or none of it in rural Canada – it is hard to find a dissenting opinion on that score. In most of urban Canada it was wildly variable, dependent on population size, the value of the tax base, the commitment of trustees, and the like. There might be supervising principals or there might not; there might be a superintendent or urban inspector whose time was mostly devoted to working with his teachers, or he might be weighed down by office work. There might be a bevy of supervisors of special subjects, or just one or two; principals might have some release time or some clerical help, or none at all – whatever the case, resources to sustain these services might disappear when times got hard. But in the main, it was only in the large towns and cities that there were supervisory staff numerous enough to provide the kind of oversight that distinguished supervision from inspection. How much effective supervision then? More, say, in 1940 than in 1890 or 1900, and certainly more in the larger urban centres – but for most Canadian schools, not much.

VI

Were the centralization of authority and increasing levels of supervision, in the cities and larger towns at least, accompanied by the growth of bureaucratic rule-making, greater degrees of regulation, or the intensification of teachers' work? Along with their pedagogical responsibilities, teachers in publicly funded school systems had always been vital cogs in the machinery of governance and administration.[174] Supervision was only one form of regulation; law and policy was another. All teachers, according to British Columbia's school legislation, were required "to call the roll morning and

afternoon, and otherwise to keep an accurate register in the manner prescribed by the Council of Public Instruction; such register to be open at
all times to the inspection of the Board, Inspectors and Superintendent
of Education." In a more general clause, to be found with near-identical
wording right across the country, teachers were to furnish on request of the
department of education *any* information it was in their power to provide.
British Columbia's regulations added that teachers were "to inquire into
the cause and record all cases of tardiness and absence of pupils" and "to
verify by affidavit, before any Justice of the Peace, the correctness of such
returns as the Superintendent of Education may from time to time require
to be verified."[175]

Universally, teachers were responsible for the "Daily Register." Produced
in a standardized format and distributed to the schools by each provincial
department of education, the register provided space, usually for a month at
a time, to enter the name, age, grade, and daily attendance record for each
pupil in the class. It might also include, in "tear-out" form, any other reports
teachers or trustees were required to submit. The instructions to teachers
in the Alberta Daily Register for 1929–30 are pretty typical. Attendance
was to be recorded for each half-day, along with "lates." On the last day
of each month, the teacher was to calculate, and enter in the register, the
total aggregate of days attendance for the month, the average attendance,
and the percentage of attendance "carried to two decimal points." Specific
instruction on how to calculate each of these figures was included. At the
close of each term, 31 December and 30 June, "the teacher shall enter a
summary of the attendance for the term on the pages provided for that purpose at the centre of the register." It was these calculations that played an
important role in estimating the government grant to each school board,
and because of their importance it was part of the duties of the inspector
to check the register each time he visited the school. Moreover, since it was
the teacher who first recorded a pupil's absence from school, it was her
responsibility to initiate a truancy investigation: "every teacher shall report
monthly, on the forms provided, to the School Attendance Branch."[176]

If not already included as part of the data collected in the attendance register, there were also likely to be, in a second register, records of enrolments
by subject, marks awarded, promotions, and the like.[177] And as this volume
of information poured in, school by school, classroom by classroom, it
became the basis for the statistical mountain each department of education
presented in its annual report. "As a technical creation," Thomas Fleming
and Helen Raptis remark, "the government's system of educational accounting was simple but elegant. Viewed from the top, one small document – the
teacher's register – contained the code for the entire management system

and served, in effect, as the Rosetta stone through which all the statistical constructions of the government's Education Office could be deciphered and understood."[178]

Technically speaking, it was the trustees, and not the teacher, who were responsible for submitting all the required reports to the department of education. But as Ontario's manual on school management warned beginners, "most of the information asked can be supplied only by the teacher ... School grants cannot be apportioned till all these reports are sent to the Department, and the inspector has the power to withhold his order for payment of the grants, if the law regarding reports is violated."[179] In some provinces this kind of clerical work was mandated. Manitoba teachers, for example, were required by law "to prepare, so far as the school registers supply the information, such reports of the corporation employing him as are required by the regulations of the Department."[180] Thus, whether explicitly or not, the teacher was on the front line when it came to ensuring that all pertinent data were complete, accurate, and filed on time.[181]

From at least the late nineteenth century, however, there was also a steady intensification of reporting and record-keeping. The same manual claimed that "school work is much more complex now than in former years, and therefore some good system of keeping records must be adopted in order to reduce the time required in preparing reports."[182] Along with the ever-present attendance register that every teacher had long been required to keep, some provinces were introducing cumulative record cards, to be kept for each pupil throughout his or her entire school career.[183] Or another example: in 1934, along with its revised issue of attendance registers, Ontario introduced a "General Register, embodying all summary data and all matters of permanent worth in relation to the school as a whole. As the latter is a ten year register it will cover the entire school history of every child as well as the statistical and financial history of the school section."[184]

In most schools, strategies to increase or improve record-keeping ran smack up against the lack of time and resources. "In Manitoba, except in the case of a few of the larger Collegiates," a high school inspector noted in the early 1940s, "the school records [and] the general administration ... are carried along as a sideline by the principal with the help of some teachers, all of whom frequently are carrying a full teaching load at the same time ... All of this cannot be done as a sideline by already overworked principals and teachers."[185] But wherever urbanization promoted sophisticated systems of supervision, there was the rapid expansion of record-keeping and rule-making as well. Strictly speaking, this was something done by the trustees through their power to make bylaws. It was associated, however, with the establishment of central administrative offices and the delegation of executive powers to senior supervisory officers. Even early in the century the burden of paperwork was growing in the big cities; as Ontario's *School Management* manual noted, "teachers are required to report to the board of trustees many facts that are not asked for by rural trustees nor by the Minister of Education. Many city boards ask for a report on the number of cases of corporal punishment each month; also the contagious diseases among the pupils and the number of cases of each. Where libraries are used in the schools, the number of books borrowed by pupils will also be reported on."[186] By 1914 Vancouver already had no less than thirty-seven formal rules governing teachers' behaviour on the job; in the mid-1930s Toronto had just over fifty. More bureaucratic administration brought work that was increasingly routinized and standardized through rules governing everything from leaves of absence for illness, discipline procedure, the supervision of fire drill, yard and hall duty, to lockstep timetabling and uniform lesson plans.[187]

In the jaundiced view of at least one teacher, who penned the following admirable jeremiad in *Maclean's* in 1937, the entire business was out of control. "To illustrate what happens in a typical school in the Toronto area," she began, there were the plethora of rules issued by the board of education and the "local codes" established by the principal.

Here are, therefore, but a few of the duties shovelled upon the members of this school staff. Besides the disciplining and the thumping of educational prescriptions into avid, stupid and fractious heads alike, they have reports to be sent to each home, desk reports to record each child's marks by the month and by the year, attendance registers to be balanced every month. Absentee slips must be filled in if a child is absent for two days, and a further special attendance form must be inscribed if his parents can't afford a telephone and his playmates can't find him. A file must be kept of excuses for absence so that the monthly register can disclose whether the dereliction is unavoidable or frivolous. If a pupil leaves the room during a class session his departure and arrival must be clocked in a special book, so that possible property damage may be properly settled on the culprit.

Then there was "the latest innovation designed to improve the country's intellectual standards," the new student record cards, "quite distinct from ordinary registration [cards]," which recorded

the name, address, age, sex, place of birth, name of parent ... his place of birth, occupation, religious denomination, etc., etc. This card must accompany the child all through school, and record each promotion mark and every medical inspection and finding. Teachers would not at all be surprised were it presently decreed that the date of each bath and haircut must also be registered.

Teachers must, furthermore, daily describe in a "plan book" what they figure on doing the following day, for the edification of the school inspector. They are required to have the room temperature "recorded on the blackboard and in a book kept for that purpose, at 9 and 9:15 a.m., and at such other times as the temperature may vary from the standard set in Subsection 8 hereof." They must also make careful record of the details of every corporal punishment in another book provided by the board.[188]

As we have argued in other chapters, the big-city school held powerful attractions for teachers in the first half of the twentieth century. But it also brought a comparatively high degree of regimentation and oversight by supervisory staff. This had advantages. A multi-classroom school is a *work community* that offers psychic and practical benefits. Effective instruction school-wide is a team effort. City teachers had at their command advice and support from colleagues and principals, as well as access to expert opinion on everything from discipline problems to advanced pedagogical techniques. Novices could be mentored in formal and informal ways, and for all teachers the staff room was more than just gossip central – it was also a place where ideas were shared and problems compared. Supervision, moreover, should not be treated, definitionally, as "a bad thing." Along with their quasi-police functions, supervisors exist to guide, assist, and co-ordinate teamwork; neither direction nor assessment are attributes to be discounted in the creation of effective professional work. But the price to be paid by the big-city teacher was a plethora of paperwork, sets of formal rules that routinized many aspects of their working lives, and much more vigorous supervision than most Canadian teachers experienced.

Care needs to be taken not to push notions of rigour, hierarchical organization, and routinized work too far. Once the classroom door was closed, teachers could still exercise a good deal of autonomy; the variety of personal and pedagogical styles and the large variations in classroom routines that teachers exhibited in the same or similar schools are reminders that the classroom was not the assembly line or the corporate typing pool replicated. Moreover, the actual effectiveness of the emerging supervisory regime should not be taken for granted. The American historian Kate Rousmaniere has drawn attention to the gap between the rationalized supervisory schemes introduced by school administrators in New York City during the 1920s and the lived experience of work in the schools. According to many of the teachers she interviewed, "their principals and other supervising administrators were often far from sight and oblivious or ignorant of teachers' work, in part because of increasing bureaucratic demands on their own time ... Oftentimes, the increasing complications of the modern school actually increased teachers' ability to control parts of their own labour. In the intensely tangled school building, teachers were often able to surreptitiously undercut or sidestep administrative regulations. Because of weak and inconsistent implementation of supervisory procedures, teachers were sometimes allowed to continue their work in the classroom, neither hindered nor helped by supervisory administrators."[189] This may or may not have been true of big-city schools in Canada; we will only know for certain when there is far more intensive research on urban school systems than exists now, but the possibility needs to be kept in mind as that research proceeds.

Rousmaniere's teachers, nonetheless, had to duck and weave to carve out spaces where elements of autonomy could be preserved. But consider the following brief quotation, cited earlier in the chapter. "You were on your own. You were completely on your own," one woman told Penelope Stephenson of her teaching experience in a remote one-room school in the Okanagan Valley during the 1920s. Proof of a level of professional isolation unimaginable in even small urban schools, it is redolent of something else as well. "Nobody interfered," another teacher reported. "I never had anybody tell me what to do." Yet another claimed she had been "absolutely autonomous ... Nobody questioned [me] at all." "With no principal to tell them what to do or from whom they could seek advice," Stephenson remarks, "they had to make their own decisions and were thus in control of the daily pedagogical activities that took place in the school. They were free to set the pace of work to meet the needs of individual students, to alter their schedules if and when it suited them, or to experiment with different kinds of teaching methods to find the approach that worked best for them. In this sense some participants viewed their professional isolation as working to their benefit rather than to their detriment."[190] While obvious limits to any teacher's autonomy were built into the system, while diversity of experience among rural school teachers needs always to be emphasized, and while learning through trial and error utterly on one's own probably had its share of disasters and produced some walking wounded, there were several generations of Canadian teachers who, once the job was mastered, thrived without close supervision and exercised their skills without the need for somebody else's rule book.

13

Questions of Quality

At least one important question remains: to what extent did the schools serve children well or badly, or not serve them at all? We begin with the quantity of educational provision; it is, after all, a prerequisite for quality. So we ask how much schooling was available to children in the first four or five decades of the twentieth century, and how inclusive was it? Next, we try to assess the quality of instruction: how well or badly did teachers do their jobs? Finally, both questions raise a related issue: the extent to which the schools lived up to the promise of equality of educational opportunity they held out to Canadian society and its children.

Between the late nineteenth century and the 1930s, two important transitions took place in English-Canadian education. One was the extension of schooling from an abbreviated and irregular experience for most children to one that stretched over a continuous period of eight or nine years. Though it occurred more slowly, the other was a steady rise in levels of educational attainment. By 1930, 45% of 14-year-olds were in grades VII and VIII, while another 22% were already in high school. Thus two-thirds of the country's young people were now achieving senior elementary school standing or better, and that figure would continue to improve through to mid-century. For the vast majority of children this marked a shift from the merest smattering of the rudiments of learning, barely assimilated and easily forgotten, to a consolidation and extension of the basic skills constituting numeracy, literacy, and the elements of citizenship. On the other hand, while completing high school was far more common in 1940 or 1950 than in earlier decades, secondary education for all was no more than in the making, still far from a Canadian commonplace. Half of those who entered grade VI in 1942 had left school by grade X and a significant minority failed to complete grade VIII. Across fifty years or more, in other words, levels of educational attainment improved substantially; but even among those adults who had grown up during the second quarter of the century, a full 46% had only eight years of schooling or less.

Compared at least to developments over the last half of the twentieth century, we have labelled this a parsimonious pattern of school-going. We went on to suggest why this was the case, distinguishing between two broad though overlapping causes, one arising from the socio-economic context, the other more narrowly focused on what we termed "school-caused" effects stemming from the organization of instruction. Expectations and aspirations always play an important role in the lives of individuals and families and have to be taken seriously as explanations for differences in patterns of school attendance or levels of educational attainment. But there were also some structural regularities that were of fundamental importance. Rural children tended to have shorter school lives than their urban counterparts – more likely to start school later, leave earlier, and have lower levels of educational attainment. Working-class youngsters, and especially those from the families of unskilled workers, were more likely to drop out of school early and less likely to make the transition from elementary to secondary school. Girls were more likely to do well in school, and to complete more years of schooling, than boys. Those of British origin were more likely to stay in school than those who were not. School credentials mattered far less in the first half of the twentieth century than they would only a few decades later, so they were not yet a near-definitive prerequisite for a successful career or even a life of modest comfort. But children's choices in life, including the experience of schooling, were materially dependent on where they lived and how prosperous or educated their parents were.

There were also children who were excluded outright by law, custom, or their incapacity to cope with a rigorous curriculum. No jurisdiction allowed 4-year-olds to attend, a matter not even canvassed in the period, within the public sector at least. Before mid-century 5-year-olds were rarely sent to school. Weather conditions in the countryside and concerns about safety on urban streets contributed to this outcome, but they were rarely welcomed in any case. High levels of irregularity among 5-year-olds disrupted teaching routines, while large numbers of repeaters increased costs; there was also a widespread conviction that they were not developmentally ready for the mental and emotional challenges of school.[1] Thus they were formally excluded in some provinces and often discouraged wherever the law permitted them to attend. The kindergarten movement made a dent in this, but provision for kindergarten within the public school system was uncommon before mid-century. While attendance at age 6 was more frequent, outside of a few large urban communities it was rarely compulsory, and many parents, especially in rural areas, chose to keep their 6-year-olds (and in Ontario even their 7-year-olds) at home. At the other end of the age spectrum, only in Ontario was the school-leaving age raised to 16 and even then only in the larger urban areas; elsewhere it was 14 or 15. While an increasing proportion of children did in fact stay in school longer each decade, they were only required to attend, even in the interwar decades, for eight years. Thus large numbers of children whom we would now consider to be of school age – at either end of the age range – were excluded from, or not expected to attend, school. Beyond that, there were other exclusions – those defined as "ineducable" due to "feeblemindedness" or other mental, behavioural, or physical conditions.[2] Others languished at the back of classrooms until they were mercifully allowed to leave school at the earliest possible moment. Even at mid-century, provision for those with special learning needs was meagre, and outside the larger cities, pitifully inadequate.[3]

The degree of inclusivity was also constrained by the selective nature of the system. Since the mid-nineteenth century, the elementary school had been the main vessel for providing all children with the elements of learning for the ordinary purposes of life; the secondary school was intended to groom an academic elite for leadership roles in society. Until at least the 1920s a winnowing process began in the earliest grades. Most children eventually reached grade v or vi, but high retardation rates meant that far fewer entered the senior elementary grades before they were old enough to leave school. Beginning at grade viii, a series of departmental examinations sifted each cohort in ever finer fashion. In contrast with long-established patterns in the United States, the Canadian organization of instruction was "unforgiving" – it posed a single standard of academic achievement grade by grade, measured by formal in-school and latterly external examinations.[4] There was little room for variations in the timing of individual maturation or the range of individual abilities or interests. Alternative programs of study hardly existed and second chances were few.

By the 1920s, however, compromise over the extent of selectivity was inevitable – and more particularly, some compromise about the role of the high school entrance examination. Apart from any other consideration, it was impossible at one and the same time to reduce retardation rates *and* raise the school-leaving age to 15 or 16 without one of two consequences. Since more and more pupils were now reaching grade viii before they were old enough to leave school, either they would have to be accommodated in the high school grades or the senior elementary grades would fill to overflowing with older children simply marking time, wasting everybody's energies and money, besides inviting massive increases in discipline problems to boot. On almost every count the latter prospect was intolerable. Thus the only real question was what to do about the high school entrance examination.

The alternative adopted right across the country during the interwar years was the recommendation system, which transferred large numbers of promotion decisions to the principals and teachers of the pupils' own schools. The transition proceeded cautiously during the 1920s, then much more rapidly in the following decade. But almost from the beginning far more children were promoted under the recommendation system than would have been the case if the high school entrance examination (HSEE) had remained in place. A similar outcome followed the abolition of external examinations in the junior high school grades. The result was to shift the selective principle from the traditional grade VIII/IX divide to the end of grade IX or X. These two grades became part of "the intermediate years," in effect a second stage of universal education – the level of schooling that all, or at least most, children could expect to attain before leaving school. Though still far less "forgiving" than American school systems in the same period, Canadian schools became at least less "unforgiving." This shift was not yet complete at mid-century, but the severity of the selective principle was substantially tempered during the interwar years. Tempered, but hardly eliminated: rather, the bar was moved upwards into the senior high school, which remained a training ground for the matriculation and normal school examinations, serving a shrinking cohort of pupils each year after grade IX or X.

"There has been a great increase in the number who remain in school for more than eight years," one school principal noted in a critical assessment of the New Brunswick secondary school curriculum. "Now we have the child staying in school and the problem is what to do with him now that he is there."[5] To many observers, including senior departmental officials and leading education academics, the dominance of a curriculum driven by matriculation standards didn't make much sense in light of a new and more diverse clientele. Thus the initiatives to introduce new options in the senior elementary and junior high school grades, as well as the creation of vocational and other program choices in the secondary schools. The pressure of numbers was not the only reason for the so-called democratization of the secondary curriculum, but it lent the movement a degree of urgency it might not otherwise have acquired. Whether or not curriculum differentiation fulfilled the promise of democratization – that is, whether it actually made schooling more inclusive or simply introduced different forms of exclusion – was left for the future to decide.

The degree of inclusivity, in any case, is only one gauge of efficacy, and it begs a different question that is at least as important, if not more so:

however long or short their stay, what can be said about the quality of instruction children might expect to receive? Any adequate answer to that question has to incorporate several dimensions ranging from the nature of the curriculum and the pedagogical prescriptions that guided practice to the institutional framework that structured teachers' activities, the academic qualifications teachers acquired in the course of their own education, the quality of their professional training, their level of experience, and the differing physical contexts they encountered in their work.

In his pioneering history of Canadian education, written just after mid-century, C.E. Phillips, who had spent a long career observing Ontario's schools, described a turn-of-the-century pedagogical environment in which elementary pupils "were able to reproduce accurately an exceptionally large number of prescribed facts, to repeat from memory an unusual quantity of approved verbal content in prose and poetry, and to make a good showing in the performance of mechanical skills in spelling, reading, arithmetic, and grammar. Those who survived the grind and the selective examinations and went on to do advanced work under better educated teachers showed equal proficiency in content requiring more intellectual ability, although power to memorize was still the greatest asset."[6] While Phillips here damned the schools with faint praise, others have been even more hostile, presenting bleak portraits of classrooms dominated, right across the first half of the twentieth century, by a stultifying round of routine marked by endless drill, reams of blackboard work to be copied, dry-as-dust memorization of disassociated facts gathered from boring textbooks – a routine broken only by teacher talk and ridden by an obsession with formal examinations. Though offering a more moderate assessment, we ourselves have described such schooling as narrowly bookish, didactic, focused on habit formation, prizing far more than we would today the role of drill, memory work, and textbooks, and depending more than would suit us on evaluation through written examinations.

But does it follow that these prescriptions and practices inevitably condemned children to an inferior form of education? Since education is, at bottom, a moral enterprise, ultimately about what one values as means and ends, people then as now will disagree not only on what constitutes worthwhile content in the curriculum, but also on the nature of the child, the conditions that promote or retard mental and emotional growth, and the appropriate pedagogy to be applied. Consensus on these issues is mostly beyond our grasp. The attainments listed by Phillips, for example, didn't persuade him that this form of pedagogy did much to train the mind. But while some might declare them modest, and while we might agree that they do not constitute the *entire* baggage of a well-trained mind, they are hardly to be dismissed as trivial. Indeed, many twenty-first-century teachers, high school and university alike, would pray to be so blessed with students who could at least "make a good showing in the performance of mechanical skills in spelling, reading, arithmetic, and grammar," who, additionally, knew a modicum of historical or other pertinent "facts," and who could draw more extensively than is now common on what used to be considered the canon of ideas and literature that constitutes the sinews of a liberal education.

In an earlier chapter we reproduced a map of Canada accompanied by an HSEE question requiring pupils to identify a large number of geographical sites. Should we declare this mindless memory work, or say rather that all young people should be required to have at least a minimal familiarity with Canadian geography? Is it worthwhile requiring children to learn that St John's is not in New Brunswick or that the Hibernia project is not part of the Athabasca oil sands? In the age of the calculator, is there any use for mental arithmetic? Is memorizing portions of Shakespeare a waste of time or good for the soul? Is it good enough that a passing reference to "blood, sweat, and tears" evokes only the name of a half-forgotten rock group, that the "dissolution of Parliament" may be taken as a reference to its porous foundations? Does it matter if pupils can't tell a gerund from a gerbil? The early twentieth century had answers to questions such as these; we may offer different answers, but are we sure they are any better? Words like "drill" or "memory work" have been largely banished from the lexicon of modern pedagogy, banned altogether, or buried in euphemism. Still, it is said that "practice makes perfect," a venerable dictum in many fields of human endeavour, including music and athletics; why not in the core curriculum? And is there anything to be said for the British Columbia inspector in 1902 who, annoyed by complaints about the undue strain allegedly caused by an excessive amount of memory work required of children, retorted that "if more were entrusted to the memory, there would be something to assimilate. There would be less dyspepsia and more muscle. Teachers and parents are over-considerate nowadays of the memory in children. In our apprehension lest pupils may turn out to be parrots, we have often turned out loons."[7]

While questions such as these may provoke disagreement, there are some things, at least, that can be resolved more conclusively. First, the best available research, that by Neil Sutherland, shows that there was no disjunction between the values of school and community about either content or methods, and this applied to middle-class and working-class families alike. Parents in particular shared the assumptions and supported the practices that animated classroom instruction throughout the first half of the twentieth century.[8] Second, one would assume, for example, that if classroom routines were nothing but a daily round of stultifying boredom, then children would generally hate school and adults remember it with distaste.

But Sutherland's survey of adults' recollections about their experience
as schoolchildren suggests the very reverse: while there were always some
who disliked school more or less intensely, most children liked it most of
the time.[9] True, nobody conducted polls of yesterday's 10-year-olds to find
out what they thought at the time, and Sutherland's adults may have mis-
remembered their own experience; still, his evidence is the most persuasive
we have on the subject. Moreover, after five or six decades of trendy pedagogical innovations, often accompanied by hysterical myth-making about
traditional modes of teaching, one can surely ask, do children like school
any better now than Sutherland's respondents did then?[10] Equally, young
people were rarely asked in the period if they thought the high school curriculum was worthwhile. But when in the 1940s, writes Rebecca Coulter,
they were invited to identify

> those subjects which had been most valuable to them since leaving
> school, a large majority opted for English (or French where that was
> the first language) and mathematics. These findings match the findings
> of a 1950 study of young people who had left school two years earlier.
> In this study boys ranked mathematics first and English second while
> shop courses came in a distant third. Girls selected English as the most
> important subject while commercial courses and mathematics ran neck-
> and-neck for second and third place ...
>
> There is something particularly significant about the high ranking
> given to English and mathematics because young workers indicated
> "that these are the subjects which have been of most value to them not
> only in their jobs but in all their activities." While young people wanted
> schooling to offer some preparation for work in terms of a good basic
> grounding in the traditional academic subjects, they rarely saw this
> preparation in terms of training in narrowly defined or job-specific
> work skills.[11]

The quality of instruction was also shaped by the institutional framework
within which teachers practised their craft. In the cities and large towns,
their work tended to be closely monitored by principals and other supervisors. "You bet the curriculum was rigid," one Calgary teacher remarked.
"Even in a subject like art. You had to teach tree drawings in September,
pencil landscape in October, and colour charts in November. You were in
trouble if the art supervisor came around and found you doing something
else."[12] Whatever its defects, such close supervision ensured a high degree
of uniformity among different teachers and different schools, as well as
specialist advice and support when needed. In the countryside or the small

urban community, teachers could expect a degree of autonomy interrupted only by an occasional visit by the inspector. This might provide latitude for imaginative experiments with methodology or more flexibility than the highly prescriptive regimen of an urban program guide, but it also allowed more room for poor teaching generally or for the incompetent presentation of an unfamiliar subject.

Since it affected all teachers, however, the most pervasive external influence on the quality of instruction was government policy. So long as the HSEE and the annual external high school examinations remained in place, for example, they had the capacity to distort pedagogical priorities. Given the stakes for pupils and teachers alike, any subject that was not examinable might get short shrift, especially in the senior elementary grades, and generally that meant subjects like music, art, hygiene, or nature study. "Several cases have recently come to notice," one Manitoba departmental memorandum warned, "where a student who passed in the Departmental Examinations has changed schools, and the new teachers find that the subjects in which there was no Departmental examination have been, in some cases, almost completely neglected. We wish to impress upon teachers that although ... the Department examines only in certain subjects, it does not mean that only those subjects are to be taught."[13] It is probably also true that, as some contemporaries complained, high-stakes external examinations invited an emphasis on teaching to the test, bred gradgrind methods of instruction, and encouraged end-of-year cramming by pupils to the detriment of daily effort.[14]

The adoption of the recommendation system probably went some way towards improving instruction. It removed the tendency to treat grade VIII solely as preparation for the HSEE and reduced the incentive to narrow down instruction to the memorization of sets of facts and formulations likely to turn up on examination papers. It allowed a more equitable distribution of time across the whole range of the curriculum. It improved evaluation by giving due weight to the quality of daily work. And though not the only factor involved, it helped shift the emphasis in the elementary school from sorting children out to encouraging all to remain in school and proceed into the high school grades.[15]

The introduction of the recommendation system, however, was also accompanied by some watering down of academic standards. This is obvious from the escalating rate of promotions in the elementary and intermediate grades as well as in the degree of unease and amount of controversy it provoked. On the other hand, too much should not be made of this. The expectations for elementary school pupils reflected in the HSEE strike us as exceptionally rigorous and the winnowing ruthless by any acceptable standard today. The program of studies continued to be challenging, and the full-scale reorientation of the elementary curriculum was just beginning in the late 1930s. Even as the HSEE and the annual external high school examinations were abandoned, moreover, there was the restraining influence of inertia, a result of the pre-established academic expectations of experienced teachers, principals, inspectors, and other supervisors that continued to shape practice in the schools.

There was as well the pervasive pressure of the matriculation examinations. Only a relatively small minority of the total school population ever wrote these exams, but they exercised a profound influence over – some critics insisted they "controlled" – both what got taught and the quality of instruction in the lower grades.[16] For example, if high matriculation standards were set for English composition or mathematics, training had to start early, remain consecutive in each grade, and become progressively more demanding. Thus the influence of the matriculation examinations cascaded down through the grades to at least the senior elementary school. They established the benchmarks for academic achievement and the range of subjects that would dominate the curriculum. Moreover, the sheer enthusiasm of parents and employers for examinations intended only to qualify for university or normal school helped undermine attempts to implement less demanding or more diversified programs of studies for those who would never go beyond one or another high school grade.

Yet changes in policies or practices could have other inimical effects on the quality of classroom instruction. In the one-room school, indeed anywhere one teacher taught two or more grades, children could proceed at their own pace and teachers could promote them at any time of the year, or deny promotion, according to their assessment of each pupil's academic progress. This individualized approach resulted in substantial minorities of "accelerants" – pupils well in advance of their age cohort – and also large numbers of those held back a year or more. Increasingly in the interwar years, however, there were declining numbers in both categories, though far greater among accelerants. This was partly due to pedagogical fashion – a growing sentiment that it was not good for children to get too far ahead or fall too far behind their age cohort. But lurking behind that notion was administrative expedience: in larger school systems where there was usually one teacher for each grade, it was simply easier to promote children all at the same time than to make individual promotions during the course of a term or even at the end of term. Thus, for both reasons, annual June promotions gradually became conventional. And inevitably, increasing urbanization brought more and more children under the sway of annual promotions.

Though far from complete during the interwar years, this pattern was one cause of the transition underway from promotion by achievement to promotion by age. But it also had other consequences for teaching and learning. It increased the tendency to lockstep learning and teaching to the average, to the middle of the class. The ablest could no longer progress at their own rate; at best "enrichment" replaced early and rapid promotion through the grades, and given high pupil-teacher ratios and heavy teaching loads, enrichment or any other form of individual attention was a some-time thing. Teachers, moreover, now had to learn to cope with not one but two sources of boredom and potential disruption – those repeating one or more grades *and* those made restless by the slower progress of their peers.

But within the institutional constraints that governed teachers' work, we can still ask, were most of them good at the job, bad, or indifferent? Assessing classroom competence is a problematic enterprise. At the very least, it has to take into account five components: academic qualifications; professional training; experience; personal characteristics; how assessment is to be done, and by whom. None of these is simple to interpret, and the extant literature is beset by problems. As T.C. Byrne, at the time chief superintendent of schools in Alberta, remarked in 1962, there were already "thousands of studies ... done on teacher competence between 1900 and 1960 ... An unkind critic might be inclined to observe that never has there been so much effort expended for so few results."[17] Despite reams of research since then, the issue remains wracked with controversy. Still, no-one doubts that it is a matter of critical importance, and we will not attempt to duck it here.

One might think that historians struggling with the question would at least be able to put to some use the annual reports generated by the inspectorate. But reports on individual teachers were confidential documents, and even when published in summary form, judgments tended to be bland. Doubtful cases, for example, fell into a range categorized as "fairly good" or "fair" rather than "weak" or "poor."[18] Nor is this surprising. Neither the inspectorate nor senior departmental officials could do much about the available pool of teachers, and they had to live with what that pool provided, tempering their judgments to fit the circumstances. Whatever they actually thought of their teachers, moreover, large numbers of negative reports in documents accessible to the public would have alarmed parents, trustees, and ratepayers alike, raising doubts about the pedagogical efficacy and financial burdens of the enterprise and, after 1920, rousing the ire of nascent teacher organizations.

Thus we are left to speculate about probabilities. We know that the vast majority of elementary school teachers had rarely completed more than a high school education, and especially before 1920, many had no more than the junior high school grades. But what does this tell us about on-the-job competence? One can probably make a plausible case that teachers with no more than junior matriculation (grade XI or XII depending on the province) might encounter difficulties teaching the more demanding subjects in the senior elementary grades – explaining concepts in mathematics or science, for example, or providing much depth in interpreting history or English literature. Still, how much difficulty remains an open question. After all, for decades large numbers of young women with the minimum requisite academic qualifications successfully prepared large numbers of pupils under the difficult pedagogical circumstances of the one-room country school to write and pass the demanding high school entrance examination. Pedagogical expectations play a very large role in how the question is answered. If the job is to drive a pupil through the basic facts of Canadian history, this can be done with little more than a textbook. (Who was Champlain? What was the date of Confederation? Identify and provide the date of the Ashburton Treaty. What were the five causes of the First World War?) More ambitious forms of pedagogy may well require more than a high school education, which was one of the usual justifications for claiming that elementary school teachers, like their secondary counterparts, needed a university degree.

Even today, on the other hand, many university-educated elementary school teachers have no more mathematics, science, history, or English than they learned in high school because their university programs did not include courses in these or other subjects that are taught in the elementary school. They will have to teach them nonetheless. If, moreover, a university degree made a decisive difference in on-the-job competence, there would not, presumably, have been the clamour in the late twentieth century over the quality of mathematics or reading instruction in the elementary schools.[19] And it is well to remember, in any case, that junior or senior matriculation was *not* a low level of attainment in an era when only a relative handful went on to any form of post-secondary education. Though this is not the place to dwell on invidious comparisons between academic standards of yesterday and today, one might at least reflect on the notion that the dramatic escalation in educational credentials and grade inflation that has taken place in both high schools and universities since the 1960s may have left today's university graduates no more competent, and perhaps less so, in both literacy and numeracy skills than yesterday's high school matriculants. And yet this is the pool that provides our only supply of elementary school teachers.

We can be somewhat more certain about one thing at least: how pupils assessed their teachers. In an influential essay on pedagogical practices in Canadian schools, Neil Sutherland draws on a large number of interviews with people who attended school between the 1920s and 1960.

Their memories of the teachers they encountered form part of that essay, and there is no substitute for Sutherland's full analysis. We attempt only the briefest of summaries here. "People's recollections" of their teachers "divided them into four rough categories," he begins.

> They gave ... their highest rating to those teachers who emphasized the fundamentals, who drilled frequently and tested often, who concentrated on having their pupils learn those things that both community and educational tradition told them were the "core" curriculum. These teachers knew their business and they taught this curriculum thoroughly and systematically ... They conveyed a sense that what they did, and what they wanted their pupils to do, was of immense importance ... They ran "no nonsense" classrooms in which routines were all-pervasive and cast in a code that itemized many "thou shalt nots." Some pupils also knew that these were good teachers because "you KNEW you'd learned a thing. The evidence was there because you could REPEAT the learning accurately – even years later." Good teachers, however, were also fair teachers. They dispensed their rebukes and punishments rarely, in an even-handed way and in strict accordance with the rules.

A second group of teachers, "remembered less sharply," were described as "nice." Though they ran more relaxed classrooms than the first group and tended to have warmer personalities, they also taught well. These two types, Sutherland continues, evoked positive memories, but there were two other sorts as well:

> One was made up of teachers and principals who were mean, nasty, sarcastic, cruel or even vicious ... Such teachers usually employed a pedagogy that was not very different from other teachers. They differed from their colleagues mostly in that, instead of being respected or liked by their pupils, they were feared and hated ...
> Finally, pupils looked on a few teachers with contempt. These unfortunates displayed their ineffectiveness or their incompetence in a variety of ways. They could not explain things clearly. The oral parts of their lessons rambled, their notes were incoherent. They could not keep order; they sometimes broke down and wept. While most disappeared in a year or less, a few persisted to become almost legendary objects to be scorned by class after class of pupils. Whether they stayed or left, they received no compassion or mercy from either pupils or parents.[20]

Relying on student assessments (and especially recollected ones) has its own problems. They are not necessarily to be privileged over other types of assessment that use different kinds of measures. And Sutherland's evidence is drawn mainly from the corps of Vancouver teachers, who were, like other big-city teachers, among those with the best formal qualifications and most experience. His account *may* not be representative of the general run of teachers in smaller communities. It draws emphatic attention, nonetheless, to the fact that competence is about more than just academic qualifications or levels of professional training – caring and concern appear here as at least of equal importance. Caring and concern, however, are not synonyms for warm and fuzzy. "The highest ratings" awarded by Sutherland's respondents went to teachers who were demanding, who ran "no-nonsense" classrooms, who taught through direct instruction, and who drilled their pupils thoroughly in the elements of learning.[21] His survey is, in any case, a collective portrait that "rings true," largely confirming what most of us already know from personal experience and from hearsay – from teachers themselves, parents, and pupils alike. There were then, as there are now, good, poor, and indifferent teachers in Canada's public schools. Nor is this to single out teachers for particular opprobrium. It simply reflects the range of aptitudes and personalities to be found in most skilled and professional occupations. In this respect, teachers are not exceptions but typical of the modern occupational order.

While adults' memories of their teachers' personalities remained sharp long after leaving school, they were less acute, we suspect, about more subtle matters, such as the varieties of methods teachers might employ. Undoubtedly there were teachers who offered no more than rigid adherence to dull routine and tedious drill. Certainly there were the inexperienced, struggling just to keep their heads above water, who could hardly be expected to have a well-developed repertoire of methodological skills. But as teachers became more experienced, more at ease and in command of their classrooms, instruction was likely to become more imaginative, and methods more varied.[22]

We say this because, in our reading of the professional press, we have been impressed by the range and variety of classroom techniques described by experienced teachers – not, we emphasize, by normal school instructors or other non-practising exponents, but by those who identify themselves as school-based practitioners, who describe, for the benefit of others, their own best practices. The pages of *The School*, the *Canadian Teacher*, the *Educational Review*, and the federation magazines are packed with these kinds of articles. Yes, there are plenty of pages that consist of model arithmetic problems, drill exercises, workbook-like fill-in-the-blanks, and so on. But there are plenty of other methods on exhibit as well. There was nothing new, for example, about projects in the late 1930s; they had been widely used long before that. Project methods suitable for individuals or groups of children existed on every conceivable topic, cutting right across the curriculum. Teachers read stories to younger pupils to catch their interest, using them as "come-ons" for seat-work. An Easter bunny story, for example, could be followed by an exercise in making Easter cards that involved construction work, drawing, and printing. Children played store to improve practical writing and arithmetical skills. Mock elections, mock councils, or mock parliaments were used to stimulate interest in government. For senior elementary and high school pupils, class debates were a staple in good social studies classes. Lessons that stressed causal relations rather than mere descriptions were outlined – in history, they might start with a physical map of Greece, for example, and then ask students to deduce how geography might shape economic, political, and social life. There were widespread experiments with variations on the Winnetka or Dalton plans, which stressed individualized instruction. There were games of all kinds that incorporated word or numerical drill.[23]

Take, for example, the methods of just one teacher, one who indeed had few of the resources available to urban teachers. Edith Van Kleek worked in Alberta's one- and two-room rural schools from the 1920s through the 1950s. Her memoir suggests she was utterly untouched by the succession of pedagogical fashions that swept across the perio d, but she was clearly an effective, though perhaps an unexceptionable, teacher among other experienced and dedicated women who enjoyed the rewards of classroom teaching. Van Kleek ran a tight ship with no-nonsense methods dominated by a successive set of daily instructional routines.[24] But she also had a repertoire of methodological approaches. She describes, for example, a series of science experiments that "never failed to fascinate the students" and a number of spur-of-the-moment nature hikes. For children slow in arithmetic, she "taught them to play cribbage (making sure first that the parents had no objections to cards). There's nothing like crib, I always thought, to sharpen up their adding skills."[25] Teaching about Canada's ocean resources, she writes, "I developed a method of teaching about fish." Reading from the encyclopedia gave no real sense of a fish and its dimensions:

So, I had a child go to the blackboard with a yardstick and draw a salmon, life-size. Others drew, life-size, herring, smelt, cod, halibut ... lobster, shrimp, every kind of fish or shellfish until the blackboard was full of them, some overlapping. Then one little boy asked, "How are we going to draw a whale?"

"Easy," I said. "We'll just push the desks aside and draw a whale, life-size, on the floor." Eager hands pushed the desks first to one side, then the other. We found there were several sizes of whales, the biggest one

being the blue whale, which would reach from corner to corner of the
schoolroom, and its tail would reach up the wall! ...

  That whale and the tuna beside it were on the floor until the chalk
got scraped off. They studied the different shapes, drawing what features they could. They even worked on their fish at recess and noon,
drawing from pictures the eyes, fins, gills, and the whale's blowhole.
They learned how the gills get oxygen out of the water, but that for the
whale the blowhole is its nose and it has to have air. Every grade learned
something about fish, whether it was for their grade or not.[26]

Even the most lively classroom or the most interesting lesson will inevitably
entail some portion of drudgery if pupils are to absorb and practise what
they are taught; but there were also a variety of techniques that experienced
teachers used to enrich learning, motivate interest, promote thought, connect schoolwork to experience, and make even the necessary drudgery
less tedious.

We dwelt at some length in an earlier chapter on the fiscal inequalities that
generated stark disparities in the quantity and quality of educational provision available in all parts of the country and that resulted in inequalities of
educational opportunity for children in different kinds of communities.
The quality of instruction is not the only determinant of equal opportunity – familial and social circumstances are obviously more important. Yet
effective instruction is not dispensable either, and to the extent that good
libraries, adequate classroom equipment and supplies, and, above all, well-
qualified and experienced teachers matter, the dramatic differences in
available resources spelled inevitable differences in the quality of teaching
and learning. These differences were endemic in early twentieth-century
Canada, distinguishing levels of educational provision in the central cities from those in their surrounding suburbs, large urban communities
from smaller ones, urban school districts from their rural counterparts,
rural school districts with rich assessment bases from those with poor ones.
But two circumstances posed particular challenges to both the quality of
instruction and equality of educational opportunity, and each deserves a
comment here.

  First, there was the multiplication of secondary-level instruction in one-
room elementary schools or in exceedingly small high schools. There is no
question about the growing demand for cheap and easy access to secondary
instruction in the rural elementary schools – enrolments expanded steadily
across the first three decades of the century and underwent mushroom
growth in the hard years of the 1930s. Justifying a long tradition in Nova
Scotia – a tradition rooted in the widespread dispersal of advanced learning

in the Scottish parish schools – its superintendent of education, Alexander MacKay, would pen this Panglossian paean as late as 1925:

> Rural High School Work is perhaps the most interesting peculiarity of the Nova Scotian School System. Unlike the European and American Systems with separate common and high school boards, a pupil in the remotest region is entitled to study in the school room up to the end of the High School program ... He studies, as it were, privately; but the teacher who has no time to treat him as a class is at hand to give momentary aid when the student fails to master a difficulty. He thus develops initiative, which as a student in a platoon-drilled high school, he might neglect ...
>
> The rural high school in this manner first selects the pupil of educational genius, for only such are disposed to work out their problems with minimum aid. In the second place he may cover twice the ground of work in a year as compared with the genius who has to keep step with a class of pupils pushed through the high school by home pressure. He can test himself with the full-staffed high school examination; and we find him often passing a grade two years earlier than an urban pupil. When such a pupil discovers his or her ability, it often leads to a year or two in a notable high school before entering a university. In such a manner have perhaps the majority of the leading men and women of the Province discovered their power. The birth of genius is not confined to the vicinity of a full-staffed high school, important as such institutions are.[27]

Two prominent American observers invited to survey the schools of Nova Scotia in 1922 offered a more tempered assessment. There were about 1,200 one-room schools, they wrote, that "profess to offer instruction in the 9th, 10th and 11th grades. The teacher, unfit as she is, is urged to do this even though it must obviously be at the expense of the earlier grades. On this lean tuition boys and girls work their way through text-books and the provincial examinations without ever attending a high school, and thereby develop enviable habits of initiative and industry to compensate for defective instruction. At Acadia University last year four out of seven prizewinners were prepared in this manner."[28]

While opinion was always somewhat divided, high school instruction in the one-room elementary school was generally condemned by schoolmen everywhere. There was the matter of academic qualifications: many teachers offered secondary-level instruction when they had no more than that level of attainment themselves. Often enough they didn't even attempt instruction, doing little more than supervising pupils' correspondence courses,

hardly a preferred mode of learning in any case. Moreover, no one-room
elementary school had the equipment required for high school science or
the requisite library facilities in other fields. But the most frequent source
of complaint, and one often heard not only from inspectors and teachers but from parents of younger children, was the effect of secondary-level
instruction on the rest of the school. Writing in 1913, James Miller, a senior
official in Alberta's Department of Education, was only one of a long line
of schoolmen to describe (and complain about) the phenomenon: "The
advice of the inspector seems to be the only restraining influence that is
brought to bear to prevent the overburdening of the one-teacher school
with junior high school work. The ambition of the parents of the particular
children concerned and their unwillingness to send their children to the
neighbouring town or village frequently force the teacher to sacrifice the
interests of the majority of pupils and centre her efforts on preparing one
or two advanced pupils for their examinations."[29] And this would be a typical response across the entire period: teaching high school pupils in rural
one-room schools served both those pupils and the rest of the school badly,
asked teachers to do work they were ill-equipped to do, and imposed additional burdens on already overburdened teachers.[30]

Pupils attending Canada's small high schools confronted conditions that
must have been almost equally discouraging. Compared to the collegiate
institutes and high schools in cities and larger towns, the small-town and village high school was far less likely to have a range of specialists responsible
for each subject. "Staffs are often so small," one observer remarked about
the state of history instruction, "that a real specialist is not to be found in
many schools, and the subject may fall into the hands of a teacher who
has no real qualifications for it, but who must take it, to fill up his or her
timetable. In such hands lessons too often take the form of 'giving notes'
or testing the reading of the book by the class."[31] But that was equally true
of any other subject, from mathematics or physics to Latin or French. The
small schools and continuation classes, moreover, were less likely to employ
university graduates and more likely to be staffed by those with first-class
elementary certificates (usually requiring only senior matriculation).

The most serious deficits, however, arose in the one-teacher, one-room
high school. Writing in 1936 about this type of school in British Columbia,
George Falconer of Lumby High School identified "four major problems:
(1) the extreme limitation of *teaching* time; (2) the difficulty of giving
options to meet individual needs; (3) the inadequacy of library facilities
and scientific apparatus; and (4) the lack of gymnasium equipment ... In
an average one-room high school there are four grades with nine or more
subjects each. Even with certain combinations of classes, this necessitates
approximately thirty-five courses. With twenty-five teaching hours per week
only forty minutes per week can be given each course. For a few students

this is sufficient, but for the majority of pupils, for whom subject matter must be taught, drilled and reviewed, *the teaching time is woefully inadequate.*" Options, Falconer went on, were out of the question. "The limitation of teaching time makes it necessary that the same slate of subjects be chosen for each pupil in each grade. This in itself is bad as it precludes any adaptation to special interests." Worse still, only a tiny minority would go on to post-secondary education, but because a handful did, the school had to meet matriculation requirements, which meant that all students had to take Latin whether or not they wanted to or benefited from it. Most of the rural high schools, moreover, were handicapped by the lack of library facilities and scientific equipment, and most had no gymnasiums even though physical education had recently been made an obligatory part of the high school curriculum. Thus Falconer's conclusion: "It seems scarcely fair that pupils prepared under such conditions must write the same departmental examinations as those with all the privileges of a larger school."[32]

Scarcely fair indeed. Effective instruction under such circumstances might not have been literally impossible, but compared with what one might reasonably expect from a larger school, they put teachers at an extreme disadvantage, where even a pedagogical genius would be hard-pressed to demonstrate competence, let alone the average teacher, and must have posed an equal challenge to all but the most able and single-minded pupils. To reiterate a passage by W.F. Dyde quoted in an earlier chapter, "The sharpest difference will be found to exist between urban and rural conditions. In all but the prescribed syllabus and textbooks the country pupil is often receiving his secondary education under conditions which are far removed from those enjoyed by the city child. The discrepancy between urban and rural secondary education presents one of the most pressing problems which the country as a whole is facing."[33]

Both the quality of instruction and equality of educational opportunity were also compromised by the nature of the workforce in Canada's one-room elementary schools. While rural schools always had a substantial corps of experienced teachers, they were mainly staffed by a succession of beginners whose professional training left them singularly ill-prepared to cope with the tasks confronting them. At best, they learned most of the necessary skills on the job. Yet teaching in the one-room rural school – the hardest, most-demanding work in the education system – was handed to the youngest, most-inexperienced people in the occupation. In 1913 James Miller summed up the problem succinctly:

Apart from the outline courses of study designed primarily for a graded school, the annual provincial examinations, the authorized text-books, and the approved library books, the rural teacher receives little aid in matters pertaining to the curriculum except such as may be given by the inspector on the occasion of his annual or semi-annual visitation. Recalling the maturity, scholarship, and professional training of the rural school teachers as indicated in the preceding chapter some idea may be formed of their ability to do for their school what a whole corps of town or city teachers, under the leadership of principals, supervisors, and superintendent, find great difficulty in doing even though the official course fits more readily into their situation. Not only are the rural teachers left almost alone to deal with the problems of finding, selecting, evaluating and organizing the detailed content for each grade of work, and of determining the questions of relative emphasis and of time distribution both between and within the various subjects, but they must also undertake to teach all the grades they may have in the same time that a town or city teacher has for a single grade.[34]

Miller was not the only one to comment on that hard reality. In 1923 one Manitoba teacher wrote that "at present the country is at once the training school of the efficient teacher and the execution yard of the inefficient ... Having stood the test, the young teacher passes on to the city or town ... and a younger and less experienced one takes the vacant place. Lack of permanence is the main reason for the inefficiency [in rural teaching] we hear so much about."[35] Yet another Manitoba teacher, this time in 1930: "In brief the ungraded school is a heavy job for an experienced and competent teacher, yet in practice we find the lowest paid, the youngest, and the least experienced condemned to work out their professional salvation in the ungraded schools while the graded schools are manned by the experienced and highly competent teachers with trained supervisors at hand to help out in any difficulty that may arise."[36] Robert England, drawing on his own and others' experience of teaching in Saskatchewan, would describe such arrangements as no less than a "crime":

There is no more difficult task than the teaching of a one-room rural school comprising 8 grades, with pupils ranging from 5 to 15. A teacher formally equipped to teach all subjects of the Saskatchewan curriculum, where the number, ages, and grades of the children differ so widely ... where school equipment is sometimes curtailed by the parsimony of school trustees ... must be prepared to suffer much disappointment, and to work ... in the face of many handicaps ...[37]

City schools refuse teachers without experience, but rural schools accept what they can get and pay the costs of the extra training and the experience needed for urban employment. The true Normal School of the city is thus the rural school. *The crime of our educational system is the sending of our weakest teachers to our hardest schools to gain experience.*[38]

Alberta's 1935 *Report of the Legislative Committee on Rural Education* had this to say: "Although the rural teachers are for the most part comparatively inexperienced, they have perhaps the most perplexing problems to be met with anywhere in the whole field of education. Working alone, they are thrown almost entirely upon their own resources, and the infrequent visits of the inspector do not afford the encouragement, direction, and advice so urgently needed in many cases."[39] These passages are only a handful among many to the same effect.[40]

Or to put it another way, during the first four decades of the twentieth century, neophyte physicians had, besides their initial years in medical school classrooms, two and a half or three years of supervised clinical experience in hospitals to learn to heal. Would-be lawyers learned not just in classrooms but also, before they were licensed to practise, in offices under the experienced eyes of senior members of a firm. Nurses-in-training were *in training* in hospitals for two or three years, closely supervised to learn their particular jobs.[41] The beginning teacher received a year or less of professional training, with most of the content geared to graded schools, and with limited opportunities – or none at all – for supervised practice in a one-room school. Mostly, she went out to teach in a rural school and was left there, without supervision or assistance, to exercise her uncertain and untested skills upon youngsters of all ages, grades, and abilities who had to depend on her alone for the basic skills of learning they would need for the rest of their lives. Such circumstances created a fundamental inequity in the Canadian school system, one that would persist so long as the one-room school provided all the education that most rural children could expect to receive.

Epitaph

We have tried in this book to portray a complex enterprise at work, to illustrate its operational assumptions, organizational structures, and pedagogical practices. Originating in the middle decades of the nineteenth century and reaching maturity in the two or three decades on either side of the turn of the twentieth, this quintessentially Victorian school system was already beginning to fray at the edges. New currents of opinion about what constituted an appropriate education for the modern age were one reason, but no less important was a series of changes in the social and economic environment. There had always been inequalities between town and country, between larger urban communities and smaller ones. But after 1900 the gaps widened, becoming more palpable every decade: inequities didn't simply persist, they got worse, and were perceived to get worse by ratepayers, teachers, academics, politicians, and the general public alike. The expansion of commerce and industry along with population growth enriched a relative handful of school boards in the cities and larger towns, enabling them to create the model for what a "modern" school system and the "good school" should look like. In everything from the most approved styles of school architecture, the elaboration of health services, or the qualifications and experience of their teachers to the introduction of special education programs, the creation of supervisory services, or innovations in pedagogy, and more besides, cities like Winnipeg set the pace and provided the template for exemplary practice. Decade by decade, smaller communities like Blairmore or Kipp School District saw themselves, as others saw them, falling further and further behind the bundle of expectations that constituted conventional ideas of educational progress.

The stresses on the system were outgrowing in other ways its capacity to cope. Child labour and compulsory attendance laws, along with the shrinking market for the labour of young adolescents, flooded the senior elementary and junior high school grades with children who had no choice but to be in school. A new mass clientele inevitably created pressures to accommodate a far wider range of abilities than Victorian assumptions allowed for. Outside of any other consideration, children could not very well be failed *en masse* when there was no other place for them to go; and if they were all required to be in school to mid-adolescence, then the school had a responsibility, one way or another, to provide a suitable education for them. Yet a great many could not meet the academic demands of the single rigorous standard of achievement that characterized Victorian programs of studies at both the elementary and secondary level. Program diversification and the elimination of most external examinations were first responses, but both presented contemporaries with unfamiliar challenges. One was the financial cost of introducing more "practical" options and programs. Larger urban communities might be able to afford these innovations but most could not. Proposals to expand the high school program, moreover, ran headlong into traditional assumptions about the purpose of a high school education that proved obdurately resistant to change. The other problem was the unresolved question of how to maintain academic standards without the mechanism of the external examination – and more fundamentally yet, unresolved questions about what constituted a meaningful academic standard when an entire generation, rather than a highly selected portion of it, was to receive a secondary-level education. Were traditional notions of excellence and academic standards compatible with greater equality of opportunity? Could a differentiated curriculum be reconciled with those notions, or was it simply a different way of separating the sheep from the goats? Or, in the last resort, did "more" simply mean "worse"?

In the mid-nineteenth century the rural school district had provided a practical solution to the organizational challenge of putting schools within reach of nearly every child in the country. But by the early twentieth century it was becoming an incubus. Once-viable school districts were gradually stripped of their populations and, with that, stripped of the resources to sustain a good elementary school. Moreover, what constituted the definition of a good elementary school was changing: increasingly it was no longer enough to provide the majority of children with the elements of literacy and numeracy; rather, the demand was for a more extended grounding that encompassed not only the senior elementary grades but some secondary school training as well. Given its meagre assessment base, the limited qualifications and experience of its teachers, and the pedagogical exigencies of the one-room school, the rural school district was singularly ill-equipped to meet these demands. And both school and school district were beginning to look expendable. As roads began to improve, especially in the interwar years, it became easier to imagine, and even in a few cases implement, innovations like the school bus, the consolidated school, the rural high school, and, with these, larger units of administration that promised to revolutionize local funding, end the isolation of the rural teacher, raise her qualifications and experience, and supplant inspection with more effective means of local supervision.

On each of these matters, and many others besides, a reform agenda had been taking shape for decades. What was good enough in 1890 or 1900 was ceasing to be so by 1920 or 1930, and year by year the critics marshalled a growing arsenal of evidence and arguments demonstrating that the existing system was failing to serve society well – or, at their most extreme, at all. Nor was this just the earnest policy talk of reform-minded bureaucrats and academic experts. Parents might be less certain of what they wanted, or less exercised – even sceptical – about grand designs, but they had concrete demands and expectations, such as the expansion of rural secondary education or, among the urban working class, the provision of advanced academic and vocational training to their children.

It took the Great Depression to fully reveal the bankruptcy of traditional arrangements and provide that agenda with real traction in the public arena. Beginning slowly and unevenly in the late 1930s and early 1940s, but gaining momentum across the two or three decades that followed, a thorough-going reconstruction would take place in the precepts and practices governing the way schools worked. New modes of administration and finance, accompanied by profound changes in program and pedagogy, would emerge, marking a final rupture with the Victorian past and creating Canada's modern system of public education. But that is another story.

Notes

1 For a pointed comment on the relative neglect of demographic characteristics of schooling compared to the attention devoted to curriculum, see
   Guppy and Davies, *Education in Canada*, xxvii.
2 Manzer, *Educational Regimes*, 10–11.
3 Sutherland, *Children in English-Canadian Society*.
4 There is very little to distinguish between the last quarter of the nineteenth
   century and the first two decades of the twentieth. Compare, for example,
   the concluding chapters of MacNaughton, *Education in New Brunswick*, with
   the New Brunswick *Annual Reports* for the next two decades; or Gidney and
   Millar, *Inventing Secondary Education*, chaps 10–15, with the Ontario *Annual
   Reports* of the early twentieth century. Or see the sense of continuity from the
   1860s to 1920 that dominates Bingay's *Public Education in Nova Scotia*. Indeed,
   some students of the subject go even further, William Haines remarking in
   the mid-1930s that "the educational system of New Brunswick has changed
   little since the Schools Act of 1871." Haines, "The Secondary School," 1.
   While the interwar years registered some new departures, we suggest that
   whatever the degree of hyperbole involved, there is much wisdom in adapting
   an observation first made by the historian G.P. de T. Glazebrook about the
   social history of Ontario: in some respects the twentieth century began for
   Canada in 1945.
5 In itself this is not a reason to exclude the English Protestant community, but
   some of the other problems we refer to here extended to it as well. It seemed
   unnecessary to pursue the subject further after publication of an account that
   explores the subject in great detail. Our own modest forays and that book,
   however, convince us that schooling in Protestant Quebec paralleled that in
   other parts of the country, though more closely resembling the Maritimes
   than provinces west of Quebec. See MacLeod and Poutanen, *A Meeting of the*

People. For a fine general survey, see chaps 4 through 14 of Magnuson, *The Two Worlds of Quebec Education.*

6 For but one example, see DBS, *Elementary and Secondary Education 1948–50,* "Secondary Education. Notes Concerning Tables 9–14," 38.

7 Goldenberg, *Municipal Finance,* 51–2. See also RCDPR, *Report,* Book 1, 227–9.

8 On this latter point, we take note of the persuasive argument made by Fahrni, "Quebec," 1–20.

9 Anyone who thinks otherwise should peruse the assembled 300 pages and 2,324 entries in Smith, *A Bibliography of Canadian Education,* published as early as 1938. A preface notes a substantial list of important sources *not* included in that bibliography.

10 The archival sources that we have used most intensively are the files of the Alberta Department of Education at the Public Archives of Alberta (PAA). Exploiting this resource in only one province, however, does not necessarily invite parochialism: one of the most valuable pan-Canadian sources at PAA consisted of the many files of "interprovincial correspondence" – a rich vein of queries, answers, exchanges of opinion, and documents on all manner of subjects, great and small, in letters between senior bureaucrats in Edmonton and other provincial capitals.

11 Smiley, *Rowell/Sirois Report.*

12 See http://www.bankofcanada.ca/en/rates/inflation_calc.html. See also our own discussion of the importance of converting current into constant dollars in chapter 6 below and in Gidney and Millar, "The Salaries of Teachers," 3.

13 Though it doesn't incorporate the literature much before 1985, the best guide since then is to be found in the successive bibliographies published in *Historical Studies in Education/Revue d'histoire de l'éducation.*

CHAPTER ONE

1 The basic structure of governance and finance in Canadian education is a staple of many texts on the history of education or educational administration. In order to try to describe the system as it existed in the early twentieth century, we have relied especially on Miller, *Rural Schools,* esp. chaps 1 and 2; Richardson, *Administration of Schools,* esp. chaps 2 and 3; Dyde, *Public Secondary Education,* chaps 2 and 3. Despite the apparent specificity of these three titles, each begins with a detailed overview of governance and finance across Canada. Richardson is very strong on the local educational authorities. Though dated 1929, Dyde's book reflects the situation earlier in the decade when the book was actually being written. See also the helpful glossary, which includes institutional terminology unfamiliar today, in DBS, *Historical Statistical Survey,* 6–7. For another thorough review of provisions for governance and finance in each province, see DBS, *Annual Survey 1934,* appendix

to Part 1, lxxii–lxxx. One brief but incisive description, a model of its kind, is Goldenberg, *Municipal Finance*, 20–5, 51–62.

2 The "exclusive jurisdiction" clause and the separate school guarantees are contained in section 93 of the British North America Act – one part of the modern Canadian constitution. In Nova Scotia and Ontario there was also a local legislative provision, emphatically not part of any constitutional guarantee, for separate schools for "coloured" children.

3 See DBS, *Education, Census, 1951*, 16. This is more than speculation on our part. As of 1941 Nova Scotia had a much lower retention rate than Alberta or British Columbia for the age group 15–19, but very close to the same number of years spent at school. See Robbins, *Youth Figured Out*, 12–13. For some commentary on other difficulties of making provincial comparisons because of policy differences alone, see DBS, *Elementary and Secondary Education 1948–50*, 13.

4 See Stone, *Urban Development*, 29, 132–3. The metropolitan regions are listed in Stone's Appendix 1. There is an excellent graphic representation of the differences in *Historical Atlas*, Plate 4. Note that in 1931 a very large percentage of the urban population of British Columbia was located in Vancouver. Ontario at that point was slightly more urbanized, but a much larger percentage of the urban population lived outside the four "metropolitan cities." Note also the much smaller percentage of urban population in each of the three Maritime provinces *and* the lack of any community over 100,000.

5 *The School* 27, no. 9 (May 1939): 811–12, citing British Columbia, *AR 1937–38*.

6 DBS, *Statistical Report on Education 1921*, 2.

7 Sandiford, *Comparative Education*, 350.

8 The figures are from New Brunswick, *Report of the New Brunswick Committee on Reconstruction*, 205, 207, citing *National Income of Canada, 1919–38*. See also Mackintosh, *Economic Development of Dominion-Provincial Relations*, chap. 8, 135.

9 DBS, *Education, Census, 1951*, 19. Similarly, between 1926 and 1940 the number employed in non-agricultural jobs increased sharply, though there was no absolute decline in the number employed in agriculture. See DBS, *National Accounts – Income and Expenditure, 1926–1956*, 8 (graphic).

10 Stone, *Urban Development*, 29. We have rounded most of the numbers in this and the next few paragraphs. For a pertinent graphic, 1891–1961, see *Historical Atlas*, Plate 4.

11 MacLean, *Illiteracy*, 142.

12 *Historical Atlas*, Plate 4. The cities were Vancouver, Winnipeg, Hamilton, Windsor, Ottawa, Toronto, Montreal, and Quebec City.

13 Cudmore and Caldwell, *Rural and Urban Composition*, 470. City ranking for each census, 1901–61, along with population figures for 1931, can be found in Artibise, "Patterns of Prairie Urban Development," 120, 124.

14 See the table in Stone, *Urban Development*, 72.

15 The meaning of "urban" has been the subject of extensive debate and the
    problematic nature of the census definition widely acknowledged. For one
    introduction, see Lucas, *Minetown, Milltown, Railtown*, chap. 1. See also
    Cudmore and Caldwell, *Rural and Urban Composition*, 443–5. Because some
    authorities draw directly from the pertinent census data and others attempt
    to create consistent historical figures by imposing a common definition of
    "urban" that modifies the changes in census definitions, urban and rural
    proportions vary somewhat depending on the source used. See Stone, *Urban
    Development*, 28, notes a and b. For the Prairies at least, Gerald Friesen, follow-
    ing the lead of Paul Voisey, suggests a dividing line of 1,000 people, but we
    are inclined to think that a distinction set at 4,000 or 5,000 is more service-
    able. On the other hand, the extent to which industries and services were
    dependent or independent of the surrounding countryside also matters. See
    Friesen, *The Canadian Prairies*, 320–1. See also the discussion in Dasgupta,
    Rural Canada, 121–5. What, indeed, was a "city"? A legally defined city in
    Ontario included only the largest urban communities; in 1930, for example,
    that province had no more than fifteen cities. At the same date, British
    Columbia had thirty-three "cities," most of which would have been catego-
    rized in Ontario as small towns or large villages.

16 Lucas, *Minetown, Milltown, Railtown*, 11–12.

17 Stone, *Urban Development*, 29.

18 Ibid.

19 Urquhart and Buckley, *Historical Statistics*, 14. The 1951 figure is based on
    the 1956 census definition of urban. If one uses the 1941 definition, the
    urban/rural population in 1951 is more evenly divided, roughly 8 million to
    6 million.

20 Cudmore and Caldwell, *Rural and Urban Composition*, 478–82.

21 That is, they lived in rural municipalities but on the edges of cities or incor-
    porated suburbs.

22 Cudmore and Caldwell, *Rural and Urban Composition*, 478.

23 Marsh, *Canadians In and Out of Work*, 109–10. More generally on the regional
    characteristics and the varieties of urban and rural communities in the 1920s
    and 1930s, see ibid., chap. 5, 103ff. For one example of the continuing estab-
    lishment of schools in frontier areas from the turn of the century on through
    the next several decades, see Lysecki, "Education in Manitoba," chap. 5. We
    are not entirely happy with "frontier" as a category meant to include, for
    example, isolated but long-established fishing villages; but because of its
    familiarity, we will adopt it anyway. The best introduction to the various pro-
    vincial "frontiers" is Coates and Morrison, *The Forgotten North*.

24 2006 figures: Statistics Canada, Summary Tables, Farm population and total
    population by rural and urban population ... , http://www40.statcan.gc.ca/
    l01/cst01/agrc42a-eng.htm (2008–11–12).

25 Our calculations from Leacy, *Historical Statistics*, Table A94-109.

CHAPTER TWO

1 For these population and enrolment figures, which include Quebec, see Leacy, *Historical Statistics*, Series A78–93 (population) and w67–93 (enrolments). This edition is also available on Statistics Canada's website. The best quick reference for enrolment increases, 1901–61, is the graphic at Plate 33, *Historical Atlas*. For an assessment of the high levels of adult literacy and school attendance in 1901, see Gossage and Gauvreau, "Canadian Fertility in 1901," 67–8, 62 (Table 2.1).

2 Our calculations from the provincial figures in Leacy, *Historical Statistics*, Series w67–93. See Table A.1 in appendix A.

3 For the numbers in this and the next paragraph, see these two tables. The age group 5–19 is a conventional grouping for estimating the "participation rate" – that is, the percentage of children and young people in school. It is normally subdivided into the categories 5–9, 10–14, and 15–19 (Table 2.2). We do not think these groupings are especially useful for the first half of the twentieth century and much prefer, whenever possible, to use participation rate by individual ages (Table 2.3). For our commentary on the shortcomings of using age groups, see appendix A, section 4 (where we also comment on the reasons why we do not use the published 1901 census data for age groups). For comparative purposes, Tables A.2 and A.3 in appendix A include Quebec. Table A.4 in appendix A provides enrolment by individual ages in each province, including Quebec. For an important study, based on the 1901 manuscript census, of patterns of school attendance by individual ages, see Mandeville, "Who Went to School?" Although it primarily focuses on local communities, it also provides provincial and national data. The national sample includes Quebec, but the patterns are very similar to those we examine and reveal the increasing degree of schooling from the beginning of the century in the core ages of school attendance (in 1901, 8 through 12), growing regularity of attendance, and differences by urban or rural residence and by gender among older children. See esp. pp. 33–42, 85–7. For her findings on immigrants, see below, note 112.

4 The census for 1951, unlike previous censuses, did not include 5-year-olds enrolled in kindergarten, so we don't know the actual numbers of 5-year-olds attending school in that year. But the figure of 6.1% in 1951 is clearly an underestimate. See *Census of Canada 1951*, vol. 10, General Review and Summary Tables, 216.

5 In 1921 the age group 8–13 attended school in the 90% range, with the 7- and 14-year-olds not far behind. By 1931 the core group included them.

6 In some provinces, pupils were required to complete the term in which that birthday occurred. By the third decade of the century, most provinces

required children to be in school until their fourteenth or fifteenth birthday. Ontario's requirement was 16, though with large numbers of exceptions after age 13. For three summaries of the changing legal requirements about compulsory attendance in each Canadian province, see DBS, *Statistical Report on Education 1921*, 8; DBS, *Annual Survey 1926*, xliii–xliv; DBS, *Annual Survey 1936*, xxxix–xl. For the best recent overview of the legal provisions right across the twentieth century, see Oreopoulos, "Canadian Compulsory School Laws," 7–12.

7 For the calculations for 1911–31, see DBS, "The Canadian School as an Increasing Social Factor." (See also the chart in DBS, *Annual Survey 1936*, xii.) For 1941, see Robbins, *Youth Figured Out*, 13. Our estimate is that ten years was still the average length of schooling in 1951. In 1911 Alberta and Saskatchewan averaged only five years, but by 1931 the two provinces matched the national average. By the latter year, Ontario and British Columbia were at nine years, while the Maritime provinces were below the national average, at about eight years.

8 *Census of Canada 1951*, vol. 10, General Review and Summary Tables, 234 (Table 12). Numbers cited exclude Newfoundland but include Quebec. The national-level figures mask a sharp regional divide. The marginal change is largely due to the fact that there was little improvement east of Manitoba. The four western provinces had larger gains for that age group.

9 This is a paraphrase of the questions; the wording changed slightly from census to census.

10 For additional commentary on the differences between census and provincial figures, see appendix A, section 1.

11 Miller, *Rural Schools*, 90. However, this conflates two provinces in the early stages of their development with the more settled province of Nova Scotia. The Nova Scotia figures were very high in the later nineteenth century; in 1895, for example, nearly 47% were in school for five months or less; but by 1910 the figure had declined to 36%. There were also very sharp differences between urban and rural Nova Scotia in this respect. See McLaren, "The Proper Education for All Classes," 75.

12 Total enrolment and ADA for Canada and each province from the 1860s to 1962 are in Leacy, *Historical Statistics*, w67-93. The figures cited here and elsewhere are derived from that table.

13 Peter Sandiford, "A Study of Non-attendance of Pupils at School," *The School* 7, no. 5 (Jan. 1919): 315. This was part one of a two-part study. The second part was published in February 1919.

14 Ibid., 7, no. 6 (Feb. 1919): 356–61.

15 If this sounds confusing, it is. For a more detailed description of the formula and our additional comments, see appendix A, section 5. This and the next

paragraph are brief summaries of a complex of problems relating to the measurement of regularity of attendance and attempt to address them. For more detailed accounts, see *The School* 7, no. 7 (May 1919): 474–5; *WSJ* 16, no. 1 (January 1921): 457; Alberta, *AR 1939*, 93; and the pertinent references in the notes that follow. The most sustained discussions are in DBS, *Historical Statistical Survey*, 22–4; DBS, *Statistical Report on Education 1921*, 16, 27; DBS, *Annual Report 1922*, 26, 39, 47; DBS, *Annual Survey 1923*, xxvii; DBS, *Annual Survey 1924*, x, xv–xvi, xxv, xxxi; DBS, *Annual Survey 1930*, xlvi.

16 On the high irregularity of 5- and 6-year-olds even in urban areas, see the figures from the 1921 census in MacLean, *Illiteracy*, 138. MacLean is not acknowledged on the title page but is identified as the author on page 5. For our commentary on this study, see section 12 in appendix A.

17 DBS, *Statistical Report on Education 1921*, 27.

18 See, for example, the complaints about this in *Proceedings, OEA, 1917*, 462–3.

19 *The School* 6, no. 9 (May 1918): 637.

20 Calgary School Board, Minutes, 1921, typescript, p. 19 (Report for 1920).

21 DBS, *Annual Report 1922*, 47.

22 Nova Scotia, *AR 1911–12*, iv. "Countries" was probably a slip of the pen. Canadian cities increasingly kept two sets of records – one calculated by the month and, if required by provincial authorities, a second set of annual returns to be added to provincial tallies. Clearly this was the practice in Calgary as the quotation in the preceding paragraph shows. Despite the implications of this first Nova Scotia reassessment, the provincial department was still using annual measures more than a decade later; see the critique in the *Educational Review*, Oct. 1922, 31. In Ontario, complaints were being registered as early as 1906, and during the second decade of the century the Ontario Educational Association nearly annually voted resolutions protesting the methods used to record ADA; see *Proceedings, OEA, 1906*, 168; *1913*, 315–16; *1917*, 52, 194; *1918*, 198.

23 DBS, *Statistical Report on Education 1921*, 27.

24 Ibid., 16.

25 See Ontario, *AR 1921*, 50; *AR 1922*, 93; *AR 1926*, 76–7; *AR 1930*, 92; *AR 1934*, 69.

26 The use of transfer cards was a critical improvement in keeping track of students who changed schools, thus eliminating duplicate counts. They began to be used in the cities and larger towns in the first or second decade of the century – in Toronto, for example, in 1918. But they were far slower to penetrate the countryside. Our thanks to Jason Ellis for the Toronto reference. See our more extended comment on this in appendix A, section 5.

27 DBS, *Annual Report 1922*, 34.

28 Alberta, *AR 1960*, 243.

29 While it is not our concern here, this also raises the question of just how accurate nineteenth-century attendance records were and how justified the conclusions of historians who have made use of them.

30 Not only are there a number of inherent problems in using age-grade tables and retention tables based on them, but marshalling our evidence in this section involves discussion of the data and presentation of too many tables to include in the text itself. Readers who are not content with our generalizations on educational attainment should consult appendix A, section 6, where we give a full account.

31 Winnipeg, for example, had been producing them since at least 1901. See Wilson, "Education in Winnipeg," 153. The London Board of Education's first table appeared in its *AR 1910*, 49. Age-grade tables for Calgary date back to at least 1914; see Calgary School Board, *AR 1916*, 49. Province-wide age-grade tables begin to appear in the late teens or early 1920s, but neither British Columbia nor New Brunswick ever produced them – in published form at least. They are conspicuously absent in the *ARs* of both provinces. For British Columbia, see also the commentary in its *AR 1938–39*, H11–13.

32 DBS, *Historical Statistical Survey*, 56.

33 Ibid.

34 Leonard, "Over-Ageness," 4.

35 DBS, *Annual Report 1922*, 10–11.

36 MacLean, *Illiteracy*, 23.

37 DBS, *Historical Statistical Survey*, 36.

38 Our calculations from ibid., 56 (Tables 37 and 39).

39 Leonard, "Over-Ageness," 4.

40 DBS, *Annual Report 1922*, 10–11.

41 DBS, *Historical Statistical Survey*, 56 (the numbers are rounded).

42 Our calculations from the figures in DBS, *Historical Statistical Survey*, 36.

43 Putman-Weir Report, 247.

44 Percentages calculated from the figures in Table 2.4 source.

45 See our comments, appendix A, section 6, and the related tables, A.7–A.9.

46 Canadian Research Committee, *Your Child Leaves School*, 36.

47 We say this because the Winnipeg School Board published only a single age-grade table after 1921 – that for 1951. To be sure that there was nothing singular about Winnipeg, we carried out a similar analysis for London, 1910 (the year the city first published an age-grade table), 1922, and 1939. London's school system was already long established at the turn of the century, it was a more homogeneous community than Winnipeg, and in the early decades of the century it was under far less expansionary stress. Thus there are fewer extremes in the early figures, but other than that, the trends are the same: a gradually diminishing number of grade-retardeds or accelerants and, concomitantly, a steady expansion of the number of those the normal age for their grade. Age homogenization, however, was far from complete in 1939.

(There are no mid-century age-grade tables for London.) See London Board of Education, AR *1910*, 49; AR *1922*, 48; AR *1939*, 14. For a comparative 1921 figure from urban New Brunswick, see Anderson, "Education in the City of Moncton," Part I, chap. 6, n.p. For age-grade tables and retardation patterns in Victoria public schools, see Hawthorne, "Victoria Public Schools," 83ff. For a mid-century comparison to Winnipeg, see McManus, "Edmonton Public Schools," 38, 48. In this study, completed in 1950, of retardation rates in two of Edmonton's elementary schools, McManus found 37.8% of pupils were over-age for their grade; of these, 66.7% were retarded by one year, 27.1% by two years, and another 5% by three or four years. He went on to demonstrate that "of the children who dropped out of school none had made normal progress [through the grades]. All had been retarded one year or more."

48 Canadian Research Committee, "First Report," 42.

49 McLaren, "The Proper Education for All Classes," 81.

50 DBS, "Recent Trends in Education in the Prairie Provinces," 3. Despite the title, this bulletin also includes data for seven provinces.

51 Our calculations from the figures given in DBS, *Annual Survey 1936*, 32.

52 On this point, see MacLean's statistical exercise in estimating the chances of 14-year-olds in the lower grades ever reaching grade VIII. MacLean, *Illiteracy*, 139.

53 DBS, "The School Standing Attained by Canadian Children" (mimeograph, 1931), 1.

54 DBS, *Annual Survey 1931*, 22 (our calculations). See also *The Year Book of Education 1934*, 605.

55 *CSJ* 15, no. 9 (Sept. 1937): 316 (1930, 1934); DBS, *Annual Survey 1931*, 24 (1931).

56 McBeath, "Education in New Brunswick," 29.

57 DBS, *Education, Census, 1951*, 52 (ten provinces). Similarly, see Canadian Research Committee, "First Report," 43–4.

58 Figure 2.1 is based on our calculations from the figures in Urquhart and Buckley, *Historical Statistics*, 590–1, 593, for elementary enrolments and for secondary enrolments above grade VIII (not just those in secondary schools). To make it possible to compare the two sets of figures, an index for each of the elementary and secondary enrolments was calculated by dividing the number, elementary or secondary, at each five-year interval by the mean of the enrolments, elementary or secondary respectively, over the entire period. (For a similar method and graph covering the period 1891 to 1923, see Dyde, *Public Secondary Education*, 74 and appendix B.) Since data for secondary school enrolments in Ontario are missing for 1920, we have substituted the numbers for 1921 in making our calculations. For comparable population indices, our calculations are from the source given for Figure 2.1. Quebec and Newfoundland are excluded.

59 Dyde, *Public Secondary Education*, 73.

60 See Table 2.6 and DBS, *Elementary and Secondary Education 1944–46*, 17.

61 Walker, "Public Secondary Education in Alberta," 159. Between 1918 and 1934, elementary enrolment in Calgary increased by 35% and high school enrolment by 400%; see Stamp, *School Days*, 60.

62 *Manitoba Teacher* 13, no. 5 (May 1932): 13.

63 DBS, *Elementary and Secondary Education 1948–50*, 39. The numbers for British Columbia, Ontario, and English Canada are rounded.

64 Our calculations from DBS, *Annual Survey 1931*, 22.

65 Our calculations from DBS, *Elementary and Secondary Education 1938–40*, 30 (Table 11) (eight provinces, excluding Quebec).

66 Our calculations from Alberta, *AR 1921*, 126; *AR 1930*, 98 (Table 9). In 1935 the percentages were much the same: 18%, 36%, and 70% respectively; and in 1940 they had decreased only somewhat, to 16%, 33%, and 61% respectively. Our calculations, Alberta, *AR 1935*, 94 (Table 9); *AR 1940*, 90 (Table 8).

67 The percentages include grades IX through to the junior matriculation year (in some provinces grade XI, in others grade XII). Our calculations from DBS, *Annual Survey 1931*, 22 (Table 9); DBS, *Elementary and Secondary Education 1938–40*, 30 (Table 11); *Census of Canada 1941*, vol. 1, 733ff. (Table 54) (figures for 1931 and 1941). Quebec is excluded in each case; British Columbia is excluded in 1931 in order to compare the two sources. Similar calculations for 1951 cannot be replicated because they require both age-grade tables and age-related population statistics, and the DBS did not produce a table that could be compared to 1951 statistics. Until the 1920s in the United States, of the age group 14 through 17 who attended school, only a minority attended secondary school and the rest were in elementary school; see Tyack and Hansot, *Learning Together*, 187–8.

68 Compare Stamp, "Canadian High Schools," 77; Comacchio, *Dominion of Youth*, 100.

69 Report, City of Halifax Schools, in Nova Scotia, *AR 1910–11*, 192.

70 Putman-Weir Report, 264. The percentages had improved only somewhat by the late 1920s and early 1930s. See Barman, "Knowledge Is Essential," 64 (Table 12). For the slippage in Toronto high schools, 1912 through 1925, see [Savage], *Secondary Education in Ontario*, 32–3.

71 Wormsbecker, "Secondary Education," 87.

72 Dyde, *Public Secondary Education*, 82. At the time, only these four provinces provided the pertinent data.

73 *The Year Book of Education 1934*, 605.

74 *CSJ* 15, no. 9 (Sept. 1937): 316. Similarly, see *CSJ* 10, no. 6 (June 1932): 211; *CSJ* 12, no. 6 (June 1934): 211.

75 For students in the academic stream alone, the figures were about 38% at the beginning of the decade and 40% by the end. Our calculations for cohorts of students going through Ontario high school grades from 1934 to 1938

and 1947 to 1950, from Ontario, *AR 1935–AR 1939* and *AR 1947–AR 1951*. See appendix A, section 8, for an explanation of how we arrived at these figures and why they differ somewhat from those in Stamp, *Ontario Secondary School Program*, esp. his Table 3.4 (p. 45). Results may differ by province: for example, in Saskatchewan, for all students in 1940, grade XII enrolment was half (48.5%) that in grade IX, a higher percentage than in Ontario, and grade XI (junior matriculation) enrolment was 65.5% of that in grade IX; these may, however, be less accurate measurements, since they do not track the progress of the same pupils as a cohort study does. Our calculations from Saskatchewan, *AR 1940*, 21.

76 Canadian Research Committee, "First Report," 42 (Table 2; the table excludes Newfoundland schools and Quebec's Catholic schools).

77 Marsh, *Canadians In and Out of Work*, 242. Compared to England, far more English-Canadian children were continuing their education into the high school grades. By the 1940s Canadian children were completing elementary school at nearly the same rate as their American counterparts, but from that point onwards, the gap widened at every grade. For the English figures from 1911 through 1950, see McKibbin, *Classes and Cultures*, 260. There is also a helpful comparison across the decades from 1870 to 1960 of British and American educational attainment that can also be used to assess the relative Canadian figures, in Goldin and Katz, *The Race between Education and Technology*, 27. See also Goldin, "America's Graduation from High School," 345–74; Goldin and Katz, "Human Capital and Social Capital," 685.

78 For province-by-province figures in 1951 for the percentage of boys and girls, rural and urban, in school, by years of age, see DBS, *Education, Census, 1951*, vol. 12, appendix, 86–9 (Table 3).

79 DBS, *Annual Survey 1934*, xviii. Though MacLean's reasoning was a little different for girls aged 15–19, he thought the same outcome applied.

80 See appendix A, section 7.

81 *Census of Canada 1951*, vol. 10, 243 (Table 16). Our calculations.

82 The figure is for the 7–14 age group only. See MacLean, *Illiteracy*, 146. For the 1921 figures, see DBS, *Annual Survey 1923*, 25 (Table 24). Donna Mandeville's national sample of the 1901 manuscript census, including Quebec, shows that rural children attended school much less regularly (or not at all) compared to urban children; both groups were less likely to attend regularly than rural or urban children, respectively, in 1921. See Mandeville, "Who Went to School?," 38–41.

83 For 1931, our calculations for the 7–14 age group are from *Census of Canada 1931*, vol. 1, 1136 (Table 72). For 1951, our calculations for two provinces, Saskatchewan and Ontario, are from DBS, *Elementary and Secondary Education 1948–50*, 30 (Table 4). The data for other provinces can also be found there.

84 Ontario, *AR 1930*, 48. A careful analysis of one southern Ontario county in the mid-1940s with a majority rural population and only a scattering of small urban communities suggests the regularity gap may have been slightly larger (9%) than our figures. See High, "Haldimand County," 61–2.

85 Canadian Research Committee, "First Report," 43–4.

86 Guppy et al., "Changing Patterns of Educational Inequality," 323 (Table 2).

87 *Census of Canada 1951*, vol. 10, 243 (Table 16). See also High, "Haldimand County," 33–6.

88 See *Census of Canada 1951*, vol. 10, 243 (Table 16). The figures for the youngest age group (15–19 not in school) with "less than 9 years of schooling" are urban 37.3%, rural non-farm 57.0%, and farm 66.5%.

89 See Meltz, *Canadian Labour Force*, 58. In 1951 these two occupations were still well below the Canadian median. For 1931, see also MacLean, "Illiteracy," 670.

90 Mark, *Ottawa*, 57; Richardson, *Administration of Schools*, 230.

91 Richardson, *Administration of Schools*, 230.

92 For all urban communities, see MacLean, *Illiteracy*, 137. For London, Montreal, and Winnipeg, see the age-grade tables in Richardson, *Administration of Schools*, 223.

93 MacLean, *Illiteracy*, 140. See our comments in appendix A, section 7.

94 Alberta, *AR 1920*, 149. Similarly, for Ontario, see *The School* 7, no. 7 (March 1919): 432.

95 For representative figures, see Calgary School Board, Minutes, 1916, p. 50; *Educational Review*, Jan. 1924, 100, 116–17 (Fredericton); Nova Scotia, *AR 1930–31*, 114; *AR 1935–36*, 116 (Halifax); Mark, *Ottawa*, 60 (Ottawa and London); Richardson, *Administration of Schools*, 230 (Montreal, London, and Winnipeg); Coulter, "Teenagers in Edmonton," 95; Putman-Weir Report, 251 (British Columbia cities); DBS, *Historical Statistical Survey*, 56; Barman, "Knowledge Is Essential," 22. For urban areas generally, see MacLean, *Illiteracy*, 138.

96 Canadian Research Committee, "First Report," 46. See Table A.12 in appendix A.

97 *Census of Canada 1951*, vol. 10, 243 (Table 16). Our calculations.

98 See DBS, *Annual Report 1922*, 14. A national sample, including Quebec, of the 1901 manuscript census shows that this pattern was already established: there was little difference between boys and girls in the core school-going age group, but older (14–16) girls were more likely to attend school for nine or more months of the year than older boys. See Mandeville, "Who Went to School?," 36–7, 86–7.

99 Quoted in DBS, *Annual Report 1922*, 48. Similarly, see the Ontario analysis for 1922–23 in Leonard, "Over-Ageness," 16b–23.

100 DBS, *Annual Report 1922*, 14.

101 Canadian Research Committee, "First Report," 43.

102 On this point, see High, "Haldimand County," 173; *The Year Book of Education 1934*, 547.

103 See *Historical Atlas*, Plate 33. For the figures themselves, see DBS, *Elementary and Secondary Education 1948–50*, 39. The figures are given by province; there are no data for Quebec. The exception is Manitoba; in the late 1940s there were more boys than girls, but not before that. For Ontario, at least, this pattern was established during the later nineteenth century. The percentage of girls attending secondary schools had risen from between a quarter and a third, in 1861, to an outright majority in the late 1890s – an edge they maintained until after 1940. For the nineteenth-century data and reasons, see Gidney and Millar, *Inventing Secondary Education*, 140, 281.

104 See appendix A, section 8, for commentary on this paragraph and for details of our cohort analysis.

105 Canadian Research Committee, "First Report," 43–7; see esp. Table 3. While we use the term "retention" here, the original table does the reverse – measuring rate of loss by grade rather than retention rate. High's analysis of one Ontario county in 1945 reaches similar conclusions on this point. See High, "Haldimand County," 150.

106 The reader needs to keep in mind that we are dealing with relatively small numbers here. The vast majority of both boys and girls did not reach grades XI or XII, and in Ontario, where grade XIII was increasingly the prerequisite for university, the numbers at that level were smaller still. In urban communities in 1931 and 1941 the percentage of boys 15–19 attending school exceeded that of girls by modest margins. This change was probably due to the larger proportion of rural girls who flocked to the towns and cities in search of work, which increased the percentage of urban girls not in school. When rural boys left school, they tended, more than girls, to stay in agricultural occupations – the two trends combining to create the long-term and much-deplored shortage of marriageable young women in the countryside. For the 1931 figures and MacLean's ruminations on the disparity, see DBS, *Annual Survey 1934*, xviii–xix. The 1941 figure for rural boys is 24.7%, and for rural girls, 32.3%; see Robbins, *Youth Figured Out*, 12. See also the comment by Kalbach and McVey, *Demographic Bases of Canadian Society*, in appendix A, section 7.

107 While the flood of immigration resumed after the First World War, the flow to Canada was smaller during the 1920s than before 1914, dried up almost entirely during the Depression and Second World War, and didn't begin again until after 1945. For the numbers and ethnic composition, see Kalbach, *Impact of Immigration*, 28–44, 71–4; Bothwell, Drummond, and English, *Canada 1900–1945*, 58–62. There are some excellent graphics on migration and ethnic origins in *Historical Atlas*, esp. Plates 17 and 27.

108 In 1911, for ages 7–14, 6.2% of children attending school were foreign-
    born; in 1921 and 1931, for ages 6–14, 4.8% and 3.3% respectively of
    children at school were foreign-born; and in 1951, for ages 5–19, 2.8%.
    See MacLean, *Illiteracy*, 146 (for 1911); *Census of Canada 1921*, vol. 2,
    702–3 (Table 108); *Census of Canada 1931*, vol. 1, 1136–7 (Table 72) (our
    calculations from the censuses). For 1951, see DBS, *Education, Census,
    1951*, 66n1. For our own commentary on this group, see appendix A,
    section 9.

109 DBS, *Census of Canada 1961*, 7.1–6, General Review: Origins of the Canadian
    Population, p. 6-64 (Table 10). The quotations are from DBS, *Census of
    Canada 1961*, 7.1–10, General Review: Educational Levels and School
    Attendance, pp. 10-26, 10-27. While we think our calculations from the fig-
    ures and our discussion illustrate the major issues, there is additional census
    commentary on the differences in 7.1–6, pp. 6-44 to 6-46.

110 See Porter, *Vertical Mosaic*, 88–9.

111 Sylvester, "Immigrant Parents," 610, 611 (Table 6).

112 Mandeville, "Who Went to School?," 96–7. These two studies of the 1901
    manuscript census – and more recently, Sager and Baskerville, *Household
    Counts* – point to the critical importance of access to the household census
    for the rest of the twentieth century for understanding, in a much more
    sophisticated manner than we have been able to accomplish, not just the
    relationship between ethnicity and school attendance but a host of other
    relationships we have attempted to describe in this chapter.

113 MacLean, *Illiteracy*, 146.

114 We suspect that if we could subdivide the adult age group 45–64, we would
    find considerable differences in educational attainment between those who
    constituted the older members of that generation.

115 See *Census of Canada 1931*, vol. 1, 1160–1 (Table 74) (our calculations).
    Here we are reviewing national-level statistics, excluding Quebec. See our
    discussion below on the attendance of francophones and other ethnic groups
    outside Quebec.

116 Our conclusions here are based on calculations from DBS, *Education, Census,
    1951*, 66 (Table 32).

117 Foght, *Saskatchewan*, 43–5.

118 England, *Central European Immigrant*, 112–14.

119 Hamilton, "Schools of Rural Manitoba," 32–4.

120 Woods, "Education in Manitoba," 100, 93 (Table 21).

121 Mandeville, "Who Went to School?," 62–3. The author notes, however, that
    when she examined only children living with a parent, "rates of school atten-
    dance soared among Victoria's visible minority community": 80% of Japanese
    and Chinese children and nearly 85% of "Indian" children. See 61n38.

122 Barman, "Knowledge Is Essential," 17, 46–50, 59.

123 Readers should consult appendix A, section 10, for our commentary and documentation for our conclusions throughout this section on French minority schooling.

124 *Census of the Prairie Provinces, 1936,* vol. 1, Table 69 for each province; our calculations. See appendix A, section 11, for our commentary on this source and analysis of the data.

125 There is a very brief introduction to the state of, and conflicts over, Franco-Ontarian education in the early twentieth century and a more detailed overview for the period after that in Gidney, *From Hope to Harris,* 142–4. Though mostly based on secondary sources, a thorough-going review that includes an extensive bibliography is Jakes and Mawhinney, *Franco-Ontarian Educational Governance;* for the years from Regulation 17 (1912) through the postwar period, see pp. 40–58. For a valuable regional study that includes an updated bibliography, see Cécillon, "Language, Schools, and Religious Conflict." For the nineteenth-century context, see Gaffield, *Language, Schooling, and Cultural Conflict.*

126 Merchant, *Report on the Condition of English-French Schools,* 36.

127 Ontario, *Report of the Committee ... the Schools Attended by French-Speaking Pupils,* 17–18.

128 Ibid., appendix H, 114–18 (age-grade tables).

129 See appendix A, section 10, for our sources and commentary on these tables.

130 Ontario, *AR 1938,* Report of the Director of French Instruction, 35. In 1939, 26% of the grade I enrolment of French-speaking pupils reached grade VIII, compared to 78% for all Ontario public schools. See Ontario, *AR 1939,* 126. See also other reports of the director of French instruction in the Ontario *ARs,* esp. *AR 1932, AR 1936,* and *AR 1937.*

131 Ontario, *AR 1938,* 36. In the general school population of Ontario, 54% of grade I enrolment entered grade IX in 1939. See Ontario, *AR 1939,* 126. Six per cent may be an underestimate, since the director could not ascertain the number of francophones who entered English-language high schools, but their number was probably very modest. For the particular circumstances of schools in the northern districts of the province, see Noël, "The Impact of Regulation 17."

132 New Brunswick, *AR 1929,* 96. Given the expense of private schools for fees, boarding, and opportunity costs, the number sent to them was not likely to have been large.

133 Savoie, *Mémoires d'un nationaliste acadien,* 279–82.

134 Fletcher Peacock, in New Brunswick, *AR 1942,* 20–8.

135 Woods, "Education in Manitoba," 93 (Table 21). For a brief description of French-language education across the country from Confederation to *c.* 1960, see Hayday, *Bilingual Today, United Tomorrow,* chap. 1. There is also a useful survey in Wilson, Stamp, and Audet, *Canadian Education,* 349–57. For

individual provinces and regions, see Forbes, "The 1930s," 283–5; *JEdNS*, March 1939, 296–9; Arsenault, *Island Acadians*, 165–81; Mombourquette, "Bilingual Schools," 37–9, 82–92; Savoie, "Education in Acadia," 402–23; Helyar, "Bureaucratic Rationalism," 178–85; Mahé, "Official and Unofficial School Inspection," 31–51; Sylvester, *Limits of Rural Capitalism*, 119–21; Russell, *Canadian Crucible*, chap. 5. See also our chapter 3, note 128.

136 For gender differences, see Woods, "Education in Manitoba," 93 (Table 21); *Census of the Prairie Provinces, 1936*, vol. 1, Table 69 for each province; Ontario, *AR 1937*, 27 (age-grade table for French-speaking pupils) compared to 152 (age-grade table for all public schools).

CHAPTER THREE

1 Winnipeg School Board, *AR 1923*, 5–6. Similarly, see Murray Report, 87; *Educational Review* (New Brunswick), Oct. 1922, 31.

2 DBS, *Historical Statistical Survey*, 36.

3 Peter Sandiford, "A Study of Non-attendance of Pupils at School," *The School* 7, no. 6 (Feb. 1919): 358–60. For other rants along similar lines, see *Educational Review*, Oct. 1922, 45–6; McLaren, "The Proper Education for All Classes," 85.

4 Ontario, *AR 1934*, 69. Similarly, see Foght, *Saskatchewan*, 42; Manitoba, *AR 1935–36*, 61–2; Stephenson, "Mrs. Gibson," 243.

5 Sandiford, "Non-attendance," *The School* 7, no. 6 (Feb. 1919): 359.

6 DBS, *Historical Statistical Survey*, 34, 36. Similarly, see *WSJ* 14, no. 3 (March 1918): 103; Prince Edward Island, *Report*, Commission on Education, 1910, 26–7; Nova Scotia, *AR 1918–19*, xxiv–xxv; UAA, John C. Charyk Fonds, 90-43-52, box 6, "School Memoirs and Correspondence," Ivah M. Anderson.

7 Hamilton, "Schools of Rural Manitoba," 39–41.

8 Manitoba, *AR 1923–24*, 43.

9 Nova Scotia, *AR 1932–33*, 104. Similarly, see Abbott, "Hostile Landscapes," 186; Stephenson, "Mrs. Gibson," 243; Alberta, *AR 1920*, 72.

10 Miller, *Rural Schools*, 89–90. Combining figures in this way masks the difference between old and new provinces. Compare the data for 1917 in DBS, *Historical Statistical Survey*, 27–8. In Nova Scotia, 97% of schools were open 150 days or more; for Alberta, the figure was 68%, but 15% were open less than five months. However, the gap between provinces in this respect was largely closed by 1920. See Patrick J. Harrigan, "Patterns of Enrolment and Attendance in Canadian Schools since Confederation," unpublished paper presented to the Canadian History of Education Association, Halifax, 1986, p. 18.

11 Alberta, *AR 1925*, 106. For the closure of the gap within the province, see ibid., *AR 1930*, 92; *AR 1935*, 89; *AR 1940*, 84.

12 See DBS, *Elementary and Secondary Education 1944–46*, 45.

13 Cited in Kinnear, *A Female Economy*, 50.

14 Abbott, "Hostile Landscapes," 186.

15 Wiebe, *Of This Earth*, 113.

16 McLaren, "The Proper Education for All Classes," 86–7. In the annual reports of New Brunswick or Nova Scotia (as in other provinces) there were always reports of schools closed for these and other reasons, usually a few hundred out of the several thousand in the province. See, for example, *Educational Review*, April 1905, 274–6 (both provinces), and April 1911, 240–1 (both provinces); Nova Scotia, AR *1931*, 51; New Brunswick, AR *1936–37*, 12.

17 On the major childhood diseases, the changes in their incidence during the interwar years, and the success in controlling some of them, see Comacchio, *"Nations Are Built of Babies,"* esp. 30–3. By the mid-1930s the first five in our list were the most serious threats, although, in much smaller numbers, children were still being attacked by pneumonia and diphtheria. See J.T. Phair, "Incidence of Disease in School Age Children," *Canadian Public Health Journal* 24 (1933): 374.

18 Nationally see DBS, *Annual Report 1922*, 88. For a vivid portrait of the impact of the 1918–19 flu on one province's attendance figures, see the chart in Saskatchewan, AR *1929*, 93. For other more localized outbreaks, see Nova Scotia, AR *1938–39*, xxiv; Ontario, AR *1928*, 47.

19 See Nova Scotia, AR *1942*, 41; Manitoba, AR *1927–28*, 32–3; *The School* 24, no. 2 (Oct. 1935): 168. For the way in which polio struck school-age children especially hard, see C.R. Donovan, "Epidemiological Features," *Canadian Public Health Journal* 28 (1937): 371 (a review of Manitoba evidence, 1927–36).

20 Sandiford, "Non-attendance," *The School* 7, no. 6 (Feb. 1919): 357.

21 British Columbia, AR *1923–24*, T27.

22 Ontario, AR *1928*, 47.

23 Manitoba, AR *1935–36*, 61; similarly, Nova Scotia, AR *1932–33*, 103.

24 *ATAM* 17, no. 6 (Feb. 1937): 9.

25 National Committee for School Health Research, *Absenteeism*, 31, 119.

26 Ibid., 103, 145.

27 See, for example, Putman-Weir Report, 47–50; Nova Scotia, AR *1932–33*, 103.

28 See Gleason, "From 'Disgraceful Carelessness' to 'Intelligent Precaution,'" 234–5.

29 Halifax City Report, in Nova Scotia, AR *1911–12*, 189.

30 Sandiford, "Non-Attendance," *The School* 7, no. 6 (Feb. 1919): 357, 359.

31 See the commentary in Nova Scotia, AR *1932–33*, 104–6, xxxi–xxxii; Race, "Compulsory Schooling in Alberta," 163.

32 Ontario, AR *1928*, 47.

33 London Board of Education, *AR 1925*, 63. Similarly, see Morton, *Ideal Surroundings*, 42.

34 Editorial comment, *Blairmore Enterprise*, 12 Feb. 1925, 3.

35 Stephenson, "Mrs. Gibson," 244. Similarly, see Stortz and Wilson, "Education on the Frontier," 278.

36 See Nova Scotia, *AR 1938–39*, xxiv. That year the Nova Scotia branch of the Red Cross, with the help of a special government grant, "provided clothing for 1,558 necessitous school children" who would not otherwise have been able to attend school. For other Depression examples, see Winnipeg School Board, *AR 1933*, 19–20; Glenbow Archives, M2004, Crowsnest Pass School Division #63, Papers, Blairmore SD No. 628, School Board Minutes, 12 Oct. 1933 and 23 Feb. 1937; Campbell, *Respectable Citizens*, 41–2.

37 See Jean, "Family Allowances," esp. 411ff.; Couturier and Johnston, "L'État, les familles et l'obligation scolaire," 1–34.

38 National Committee for School Health Research, *Absenteeism*, 103.

39 E.W. Henry, "Nutrition in Canada," *Canadian Public Health Journal* 30 (1939): 431–2. The study is reported in more detail in E.W. Henry, "Nutrition in Toronto," *Canadian Public Health Journal* 30 (1939): 4–13.

40 Report of Superintendent of Schools, Saskatoon, in Saskatchewan, *AR 1930*, 95.

41 Barman, "Knowledge Is Essential," 48. For two other examples from greater Vancouver in the early 1920s, see British Columbia, *AR 1919–20*, C45; Thompson, with Seager, *Canada 1922–1939*, 76. Early in the century, malnutrition was assumed to be linked to poor school performance and to "feeble-mindedness." But research in the 1920s produced conflicting evidence, and the use of height/weight scales (rather than caloric intake) led some researchers to conclude that malnutrition was as common among the well-off as among the poor (or even more common!) and that huge numbers of school-age children were malnourished – percentages as high as 25% or 33%. See, for example, Alan Brown and G. Albert Davis, "The Prevalence of Malnutrition in the Public School Children of Ontario," *Public Health Journal* 12, no. 2 (Feb. 1921): 66–9; E.J. Pratt, "Mental Measurements as Applied to a Toronto School," *Public Health Journal* 12, no. 4 (April 1921): 150–2; Chas. S. Macdougall, "Malnutrition in Children of School Age," *Public Health Journal* 16, no. 1 (Jan. 1925): 25–35. Both the measurement and extent of malnutrition in the interwar years have recently become subjects of debate and historical revisionism. "Paradoxically," Aleck Samuel Ostry remarks, food supply for the general population was probably better in the 1930s than in the 1920s, and so, he suggests, was the general health of the population, including the less well-off. But "vulnerable sub-populations, particularly the urban unemployed, struggled to find enough money to buy food." Ostry, *Nutrition Policy*, 102. For undernourishment among schoolchildren in the late teens

and early 1920s, see Ostry, *Nutrition Policy*, 23–4. See also Mosby, "Making and Breaking Canada's Food Rules." For a revisionist American interpretation, see Levenstein, *Paradox of Plenty*, chap. 4.

42 For references to and summaries of these surveys, see Greenway, *Housing in Canada*, 434–8 (covering the period 1912 through 1934); League for Social Reconstruction, *Social Planning for Canada*, 9–12. On housing, overcrowding, and children's spaces, see Sutherland, *Growing Up*, 35–40. More generally, see Harris, *Unplanned Suburbs*, 248–9 (for the 1940s); Purdy, "It was tough on everybody," 459–60 (1900 through 1950).

43 Greenway, *Housing in Canada*, 414–15.

44 See *Census of Canada 1941*, vol. 9, xxxiii–xxxvii. For a particularly stark portrait, see Lotta Dempsey, "Housing Headache," *Maclean's*, 1 June 1943, 17ff.

45 In England, where the research on the linkage between home conditions for working-class children and school performance is much richer, these features were of substantial importance in the first half of the twentieth century; see McKibbin, *Classes and Cultures*, 264.

46 British Columbia, *AR 1923–24*, T27. Similarly see Calgary School Board, *AR 1916*, 50.

47 Manitoba, *AR 1929–30*, 124.

48 Friesen, *Canadian Prairies*, 287–8. Similarly, see the discussion of intra- and extra-city mobility in Hawthorne, "Victoria Public Schools," 100, 106–19.

49 Quoted in Dunn, "Mass Schooling in British Columbia," 31.

50 Cited in Canada, *Employment of Children and Young Persons*, 31.

51 National Committee for School Health Research, *Absenteeism*, 21, 119. On the paid and unpaid work of both urban and rural children, see also Sutherland, *Growing Up*, chaps 6 and 7.

52 See Halifax City Report, in Nova Scotia, *AR 1911–12*, 189.

53 Prince Edward Island, Royal Commission on Education, *Report*, 1910, 26. Similarly, for PEI, see *The School* 16, no. 4 (Dec. 1927): 416; and 18, no. 5 (Jan. 1930): 450.

54 Cited in Canada, *Employment of Children and Young Persons*, 35. For other examples, see ibid.; Alberta, *AR 1920*, 72; *AR 1930*, 46–7; Foght, *Saskatchewan*, 42.

55 Canada, *Employment of Children and Young Persons*, 34. Only PEI had the good sense to provide for the closure of rural schools for two or three weeks during "potato picking time," although it did have the temerity to label it "Fall Vacation." DBS, *Statistical Report on Education 1921*, 8; *The School* 18, no. 5 (Jan. 1930): 450.

56 Canada, *Employment of Children and Young Persons*, 31.

57 Ibid., 35. For examples of the way in which irregular attendance among older children encouraged early school-leaving, see Sutherland, *Growing Up*, 74–5; Baillargeon, *Making Do*, 33.

58 For these reasons the study found rural children two or three years behind their urban counterparts in reading and arithmetic. Mowat, *School Achievement of Nova Scotia Pupils*, 34–5. Similarly, see the analysis of the effects of late entry and irregularity in Leonard, "Over-Ageness," 33–5.

59 Barman, "Knowledge Is Essential," 55 (Table 1). For the sharp decline in employment of children 10–14 between 1891 and 1911, see Canada, *Employment of Children and Young Persons*, 19 (Table 5). See also Hurl, "Restricting Child Factory Labour," 87–121; and for 1901, see Mandeville, "Who Went to School?," 53–5.

60 Canada, *Employment of Children and Young Persons*, 27 (Tables 11 and 12), 26–7.

61 For the details on these points see ibid., 76–80 (summary section); 30 (Table 15), 31ff. (agricultural employment), 38ff. (other industries). For the focus of unease on rural areas, see pp. 32–5.

62 Compare, for example, the 1911 figures in the previous paragraph for the percentage employed with the percentage of non-attenders in MacLean, *Illiteracy*, 84 (Table 56).

63 See Canada, *Employment of Children and Young Persons*, 11–12.

64 MacLean, "Illiteracy," 587.

65 Ibid., 675. The limited evidence from an analysis of Victoria public school attendance, drawn from the 1901 manuscript census, tends to confirm MacLean's argument; see Mandeville, "Who Went to School?," 61, 61n38.

66 MacLean, "Illiteracy," 675. In contrast, according to Mandeville, a national sample of the 1901 manuscript census (including Quebec) shows that children from larger families were more likely to attend school than those from smaller families. Mandeville, "Who Went to School?," 90–1. Since thirty years separate these two findings and they use very different kinds of analysis, we await further research on this topic.

67 MacLean, "Illiteracy," 673. There were also a significant number of non-attending children who were "not attached to families": 31,218 were either homeless or in institutions (672).

68 Ibid., 679. Our italics.

69 For this paragraph, see ibid., 679–81.

70 For this paragraph, see MacLean, *Illiteracy*, 136–44. The quotations appear on p. 144.

71 In his study of the 1931 census ("Illiteracy and School Attendance"), MacLean didn't replicate this urban analysis.

72 For further commentary on both MacLean reports, including our reservations about the value of the 1926 report (*Illiteracy and School Attendance*), see appendix A, section 12.

73 Robbins, *Youth Figured Out*, 15.

74 Ontario, AR *1924*, 24.

75 For the numbers 1900 through 1950, see DBS, *Annual Survey 1935*, Table 21; and DBS, *Elementary and Secondary Education 1948–50*, Table 9. For a graphic illustration of the impact of the First World War on the Ontario high school, see Ontario, *AR 1932*, 61. Despite population decline and a concomitant decline in total enrolments in Saskatchewan every year from 1932 to 1940, high school enrolments actually rose in each of those years. See Lyons, "Ten Forgotten Years," 119. On the expansion of high school enrolments in the Great Depression, see also DBS, *Annual Survey 1932*, xxiv; RCDPR, Report of Hearings, Manitoba, vol. 3, 1010; *The School* 24, no. 8 (April 1936): 708 (Ontario); *JEdNS*, Jan. 1932, 124–5; Marsh, *Canadians In and Out of Work*, 293.

76 Putnam-Weir Report, 270.

77 See Ontario, *AR 1921*, 34; Alberta, *AR 1922*, 87.

78 DBS, *Annual Survey 1927*, xi–xii.

79 Heron, "The High School," 229–32, 246.

80 *The School* 31, no. 10 (June 1943): 882 (Report of DBS Education Branch). For a graphic illustration of the impact on Alberta high school enrolments, see Walker, "Public Secondary Education in Alberta," 243.

81 Ontario, *AR 1941*, 108; *AR 1945*, 60. See also Keshen, "Wartime Jitters over Juveniles," 367–8.

82 See, for example, PAA, 79.334, box 10, Canada-Newfoundland Education Association, 1942, 1943, and 1944: DM, Education, Alberta, to Director, National Selective Service, Dept of Labour, Ottawa, 18 Aug. 1942; same to Dr S.J. Willis, President CNEA, Dept of Education, Victoria, 25 Aug. 1942; Charles Phillips, Secretary Treasurer, CNEA, to Fred McNally, DM, Education, Alberta, 8 Dec. 1943; Clayton Adams, Chairman, Board of Industrial Relations [Alberta], to W.D. King, Deputy Minister, Dept of Trade and Industry, "Re the Labour Welfare Act – Employment of Children," 20 Jan. 1944.

83 Coulter, "The Working Young of Edmonton," 144.

84 See Synge, "The Transition from School to Work," 249–69; Heron, "The High School," 217–59, esp. the summary paragraph, 233; Coulter, "The Working Young of Edmonton," 156; Strong-Boag, *New Day Recalled*, 48; Gagnon, "Work and Schooling of Franco-Albertan Women," 171–3; Comacchio, *Dominion of Youth*, 48–51.

85 Manitoba, Legislative Assembly, Sessional Papers No. 3, 1912, appendix A, Royal Commission on Industrial Training and Technical Education, *Report*, 333–4.

86 See the analysis of family incomes during the 1920s in League for Social Reconstruction, *Social Planning for Canada*, 5–7; Barman, "Knowledge Is Essential," 27–8.

87 Marsh, *Canadians In and Out of Work*, 196–7.

88 Ontario, *AR 1919*, 95 (Table 3). For the actual fees, which varied from school
    to school, see Ontario, *AR 1920*, 217. "How can persons in various occupa-
    tions who receive only $400 or $500 a year, send their children to a high
    school or collegiate institute if they have to pay for each one of them $20 or
    $30 a year?" asked Ontario's deputy minister of education, in *Proceedings, OEA,
    1901*, 71.

89 See Ball and Reid, *School Administration*, 142–3, 145.

90 For the law in British Columbia, see British Columbia, *School Law Manual
    1932*, 73 (sec. 140[1]); *School Law Manual 1937*, 30 (sec. 47[1]). For the
    grade XII fee, see British Columbia, *AR 1926*, R29; *ATAM* 12, no. 9 (May
    1932): 25; *The School* 25, no. 2 (Oct. 1936): 160 (Saint John); DBS, *Annual
    Survey 1934*, lxxvii.

91 Textbook policies varied by province and date and can only be followed by
    reference to the annual reports of each province. For examples of the devel-
    opment of free textbook policies (and, in some cases, free supplies), see New
    Brunswick, *AR 1928*, lxiv–lxv; Putman-Weir Report, 303; *The School* 24, no.
    9 (May 1936): 800–1 (Nova Scotia). See also Richardson, *Administration of
    Schools*, 188; Clark and Post, "A Natural Outcome of Free Schools," 23–42.

92 See G.R. Dolan, "The Case for Uniform Textbooks," *School Progress* 3, no. 2
    (Sept. 1934): 11–12.

93 Marsh, *Canadians In and Out of Work*, 248.

94 Canadian Research Committee, *Your Child Leaves School*, 54.

95 Morton, *Ideal Surroundings*, 97. For a similar Canada-wide pattern at the turn
    of the century, see Bradbury, "Children Who Lived with One Parent in 1901,"
    281–4.

96 For the occupational distribution of unemployment, see Marsh, *Canadians In
    and Out of Work*, 335.

97 See Lloyd, *Woodrow*, 18; *Maclean's*, 15 Jan. 1934, 24.

98 For a succinct American summary of the research on the decline in jobs for
    children and young people, see Zelizer, *Pricing the Priceless Child*, 62–3. For
    a Canadian commentary, see Canadian Youth Commission, *Youth and Jobs*,
    84–7.

99 Canada, *Employment of Children and Young Persons*, 62. Similarly, see the com-
    mentary by Vancouver school officials in the early 1920s, cited in Barman,
    "Knowledge Is Essential," 28, 28n71.

100 Marsh, *Canadians In and Out of Work*, 223–5. By 1930 Toronto employers
    were unwilling to hire young teenage girls even for jobs requiring little skill
    or education. A wide-ranging city survey found, for example, that employers
    wanted waitresses and those tending power machinery in the textile industry
    to be at least 18. The only corporate jobs the survey located for 16-year-olds
    (i.e., those leaving school at the earliest legal opportunity) were in the laun-
    dry rooms of the big hotels. E.I. McKim, "Report of a Survey," *Proceedings, OEA,
    1931*, 133–9.

101 Ostry, *Occupational Composition*, 12–13.

102 Manitoba, AR *1925–26*, 84.

103 See Bothwell, Drummond, and English, *Canada 1900–1945*, 171–2, 214–15, 248–53. Using data from the 1931 census, Leonard Marsh demonstrated the substantial differences in income that existed between skilled and unskilled workers, many of the former with incomes well above the subsistence level. See Marsh, *Canadians In and Out of Work*, 195–6.

104 While the linked growth of white-collar work and formal schooling is familiar, the growth, in the later nineteenth and early twentieth centuries, of techno-logically advanced industrial and service jobs that required secondary school for entry has now been persuasively demonstrated for the United States in Goldin and Katz, *The Race between Education and Technology*, esp. 102–18, 168–71. There may have been proportionally fewer of these types of jobs in Canada, but there is no reason to think that the same thing wouldn't have been true in this country as well.

105 Ostry, *Occupational Composition*, 9, 51.

106 *Educational Review*, April 1910, 272; June 1910, 12.

107 Ontario, AR *1922*, 21–7.

108 *WSJ* 26, no. 1 (Jan. 1931): 14. "The larger offices" and the best jobs are key qualifiers; more generally, a couple of years of high school with good commercial training was probably a far more common requisite. As Goldin and Katz point out, in any case, the deskilling thesis is not at issue here; any decrease in overall skill demands was more than compensated for by the gross expansion of office jobs, all of which required some modicum of secondary education. See Goldin and Katz, *The Race between Education and Technology*, 174–5.

109 For the labour force generally, including male and female clerks, 1901–31, see Lowe, *Administrative Revolution*, 160 (Fig. 7.1). It is unusual to find calcu-lations that isolate young people, but for wages for those under 20 in 1930–31, see Marsh, *Canadians In and Out of Work*, 188–91, esp. Fig. 17. For 1941, see Robbins, *Youth Figured Out*, 17–21, and for mid-century, see Canadian Research Committee, *Your Child Leaves School*, 28 and Chart 13. The latter two sources do not provide earnings by occupations but do indicate that earnings were related to length of time in school. American estimates were that by 1915 the financial premium for each high school year completed was of the order of 12%. After 1915, however, the premium declined through to mid-century because of the growing supply of secondary school graduates and wage improvements among some sectors of the working class. The extent of the premium in Canada is a matter for further research, but it is plausible to think that any decline was much delayed because of the much smaller cohort of secondary-level students. See Goldin and Katz, "Human Capital and Social Capital," 691; Goldin and Katz, *The Race between Education and Technology*, 287–9, 304ff. For a recent helpful Canadian review of the state of the debate

on the school/skills/jobs nexus, see Riddell, "Education, Skills, and Labour Market Outcomes," 40–51.

110 *The School* 24, no. 4 (Dec. 1935): 354. Similarly, see the survey of Toronto employers in Ontario, *AR 1922*, 23; *Proceedings, OEA, 1931*, 164–5.

111 Marsh, *Canadians In and Out of Work*, 81. For a comparison of the range of occupations available to males and females, see ibid., 70–5, 81–5, 95–7.

112 Ibid., 82.

113 Weir, *Nursing Education*, 52–3, 55. The count excluded the "so-called 'practical nurse'" and various types of semi-trained nurses in the different provinces.

114 Statistics Canada, *Historical Compendium of Education Statistics*, 154. The figures are for nine provinces and include women teachers in both elementary and high school.

115 Lowe, *Women in the Administrative Revolution*, 6–7.

116 Weir, *Nursing Education*, 56–7, 62, 379. By the mid-1940s a full three- or four-year high school course had become a standard prerequisite. See "How to Become a Nurse," *JEdNS*, Sept. 1946, 408.

117 See Lowe, *Administrative Revolution*, 77–8; Canadian Youth Commission, *Youth and Jobs*, 154.

118 For an example of the preferred standard, see the survey of Toronto businessmen carried out by the department of education, in Ontario, *AR 1922*, 27. On the link between formal education and girls' occupational opportunities, see also the commentary in [Savage], *Secondary Education in Ontario*, 28; Guppy and Davies, *Education in Canada*, 85.

119 Marsh, *Canadians In and Out of Work*, 234. See particularly the breakdown of female occupations by type, 235. Marsh comments on Manitoba's representativeness on pp. 487–8.

120 For an illuminating contemporary discussion of the complex interactions between the forces at work, see Davies and Guppy, *Schooled Society*, 134ff.

121 Canadian Research Committee, *Your Child Leaves School*, 55.

122 On this point, see Sutherland, *Growing Up*, 138–9; Morton, *Ideal Surroundings*, 109–10.

123 See Canadian Research Committee, *Your Child Leaves School*, 18; Gushaty, "High-School Drop-outs," 33–4.

124 Garner, *Cabbagetown*, 11. See also on this point Tyack, Lowe, and Hansot, *Public Schools in Hard Times*, 169.

125 For an example, see Morton, *Ideal Surroundings*, 145. More generally, see McKibbin, *Classes and Cultures*, 264–5. Both examples in the text might be termed "the hidden injuries of class," the latter as much as the former.

126 British Columbia, *AR 1923–24*, T27.

127 See Barman, "Knowledge Is Essential," 48; Hoerder, *Creating Societies*, 128–9; Wiebe, *Of This Earth*, 36–7; Stephenson, "Mrs. Gibson," 240–1. This might also apply to French-Canadian children forced to attend English-language schools; see Gagnon, "Work and Schooling of Franco-Albertan Women," 174.

128 "In 1900, of the 250 French schools in New Brunswick, 240 were one-room rural schools. Of the 273 Acadian teachers, 242 held third-class licences." Hody, "Bilingual Schools," 133. On the need for labour generated by market gardening in Essex and Kent Counties, Ontario, see Merchant, *Report on the Condition of English-French Schools*, 21. On the difficulties presented by attempting to master two languages, see ibid., 70, and "Report of Subcommittee on ... French-Speaking Children, " in New Brunswick, *Report of the Commission on Education*, 38; Savoie, "Education in Acadia," 405–17, passim; Russell, *Canadian Crucible*, 201–2. On the shortage of qualified teachers, see Mahé, "Bilingual School Teachers' Cultural Mission," 142ff., and "French Teacher Shortages and Cultural Continuity," 219–46; Arsenault, *Island Acadians*, 178–81; Ontario, *AR 1932*, "Report ... on French-Speaking Pupils," 22; Helyar, "Acadian Teacher Identity"; Hody, "Bilingual Schools," 143: though primarily focused on New Brunswick, this thesis offers an all-round discussion of policies, practices, and consequences pre-1960 and is much broader than its title might suggest. For an overview of francophone schooling difficulties in New Brunswick in the interwar years, see also Wilbur, *Rise of French New Brunswick*, chap. 11. See also our chapter 2, note 135.

129 *Census of Canada 1941*, vol. 9, 63–5 (Table 13). For those who may consider this a trivial matter, we recommend, on the basis of personal experience, that they try doing academic work in the evening with the aid only of old-fashioned kerosene or oil lamps, let alone in front of the fireplace!

130 See DBS, *Annual Survey 1928*, xi; *Annual Survey 1927*, xiii (data available only for Nova Scotia, Ontario, Saskatchewan, and Alberta). These declines were not due to children starting school at earlier ages. See DBS, *Annual Survey 1935*, viii.

131 Winnipeg School Board, *AR 1929*, 9.

132 See Canadian Research Committee, *Your Child Leaves School*, 103; Gushaty, "High-School Drop-outs," 33; Stephenson, "Mrs. Gibson," 240–2.

133 For one good example, see Morton, *Ideal Surroundings*, 145. For surveys of farm opinion on this point, see Whyte, "Rural Canada in Transition," 74–5.

134 The best discussion of these variations is in Sutherland, *Growing Up*, 74ff. But see also examples in Harris, *Unplanned Suburbs*, 269; Coulter, "Teenagers in Edmonton," 102; Comacchio, *Dominion of Youth*, 103–4; Millar, "Jewish Medical Students," 113–17; Iacovetta, *Such Hardworking People*, 72–3. On expectations in rural communities, see Whyte, "Rural Canada in Transition," 73–5. For two American articles that illuminate the clash in values between the schoolmen and many working-class or immigrant families, see Lassonde, "Learning and Earning," 839–70, and "Should I Go or Should I Stay?," 37–60.

135 See Zelizer, *Pricing the Priceless Child*, chaps 2 and 3, esp. 63ff.

136 Sylvester, "Immigrant Parents," 610. See also Mandeville, "Who Went to School?," 92.

137 See Gaffield, "Children, Schooling, and Family Reproduction," 157–91. For a suggestive piece of theorizing around this matter, see Phillips and Norris, "Literacy Policy," 220–7.

138 Canadian Research Committee, *Your Child Leaves School*, 24.

139 See Gray, "Our World Stopped," 635–6.

140 Mowat, *School Achievement of Nova Scotia Pupils*, 28–9. Though it covers a later period than we are concerned with here, a suggestive piece of work based on intensive interviews, *Learning to Leave*, by Michael Corbett, develops the pertinence and patrimony themes, including the way in which they differed by gender.

141 Friesen, *Citizens and Nations*, 92–3. For Goudie's background, see 58ff.

142 Marsh, *Canadians In and Out of Work*, 230.

143 See ibid., 229, 178–9, 243.

144 Ibid., chaps 9 and 10.

145 Canadian Research Committee, *Your Child Leaves School*, 24.

146 LaZerte, "The Selective Nature of Secondary Education," 5.

147 Marsh, *Canadians In and Out of Work*, 157–8.

148 For relative incomes, see ibid., 181.

149 Woods, "Education in Manitoba," 86. Woods's point about "secondary lands" is substantially confirmed, for Manitoba at least, by Martynowych, *Ukrainians in Canada*, 85–7. See also the similar commentary by one school inspector in Manitoba, *AR 1921–22*, 63–4. Trying to distinguish the relative influence of cultural and structural factors in promoting or retarding social mobility or educational attainment is complex and controversial. For a set of international essays that probe these problems, see Vermeulen and Perlmann, *Immigrants, Schooling, and Social Mobility*. See also Warikoo and Carter, "Racial and Ethnic Stratification," 366–94; Miller, "Italian Australians and School Success," 185–98.

150 The data are included in the Ontario *AR*s. For annual figures, 1900 to 1930, see DBS, *Annual Survey 1933*, 57 (Table 36). In 1900 the manual workers' category is "The Trades"; for 1921–22 and 1929–30, we have combined the categories "trades" and "labouring occupations." In the latter two years the "other occupations" category accounted for 10% and 14% respectively. All calculations are our own.

151 See *Historical Atlas*, Plate 33.

152 Heron, "The High School," 246. Heron's study is especially useful because it provides charts of the rising and falling numbers, by occupation, from 1900 to 1930, and separates academic from vocational enrolments.

153 Goodson and Anstead, *Through the Schoolhouse Door*, 168.

154 Millar, "Jewish Medical Students," 113–17; Millar, Heap, and Gidney, "Degrees of Difference," 160–5, 169–70.

155 Guppy et al., "Changing Patterns of Educational Inequality in Canada," 329.

156 See Gidney and Millar, *Inventing Secondary Education*, 126ff., 279–80. We are, however, referring to secondary enrolments only. For a less optimistic view of the later nineteenth century, see Darroch, "Families, Fostering, and Flying the Coop," 231–2. The difference probably lies in distinguishing between the children of skilled and unskilled workers, the former constituting by far the larger group staying in school.

157 There is now a large international literature on the cultural and economic meaning in the shifts taking place in the occupational order, but for the first half of the twentieth century especially, in part just because of its publication date but also because of its rich fund of insight, a basic source is Mills, *White Collar*. Mills, on the other hand, shouldn't be given the last word. See Jerome P. Bjelopera's commentary, not so much a fundamental criticism as a significant qualification, in his *City of Clerks*, 4–5.

158 Weir, *Nursing Education*, 70, 98, 119, 168. The only exception was for public health nursing, which generally required more education, though even here farmers' daughters ranked a close second to those with fathers in "business and other" occupations.

159 See Alberta, *AR 1937*, 39, 42 (Alberta Normal School reports).

160 Robbins, *Youth Figured Out*, 7, 11.

161 Giffen, *Rural Life*, 172–3. Of the 256 students, 20 boys and 34 girls remained in or returned to the community. The author does not indicate the careers of the remaining 34 girls.

162 Gagnon, "Work and Schooling of Franco-Albertan Women," 178–9.

163 Loewen, *Family, Church, and Market*, 228–9.

164 We will return to this matter in chapter 5.

165 Manitoba, *AR 1921–22*, 65.

166 The source is Glenbow Archives, M2017, Pincher Creek S.D. No. 29, "Truancy," 1946–49. We have not added the precise correspondence references to avoid identifying by name the children or parents involved. Where necessary, the names have been changed or deleted for the same reason.

CHAPTER FOUR

1 See Artibise, "Patterns of Prairie Urban Development," 121–2 (Tables 2 and 3). By 1911 Winnipeg also had the highest percentage of non-British immigrants of any city in Canada. See Artibise, *Winnipeg*, 46.

2 Wherever there are no additional endnotes, this sketch of the Winnipeg system draws on the following sources: the solid work of Wilson, "Education in Winnipeg," chaps 4 and 5; and Winnipeg School Board, *AR 1920*. We have also made occasional use of Chafe, *An Apple for the Teacher*; and Lucow, "Public School System in Winnipeg."

3 There is a good example of this continuing campaign in Winnipeg School Board, *AR 1921*, 93–8.

4 This may seem a trivial feature to note, but it was in fact singled out by the public health movement from early in the twentieth century as a vital improvement. Drinking from a common cup or dipper was considered a major contributor to the spread of disease. On the problem and the campaign for individual drinking cups and water fountains, see Tomes, *Gospel of Germs*, 179–82.

5 For an early description of his aims and procedures, see W.J. Sisler, "The Immigrant Child," *WSJ* 1, no. 3 (March 1906): 4–6. Sisler later wrote a detailed account of his experiences teaching immigrant children; see esp. chap. 4, "Methods of Language Teaching," in his *Peaceful Invasion*.

6 On the background and development of the collegiate institute, see Osborne, *Daniel McIntyre Collegiate Institute*, chaps 1–3. The budget imposed limits to the original vision, and among other compromises, the school went without a proper gymnasium for decades.

7 For Crawford's retirement, see Winnipeg School Board, *AR 1941*, 35.

8 Winnipeg School Board, *AR 1940*, 36.

9 One can trace and date the developments referred to in the next few pages through successive annual reports, but this is an excellent synthesis. See Manitoba, *Report of the Royal Commission on ... Municipal Finances*, chap. 4, esp. 86–97.

10 There are many descriptions of Canada's urban schools in the period. In most cases the annual reports of the provincial departments of education carry reports by inspectors assigned to urban areas by town and city school superintendents or by the chairmen of urban school boards. This is the case, for example, in the British Columbia annual reports, not just for Vancouver and Victoria but for other urban communities in the province; in the Saskatchewan annual reports for cities like Regina, Saskatoon, and Moose Jaw; in the Manitoba annual reports for communities such as Brandon; and for Halifax in the Nova Scotia annual reports. Most boards in large communities also published their own annual reports. A partial list of secondary sources would include the following. For an indispensable study on the state of things *c.* 1920 that indicates policies and programs put in place during the first two decades of the century, see the collective portrait of some fifty larger towns and cities in Richardson, *Administration of Schools*. The content is much broader than the title suggests. Chapter 25 of the Putman-Weir Report provides an excellent overview of the Vancouver school system as of the early 1920s. There is also a brief factual summary of the development of Vancouver's system, written to celebrate the city's fiftieth anniversary, in *The School* 24, no. 7 (March 1936): 634–8. For Calgary, see Stamp, *School Days*. For Protestant Montreal, see the pertinent sections of MacLeod and Poutanen, *A*

Meeting of the People. See also Cochrane, *Board of Education for the City of Toronto*;
Blashill, *Saskatoon Public School System*; Archer, *Regina Board of Education*;
Anderson, "Moncton"; Hawthorne, "Victoria Public Schools," 134.

11 For city rankings, see Artibise, "Patterns of Prairie Urban Development," 122
(Table 3). In 1931 London ranked tenth, just below Calgary and Edmonton.
Our comment here on the London system is based on a reading of the city's
Board of Education annual reports from 1900 onwards. Ottawa in 1921
ranked sixth; for the progress of its school system to *c.* 1920 and especially
the plethora of programs (including kindergarten) introduced during the
second decade of the century under the dynamic leadership of J.H. Putman,
see Mark, *Ottawa.* Though the Winnipeg board gave financial assistance to
privately organized kindergartens in the 1920s, it didn't begin its own regular
kindergarten program until 1943. By 1949 access was near-universal. See
Winnipeg School Board, *AR 1943,* 20; *AR 1949,* 20.

12 Alberta, *AR 1922,* 70.

13 For one detailed description of the provision of core educational programs
and the variety of special programs routinely offered in the city, see Calgary
School Board, *AR 1927,* 3–19.

14 The description that follows is drawn from reports of the Fredericton Board
of School Trustees, in New Brunswick, *AR 1905* through *AR 1939,* and, infrequently, from the *Educational Review,* 1900 through 1931.

15 Though not the only cause, this pressure resulted in moving the manual
training department to the Smythe Street School, located near the western
edge of the city, "which makes attendance rather difficult for the pupils living at the other end of the city. As a result, it is possible to give these classes
instruction only once a week."

16 See Manitoba, *Report of the Royal Commission on … Municipal Finances,* 112.

17 Calgary School Board, *AR 1930,* 18.

18 Chiang, "School Principalship in Vancouver," 14 (Table 2.4); British
Columbia, *AR 1919–20,* C39 (Report, Municipal Inspectors, Vancouver).
For expedients in London ranging from turning hallways into classrooms
to renting rooms in residential houses, see London Board of Education, *AR
1919 and 1920,* 8. On the use of tents to cope with overflows in Victoria, see
Hawthorne, "Victoria Public Schools," 50.

19 See Report, Board of Trustees, Fredericton, in New Brunswick, *AR 1916–17,*
72; *AR 1917–18,* 71; *AR 1919–20,* 53; *AR 1920–21,* 58.

20 Halifax Report, in Nova Scotia, *AR 1930–31,* 106–7. For other examples,
see Heron, "The High School," 221–3; Report, Brandon Superintendent of
Schools, in Manitoba, *AR 1919–20,* 100; *AR 1924–25,* 54. For Edmonton, see
Alberta, *AR 1922,* 71; and Coulter, "Teenagers in Edmonton," 94–5.

21 *ATAM* 7, no. 4 (Oct. 1926): 12–13.

22 Ontario, *AR 1932,* vi.

23　*The School* 2, no. 7 (March 1914): 410.

24　Mark, *Ottawa*, 41.

25　*The School* 9, no. 1 (Sept. 1920): 17, citing a local report on the city schools.

26　Winnipeg School Board, *AR 1934*, 6; Report, Superintendent, Winnipeg Schools, in Manitoba, *AR 1934–35*, 105.

27　British Columbia, *AR 1929–30*, Q34. For the numbers in Victoria in the first two decades of the twentieth century, see Hawthorne, "Victoria Public Schools," 70–5.

28　Coulter, "Teenagers in Edmonton," 94.

29　James Bingay, "The Schools of Glace Bay, 1909–1930," *JEdNS*, March 1931, 33–4.

30　*Educational Review*, March 1929, 153.

31　Anderson, "Moncton," chap. 2, n.p.

32　The figure for 1939 was actually 39, but the overall average was pulled down sharply by the sanatorium school, which had only 11 pupils. Class sizes were given annually in London Board of Education annual reports.

33　For some typical examples, see *The School* 4, no. 9 (May 1916): 804–6 (London's path-breaking one-storey Ryerson elementary school); 19, no. 3 (Nov. 1930): 284–5 (Hamilton's composite Westdale Secondary); Ontario, *AR 1924*, 25–7 (several new Ontario high school buildings, including Jarvis Collegiate Institute); *JEdNS*, Jan. 1933, 53–4 (Saint John Vocational School); Calgary School Board, *AR 1935*, 5; Stamp, *School Days*, 84–5 (Western Canada Composite High School). In the local annual reports and histories of urban schools there are usually descriptions and often pictures of these new schools. For an assessment and critique of Vancouver's physical plant *c.* 1925, see Putman-Weir Report, 376ff. For more details here, see Johnson, *Pursuing Higher Education*, 9–10. Despite the title, this is primarily about changes in school architecture.

34　Manitoba, *Report of the Royal Commission on ... Municipal Finances*, 86.

35　Cited in *Maclean's*, 15 April 1951. The report was done in 1948.

36　The best general account is Cousins, *A History of the Crow's Nest Pass*. For the population figures, see ibid., 119; *Blairmore: Hub of the Crow's Nest Pass*, 3.

37　Our main source for this section on Blairmore consists of the school board minutes, read through from 1920 to 1957. These are located within a larger record group at Glenbow Archives, M2004, Crowsnest Pass School Division #63, Papers. The inventory contains a brief outline of the history of the Pass schools, including Blairmore. For the minute books, see Blairmore SD No. 628, School Minutes, 1914–57, files 169–176A. These also include minutes of the annual ratepayers meetings, nearly always useful for enrolments, staff, finance, and other details. We do not provide specific citations for our summaries or quotations from the minutes themselves. The record group includes a variety of other useful files on Blairmore, and we have also read through the local newspaper, the *Blairmore Enterprise*, these we cite in conventional fashion.

38 See *Blairmore Enterprise*, 5 March 1925, and for the most detailed description of school finances, see the auditor's report for 1932 in ibid., 2 March 1933.

39 Ibid., 16 July 1925. For an introduction to the state of the industry in the Pass and additional references to the secondary literature, see Seager, "The Pass Strike of 1932," 1–11.

40 On the collapse of the Home Bank, see Bliss, *Northern Enterprise*, 386–7.

41 In the 1920s the inspectors usually met with the board to go over their assessment of the school, so the gist of the reports is incorporated in the minutes.

42 For the contract, see Glenbow Archives, M2017, Pincher Creek School Division No. 29, file 841, Contract with Dr R.K. Lillie, "Agreement for Dental Services," 15 March 1935 to 30 June 1936.

43 Ibid., M2004, Blairmore, file 877, "Inspectors' Reports," H.J. Sparby, 22 May 1942.

44 Ibid., file 876, "Principal's Reports," n.d. [probably 1941 or 1942].

45 There is a nice description of facilities and arrangements for both domestic science and manual training in ibid., file 845, Director of Technical Education to Secretary Treasurer, Blairmore SD, 9 Jan. 1942 (probably a copy of a letter to department of education).

46 See the inspector's comments, ibid., file 877, 16 May 1945 and 26 May 1947.

47 See ibid., 26 May 1947 and 25 Jan. 1949.

48 See ibid., Inspector James McKay's comments, 31 Jan. 1950.

49 Departmental pressures on the Pass boards to reorganize went back to at least the 1940s, but for one good example, see ibid., file 874, letter from H.E. Balfour, Director of School Administration, Alberta, Dept of Education, to Secretary Treasurer, Coleman SD, 15 Nov. 1950 (copy to Blairmore board).

50 The detail in this and the next paragraph is from UAA, John C. Charyk Fonds, 90-43-83, box 10, Mrs Dorothy M. Willner, Davidson, Saskatchewan, Records relating to Kipp School District No. 1589. The teacher's salary is given for each year but not the total budget. But "something over $1,200" appears to be approximately right.

51 Glenbow Archives, M2017, Pincher Creek School Division No. 29, School Census, Chipman Creek SD No. 863, "Distances from School on Van Route."

52 Alberta, *AR 1920*, 153.

53 Our calculations, DBS, *Annual Survey 1923*, 53 (Table 81; six provinces).

54 Ontario, *AR 1944*, 107.

55 In 1923 the DBS estimated that about 600 graded schools were essentially rural schools. Along with the one-room rural schools in Ontario in 1944–45, there were another 456 two-room schools. See ibid. and DBS, *Annual Survey 1923*, 53 (Table 81).

56 See also the equally illuminating map of Saskatchewan in *Historical Atlas*, Plate 33.

57 Ontario, *AR 1922*, 43.

58 See New Brunswick, *AR 1909–10*, xv; *AR 1930*, xx.

59 Alberta, *AR 1945*, 78, 88. There are discrepancies because of different definitions of what one means by a rural school. Our Table 4.1 gives a rural figure for Alberta of only 46%, but Fred McNally's estimate in 1928 was that "approximately three-fifths of all children attend one-room rural schools or village schools of two rooms." See his article "Education in Alberta," *The School* 16, no. 10 (June 1928): 1026.

60 Ontario, *AR 1945*, 103 (Table 4).

61 A second frequency distribution, for 1944, suggests enrolments fell in the intervening years. At that point 26% of rural schools with more than one room had 19 pupils or fewer, and 48% of the one-room schools had 19 or fewer (20% had under 10), for a total of nearly 69% of all rural schools with 19 or fewer pupils. See DBS, *Elementary and Secondary Education 1943–44*, 18.

62 Stortz and Wilson, "Education on the Frontier," 273.

63 Alberta, *AR 1920*, 88; Glenbow Archives, M2017, Pincher Creek School Division No. 29, file 678, "Superintendent's Term Return," 30 June 1941.

64 DBS, *Annual Report 1922*, 31.

65 Our calculations from Nova Scotia, *AR 1927–28*, 12 (Table 6).

66 Nova Scotia, *AR 1920*, xxvi–xxviii.

67 *Maclean's*, 15 April 1951, 8–9, 61.

68 For a matching piece in the popular press that is even more savage, see the article by Max Braithwaite and Craig Mooney, "School Drought," *Maclean's*, Nov. 1937. For an early example, see Miller, *Rural Schools*, appendix C.

69 Ontario, *AR 1921*, 128. Similarly, see Manitoba, *AR 1939–40*, 138 (Table 4), which gives statistics for 1925 through 1940. The province had only a handful of log schools, but compared to Ontario, far more schools were frame rather than brick.

70 Foght, *Saskatchewan*, 52.

71 Miller, *Rural Schools*, appendix C. See also Putman-Weir Report, 20; New Brunswick, *AR 1931*, 33. From early on, all provinces developed elaborate sets of regulations regarding minimum levels of accommodation, grounds, classroom equipment, water supply and sanitation, etc. But enforcing the law was up to inspectors, and while they had the power to do so, it was the better part of wisdom to make compromises based on their estimates of the ability and willingness of trustees and ratepayers to comply with departmental standards and expectations. Large numbers of school buildings violated both the letter and spirit of the regulations. Compare, for example, the description of the Pelham school offered by Norman High a few pages below with the three

full pages of building and equipment requirements in Ontario's regulations published in *CSJ* 5, no. l (Jan. 1927): 9–11.

72 Report, Chief Inspector of Schools, Alberta, *AR 1937*, 69. A Manitoba report in 1932 declared (*pace* Camrose) that of 1,000 one-room schools surveyed, only 12% had a piano though 36% had an organ. "A school in a northern mining district reports the presence in the school house of a radio, a piano, an organ and a gramophone. Another reports that the gramophone was won by a spelling match. A number report that the gramophone is 'broken' and one states that the organ is 'lame.'" *Manitoba Teacher* 13, no. 4 (April 1932): 6.

73 Quoted in Hallman, "A Thing of the Past," 113. Similarly, see the description in E.W. Nichols, "The Little White Schoolhouse," *JEdNS*, Dec. 1933, 81–4.

74 High, "Haldimand County," 1–2.

75 Nova Scotia, *AR 1929*, 41.

76 Aside from the many individual memoirs, there are some excellent sources that offer collective portraits. See (among others) Charyk, *Little White Schoolhouse: Pulse of the Community* [vol. 1], *Little White Schoolhouse: Those Bittersweet Schooldays*, and *Syrup Pails and Gopher Tails*; McLachlan, *With Unshakeable Persistence* and *With Unfailing Dedication*; Peabody, *School Days*. Charyk provides no sources in any of his books, but the Charyk collection at UAA contains all of his source material, with much good material that didn't get used in his books. See also Cochrane, *One-Room School*, a delightful book with fine photographs but less rich in information than the books cited above. Another valuable source on nearly all the subjects touched on in this chapter – and especially on "the pioneer fringe" – is Stortz's MA thesis "The Rural School Problem in British Columbia." Most of Stortz's generalizations are to be found in his articles that we cite in various chapters of this book, but the thesis itself is rich in detail. On rural school buildings, for example, see pp. 105–8.

77 Flin Flon is an example where a modern multi-classroom elementary and high school built by the Hudson Bay Mining and Smelting Company was rented to the school board for one dollar a year. See Lysecki, "Education in Manitoba," 121–2, 126. For an example where a company not only built but maintained a private school for its employees, see ibid., 134. See also Goltz, "Copper Cliff," 29, 36–7.

78 McDougall, *Building the North*, 143–4.

79 Adams and Thomas, *Floating Schools*, 18ff.; Barman, *The West beyond the West*, 184–5.

80 Nova Scotia, *AR 1931*, 37.

81 For a description of the original initiative, see "A School on Wheels," *The School* 15, no. 3 (Nov. 1926): 222–5. See also Charyk, *Little White Schoolhouse:*

Bittersweet Schooldays, 147–8; Burnham Wyllie, "A Schoolroom on Wheels," *Maclean's*, 15 April 1929, 21, 53–4.

82 Lysecki, "Education in Manitoba," 119. For another example, see ibid., 97.

83 *ATAM* 27, no. 6 (Feb. 1946): 2.

84 William A. Plenderleith, "The Peace River Experiment," *The School* 25, no. 3 (Nov. 1936): 187.

85 The situation in Ontario's separate schools was even worse. See the matching graph in Ontario, *AR 1942*, 164.

86 "A Health Survey of Canadian Schools, 1945–1946: A Survey of Existing Conditions in the Elementary and Secondary Schools of Canada," *Canadian Education* 2, no. 2 (Feb. 1947): 9–87. The report was primarily designed to investigate the state of health and physical education instruction in the schools as well as their contribution to child nutrition. But a preliminary chapter surveyed the physical environment of the schools.

87 Report of a Committee of the Canadian Education Association, "The Status of the Teaching Profession," *Canadian Education* 5, no. 1 (Dec. 1949): 104–8. These pages deal specifically with conditions in the rural schools.

88 Five per cent of the schools sampled by the Canadian Teachers' Federation drew their water "from a stream or lake or depend on melted ice."

89 *Census of Canada 1941*, vol. 9, 11–83 (Tables 3–19).

90 See Charyk, *Little White Schoolhouse: Those Bittersweet Schooldays*, 33ff. This book by Charyk is itself a kind of contextualization of his earlier books, which focus primarily on the school itself.

91 See McLachlan, *With Unshakeable Persistence*, 36.

92 *The School* 25, no. 8 (April 1937): 658. The school was in Markham Township.

93 Using the legal or regulatory nomenclature adopted by the various provinces to describe the provision of secondary education is daunting and largely fruitless. Not only did terminology change over the decades, but different provinces used different terms for the same thing or, vice versa, used the same terms for different kinds of institutions. We've attempted to piece together a composite picture. For a careful description of the specific designations used in each province and the range of grades they taught, see DBS, *Historical Statistical Survey*, 11–13. But for the best analysis of the different types of secondary schooling, by province, which also groups institutions so that comparison of provision can be made, see Dyde, *Public Secondary Education*, 33–51. For a compilation that lists all the secondary schools by province (though it omits some of the one-department schools), see DBS, *List of Public Secondary Schools in Canada*.

94 An Ontario "collegiate institute" was a high school with large enrolments, a highly qualified staff of specialists, a broader curriculum, and superior facilities. For the development of secondary education in the province, including the reasons for the spread of high schools into some very small communities, see Gidney and Millar, *Inventing Secondary Education*, passim.

95 See Jackson and Gaskell, "White Collar Vocationalism," 167–96. For provincial-level accounts of the origins of the vocational education movement, see, for example, Johnson, *Public Education in British Columbia*, 63–8; Chalmers, *Schools of the Foothills Province*, 211–19; Stamp, *Schools of Ontario*, chaps 3 and 4.

96 We are referring here to regularly organized, full-time secondary school programs. During the first half of the twentieth century, and in several cases early on, most provinces established technical and/or agricultural colleges devoted to high-level vocational training. These operated at roughly senior high school level or beyond. Some were residential, some were not. Nova Scotia is one good example; though it had no secondary day vocational schools, it did have an extensive network of vocational evening schools, a large college of technology in Halifax, and an agricultural college in Truro. We will not deal with these forms of vocational training here.

97 Dyde, *Public Secondary Education*, 61. For a helpful graphic on the establishment of vocational schools from the early twentieth century onwards, see *Historical Atlas*, Plate 33. There is a comprehensive list of Canadian secondary schools offering vocational programs (including enrolments) in DBS, *Elementary and Secondary Education 1938–40*, 52ff. (Table 31).

98 See, for example, Seath, *Education for Industrial Purposes*, 340; Dyde, *Public Secondary Education*, 62–4; British Columbia, *AR 1925–26*, Report on Technical Education, R59.

99 *The School* 1, no. 5 (Jan. 1913): 388–9. Similarly, see the description and picture of the Saint John Vocational School in *Educational Review*, June 1930, 218; London Board of Education, *AR 1919 and 1920*, 38–40; J.G. Lister, "Vancouver Technical High School," *BC Teacher* 8, nos 7 and 8 (March and April 1929): 40–1 and 14–15.

100 *The School* 18, no. 1 (Sept. 1929): 69.

101 In New Brunswick the first vocational school, in Saint John, was stand-alone, but by the 1930s most were identified as parts of "composite schools." New Brunswick, *AR 1935–36*, 298. For Alberta's first composite high school – Western Canada Composite High School in Calgary – see Stamp, *School Days*, 84–5.

102 See the enrolment figures by program and school, Winnipeg School Board, *AR 1920*, 41; *AR 1926*, 43–4.

103 DBS, *Statistical Report on Education 1921*, 6.

104 Dyde, *Public Secondary Education*, 32. Italics added.

105 Fred Clarke, "Secondary Education in Canada: Past and Present," *The Year Book of Education 1934*, 565. Italics in original.

106 For one good early description, see Foght, *School System of Ontario*, 14–15. There were regulations that allowed growing communities to upgrade continuation schools to high schools. See *The School* 24, no. 1 (Oct. 1935): 161.

107 See, for example, British Columbia, "Course of Study and Regulations for Superior Schools," in *Manual of School Law, 1910*, 68; Ball and Reid,

School Administration, 142–5 (Saskatchewan); New Brunswick, *AR 1919–20*, "Superior Schools," A29; McBeath, "Education in New Brunswick," 16.

108 Manitoba, Murray Report, 45. While the terminology had changed, the same categorization was still in place in the late 1930s; see Manitoba, *AR 1937–38*, 133.

109 Though in other provinces "common schools" was an antiquated term by 1900, Nova Scotia remained attached to it just because they were not conceived to be simply "elementary" in terms of the curriculum.

110 Bingay, *Public Education in Nova Scotia*, 97.

111 See *The School* 24, no. 4 (Dec. 1935): 350.

112 DBS, *Historical Statistical Survey*, 11. Beginning in the 1930s a few of the larger towns added grade XI (the junior matriculation year) to their curriculum. See McKenna, "Higher Education in Transition," 208.

113 Ontario, *AR 1925*, 3.

114 See New Brunswick, *AR 1927*, lv, A10; Stratton, "Public Secondary Education in the Rural Areas of New Brunswick," 29; Lyons, "Ten Forgotten Years," 118; Manitoba, Dept of Education, *Regulations Effective July 1, 1934*, s. 20.

115 In Alberta, as in most other provinces, there were, however, restrictive policies, enforced by the inspectorate, to limit such instruction, such as the pupil-teacher ratio in the elementary grades, the qualifications of the teacher, the accessibility of alternatives, and the like. For a brief but thorough description of Alberta's policies on the circumstances that permitted high school instruction in one-room schools and in one- and two-teacher departments of village and small-town schools, see PAA, 79.334, box 2, "Interprovincial Correspondence: Maritime Provinces," DM, Alberta, to H.P. Moffatt, Education Office, Nova Scotia, 13 Oct. 1933.

116 We say "near-exclusively" because by the 1930s at least there were clearly exceptions. In 1933, 54 elementary schools in rural districts enrolled 85 students in grade IX and 17 in grade X. See Gordon, "Secondary Education in Rural British Columbia," 45. The regulations established for superior schools and high schools can be found in British Columbia, *Manual of School Law*, various editions. Similarly, see Cameron, "The Small High School," 6–7.

117 DBS, *Annual Report 1922*, 30; DBS, *Annual Survey 1927*, xxi. The latter figure includes fifty-six collegiate institutes.

118 Saskatchewan, *Report, Committee on School Finance and School Grants*, 12. For the numbers in British Columbia, see Cameron, "The Small High School," 5–6.

119 Alberta, *Report of the Legislative Committee on Rural Education*, 2.

120 Ibid. For the equivalent figures in Saskatchewan, see Saskatchewan, *AR 1927*, 14.

121 Learned and Sills, *Education in the Maritime Provinces*, 9.

122 Stamp, *Schools of Ontario*, 124.

123 Dyde, *Public Secondary Education*, 39.

124 Stamp, *Schools of Ontario*, 124.

125 Conrad, "Henry Fraser Munro," 28; Davis, "Secondary Education in Nova Scotia," 71.

126 Woods, "Education in Manitoba," 1:111–12.

127 Johnson, *Public Education in British Columbia*, 69.

128 British Columbia, AR *1929–30*, Q11–12 (statistics for both 1928–29 and 1929–30).

129 Cameron, "The Small High School," 7–12.

130 British Columbia, AR *1939–40*, B15.

131 Alberta, AR *1955–56*, 9.

132 PAA, 79.334, box 2, Interprovincial Correspondence: Maritime Provinces, Chief Inspector of Schools, Alberta, to H.P. Moffatt, Assistant Superintendent of Education, Halifax, 6 Oct. 1941.

133 Prince Edward Island, Royal Commission on Education, *Report*, 1930, 24.

134 Ontario, AR *1941*, 114 (Table 10).

135 Cameron, "The Small High School," 13, 37–8.

136 Woods, "Education in Manitoba," 47.

137 DBS, *Annual Report 1922*, 14.

138 Nova Scotia, AR *1929–30*, xiv.

139 Saskatchewan, AR *1935*, 9. See also the statistical tables in ibid., AR *1930*, 54A; AR *1935*, 24–5; AR *1939*, 20–1.

140 Our calculations from data in Ontario, AR *1925*, AR *1926*, AR *1935*, AR *1936*.

141 Our calculations, excluding Prince Edward Island and Quebec, from DBS, *Annual Report 1922*, 108 (Table 55); DBS, *Elementary and Secondary Education 1938–40*, 50–1 (Table 30). This is our best estimate from the available data, but it may be somewhat too high or too low because of the way different provinces classified enrolments. For the difficulties of arriving at a hard figure, see Dyde, *Public Secondary Education*, 45–8. Dyde's own estimate, as of the mid-1920s, of those enrolled in secondary programs that were taught within graded and ungraded elementary school buildings was, excluding Ontario, 40% of Canadian high school pupils. In 1940 high school enrolment in the ungraded elementary schools of Alberta was 27% of total secondary enrolment; in Saskatchewan, 24%; in Nova Scotia, 42%.

142 Glenbow Archives, M2004, Crowsnest Pass School Division 63, Papers, box 106, file 877, Blairmore SD No. 628, 1941–56, High School Inspector's Report, H.J. Sparby, 22 May 1942.

143 PAA, 79.334, box 17, file 272, H.C. Balfour to Chief Inspector, 13 June 1935; Chief Inspector to Secretary Treasurer, Ewelme SD No. 2829, 24 June 1935.

144 Glenbow Archives, M2004, Crowsnest Pass School Division #63, Papers, box 106, file 831, W. Skelton to Secretary Treasurer, Blairmore SD, 22 April

1940. The letter was accompanied by a 8" × 11", fourteen-page, multicolour brochure showing designs for schools and their mechanical facilities and pictures of schools the company had built.

145 Nova Scotia, AR *1931*, 70. For an earlier example, see "The New County Academy Building at Truro," *Educational Review*, June 1903, 17. Moncton rebuilt in 1934; see the description in Anderson, "Moncton," appendix A, "The Moncton High School Building."

146 Ontario, AR *1919*, 34.

147 Ontario, AR *1919*, 35; AR *1920*, 48. In 1929 the chief inspector of schools for Nova Scotia carried out a first "visitation" of that province's academies and high schools, and though generally positive, his report noted the range of accommodation and facilities available.

148 Galbraith, *The Scotch*, 125–6. On rural high school buildings and facilities, see also Johnson, *Pursuing Higher Education*, 10–12; Gordon, "Secondary Education in Rural British Columbia," 107–15.

149 DBS, *Annual Survey 1923*, 53 (Table 81, note 2).

150 Manitoba, Murray Report, 50.

151 R.G. Gemmell, "Vocational Training in the Small High School," *The School* 25, no. 1 (Sept. 1936): 13. For some Saskatchewan figures, see DBS, *Annual Survey 1923*, 52 (Table 79). We assume this also helps account for the considerable numbers of young people attending school away from home in the later nineteenth century. See Darroch, "Families, Fostering, and Flying the Coop," 221–5.

152 *CSJ* 11, no. 4 (April 1933): 145; *CSJ* 6, no. 1 (Jan. 1928): 7.

153 The issue is complex because the evidence often doesn't help in distinguishing between charges to individual parents and those to public authorities. In several provinces, for example, school board receipts include "non-resident fees" but don't indicate who is paying them. The legislation is often phrased in ambiguous terms – boards "could" charge fees but didn't necessarily do it, or school districts "could" pay fees to a host school district. Government regulations might stipulate the amount of a fee but allow boards to exceed it. During the interwar period, moreover, policies changed in several provinces from restrictive to more laissez-faire approaches to non-resident fees. The more evidence we gathered on this issue, the more murky the matter became. In Saskatchewan, for example, government grants to subsidize non-resident pupils were abolished in 1926 and boards allowed to charge fees to parents; some boards did, others did not. See Saskatchewan, Committee on School Administration, *Report*, 54–5; *The School* 21, no. 2 (Oct. 1932): 165. Something similar happened during the 1930s in Manitoba; see Manitoba, AR *1934–35*, 13. On Alberta, see Walker, "Public Secondary Education in Alberta," 115–16, 131; *Alberta School Trustees Magazine* in ATAM 12, no. 9 (May 1932): 24–7. For Nova Scotia, see Nova Scotia, AR *1930*, 107. In British

Columbia it appears that non-resident fees were charged to the municipality, not to the parent. See British Columbia, *Manual of School Law*, 1910, p. 14, ss 14A, 14B; ibid., 1919, p. 12, s. 15; ibid., 1937, pp. 45–6, s. 68.

154 *Proceedings, OEA, 1922,* 176.

155 Glenbow Archives, M2017, Pincher Creek School Division, file 722, Secretary Treasurer, Pincher Creek SD, to Mrs White, 23 Sept. 1943.

156 See DBS, *National Income of Canada, 1919–1938,* 106–10.

157 Lloyd, *Woodrow,* 15.

158 Parker, *Galbraith,* 31.

159 Galbraith, *The Scotch,* 129–32. Clearly, various psychic costs were not isolated problems. For other examples, see Saskatchewan, *AR 1923,* 97; Comacchio, *Dominion of Youth,* 110–11.

160 Lloyd, *Woodrow,* 16; Parker, *Galbraith,* 32.

161 The best evidence here is the numbers themselves, which we have taken note of in an earlier paragraph. But for reiterated statements throughout the interwar years, one good source is the Alberta annual reports. Each year the report of the chief inspector of schools included a section labelled "Advanced Instruction," which contains a running overview that is followed by extracts from the inspectors' reports. For views from the other side of the country, see New Brunswick, *AR 1932–33,* s11; *AR 1938–39,* 26.

162 Saskatchewan, *Report, Committee on School Finance and School Grants,* 11. For a sampling of opinion on the advantages of keeping children close to home rather than sending them off to the nearest high school, see *CSJ* 10, no. 6 (June 1932): 210–13.

163 Jones, "A Strange Heartland," 94.

164 Ontario, *AR 1941,* 114 (Table 10); New Brunswick, *AR 1933–34,* 10; Saskatchewan, *AR 1935,* 45–6.

165 Alberta, *AR 1932,* 15.

166 See Glenbow Archives, M2004, Crowsnest Pass School Division #63, Papers, Blairmore, School Minutes, 15 Aug. 1923, 10 Oct. 1923, 27 June 1924, 1 June 1925.

167 Ibid., Minutes, 8 and 18 Aug. 1930.

168 Ibid., Minutes, 19 June 1931.

169 Ibid., Minutes, 31 July and 28 Aug. 1931.

170. See ibid., Minutes, 16 June 1932, 5 Sept. 1934, 1 Sept. 1937; file 864, Report of Annual Meeting, Blairmore SD, 3 Jan. 1941.

171 Glenbow Archives, Pincher Creek School Division No. 29 Fonds, M2017, file 676, C.W. Thomas, Fishburn, Alberta, to Mr W. Aberhart, Minister of Education, 2 Sept. 1939; Chief Inspector of Schools to C.W. Thomas, 11 Sept. 1939. For other examples, see PAA, 79.334, box 13, file 122, J. Leech to DM, Dept of Education, 4 Aug. 1938; ibid., box 17, file 272, R.B. Boyce to E.C. Fuller, Chief Inspector, 28 Sept. [n.d.]; UAA, John C. Charyk Fonds,

90-43-75, box 9, "W.A. Olive"; ibid., box 8, "Anne Ismond." Even before the Depression such pressures were apparent. Despite their own regulation requiring three teachers before the two senior high school grades were undertaken, Saskatchewan authorities "seldom, if ever," enforced it "where trustees and ratepayers seemed to be reasonably unanimous in the desire to include Grade XII." Saskatchewan, *AR 1928*, 87.

172 *The School* 19, no. 6 (Feb. 1931): 591. See also the inspectors' commentary in Saskatchewan, *AR 1934*, 41–2. For an article describing the actual process of conducting such courses, see "The Saskatchewan Correspondence School," *The School* 20, no. 4 (Dec. 1931): 314–19.

173 Archer, *Saskatchewan*, 238.

174 Manitoba, *AR 1935–36*, 15.

175 *The School* 24, no. 4 (Dec. 1935): 350.

176 RCDPR, *British Columbia in the Canadian Confederation*, 153. See also the description of its policies in British Columbia, *AR 1929–30*, Q40–3; J.W. Gibson, "Why Stop Learning?," *BC Teacher* 15, no. 4 (Dec. 1935): 23–7.

177 Ontario, Committee on the Costs of Education, *Report*. The text reflects the major problems, but see also the appendices, which include briefs from various interested parties.

178 Woods, "Education in Manitoba," 108.

179 On the different ratios of high school pupils to elementary pupils between town and country – one indicator of accessibility – see Dyde, *Public Secondary Education*, 50.

180 Ibid., 32.

CHAPTER FIVE

1 The quantitative data for much of this chapter have a variety of limitations, and our generalizations and conclusions have to be understood in that light. Those who want to pursue these issues beyond what is contained in the text and notes should consult appendix B.

2 The figure of 75% would be even higher if one included teachers in continuation and vocational schools. For the entire period, see, in the Ontario *ARs*, the relevant tables showing the number of elementary school teachers and the number of teachers in high schools and collegiate institutes, 1900 to 1940. The rates of increase in British Columbia diverged even more: between 1920 and 1930, they were 33% for elementary school teachers and 137% for high school teachers (see the relevant tables in British Columbia *ARs* for 1920 and 1930). The high school figure does not include teachers in superior and junior high schools, a fast-growing sector in British Columbia but one for which we lack comparable data. Calculations of rates of increase are our own. As in Ontario, in British Columbia the growth rate for high school teachers

is exaggerated by their small numbers; in 1930 elementary school teachers composed 80% of the workforce even when superior and junior high school teachers were included among all high school teachers. There is no compilation of national figures that separates elementary from high school teachers. For further discussion of the British Columbia data, see appendix B.

3 It is difficult to describe matriculation standards across Canada in the first half of the twentieth century because they vary by province and by decade. To the 1920s, all provinces except Ontario set junior matriculation at grade XI and senior matriculation at grade XII. But during the 1930s especially, entry standards to university (and the normal schools) crept upwards towards four years, which in some provinces became senior matriculation and in others an extension of the regular high school program to four years. In the Maritimes, junior matriculation remained at grade XI even at mid-century. While difficult to describe, its meaning is not trivial because a four-year junior matriculation program required one full year of additional high school work and thus an extra year of maturity for those entering teaching.

4 "Normal school" was a literal translation of the French phrase *école normale* and was meant to indicate a school that modelled, or set the norm for, exemplary pedagogical practice. These schools were increasingly designated "teachers' colleges."

5 We are ignoring here distinctions between interim and permanent certificates, finer subdivisions than three or four categories (New Brunswick and Nova Scotia had six levels), subcategories such as "first-class A" or "B," and a variety of specialist certificates for such areas as music, art, kindergarten, or vocational subjects.

6 Until 1927 one could qualify as a third-class teacher in Nova Scotia by writing a professional examination rather than attending normal school.

7 Miller, *Rural Schools*, 52–3. For the standards c. 1920, there is a detailed description province by province in DBS, *Historical Statistical Survey*, 67–9, and for 1922, a tabular description in DBS, *Annual Report 1922*, insert at 128–9.

8 Harrigan, "Public School Teachers," 496–7 and Table 6.

9 Miller, *Rural Schools*, 63 (Table 6). Our calculations, excluding Quebec, from Miller's data.

10 Ibid., 56. For a nice description of this short-lived migration of university students, see Rosalind Rowan, MA, "The Eastern Student as a Western Teacher," *The School* 5, no. 2 (Oct. 1916): 97–101.

11 Our commentary here is based on a source that is not itself easy to interpret, and we have also made our own modifications. We discuss both the data and interpretive issues at length in appendix B, sections 2 and 3.

12 While Ontario and Manitoba experienced losses to the western provinces, the exodus was a particular source of complaint in the Maritimes, which annually lost some of their best-qualified teachers to better-paying jobs in the

West. See New Brunswick, *AR 1905–06*, 1; *AR 1908–09*, xv; *AR 1909–10*, xxxvii; Nova Scotia, *AR 1919–20*, v. The western migration declined after 1920 when those provinces began to generate an adequate supply of their own. For the war-induced teacher shortage, see Sheehan, "World War I and Provincial Educational Policy," 254–7.

13 See, for example, Saskatchewan, *AR 1926*, Report, DM, Education, 12–13.

14 Chalmers, *Schools of the Foothills Province*, 423.

15 For the changes in required standards, compare the references in note 7 with those laid out in DBS, *Annual Survey 1930*, insert between pp. 60 and 61; DBS, *Annual Survey 1936*, insert between pp. viii and ix. For other evidence for the claims made in this paragraph, see (for Alberta) Alberta, *AR 1925*, 31; DBS, *Annual Survey 1930*, xiii; Alberta, *Report of the Legislative Committee on Rural Education*, 9; (British Columbia) Johnson, *Public Education in British Columbia*, 86, 210–14; (New Brunswick) New Brunswick, *AR 1926*, xliii; *AR 1928–29*, 7; *AR 1930*, xi; *AR 1936*, 15; (Nova Scotia) *JEdNS* (Sept. 1931), 7; Nova Scotia, *AR 1940*, xxvi; Nova Scotia, *Report of the Royal Commission on Provincial Development and Rehabilitation*, Part 5, Education, 24; (Saskatchewan) Lyons, "Ten Forgotten Years," 117; Saskatchewan, *AR 1938*, 22. For three particularly good graphics showing the improvement in qualifications, see Ontario, *AR 1939*, 174 (1860–1938); *Manitoba Teacher* 10, no. 4 (April 1929): 1 (1920–28); Saskatchewan, *AR 1929*, 87 (1912–29). For examples of the optimism of the late 1930s, see Nova Scotia, *AR 1940*, xxvi; RCDPR, Report of Hearings, Saskatchewan, vol. 3, 1903–4 (President, Saskatchewan Teachers' Federation, commenting on STF brief).

16 For the evidence on interprovincial differences, 1910–40, see appendix B, tables for Nova Scotia, Saskatchewan, and British Columbia (Tables B.1, B.2, B.3). We offer these as illustrations. We have created tables for all eight provinces, and these tables consistently illustrate the trends we identify here.

17 Miller, *Rural Schools*, 63 (Table 6).

18 Although his calculations differ from our own, Harrigan identifies the same east-west pattern; see Harrigan, "Public School Teachers," 500–1. In most provinces the third-class certificates were abolished outright, mostly in the 1920s, but there were exceptions: for example, they lingered on in New Brunswick. There were enough surplus applicants to the New Brunswick normal school in the 1930s to allow higher standards of entry, but the normal school was required to admit quotas for each level of certificate, including third class, to ensure that the poorest school districts had a supply of licensed teachers. See, for example, New Brunswick, *AR 1930*, x. Between 1920 and 1940, in any case, the number of third-class certificates shrank from 20% to 7% of all certificates; see New Brunswick, *AR 1934–35*, 23 (1910–35); *AR 1939*, 185; *AR 1940*, 17.

19 Charyk, *Those Bittersweet Schooldays*, 141. The relationship between qualifi-
    cations, experience, salaries, and geographical location is knotty. We have
    attempted to unravel it in Gidney and Millar, "The Salaries of Teachers in
    English Canada," 9–18.

20 Miller, *Rural Schools*, unpaginated fold-out sheet at p. 60.

21 Ibid., 56.

22 Richardson, *Administration of Schools*, 161.

23 See, for example, the comparison between 1916 and 1926 in Winnipeg
    School Board, *AR 1926*, 15.

24 New Brunswick, *AR 1911*, 76.

25 Anderson, "Moncton," Part 1, chap. 5 (n.p.).

26 New Brunswick, *AR 1925*, iv.

27 Teachers' certificates are recorded annually in the London Board of
    Education ARs.

28 Alberta, *AR 1911*, 68. Similarly, see Alberta, *AR 1915*, 89; *WSJ* 17, no. 5 (May
    1922): 183; *Manitoba Teachers' Federation Bulletin*, Dec. 1923, 495.

29 Our calculations from DBS, *Elementary and Secondary Education 1938–40*,
    68–77. The first good DBS data on this point are for 1938, and the percent-
    ages are somewhat lower than those cited here for 1940. But we have chosen
    to use the data for 1940 in order to be consistent with the comparison drawn
    earlier between 1920 and 1940, which was based on Table 5.1. The DBS fig-
    ures include high school teachers. However, figures for Ontario and British
    Columbia, for elementary teachers alone, confirm these trends (our calcula-
    tions from the relevant tables in Ontario and British Columbia ARs).

30 Teacher qualifications were the one significant topic missing from W.F.
    Dyde's thorough-going 1929 study of the Canadian high school, precisely
    because, as he pointed out, there were no data to allow him to cover the sub-
    ject. See his comment in his *Public Secondary Education*, 131. In Saskatchewan,
    for example, there are good data for those high schools and collegiate
    institutes established under the Secondary Education Act, but no data on
    the qualifications of those who taught continuation or high school rooms
    established under the [Public] School Act or who taught high school subjects
    in ordinary rural schools, and these latter types of schools had as many high
    school pupils as did the former. See, for example, the table in Saskatchewan,
    AR 1930, 54A. What we most want here is exactly that comparison, which is
    why we use the Ontario data.

31 Compare the qualifications of Halifax's high school teachers, in Nova Scotia,
    AR 1920, 161–2, and the limited qualifications of Nova Scotia's rural school
    teachers, in Learned and Sills, *Education in the Maritime Provinces*, 8. Two
    decades later the disparity still existed: see Mowat, *School Achievement of Nova
    Scotia Pupils*, 3.

32 See, for example, British Columbia, *AR 1926*, R30; DBS, *Annual Survey 1930*, 69. The only two provinces that clearly separate elementary and high school teachers in their statistics are Ontario and British Columbia, and the latter doesn't begin to make the pertinent distinctions by geographical location until the late 1920s. Thus Ontario statistics remain the best guide we have.

33 Gordon, "Secondary Education in Rural British Columbia," 117–18. See also appendix B, sections 1 and 8, for our discussion of the British Columbia data on this point.

34 Walker, "Public Secondary Education in Alberta," 165–6.

35 Alberta, *AR 1939*, 71.

36 Alberta, *AR 1935*, 54.

37 For the importance of experience in developing expertise and for some of the differences between the novice practitioner and the expert, see Berliner's review of the research in "Teacher Expertise," 46–51; Bransford, Brown, and Cocking, *How People Learn*, 19–38.

38 Prince Edward Island, Royal Commission on Education, *Report* (1910), 35.

39 Manitoba, Murray Report, 87.

40 Nova Scotia, *Report of the Royal Commission on Provincial Development and Rehabilitation*, Part 5, Education, 22. There is no shortage of similar statements across the twentieth century. See *Proceedings, OEA, 1901*, 349; Wilson and Stortz, "The Rural School Problem in British Columbia," 216; RCDPR, Report of Hearings, Saskatchewan, vol. 3, Testimony of President of Saskatchewan Teachers' Federation, 1906–07. For a perceptive assessment of the negative consequences of teacher turnover, see Calam and Fleming, "Rural Inequality," 24–5.

41 Miller, *Rural Schools*, 65.

42 Ibid., 66.

43 Foght, *Saskatchewan*, 104–13. The percentages are our calculations.

44 *WSJ* 11, no. 2 (Feb. 1916): 61.

45 Perry, "A Concession to Circumstances," 340, Fig. 4.

46 Learned and Sills, *Education in the Maritime Provinces*, 8.

47 Ontario, *AR 1911*, 26; *AR 1921*, 124. From 1886, New Brunswick also kept a continuous record. However, it included only first- and second-class teachers, not its third-class or local licences. Thus it is an incomplete record of the total workforce. But among second-class teachers in 1910, for example, 28% taught for two years or less and 55% five years or less. Again, these figures hardly changed to 1920. Our calculations from New Brunswick, *AR 1910*, A19; *AR 1920*, A19. Figures for Nova Scotia teachers from 1886 to 1919, for New Brunswick teachers from 1886 to 1919, and for Ontario teachers from 1905 to 1918 are in DBS, *Historical Statistical Survey*, 79–81.

48 Richardson, *Administration of Schools*, 161.

49 Putman-Weir Report, 404; Stamp, *School Days*, 44.

50 Winnipeg School Board, *AR 1920*, 39. Similarly, see Regina's three-year rule, in Saskatchewan, *AR 1927*, 96.

51 DBS, *Annual Survey 1933*, xxi.

52 Ontario, *AR 1921*, 124; *AR 1926*, 106; *AR 1930*, 142.

53 Perry, "A Concession to Circumstances," 340, Fig. 4.

54 Compare the figures in Ontario, *AR 1930*, 142; *AR 1938*, 114; DBS, *Annual Survey 1930*, 62–4; DBS, *Annual Survey 1931*, 75–80; DBS, *Annual Survey 1936*, 54–5; DBS, *Elementary and Secondary Education 1938–40*, 70–7 (Tables 42–5).

55 Our calculations from DBS, *Elementary and Secondary Education 1936–38*, 60–7. Table 5.4 presents the data in a different format.

56 We use these 1941 medians and percentages because they include Ontario and Quebec and thus give a genuinely national portrait. But we suspect that both medians and percentages were already being affected by the war and reflect declines in experience from higher figures for, say, 1938 or 1939. *CEA*, *Report of the Survey Committee*, 34–5 (Tables 3 and 4). We say "probably" for New Brunswick because, to reiterate, we have reservations about the data being complete.

57 The evidence here is limited to Ontario, 1910 to 1936/37, and Ontario plus three other provinces for the 1930s (Nova Scotia, New Brunswick, and Manitoba).

58 Putman-Weir Report, 188.

59 Calculated from British Columbia, *AR 1937*, 19, 112. See also, for British Columbia teachers in 1932, the Report of the People's Panel, Provincial Salary Committee, *BC Teacher* 12, no. 4 (Dec. 1932): 38–9.

60 Ontario, *AR 1921*, 124; *AR 1926*, 106; *AR 1930*, 142.

61 The data are not complete. In the early 1930s only four or five provinces reported but Ontario was included; from 1938, seven provinces reported, not including Ontario (or Quebec). We think this is a tolerably good national picture because, with or without Ontario, all of the returns include a majority of Canadian teachers. For the figures, see references cited in note 54. The DBS data include both elementary and high school teachers. However, the evidence for British Columbia's *elementary* teachers in 1936 is similar: 84% of city teachers had six or more years' experience, while two-thirds in one-room rural schools had five years or less and over a third had two years or less; these figures are consistent with Table 5.4. Calculated from British Columbia, *AR 1937*, 19, 112.

62 *Proceedings, OEA, 1904*, 295 (Chairman, Inspectors Section); London Board of Education, *AR 1910*, 32. Similarly, see *Proceedings, OEA, 1901*, 349.

63 Foght, *Saskatchewan*, 104–13 (our calculations).

64 Putman-Weir Report, 186. For even higher levels of transiency in one frontier region of British Columbia, see Stortz and Wilson, "Education on the Frontier," 275.

65 Manitoba, Murray Report, 88.

66 New Brunswick, *AR 1928–29*, 22.

67 Saskatchewan, *AR 1927*, 73. Similarly, see *Manitoba Teacher* 12, no. 8 (March 1931): 2; Manitoba, *AR 1937–38*, 43.

68 Fletcher, *Next Step in Canadian Education*, 25.

69 PAA, 90.174, "GSE," *Educational-Personnel Problems in Alberta*, Report of a Special Committee appointed by Dr Robert Newton, Chairman, Sub-committee on Education and Vocational Training of the Alberta Post-War Reconstruction Committee, 1 Dec. 1943, 14.

70 Calculated from British Columbia, *AR 1937*, 110, 112–13.

71 For the DBS interpretation of "where teaching," see DBS, *Elementary and Secondary Education 1938–40*, 61. For the data, see DBS, *Elementary and Secondary Education 1936–38*, 66–7. The only close study of the paradox – comparatively greater total experience than experience levels at the same school – is Corman, "Seeking Greener Pastures," 181–93.

72 "Eastern European" is the designation given in the 1931 census; we have included in it the "Hebrew" category (most prewar Jewish immigrants came from Eastern Europe, and according to the DBS analysis of the "mother tongue" of Canadian teachers for 1931, "Russian" accounted for the same percentage of teachers as "Hebrew" in the 1931 census). For 1941 we have included, in the category "Eastern European," Jewish, Polish, Russian, and Ukrainian teachers. Our calculations from *Census of Canada 1931*, vol. 7, 452ff. (Table 49); DBS, *Elementary and Secondary Education 1944–46*, 25–6.

73 For the Ontario figures in 1931 and 1941, see Reynolds, "Hegemony and Hierarchy," Table 12. For the late nineteenth century, see Sager, "Women Teachers in Canada," 210–11.

74 Saskatchewan, *AR 1930*, 13; *AR 1929*, 99; *AR 1937*, 38.

75 Reid, "Secondary and Higher Educational Interests," 22.

76 PAA, *Educational-Personal Problems in Alberta* ... , Sub-committee on Education and Vocational Training of the Alberta Post-War Reconstruction Committee, 1 Dec. 1943, 2 (in 1943–44 those of non-British origin constituted 65%: ibid.); Stamp, *Becoming a Teacher*, 30, 38, 50.

77 Sager, "Women Teachers in Canada," 233.

78 Saskatchewan, *AR 1930*, 77. Similarly, see Saskatchewan, *AR 1926*, 80; *AR 1932*, 47, 49; *AR 1933*, 45, 48.

79 In one small Ontario sample created for a study in collective biography, teachers reported "that their fathers were labourers, clerical workers, or farmers." Reynolds, "Hegemony and Hierarchy," 100.

80 Weiler, *Country Schoolwomen*, 265n35, reporting on a major 1911 survey of American teachers. Similarly, see Rousmaniere, *City Teachers*, 36.

81 For example, while the various teachers' federations ferociously guard access to their records, these may very well provide this kind of alternative source. Another possibility is the discovery of a cache of normal school records. What

is needed, in any case, are studies of teachers or student teachers like the probes made by ourselves and others into the student records at Canadian universities.

82 Copelman, *London's Women Teachers*, 4, 31–45.

83 These changes are not reflected in Table 5.5, which gives the data at five-year intervals only. Here we are drawing on a table and commentary by the DBS; see *Annual Survey 1930*, xiv. For the late nineteenth-century background and an introduction to the historiography, see, most recently, Sager, "Women Teachers in Canada."

84 This change in the proportion of men versus women teachers in the 1930s was an unusual occupational pattern. See, for example, Sager, "Women in the Industrial Labour Force," 46–9.

85 While the statement is true for the occupation as a whole, it needs some qualification. Table 5.5 includes both elementary and secondary school teachers and the long-term trend might well be explained, after mid-century, by the expansion of high school enrolments and thus an increase in the number of male secondary school teachers. But if the Ontario figures in Table B.4 are representative, this does not seem to apply to the period to 1940, since there was clearly an increase in the proportion of male elementary teachers. As we indicate in a subsequent paragraph in this chapter, moreover, by 1930 the number of women who taught in the secondary schools was about the same as the number of men.

86 The province-by-province figures, along with the combined provincial mean, 1870–1980, are given in Harrigan, "Public School Teachers," Table 5. See also his discussion (493) and DBS, *Annual Survey 1930*, xiv. In the only two provinces (Ontario and British Columbia) where the numbers of elementary and secondary teachers can be separated, the percentage of female teachers in the elementary schools was somewhat higher than these figures indicate. See appendix B, section 7.

87 However, once again Prince Edward Island is an anomaly, with a much higher percentage of males than the other two Maritime provinces. We have no explanation for this.

88 For the data and analysis, see appendix B, section 8.

89 In this case we cannot use a measure similar to that for Table 5.1 because the Jackson data did not include gender breakdowns. And because certification schemes varied so much from province to province, we cannot make provincial comparisons.

90 See Table B.7, appendix B. There are some data for certificates by gender dating back to the early twentieth century or even earlier, but we think they are too problematic in several ways to be helpful here.

91 Our calculations; see appendix B, Table B.8. There are two problems with the data, however: they are only for 1938, and they include both elementary and secondary school teachers. In order to be sure that our generalizations here

are tolerably well grounded, we offer, in Table B.9, Ontario data for elementary teachers only and for five points of time across the interwar period.

92 In our opinion, the explanation sometimes offered, that women didn't bother upgrading because they didn't expect to be promoted to principalships, etc., seems unlikely. Many men would not expect to be promoted either – they were surely able to see that there were fewer of these managerial positions than there were male teachers. And those women who treated teaching as a career had similar salary incentives to upgrade.

93 The figures in this paragraph are our calculations from DBS, *Elementary and Secondary Education 1936–38*, 68–77.

94 Ontario, *AR 1937*, 105 (retrospective table).

95 The documentation for this, Table B.10, is included in appendix B. It gives percentages rather than averages. The 1936 data for British Columbia elementary teachers tend to confirm this Ontario pattern: both men and women teachers in cities had much more experience than their counterparts in one-room rural schools; and more women than men in both places had six or more years of teaching experience. See British Columbia, *AR 1937*, 19, 112.

96 This is true even in those provinces where the median experience in rural schools was lowest. In 1940 the rural median for women in Nova Scotia was 3.7 years but 42% had six or more years of experience. In several provinces a majority of rural teachers had six or more years. See DBS, *Elementary and Secondary Education 1938–40*, 74–7.

97 Our calculations from *Census of Canada 1921*, vol. 4, 116–17; *Census of Canada 1941*, vol. 7, 52, 60. The figures include Quebec.

98 Except where noted, for the Ontario figures in this paragraph see Gelman, "Women Secondary School Teachers," 283 (Table 2.5), 285 (Table 2.7); Ontario, *Schools and Teachers in the Province of Ontario ... November 1930* (Toronto, 1930), 673, 696. For British Columbia, our calculations are from the tables in British Columbia, *AR 1921–22*, C19; *AR 1924–25*, M12; *AR 1929–30*, Q8; *AR 1934–35*, S11; *AR 1939–40*, B9.

99 By 1938–39 the staffs, excluding principals, of the collegiate institutes were 44% female; in high schools, 63%; in continuation schools, 64%. See Ontario, *AR 1939*, Table 25.

100 See, for example, the retrospective table in Ontario, *AR 1940*, 120. Our conclusions in this paragraph are based in addition on calculations made from the following sources: Ontario, *AR 1935*, 80–1; *AR 1936*, 96–7; *AR 1937*, 107–8; British Columbia, *AR 1937*, 19, 112.

101 Gelman, "Women Secondary School Teachers," 79.

102 Although the terminology had long been abandoned, at one point in the late nineteenth century the pertinent statistical tables were labelled, for secondary school teachers, "Gentlemen" and "Ladies," and for elementary school teachers, "Male" and "Female." See Gidney and Millar, *Professional Gentlemen*, 245.

103 On the role of the secondary school in this matter and more generally the reshaping of professional education in the late nineteenth and early twentieth centuries, see Gidney, "Madame How and Lady Why," 13–42; Millar, Heap, and Gidney, "Degrees of Difference," 155–87.

104 The figure varies somewhat by decade. For the late nineteenth century, see Sager, "Women Teachers in Canada," 204. For the twentieth century, our calculations are from *Census of Canada 1921*, vol. 4, xv, 6–7 (1881–1921); DBS, *Annual Survey 1926*, 78 (1921 census); *Census of Canada 1931*, vol. 7, 310, 320; *Census of Canada 1941*, vol. 7, 26–7, 32–3. See also Harrigan, "Public School Teachers," 492 (Table 4).

105 See also Marsh, *Canadians In and Out of Work*, 71 (Table 16). His 1931 estimate is 54%. The census routinely placed teachers in the category of "professionals," and percentages can be calculated from that set of figures. But there were jobs in other classifications that also required a good deal of education, so we are reluctant to be much more specific than this.

106 Saskatchewan, *AR 1930*, 23, 51.

107 These were regular certificates, elementary and secondary, and do not include several thousand additional "temporary" certificates. See Ontario, *AR 1948*, 118 (Table 4); for the number of teaching jobs in Ontario, see Leacy, *Historical Statistics*, Series w170. For two other provincial-level examples, see Perry, "A Concession to Circumstances," 341–5; PAA, 90.174, "GSE," Report of a Special Committee ... of the Alberta Post-War Reconstruction Committee, 1 Dec. 1945, 14. The data here are for the interwar years.

108 Harrigan, "Public School Teachers," 487. In this instance his data do not include Quebec.

109 For some suggestive implications from two American scholars, see Perlmann and Margo, *Women's Work?*, 129–31.

CHAPTER SIX

1 Warren, "Beginnings Again," 405.

2 DBS, *Annual Survey 1934*, xiii. This is a good example of some of the stark differences between then and now. In 1940 Ontario had approximately 6,600 school districts; it now has 72. See DBS, *Elementary and Secondary Education 1940–42*, 57; Gidney, *From Hope to Harris*, 247. Similar reductions have been made in other provinces.

3 In six Canadian provinces in the late 1920s it was a little more or a little less than that. See Table 6.2.

4 The fine detail of municipal and school district taxation was a good deal more complicated than we suggest here. "Property" for our purposes throughout the text refers to the taxation of "real property" – that is, lands and buildings. While most provinces had abandoned the taxation of "personal property" (other than lands and buildings) by the 1930s, some still

raised modest amounts this way. The way in which land was taxed varied and municipalities might also levy other kinds of taxes. But most local revenue came from property taxation. There is a description of the sources of school district revenue in Goldenberg, *Municipal Finance*, 54–62, 82ff. For a much more detailed historical review of provincial and municipal tax systems, see the pertinent sections of Perry, *Taxes, Tariffs, and Subsidies*, vol. 1 and vol. 2, esp. chap. 30.

5 It is not easy to get a fix on actual total cash outlays for individual rural schools, and there were great variations in any case. In Ontario in 1907, ss No. 7, Stamford Township (Falls View School), spent $550 for the teacher's salary, $65 for a caretaker, and $224.64 on miscellaneous expenses, for a total of $839.64. Martha Black records, in possession of the authors. In the first two decades of the twentieth century one could buy a prefabricated one-room schoolhouse through Eaton's catalogue in any of three sizes, with the cost ranging from $683.63 to $829.99. See Cochrane, *The One-Room School*, 25. The average operating cost in Alberta in 1925 was about $1,300. *ATAM* 6, no. 7 (Dec. 1925): 22. In Saskatchewan, *c.* 1930, one estimate for a typical budget was as follows: teacher's salary $1,000, janitor $100, official's salary $50, debenture payment $300, miscellaneous $300, or $1,800 in all; at about the same time in that province it cost anywhere from $2,500 to $4,500 to build and equip a one-room school, depending on the type of construction. Saskatchewan, *Report, Committee on School Finance and School Grants*, 6, 9. In a pioneer area of British Columbia the average total operating budget for one-room schools during the 1920s was $1,179.49. See Wilson and Stortz, "May the Lord Have Mercy on You," 211.

6 There is a detailed description of the organization and finance of local schools, both urban and rural, province by province, in DBS, *Annual Survey 1934*, "Appendix to Part I: The Mechanism of Administration and Support of the Provincial School System in Canada," lxxii–lxxx. There is an overview for the early twentieth century in Miller, *Rural Schools*, chap. 2. See also the crisp account provided by Goldenberg, *Municipal Finance*, 22–5, 51–62. In some provinces, though not in others (Ontario versus Saskatchewan, for example), the school rate had to be formally approved at the annual meeting of the ratepayers in each rural school district. Any of the provincial school acts provide the fine detail of funding arrangements in each province, and sometimes, as in the case of British Columbia, these are codified in a series of *Manuals of School Law* that also includes the general and funding regulations. For one good guide for Saskatchewan in which the technical language of the law is translated into lay terms, see Ball and Reid, *School Administration*.

7 For one good example, see Report, Inspector, Cape Breton West, in Nova Scotia, *AR 1925*, 83: "It is utterly indefensible that the farmers in a school

section should bear nearly the whole burden of maintaining the school while miners or fishermen beside them should be allowed off on payment of a trifle" – particularly miners, the inspector added, who generally enjoyed a better income than the average farmer.

8 See Woods, "Education in Manitoba," Part 2, chap. 7. Woods provides breakdowns for cities and towns, clearly showing the large gaps in resources that existed among urban areas. Similarly, see Cameron, *Financing of Education*, chap. 11 and 155ff.

9 Putman-Weir Report, 277. The figures are for the regularly organized schools, not the assisted schools.

10 RCDPR, Report of Hearings, New Brunswick, vol. 1, 8620. Fletcher Peacock, the provincial director of educational services, was citing data from the New Brunswick Commission on Education of 1932. For the full analysis see that commission's report, esp. 13ff.

11 Ontario, Committee on the Costs of Education, *Report*, 10. Similarly, see Cameron, *Financing of Education*, 156.

12 See Nova Scotia, AR *1926–27*, xix–xx; Saskatchewan, *Report, Committee on School Finance and School Grants*, 6; *The School* 18, no. 8 (April 1930): 671 (McNally on Alberta).

13 This was also the system used in Quebec, though in that province there were also minority-religion schools organized on the school district model.

14 *Manitoba Teacher* 10, no. 4 (April 1929): 14. The differences between municipalities and the consequences for education in Manitoba were thoroughly canvassed in Manitoba, Murray Report, 18–20. A great boon to the poor school district in a prosperous municipality, equalization did nothing to help the schools if a large part or the entire municipality was assessment poor.

15 Report of the Commission on the Larger School Unit, in Nova Scotia, AR *1939*, xlviii.

16 Saskatchewan, *Report, Committee on School Finance and School Grants*, 10–11. See also the extended discussion in High, "Haldimand County," 108–16.

17 See RCDPR, *The Case for Alberta*, 268. In 1930–31, one-fifth of Nova Scotia's rural schools "cannot finance even the minimum programme without government support." Nova Scotia, AR *1930–31*, xxix.

18 See Ontario, Committee on the Costs of Education, *Report*, 10.

19 See the commentary in DBS, *The Size Factor in One-Room Schools*, 3. For the range in class sizes, see our chapter 4.

20 Galbraith, *The Scotch*, 87–8.

21 Stortz and Wilson, "Education on the Frontier," 279–80.

22 John Field, "Educational Conditions in Rural Schools," *The School* 1, no. 2 (Oct. 1912): 115. Field was a public school inspector in East Huron County.

23 William A. Plenderleith, "The Peace River Experiment," *The School* 25, no. 3 (Nov. 1936): 189. For a like example, see Report, Inspector, Cape Breton West, in Nova Scotia, *AR 1929*, 65.

24 There was yet another reason why mill rates might vary greatly, however: assessment values were established in a haphazard and idiosyncratic manner, municipality by municipality, right across Canada. For an extended commentary on this matter, see appendix C, section 3.

25 *ATAM* 6, no. 7 (Dec. 1925): 22. The original text gives a figure of $40 raised by a tax of 10 mills – clearly a typo. For a general commentary on how new settlements might produce low assessment bases, see RCDPR, *The Case for Alberta*, 268.

26 Cited in Abbott, "Hostile Landscapes," 182.

27 Nova Scotia, *AR 1931*, 39. Similarly, see Report, Inspector, Colchester and Hants East, in Nova Scotia, *AR 1924–25*, 84. Generally, see RCDPR, *Report*, Book 1, 118; New Brunswick, *Report of the New Brunswick Committee on Reconstruction*, appendix A, "The Regional Economy of New Brunswick," by J.R. Petrie, 158–60.

28 Ontario, Committee on the Costs of Education, *Report*, 41. For helpful graphics on the location and extent of rural depopulation, see *Historical Atlas*, Plate 28.

29 Manitoba, *AR 1930–31*, 72. The figures are given on pp. 72–4.

30 Jones, *Empire of Dust*, 117. For the Saskatchewan figures, see Waiser, *Saskatchewan*, 257.

31 For Nova Scotia, a 1949 study by D.C. Rowat, cited in Graham, *Fiscal Adjustment*, 67; for Saskatchewan in 1945, see Johnson, *Dream No Little Dreams*, 113; for Ontario, *c.* 1941, see Staples, "The Ontario Rural Teacher," 29.

32 Though aggravated by the Great Depression, pressures on municipalities to provide a wide variety of services had been growing across the first three decades of the century and especially after the Great War, so that even relatively prosperous municipalities were under stress and those with weak assessment bases even more so. See Goldenberg, *Municipal Finance*, 3–9.

33 Ontario, Committee on the Costs of Education, *Report*, 11. For a Nova Scotia example, see Report, Inspector, Cumberland County, in Nova Scotia, *AR 1927*, 75.

34 Wilbur, *The Rise of French New Brunswick*, 131 and, generally, 130–3.

35 *The School* 14, no. 3 (Nov. 1925): 213. For an introduction to the growth of suburban communities around all of Canada's larger cities, see the commentary and the metropolitan region maps in Cudmore and Caldwell, *Rural and Urban Composition*, 470–2. For a study that rarely touches on education but is very helpful on developments in a single region, see Harris, *Unplanned Suburbs*.

36 Cameron, *Financing of Education*, 160, 145.

37 See Goldenberg, *Municipal Finance*, 57. An expert on the subject, Goldenberg considered the problem to be at crisis levels in all ten of Canada's major metropolitan areas.

38 *Manitoba Teacher* 10, no. 4 (April 1929): 14. Similarly, see the grievance expressed by another Winnipeg suburb, in RCDPR, Submissions, vol. 2, *Brief of the Rural Municipality of St James*, 5.

39 Many scholars have pointed out the flaws in such measures. One Canadian example is to be found in Brown, "Education Finance." Brown notes that per-pupil expenditure is "a relatively crude measure of variation in financial effort because spending per pupil does not take into account variation in financial ability [to support education]" (70). He goes on to advocate measures of relative effort that more adequately reflect capacity to pay rather than what is actually paid (70–3). For a critique of international comparisons that is largely dismissive of per-pupil expenditure, see Lindert, *Growing Public*, 142–3. The early twentieth-century Canadian data, however, would be hopelessly inadequate to sustain his preferred alternatives.

40 We provide the documentation for this paragraph in appendix C, section 2. There was nothing uniquely Canadian about the much higher rate of expenditure on secondary education; the same was true in the United States. See Goldin and Katz, "Human Capital and Social Capital," 685.

41 The figures are from Leacy, *Historical Statistics*, Series W275–300. They include Quebec. Table 6.1 provides annual total expenditure figures, 1914 through 1930, which exclude Quebec. These combine both operating and capital expenditure but include only provincial government grants to school boards and not other education-related spending by provincial governments (for more explanation, see appendix C, section 2).

42 The reader may note here and elsewhere the considerable lags between downturns in the economy and declines in educational spending. We think that this is due to the fact that most of the data are based on calendar years rather than the school years that drove budgeting, and to the lag between anticipated resources and the subsequent recognition of new economic circumstances. We return to this issue in the next chapter.

43 On rates of increase see the tables and commentary in DBS, *Annual Survey 1929*, xii–xiv.

44 Our calculations from RCDPR, *Report*, Statement by the Government of Ontario, April 1938, Book 3, Table 16.

45 Calculated from Nova Scotia, *AR 1934*, li–liii.

46 Foght, *Saskatchewan*, 166–8.

47 Our calculations from RCDPR, *British Columbia in the Canadian Confederation*, 143–4.

48 Based on 100 in 1935–39, the cost of living index stood at 79.5 in 1913, rose to 118.1 in 1918, and reached 150.4 in 1920. Sharp declines followed

between 1921 and 1924, and it rose only slightly, to 121.6, by 1929. See Leacy, *Historical Statistics*, series K1–7. The index was intended to measure "retail prices and living costs" and is not necessarily a very good indicator of the cost of goods and services for public authorities or other sectors of the economy. In the early twentieth century, economic data generally, not just those related to education, are problematic. For a comment on the difficulties, see Bothwell, Drummond, and English, *Canada 1900–1945*, 81–2.

49 DBS, *Expenditure for Schools in 1931 as Compared with 1913*, 1.

50 Manzer, *Public Schools and Political Ideas*, 129 (Table 7.9). Both the DBS and Manzer tallies include Quebec.

51 Annual provincial tallies are given for 1901–19 in DBS, *Historical Statistical Survey*, 99–104, and for 1914–30 in Tables C.1 and C.2 in appendix C. Where they overlap, the two sets of data give different figures but the trends are the same. There is also a useful DBS analysis of provincial differences in spending, 1913–29, that takes account of gross expenditure, expenditure in 1913 dollars, and per-pupil expenditure. See DBS, *Annual Survey 1929*, xiv–xv.

52 See Kendle, *John Bracken*, 26–39. On the provincially imposed restrictions on educational spending in the later 1920s, see Gregor and Wilson, *Education in Manitoba*, 107. The restrictions, however, did not make Manitoba the poor man in Confederation. Despite the decline, per capita expenditure on education still put it above the national average every year and above Ontario every year but 1930. In New Brunswick there was a very sharp spending spike in 1925; if one excludes that year, per capita spending increased modestly from about 1924 to 1931, though not to its 1925 peak.

53 Strictly speaking, government grants in the Maritimes went to teachers, not local boards, but to keep our usage uniform we will treat them as one and the same thing.

54 See the table in DBS, *Annual Survey 1929*, xiv.

55 Ibid., xiii.

56 RCDPR, *Report*, Book 1, 205–6.

57 British Columbia began with a system of public education fully funded by the provincial government, but in the late nineteenth and early twentieth centuries the province gradually devolved more and more fiscal responsibility on local authorities. The provincial government, nonetheless, generally carried a greater share of the burden than most other Canadian provinces. For an overview, see King Report, 7–13.

58 Richardson, *Administration of Schools*, 69. Richardson did not break these figures down further, but we assume that most of these large increases took place prior to 1914, since rates of expenditure decreased after that.

59 DBS, *Expenditure for Schools in 1931 as Compared with 1913*, 1–2.

60 This and the next paragraph summarize an extensive literature on the economic context of the period and, more particularly, on the problems

of capital expenditure. The two indispensable secondary sources are Perry, *Taxes, Tariffs, and Subsidies*, vol. 1, chap. 12, esp. 178–81, 185–7; Artibise, "Patterns of Prairie Urban Development," 122–32. Both deal with municipal finance generally and not just school finance, but they make it clear that the fiscal problems originated from the impact of the 1913 depression and, initially at least, much less so from the Great War. Artibise is especially good on the way in which municipal debt remained a problem for Prairie cities long after 1920. There is also an important analysis of school indebtedness on the three Prairie provinces in DBS, "Recent Trends in Education in the Prairie Provinces." More generally on the period, see Norrie, Owram, and Emery, *A History of the Canadian Economy*, Part 5, 26off. The legal provisions governing "Extraordinary or Capital Expenditures" are outlined province by province in Richardson, *Administration of Schools*, 79–84. In some cases school boards had the power to issue bonds and debentures directly, but mostly this was done by the municipality. As well, in some cases plebiscites were required to approve them. Provincial figures for "Debenture Indebtedness," 1914 through 1933 or 1934, are given in DBS, *Financial Statistics of the Provincial School Systems in Canada 1914–1934*. (There are no figures for the three Maritime provinces.) Winnipeg School Board, *AR 1930*, 43, lists its debentures by date of issue, date of maturity, and amount, from 1895 through 1930. There is a nice brief summary of the debt problem in DBS, *Annual Survey 1923*, xiii. For British Columbia, see Putman-Weir Report, 294–8; for Ontario, see Ontario, Committee on the Costs of Education, *Report*, 20–1.

61 Between 1913 and 1916, expenditure on the category "school building and repairs" dropped in Alberta by 82% and in Saskatchewan by 48%. Expenditure on construction began to rise in 1917 but in 1919 was still well below 1913 figures. Our calculations from DBS, *Historical Statistical Survey*, 102–3.

62 Our calculations from ibid., 100–1. The Ontario figures are for the elementary schools only.

63 Between 1914 and 1920 the price of building and construction materials alone had more than doubled. They declined somewhat during the 1920s but never to pre-1914 levels. See Urquhart and Buckley, *Historical Statistics*, 296 (col. J68).

64 DBS, *Annual Survey 1929*, xii–xiii.

65 Calgary School Board, *AR 1930*, Report, Secretary-Treasurer, n.p.

66 Ontario, Committee on the Costs of Education, *Report*, 76 (Table 4).

67 See Winnipeg School Board, *AR 1920*, 17–19; and compare ibid., *AR 1930*, 46–51. The costs of new innovations in curriculum, pedagogy, and auxiliary services were noted by virtually anyone commenting on rising costs during the period. See, for example, DBS, *Annual Survey 1923*, xiii; James Bingay, "The Schools of Glace Bay," *JEdNS*, March 1931, 35–6; *ATAM* 7, no. 4 (Oct. 1926): 12; DBS, "Recent Trends in Education in the Prairie Provinces," 1.

68 Because of a lack of clarity in the data, it is not easy to determine the percentage of board budgets spent on teachers' salaries. Those percentages also vary not only board by board but by what is excluded or included by the accounting procedures. In 1920 "the percentage of General Maintenance Expenditure absorbed by teachers' salaries" in Ontario was 73% and 76% for public and high schools respectively. See Ontario, Committee on the Costs of Education, *Report*, 19. A national estimate proposed by the DBS in 1929 was substantially lower: "On average ... the money devoted to payment of teachers' salaries accounts for little more than one-half of the entire outlay for education. The greater part of the balance is devoted to school accommodation, equipment and maintenance." This calculation, however, was based on total provincial expenditure, not on local board budgets. DBS, *Annual Survey 1929*, xiii.

69 Gidney and Millar, "The Salaries of Teachers," 2, 8–9, appendix, section 6.

70 Our calculations for total salary bills from DBS, *Annual Survey 1926*, 100–3. The percentages for Manitoba were 72%, 1907–13; 28%, 1914–18; and 86%, 1919–25.

71 Prince Edward Island, Royal Commission on Education, *Report*, 1930, 42–3.

72 DBS, *Annual Survey 1929*, xiii.

73 The figures for each province are in Gidney and Millar, "The Salaries of Teachers," Table 3.

74 For the percentage of each provincial budget devoted to education, 1913–38, see RCDPR, appendix 1, Statement 36. This includes, however, all education expenditure, not just grants in aid of schools.

75 See New Brunswick, *Report of the New Brunswick Committee on Reconstruction*, 203–11, and esp. the retrospective graph, 204 (Chart 13). For a recent overview and bibliographical guide, see Conrad and Hiller, *Atlantic Canada*, chap. 10, 161ff. See also Forbes and Muise, *The Atlantic Provinces in Confederation*, esp. chap. 7; RCDPR, *Report*, Book 1, 117–20. A third basic source is the discussion in Norrie, Owram, and Emery, *A History of the Canadian Economy*, 281, 309–14.

76 On the comparatively limited revenues available from real estate taxation (and other sources as well), see RCDPR, *Report*, Book 1, 219ff., "Revenue Systems" for Prince Edward Island, Nova Scotia, and New Brunswick.

77 For a full account, including of the annual revenues derived from the lands in each province as late as the 1930s, see Miller, *National Government and Education*, 64–92. None of the revenues were transferred directly to local school districts but rather formed part of provincial expenditure for education. Saskatchewan's deputy minister, for example, wrote that "the chief source of Government revenue in relation to its expenditure for education is the School Lands Fund." *The School* 15, no. 5 (Jan. 1927): 504. Similarly, for Alberta see *The School* 17, no. 4 (Dec. 1928): 396. The amounts generated by

the sale of school lands were substantial; in 1932 the account in Alberta stood at $9.5 million. *ATAM* 12, no. 9 (May 1932): 25. For a nice description of the way lots were reserved for various purposes, including the support of education, see Waiser, *Saskatchewan*, 102–5. For a summary of the Saskatchewan legislation relating to the school lands, see Ball and Reid, *School Administration*, 178–80. For Alberta, see UAA, #74-169-467, William Pearce Manuscript, vol. 1, 43–4 (our thanks to Jeremy Schmidt for this reference).

78 Nova Scotia, *AR 1929*, xxv.

79 Prince Edward Island, Royal Commission on Education, *Report*, 1930, 41. For typical invidious comparisons on the spending gap, see ibid., 41–2; Nova Scotia, *AR 1925–26*, xviii–xix.

80 Henry Munro, "School Finance," *JEdNS*, March 1938, 218.

81 King Report, 70. We are taking Major King at his word that the American and Canadian figures are comparable, and if push came to shove, we would probably opt for Ronald Manzer's comparisons below. King's figures, however, are consistent with a set of 1951 calculations carried out by the Canadian Teachers' Federation in *Educational Finance*, 16.

82 Manzer, *Educational Regimes*, 349 (Fig. 1), 356 (Table 1). A second calculation gives "government expenditures per student enrolled ... as a percentage of gross domestic product per capita." Again, the 1925 Canadian percentage is higher than those for the United States and Australia but lower than those for the United Kingdom and New Zealand. Ibid., 350 (Fig. 2), 356 (Table 2).

83 RCDPR, *Report*, Book 1, 126.

CHAPTER SEVEN

1 The literature on the Great Depression is extensive. For three good overviews, see Thompson with Seager, *Decades of Discord*, esp. chap. 9; Bothwell, Drummond, and English, *Canada 1900–1945*, chap. 15; Norrie, Owram, and Emery, *A History of the Canadian Economy*, chap. 17. For a comparative view of the Depression's impact on education in the United States, see Tyack, Lowe, and Hansot, *Public Schools in Hard Times*, 27–41.

2 For the national-level figures, see Tables 6.1, 6.3, and 6.4. The 1930s were a period of very sharp price deflation, but even in constant dollars the decline in spending was steep. See McCordic, *Financing Education*, 8–9.

3 RCDPR, *Report*, Book 1, 205–6.

4 The figures for each province are included in Tables C.1 and C.2, appendix C. For a province-by-province description of the overall impact of the Depression and interprovincial comparisons, see RCDPR, *Report*, Book 1, 165ff., 218ff.

5 Thompson with Seager, *Decades of Discord*, 195.

6 RCDPR, *Report*, Book 1, 237. For the impact of the Depression on Saskatchewan generally, see Waiser, *Saskatchewan*, 278ff. The impact on all three of the Prairie provinces is best illuminated by the graphics on farm income, wheat yields, and market value of wheat, *Historical Atlas*, Plate 43.

7 Ontario, Committee on the Costs of Education, *Report*, 17.

8 The city figures are from RCDPR, Report of Hearings, Manitoba, vol. 3, 1003, and were compiled by the "Citizens' Research Bureau." The provincial figures are from Table C.1, appendix C.

9 RCDPR, Submissions, vol. 1, *Manitoba's Case*, 23.

10 Goldenberg, *Municipal Finance*, 51–2.

11 Calculated from Goldenberg, *Municipal Finance*, 53. The phrase "almost exclusively" is used because London's spending went up in the years 1929–33, then dropped in 1934–36. The figures for Winnipeg given in this paragraph and the last are not inconsistent. Spending dropped sharply between 1931 and 1933, then began to rise from $1.4 million in 1933 to $1.7 million in 1937. See Manitoba, *Report of the Royal Commission on … Municipal Finances*, 117. On the desperate situation of Prairie cities during the Depression, see Artibise, "Patterns of Prairie Urban Development," 132–7.

12 RCDPR, Submissions, vol. 2, *Brief of the Rural Municipality of St James*, 7.

13 Cited in a historical retrospective, *Manitoba School Journal* 16, no. 5 (Jan. 1955): 16.

14 Ontario, Committee on the Costs of Education, *Report*, 4. In Ontario nearly all of the municipalities that went bankrupt, 1931–34, were suburban municipalities. See *Historical Atlas*, Plate 42.

15 For the figures, see Goldenberg, *Municipal Finance*, 53.

16 RCDPR, Report of Hearings, New Brunswick, vol. 1, 8637.

17 We are summarizing in these paragraphs explanations of the impact of the Depression on municipal finance offered, in various passages, by Goldenberg, *Municipal Finance*; by the RCDPR; by Perry, *Taxes, Tariffs, and Subsidies*, vol. 1, esp. 253–5.

18 For the differential impact of the Depression on different categories of individuals and industries, see RCDPR, *Report*, Book 1, 147–50. For a table showing the major categories of employment marked by "employment decline, improved employment, and those where numbers were stationary," see Marsh, *Canadians In and Out of Work*, 298. For helpful graphics on wage rates and purchasing power, see *Historical Atlas*, Plate 41. On the rising consumption of consumer goods *during* the Depression, see Bothwell, Drummond, and English, *Canada 1900–1945*, 251–2.

19 See Thompson with Seager, *Decades of Discord*, 215, 350 (Table 13a).

20 Except where otherwise noted, the figures and percentages in this paragraph are our calculations from RCDPR, appendix 1, Statements 35 and 36.

21 Kendle, *John Bracken*, 130.

22 W.E. MacPherson, "Canada," in *The Year Book of Education 1934*, 281–2.

23 *CSJ* 13, no. 5 (May 1935): 153; and 14, no. 1 (Jan. 1936): 16.

24 Clark and Post, "A Natural Outcome of Free Schools," 36.

25 Bothwell, Drummond, and English, *Canada 1900–1945*, 255.

26 Annual figures for local tax revenues and for government grants, including the peak years in the late 1920s and early 1930s, and the subsequent declines are recorded in DBS, *Elementary and Secondary Education 1942–44*, 73–4.

27 Saskatchewan, *Report, Committee on School Finance and School Grants*, 24.

28 Comparatively speaking, its cities did much better. For the figures, see Saskatchewan, *AR 1933*, 8.

29 DBS, *Annual Survey 1934*, xxv–xxvi. Similarly, see Nova Scotia, *Report of the Commission on the Larger Unit*, in Nova Scotia, *AR 1939*, lx.

30 See, for example, Saskatchewan, *AR 1933*, 8; Saskatchewan, Committee on School Administration, *Report*, 13–14; RCDPR, *The Case for Alberta*, 271.

31 *CSJ* 11, no. 10 (Oct. 1933): 351. Similarly, see the brief by the Manitoba Teachers' Society in *The School* 22, no. 2 (Oct. 1933): 165.

32 RCDPR, Report of Hearings, New Brunswick, vol. 1, F. Peacock, Director of Educational Services, New Brunswick, 8626.

33 RCDPR, Report of Hearings, Nova Scotia, vol. 1, Hon. Mr Macdonald [premier and minister of education], 4069; Nova Scotia, *Report of the Commission on the Larger Unit*, in Nova Scotia, *AR 1939*, xlix. For a description of the various types of "grants to Assisted Sections," see Nova Scotia, *AR 1933*, xix–xxiii. The most severely affected sections were "in the fishing districts and Cape Breton." Ibid., xxi.

34 RCDPR, Report of Hearings, Saskatchewan, vol. 3, President, Saskatchewan Teachers' Alliance, 1905.

35 PAA, 79.334, file 117, G.W. Cordell, Secretary, Oyen Trustees Association, to DM, Edmonton, 26 June 1933.

36 See, for example, RCDPR, *Brief, Manitoba School Trustees Association*, 10–11; Jones, "Schools and Social Disintegration," 268–72.

37 See, for example, the "vigorous protest" by the Vancouver City Council and School Board. *The School* 21, no. 7 (March 1933): 638–40.

38 Ibid., 24, no. 7 (March 1936): 631. For new school construction in Ontario, see Ontario, *AR 1935*, 15; for Nova Scotia, Nova Scotia, *AR 1939*, xxxv.

39 See, for example, *The School* 24, no. 7 (March 1936): 631 (programs in Calgary and Edmonton); Nova Scotia, *AR 1939*, xxiii–xiv.

40 See *The School* 22, no. 2 (Oct. 1933): 169 (Calgary); ibid., 173 (North Vancouver).

41 Saskatchewan, *AR 1932*, 8; for an Alberta example, see *The School* 20, no. 6 (Feb. 1932): 586.

42 Ontario, Committee on the Costs of Education, *Report*, 21.

43 *CSJ* 15, no. 4 (April 1937): 127.

44 RCDPR, *Submission by the Government of New Brunswick*, 132.

45 There were in fact plenty of school closures during the 1930s, but they appear to have been mostly due to declining population or cases where a handful of children – too few to sustain the school – were sent to nearby school districts.

46 See, for example, RCDPR, Report of Hearings, New Brunswick, vol. 1, F. Peacock, Director of Educational Services, 8627; RCDPR, *Brief, Manitoba School Trustees Association*, 6; *Manitoba Teacher* 13, no. 5 (May 1932): 3; Saskatchewan, *AR 1932*, 35 (which includes a statistical breakdown for the shift to a shorter school year in rural schools); *The School* 21, no. 5 (Jan. 1933): 458.

47 *The School* 24, no. 10 (June 1936): 836–8; *WSJ* 27, no. 7 (Sept. 1932): 287–8 (reporting a high school reorganization scheme in London, Ontario); on the elimination of vocational subjects, see, for example, *The School* 22, no. 4 (Dec. 1933): 362–3 (British Columbia); *The School* 19, no. 8 (April 1931): 804 (Alberta); *The School* 21, no. 8 (April 1933): 715 (Newcastle, NB). In Vancouver both manual training and home economics were cut back but not eliminated from the elementary schools; see *BC Teacher* 13, no. 10 (June 1934): 18–19.

48 *CSJ* 12, no. 5 (May 1934): 192. Writing for an international audience, W.E. MacPherson offered a particularly good brief overview of the impact of the Depression on facilities and programs across Canada, in *The Year Book of Education 1934*, 281–6.

49 See *The Year Book of Education 1935*, 255–6; *CSJ* 11, no. 11 (Nov. 1933): 393–4; our chapter 4.

50 *CSJ* 11, no. 1 (Jan. 1933): 36; *CSJ* 11, no. 10 (Oct. 1933): 371. Similarly, see *CSJ* 12, 6 (June 1934): 243–4 (Kitchener).

51 Manitoba, *Report of the Royal Commission on ... Municipal Finances,* 117 (Table 10).

52 This summary is based on our reading of the annual reports, Winnipeg School Board, 1930–39.

53 See the protest by the Vancouver and New Westminster Trades and Labour Council against cuts affecting "backward children and ... medical, dental and nursing services" in the schools, cited in *The School* 21, no. 8 (April 1933): 732.

54 Ontario, Committee on the Costs of Education, *Report*, 22.

55 Chalmers, *Schools of the Foothills Province*, 84–5; *The School* 19, no. 10 (June 1931): 992. For Manitoba, see *The School* 24, no. 2 (Oct. 1935): 165. By the mid-thirties, the scarcity of jobs and department of education policies restricting the numbers of entrants and/or raising entry standards reduced enrolments in nearly every province.

56 *The School* 23, no. 4 (Dec. 1934): 349. Similarly, see *Manitoba Teacher* 12, no. 9 (Nov. 1931): 1.

57 Cited in Strong-Boag, *New Day Recalled*, 45.

58 *The School* 19, no. 8 (April 1931): 796.

59 *CSJ* 15, no. 4 (April 1937): 127.

60 The 1931 Canada census reported that only about 3% of women teachers were married. It may be that the census was taken too early to reflect the influx. But other sources took note of large numbers. In 1931 in Saskatchewan, for example, there were "fully one thousand" married women teachers. *The School* 19, no. 8 (April 1931): 796. Similarly, see *Manitoba Teacher* 12, no. 1 (Jan. 1931): 2; Saskatchewan, *AR 1934*, 38; *ATAM* 11, no. 9 (May 1931): 3; *ATAM* 14, no. 2 (Oct. 1933): 13 (the estimate here was "1800 of these farmers' wives in active teaching"); Chalmers, *Schools of the Foothills Province*, 84. For the phenomenon in parts of Nova Scotia, see Nova Scotia, *AR 1933*, 41. By 1941, in any case, the census recorded that 10.5% of women teachers were married; see DBS, *Elementary and Secondary Education 1944–46*, 28–9.

61 *The School* 21, no. 9 (May 1933): 812. For sources and commentary here, see Gidney and Millar, "The Salaries of Teachers," appendix, section 17.

62 RCDPR, *The Case for Alberta*, 269.

63 RCDPR, Report of Hearings, Manitoba, vol. 1, 331–2.

64 DBS, *Annual Survey 1936*, viii. The extent of the salary reductions during the Depression varies depending on the dates selected and the categories used, so figures cited by both contemporaries and historians will vary (as do our own sources). For other comparisons, see, for example, two good graphics that trace salary declines, breaking them down more finely: for Ontario, by men, urban and rural, and women, urban and rural (Ontario, *AR 1939*, 174); for Alberta, by towns and cities, all urban, village, separate, and rural schools, and all schools (*ATAM* 20, no. 9 [May 1940]: 8). Most other provinces provide helpful tabular breakdowns: for British Columbia, for example, in the ARs (city, rural municipality, rural and assisted, though not by gender); Nova Scotia, *AR 1935–36*, xxiii (all teachers, all men, all women, and then urban and rural by gender).

65 Goldenberg, *Municipal Finance*, 54.

66 See Table 3 in Gidney and Millar, "The Salaries of Teachers."

67 RCDPR, *Report*, Book 2, 51, and Report of Hearings, Saskatchewan, vol. 3, President, Saskatchewan Teachers' Alliance, 1898.

68 UAA, John C. Charyk Fonds, box 10, Records from Mrs Dorothy Willner, Minutes and related records, Kipp School District No. 1589.

69 *The School* 24, no. 8 (April 1936): 718.

70 Our thanks to Vicki Wallace, editor of the *Southern Manitoba Review* (Cartwright) for the reference from that paper, 18 June 1931, and to Mac Watts for drawing our attention to it.

71 See Gidney and Millar, "The Salaries of Teachers," 12 and note 54. See also the summary in MacPherson, "Canada," *The Year Book of Education 1934*, 286.

72 *The School* 26, no. 9 (May 1938): 813–14. See also *The School* 21, no. 9 (May 1933): 815–16; Picot, *Teacher Training in New Brunswick*, 78–9.

73 Alberta's deputy minister of education estimated that, by 1932, 15% of the province's rural teachers were earning less than the minimum. PAA, 79.334, Dept of Education, correspondence with other provinces, Saskatchewan, 1928–34, DM Alberta to DM Saskatchewan, 22 April 1932.

74 For suspension of the legislation, see *The School* 21, no. 9 (May 1933): 815–16; for the 1938 figures (our calculations), see "A Skinning 'Em Wage for Teachers," CTF Bulletin No. 1, *ATAM* 20, no. 2 (Oct. 1939): 10.

75 PAA, 79.334, file 117, Marion Rogers, Secretary Treasurer, Alberta Teachers' Federation, to V.H. Shaw, Dept of Education, 20 March 1933. This was not an isolated case. See the general comment, *ATAM* 14, no. 6 (Feb. 1934): 2.

76 Nova Scotia, *AR 1932*, 41.

77 RCDPR, *Submission by the Government of Nova Scotia*, 132. Similarly, see Nova Scotia, *AR 1934*, 63.

78 RCDPR, *The Case for Alberta*, 270.

79 Saskatchewan, *AR 1935*, 33; *The School* 27, no. 7 (March 1939): 624.

80 Saskatchewan, Committee on School Administration, *Report*, 14.

81 *CSJ* 12, no. 10 (Oct. 1934): 358. See also Broadfoot, *Ten Lost Years*, 76; Horn, *The Dirty Thirties*, 244, 261–2; *JEdNS*, Oct. 1940, 932; Calgary School Board, Minutes, 17 April 1934 and 21 Nov. 1935; Winnipeg School Board, *AR 1933*, 19–20; *AR 1934*, 20. On Ontario, see Campbell, *Respectable Citizens*, 28, 32, 41–2, 90–5, 123–4, 167–8.

82 Broadfoot, *Ten Lost Years*, 79.

83 Ibid., 51–2.

84 *The School* 21, no. 9 (May 1933): 808; 25, no. 8 (April 1937): 712.

85 Ibid., 22, no. 2 (Oct. 1933): 167.

86 Winnipeg School Board, *AR 1933*, 18–19; Glenbow Archives, M2004, Crowsnest Pass School Division #63, Papers, Blairmore SD No. 628, School Board Minutes, 9 Sept. 1932. Similarly, see, for London, *CSJ* 14, no. 1 (Jan. 1936): 19.

87 PAA, 79.334, IODE 1930-43, file 72, LeMay to Aberhart, 13 May 1936; ibid., enclosure, DM to Mrs C.T. Woodside, 1 June 1936. Both letters were forwarded to the IODE and Woodside outlined the association's efforts and general procedures for textbook distribution in a reply of 30 Sept. 1936.

88 For a Cape Breton example, see Nova Scotia, *AR 1934*, 63.

89 Hudson, *Taxation in Rural Ontario*. For national and provincial estimates of the comparative declines in agricultural incomes, see Mackintosh, *The Economic Background of Dominion-Provincial Relations*, 124–34 (Table 13).

90 Woods, "Education in Manitoba," Part 2, 135 (italics added). In 1933 property taxes for all Alberta residents equalled about 12% of personal income,

compared to 6% in 1926 and 5% in 1955. Hanson, *Local Government in Alberta*, 101.

91 RCDPR, *Report*, Book 1, 146. "Men were forced into the fishery," R.A. Young writes of New Brunswick, "where, despite lower prices and variable catches, the number trying to make a living rose from 29,593 in 1930 to 34,797 in 1939." Young, "Maritimes Rise to War," 148. On the impact of the Depression on the Maritimes generally, see also the revisionist essay "Cutting the Pie into Smaller Pieces ... ," in Forbes, *Challenging the Regional Stereotype*, esp. 148–59.

92 RCDPR, *Report*, Book 1, 187.

93 Nova Scotia, *AR 1933*, 66.

94 RCDPR, *Report*, Book 1, 197.

95 Friesen, *The Canadian Prairies*, 388.

96 RCDPR, *Report*, Book 1, 148.

97 Marsh, *Canadians In and Out of Work*, 298 (Table 46).

98 For a graphic representation of wage and price indices, 1926–40, see *Historical Atlas*, Plate 41. For a sample of Canadian cities, see Emery and Levitt, "Cost of Living," esp. Tables 2a and 2b.

99 See Gidney and Millar, "The Salaries of Teachers," 22, 26 (Table 2), and Appendix, Table A.2.

100 Canadian Teachers' Federation, *Trends*, 23–8, 133 (Table 5 – in constant dollars). See esp. the graphic, 27.

101 Ibid., 48–9 (Tables 1.1, 1.3), 132 (Table 4). The figure for farm income is for owner/operators only; it does not include family members. Even using 1929 as a comparison is misleading for farm income, which peaked at $947 in 1928 and then experienced a sharp drop the next year. The decline in farm income we cite here may seem extreme, but other data confirm it. See DBS, *National Accounts – Income and Expenditure, 1926–1956*, 96 (Table 52). Accrued net income of farm operators from farm production fell from $636 million in 1928 to $66 million in 1933. See also the graph showing the trend in wholesale prices of agricultural products in DBS, *Handbook of Agricultural Statistics*, Part 2, Farm Income 1926–57, 23; *Historical Atlas*, Plate 43 (three Prairie provinces only).

102 Hallman, "A Thing of the Past," 119. Italics in original.

CHAPTER EIGHT

1 Alberta, *AR 1910*, appendix A, Regulations of the Dept of Education Approved in 1906, Regulation 24. This basic structure of control was fundamentally different from policy and practice in the United States, not only for the curriculum but for the centralized examination system as well. For comparative purposes, see Goldin and Katz, *The Race between Education and Technology*, 343–5.

2 Nova Scotia, *Manual of School Law, 1901*, 115ff.; *Statutes and Regulations Respecting Public and High Schools, Ontario, 1901*, 122–5.

3 British Columbia, *Manual of the School Law and Regulations, 1910*, 64–6. Authorized textbooks were routinely listed in the program of studies. See ibid., 77–9, which provides a complete list of authorized texts for elementary and high school.

4 Nova Scotia Public School Programme, *JEdNS*, April 1921, 141, 144–5.

5 Osborne, "100 Years of History Teaching," 9. But there were also variations between provinces. See the comment by G. Fred McNally about his shift from teaching in New Brunswick to Alberta, in Coutts and Walker, *G. Fred*, 60.

6 On the development of this sequential pattern, replacing the more traditional overlapping curriculum of the common and grammar schools, see Gidney and Millar, *Inventing Secondary Education*, passim.

7 The term "grade" was also common parlance elsewhere and was often in formal use in urban areas before being adopted in a province's program of studies.

8 See the review in Alberta, *AR 1937*, 15. For the program itself, see Alberta, *Programme of Studies*, 1910, standards I–V. Saskatchewan changed its elementary classification from "standard" to "grade" in 1907; see Langley, "Programmes of Study," 34.

9 See British Columbia, *Manual of School Law 1910*, 64–6; British Columbia, *AR 1922–23*, F10.

10 This continued into the 1930s. See McBeath, "Education in New Brunswick," 15. But when the DBS started collecting nation-wide statistics, it persisted in classifying the province's standards as equivalent to five grades, thus blackening its reputation as the worst province in the country for pupil retention. Under protest, New Brunswick switched in the late 1920s for reporting purposes, since the DBS "requires reports in grades – that the five standards be reduced to four, as in Nova Scotia – each standard to embrace two grades and to cover two years." See New Brunswick, *AR 1920*, lii–liii; *AR 1927*, lv.

11 See DBS, *Historical Statistical Study*, 11–13, 29.

12 Miller, *Rural Schools*, 69. Similarly, see *Proceedings, OEA, 1895*, 156–7, or the comment, three decades later, by New Brunswick's superintendent of schools in the *Educational Review*, April 1927, 171.

13 Miller, *Rural Schools*, 68. For a similar summary of the Canadian elementary curriculum, see Sandiford, *Comparative Education*, 364–5.

14 *JEdNS*, April 1921, 140.

15 This was the pattern in Ontario from early on. See, for example, *Regulations and Course of Study of the Public Schools of Ontario, 1911*, Regulation 14, note 1; Ontario, Dept of Education, *Courses of Study, Public and Separate Schools, 1926*, 8.

16 Alberta, *English and Citizenship. Part I of the Course of Studies ... Grades I to VIII Inclusive*, 1922, 4. Similarly, see the two groupings of subjects – one list examinable and the other not – in Ontario, Dept of Education, *Courses of Study, Public and Separate Schools, 1926*, 33. For another example, see Saskatchewan, *Programme of Study for Public Schools, 1929*, 5.

17 *JEdNS*, April 1921: compare 140–5 and 149–54.

18 Ontario, *Ontario Normal School Manuals – School Management*, 175. For other examples that reflect the same kind of weightings, see Alberta, *English and Citizenship*, 5; Manitoba, *School Curriculum and Teachers' Guide, Grades I–VI*, 1928, 5; Manitoba, *The Interim Programme of Studies, Grades I–VI*, 1939, 21; Mark, *Ottawa*, 78 (Ottawa, Ontario, and American cities); Nova Scotia, *Manual of School Law, 1901*, Regulation 155; Fleming, *The Principal's Office*, vol. 1, chap. 4, 252–3 (Figs. 2 and 3).

19 British Columbia, Dept of Education, *Programme of Studies for the Junior High Schools*, 1936, 20–1.

20 Compare *Programme of Studies for the Elementary Schools of Manitoba, July 1912* and the near-identical *Programme of Studies for the Schools of Manitoba, July 1, 1920* with Manitoba, *School Curriculum and Teachers' Guide, Grades I–VI*, 1928. The *Programme of Studies for the Schools of Manitoba, 1930–31, Grades VII to VIII* took another 80 pages. Similarly, for Nova Scotia, see "Report of the Committee on Studies," covering only grades I–VI, which runs to several hundred pages, in *JEdNS*, March–May 1933, and became the basis for the first major revision of the elementary curriculum since the turn of the century.

21 See, for example, Miller, *Rural Schools*, 69–70, 77.

22 See DBS, *Annual Survey 1936*, xl.

23 Beginning in 1919, Winnipeg gradually converted its entire system to a 6-3-3 pattern. Other city systems – Saint John, Ottawa, Brandon, Calgary, and Vancouver, for example – also introduced "intermediate schools" or "junior high schools" during the 1920s and 1930s, usually before it became *de rigueur* in their provincial programs of studies.

24 It is impossible to provide a definitive national description of what was actually taught because several departments of education either didn't collect or didn't publish grade-by-grade enrolment lists for elementary subjects. See the complaint registered on this score by the DBS, *Annual Survey 1930*, xvi. Moreover, some subjects were compulsory in some provinces and optional in others (music, physical training, and agriculture are examples). But our summary here of the situation *c.* 1930 is drawn from New Brunswick, *AR 1929–30*, 6ff. (Table 3); Ontario, *AR 1931*, 105 (Table 1 [b]); DBS, *Annual Survey 1930*, xvi (Saskatchewan). See also British Columbia, *AR 1925–26*, Part 2, R20ff.; this was the last year the province published elementary enrolments by subject. We take up the actual extent of manual training and domestic science instruction in the elementary schools in chapter 10.

25 This was a period when pedagogical theory was being radically transformed and a multitude of conflicting voices could be heard. In the paragraphs that follow, however, we are trying to capture only the mainstream opinion reflected in the authoritative voices shaping provincial policies and prescriptions. For descriptions of actual classroom routines and practices, see Sutherland, *Growing Up*, chap. 9, and chap. 11 in this volume, "The Teacher's Work." (A slightly different version of Sutherland's essay, first published in 1986, is available in *Children, Teachers, and Schools*, 1st edn, ed. Barman, Sutherland, and Wilson, and 2d edn, ed. Barman and Gleason.)

26 We are referring here more particularly to the elementary school; they lingered longer at the secondary and college levels. For an explanation of these nineteenth-century doctrines in the Canadian context, see Gidney and Millar, *Inventing Secondary Education*, 234ff. We do not think that Sutherland's references to mental discipline, disciplinary formalism, or faculty psychology actually explain the theories or prescriptions underpinning the twentieth-century practices he describes in his otherwise indispensable and finely honed essay cited in note 25 above.

27 Cited in *The School* 24, no. 1 (Sept. 1935): 27.

28 Saskatchewan, Dept of Education, *Programme of Studies for Public Schools, 1929*, 8.

29 Ontario Teachers' Manual, *Composition and Spelling*, "Spelling," 2.

30 *JEdNS*, April 1921, 136.

31 Mark, *Ottawa*, 81. Similarly, see *Manitoba Teacher* 12, no. 6 (June 1931): 24.

32 *JEdNS*, April 1921, 135.

33 Saskatchewan, *Programme of Studies for Public Schools 1929*, 7.

34 The *Third Book* was authorized in Ontario from 1925 to 1935. In its poetry and prose selections it is typical of the entire series.

35 Ontario, *Principles of Method*, 102–3. The principles of habit formation are explained at length in chapter 8 and briefly reiterated on 102.

36 Ibid., 139.

37 Ontario, *Ontario Normal School Manuals – School Management*, 57, 75.

38 Manitoba, *Programme of Studies for the Elementary Schools of Manitoba, July 1912*, 3. See also *Programme of Studies for the Schools of Manitoba, July 1, 1920*, where the emphasis is, if anything, even stronger. Similarly, see Mark, *Ottawa*, 87, citing the Ontario program on oral and written composition.

39 Saskatchewan, *Programme of Studies 1929*, 8.

40 Mark, *Ottawa*, 93.

41 *JEdNS*, April 1921, 134.

42 Ibid., 136–7. Similarly, see *The School* 31, no. 7 (March 1943): 583; 32, no. 3 (Nov. 1943): 252.

43 Stanley A. Watson, "Arithmetic: Junior Third to Senior Fourth (Grades V–VIII)," *The School* 24, no. 1 (Sept. 1935): 27. Similarly, see Saskatchewan,

Programme of Studies 1929, 17; *The School* 31, no. 7 (March 1943): 583; 32, no. 3 (Nov. 1943): 252; Ontario, *Ontario Normal School Manuals – School Management*, 259–60.

44　New Brunswick, AR *1915–16*, l–li.

45　Saskatchewan, *Programme of Studies 1929*, 16–17. Similarly, see "General Prescriptions," *JEdNS*, April 1921, 135.

46　Ontario, *Principles of Method*, 138, 142.

47　Ontario Teachers' Manual, *Composition and Spelling*, "Composition," 31–2.

48　Ontario, *Ontario Normal School Manuals – School Management*, 33, 41.

49　von Heyking, *Creating Citizens*, 13.

50　Ontario, *Principles of Method*, 118–19. On the central role of the textbook, see also von Heyking, "Shaping an Education," 117–24.

51　See, for example, "General Prescriptions," *JEdNS*, April 1921, 137.

52　These are often to be found in the "teachers' helps" department of the various professional magazines. See, for example, "June Tests, Spelling and Arithmetic, Grades I–IV," *Manitoba Teacher* 12, no. 6 (June 1931); "Outline for October," *ATAM* 10, no. 2 (Oct. 1929): 20–1; "Outline for February" [from Calgary School Board], *ATAM* 14, no. 5 (Jan. 1932): 13–20.

53　See, for example, *The School* 17, no. 2 (Oct. 1928): 157ff.; 17, no. 3 (Nov. 1928): 257ff.; 17, no. 10 (June 1929): 978ff.; 20, no. 1 (Sept. 1931): 37ff. For a slightly different format, see "Grammar for Grades VII and VIII," *The School* 24, no. 7 (March 1936): 586–8.

54　Ontario, *Ontario Normal School Manuals – School Management*, 55–6.

55　Ibid., 28. Similarly, see J. Elgin Tom, "In Graded Schools can More Efficient Work be done with Two Classes in a Room than with One?," *Proceedings, OEA, 1903*, 386–7.

56　Ontario, *Principles of Method*, 126.

57　Nova Scotia, *Manual of School Law, 1901*, s. 105; *Statutes and Regulations Respecting Public and High Schools, Ontario, 1901*, s. 80 (1) of Act Respecting Public Schools. This clause was still in Nova Scotia's school law as late as 1939, and remained in the Ontario legislation throughout the twentieth century with the single addition of "Judeo-Christian morality."

58　New Brunswick, AR *1928–29*, Regulation 23, xiv.

59　See Alberta, *Programme of Studies, 1910, Standards I–VI*, 19; Saskatchewan, "Programme of Studies for Saskatchewan Schools," AR *1906*, 71.

60　See "Courses of Study and Examinations," in Prince Edward Island, AR *1925–26*, 6c–21c. The topics in grade II, for example, were very similar to those listed for Manitoba in Figure 8.1.

61　If it were true, in any case, that the job of the school was primarily moral training at the expense of academic goals, one would expect to find the very extensive contemporary literature on teacher training focusing on moral rather than academic qualities. But the reverse is the case. Moral qualities in teachers were certainly never discounted, but the focus of the literature is on improving teachers' academic knowledge and their skills in teaching it. For two examples of our point here, see D.J. Goggin, "Some Problems in the Training of Teachers," in *Proceedings, OEA, 1903*, 352–8; J.H. Putman, "Reorganization of Professional Schools," in *Proceedings, OEA, 1904*, 282–94.

62 *JEdNS*, Apr. 1921, 139. While virtue could always exist without learning, the view that mental culture contributed to or enhanced the virtuous life was a conventional and long-standing view. See the quotation from Cicero in *The School* 3, no. 2 (Oct. 1914): 73. For turn-of-the-century opinion on this point, see the articles by T.B. Kilpatrick and E.M. Keirstead in *Proceedings, OEA, 1906*, 272–84.

63 von Heyking, *Creating Citizens*, 16. See also Sheehan, "Indoctrination," 222–33.

64 See Nova Scotia, *Manual of School Law, 1901*, 61, Regulations 21 and 22.

65 *Statutes and Regulations, Public and High Schools, Ontario, 1901*, 119, Regulation 119. The authorized prayer is printed on p. 138. There was a "conscience clause" for teachers included in the regulation. More generally on Ontario see Gidney and Millar, "The Christian Recessional," 275–93.

66 PAA, 79.334, Dept of Education Correspondence, Religious Instruction in Schools, file 192, DM to Mr Howard Murray, 10 Jan. 1922. For a later survey that confirms his opinion, see PAA, 79.334, file 664, Memorandum by Chief Inspector of Schools, "Religious Instruction in Schools." For practices in British Columbia, see Putman-Weir Report, 53–6; Sutherland, *Growing Up*, 191. For the law respecting local option, see, for example, Manitoba, *The Public School Act. Being Chap. 165 of the Revised Statutes of Manitoba, 1913. With all Amendments ... 1925*, ss. 8, 247, 248; Nova Scotia, *Manual of School Law, 1901*, 61, Regulations 21 and 22. See also British Columbia, *Manual of School Law 1910*, 6, s. 3. Despite the fact that British Columbia's schools were by law "strictly secular," the 1910 "Regulations respecting School Libraries" began with the injunction that "no book hostile to the Christian Religion ... shall be permitted in the School Library." Ibid., 91.

67 See *Ontario Readers, Second Book* or *Third Book*, for examples of hymns and Bible extracts to be taught as literature (e.g., in the *Second Book* [*c.* 1923], "O Little Town of Bethlehem," 88–9; "The Story of Joseph," 74–8; "The Good Samaritan," 65–6).

68 See, for example, London Board of Education, *AR 1922*, 40.

69 Osborne, "100 Years of History Teaching," 9. See also an indispensable contribution by Osborne that covers the entire century, "Public Schooling and Citizenship Education," 8–37.

70 Stanley, "White Supremacy," 42.

71 James L. Hughes in *Proceedings, OEA, 1908*, 124.

72 See, for example, "The Use and Salutation of School Flags" in New Brunswick, *AR 1908–9*, xlviii–xlix; *Regulations and Course of Study of the Public*

Schools of Ontario, 1911, Regulation 6, 6; Manitoba, *The Public School Act ... 1925*, s. 156 (l).

73 Stamp, "Empire Day," 100–15. Between 1899 and 1920 the *Educational Review* (New Brunswick) devoted huge portions of its April or May issues to outlines of Empire Day programs and appropriate passages to be read or sung. In British Columbia, Empire Day was an official school holiday, and on the day before, the schools were ordered to devote "the lessons, recitations and other exercises" to celebrating it. See British Columbia, *Manual of School Law 1910*, 49; *1919*, 43–4; *1929*, 89.

74 Alberta, AR *1910*, appendix A, Regulations of the Dept of Education Approved in 1906, Regulation 14.

75 Morton, "The Cadet Movement," 56–68. Though limited to Ontario, a helpful account of most of the subjects raised in this section is offered by Moss, *Manliness and Militarism*, esp. chap. 5.

76 The best account of the schools' response to the Great War is Sheehan, "World War I and Provincial Educational Policy," 253–79. A fine study that regretfully came to our notice too late to influence our analysis is Fisher, *Boys and Girls*, esp. chaps 2 and 3.

77 Stanley, "White Supremacy," 39–56.

78 Bercuson, "Regionalism and 'Unlimited Identity,'" 124–5.

79 See, for example, "Agricultural Education in the Primary Schools," in Seath, *Education for Industrial Purposes*, 313; Peabody, *School Days*, chap. 10 ("School Gardens").

80 Osborne, "Public Schooling and Citizenship Education," 26.

81 Sutherland, *Growing Up*, 223. We say "only one" because Sutherland emphasizes not only that other adults and institutions were important to the formation of this culture but also that there were semi-autonomous sites of learning like the playground and the street. See 222–3 and, more generally, 220ff. On the range of elementary school extracurricular activities in one part of northeastern Ontario, see Noel, *Family and Community Life*, 149–54.

82 *JEdNS*, May 1931, 69.

83 Manitoba, *School Curriculum and Teachers' Guide ... 1928*, 225–6, 231–2. Similarly, see Alberta, *English and Citizenship ... 1922*, 128ff. Note under "Self-government" "the application of Christian principles and the practise of the Golden Rule" (129) and the values to be inculcated (e.g., 131–5). A 1929 revision under the same title is even more explicit in specifying the values to be taught (128–31). The same sort of shift took place in Saskatchewan, where the traditional reference to instruction in morals and manners was abandoned in the program revision of 1921. See Langley, "Programmes of Study," 44.

84 *CSJ* 6, no. 1 (Jan. 1928): 7.

85 *BC Teacher* 16 (Nov. 1936): 122. Similarly, see British Columbia, *Programme of Studies for the Junior High Schools ... 1936*, "Education for Moral Character,"

12. For Saskatchewan, see the article by Elmer W. Reid citing that province's revised program, in *BC Teacher* 14, no. 3 (Nov. 1934): 13.

86　On the context, see PAA, 79.334, box 16, file 221, Mrs M. French to Perrin Baker, Minister of Education, Alberta, 17 April 1926. For examples, see *Manitoba Teacher* 9, no. 5 (May 1928): 15; 10, no. 4 (April 1929): 17; *WSJ* 21, no. 4 (April 1926): 741–2; *ATAM* 15, no. 6 (Feb. 1935): 19–21; *BC Teacher* 5, no. 1 (Sept. 1925): 18–21; 6, no. 8 (April 1927): 2–3.

87　See Sheehan, "The Junior Red Cross Movement," 66–86. For an instructive sampling of the emphases, causes espoused, and pedagogical methods adopted, see any series of issues during the interwar years of the movement's monthly magazine, the *Canadian Junior Red Cross Magazine*. On the sheer volume and variety of health propaganda, see the three cumulative "health indexes" published in March, April, and May 1934.

88　On the remarkably elaborate observances proposed by the Alberta Dept of Education for each school on the occasion of the coronation, see *ATAM* 17, no. 8 (April 1937): 29–32. On the continuing strength of the imperial tie during the interwar years, see "Introduction," in Buckner, *Canada and the End of Empire*, 4–5. By the 1930s, in some provinces, Empire Day had morphed into Victoria Day but the imperial emphasis remained. See British . Columbia, *Manual of School Law, 1937*, 115. Similarly, the Diamond Jubilee of Confederation was formally celebrated in several provinces by special programs in the schools. See, for example, British Columbia, Dept of Education, *Diamond Jubilee of Confederation, 1867–1927: Schools Celebration*. The pamphlet included the words to *O Canada* and *The Maple Leaf Forever* but also *Rule Britannia* and *God Save the King*. For a revisionist piece reflecting on the "imperialist counter-offensive" of the 1920s and the nationalist-imperialist tensions, see Cupido, "The Puerilities of the National Complex," 81–110.

89　The most recent and best account of patriotism and citizenship in the schools is von Heyking, *Creating Citizens*, chaps 1 and 2. She is especially helpful on the changing emphases and their limits during the interwar years. However, readers should be aware that the book is a much pared-down version of her doctoral thesis and, for our entire section on the moral content of the curriculum, her thesis (which is broader than the title might suggest) offers a rich array of material not available in her book. See von Heyking, "Shaping an Education," chaps 1–4.

90　On the three-year high school, see, for example, Nova Scotia, *Manual of School Law, 1901*, Regulation 164, "Special Prescriptions for High Schools"; S.J. Willis, "The Public School System of British Columbia," *The School* 16, no. 5 (Jan. 1928): 503; DBS, "Recent Trends in Education in the Prairie Provinces," 1; Alberta, *AR 1926*, 17; A.H. Ball, "An Outline of Education in Saskatchewan," *The School* 15, no. 6 (Feb. 1927): 607. For continuing practices even after the introduction of four-year programs, see Wormsbecker, "Secondary Education in Vancouver," 242–3; PAA, 79.334, Alberta Dept of Education, Interprovincial Correspondence, box 2, file 14, H.C. Newland to Director, Educational and Vocational Guidance, Dept of Education, Victoria, BC, 26 Oct. 1944. In Manitoba and the Maritime provinces the three-year high school continued to be the norm well beyond the interwar years. British Columbia added its own grade XIII in the 1930s and began requiring it for normal school admission in 1937. See DBS, *Annual Survey 1936*, xxxiv.

91 The territorial program is given in full in Walker, "Public Secondary Education in Alberta," 279 (Table 11). For the minor revisions in Alberta in 1912, see ibid., 142. For the secondary program in Saskatchewan, see its *AR 1911*, 101–8. For the early Ontario program, see Pullen, "Secondary School Curriculum Change," 70–80. For Nova Scotia, see *Manual of School Law, 1901*, 128–31. For Manitoba, see *Programme of Studies for the Secondary Schools of Manitoba, 1 July 1912*. For an interesting comparison of the programs in Ontario, Saskatchewan, and British Columbia, see Sandiford, *Comparative Education*, 405–9.

92 For the Ontario commercial program, see *Statutes and Regulations, Public and High Schools, Ontario, 1901*, 137–8. For British Columbia, see *Manual of School Law 1910*, 74–6. The Alberta standards of 1910 did not list a commercial program, but compare Walker, "Public Secondary Education in Alberta," 279–81. Saskatchewan had a commercial course from at least 1908, along with a general course, teachers' course, university course, and agricultural course, though at that point the commercial and agricultural courses were rarely offered. See Saskatchewan, *AR 1908*, 9.

93 By 1917, for example, Ontario had seven different courses in its high school program of studies: matriculation, normal school, household science, agriculture, commercial, manual training, and middle school art. See Sandiford, *Comparative Education*, 405. Most of these, however, were "paper programs" with minuscule enrolments or none at all, since most secondary schools didn't offer them. We pursue this point further in chapter 10.

94 See Green, "Development of the Curriculum," 109–13. A similar arrangement was introduced in Manitoba – four programs, including "Normal Entrance," "Matriculation," "Commercial," and "High School Leaving." The last was the least prescriptive; only English and history were required, "and the student may choose the remainder of his subjects from those which the School is able to offer." *Programme of Studies for the Schools of Manitoba, 1930–31, Grades VII–XIII*, 51. For revisions in other provinces, see *WSJ* 17, no. 5 (May 1922): 198–9; Walker, "Public Secondary Education in Alberta," 148–9 and Table 14; Pullen, "Secondary School Curriculum Change," 81–5; Ontario, *Interim Report of the Committee on High School Education*. In contrast to the major rethinking of the curriculum for grades I–IX, Nova Scotia made only modest

revisions during the 1930s in its high school program; see *JEdNS*, March 1937, 146–9.

95 Federal funding began with the federal Technical Education Act of 1919. On the time allocations, see Dyde, *Public Secondary Education*, 59. The 50% vocational content rule was also met by allowing some academic subjects, such as math or science, to be included in the count for those students registered in a vocational program. Generally, see Fluxgold, *Federal Financial Support*, chap. 1.

96 The larger technical schools, however, also tended to offer a matriculation program that allowed pupils a broader range of academic subjects, at least enough to qualify for science or engineering programs in the universities.

97 See Ontario, Dept of Education, *Recommendations and Regulations ... Vocational Schools*, 9–11, 34–9. We are referring here to full-time day school programs only.

98 See, for example, Ontario, *AR 1930*, 352–60. For a full description and time-table examples, see Dyde, *Public Secondary Education*, 204–8. For the program at the Calgary Technical High School, see *ATAM* 10, no. 6 (Feb. 1930): 15. On Vancouver, see Wormsbecker, "Secondary Education in Vancouver," 268–70. On vocational training for girls (as opposed to courses emphasizing home-making only), see Heap, "Schooling Women for Home or Work," 195–243.

99 On the availability of commercial training, see John E. Casson, "The Advance of Commercial Education in Canada," *The School* 26, no. 10 (June 1938): 884–7. For the sheer range of vocational options available, school by school, in Ontario, see the tables in Ontario, *AR 1920*, 258–61; *AR 1925*, 218–23; *AR 1930*, 352–61. For a New Brunswick description, see "18th Annual Report of the New Brunswick Vocational Education Board," in New Brunswick, *AR 1935–36*, 299ff. See also Weeks, "Business Education in British Columbia."

100 Comacchio, *Dominion of Youth*, 112–25. See also Noel, *Family and Community Life*, 165–71.

101 For one example, see the extensive discussion in *A History of the Ottawa Collegiate Institute*, chaps 6 and 7. Similarly, see *Owen Sound Collegiate and Vocational Institute*, chapters covering the 1890s through 1920.

102 For this pattern in Saskatchewan, see Dyde, *Public Secondary Education*, 114. For Alberta, see *ATAM* 9, no. 3 (Nov. 1928): 1–3. In our own exploration of the qualifications of applicants to the professional schools at the University of Toronto, we found large numbers of Ontario students taking more than the minimum number of years to complete the junior or senior matriculation requirements; see Millar, Heap, and Gidney, "Degrees of Difference," 173–5; Millar and Gidney, "Medettes," 219–20; Millar, "Jewish Medical Students," 117.

103 See, for example, PAA, 79.334, box 2, Interprovincial Correspondence, DM, Alberta, to A.S. McFarlane, Chief Superintendent of Education, Fredericton,

NB, 12 Dec. 1933; *The School* 23, no. 10 (June 1935): 904–5 (Saskatchewan); 25, no. 10 (June 1937): 903 (British Columbia).

104 DBS, "Recent Trends in Education in the Prairie Provinces," 1.

105 See, for example, the opposition in British Columbia: Gordon, "Secondary Education in Rural British Columbia," 72; *BC Teacher* 10, no. 10 (June 1931) [*sic*: 10, no. 9 (May 1931)]: 41; 12, no. 5 (Jan. 1933): 35. For a defence of the four-year program and an explanation of why it represented an improvement, see "Editorial," *BC Teacher* 9, no. 7 (March 1930): 3–7.

106 For Alberta and Manitoba, see PAA, 79.334, Interprovincial Correspondence, box 1, file 6, Andrew Moore [high school inspector, Manitoba] to G.F. McNally, 16 Dec. 1943, and H.C. Newland (replying for McNally) to Moore, 7 Jan. 1944. In the Maritimes, grade XI remained the norm until at least mid-century. Students in Manitoba or the Maritimes might, however, take four years to complete the three-year program.

107 See citations in note 105 above and *The School* 25, no. 10 (June 1937): 903.

108 Axelrod, *Making a Middle Class*, 45. The University of Saskatchewan followed suit in 1934 in requiring senior matriculation for entrance (albeit after four years of high school); the University of Alberta in 1937. Ibid., 46, 204n31.

CHAPTER NINE

1 Ontario, *Ontario Normal School Manuals – School Management*, 286–7.

2 DBS, *Historical Statistical Survey*, 29–30. In British Columbia it was provincial policy throughout the period that promotion examinations below grade IV "shall be entirely oral," but in all classes from grade I through VII, "the judgement of the teachers who have respectively taught the pupils during the term shall chiefly determine the promotion list." See British Columbia, *Manual of School Law 1910*, 67; *1932*, 111; *1937*, 128.

3 *Manitoba Teacher* 7, no. 1 (June 1926): 13.

4 Anderson, "Moncton," Part 2, chap. 5 (n.p.).

5 Contemporary observers often asserted that in the elementary grades, promotions were primarily the responsibility of the local school. See DBS, *Historical Statistical Survey*, 19–20; Dyde, *Public Secondary Education*, 85; *The School* 16, no. 10 (June 1928): 28. But this is clearly misleading. The reports of inspectors, and the law and regulations, make it clear that while, *in the first instance*, promotion decisions probably did lie with teachers and principals, the inspectorate was not only the final authority but was actively engaged in approving, reviewing, and setting standards for promotion. For one example of the inspector's authority in this respect, see Alberta, *AR 1910*, appendix A, Regulations of the Dept of Education Approved in 1906, Regulation 19: "All promotions shall be made by the teacher subject to the approval of the

inspector." Similarly, see Saskatchewan, AR 1907, 57, Regulations of the Dept of Education, 6 (5).

6 "In the rural schools it is customary for the inspector to set uniform examination papers for the promotion of pupils in his inspectorate." Ontario, *Ontario Normal School Manuals – School Management*, 147. Similarly, see Saskatchewan, AR 1927, 75; Ontario, AR 1928, Report of the Chief Inspector, 12; Nova Scotia, AR 1933, 38.

7 Winnipeg School Board, AR 1934, 13–14. A similar method was in use a decade earlier; see ibid., AR 1924, 8. For another example, see Manitoba, AR 1924–25, Report, Superintendent of Brandon Schools, 53.

8 London Board of Education, AR for 1919 and 1920, 7. For the procedures at the turn of the century in various urban communities in New Brunswick, see *Educational Review*, Jan. 1899, 161–2.

9 Foght, *Saskatchewan*, 157.

10 On the origins and development of the HSEE in Ontario, see Gidney and Millar, *Inventing Secondary Education*, chaps 7–15. On the rise of, and the presuppositions underlying, the examination system generally, see Gidney and Millar, "Schooling and the Idea of Merit," 109–30. That article includes a broad introduction and a range of references to the British context for Canadian developments.

11 The exception was Prince Edward Island, where the examination was held at the end of grade x for entrance to Prince of Wales College.

12 See Dyde, *Public Secondary Education*, 87.

13 On the restrictions in Ontario and Nova Scotia, see Ontario, Dept of Education, *Courses of Study, Public and Separate Schools*, 1926, Regulations 1 (c) and 8, pp. 33–4; *The School* 24, no. 1 (Sept. 1935): 74. In Saskatchewan, pupils had the legal right to write if they wished. Saskatchewan, AR 1910, 74. In British Columbia "it was the practice of teachers to hold back all but those students who stood a good chance of passing." Johnson, *Public Education in British Columbia*, 69.

14 On the influence fees exercised over numbers who might sit the examination, see *Proceedings, OEA, 1897*, 52. According to the Bank of Canada inflation calculator, the $5 fee to sit the HSEE in 1914 was the equivalent of $102.20 in 2011 dollars; $2 in 1925 equalled $26.80 in 2011 dollars. Thus these fees were not trivial. For representative exam fee schedules, see *Statutes and Regulations, Public and High Schools, Ontario, 1901*, 109; Saskatchewan, AR 1922, 62; WSJ 18, no. 2 (Feb. 1923): 489; ATAM 6, no. 11 (April 1926): 11; *Manitoba Teacher* 10, no. 3 (March 1929): 6; *The School* 21, no. 7 (March 1933): 554 (Ontario); RCDPR, *Brief Presented by the Canadian Teachers' Federation*, 9. From at least the turn of the century, Nova Scotia charged fees only for supplemental examinations. Nova Scotia, *Manual of School Law, 1901*, 89; JEdNS, April 1920, 106, Regulations 95 (b) and 105. With the spread of

the recommendation system, provinces either abolished the examination fee altogether or imposed it only on those actually writing the examination. Even in the interwar years, high school examination fees tended to be substantially higher than those for the HSEE.

15 See, for example, Alberta, *AR 1921*, 31; *AR 1926*, 17; Charyk, *The Little White Schoolhouse*, 287.

16 The number enrolled in grade VIII was always considerably larger than the number of candidates for the HSEE.

17 For the arrangements in Alberta, see Dyde, *Public Secondary Education*, 86, 118; *ATAM* 5, no. 6 (Nov. 1924).

18 Nova Scotia, *Manual of School Law*, 1901, 81.

19 On the constitution of the local examining boards, see *Statutes and Regulations respecting Public and High Schools, Ontario, 1901*, 101–2. On departmental review, see *The School* 4, no. 5 (Jan. 1916): 433–4. The review by the high school inspectors had been instituted by John Seath early in the century and continued long after; see *The School* 8, no. 10 (June 1930): 88.

20 Charyk, *Syrup Pails and Gopher Tails*, 132.

21 Ibid., 132–5. For Nova Scotia's intimidating set of rules, see Nova Scotia, *Manual of School Law, 1901*, 90–2.

22 Saskatchewan, *AR 1930*, 65 (figures for 1926 through 1930; both the number of papers and costs increased each year).

23 Nova Scotia, *Manual of School Law*, 1901, 93. "General knowledge" drew on a grouping of subjects and dealt with aspects of Nova Scotia's flora and fauna, geology, and the course in hygiene. See *JEdNS*, April 1920, 123.

24 Ontario, Dept of Education, *Examination Papers, 1901. High School Entrance.* The number of papers, however, dwindled over the years. By 1920, five or six were more common, and by 1940 there were only four. See *The School* 28, no. 8 (April 1940), 740 and examination schedule inside front cover.

25 *WSJ* 8, no. 4 (June 1913): inside front cover, "Entrance Timetable."

26 See British Columbia, *Manual of School Law 1910*, 184; British Columbia, *AR 1926*, R135–42.

27 Since the examinations were printed and widely distributed, copies survive in various places and even turn up, in booklet form, in used bookstores. In some cases they were printed in the departmental *AR*s. Complete sets are often preserved in provincial archives or university libraries. There is, for example, a nearly complete run of all departmental examinations – high school entrance, annual high school, and matriculation examinations alike – in the Faculty of Education library at the University of Manitoba.

28 Saskatchewan, *AR 1910*, 93, 96, 100–1.

29 British Columbia, *AR 1925–26*, R135–7.

30 Manitoba, Dept of Education, *Entrance Examination 1922: History.*

31 Ontario, Dept of Education, *Entrance Examination 1901. Reading.*

32 The map is from British Columbia, *AR 1928–29*, appendix B, R137. The question is printed on R136. The map is reproduced as distributed to thousands of pupils writing the HSEE; one wonders how many found it hard to read or missed identifications because of that.

33 The marks required for a pass varied over the years. For brief descriptions on this point, see Phillips, *Education in Canada*, 518; Haines, "The Secondary School," 8.

34 See, for example, *Statutes and Regulations for Public and High Schools, Ontario, 1901*, 102, Regulation 26.

35 Ontario, Dept of Education, *Courses of Study, Public and Separate Schools, 1926*, 34.

36 As Neil Sutherland has pointed out, by the early twentieth century the entrance certificate and similar high school certificates were increasingly used as proof of accomplishment for entry to various jobs that didn't formally require them; see Calam, *Alex Lord's BC*, 170n4. Similarly, see the comment by Ontario's minister of education, *Proceedings, OEA, 1908*, 106.

37 The most significant difference between the matriculation and high school entrance examinations lay in university involvement. Because the universities had a stake in matriculation standards, they were usually participants in setting and marking the examinations through joint university-departmental committees. For the organization of the high school matriculation examination, see, for example, Fleming, *Ontario's Educative Society*, vol. 5, 292–4; *The School* 8, no. 5 (Jan. 1920): 237–8; *WSJ* 23, no. 5 (May 1928): 169; Dyde, *Public Secondary Education*, 117–18; Johnson, *Public Education in British Columbia*, 159. See also the historical introduction in R.W. Kane, "The Atlantic Provinces Examining Board," *Canadian Education* 13, no. 2 (March 1958): 25–9.

38 The number of papers or subjects a senior student might write depended on normal school entrance requirements or the matriculation requirements of particular universities, both of which might vary by province, by university, and over time. For two matriculation standards, see *The School* 10, no. 7 (March 1922): 426–8 (the Ontario matriculation requirements at this point); *Programme of Studies for the Schools of Manitoba ... July 1, 1920*, 30–5. The time allowed for examinations is nearly always printed at the top of each subject paper. For a typical Ontario examination schedule, see *The School* 5, no. 9 (May 1917): 586–90; *The School* 25, no. 7 (March 1937): 643–4. Similarly, see British Columbia, *AR 1925–26*, appendix B, R143ff; *JEdNS*, Sept. 1932, 32–53. For marking standards and analyses of the quality of the answer papers, see [Ontario], "Composition Standards in the Middle School," *The School* 22, no. 4 (Dec. 1933): 323–33, and the extensive commentary by the "Common Examining Board for the Maritimes and Newfoundland," *JEdNS*, Sept. 1932, 44ff.

39 *Proceedings, OEA, 1929*, 37. For another description of the process, Regina
   in this case, see *The School* 21, no. 1 (Sept. 1932): 72. That year, with only
   grade XI and XII papers to be marked centrally, the Saskatchewan department employed 235 sub-examiners to mark 76,991 answer papers. Similarly,
   see, for Alberta, ibid., 84. In 1932 the "Common Examining Board for
   the Maritime Provinces" (conducting examinations for Nova Scotia and
   Newfoundland only) read "over 34,000 answer papers." *JEdNS*, Dec. 1932, 23.

40 Beginning in the second decade of the century, the effective enforcement of
   the compulsory attendance laws in most provinces kept nearly all children
   in school until they were 14 or 15 – including that small minority who would
   never reach the senior elementary grades no matter how often they repeated
   lower grades. As we suggested in chapter 3, in the larger towns and cities
   these children were increasingly shunted into "pre-vocational," "opportunity,"
   or "auxiliary" classes (or into entirely separate buildings) and offered an
   alternative to the regular program of studies that incorporated, along with a
   much modified program of academic work, a heavy dose of manual activities.
   Outside of the large urban centres such children were most likely to be left to
   vegetate at the back of the class or, if local authorities were prepared to turn
   a blind eye, allowed to leave school early. Although the number of children
   actually segregated in special classes was very modest, there is an enormous
   literature on the subject in the educational press as well as in the medical
   and public health journals. For one contemporary sampling of ideas and
   programs, see Sinclair, *Backward and Brilliant Children*. Two recent articles that
   contain many references to the Canadian and international literature are
   Clarke, "Sacred Daemons," 61–89; Thomson, "Josephine Dauphinee," 51–73.
   See also Ellis, "Backward and Brilliant Children."

41 UAA, John C. Charyk Fonds, 90-43-83, box 10, Rosalie M. Zenner.

42 See Sinclair, *Backward and Brilliant Children*, 71; Saskatchewan, *Programme of
   Study for Public Schools, 1929*, 5. See also Rudy Wiebe's experience, in Wiebe,
   Of This Earth, 215.

43 One report card from a one-room Alberta school illustrates the process
   (see Fig. 11.4). The young girl began grade I in September 1931, received
   excellent marks each month, and was promoted to grade II in April. By the
   end of June she was "not yet ready for grade III" but would, presumably, have
   been given that promotion by Christmas 1932, or even earlier. Our thanks to
   Jeremy Schmidt for lending us this document.

44 See, for example, DBS, *Historical Statistical Survey*, 29–31; Ontario, *Ontario
   Normal School Manuals – School Management*, 150–3. On double promotions
   in Winnipeg schools, see Manitoba, *AR 1919–20*, 105–6; Winnipeg School
   Board, *AR 1937*, 9. Similarly, see London Board of Education, *AR 1919 and
   1920*, 13; G.F. McNally, "Education in Alberta," *BC Teacher* 10, no. 8 (April
   1931): 22; *Educational Review*, Aug.–Sept. 1924, 7 (Moncton). In British

Columbia, highly flexible promotion procedures for grades I through VII were provincial policy across the period; see British Columbia, *Manual of School Law 1910*, 67; *1937*, 128. Similarly, see Saskatchewan, *Programme of Study for Public Schools, 1929*, 5. While critical voices were already beginning to be heard early in the century, most schoolmen remained supportive of acceleration for the ablest pupils, indeed saw it as the best antidote to the rigidities of the urban graded school. See, for example, British Columbia, AR *1923–24*, T27; Ontario, *AR 1926*, 9; Winnipeg School Board, *AR 1924*, 8–9; *WSJ* 31, no. 6 (June 1936): 179–80. Canadians would make the shift to social promotion much later than Americans, but the best account of changing attitudes, policies, and practice on this subject is Angus, Mirel, and Vinovskis, "Age Stratification in Schooling," 211–36.

45 Van Kleek, *The Way It Was*, 2, 10.

46 *Proceedings, OEA, 1914*, 214.

47 Ontario, *Ontario Normal School Manuals – School Management*, 286.

48 See B.L. Newcombe and M.V. Marshall, "A Study in School Careers," *JEdNS*, Sept. 1944, 589–93. This study of the community of Canning covered the years 1925 through the early 1940s. In 1924 the estimate for Fredericton was that 43% of all children had failed a grade at some time in their school life. *Educational Review*, Jan. 1924, 116. See also Leonard, "Over-Ageness," 36–7. Leonard gives failure rates in the early 1920s for Toronto, Winnipeg, Brandon, Lethbridge, and Regina. The overall figures tended towards the 10% range except in grade I, where they ran between 20% and 30%; generally, however, failure rates were lower in the larger cities than in other communities.

49 Ontario, *AR 1930*, 100 (Table 12); Walker, "Public Secondary Education in Alberta," 295 (Table 22); Putman-Weir Report, 264 (Table 2); *JEdNS*, Oct. 1920, 63 (figures are given for each county academy only and they range from no failures on up).

50 Walker, "Public Secondary Education in Alberta," 297 (Table 24).

51 Dyde, *Public Secondary Education*, 116. The five provinces were British Columbia, Alberta, Saskatchewan, Manitoba, and Nova Scotia; Ontario had to be calculated separately. Dyde provides tables and commentary for each province (104–9).

52 Ibid., 113–15. Saskatchewan had substantially lower failure rates than did most of the other provinces because "the great majority of pupils" took two years to write all their grade XI examinations.

53 Learned and Sills, *Education in the Maritime Provinces*.

54 At the turn of the century this was very much a minority opinion, although the view that a pupil's daily work should form a significant portion of assessment for promotion was more common. See, for example, the comments of two Ontario ministers of education, in *Proceedings, OEA, 1896*, 32; *1900*, 72.

55 This kind of criticism first appeared during the second decade of the century but gained great momentum during the interwar years, accompanied by enthusiasm for various kinds of standardized and "objective" achievement tests. For examples of the critique see *The School* 3, no. 2 (Oct. 1914): 73–5; *ATAM* 5, no. 6 (Nov. 1924): 22–6; 7, no. 4 (Oct. 1926): 5–10; Saskatchewan, *AR 1927*, 75–6.

56 For one unusually illuminating exposition, see the Registrar's Report, Manitoba, *AR 1923–24*, 55–8.

57 *Proceedings, OEA, 1929*, 37.

58 The details by province are given in Dyde, *Public Secondary Education*, 100–3. After a brief flirtation with recommendations, Alberta reverted to annual departmental examinations until 1931. See Alberta, *AR 1920*, 42–3; Walker, "Public Secondary Education in Alberta," 151–5; *ATAM* 11, no. 2 (Oct. 1930): 4; Calgary School Board, *AR 1931*, 7.

59 For example, for private school and out-of-province students and in some provinces for pupils applying to the normal schools after grade x. Initially, at least, there were also restrictions in some provinces on the type of high school that could recommend. See, for example, *The School* 11, no. 9 (May 1923): 656 (Ontario); 16, no. 5 (Jan. 1928): 504 (British Columbia); *Manitoba School Journal* 4, no. 6 (Feb. 1942): 18 (retrospective on Manitoba school policies).

60 The early arrangements in each province are given in Dyde, *Public Secondary Education*, 85–6.

61 See, for example, the Alberta initiative in Alberta, *AR 1920*, 42; Manitoba, *Programme of Studies for the Schools of Manitoba. Authorized by the Advisory Board, July 1, 1920*, 26.

62 Dyde, *Public Secondary Education*, 87.

63 Nova Scotia abandoned its HSEE altogether after 1928. *JEdNS*, April 1929, 207. For British Columbia, see Johnson, *Public Education in British Columbia*, 110–11. See also Saskatchewan, Dept of Education, *Programme of Study for Public Schools 1929*, "Departmental Examinations for Grade VIII Diplomas," 51–2. New Brunswick, on the other hand, didn't even introduce recommendations until 1936, although it held its last HSEE only three years later. See *The School* 24, no. 8 (April 1936): 716; New Brunswick, *AR 1938–39*, 27–8. For Ontario, see *The School* 21, no. 7 (March 1933): 533. There are brief summaries of the changes in provincial policies on external examinations in W.E. MacPherson, "Canada," in *The Year Book of Education 1934*, 291–2; Haines, "The Secondary School," 31–3. A longer review by A.E. Ault is "Examinations in Canada," in *The Year Book of Education 1938*, 154–71.

64 Manitoba, *Programme of Studies ... July 1, 1920*, 26.

65 Ontario, Dept of Education, *Courses of Study, Public and Separate Schools, 1926*, 34.

66 British Columbia, *Manual of School Law, 1932*, 111–12.

67 For Saskatchewan, see *The School* 20, no. 1 (Sept. 1931): 88; 20, no. 10 (June 1932): 926–7; Saskatchewan, *AR 1939*, 23. For Manitoba, see *AR 1931–32*, 11; *Manitoba School Journal* 4, no. 6 (Feb. 1942): 18 (retrospective review of policy). In Alberta a similar policy was introduced but teachers were only "advised" to use the departmental papers. See Alberta, *AR 1931*, 19; Alberta, Dept of Education, *Programme of Studies for Intermediate Schools, 1935*, 13.

68 *The School* 2, no. 10 (June 1914): 599; see also the comment in London Board of Education, *AR 1914*, 48.

69 London Board of Education, *AR 1919 and 1920*, 7.

70 *The School* 18, no. 10 (June 1930): 883.

71 Blashill, *Saskatoon Public School System*, 50.

72 Wormsbecker, "Secondary Education in Vancouver," 247–8.

73 Dyde, *Public Secondary Education*, 88.

74 Our calculations from Ontario, *AR 1926*, appendix Q, 286–91.

75 In some provinces there was also a public school leaving certificate that students could obtain, though it did not represent promotion standing. See Ontario, *Regulations and Course of Study of the Public Schools of Ontario, Amended and Consolidated, 1911*, Regulation 19.

76 The calculations in this paragraph are made from the data in DBS, *Annual Survey 1930*, 52–3 (Table 61), and *Annual Survey 1935*, 78–82 (Table 23).

77 Alberta, *AR 1922*, 55. See also the justification for Ontario's system of external examinations penned in the 1890s by the deputy minister of education, John Millar, cited in [Sadler], *Special Reports on Educational Subjects*, 22–3; and the justification for introducing New Brunswick's HSEE, new in 1899, by its superintendent of education, cited in Warner, "Secondary Education in New Brunswick," 287–8. On the accountability uses of provincial examinations, see also Fleming and Raptis, "Government's Paper Empire," 179–82.

78 *The School* 17, no. 4 (Dec. 1928): 1. Exams were serious business, indeed well nigh a craze, beyond the schoolroom. Even some of Canada's small but hardy bands of socialists required party "entrance examinations" as proof of commitment, capability, and knowledge of pertinent dogma. See McKay, *Reasoning Otherwise*, 52, 156.

79 Saskatchewan, *AR 1924*, 97.

80 Inexperience and variable marking standards were commonly cited by inspectors and other officials as reasons for maintaining a system of external exams. See Alberta, *AR 1923*, 59; Saskatchewan, *AR 1927*, 75; *Educational Review*, March 1927, 156–7; *Proceedings*, OEA, *1897*, 52, 374; *1899*, 365; *1908*, 12–13.

81 Dyde, *Public Secondary Education*, 112.

82 Ontario, *AR 1921*, 99; *AR 1925*, 70 (Table 3).

83 British Columbia, *AR 1922*, C9–10.

84 Cited in Walker, "Public Secondary Education in Alberta," 154. Similarly, see Fred McNally's assessment in *The School* 16, no. 10 (June 1928): 1028.

85 *JEdNS*, Sept. 1932, 44.

86 The exception was grade I, where retardation rates were nearly 34%.

87 Hamilton, "Schools of Rural Manitoba." Hamilton was interested in a broader range of retardation problems than just promotion rates, but the analysis cited here is from pp. 21–5 and 60. The published reports of inspectors are generally more upbeat than Hamilton's assessment, but they too offer mixed views about the success of the recommendation system, mostly for the same reasons. See Manitoba, *AR 1935–36*, 22–7.

88 Hamilton, "Schools of Rural Manitoba," 25. For examples of the additional burdens the transition to the recommendation system imposed on the inspectorate, see Manitoba, *AR 1932–33*, 14–15. By 1937, when British Columbia had moved to a much more liberalized recommendation system, the inspectors alone became responsible for vetting the quality of grading and the efficiency of the teachers in all those elementary schools outside a district where a high school or superior school was located – in effect, all the rural schools in the province. See British Columbia, *Manual of School Law, 1937*, 128, note 2b. Similarly, the high school inspectors were instructed to maintain their own testing regimes in lieu of the abandoned departmental exams in grades IX to XI. See *BC Teacher* 15, no. 6 (Feb. 1936): 19.

89 *ATAM* 11, no. 2 (Oct. 1930): 4.

90 The figures are given in the London Board of Education *AR*s. Even city boards, however, could change their minds, reverting to regular examinations in the face of recommendation results they believed too lax. For an example for Moncton, see *Educational Review*, Oct. 1928, 40.

91 Our calculations from figures given in *The School* 26, no. 1 (Sept. 1937): 78.

92 Ontario, *AR 1941*, 155 (Table 12). No results are given for the rural schools. See also the table and commentary in J.E. Robbins, "Canadian Education," in *The Year Book of Education 1936*, 610–11.

93 Alberta is the exception. Having abandoned its HSEE in 1931, it effectively reintroduced the HSEE in 1935, requiring all pupils to write an entrance examination at the end of grade IX. Thus Alberta had departmental examinations for both high school entry and at the end of high school. See Alberta, Dept of Education, *Programme of Studies for the Intermediate Schools, 1933*, 14; Alberta, *AR 1939*, 42–3. On failure rates: in Manitoba the 1938 failure rate on the grade XI externals was 29%, and in 1940, 24% (*Manitoba School Journal* 3, no. 2 [Oct. 1940]: 12–13); in Ontario in the early 1940s about 25% failed the Upper School externals (Ontario, *AR 1944*, 182).

94 *The School* 2, no. 1 (Sept. 1913): 2. Similarly, see British Columbia, *AR 1913–14*, A42; Putman-Weir Report, 262.

95 Glenbow Archives, M2004, Crowsnest Pass School District #63, Papers, Blairmore SD No. 628, School Board Minutes, 28 May 1926.

96 See, for example, ibid., 29 June 1923, 4 July 1927, and 29 June 1933. Similarly, see WSJ 19, no. 7 (Sept. 1924): 1.

97 *Manitoba Teacher* 5, no. 8 (Nov. 1924): 1–2. See also WSJ 23, no. 3 (March 1928): 83. For a British Columbia example, see Fleming and Raptis, "Government's Paper Empire," 181–2.

98 Manitoba, *AR 1940–41*, 25.

99 Hamilton, "Schools of Rural Manitoba," 25.

100 *ATAM* 11, no. 10 (June 1931): 12–13.

101 Ibid., no. 5 (Jan. 1931): 15.

102 Saskatchewan, *AR 1934*, 42. The evidence on this point is substantial. See, for example, Saskatchewan, *AR 1923*, 59; *AR 1924*, 97; *AR 1926*, 99; *AR 1928*, 18–19; *AR 1935*, 46–7; *The School* 17, no. 4 (Dec. 1928): 319; WSJ 29, no. 1 (Jan.1934): 34; Alberta, *AR 1923*, 59; *ATAM* 6, no. 11 (April 1926): 11; *BC Teacher* 14, no. 10 (June 1935): 23; 15, no. 7 (March 1936): 47; 15, no. 9 (May 1936): 43; 19, no. 5 (Jan. 1940): 249–50; Ault, "Examinations in Canada," in *The Year Book of Education 1938*, 161, 171 (Ontario and Nova Scotia). Similar fears arose over proposals by the Ontario Dept of Education to abolish the Middle School examinations, and led to vociferous protests and a "decisive rejection" of the idea at the 1930 and 1931 secondary school teachers' conventions. See *CSJ* 9, no. 11 (Nov. 1931): 21–2; Langford, *Educational Service*, 117–19.

103 Nova Scotia, *AR 1933*, 44.

104 On the renewed debate in Manitoba, see the departmental discussion paper, which summarizes opinion on both sides, in *Manitoba School Journal* 4, no. 6 (Feb. 1942): 18–19, 22. See also *BC Teacher* 13, no. 6 (Feb. 1934): 20–1; 13, no. 8 (April 1934): 12; 15, no. 6 (Feb. 1936): 34–5; 15, no. 8 (April 1936): 32.

105 For an illuminating modern introduction to assessment issues and debates over testing, see Osborne, *Education*, chap. 8.

CHAPTER TEN

1 G. Fred McNally, "Education in Alberta," *The School* 16, no. 10 (June 1928): 1027. Italics added. For some reason, McNally didn't include the "general course" introduced, along with the others, in 1922.

2 Dyde, *Public Secondary Education*, 121, 123, 187. Dyde's analysis of the curriculum is much more detailed and sophisticated than this passage might suggest, and he offers an impressive statistical analysis to support his argument about the narrowly academic curriculum. See esp. chap. 8, "Articulation with Higher Schools," and chap. 11, "The Curriculum." Although his analysis was

restricted to Ontario, a visiting inspector from England reached exactly the same conclusion; see [Savage], *Secondary Education in Ontario*, 54–5.

3 Green, "Development of the Curriculum," 156–7.

4 DBS, *Annual Survey 1930*, xii. Manitoba, Quebec, and Prince Edward Island were not included. For the figures by province based on the same data, see *ATAM* 11, no. 10 (June 1931): 9. On the very high standing of French and Latin in Canada compared to the United States, see the graphic in DBS, *Annual Survey 1936*, xiv.

5 Ontario, *AR 1942*, 167.

6 Alberta, *AR 1935*, 98.

7 DBS, *Annual Survey 1935*, 77.

8 Dyde, *Public Secondary Education*, 61. Dyde gives the figures by province: 15,500 of the 24,000 were located in Ontario; British Columbia was a distant second with 2,100. Nova Scotia and Prince Edward Island were exceptions; neither had vocational day schools during the interwar years. New Brunswick, however, began its vocational program in 1920 and by 1939 had over 2,200 full-time day students enrolled in eight vocational or composite schools. See *21st Annual Report of the New Brunswick Vocational Education Board, 1939*, 37 (Table 1).

9 Wormsbecker, "Secondary Education in Vancouver," 282. The author notes that this includes those in the matriculation course at the technical school and on that account suggests a more likely figure of 25%; see p. 283.

10 Winnipeg School Board, *AR 1933*, 8. The figure is probably too high, since it includes students in the general program and a certain percentage who would transfer to a straight academic program.

11 Our calculations from Ontario, *AR 1930*, 222–3 (Table 14), 354 (Table 21).

12 Winnipeg School Board, *AR 1926*, 43 (our calculations).

13 Calgary School Board, *AR 1931*, 13.

14 For Edmonton, see Coulter, "Teenagers in Edmonton," 80; for Vancouver, see Wormsbecker, "Secondary Education in Vancouver," 282–3. For Vancouver figures for the 1920s, see Barman, "Knowledge Is Essential," 58 (Table 5).

15 Langley, "Programmes of Study," 204.

16 Walker, "Public Secondary Education in Alberta," 149.

17 Our calculations from Ontario, *AR 1935*, 161–3 (Table 23), 188 (Table 36).

18 Ontario, *AR 1944*, 116.

19 Our calculations from Ontario, *AR 1935*, 161–3 (Table 23), 188 (Table 36). Toronto schools accounted for 11,172 of the 32,551 vocational students in these communities, and that unduly weights the provincial average; without Toronto the figure would be much lower than 44%. Our 1930 figure for Hamilton for the combined technical and commercial programs is 55% of enrolments – about 10% higher than Craig Heron's. His is probably a better reflection of what was actually happening on the ground, since it is based

on average attendance data in the Hamilton Board of Education records. Our figures are for enrolments, and we use them here only in order to allow comparison with other towns and cities. See Heron, "The High School," 256 (Table 5).

20 In other provinces it is much harder to identify a distinct vocational track or distinguish it from a vocational subject option taken as part of another program. Even in Ontario, however, there are problems on this score and it would probably be better to use the phrase "quasi-distinct." Because we want to avoid misleading the reader or substituting speculation for hard numbers, we report the statistics cited in this paragraph as we have calculated them from the original published figures. But in our view, the percentage enrolled in vocational programs is at least somewhat inflated. From 1921 in Ontario, options in the academic program included agriculture, manual training, domestic science, and various commercial subjects. Thus numbers of academic students took one or two practical options to fill out a predominantly academic program, substituting typing or shop for Latin or algebra, or simply taking a useful subject like typing as an additional elective. But where a high school or collegiate institute building included a vocational department, these students were frequently counted as vocational enrolments and vocational percentages are therefore inflated. For the Ontario figures, we reach this conclusion through a chain of inferential reasoning, but in other circumstances the point is explicit. For example, in 1913 the various technical subjects in Winnipeg enrolled 831 boys: "of these, 231 are taking Technical or Engineering courses, while the remaining 600, enrolled in other courses, are taking selected technical work." The same was true for domestic science subjects for girls. (See Winnipeg School Board, *AR 1913*, 25.) It was much the same for commercial enrolments in British Columbia, where large numbers were simply picking up a year or two of typing, for example, as one option within an academic program rather than enrolling in a full commercial program. See Bruce, "Business Education in British Columbia," 37, 40; Weeks, "Business Education in British Columbia," xi, 8–9, 96. The second problem is that even within the technical school a minority might be enrolled in matriculation programs, which gave students exposure to specialized commercial or technical areas but also required a substantial amount of academic work and kept options open for post-secondary education. One could with some justification include these students in the academic stream. At the London Technical School during the interwar period, for example, 5–10% of pupils (depending on the year) entered the matriculation program (see Goodson and Anstead, *Through the Schoolhouse Door*, 7; similarly see Wormsbecker, "Secondary Education in Vancouver," 282–3; Winnipeg School Board, *AR 1933*, 11).

21 This didn't mean, however, that admission to an Ontario vocational school was promiscuous. The regulations gave automatic admission to those with a high school entrance certificate, but others were required to have "4th form standing" and a recommendation from the principal that they were "able to take up the courses selected," which might mean completion of grade VII and all or part of grade VIII, though without being recommended for admission to an academic high school or passing the HSEE. See Ontario, Dept of Education, *Recommendations and Regulations ... Vocational Schools*, 14–15.

22 See H.B. Beal, "Vocational and Industrial Classes," *Proceedings, OEA, 1924*, 295 (figure for 1924); Goodson and Dowbiggin, "Vocational Education," 55 (figure for 1927).

23 Goodson and Dowbiggin, "Vocational Education," 55.

24 British Columbia, *AR 1927–28*, Part 1, Report, Municipal Inspector, Vancouver, v35.

25 Stamp, *Ontario Secondary School Program*, 21–2, 37. For a similar conclusion based on a different set of figures, see Heron, "The High School," 252–3. See also our cohort retention table, Table A.13. For American vocational retention figures, which were also far lower than one might expect from the volume of rhetoric on the subject, see Tyack and Hansot, *Learning Together*, 189–92; Angus and Mirel, *Failed Promise*, 44–53.

26 Ontario, *AR 1937*, 76 (Table 4).

27 See Fluxgold, *Federal Financial Support*, 46–9.

28 According to the DBS, Canadian vocational enrolment stalled during the 1930s but the bureau's explanation was that it was "probably due to the technical schools being filled to capacity with no money available for their expansion." *Canada Year Book 1939*, 1015.

29 R.G. Gemmell, "Vocational Training in the Small High School," *The School* 25, no. 1 (Sept. 1936): 13. The total number of 426 includes the continuation schools.

30 In 1925–26, for example, domestic science enrolled just over 19% of female enrolments in the collegiate institutes but only 3.7% in the high schools; in 1931 the figures had shrunk to 10% and 1.5% respectively. See Danylewycz, "Domestic Science Education," 134. For the continuation schools, see Ontario, *AR 1925*, 152–3.

31 Ontario, *AR 1930*, Tables 14, 18, and 21. The figures were even lower in 1926; see Ontario, *AR 1926*, Tables J, N, and P.

32 British Columbia, *AR 1924–25*, M16–17. This, however, was not the case with the "rural municipal high schools," which were more likely to offer some of these subjects.

33 DBS, *Elementary and Secondary Education 1938–40*, 58 (our calculations). The only other provinces for which enrolments are given subject by subject, urban

and rural, are Nova Scotia and Saskatchewan (56, 58). Even a cursory glance will show the similar differences in available options between urban and rural schools.

34 Glenbow Archives, M2004, Crowsnest Pass School Division #63, Papers, Blairmore SD No. 628, School Board Minutes, 28 Aug. and 6 Sept. 1933.

35 M.A. Cameron, "The Small High School," *The School* 30, no. 1 (Sept. 1941): 26. Cameron's MA thesis, "The Small High School in British Columbia," offers an extended version of his argument. See particularly the telling graphic where he compares the range of subjects offered in large and small high schools, opposite p. 68, and the summary, pp. 73–6. For yet another incisive analysis of the problems, written in 1933 by a rural high school principal, see the lengthy quotation in Gordon, "Secondary Education in Rural British Columbia," 168–70. Similarly, see *BC Teacher* 16, no. 5 (Jan. 1937): 241. For a stunning example of one high school teacher's struggle to provide the entire curriculum for some thirty students spread across each grade, IX through XII, see the plaintive plea for help in PAA, 79.334, box 17, file 272, Percy Page, Principal, Elnora, Alberta, to H.E. Balfour [high school inspector], 11 June 1935. For the difficulties of timetabling a full slate of subjects in a two-teacher Ontario continuation school, see *The School* 10, no. 4 (Dec. 1921): 219–21.

36 Alberta, *Report of the Legislative Committee on Rural Education*, 21.

37 See the article by S.J. Willis, *BC Teacher* 14, no. 2 (Oct. 1934): 8. British Columbia introduced this system at the same time as it introduced its broadened high school program of studies, in 1929. But the high school graduation diploma was "not accepted as a certificate of qualification for admission to the local University or to one of the Provincial Normal Schools." For arrangements in Alberta, see PAA, 79.334, box 2, file 14, Supervisor of Schools, Alberta, Dept of Education, to S.J. Willis, telegram, 31 Jan. 1939. Similarly, see Ontario, *Interim Report of the Committee on High School Education*, 5.

38 Winnipeg School Board, *AR 1937*, 14.

39 Langley, "Programmes of Study," 204.

40 New Brunswick, *AR 1930–31*, Report, Moncton Board of Trustees, 107.

41 *The School* 23, no. 2 (Oct. 1934): 94. For other examples, see Ontario, *AR 1919*, 60; Ontario, *Interim Report of the Committee on High School Education*, 5; Manitoba, *AR 1925–26*, 84; *WSJ* 26, no. 1 (Jan. 1931): 14; G.O. Smith, "Compulsory Latin in Ontario," *Canadian Forum* 13, no. 156 (Sept. 1933): 464; *CSJ* 13, no. 10 (Oct. 1935): 281–2; *The School* 29, no. 9 (May 1941): 848; LaZerte, "The Selective Nature of Secondary Education," 20.

42 Cited in Langford, *Educational Service*, 21.

43 *Maclean's*, 1 Dec. 1934, 18. See also the more tempered strictures in Marsh, *Canadians In and Out of Work*, 241–2.

44 Ontario, *AR 1932*, appendix A, "The Schools and the Universities," 3.

45　See, for example, *The School* 7, no. 6 (Feb. 1919): 416 (Manitoba); *WSJ* 13, no. 9 (Nov. 1918): 363 (Alberta and British Columbia).

46　Glenbow Archives, M2004, Crowsnest Pass School District #63, file 826, C. Samson to Secretary, Blairmore School Board, 18 March 1935: encl.: "A Proposal for the Re-organization of the Secondary Schools, Submitted by the Educational Progress Club of Calgary," 1.

47　*BC Teacher* 9, no. 1 (Sept. 1929): 8.

48　Seath, *Education for Industrial Purposes*, 265.

49　Bingay, *Public Education in Nova Scotia*, 112–13. Similarly, see the jeremiad in Anderson, "Moncton," Part 2, chap. 4 [n.p.], "The Curriculum Lacks Elasticity."

50　*CSJ* 9, no. 8 (Aug. 1931): 15. Similarly, see *CSJ* 10, no. 1 (Jan. 1932): 17.

51　Bruce, "Business Education in British Columbia," 68–9; similarly, see ibid., 71–2.

52　Weeks, "Business Education in British Columbia," 61.

53　F.H. Sexton, "Technical Education in Canada," in *The Year Book of Education 1939*, 613–14.

54　Despite the enormous volume of rhetoric in the educational press (and elsewhere) about the cultural values of a liberal education, most students didn't take Latin, French, or the higher mathematics for the good of their souls or the cultural benefits such studies purportedly conferred. If Sanscrit had suddenly replaced Latin as a matriculation requirement, Sanscrit enrolments would have soared and Latin declined precipitously, as had already happened to Greek when it ceased to be a required subject for university matriculation. For a good example of the tight fit between matriculation requirements and subject enrolment levels, see John Henderson, "Should Greek and Latin Be Retained?," *Proceedings, OEA, 1902*, 239–40.

55　Alberta, *Report of the Legislative Committee on Rural Education*, 21.

56　The memorandum is quoted in full in Wormsbecker, "Secondary Education in Vancouver," appendix E, 474–6.

57　Winnipeg School Board, *AR 1926*, 20.

58　Wormsbecker, "Secondary Education in Vancouver," 475.

59　*ATAM* 9, no. 3 (Nov. 1928): 1.

60　Nova Scotia, *AR 1929*, 82–3. Italics added.

61　"Problems of a Small High School," *BC Teacher* 15, no. 9 (May 1936): 19.

62　Arn, "Extra-Curricular Activities," MED thesis, 7–9.

63　Ibid., 12. The following analysis is based on pp. 12ff.

64　Arn, "Extra-Curricular Activities," Research Bulletin, 21.

65　Watkin, "Extra-Curricular Activities."

66　Ibid., 8–9.

67　Ibid., 15–19, 25–34, 41–51.

68　Cameron, "The Small High School," 28, 30.

69 Ibid., 120–2. On time constraints for rural children, see also Watkin, "Extra-Curricular Activities," 50. The point is important. Before the establishment of the rural or district high school, a great many rural adolescents in all parts of Canada attended urban high schools. In 1923, for example, the DBS estimated that 14% of all rural pupils were in attendance at urban schools, mostly high schools. DBS, *Annual Survey 1923*, 53 (Table 81, note 2). In village and small-town high schools in Ontario the figure could run as high as 50%. See Gemmell, "Vocational Training in the Small High School," 13; *CSJ* 11, no. 4 (April 1933): 145; 6, no. 1 (Jan. 1928): 7. Similarly, see the estimate of one-sixth in 1924 for Manitoba, in Murray Report, 50.

70 For the analysis in this paragraph, see *Survey of the Schools of the Greater Victoria Area*, 40–52. For similar earlier commentary, see Anderson, "Moncton," 2.

71 *Survey ... Greater Victoria Area*, 55. For comments on the lack of a music program and extracurricular activities in Ontario, see *CSJ* 13, no. 2 (Feb. 1935): 39–40; 14, no. 9 (Sept. 1936): 187–8. In 1937 two secondary schools in cities, seven in towns, five in villages, and six in rural areas taught music: *CSJ* 15, 3 (March 1937): 89.

72 C.C. Goldring, "After School Activities in Toronto Schools: A Report Submitted to the Toronto Board of Education, Dec. 18, 1935," *The School* 24, no. 5 (Jan. 1936): 373–8.

73 The survey counted up the total numbers in all activities and concluded that "the typical high school boy or girl participates in three or four organized after-school activities," two of which were sports. Ibid., 374–5. But this average figure assumes that every high school pupil engaged in that many, which seems unlikely in light of the other commentaries cited.

74 Compare Cynthia Comacchio's *Dominion of Youth*, chap. 4. The quotations are on pp. 99 and 113. The reader familiar with her book will be aware that we are taking some exception to her account of the place of "modern high" in the rise of a distinctive youth culture. We think her argument needs more nuance and some tempering of the conclusions. A better formulation, we think, might be a central institution for *some* high school students, and a distinct minority at that. Nonetheless, Comacchio convinces us that even in the interwar years, there were many places where "modern high" indubitably existed, and she offers a rich narrative to describe it, identifying a set of institutions that represent the vanguard of modernity – models, as we suggest here, for what in the future all high schools would become. Our commentary in this section, moreover, does not represent a substantive challenge to the thrust of the book, which we find persuasive. Indeed, some research of our own offers a modest supplement. In Blairmore, for example, there appear to have been virtually no extracurricular activities in the high school itself. But a whole raft of sports, music, and other youth activities were sponsored by the churches, miners' unions, and other groups in Blairmore or by inter-urban

organizations in the Crowsnest Pass. One doesn't even need the high school to sustain the general thrust of her argument.

75 Davies and Guppy, *The Schooled Society*, 46; similarly, see Comacchio, *Dominion of Youth*, 108.

76 Despite our caveat in note 20 about Ontario data on total enrolments in vocational versus academic programs, the data on parents' occupations give what we think are reasonably good comparisons.

77 The data begin in 1896 but are not adequate for comparisons between types of school until the early 1920s. Similarly, partial data on parental occupations are available after 1933 but either only in summary form for the province or only for a few schools. In the category of "professions" we are combining the two original categories of "law, medicine, dentistry, or the church" and "teaching." By "parents" we mean the title given in the reports as "heads of families."

78 There are two significant problems with the data. First, we do not know which particular occupations were slotted into each category. For example, does "agriculture" include farm owners only or farm labourers as well? Does "trades" include only skilled manual worker employees or also owner-operators of electrical repair shops or auto repair garages, etc.? Does "commerce" include pedlars and bankers, and if so, does the category have any coherence? The second problem is the large percentage of "other occupations"/no occupation, which runs as high as 20%, 25%, or even 35% (usually the higher percentages are in the vocational schools). To ignore these and do the calculations with only the known occupations is very misleading. For example, by excluding others/none, the category of skilled manual or "trades" would, in 1930, look like this: collegiate institutes 36%, high schools 34%, vocational 50%. With others/none added, skilled manual or "trades" in collegiate institutes constituted 25%, high schools 18%, and vocational schools 35%. The implications are quite different. It seems to us a dubious and misleading quantitative device to ignore others/none. Compare Goodson and Anstead, *Through the Schoolhouse Door*, 133n26, 134 (Table 2).

79 Compare Comacchio, *Dominion of Youth*, 108–9.

80 All of the calculations in this and the next section (on subject enrolment) are our own, unless otherwise indicated. Calculations on social origins in this paragraph are from Ontario, *AR 1930*, 230–1 (Table 14), 354–5 (Table 21). We have also done similar calculations for 1920 and 1925 to assure ourselves that only modest changes took place. The distribution of the Ontario labour force in 1931 is from *Historical Atlas*, Plate 33. Plate 33 also provides an easy way to illustrate the consequences of leaving out the "other occupations" and "without occupation." The general labour force in 1931 adds up to *c.* 100% but enrolments to only *c.* 80%. If one were to assume that the remaining 20% was mainly made up of labourers' children and assign them to that

category, the labouring group would be over-represented in Ontario high
school classrooms.

81 Though we put the volume by Goodson and Anstead, *Through the Schoolhouse
Door*, to good account elsewhere, its exclusive focus on the London Technical
School makes comparison with the London collegiate institutes difficult;
where possible, we have contrasted figures for the latter drawn from the
Ontario *AR*s. One must also keep in mind that many of Goodson and
Anstead's figures are only for an entry cohort, whereas the *AR*s record the
total enrolments of the schools. See also our comment in note 78.

82 Heap, "Schooling Women for Home or for Work," 226.

83 In the years 1905, 1910, and 1915, working-class youngsters at Toronto
Technical High School formed, respectively, 36%, 55%, and 51% of enrolments. Heap, "Schooling Women for Home or for Work," 229 (Table 6). The
1915 percentage may be somewhat higher than it should be because of data
inadequacies. In Toronto's collegiate institutes and high schools the comparable figures were 33%, 30%, and 29% respectively; our calculations from
Ontario, *AR 1906* (1905 figures), 40–1, 44–5; *AR 1911* (1910 figures), 70–1,
78–9; *AR 1916* (1915 figures), 230–1, 238–9. A figure for Toronto Technical
in 1920 is unavailable because there is a serious under-enumeration of
occupations compared to enrolments, but in 1922, 41% of its students were
working class, compared to 31% in the other Toronto secondary schools.
It should be noted that a large number of parents were classified as having
unspecified "other occupations" or as "without occupations" in some years;
for example, in 1922 these categories accounted for 21% of students in the
collegiate institutes and high schools and 32% at Toronto Technical. Ontario,
AR 1922, 229, 261. Working-class students in the London Technical School in
1922 constituted 57% of enrolments, but only 3% were from families in the
"other" or "without" occupational category, which may account for the difference from Toronto. The comparable figure for working-class enrolments
in London Collegiate Institute was 29%. Our calculations from Ontario, *AR
1922*, 229, 261.

84 Heron, "The High School," 246, 230, 247. Our own calculations for 1930
are that 37% of academic enrolments were from blue-collar families (27%
from "trades" and 10% from "labour"); in the vocational programs, 57% of
students had blue-collar backgrounds (36% "trades" and 22% "labour"). By
way of comparison, the figure for enrolment from trades and labouring families for all Ontario collegiate institutes and high schools was 33%; and for all
vocational enrolments, 51%. Ontario, *AR 1930*, 230–1, 354; our calculations.

85 For example, in some industrial towns like Brantford and St Catharines, just
as in Hamilton, vocational schools had high enrolments of working-class
youngsters compared to those of the collegiate institutes; but in Toronto, with
its six large stand-alone vocational schools in 1930, the proportion was not

nearly so high. Conversely, in places such as St Thomas and Owen Sound the social origins of students were nearly the same in both academic or vocational schools. Compare figures in Ontario, *AR 1930*, Tables 14 and 21.

86 Goodson and Anstead, *Through the Schoolhouse Door*, 151; our calculations for Hamilton from Ontario, *AR 1931*, 298–9. The social origins of commercial and technical students are distinguishable in Ontario, *AR 1930*, for five schools: 28% of commercial students came from non-manual backgrounds versus 19% of technical students; and 47% versus 55% respectively from manual backgrounds. Our calculations from Ontario, *AR 1930*, 354 (Table 21).

87 Aside from the two Ontario studies already cited, we have also located an analysis of Edmonton high school students in 1941–42 (effectively covering students who entered high school from 1939 to 1941). All students were required to take some compulsory academic subjects, which made up 28% of the high school curriculum; the rest, or 72%, were elective subjects (divided into academic, general, commercial, technical, and home economics). Students whose parents were labourers chose 19% of their electives from commercial, technical, or (a small number of) home economics subjects; the children of skilled tradesmen selected 15% of their electives from these options. The equivalent figure for professionals' children was 7%; for those of managers, proprietors, clerical, or commercial workers, 10%; for farmers' children, 11%. Conversely, students from labouring families chose only 30% of their elective courses from academic subjects, and those from tradesmen's families, 37%. Those from the other groups mentioned above took 40% or more of their subjects in academic options. There was thus a clear bias in the kinds of subjects that students from varying occupational backgrounds chose. Lazerte, "The Selective Nature of Secondary Education," 2, 7.

88 In 1930 the figure for "labouring occupations" in collegiate institutes and high schools was 6,296; in vocational schools, 3,795. "Trades" in collegiate institutes and high schools accounted for 12,787; in vocational schools, 8,281. See Ontario, *AR 1930*, 222–3 (Table 14), 354 (Table 21).

89 To 1920, physical training was not commonly taught in Canadian high schools. But in the major curriculum revisions during the interwar years it was increasingly introduced as a compulsory subject, in some cases in each year, in others only for grades IX and X. In Ontario high schools, for example, it became compulsory in Lower and Middle School in 1922, and in British Columbia in 1930. But until the late 1930s, in Nova Scotia it was not even listed as a high school subject. Thus, even in the interwar years, it was not universally taught and levels of enrolment varied over time and by province. Moreover, pupils might be segregated for physical education for each year of high school, for only one year, or, if it wasn't offered, not at all. For enrolment statistics in physical education, Canada-wide and by province

as of 1923, see Dyde, *Public Secondary Education*, 186–8. Similarly, see Alberta, *AR 1924*, 126–7; *AR 1934*, 90; Saskatchewan, *AR 1922*, 44–5; *AR 1925*, 40–1; British Columbia, *AR 1929–30*, Q116–17.

90 Richardson, *Administration of Schools*, 195–6. We are referring in this section to formal instruction that required at least a modicum of specialized equipment and teachers. At the turn of the century terms such as "manual arts" were also used in programs of studies to cover "constructive work," including paper cutting, sewing, and the like, that was begun in the primary grades and might be subsumed within other subjects, including drawing, or given a subject heading of its own.

91 *The School* 20, no. 6 (Feb. 1932): 195–6.

92 Ibid., 16, no. 6 (Feb. 1928): 605. "Rural municipalities" were areas where many schools were consolidated and large enough to maintain specialized facilities for teaching both subjects.

93 Saskatchewan, *AR 1927*, 109.

94 Alberta, *AR 1929*, Report of Inspector for Calgary, 34.

95 Anderson, "Moncton," Part 2 [n.p.], "Household Science Department."

96 Danylewycz, "Domestic Science Education," 133 (Table 1). For manual training enrolments, see Ontario, *AR 1926*, 96.

97 DBS, *Annual Survey 1930*, xvi.

98 Ibid. The percentages are either lower or no better for grade VIII pupils.

99 Danylewycz, "Domestic Science Education," 133 (Table 1).

100 In 1927 and again in 1930 Ontario's inspector of manual training and domestic science pointed to the rapid spread of domestic science in the rural elementary schools. But it is clear from his commentary that this was closely associated with the hot lunch movement. The subject appears, moreover, to have been taught to both boys and girls. Manual training was taught far less frequently simply because it demanded special equipment. See Ontario, *AR 1927*, 62; *AR 1930*, 43.

101 RCDPR, *Brief Presented by the Canadian Teachers' Federation*, 9–10.

102 The contrast between Winnipeg and Blairmore recounted in chapter 4 is one good example.

103 See the commentary about the difficulties of introducing domestic science in New Brunswick in Carolyn Currie, "The Value of Home Economics in Rural Schools," *Educational Review*, Nov. 1925, 55. Similarly, see the comment in British Columbia, *AR 1925–26*, R64, Report, Director of Agricultural Education, on the reluctance of local boards to introduce instruction in manual training, domestic science, or agriculture: "It seems passing strange that, although these three subjects have more intimate connection with everybody's life than have any of the other school subjects, many School Boards have to be urged, and even persuaded, seemingly against their will, to make this highly important field of instruction available to the boys and girls

of their respective districts. This is particularly noticeable in the smaller towns and cities."

104 British Columbia, *Programme of Studies for the Junior High Schools, 1936*, 20. See also British Columbia, AR *1938–39*, H48–9.

105 See *JEdNS*, April 1942, 303–4.

106 Here again we are dealing with data that are sparse in respect to both time and space. Only four provinces – British Columbia, Alberta, Saskatchewan, and Nova Scotia – provide data on secondary subject or program enrolments by gender, and they fail to do it with any consistency over time. British Columbia, for example, offers this information for the years 1926–27 to 1929–30 only, Saskatchewan for 1922 to 1925, and Alberta for 1922 to 1925 and then not again until the mid-1930s. Saskatchewan and Nova Scotia provide the data grade by grade but without totals, Alberta offers only provincial totals, and British Columbia gives totals by groupings of geographical places. The only other useful pertinent data, which are much more common, are total enrolments in particular subjects that were conventionally gendered, such as domestic science or manual training, etc.

107 Dyde, *Public Secondary Education*, 186–8.

108 They are not listed in the Nova Scotia subject enrolment tables until the mid-1930s.

109 See Alberta, AR *1924*, 126; AR *1934*, 90; AR *1935*, 98.

110 Ontario, AR *1930*, Tables 14, 18, and 21; our calculations. Precise percentages are not possible because there is no overall figure in the vocational schools for enrolments in "domestic science"; these percentages are calculated from enrolments in particular subjects, such as cooking or home economics. Domestic science enrolments had declined from 1926, when they stood at 13%–17%; see Ontario, AR *1926*, Tables I, N, and P.

111 Saskatchewan, AR *1925*, 40–1.

112 Nova Scotia, AR *1936*, 20–1.

113 Saskatchewan, AR *1925*, 40–1.

114 See British Columbia, AR *1929–30*, Part 2, Q116–17; see also AR *1926–27*, Part 2, M108–9. Although junior high schools were still uncommon in British Columbia at this point, wherever they were established, domestic science was a high-enrolment subject, as it was in urban elementary schools.

115 Ontario, AR *1926*, Table P; AR *1930*, Table 21; AR *1936*, 218. Precise figures are available for 1930: 75% of vocational girls enrolled in the commercial program. For 1926 and 1936, we have estimated the number of girls.

116 See Saskatchewan, AR *1935*, 23; for British Columbia, see *The School* 17, no. 6 (Feb. 1928): 605; British Columbia, AR *1929–30*, Part 1, Q28; AR *1930–31*, L37; AR *1938–39*, H51, H54.

117 For similar conclusions for the United States, see Powers, *The "Girl Question" in Education*, 94–7.

118 British Columbia, AR *1926–27*, M13. In 1939, 25% of students in Vancouver's
     two commercial high schools were boys. British Columbia, AR *1938–39*, H97.

119 Saskatchewan, AR *1929*, 51.

120 Goodson and Anstead, *Through the Schoolhouse Door*, 128; Strong-Boag, *The
     New Day Recalled*, 20–1.

121 Goodson and Anstead, *Through the Schoolhouse Door*, 128, 132. The figure
     for boys in the commercial departments of all Ontario vocational schools in
     1930 was 22.5%; see Ontario, AR *1930*, 352–3.

122 DBS, *Elementary and Secondary Education 1938–40*, 58.

123 Much is occasionally made of the internal stratification of courses in the com-
     mercial schools – boys taught "business" and girls taught "typing," etc. This
     was indisputably the case in a handful of big-city, large-enrolment programs,
     but it was not typical of most commercial courses, which rarely included
     more than typing, shorthand, and bookkeeping or general business practice.
     Goodson and Anstead note that at the London Technical School efforts
     were made to maintain sexually segregated commercial classes (*Through
     the Schoolhouse Door*, 149). But this was unsuccessful in the early years when
     enrolments were small. It was never possible in smaller schools. There is no
     evidence, for example, that typing classes in the academic high schools were
     segregated in this manner.

124 For example, in 1928 St Patrick's Girls' High School in Halifax had a com-
     mercial class accounting for 5% of enrolments in grades IX to XII; only
     one other high school offered a commercial class, which had similar small
     enrolments, out of the eight schools in the city offering some instruction
     in high school subjects. See Nova Scotia, AR *1928–29*, Report, Chairman of
     School Commissioners, Halifax, 114. Commercial subjects began to be listed
     among the high school subjects during the 1930s, but very few students were
     enrolled. See Nova Scotia, AR *1936*, 22–5; AR *1939*, 22, 28. In 1939, even in
     the urban high schools, only 4.2% of high school girls were enrolled in com-
     mercial subjects (for boys the figure was 3.6%). The subjects were taught in
     urban high schools in only seven out of eighteen counties and in a handful of
     rural and village high schools in three counties.

125 Our calculations from Saskatchewan, AR *1925*, 38, 40.

126 Our calculations from Alberta, AR *1924*, 126–7; AR *1934*, 90.

127 British Columbia, AR *1926–27*, M13; AR *1929–30*, Q96–7.

128 Heron, "The High School," 256 (Table 5); his calculations. These percent-
     ages are based on average attendance figures and thus differ from those
     based on the enrolment figures we use, but the trends are similar.

129 Our calculations from Ontario, AR *1922*, AR *1930*, and AR *1935*, relevant sta-
     tistical tables. Subject enrolments are not provided for the academic schools
     by gender, but we have estimated the number of boys taking commercial at
     20%, which is consistent with the proportions found in studies where the
     precise figures are known; see Goodson and Anstead, *Through the Schoolhouse*

Door, 132. Estimating the proportion of boys at 25% gives almost the same results. Total enrolments by gender for commercial subjects in the vocational schools exist only for 1929 and 1930. The percentages are derived therefore from estimated figures for girls taking commercial subjects in collegiate institutes, high schools, and continuation schools. Girls' enrolments in commercial subjects in vocational schools are estimated for 1922 and 1935, but percentages for 1930 are based on the actual figures.

130 See Goodson and Anstead, *Through the Schoolhouse Door*, 135–6, 155 (Table 9). The figures for those taking the general commercial course are for the entry cohort for the respective years. There was also a significant minority of boys enrolled in the commercial course in London.

131 In the mid-1920s E.G. Savage estimated that it wasn't possible to offer a commercial course in schools with enrolments "much less than 250" and with staffs of only eight or nine teachers, including the principal; but 110 of 176 collegiate institutes and high schools had enrolments of *less* than 200 and another significant group fell between 200 and 250. See [Savage], *Secondary Education in Ontario*, 55, and his figures on school size (10–27).

132 Nova Scotia, AR *1925*, 26–31; AR *1931*, 20–5; British Columbia, AR *1926–27*, M108–9; AR *1929–30*, Q116–17. While an equal number of grade XI girls and boys in Saskatchewan in 1925 took chemistry (66%), 62% of the boys but only 52% of the girls took physics. A higher percentage of boys also took Latin and French. Our calculations from Saskatchewan, AR *1925*, 38–41.

133 See Alice Wilson, "Co-education," *The School* 10, no. 3 (Nov. 1921): 160–4; editorial, *The School* 11, no. 10 (June 1923): 668–9.

134 For one nice example, see Ontario, *Principles of Method*, 319–20. On embedded forms of gender differentiation, see also Sutherland, *Growing Up*, 214–16. Extracurricular activities might be gender segregated, at least in the larger schools, though even this point should not be exaggerated. Goodson and Anstead give examples of extracurricular activities at London Technical School that involved both sexes. Before the gymnasium and auditorium were built, teachers organized hikes, sleigh rides, and skating parties; later, there was a school orchestra, big school shows annually, dances, and annual school or class picnics. *Through the Schoolhouse Door*, 192–4. Moreover, studies based on the big-city high school that stress the development during the interwar years of sophisticated and segregated extracurricular programs take no account of the fact that most Canadian high schools were far too small to provide anything like these kinds of programs.

CHAPTER ELEVEN

1 There is already an analysis of the urban elementary classroom in Sutherland, *Growing Up*, 186–201. In order to keep the comparison sharply focused, we will ignore the two- or three-teacher schools that existed in a few rural areas

or more commonly in hamlets and small villages. But for commentary on teaching and timetabling in these schools, see Ontario, *Ontario Normal School Manuals – School Management*, 180ff.; "Public School Programme," *JEdNS*, April 1921, 133ff. For an introduction to the nineteenth-century context, see Danylewycz and Prentice, "Teachers' Work," 137–59. Compared to the elementary school there is surprisingly little secondary literature or primary source material on pedagogic routines and the teacher's work in secondary schools. Though the focus is on one vocational school only, for an account that touches on these matters, see Goodson and Anstead, *Through the Schoolhouse Door*, chap. 8. For two good articles on the tribulations of teaching in one- or two-teacher rural high schools, where the problems closely resembled those in the one-room elementary schools, see *BC Teacher* 15, nos 8 and 9 (April and May 1936): 19–20, 39–40.

2　For illuminating comparisons of teachers' work in the late twentieth century, see King and Peart, *Teachers in Canada*, esp. chap 3, "The Work Day."

3　Nova Scotia, *Manual of School Law, 1901*, Education Act, s. 105 (e) and (f).

4　Ontario, *Regulations and Course of Study, 1911*, extracts from Education Act, 29–30.

5　British Columbia, *Manual of the School Law, 1929*, Regulations, Article 6 (3).

6　Alberta, School Act, 1930, s. 202 (c).

7　Tyack and Cuban, *Tinkering toward Utopia*, 8–9, 85–94. The quotation is on p. 94.

8　Wilson and Stortz, "May the Lord Have Mercy on You," 2nd edn, 246; similarly, see McLachlan, *With Unshakeable Persistence*, 9–10, 126–7. This doesn't mean that trustees exercised a free hand in imposing such tasks, however. In New Brunswick, for example, the law specified that such janitorial services "form no part of the duty of any teacher (or pupil)." But "any teacher or pupil may be employed by the Trustees to attend to … these matters, at a suitable compensation." See the amended regulation printed in *Educational Review*, Feb. 1918, 228.

9　Van Kleek, *The Way It Was*, 161.

10　See, for example, Stephenson, "Mrs. Gibson," 245–6; Patterson, "Voices from the Past," 108.

11　Van Kleek, *The Way It Was*, 198. Impetigo is a nasty, highly contagious pustular skin infection that most commonly affects children. Treatment involves antiseptic ointment (which may have been what Van Kleek used) or antibiotics (obviously not available before the 1940s) and strict hygienic measures, as the infection is easily passed from one child to another, a characteristic that would have increased the chances of an epidemic under the conditions in many rural schools.

12　While his books are useful compilations, we have found his archival collection far more valuable. See UAA, John C. Charyk Fonds, 90-43-52, boxes 6ff., "School Memoirs and Correspondence."

13 Ibid., box 7, Mrs H. Clews, 18 Nov. 1964, p. 12.

14 Ibid., box 10, Mrs. Van Kleek, 25 Nov. 1969.

15 See Charyk, *The Biggest Day of the Year.* Similarly, see Cochrane, *The One-Room School*, chap. 6. For the intimidating challenge that organizing the Christmas concert could pose for the rural teacher, see Harriette MacPherson, "Getting Ready for the Christmas Concert," *The School* 19, no. 3 (Nov. 1930): 218–20; *Canadian Teacher* 33, no. 5 (16 Nov. 1928): 345–50.

16 For one good example, see the description in London Board of Education, AR *1930*, 16–17.

17 For the typical numbers and the comparisons, see chapter 4 of this volume.

18 Stephenson, "Mrs. Gibson," 239.

19 Glenbow Archives, M2017, Pincher Creek SD No. 29, file 678, "Superintendent's Term Return," 30 June 1941; file 29, "School Census 1941." The census exists for each school and links children and parents by name and address. Though we've given only three examples here, they are typical of nearly all the schools in the division.

20 UAA, Charyk Fonds, 90-43-52, box 6, Rose Anderson.

21 See High, "Haldimand County," 82, 67–8. Percentages are rounded.

22 Stephenson, "Mrs. Gibson," 239. Similarly, see Corman, "Seeking Greener Pastures," 186.

23 Manitoba, AR *1950–51*, 36.

24 For descriptions of the basic pedagogical routines, see Stephenson, "Mrs. Gibson," 236–9; Charyk, *Little White Schoolhouse*, 255–61; Peabody, *School Days*, 53–7. For a helpful description of the pedagogy in American one-room schools – one that parallels the evidence in Canada – see Cuban, *How Teachers Taught*, 123–30. For an extended discussion of the "recitation" or lesson, see Salisbury, *School Management*, 164.

25 Dorothy Lane, "36 Lessons in One Day," *The School* 7, no. 5 (Jan. 1919): 327. For an even more extreme calculation, see C.R. Tate, "A Rural School Timetable," *BC Teacher* 18, no. 8 (April 1939): 427.

26 Nova Scotia, *Manual of School Law, 1901*, 124.

27 Ontario, *Ontario Normal School Manuals – School Management*, 175–6. For similar advice that takes account of the differences between graded and ungraded schools, see *JEdNS*, April 1921, 133 ff., esp. 149–54.

28 UAA, Charyk Fonds, 90-43-52, box 7, Mrs R. (Kathleen) Christie, 9 Feb. 1965.

29 *WSJ* 18, no. 4 (April 1924): 534–5. Grouping for reading in the primary classes was usual in urban and rural schools alike, but in rural schools the necessity of dividing beginners into subgroups multiplied even further the number of lessons teachers had to prepare. See also *BC Teacher* 13, no. 6 (Feb. 1934): 31; *Educational Review*, Feb. 1929, 128.

30 In Ontario this was official policy; see Ontario, *Ontario Normal School Manuals – School Management*, 175–6. At least one authority, however, contended that in rural areas this was in fact a dangerous practice, exposing young children

to long walks home without the protection or supervision of older children. See "Presidential Address," *Proceedings, OEA, 1919,* 198.

31 *Manitoba Teacher* 12, no. 4 (April 1931): 21. The educational press records many additional shortcuts and time savers. See *Educational Review,* March 1902, 211; *BC Teacher* 18, no. 8 (April 1939): 427–8; *Canadian Teacher* 30, no. 6 (5 Dec. 1925): 386.

32 For some examples, see *JEdNS,* series 5, 1, no. 1 (Oct. 1951): 18–20; Alex Stockwell, "The Time Table and Classroom Management," *ATAM* 5, no. 10 (March 1925): 31–2; New Brunswick, *AR 1925–26,* "Time Table in Ungraded Schools," 162–6. See also Alberta, *AR 1925,* 56; *WSJ* 18, no. 4 (April 1924): 535–6; *The School* 17, no. 3 (Nov. 1928): 242–3.

33 Ontario, *Ontario Normal School Manuals – School Management,* 175–6. The suggested timetable for ungraded schools accompanying the Nova Scotia program of studies of 1921 is higher than twenty recitations; see Figure 11.2. In one American survey of 1920, the *median* number of recitations per day was twenty-six. See Cuban, *How Teachers Taught,* 123.

34 Nova Scotia, *Manual of School Law, 1901,* 122.

35 Quoted in Kinnear, *A Female Economy,* 128.

36 UAA, Charyk Fonds, 90-43-52, box 10, Grace M. Thurlin, n.d.

37 *WSJ* 21, no. 8 (Oct. 1926): 926; 22, no. 1 (Jan. 1927): 5. Similarly, see Ontario, *Ontario Normal School Manuals – School Management,* 26. Yet another estimate placed the figure as high as seven-eighths; see Ontario, Dept of Education, *Public School Manual Training,* 22.

38 Alberta, *AR 1931,* 52.

39 Ontario authorities recommended that "from 30 to 50% of the total time allotted to any subject" should be given over to independent seat-work. "During this time occasional individual instruction should be given to those who need it." See Ontario, *Ontario Normal School Manuals – School Management,* 180.

40 See *The School* 7, no. 5 (Jan. 1919): 329; *WSJ* 15, no. 6 (June 1920): 227; 22, no. 1 (Jan. 1927): 5; Ontario, *Ontario Normal School Manuals – School Management,* 26, 28–9, 177.

41 See, for example, Henry Conn, "The Unemployment Problem in Primary Classes," *The School* 18, no. 1 (Sept. 1929): 31–3. See also the use of simple games as a means of drilling pupils in number work. *BC Teacher* 5, no. 5 (Jan. 1926): 101.

42 See, for example, *WSJ* 15, no. 6 (June 1920): 226–9; 21, no. 8 (Oct. 1926): 926–7; 23, no. 2 (Feb. 1928): 57–9; *Manitoba Teacher* 9, no. 6 (June 1928): 21–2; 12, no. 4 (April 1931): 21–4; *Proceedings, OEA, 1925,* 173–6; *Educational Review,* July–Aug. 1903, 2–3; Feb. 1904, 224; Nov. 1913, 111–13; *Canadian Teacher* 33, no. 4 (29 Oct. 1928): 63–4.

43 Van Kleek, *The Way It Was,* 46–7.

44 *ATAM* 10, no. 2 (Oct. 1929): 22–3.

45 *Canadian Teacher* 30, no. 7 (24 Dec. 1925): 457.

46 *Educational Review*, Dec. 1900, 138. Similarly see the editorial in ibid., Jan. 1901, 192; Nov. 1904, 144; Jan. 1911, 167; John Millar, Ontario's deputy minister of education, *Proceedings, OEA, 1901*, 70–1.

47 Editorial, *JEdNS*, Sept. 1934, 635.

48 For examples, see, for Manitoba, *WSJ* 16, no. 1 (Jan. 1921): 465–7; 19, no. 9 (Nov. 1924): 117–19; 23, no. 3 (March 1928): 83–5; New Brunswick, *AR 1923*, lxiv; *Blairmore Enterprise* (Alberta), 9 Oct. 1924, 3; 16 Oct. 1924, 3; Glenbow Archives, M2004, Crowsnest Pass School Division #63, Papers, Blairmore SD No. 628, School Board Minutes, 30 Jan. 1931, 25 Feb. 1935, 27 Oct. 1936, 29 Jan. 1937, 25 Feb. 1937; *ATAM* 12, no. 5 (Jan. 1932): 32; *CSJ* 10, no. 11 (Nov. 1932): 375; 12, no. 10 (Nov. 1934): 392; 14, no. 3 (March 1936): 72; 14, no. 9 (Sept. 1936): 256; 15, no. 3 (March 1937): 115.

49 See, for example, "Report of the Committee on Homework," *ATAM* 17, no. 10 (June 1937): 8–11; "Department of Education Memorandum ... Regarding the Course of Study," *The School* 13, no. 3 (Nov. 1924): 233–4. For British Columbia policies, see *Manual of School Law 1910*, Regulation 3 (c); *1929*, Regulation 4 (c); and the more peremptory 1937 Regulation 1 (5).

50 On parental views, see *Educational Review*, Dec. 1900, 138; *WSJ* 16, no. 1 (Jan. 1921): 465; 23, no. 3 (March 1928): 83–4; *Blairmore Enterprise*, 9 Oct. 1924, 3 (reprint of editorial from the *Winnipeg Tribune*); *ATAM* 12, no. 5 (Jan. 1932): 32 (citing views of Dr Helen McMurchy).

51 In British Columbia and Prince Edward Island, monthly reports were a legal requirement. See British Columbia, *Manual of School Law 1910*, section 10 (d); *1929*, Regulation 5; Prince Edward Island, *AR 1925–26*, xxxii. In Alberta, monthly reports had to be made if required by trustees. Alberta, School Act, 1930, s. 202 (g). For Ontario, see Ontario, *Ontario Normal School Manuals – School Management*, 206. Similarly, see Anderson, "Moncton," Part 2, chap. 5. It was during the interwar years that departments began to encourage elementary teachers to switch from numeric to alphabetical indicators for grades, that is, "C–" instead of "61." See *BC Teacher* 15, no. 6 (Feb. 1936): 19, citing a September 1935 memorandum from the minister of education.

52 *BC Teacher* 19, no. 5 (Jan. 1940): 249.

53 Some of Stephenson's Okanagan teachers complained about the extra work caused by the lack of texts. See "Mrs. Gibson," 237–8.

54 See Ontario, *Ontario Normal School Manuals – School Management*, 185; Reta L. McBratney, "Seat Work in the Lower Grades," *Manitoba Teacher* 12, no. 4 (April 1931): 24; London Board of Education, *AR 1911*, "Value of Blackboards," 36; J.M. Niven, "Arithmetic on the Blackboard for Senior First Book Children," *Educational Review*, Oct. 1913, 88 (this article also includes a picture of group work at the blackboard).

55 For the various types of blackboard and their relative effectiveness, see
    Charyk, *Little White Schoolhouse*, 126; Peabody, *School Days*, 38; Salisbury, *School
    Management*, 23–4. "Hyloplate," a popular and relatively effective substitute
    for slate, was liquid slating applied to large boards of cemented wood pulp.
    According to one school supply company's ad, it was half the price of slate,
    less costly to ship, less likely to break through shipping or installation, could
    be easily installed simply by nailing the large slabs to a wall, and took chalk
    and erasure well. See *Educational Review*, June 1900, 2.

56 Charyk, *Little White Schoolhouse*, 126.

57 See Ontario, *Ontario Normal School Manuals – School Management*, 128–9;
    Alberta, *AR 1910*, appendix A, Regulation 8. Windows were to be placed to
    the left of pupils' desks, or if necessary behind, near the left corner.

58 See *WSJ* 23, 2 (Feb. 1928): 58.

59 McLachlan, *With Unshakeable Persistence*, 28. The "cookie sheet" would have
    had to have sides – like a cake or baking tin – to prevent the gel running out,
    and McLachlan does not adequately describe the chemical composition. For
    detailed recipes for making and using a hectograph pad, see *ATAM* 18, no. 3
    (Nov. 1937): 14; *WSJ* 23, no. 2 (Feb. 1928): 58–9; *BC Teacher* 14, no. 9 (May
    1935): 5; Van Kleek, *The Way It Was*, 69. For examples of what hectograph
    masters looked like, see *The School* 25, no. 1 (Sept. 1936): 44–5; 25, no. 2
    (Oct. 1936): 133–5. The hectograph was the cheapest duplicator available,
    which added to its attractions. In the late 1930s, for example, a commercial
    kit could be had for $5.50 and a homemade version for half that. See *The
    School* 26, no. 1 (Sept. 1937): back cover advertisement; *ATAM* 19, no. 5 (Jan.
    1939): inside front cover advertisement.

60 See Joyce Boyle, "Primary Seat Work Again," *The School* 25, no. 2 (Oct. 1936):
    133; *BC Teacher* 14, no. 9 (May 1935): 5.

61 Van Kleek, *The Way It Was*, 70.

62 McLachlan, *With Unfailing Dedication*, 124.

63 In 1939, for example, a Ditto machine cost $125 and that did not include the
    cost of Ditto masters or duplicating fluid. See the ad in *The School* 27, no. 7
    (March 1939): iii.

64 Van Kleek, *The Way It Was*, 70. Carbon paper was most commonly associ-
    ated with use in typewriters, but it could just as easily be used with a pen or
    pencil and could make up to four or five good-quality copies. Carbon paper
    was interleaved with writing paper, one sheet on top of the other, and you
    wrote directly on the top sheet, pressing firmly (or put all the interleaved
    sheets into the roller of a typewriter). If a teacher needed eight or ten copies,
    she would have to repeat the process at least once. Carbon paper could be
    reused a limited number of times. Cumulatively the hectograph was probably
    cheaper, since each piece of carbon paper had to be purchased. Typewriters
    were widely advertised in the educational press but they were not cheap. In

the mid-1920s a portable Corona cost $65 and a portable Remington $77.50. See *Manitoba Teacher* 5, no. 4 (April 1924): 19; 5, no. 6 (June 1924): 16. By 1930 large numbers of London teachers were taking board-sponsored typing lessons "in order to acquire sufficient skill to make effective use of the typewriter and [mechanical] duplicators in the schools"; but the board had also recently distributed hectographs as well. See London Board of Education, AR *1930*, 14, 42. Simply from seeing the original materials generated by school boards and principals' offices, we have the impression that mimeograph machines with their typed stencils were increasingly used by administrators or for any general purpose where large numbers of copies had to be produced, but rarely put to use by individual teachers for their own classrooms.

65 There is a substantial literature in the educational press on the development of school broadcasting but very little evidence on the actual number of radios in rural schools. What we have been able to locate suggests that in the interwar years they were still uncommon. See, for example, *Manitoba Teacher* 13, no. 4 (April 1932): 6; Manitoba, AR *1939–40*, 22; PAA, 79-334, box 10, Canadian Education Association 1946, Memo, Director of Curriculum, Alberta, to C.E. Phillips, 3 June 1946. For Ontario, see Figure 4.2 in chapter 4 of this volume,. Relatively inexpensive radios powered by 6- or 12-volt batteries were widely advertised but probably little used because batteries had to be purchased separately and then kept charged. Because they could be wound by hand, gramophones appear to have been more common, although one still had to purchase records to make them useful. A 1932 Manitoba study reported that of 1,000 one-room schools surveyed, only 30 had a radio, though 37.5% had a gramophone. *Manitoba Teacher* 13, no. 4 (April 1932): 6. For ads with prices, see *The School* 11, no. 5 (Jan. 1923): 280; 19, no. 8 (April 1931): 799; BC *Teacher* 9, no. 7 (March 1930): advertisement between table of contents and editorial. In 1940 Bell and Howell was advertising a "12 volt motor driven projector for Rural Schools," run by two 6-volt car batteries. ATAM 20, no. 9 (May 1940): 20. We've found no references to its use in Canadian schools.

66 A flash card is a small rectangular sheet that contains a short problem, such as "$3 \times 5 = ?$"

67 Peabody, *School Days*, 64.

68 BC *Teacher* 7, no. 6 (Feb. 1928): 37–8. In Manitoba one inspector reported in 1916 that 33 of the 41 schools in his district had libraries, and 12 schools reported "extensive" use of the library while 6 reported "little or none." "Several of the libraries," he noted, "have little that is of value in the school – one of 28 books is quite suitable for a college professor." WSJ 11 (Feb. 1916): 61–2. By 1931, however, good school libraries were far more common in Manitoba. A survey of 1,000 one-room schools that year showed that almost half had libraries of 200 to 300 books and many had more than that.

Manitoba Teacher 12, no. 5 (May 1931): 13. On the other hand, see the comment by the Camrose, Alberta, inspector quoted in chapter 4.

69 Stephenson, "Mrs. Gibson," 237.

70 Report, Chief Inspector of Schools, Alberta, AR *1937*, 69. For the full description, see chapter 4.

71 Saskatchewan, AR *1934*, 43–4.

72 In a previous chapter we've already noted the teachers' consortiums formed to produce promotion exams. For good descriptions of more broadly based co-operative schemes, see *BC Teacher* 6, no. 6 (Feb. 1927): 35 (co-operative activities by Biggar [Saskatchewan] Inspectorate, Teachers' Association); O.E. Wahl, "Co-operation in McBride District," *BC Teacher* 19, no. 5 (Jan. 1940): 249–51.

73 For a typical monthly outline, in this case for February, see *ATAM* 14, no. 5 (Jan. 1934): 13–20.

74 *BC Teacher* 20, no. 1 (Sept. 1940): 37. A month later the editor of "The Question Box" noted that while colleagues were offering up good answers to a wide range of other questions, "no one has come to the assistance of the teacher whose school is on a raft." *BC Teacher* 20, no. 2 (Oct. 1940): 90.

75 Since this was the bread-and-butter content of the federation journals and one of the chief purposes in publishing *The School* or the *Educational Review*, the best source is the table of contents of any of these journals. While we have not tried to quantify the subject, our impression is that this kind of material would constitute 40% or 50% or more of most issues of any of the professional journals.

76 See the ad in *Educational Review*, Nov. 1918, 91.

77 See the ad in *BC Teacher* 18, no. 1 (Sept. 1938): 46.

78 *Canadian Teacher* 29, no. 16.

79 We have lifted these examples from a remarkable swathe of similar ads in the *Canadian Teacher*, 1925–28.

80 For other evidence that such magazines were in high demand, see the commentary about Saskatchewan's *The Modern Instructor* in Gagné, "Print, Profit, and Pedagogy," 19.

81 See the full-page ads from Nelson and Dent, *BC Teacher* 2, no. 8 (April 1923): inside back cover; 20, no. 1 (Sept. 1940): opposite p. 1. Similarly, see the Macmillan Company ad for kindergarten and primary teaching aids, *Canadian Teacher* 29, no. 4 (28 Oct. 1924): 209.

82 *ATAM* 8, no. 2 (Sept. 1927): 3. The Alberta report card reproduced in Figure 11.4 was purchased from Moyer's.

83 See, for example, the splashy four-page coloured insert from *The World Book* in *BC Teacher* 5, no. 8 (April 1926); and free projects book, *BC Teacher* 5, no. 3 (Nov. 1925): 57.

84 For other examples and extended analysis of this phenomenon, see Gidney and Gidney, "Branding," 345–79. There is also a picture of a classroom with the Neilson chocolate bar map of Canada, in Lawr and Gidney, *Educating Canadians*, 123.

85 See *Educational Review*, Feb. 1927, 129–30; March 1927, 159–60; May 1927, 197–8; Sept. 1927, 7–8; Dec. 1927, 79–80. For other examples, see Gidney and Gidney, "Branding."

86 Lane, "36 Lessons in One Day," *The School* 7, no. 5 (Jan. 1919): 329.

87 *WSJ* 18, no. 4 (April 1924): 536.

88 T.R. Hall, inspector of schools, Kelowna, "Time Economy in the Rural School," *BC Teacher* 13, no. 6 (Feb. 1934): 36.

89 "A Time Table for Rural Schools," *JEdNS*, new series, 1, no. 1 (Oct. 1951): 21–2.

90 For another good example, see Lucile Elder, "Economy of Time in School Management," *WSJ* 15, no. 5 (May 1920): 189–91. Some readers may feel that an essential requisite is missing from our discussion thus far – establishing and maintaining discipline. We agree it is fundamental; without it, orderly learning is impossible. But aside from the use of the strap and law cases involving assault, both well documented, the sources are very thin. The use of the strap, after all, is usually a sign that discipline has broken down, and large numbers of individual accounts suggest that most teachers never resorted to it. Yet there is almost a blanket silence on how teachers, in ordinary circumstances, established and maintained order, or how they learned to do so. There is some helpful material in Sutherland, *Growing Up*, 204–12, and in Charyk, *Pulse of the Community*, 29–57. Though less helpful on practice, a comprehensive and valuable survey of policy is Johnson's "Changing Conceptions."

91 Stephenson, "Mrs. Gibson," 237. Elder is also emphatic on this point. See previous note.

92 *Canadian Teacher* 30, no. 10 (19 Feb. 1926): 660. For another similar account, but one that also includes how, as she gained experience, a teacher learned to manage her preparation time, see ibid., 30, no. 6 (5 Dec. 1925): 386.

93 Corman, "Seeking Greener Pastures," 185–7.

94 UAA, Charyk Fonds, 90-43-45, box 6, Katie Baker, 14 May 1971. For another example and a similar story, see McLachlan, *With Unshakeable Persistence*, 102–3.

95 *Proceedings, OEA, 1914*, 213.

96 Alberta, *AR 1915*, 34.

97 Saskatchewan, *AR 1930*, 13, 77–8.

98 New Brunswick, *AR 1934–35*, 103. Similarly, see Alberta, *AR 1922*, 45; *AR 1925*, 46.

99 This does not mean that the normal schools did a superlative job at training urban teachers, only that the type of training was more suited to urban
schools. For a critique by a group of inspectors of the work of the Ontario
normal schools generally, see W.J. Karr, "Possibilities of Improvement in the
Training of Teachers," *Proceedings, OEA, 1915*, 290–1.

100 *ATAM* 7, no. 8 (Feb. 1927): 11.

101 Ontario, *Ontario Normal School Manuals – School Management*, 188, 190.

102 See ibid., chap. 4. The gap between the realities and what the leadership
envisioned as the model physical plant for the rural school was extreme.
Compare the descriptions of actual schools offered here and in chapter
4 with such articles as "A Model Rural School," *WSJ* 11, no. 5 (May 1916):
164–6 – a description of "one of the most striking exhibits at the Teachers'
Association in Winnipeg [of] the properly equipped rural school." Similarly,
see ibid., 18, no. 8 (Oct. 1923): 696.

103 Ontario, *Ontario Normal School Manuals – School Management*, 37.

104 See ibid., 28–30.

105 Jones, *Empire of Dust*, 179. Ontario was an exception. By 1915 its normal
schools were required to provide one week of observation and practice lessons in a rural school; however, this was considered by several observers to be
little more than tokenism. See O.J. Stevenson, "The Training of Teachers for
Rural Schools," *Proceedings, OEA, 1917*, 497.

106 Stephenson, "Mrs. Gibson," 248.

107 *Manitoba Teachers' Federation Bulletin*, May 1923, 377. For a similar comment,
see Saskatchewan, *AR 1928*, 113–14.

108 McBeath, "Education in New Brunswick," 100.

109 Alberta, *AR 1925*, 56.

110 Alberta, *AR 1927*, 43. Similarly, see ibid., 41–2; *AR 1926*, 29.

111 On the level of concern about the lack of rural practice teaching in Alberta in
the 1920s, see, for example, Alberta, *AR 1921*, 45; *AR 1922*, 45; *AR 1925*, 40;
AR 1927, 36. On the attempt to replicate an ungraded classroom in a normal
school model school, see Alberta, *AR 1931*, 31; New Brunswick, *AR 1932*, 5; *AR
1935*, 103; Calam, *Alex Lord's British Columbia*, 9.

112 *The School* 26, no. 6 (Feb. 1938): 479.

113 New Brunswick, *AR 1934–35*, 103–4.

114 For developments in Alberta, see Mann, "Alberta Normal Schools," 87–8,
106, 124, 137, 237–8. For Ontario, see Ontario, *AR 1936*, 27; *AR 1945*,
33. For provision in British Columbia in the 1920s, see Wilson, "Lottie
Bowron," 219; Manitoba, *AR 1929–30*, 81; Saskatchewan, *AR 1929–30*, 13.
Nova Scotia made provision for rural school experience from 1929 or 1930,
though it may not have survived in the later years of the Depression; see
Nova Scotia, *AR 1932*, 91; *JEdNS*, Jan. 1941, 94; J.P. McCarthy, "100 Years of
Teacher Education," Part 2, *JEdNS*, new series, 5, no. 2 (March 1956): 11.

New Brunswick introduced one week in 1938 and two the next year. See New Brunswick, *AR 1935*, 103; *The School* 27, no. 6 (Feb. 1939): 537.

115 PAA, 79.334, box 1, Dept of Education, Correspondence with Other Provinces, Saskatchewan, 1939–46, H.C. Newland to Principal, Normal School, Saskatoon, 9 Feb. 1940.

116 Alberta, *AR 1937*, 41. Similarly, see Alberta, *AR 1935*, 28.

117 On this point, see Dorothy Lane's comment in "36 Lessons in One Day," *The School* 7, no. 5 (Jan. 1919): 329–30.

118 See, for example, the quotations from Saskatchewan teachers and June Corman's commentary on the advantages of moving on each year, in Corman, "Seeking Greener Pastures," 187.

119 Generally on this point, see Coulter, "Girls Just Want to Have Fun," 211–29. For other examples, see Stephenson, "Mrs. Gibson," 252–3; UAA, Charyk Fonds, 90-43-52, box 7, Mrs H. Clews to Charyk, 18 Nov. 1964. Compare Weiler, *Country Schoolwomen*, 191–5.

CHAPTER TWELVE

1 Just because of this, as early as 1930 some provinces began to abandon the term "inspector," adopting the purportedly more nurturing term "superintendent" instead. However, this new terminology did not substantially alter their duties or loyalties to the central authority. On the role of the central authority itself, see chapter 1 and Manzer, *Public Schools and Political Ideas*, 135–9.

2 See Fleming, *The Principal's Office*, vol. 1. This volume is much broader than the title might suggest and offers the best available study of the context and development of supervision in Canada. Other important sources on Canadian school administration in the early twentieth century are Miller, *Rural Schools*, chap. 10; Richardson, *Administration of Schools*; and Fleming, *School Leadership*. Two classic American studies are Tyack and Hansot, *Managers of Virtue*; and Campbell, Fleming, Newell, and Bennion, *Educational Administration*. For a useful introduction to the differences between Canada and the United States that also incorporates references to much of the pertinent literature, see Allison, "Pride and Privilege," 209–38.

3 There were exceptions, notably in Ontario, where until 1930 public school inspector appointments were made by county councils in southern Ontario and by city boards of education. However, qualifications and duties were controlled by the province and the minister of education exercised a veto power over appointments. For the details and formal procedures in all provinces, see Miller, *Rural Schools*, 133–4; DBS, *Annual Survey 1934*, appendix to Part 1, "The Mechanisms of Administration ... of the Provincial School Systems," lxxiii.

4 Ontario, *AR 1921*, 297–8. For arrangements in British Columbia about the same time, see Putman-Weir Report, 235. For an example of the daily work routines and expectations of the high school inspectorate, see the description provided by a visiting English inspector, [Savage], *Secondary Education in Ontario*, 35–6.

5 The outstanding historical study of the twentieth-century inspectorate is Fleming, "Our Boys in the Field," 55–76. But see also the introduction in Calam, *Alex Lord's British Columbia*. These two fine essays are complemented by the valuable thesis by Stairs Quinn, "Sympathetic and Practical Men?" Stairs Quinn is especially enlightening on the collective beliefs of the inspectorate about the good school and the good school system, along with their conception about their roles in shaping both; see esp. chap. 2.

6 On recruitment, see Fleming, "Our Boys in the Field," 61. There is no reason to think this wasn't typical across the country.

7 On their qualifications, see Miller, *Rural Schools*, 144–5; Foght, *Saskatchewan*, 35; Saskatchewan, *AR 1930*, 55–6; Alberta, *AR 1921*, 53; *AR 1929*, 32; Ontario, *AR 1922*, 2–3. On their backgrounds, see Miller's large Canada-wide sample, *Rural Schools*, 146–8.

8 Miller, *Rural Schools*, 149–50; Collins, "Provincially Appointed Superintendents," 127.

9 Nova Scotia, *AR 1924*, xx. For a detailed exposition on the work of "educational propaganda," see Stairs Quinn, "Sympathetic and Practical Men?," 168ff. For quite explicit instructions from a minister of education to his inspectors about vigorous salesmanship for departmental policies, see, for example, G.M. Weir's memo of 13 Sept. 1935 in *BC Teacher* 15, no. 6 (Feb. 1936): 18–19. For typical lists of the inspector's duties, see Miller, *Rural Schools*, 149–50; Nova Scotia, *Manual of School Law, 1901*, School Act, 27–8, and "Regulations and Comment," 58–9; *Statutes and Regulations Respecting Public and High Schools, Ontario, 1901*, School Act, s. 87; Manitoba, *Regulations of the Department of Education, Effective 1 July 1934*, Regulation 14. For some good general description by departmental officials of the work of the inspectorate, see also Alberta, *AR 1921*, 49; *AR 1922*, 52; *AR 1930*, 47–8; Saskatchewan, *AR 1922*, 91–2.

10 Alberta, *AR 1930*, 47. Just because they were the "eyes and ears," the relationship between the central office and the inspectorate was reciprocal. Individually and collectively the inspectorate could also exercise a role in policy-making. See Stairs Quinn, "Sympathetic and Practical Men?," 130ff.

11 Depending on the province, for example, the inspector might or might not have the power to withhold the grant for infractions, but if not, he could recommend that the department do so. Similarly, in some provinces rural inspectors were required to help enforce compulsory attendance laws and after investigation refer truancy cases to a magistrate.

12 Miller, *Rural Schools*, 150. The internal quotation is from Ontario's instructions to inspectors. For other examples of the dual role that department of education inspectors were expected to perform – both inspection and supervision – see Nova Scotia, *Manual of School Law, 1901*, Regulation 15 (a) through (d); British Columbia, *Manual of School Law 1910*, School Act, s. 8 (a) through (c).

13 Ontario inspectors were not offered funding assistance until 1930, though this was probably true only for rural inspectors who didn't have the advantage of city central offices. As late as 1940 Saskatchewan's inspectors were still "doing all their own office and stenographic work," and similar conditions held in New Brunswick. See Ontario, *Report of the Royal Commission on Education, 1950*, 329; Saskatchewan, AR *1940*, 33; New Brunswick, AR *1941–42*, 19. Indeed a national survey in the early 1940s reported that in five of the nine provinces, the inspectorate operated without office and stenographic assistance. CEA, *Report of the Survey Committee*, 21. For examples of the types of correspondence between the inspectorate and central office, see PAA, 79.334, box 22, Dept of Education Correspondence with School Superintendents and Inspectors.

14 *Regulations and Course of Study of the Public Schools of Ontario, 1911*, Regulation 20 (2). In Nova Scotia it was at least once a year, and at least one and a half hours for a small school, but most would require more, up to half a day. Nova Scotia, *Manual of School Law, 1901*, 59. In Saskatchewan the rule of thumb was half a day per room. Saskatchewan, AR *1929*, 69.

15 Manitoba, *Regulations ... Effective 1 July 1934*, Regulation 14 (o). Similarly, see Alberta, AR *1910*, "Regulations of the Department of Education, Approved 1906," Regulation 31; *Regulations and Course of Study of the Public Schools of Ontario, 1911*, s. 20. In Nova Scotia and British Columbia there were no parallel explicit instructions of this sort, but the authority was implicit in the powers to inspect included in the school acts.

16 John Dearness, "The Best Methods of Inspecting Public Schools," *Proceedings, OEA, 1906*, 306–9. For other descriptions of the school visit, see ibid., *1897*, 367–71; *1914*, 219–24; WSJ 9, no. 1 (March 1914): 11; New Brunswick, AR *1932–33*, 50–1. For "Methods of Inspection and Supervision" reported by Miller's sample of Canadian inspectors, see *Rural Schools*, 162ff. – a very useful overview of procedures commonly used and also some of the variations.

17 For one classic case of a near-intractable dispute, see Calam, *Alex Lord's British Columbia*, 55–7. For an example of the kinds of issues that routinely caused difficulties within school districts, see New Brunswick, AR *1932–33*, 51.

18 *JEdNS*, Jan. 1939, 25–8. This doesn't mean that an inspector's recommendations were necessarily adopted. See Stairs Quinn, "Sympathetic and Practical Men?," 153–4.

19 For an example of the categories of information required in monthly reports by each inspector and the uses to which the information was put, see Alberta, *AR 1922*, 54.

20 These individual reports were never published and were usually considered confidential information, but for years Alberta published summary ratings by inspectorate; see Alberta, *AR 1930*, 49.

21 Glenbow Archives, M2004, Crowsnest Pass School Division #63, Papers, Blairmore SD No. 628, School Board Minutes, 11 Jan. and 24 Feb. 1922. This was not the only time it happened. An adverse report of 1928 on the vice-principal resulted in his contract not being renewed. Ibid., 19 June 1928.

22 Ibid., 10 Dec. 1926 and 4 March 1927. See also the board's reaction when one high school inspector insisted they hire a third teacher for the high school, in ibid., 26 Dec. 1925; *Blairmore Enterprise*, 31 Dec. 1925.

23 Blairmore School Board Minutes, 19 June 1928. Similarly, see ibid., 20 Dec. 1926.

24 Foght, *Saskatchewan*, 36.

25 McDougall, *Building the North*, 108–9.

26 Calam, *Alex Lord's British Columbia*, 36.

27 PAA, 79.334, file 6, Chief Inspector of Schools, Alberta, to same, Manitoba, 11 June 1935.

28 Calam, *Alex Lord's British Columbia*, 37.

29 McDougall, *Building the North*, 122, 125.

30 PAA, 79.334, box 22, F.L. Aylesworth to Chief Inspector, 11 Sept. 1915, and Chief Inspector to Aylesworth, 16 Sept. 1915.

31 See, for example, the comment by the chief inspector in Saskatchewan, *AR 1929*, 69.

32 *The School* 17, no. 1 (Sept. 1928): 98.

33 Saskatchewan, *AR 1922*, 92.

34 Saskatchewan, *AR 1929*, 69.

35 Saskatchewan, *AR 1932*, 42.

36 Alberta, *AR 1910*, 30; *AR 1922*, 54.

37 *ATAM* 4, no. 2 (July 1923): 7.

38 Race, "Compulsory Schooling in Alberta," 158, 160.

39 Alberta, *AR 1930*, 33.

40 PAA, 79.334, box 1, file 6, Chief Inspector of Schools, Alberta, to same, Manitoba, 11 June 1935.

41 Nova Scotia, *AR 1926–27*, xxiv.

42 New Brunswick, *AR 1939*, 8. On the "superficial" level of inspectors' visits to rural schools in remote parts of British Columbia, see Stortz, "The Rural School Problem in British Columbia," 127.

43 Miller, *Rural Schools*, 158.

44 Putman-Weir Report, 238; PAA, 79.334, box 1, file 6, Chief Inspector of
   Schools, Alberta, to same, Manitoba, 11 June 1935.

45 For an illuminating and thoughtful response by one inspector to a call by the
   British Columbia Trustees Association for twice-yearly visits to all high school
   classrooms, see British Columbia, *AR 1920*, C18.

46 The best account is Fleming, *The Principal's Office*, vol. 1, chaps 3 and 4.

47 On this point, see, for example, Miller, *Rural Schools*, 207–8, and the pointed
   comments on the sharp contrast between urban and rural classrooms by New
   Brunswick's Director of Educational Services, in New Brunswick, *AR 1942*,
   18–20.

48 Black, *School Administration*, 106; similarly, see Putman-Weir Report, 238.

49 Prince Edward Island, Royal Commission on Education, *Report*, 1930, 23.

50 S. Silcox, "Modern Rural Schools," *Proceedings*, OEA, *1918*, 375.

51 "Observation on Supervision," ATAM 18, no. 6 (Feb. 1938): 17. The citations
   on this point only scratch the surface of concern about the issue. For other
   examples – again, just a sample of the sources – see Miller, *Rural Schools*,
   202–3; Bingay, *Public Education in Nova Scotia*, 72; Murray Report, 88–9; Davis,
   "Secondary Education in Nova Scotia," 182–3; MacDiarmid, "Functions of
   a School Principal," 19–20 (New Brunswick); New Brunswick, *AR 1941–42*,
   19–23; C.E. Little, "Better Education through Better Supervision," *CSJ* 9, no. 2
   (Feb. 1930): 14–15 (Ontario and Saskatchewan); *Manitoba Teachers' Federation
   Bulletin*, May 1923, 377–8; Foght, *Saskatchewan*, 33–5; Saskatchewan, *AR 1922*,
   93; *AR 1939*, 32; Alberta, *AR 1922*, 53–4; ATAM 5, no. 2 (July 1924): 5; G. Fred
   McNally, "Education in Alberta," *The School* 16, no. 10 (June 1928): 1029;
   Putman-Weir Report, 238–9; *BC Teacher* 16, no. 2 (Oct. 1936): 89–90.

52 Stephenson, "Mrs. Gibson," 249.

53 Ibid., 251. Similarly, see the assessment of the value of inspectoral visits and
   the sense of isolation in Harper, "Personal and Professional Freedom," 65–6.

54 In the early twentieth century these two terms were still in common use, the
   elision to "principal" still in process. Until Fleming's indispensable study,
   The Principal's Office, there was very little literature in Canada on the principal. For earlier work that remains useful, however, see Fleming, "British
   Columbia Principals," 249–85. For a rare survey of one city, see Chiang,
   "School Principalship in Vancouver." An overview that covers both Canada
   and the United States is Rousmaniere, "Go to the Principal's Office," 1–22.
   Rousmaniere overestimates the similarities in the administrative structures
   of the two countries and her Canadian research doesn't probe very deeply;
   still, it is a helpful introduction to the subject. See also Rousmaniere, "The
   Great Divide," 17–27. The two most accessible and useful contemporary
   sources for the period we are concerned with are Richardson, *Administration
   of Schools*, chap. 5, and Dyde's chapter 10 on high school principals in *Public*

Secondary Education. Because of his political career, one principal's professional career is well documented and illuminating on the career trajectory,
work, and educational environment of the Canadian high school principal
in the early twentieth century. See Irving, *The Social Credit Movement*, chap. 2;
Elliott and Miller, *Bible Bill*, 14–15, 23–5, and chap. 5. For another example,
see Kirkconnell, *A Canadian Headmaster*, esp. chaps 2, 3, and 10.

55 On education and experience, see Richardson, *Administration of Schools*,
   155–6, 160; Dyde, *Public Secondary Education*, 161–7, 170; Harris, "Graded
   Schools in Rural Manitoba," 22; Fleming, "British Columbia Principals," esp.
   252.

56 Alberta, *The School Act ... 1930*, s. 204. Similarly, see *Manual of School Law
   for British Columbia, 1910*, Rules and Regulations, Article 9; *Regulations and
   Course of Study ... Ontario, 1911*, 3 (b); Manitoba, *Regulations 1930*, 15 (b);
   MacDiarmid, "Functions of a School Principal," 36, citing New Brunswick's
   Regulation 26.

57 In the various school law manuals for British Columbia, 1910 through 1937,
   there is nothing in the legislation pertaining specifically to principals, and
   in the regulations only two brief references. Much the same is true in the
   early twentieth-century Ontario legislation. See, for example, "The Public
   School Act" in *Acts of the Department of Education, Ontario, 1909*, where there is
   no entry for "principal" at all, and *Regulations and Course of Study of the Public
   Schools of Ontario, 1911*, where there is only the briefest four-line entry. By
   the interwar years, however, Ontario had introduced a wide variety of rules
   (see Dyde, *Public Secondary Education*, 179–81) and Manitoba spelled out the
   duties of the job in considerable detail. These kinds of province-wide duties
   were in addition to any assigned by local trustees. When duties were prescribed in the acts and regulations, the law usually designated the teacher in
   a one-room school as principal. See Nova Scotia, *Manual of School Law, 1901*,
   61; Manitoba, *Regulations ... Effective 1 July 1934*, Regulation 15 (a).

58 See Chiang, "School Principalship in Vancouver," 52–4, and appendix 3; 96–7.

59 For the list, see Anderson, "Moncton," Part 1, chap. 5 ("The Principal").

60 Along with the references in the previous notes on the core tasks and sheer
   variety of duties, see Richardson, *Administration of Schools*, 152–5; Dyde, *Public
   Secondary Education*, 179–81; Manitoba, *Regulations ... Effective 1 July 1934*,
   Regulation 15, which includes twenty-three specified tasks; Saskatchewan, AR
   1910, Part 4, Regulations Governing the Public Schools, 70–1, Regulations
   6 (a) and 14; British Columbia, *Manual of School Law, 1910*, Articles 9 and
   10. The multifarious duties and activities of the principal of the Blairmore
   school, *c.* 1920–40, can be gathered in a reading of the Blairmore School
   Board Minutes. Fleming, *The Principal's Office*, is strong on the overall managerial role; see vol. 1, chaps 3 and 4. We are almost exclusively concerned
   here with the supervision of teachers.

61 London Board of Education, *AR 1910*, 32.

62 Richardson, *Administration of Schools*, 153.

63 Dyde, *Public Secondary Education*, 176–7.

64 Richardson, *Administration of Schools*, 153; Dyde, *Public Secondary Education*, 175.

65 Richardson, *Administration of Schools*, 153.

66 Ibid., 152.

67 Nova Scotia, *AR 1931*, 106.

68 Winnipeg School Board, *AR 1933*, 15.

69 Ontario, Dept of Education, *Schools and Teachers in the Province of Ontario* (Ontario Blue Book), 1930, 36ff. (This is one of the annual publications called "Blue Books" because of the colour of their covers; it lists all Ontario teachers and principals, etc., by name and school, by city, county, and districts, and identifies supervisory roles.) For the similar pattern in Calgary and Edmonton, see Alberta, *AR 1920*, 107–8; *AR 1929*, 34; *ATAM* 8, no. 3 (Nov. 1927): 23. See also London Board of Education, *AR 1922*, 68; Mark, *Ottawa*, 75; New Brunswick, *AR 1941–42*, 18.

70 London Board of Education, *AR 1930*, 9.

71 Blashill, *Saskatoon Public School System*, 67, 73. Similarly, compare the statistics for Regina, in Saskatchewan, *AR 1934*, 52; *AR 1941*, 39.

72 Blairmore School Board Minutes, 26 Dec. 1925. Italics added. For other examples of full-time or nearly full-time teaching loads, see Harris, "Graded Schools in Rural Manitoba," 22; W.J. Bond, "The Village Principal as Supervisor," *WSJ* 31, no. 5 (May 1936): 153.

73 Harris, "Graded Schools in Rural Manitoba," 20–3.

74 Bond, "The Village Principal," 153.

75 Anderson, "Moncton," Part 1, chap. 5 ("The Principal"). For yet another analysis that reached similar conclusions, see Spencer, "Supervising Activities of School Principals," 10–16, 54–5.

76 The distinction between non-teaching principals and those who taught can be made because the reports give enrolments by subject or grade for each teacher. Those we identify as non-teaching principals carried no student load. Though it's more of a guestimate, we can also get some sense of partial release time by estimating teaching loads. We think we are on solid ground in the first case, less so in the second. The Ontario Blue Books don't provide equivalent data that would allow for a direct and systematic comparison. The sources of the data here are the lists of teachers by school that were published in the British Columbia *Annual Reports*. The most useful of the records begin in 1917–18.

77 See Chiang, "School Principalship in Vancouver," 84, 74ff. (generally). See also Fleming, *The Principal's Office*, vol. 1, chap. 3; Davy, "The Function of the Principal of the Elementary School," 5–6.

78 Our guess is that in most cases it did not. The Depression also wiped out the substantial cadre of supervisors Vancouver had had in the late 1920s, and there is no evidence of auxiliary teachers until the late 1930s, when a long list of highly qualified and salaried "relief teachers" appears. These, we suspect, allowed the resumption of at least partial release time.

79 Dyde, *Public Secondary Education*, 182.

80 Davis, "Reorganization of Secondary Education," 176.

81 [Savage], *Secondary Education in Ontario*, 38.

82 Gordon, "Secondary Education in Rural British Columbia," 27. We have carried out the same kind of analysis for British Columbia's high school principals as we did for the elementary schools, and Gordon's estimate for the late 1930s appears to be not only correct but also applicable to the 1920s. Unlike the elementary schools, there was a steady expansion in the number of full-time principals in secondary schools in the larger towns; in Vancouver by 1929–30 all high schools had full-time principals, and there was no lost ground during the Depression. By 1938–39 six schools even had vice-principals. Thus the high school was better provided for than the elementary school, but even then, most high schools did *not* have principals on full-time release and in other cases the high school principal was also supervising principal for the town school system.

83 Saskatchewan, *AR 1907*, Regulations of the Dept of Education, 7 (1). By 1944 the regulation had changed to twenty-five teachers. Saskatchewan, *Regulations under the School Act, 1944*, s. 15 (1).

84 Manitoba, *The Public School Act, 1925*, s. 134.

85 The county inspector sometimes played a similar role in the larger county towns, though he was also responsible for the regular inspection of the rural schools within the county. British Columbia had an optional system of city (or municipal) inspector-superintendents. See British Columbia, *Manual of School Law, 1910*, School Act, s. 8, and *1919*, s. 10.

86 Nova Scotia, *Manual of School Law, 1901*, "Comments and Regulations," 61–2.

87 Richardson, *Administration of Schools*, 114.

88 Stamp, "The Response to Urban Growth," 119; Calgary Board of Education, *AR 1935*, 8.

89 Trueman, *A Second View of Things*. On his years as superintendent, see chap. 9.

90 On the aura of authority and competence that arose from a liberal education and high social status rather than technical expertise *per se*, see Gidney and Millar, *Professional Gentlemen*, passim.

91 Manitoba, *Report of the Royal Commission on ... Municipal Finances*, 82. For a full description of the entire structure, see 79–84.

92 See V.K. Greer, "Re-organization of Educational Administration in London," *The School* 13, no. 7 (March 1925): 546. In fall 1934 the Toronto board

debated the idea of centralizing authority in the hands of its superintendent, making him in effect CEO, in charge of academic and business affairs alike, but then decided against it. See *CSJ* 12, no. 10 (Nov. 1934): 384; *CSJ* 13, no. 1 (Jan. 1935): 25.

93 See Greer, "Re-organization of Educational Administration," 545–8; but the changes are best traced over time through the London Board of Education *AR*s, which include as a frontispiece a list of officers and titles.

94 Richardson, *Administration of Schools*, 117. On the relationship between the board of trustees and the municipal inspector (i.e., superintendent) in Vancouver, on the one hand, and the municipal inspector and his principals, on the other, see Chiang, "School Principalship in Vancouver," 54ff. For the bureaucratizing effects of this centralization of authority on the role of the principal, see Fleming, *The Principal's Office*, vol. 1, chap. 3.

95 On the latter three tasks, see the rules established for the Regina schools, cited in Archer, *Honoured*, 67–9.

96 Our summary here is based on Richardson, *Administration of Schools*, 114–28; the quotation is from p. 120. For a later example of the superintendent's duties in one city, see Anderson, "Moncton," Part 1, chap. 4 ("Duties and Powers of the Superintendent").

97 Richardson, *Administration of Schools*, 120.

98 *BC Teacher* 13, no. 3 (Nov. 1933): 30.

99 Ontario Blue Book, 1930, 262–3. Similarly, see Spencer, "Supervising Activities of School Principals," 12 (Melville, Saskatchewan).

100 Winnipeg, for example, created the superintendent's office in 1876, began adding subject supervisors in 1891, and appointed an assistant superintendent early in the next century's second decade. See Lucow, "Public School System in Winnipeg," chap. 4 ("The Organization of Administration"), 23ff. Toronto appointed its first assistant superintendent and specialist subject supervisor in the early 1890s; see Danylewycz and Prentice, "Teachers' Work," 145, 157n25. For Vancouver, see British Columbia, *AR 1913–14*, A62–3. Regina appointed its first specialist supervisors in 1911; see Archer, *Honoured*, 44.

101 See Richardson, *Administration of Schools*, 121–3, 298 (Table 16). The figures for Toronto are for the public school board only. The original table also includes four school systems in the province of Quebec.

102 Mark, *Ottawa*, 70.

103 Richardson, *Administration of Schools*, 122.

104 Cited in Kostek, *A Century and Ten*, 310.

105 London Board of Education, *AR 1922*, 7, and "Reports of Supervisors: Art," 69.

106 British Columbia, *AR 1913–14*, A62–3.

107 Winnipeg, AR *1933*, 14. For other examples of the work of subject supervisors, see Mark, *Ottawa*, 72; Saskatchewan, AR *1938*, "Report of Superintendent of Schools, Regina," 38.

108 Shack, "The Making of a Teacher," 465–6.

109 Putman-Weir Report, 403. For the supervisory staff in Calgary during the 1930s, see Calgary Board of Education, AR *1935*, 7; AR *1936*, 19; AR *1938*, 9.

110 For a flow chart that incorporates all of the departments involved in managing one big-city school system by 1928, see Chiang, "School Principalship in Vancouver," 15A, and compare the late nineteenth-century chart on p. 16A.

111 New Brunswick, AR *1941–42*, "Report, Director of Educational Services," 18.

112 Our estimates here are drawn from Ontario Blue Book, 1930.

113 See, for example, New Brunswick's *Educational Review*, Sept. 1918, 44, which lists the appointment of ten women principals. This figure is abnormally high, but there are near-monthly references of this sort in the "School and College" column. For other examples, see *Educational Review*, Aug. 1918, 21; *BC Teacher* 7, no. 8 (April 1928): 43; 11, no. 3 (Nov. 1931): 5; *The School* 21, no. 5 (Jan. 1933): 440. Most ARs do not provide lists of elementary principals (though those for secondary schools are somewhat more common), so it is not possible to put together a systematic national portrait. The richest sources are the Ontario Blue Books and the British Columbia ARs.

114 Our calculations from Manitoba, AR *1928–29*, 120–2.

115 Calgary School Board, AR *1930*, 10.

116 Kinnear, "Mostly for the Male Members," 4–5. For references to specific appointments, see, for example, Winnipeg School Board, AR *1930*, 8–9, or AR *1931*, 8–9.

117 New Brunswick, AR *1935–36*, 172–3.

118 Small, "Principals in Southwestern Ontario," 13.

119 Ontario Blue Book, 1930, our calculations.

120 Our calculations from British Columbia, AR *1928–29*, Part 2, Statistical Returns.

121 See Fleming, *The Principal's Office*, vol. 1, 305–6 (Table 14), and more generally his discussion and tables on 197–200 and 294–307; see also vol. 2, chap. 4.

122 Dyde, *Public Secondary Education*, 156.

123 Our calculations from Ontario Blue Book, 1930, 605ff. Susan Gelman found that between 1900 and 1930 twenty-one women held secondary school principalships but all were appointed to small high schools. See Gelman, "Women Secondary School Teachers," 88–9. In Table 1 in her article, "Hegemony and Hierarchy," 111, Cecilia Reynolds includes two women who were Toronto secondary school principals in 1930. However, they were principals of girls' schools for slow learners and not regular secondary schools. Compare pp. 629–37 (list of Toronto collegiate institutes) in Ontario Blue Book, 1930 with p. 735 (Toronto "Special Industrial Schools").

124 Ontario Blue Book, 1930, our calculations from 675ff.

125 Our calculations from British Columbia, *AR 1928–29*, Part 2, Statistical Returns.

126 Our calculations from Manitoba, *AR 1928–29*, 120–2.

127 Kinnear, "Mostly for the Male Members," 4–5.

128 Personal communication, Thomas Fleming, 10 Feb. 2010, based on his systematic survey, 1889–1975.

129 Morgenroth, "Saskatoon School System," 66–8a (Table 9).

130 Reynolds, "Hegemony and Hierarchy," 111 (Table 1).

131 For Trail, see, for example, British Columbia, *AR 1921–22*, Statistical Returns, C30; for Moncton, see New Brunswick, *AR 1928–29*, 99; for Fredericton, see New Brunswick, *AR 1935–36*, 172–3; for Calgary, see Calgary School Board, *AR 1930*, 10.

132 Compare for example the villages of Blenheim and Ridgetown in Ontario Blue Book, 1930, Kent Inspectorate No. 1, p. 180. Both had a single eight-teacher school but the principal in one was a woman and in the other, a man.

133 See Chiang, "School Principalship in Vancouver," 6, 40–3; Goodson and Anstead, *Through the Schoolhouse Door*, 131.

134 See, for example, Ontario Blue Book, 1930, entries for Woodstock, Paris, Whitby, Petrolia, and Oakville.

135 While women principals in the two inspectorates of Huron West and Leeds-Grenville No. 1 outnumbered men, the women were principals in rural schools, while the men held most of the positions in urban schools. Similarly, see Small, "Principals in Southwestern Ontario," 30–4.

136 Our calculations from the Statistical Returns in British Columbia, *AR 1920–21*, *AR 1928–29*, *AR 1938–39*.

137 See Small, "Principals in Southwestern Ontario," 14 (Fig. 2.1).

138 The decline for city elementary schools outside Vancouver was from 37% to 33%; in the rural municipality schools, from 43% to 36%; in rural district schools, from 40% to 22%. Our calculations from the Statistical Returns in British Columbia, *AR 1928–29*, *AR 1938–39*.

139 See, for example, Alberta, *AR 1910*, list of "City and Town Districts," 31, which includes the principals and school size, both public and separate; Ontario Blue Book, 1930, 477–604 – in this list of over a hundred pages one is hard-pressed to find *any* male separate school principals except in the single-sex boys' schools. And women religious were in charge of the largest as well as the smallest co-educational schools.

140 Our calculations from Manitoba, *AR 1932–33*, 85ff. Similarly, consider the consequences of adding together the public and separate school lists in Alberta, *AR 1910*, 31. See also Small, "Principals in Southwestern Ontario," 47–8. Combining all of the elementary school principals in Ontario, public

and separate alike, would give a positively panglossian picture of women's place in educational administration in that province.

141 For her career, see Fleming and Craig, "Margaret Strong," 323–44.

142 Marty had a long and distinguished career, however. Possessed of a graduate degree in modern languages, she gave a paper to the Ontario Educational Association as early as 1895, was the subject of a flattering article in *Maclean's* (15 Feb. 1920, 74), and was author of *An Educational Creed*. Her obituary is in Ontario, *AR 1929*, 2.

143 See the obituary in *Manitoba School Journal* 17, no. 5 (Jan. 1956): 4.

144 See Weiler, *Country Schoolwomen*, 21; Rousmaniere, *City Teachers*, 140n45; Tyack and Hansot, *Managers of Virtue*, 182–3.

145 See Gidney, *From Hope to Harris*, 161–3; Small, "Principals in Southwestern Ontario," 14.

146 The presence of substantial numbers of women principals and supervisors, even though mostly among the lower echelon of administrators, rather nicely parallels Peter Baskerville's more surprising findings about their role in business and finance. Baskerville comments on the importance of looking for women "below the top level of economic activity. Thousands of individual women demonstrated that they could function quite well in the public (masculine) spheres of finance and business." *A Silent Revolution*, 247, 236–47 (generally).

147 See Sylvester, *The Limits of Rural Capitalism*, 121; Ontario, *Report of the Committee Appointed to Enquire into the Condition of the Schools Attended by French-Speaking Pupils*, 23; Mahé, "Bilingual School District Trustees," 65–82, and "Official and Unofficial School Inspection," 31–51; Noël, "The Impact of Regulation 17."

148 See, for example, the work of the special inspectors: Alberta, *AR 1913*, "Report of Robert Fletcher, Supervisor of Foreign Schools," 39–49; Manitoba, *AR 1915–16*, Report, Ira Stratton, 213–19. On the regular inspectorate, see Alberta, *AR 1914*, 24–5; *AR 1919*, 66; *AR 1922*, 66.

149 For one good example of petty tyranny, see Wiebe, *Of This Earth*, 177. See also *ATAM* 5, no. 2 (July 1924): 5; Fleming, "Our Boys in the Field," 59; Abbott, "Accomplishing 'a Man's Task,'" 51–72. For a particularly harsh judgment, see Craig M. Mooney and J.M. Braithwaite, "School Drought," *Maclean's*, 1 Nov. 1937, 47.

150 See Van Kleek, *The Way It Was*, 26; *Educational Review*, March 1924, 155; Fleming and Smyly, "The Diary of Mary Williams," 266; Fleming, "Our Boys in the Field," 60; interview by Helen Raptis of a British Columbia teacher (personal communication, 5 June 2009); Fleming, *Schooling in British Columbia*, 179–83.

151 See, for example, McLachlan, *With Unshakeable Persistence*, 99–100.

152 Fleming, "Our Boys in the Field," 59.

153 Ibid., 60. Similarly, see, in the same volume, Fleming, Smyly, and White, "Beyond Hope and Past Redemption," 127; Calam, *Alex Lord's British Columbia*, 26. See also the commentary in Fleming, *The Principal's Office*, vol. 2, 179.

154 Stairs Quinn, "Sympathetic and Practical Men?," 105–6.

155 Wilson and Stortz, "May the Lord Have Mercy on You," 2nd edn, 238–9.

156 Compare, for example, the assessments of the success of the recommendation system for promotions in Manitoba, *AR* 1935–36, 22–7, with the analysis in Hamilton, "Schools of Rural Manitoba," 21–5, 60. We deal with Hamilton's analysis in chapter 9.

157 See Abbott, "Accomplishing 'a Man's Task,'" passim; Prentice, "Multiple Realities," 133.

158 Putman-Weir Report, 168.

159 Miller, "A Comparative Study," 194.

160 See the discussion and references in Gidney, "Madame How and Lady Why," 13–42.

161 See *Educational Review*, March 1924, 155.

162 See, for example, editorial, *ATAM* 8, no. 4 (Nov. 1927): 23.

163 See *Proceedings, OEA, 1910*, 156–60; *ATAM* 3, no. 6 (Nov. 1922): 20.

164 Teacher evaluation by *any* method is a mare's nest. On evaluation by inspectors or local supervisors, see the summary of the literature and critique in Fleming, *Schools, Pupils, and Teachers*, 440–6; Byrne, "Good Teaching and Good Teachers," 20–1, 23–4; Young, Levin, and Wallin, *Understanding Canadian Schools*, 206. For an international review of the literature that points to the strengths and weaknesses in nearly every known form of evaluation, see Medley, "Teacher Evaluation," 1345ff. See also Osborne's thoughtful comment on the value of the inspectorate in his *Education*, 119.

165 See Sutherland, *Children*, 169; CEA, *Report of the Survey Committee*, 21.

166 See Miller, *Rural Schools*, 153; CEA, *Report of the Survey Committee*, 21. For the data on Alberta and Nova Scotia, see p. 308, this chapter.

167 CEA, *Report of the Survey Committee*, 21.

168 See as well the pertinent comments in Sutherland, *Children in English-Canadian Society*, 168–71; Calam, *Alex Lord's British Columbia*, 26–7.

169 In 1871 Canada had only three communities with more than 30,000 people; by 1901 there were ten, by 1921, eighteen, and by 1941, twenty-seven. Stone, *Urban Development*, 72 (Table 4.2).

170 CEA, *Report of the Survey Committee*, 20.

171 On the numbers, see Stone, *Urban Development*, 72 (Table 4.2). Even Stone's figures minimize the contrast because he includes only urban communities with 5,000 or more people.

172 *ATAM* 8, no. 4 (Nov. 1927): 23.

173 The differences between Toronto and the school districts in southern York County (in Ontario Blue Book, 1930) can be identified by comparing the number of inspectors and other supervisors in each. Despite the very many large schools in parts of York County, its school districts clearly had fewer supervisors than Toronto. For Vancouver and its suburbs, see the lists of teaching personnel in British Columbia, *AR 1923–24* or *AR 1929–30*.

174 See Danylewycz and Prentice, "Teachers' Work."

175 British Columbia, *Manual of School Law, 1929*, School Act, s. 152 (b) and (c); Regulations, Article 6 (4) and (16).

176 Glenbow Archives, M2017, Pincher Creek SD No. 29, file 79; Alberta, Dept of Education, *Daily Register ... 1929–30*. The instructions are on the inside cover. For a description of the Ontario registers, see Ontario, *Ontario Normal School Manuals – School Management*, 195–7. For British Columbia, see Fleming and Raptis, "Government's Paper Empire," 178–9.

177 By the interwar years some provinces had introduced two distinct registers – the attendance register plus a "general register," where everything else but attendance was recorded. Thus the pertinent sections of the school acts refer to "registers" rather than "register."

178 Fleming and Raptis, "Government's Paper Empire," 179.

179 Ontario, *Ontario Normal School Manuals – School Management*, 205.

180 Manitoba, *The Public Schools Act, 1925*, s. 156 (i).

181 This is not to say that there weren't plenty of other legal duties that devolved on teachers. All provinces had idiosyncratic requisites ranging from the promotion of Arbour Day (Alberta) to the seizure "of any rifles, guns or other offensive and dangerous weapons which are brought to school by pupils" (Manitoba).

182 Ontario, *Ontario Normal School Manuals – School Management*, 206.

183 See, for example, *BC Teacher* 6, no. 8 (April 1927): 27–8. This type of record had been under discussion in educational circles since early in the century, and some urban systems had begun to introduce it well before any province-wide initiative. See *WSJ* 8, no. 2 (Feb. 1913): 75; Alberta, *AR 1913*, "Special Committee on Standardization of School Records and Reports," 52–6; C.B. Edwards, "Pupils' Record Cards," *Proceedings*, OEA, 1915, 325–7.

184 *School Progress* 3, no. 2 (Sept. 1934): 10.

185 Manitoba, *AR 1943–44*, 38. Similarly, see Cameron, "The Small High School," 114.

186 Ontario, *Ontario Normal School Manuals – School Management*, 206.

187 See Chiang, "School Principalship in Vancouver," 52; "The School Marm a Menace? A Reply to Mr Woollacott by a Woman Schoolteacher," *Maclean's*, 1 Jan. 1937, 33. For one description of standardized pedagogical procedures and central office oversight, see Mark, *Ottawa*, 71–3.

188 "Reply to Mr Woollacott," *Maclean's*, 1 Jan. 1937, 33.

189 Rousmaniere, *City Teachers*, 95.

190 Stephenson, "Mrs. Gibson," 252–3. Similarly, see Harper, "Personal and Professional Freedom," 66–7.

CHAPTER THIRTEEN

1 On these points, see *Proceedings, OEA, 1906*, 63; MacLean, "Illiteracy," 585, 647, 655; W.A. Swift, "The Case against the Five Year Old Pupil," *ATAM* 13, no. 4 (Dec. 1932): 26. For local pressures to exclude 5-year-olds in Ontario, see the resolutions moved at Ontario trustees' conventions, in *CSJ* 11, no. 10 (Oct. 1933): 377–8; 12, no. 1 (Jan. 1934): 38; 13, no. 5 (May 1935): 151; 19, no. 1 (Jan 1941): 22.

2 See Pletch, *Not Wanted in the Classroom*, chap. 1; Sutherland, *Growing Up*, 90ff.; Gleason et al., *Lost Kids*.

3 See National Committee for School Health Research, *A Health Survey of Canadian Schools*, chap. 6, esp. Table 28. In the early 1930s, Ontario, better provided than most provinces, had only 317 special classes in urban areas and a mere 61 in rural areas, despite the existence of several thousand public school boards. See *CSJ* 12, no. 6 (June 1934): 222.

4 The phrase is borrowed from Goldin and Katz, *The Race between Education and Technology*, 129–31.

5 Haines, "The Secondary School," 2.

6 Phillips, *Education in Canada*, 508.

7 Cochrane, *The One-Room School*, 57.

8 Sutherland, *Growing Up*, 218. See also the discussion of the rural schools in Noël, *Family and Community Life*, 138–43.

9 Sutherland, *Growing Up*, 217.

10 For examples of this sort of mythmaking, see Gidney, *From Hope to Harris*, 72–4, 77. More generally, on the way mythmaking shapes what gets remembered, see Todman, *The Great War*, 158–73.

11 Coulter, "Schooling, Work and Life," 81–2. Coulter is summarizing views expressed in two large-scale surveys.

12 Cited in Stamp, *School Days*, 74.

13 *WSJ* 20, no. 3 (March 1925): 281. The warning was reissued in the following year. See *Manitoba Journal* 7, no. 2 (Feb. 1926): 3. Similarly, see British Columbia, *AR 1924–25*, M15.

14 See, for example, Putman-Weir Report, 260; Davis, "Secondary Education in Nova Scotia," 107; Ontario, *Principles of Method*, 263.

15 For inspectoral commentary on how the recommendation system operated to improve instruction, see Manitoba, *AR 1932–33*, 13–15; *AR 1934–35*, 23–5.

16 For complaints on this score, see Spence, *Education as Growth*, 79ff.

17 For the quotation and Byrne's own survey of that literature, see Byrne, "Good Teaching and Good Schools," 20–1, 23–4. For an excellent non-technical overview, see Osborne, *Education*, 81–108. For one interpretive essay summarizing the international literature, see Medley, "Teacher Evaluation," 1345ff.

18 It is only in Alberta that one finds such summaries and then only sporadically. In the early 1920s there was a "weak" category but *very* few teachers fell into it. By the later 1920s, in any case, the bottom category was "fair." See Alberta, *AR 1923*, 60; *AR 1929*, 50–1; *AR 1931*, 50; *AR 1935*, 55.

19 For the furore over education standards – at a time when most teachers had university degrees – see Gidney, *From Hope to Harris*, 170–9 and chap. 12; Nikiforuk, *School's Out*; Lewington and Orpwood, *Overdue Assignment*.

20 Sutherland, "The Triumph of 'Formalism,'" 113–15 (capitalization in original). This first version of the essay draws primarily on Vancouver schools. A slightly longer version of the same passage is included in Sutherland's *Growing Up*, 205–7. Here Sutherland broadens his research base to cover Canada as a whole; his framework of four kinds of teachers, however, remains the same.

21 For a stimulating study that privileges such personal traits as "humility, courage, impartiality, empathy, enthusiasm, judgement, and imagination" over technique or more easily measurable behaviours, see Hare, *What Makes a Good Teacher*.

22 On this point we think Sutherland's portrait is rather flat, tending to emphasize a degree of uniformity and uniformly dull routine that underestimates the skills and "bag of tricks" that experienced teachers had at their disposal to make learning routines interesting and varied. The reason, we suggest, is that while teachers' personalities remain vivid memories decades later, the relatively subtle variations in the methodology they employ are either not recognized by pupils or don't leave much mark on the memory. On this, see also the comments by Osborne, "Education Is the Best National Insurance," 35–6; Labaree, *The Trouble with Ed Schools*, 57.

23 For a few examples drawn from this mass of material, illustrating the full range of methods, see *The School* 20, no. 5 (Jan. 1932): 400–6; 24, no. 1 (Sept. 1935): 27–60; 24, no. 8 (April 1936): 686–94, 697–8; *WSJ* 29, no. 5 (May 1934): 164; *Manitoba Teacher* 13, no. 7 (Sept. 1932): 19–21; *BC Teacher* 5, no. 3 (Nov. 1935): 57, 61.

24 For one description of the daily round of instruction, see Van Kleek, *The Way It Was*, 162–3.

25 Ibid., 163.

26 Ibid., 88–90.

27 Nova Scotia, *AR 1924–25*, xxii. Though the date makes it difficult to be sure, this was almost certainly penned by Alexander MacKay, who had been superintendent of education in Nova Scotia since the late nineteenth century. His

successor, Henry Munro, who took over that year, held no such high-faluting view of offering high school subjects in the one-room school. See his editorial comment in *JEdNS*, Sept. 1934, 634.

28 Learned and Sills, *Education in the Maritime Provinces*, 9.

29 Miller, *Rural Schools*, 118.

30 See, for example, President's Address, *Proceedings, OEA, 1900*, 381; Ethel J. Cossitt, "High School Work in the Miscellaneous School," *Educational Review*, June–July 1915, 34; canvass of inspectoral opinion, Saskatchewan, *AR 1934*, 41–2; *CSJ* 9, no. 12 (Dec. 1931): 23–4.

31 [Savage], *Secondary Education in Ontario*, 77.

32 *BC Teacher* 15, no. 9 (May 1936): 19–20. Italics added. For other commentary on the problems, see British Columbia, *AR 1912–13*, A28; Gordon, "Secondary Education in Rural British Columbia," 24, 45–54; Cameron, "The Small High School," 27–31, 60–9; PAA, 79.334, file 272, Percy Page, Principal, Elnara, Alberta, to H.E. Balfour [HS1], 11 June 1935; Nova Scotia, *AR 1930*, 72.

33 Dyde, *Public Secondary Education*, 32.

34 Miller, *Rural Schools*, 69.

35 *Manitoba Teachers' Federation Bulletin*, Dec. 1923, 495.

36 *WSJ* 25, no. 3 (March 1930): 110.

37 England, *The Central European Immigrant*, 118–19.

38 Ibid., 130–1. Italics added.

39 Alberta, *Report of the Legislative Committee on Rural Education*, 22.

40 See, for example, CEA, *Report of the Survey Committee*, 21; Murray Report, 88–9; New Brunswick, *Report of the Commission on Education*, 10; *CSJ* 9, no. 2 (Feb. 1930): 13; 9 [*sic*], no. 12 (Dec. 1931): 23.

41 On the development, varieties, and organization of professional training in the nineteenth and early twentieth centuries, see Gidney and Millar, *Professional Gentlemen*, chaps 8, 17, 18; Gidney, "Madame How and Lady Why," 13–42.

Bibliography

This bibliography includes government reports and publications, periodicals, books, theses, and articles published as secondary literature, and is mainly confined to works cited in the text and appendices. It does not include archival sources, school legislation, manuals of school law, regulations and related policy documents, or provincial programs of study.

GOVERNMENT REPORTS AND PUBLICATIONS

See also "List of Abbreviations," page xiii.

Alberta. *Report of the Legislative Committee on Rural Education.* April 1935

– *Report of the Royal Commission on Education in Alberta, 1959* [Cameron Report]

British Columbia. *School Finance in British Columbia,* by H.B. King [King Report]. Victoria, 1935

– *Survey of the School System,* by J.H. Putman and G.M. Weir [Putman-Weir Report]. Victoria: King's Printer, 1925

Canada, Department of Labour. *The Employment of Children and Young Persons in Canada.* Ottawa: King's Printer, 1930

Canada, Royal Commission on Dominion-Provincial Relations (RCDPR). Briefs, submissions, statements, reports, including:

– *Brief, Manitoba School Trustees Association.* 1937

– *Brief of the Rural Municipality of St James.* 1938

– *Brief Presented by the Canadian Teachers' Federation to the Royal Commission on Dominion-Provincial Relations.* 1938

– *British Columbia in the Canadian Confederation. A Submission Presented to the RCDPR by the Government of the Province of British Columbia.* Victoria, 1938

– *The Case for Alberta. Submission of the Government of Alberta to the RCDPR.* 1938

– *Manitoba's Case.* 1938

– *Public Accounts Inquiry, Dominion of Canada … and Provincial Governments, Comparative Statistics of Public Finance.* Ottawa, 1939

– *Report.* 1940

– Report of Hearings. 3 vols
– *Submission by the Government of New Brunswick.* 1938
– *Submission by the Government of Nova Scotia.* 1938

Canada, Royal Commission on Industrial Training and Technical Education. *Report of the Commissioners.* 1913

Census of Canada. Decadal, 1901–61

Census of the Prairie Provinces, 1936

Dominion Bureau of Statistics (DBS). *Annual Report on Education Statistics in Canada 1922*

– *Annual Survey of Education in Canada* (1923–36)
– "The Canadian School as an Increasing Social Factor, 1931." Mimeograph
– *Expenditure for Schools in 1931 as Compared with 1913.* Cost of Education Bulletin No. 3. 1934
– *Financial Statistics of the Provincial School Systems in Canada 1914–1934.* Cost of Education Bulletin No. 5. 1935
– *Historical Statistical Survey of Education in Canada* (1921)
– *List of Public Secondary Schools in Canada.* Education Bulletin No. 7. 1937
– *National Accounts – Income and Expenditure, 1926–1956.* Ottawa, 1958
– *National Income of Canada, 1919–1938*
– "Recent Trends in Education in the Prairie Provinces." Mimeograph, 1932
– "The School Standing Attained by Canadian Children." Mimeograph, 1931
– *The Size Factor in One-Room Schools.* Education Bulletin No. 3. 1938
– *Statistical Review of Canadian Education, Census, 1951*
– *Statistical Report on Education in Canada, 1921*
– *Student Progress through the Schools by Grade.* 1960
– *Survey of Elementary and Secondary Education in Canada* (1936/38–)

DBS, Agriculture Division, Farm Finance Division. *Handbook of Agricultural Statistics.* Ottawa, 1958

MacLean, M.C. "Illiteracy and School Attendance." *Census of Canada 1931.* Vol. 12, Monographs

– *Illiteracy and School Attendance in Canada: A Study of the Census of 1921 with Supplementary Data.* Ottawa: DBS, 1926

Manitoba. *Report of the Royal Commission on the Municipal Finances and the Administration of the City of Winnipeg, 1939*

Manitoba, Department of Education. *Report of the Educational Commission* [Murray Report]. Winnipeg: King's Printer, 1924

Merchant, F.W. *Report on the Condition of English-French Schools in the Province of Ontario.* Toronto, 1912

New Brunswick. *21st Annual Report of the New Brunswick Vocational Education Board, 1939*

– *Report of the Commission on Education for New Brunswick.* Fredericton, 1932
– *Report of the New Brunswick Committee on Reconstruction.* 1944

Nova Scotia. *Report of the Royal Commission on Provincial Development and Rehabilitation*. 1944

Ontario. *Interim Report of the Committee on High School Education*. Toronto, 1921

– *Report of the Committee Appointed to Enquire into the Condition of the Schools Attended by French-Speaking Pupils*. F.W. Merchant, chairman. Toronto, 1927

– *Report of the Royal Commission on Education in Ontario, 1950*. Toronto, 1950

Ontario, Committee on the Costs of Education. *Report*. 1938

Ontario, Department of Education. *Ontario Normal School Manuals – School Management*. Toronto: Wm Briggs, 1915

– *Ontario Teachers' Manuals: Composition and Spelling*. 1916

– *Ontario Teachers' Manuals: Principles of Method*. Toronto: Copp Clark, 1930

– *Public School Manual Training*. Toronto, 1920

– *Recommendations and Regulations for the Establishment, Organization and Management of Vocational Schools*. Toronto, 1922

– *Schools and Teachers in the Province of Ontario* [Blue Books]

Prince Edward Island, Royal Commission on Education in Prince Edward Island. *Report*. 1910

Prince Edward Island, Royal Commission on Education in Prince Edward Island [Macmillan Commission]. *Report*. 1930

Saskatchewan, Committee on School Administration. *Report* [Martin Report]. 1939

Saskatchewan, Department of Education. *Report, Committee on School Finance and School Grants, 1933*

Statistics Canada. *Historical Compendium of Education Statistics from Confederation to 1975*. Ottawa 1978

PERIODICALS

Except where indicated, these were read between 1900 and *c.* mid-century, or for the period of their existence.

ATA Magazine

BC Teacher

Blairmore Enterprise

Canada Year Book, selected years

Canadian Education

The Canadian Forum, selected years

The Canadian Junior Red Cross Magazine

Canadian School Board Journal/Canadian School Journal

The Canadian Teacher

The Educational Review

The Journal of Education for Nova Scotia

Maclean's, selected years

The Manitoba School Journal

Manitoba Teachers' Federation Bulletin/The Manitoba Teacher
Proceedings of the ... Ontario Educational Association
Public Health Journal/Canadian Public Health Journal
The School
School Progress, selected years
Western School Journal
The Year Book of Education

SECONDARY SOURCES

Abbott, John. "Accomplishing 'a Man's Task': Rural Women Teachers, Male Cul-
ture, and the School Inspectorate in Turn of the Century Ontario." In *Gender
and Education*, edited by Heap and Prentice
– "Hostile Landscapes and the Spectre of Illiteracy: Devising Retrieval Systems for
'Sequestered' Children in Northern Ontario, 1875–1930." In *An Imperfect Past:
Education and Society in Canadian History*, edited by J. Donald Wilson. Vancouver:
Centre for the Study of Curriculum and Instruction, University of British Col-
umbia, 1984
Adams, Joan, and Becky Thomas. *Floating Schools and Frozen Inkwells: The One-Room
Schools of British Columbia*. Madeira Park, BC: Harbour Publishing Co., 1985
Allison, Derek J. "Pride and Privilege: The Position and Role of the Chief Educa-
tion Officer in the United States and Canada." In *Understanding School System
Administration: Studies of the Contemporary Chief Education Officer*, edited by Ken-
neth Leithwood and Donald Musella. London, ON: The Falmer Press, 1991
Anderson, A.M. "Education in the City of Moncton." [MA thesis?], University of
New Brunswick, 1935, thesis no. 40
Angus, David L., and Jeffrey E. Mirel. *The Failed Promise of the American High School,
1890–1995*. New York: Teachers College Press, 1999
Angus, David L., Jeffrey E. Mirel, and Maris A. Vinovskis. "Historical Development
of Age Stratification in Schooling." *Teachers College Record* 90, no. 2 (Winter
1988)
Archer, John. *Honoured with the Burden: A History of the Regina Board of Education*.
Regina: Regina Board of Education, 1987
– *Saskatchewan: A History*. Saskatoon: Western Producer Prairie Books, 1980
Arn, Elmer Howard Robert. "Extra-Curricular Activities in Saskatchewan High
Schools." MED thesis, University of Manitoba, 1939
– "Extra-Curricular Activities in Saskatchewan High Schools." University of Mani-
toba, Faculty of Education, Research Bulletin, March 1941
Arsenault, Georges. *The Island Acadians, 1720–1980*. Charlottetown: Ragweed
Press, 1989
Artibise, Alan. "Patterns of Prairie Urban Development, 1871–1950." In *Eastern
and Western Perspectives: Papers from the Joint Atlantic Canada/Western Canadian*

Studies Conference, edited by David Jay Bercuson and Phillip A. Buckner. Toronto: University of Toronto Press, 1981

– *Winnipeg: An Illustrated History*. Toronto: Lorimer, 1977

Axelrod, Paul. *Making a Middle Class: Student Life in English Canada during the Thirties*. Montreal and Kingston: McGill-Queen's University Press, 1990

– *The Promise of Schooling: Education in Canada, 1800–1914*. Toronto: University of Toronto Press, 1997

Baillargeon, Denyse. *Making Do: Women, Family and Home in Montreal during the Great Depression*. Waterloo, ON: Wilfrid Laurier University Press, 1999

Ball, A.H., and N.L. Reid. *School Administration*. Toronto: Gage, 1933

Barman, Jean. "'Knowledge Is Essential for Universal Progress but Fatal to Class Privilege': Working People and the Schools in Vancouver during the 1920s." *Labour/Le Travail* 22 (Fall 1988)

– *The West beyond the West: A History of British Columbia*. Toronto: University of Toronto Press, 1991 (rev. ed., 1996; 3rd ed., 2007)

Barman, Jean, and Mona Gleason, eds. *Children, Teachers, and Schools in the History of British Columbia*. 2nd ed. Calgary: Detselig Enterprises, 2003

Barman, Jean, Neil Sutherland, and J. Donald Wilson, eds. *Children, Teachers, and Schools in the History of British Columbia*. 1st ed. Calgary: Detselig, 1995

Baskerville, Peter. *A Silent Revolution? Gender and Wealth in English Canada, 1860–1930*. Montreal and Kingston: McGill-Queen's University Press, 2008

Bercuson, David. "Regionalism and 'Unlimited Identity' in Western Canada." *Journal of Canadian Studies* 15, no. 2 (Summer 1980)

Berliner, D.C. "Teacher Expertise." In *International Encyclopedia of Teaching and Teacher Education*, edited by Lorin W. Anderson. 2nd ed. Oxford: Pergamon Press, 1995

Bingay, James. *Public Education in Nova Scotia: A History and Commentary*. Kingston: Jackson Press, 1919

Bjelopera, Jerome P. *City of Clerks: Office and Sales Workers in Philadelphia, 1870–1920*. Urbana: University of Illinois Press, 2005

Black, Norman, ed. *Peace and Efficiency in School Administration*. London and Toronto: J.M. Dent, 1926

Blairmore: Hub of the Crow's Nest Pass … 1905–1950; 50 Golden Years. N.p., n.d. [1955?]

Blashill, Lorraine. *From a Little Stone School: The Story of the Development of the Saskatoon Public School System over the Past One Hundred Years*. Saskatoon: Saskatoon Board of Education, 1982

Bliss, Michael. *Northern Enterprise: Five Centuries of Canadian Business*. Toronto: McClelland and Stewart, 1987

Bothwell, Robert, Ian Drummond, and John English. *Canada 1900–1945*. Toronto: University of Toronto Press, 1987

Bradbury, Bettina. "Children Who Lived with One Parent in 1901." In *Household Counts*, edited by Sager and Baskerville

Bransford, John D., Ann L. Brown, and Rodney R. Cocking, eds. *How People Learn: Brain, Mind, Experience, and School.* Washington, DC: National Academy Press, 1999

Broadfoot, Barry. *Ten Lost Years, 1929–1939: Memories of Canadians Who Survived the Depression.* Toronto: Doubleday, 1973

Brown, Wilfred J. "Education Finance and the Interplay of Competing Goods." In *Scrimping or Squandering? Financing Canadian Schools*, edited by Stephen B. Lawton and Rouleen Wignall. Toronto: OISE Press, 1989

Bruce, Graham. "Business Education in British Columbia." MA thesis, University of British Columbia, 1941

Buckner, Phillip, ed. *Canada and the End of Empire.* Vancouver: University of British Columbia Press, 2005

Byrne, T.C. "Good Teaching and Good Teachers." *Canadian Administrator* 1, no. 5 (Feb. 1962)

Calam, John, ed. *Alex Lord's British Columbia: Recollections of a Rural School Inspector, 1915–1936.* Vancouver: University of British Columbia Press, 1991

Calam, John, and Thomas Fleming. "Rural Inequality." In British Columbia, Royal Commission on Education, *British Columbia Schools and Society.* Research Paper No. 3. Commissioned Papers, vol. 1, May 1988

Cameron, Maxwell A. *The Financing of Education in Ontario.* Toronto: Department of Educational Research, University of Toronto, 1936

– "The Small High School in British Columbia." MA thesis, University of British Columbia, 1932

Campbell, Lara. *Respectable Citizens: Gender, Family, and Unemployment in Ontario's Great Depression.* Toronto: University of Toronto Press, 2009

Campbell, Roald F., Thomas Fleming, L. Jackson Newell, and John Bennion. *A History of Thought and Practice in Educational Administration.* New York: Teachers College Press, 1987

Canadian Education Association. *Report of the Survey Committee Appointed to Ascertain the Chief Educational Needs in Canada.* March 1943

Canadian Research Committee on Practical Education. "First Report of the Canadian Research Committee on Practical Education." *Canadian Education* 4, no. 2 (March 1949)

– *Your Child Leaves School.* Report No. 2. Toronto, 1950

Canadian Teachers' Federation. *Educational Finance in Canada.* CTF Information Bulletin, Dec. 1954

– *Information Bulletin 56-1*, March 1956

– *Information Bulletin 56-1, Revision*, 1956

– *Trends in Certification Standards, 1939–1957; Information Bulletin 58-2*, 1958

‒ *Trends in the Economic Status of Teachers, 1910–1955.* Research Study No. 2. Ottawa: CTF, 1957

Canadian Youth Commission. *Youth and Jobs in Canada.* Toronto: Ryerson Press, 1945

Cécillon, Jack D. "Language, Schools, and Religious Conflict in the Windsor-Border Region: A Case Study of Francophone Resistance to the Ontario Government's Imposition of Regulation 17, 1910–1928." PhD diss., York University, 2008

Chafe, J.W. *An Apple for the Teacher: A Centennial History of the Winnipeg School Division.* Winnipeg: n.p., 1967

Chalmers, John W. *Schools of the Foothills Province: The Story of Public Education in Alberta.* Toronto: University of Toronto Press, 1967

Charyk, John C. *The Biggest Day of the Year.* Saskatoon: Western Producer Prairie Books, 1985

‒ *The Little White Schoolhouse.* [Vol. 1]. Saskatoon: Western Producer, 1968

‒ *The Little White Schoolhouse: Pulse of the Community.* Vol. 2. Saskatoon: Western Producer, 1970

‒ *The Little White Schoolhouse: Those Bittersweet Schooldays.* Vol. 3. Saskatoon: Western Producer, 1977

‒ *Syrup Pails and Gopher Tails: Memories of the One-Room School House.* Saskatoon: Western Producer Prairie Books, 1983

Chiang, Po-Yu Emmy. "The Development of School Principalship in Vancouver, 1886–1928." MA thesis, University of British Columbia, 1990

Clairmont, Donald H., and Dennis William Magill. *Africville: The Life and Death of a Canadian Black Community.* Toronto: McClelland and Stewart, 1974

Clark, Penney, and Yesman Post. "'A Natural Outcome of Free Schools': The Free Text-book Branch in British Columbia, 1908–1949." *Historical Studies in Education* 21, no. 2 (Fall 2009)

Clarke, Nic. "Sacred Daemons: Exploring British Columbia Society's Perceptions of 'Mentally Deficient' Children, 1870–1930." *BC Studies*, no. 144 (Winter 2004/05)

Coates, Kenneth, and William Morrison. *The Forgotten North: A History of Canada's Provincial Norths.* Toronto: Lorimer, 1992

Cochrane, Honora M., ed. *Centennial Story: The Board of Education for the City of Toronto, 1850–1950.* Toronto: Nelson, 1950

Cochrane, Jean. *The One-Room School in Canada.* [Don Mills, ON]: Fitzhenry and Whiteside, 1981

Collins, Cecil Patrick. "The Role of Provincially Appointed Superintendents of Schools in Large Units of Administration in Canada." PhD diss., University of Alberta, 1958

Comacchio, Cynthia. *The Dominion of Youth: Adolescence and the Making of a Modern Canada, 1920 to 1950.* Waterloo, ON: Wilfrid Laurier University Press, 2006

– *"Nations Are Built of Babies": Saving Ontario's Mothers and Children, 1900–1940.*
   Montreal and Kingston: McGill-Queen's University Press, 1993

Conrad, Arthur Thomas. "Educational Development in Nova Scotia under Henry
   Fraser Munro." MA thesis, St Mary's University, 1960

Conrad, Margaret R., and James K. Hiller. *Atlantic Canada: A Region in the Making.*
   Don Mills, ON: Oxford University Press, 2001

Copelman, Dina. *London's Women Teachers: Gender, Class, and Feminism, 1870–1930.*
   London: Routledge, 1996

Corbett, Michael. *Learning to Leave: The Irony of Schooling in a Coastal Community.*
   Halifax: Fernwood Publishing, 2007

Corman, June. "Seeking Greener Pastures: Rural Women Teachers in Southern
   Saskatchewan." In *A History of Education in Saskatchewan: Selected Readings,* edited
   by Brian Noonan, Dianne Hallman, and Murray Scharf. Regina: Canadian
   Plains Research Center, University of Regina, 2006

Coulter, Rebecca Priegert. "'Girls Just Want to Have Fun': Women Teachers and
   the Pleasures of the Profession." In *History Is Hers,* edited by Coulter and Harper

– "Schooling, Work and Life: Reflections of the Young in the 1940s." In *Rethinking Vocationalism: Whose Work/Life Is It?,* edited by Rebecca P. Coulter and Ivor F.
   Goodson. Toronto: Our Schools/Our Selves, 1993

– "Teenagers in Edmonton, 1921–1931: Experiences of Gender and Class." PhD
   diss., University of Alberta, 1987

– "The Working Young of Edmonton, 1921–1931." In *Childhood and Family in
   Canadian History,* edited by Joy Parr. Toronto: McClelland and Stewart, 1982

Coulter, Rebecca Priegert, and Helen Harper, eds. *History Is Hers: Women Educators
   in Twentieth-Century Ontario.* Calgary: Detselig Enterprises, 2005

Cousins, William James. *A History of the Crow's Nest Pass.* Calgary: Historic Trails
   Society of Alberta, 1981

Coutts, H.T., and B.E. Walker. *G. Fred: The Story of G. Fred McNally.* Don Mills, ON:
   Dent and Sons, 1964

Couturier, Jacques-Paul, and Wendy Johnston. "L'État, les familles et l'obligation
   scolaire au Nouveau-Brunswick dans les années 1940." *Histoire sociale* 35 (May
   2002)

Cuban, Larry. *How Teachers Taught: Constancy and Change in American Classrooms,
   1890–1990.* 2nd ed. New York: Teachers College Press, 1993

Cudmore, S.A., and H.G. Caldwell. *Rural and Urban Composition of the Canadian
   Population.* Monographs, *Census of Canada 1931,* vol. 13. Ottawa: DBS 1942

Cupido, Robert. "'The Puerilities of the National Complex,' English Canada, the
   Empire, and the Diamond Jubilee of Confederation." In *Beyond National Dreams:
   Essays on Canadian Citizenship and Nationalism,* edited by Andrew W. Nurse and
   Raymond B. Blake. Markham, ON: Fitzhenry and Whiteside, 2009

Danylewycz, Marta. "Domestic Science Education in Ontario, 1900–1940." In
   Gender and Education, edited by Heap and Prentice

Danylewycz, Marta, and Alison Prentice. "Teachers' Work: Changing Patterns and Perceptions in the Emerging School Systems of Nineteenth- and Early Twentieth-Century Central Canada." In *Women Who Taught*, edited by Prentice and Theobald

Darroch, Gordon. "Families, Fostering, and Flying the Coop: Lessons in Liberal Cultural Formation, 1871–1901." In *Household Counts*, edited by Sager and Baskerville

Dasgupta, S. *Rural Canada: Structure and Change*. Lewiston, NY/Queenston, ON: Edward Mellen Press, 1988

Davies, Scott, and Neil Guppy. *The Schooled Society: An Introduction to the Sociology of Education*. 2nd ed. Don Mills, ON: Oxford University Press, 2010

Davis, David Gray. "Reorganization of Secondary Education in Nova Scotia." DEd diss., Harvard University, 1926

Davy, John Gregory. "The Function of the Principal of the Elementary School with Particular Reference to British Columbia." MA thesis, University of British Columbia, 1938

Dunn, Timothy A. "The Rise of Mass Schooling in British Columbia, 1900–1929." In *Schooling and Society in 20th Century British Columbia*, edited by J. Donald Wilson and David C. Jones. Calgary: Detselig, 1980

Dyde, W.F. *Public Secondary Education in Canada*. New York: Teachers College Press, 1929

Elliott, David, and Iris Miller. *Bible Bill: A Biography of William Aberhart*. Edmonton: Reidmore, 1987

Ellis, Jason. "'Backward and Brilliant Children': A Social and Policy History of Disability, Childhood, and Education in Toronto's Special Education Classes, 1910 to 1945." PhD diss., York University, 2011

Emery, J.C. Herbert, and Clint Levitt. "Cost of Living, Real Wages and Real Incomes in Thirteen Canadian Cities, 1900–1959." *Canadian Journal of Economics* 35, no. 1 (Feb. 2002)

England, Robert. *The Central European Immigrant in Canada*. Toronto: Macmillan, 1929

Fahrni, Magda. "Reflections on the Place of Quebec in Historical Writing on Canada." In *Contesting Clio's Craft: New Directions and Debates in Canadian History*, edited by Christopher Dummitt and Michael Dawson. London: Institute for the Study of the Americas, 2009

Fisher, Susan R. *Boys and Girls in No Man's Land: English-Canadian Children and the First World War*. Toronto: University of Toronto Press, 2011

Fleming, Thomas. "British Columbia Principals: Scholar-Teachers and Administrative Amateurs in Victorian and Edwardian Eras, 1872–1918." In *School Leadership*, edited by Fleming

– "'Our Boys in the Field': School Inspectors, Superintendents and the Changing Character of School Leadership in British Columbia." In *School Leadership*, edited by Fleming

- *The Principal's Office – And Beyond.* Vol. 1: *Public School Leadership in British Columbia, 1849–1960.* Vol. 2: *Public School Leadership in British Columbia, 1961–2005.* Calgary: Detselig Enterprises, 2010
- ed. *Schooling in British Columbia, 1849–2005: Voices from the Past.* Mill Bay, BC: Bendall Books, 2010
- ed. *School Leadership: Essays on the British Columbia Experience, 1872–1995.* Mill Bay, BC: Bendall Books, 2001

Fleming, Thomas, and Madge Craig. "The Anatomy of a Resignation: Margaret Strong and the New Westminster School Board, 1911–1915." In *School Leadership*, edited by Fleming

Fleming, Thomas, and Helen Raptis. "Government's Paper Empire: Historical Perspectives on Measuring Student Achievement in British Columbia Schools, 1872–1999." *Journal of Educational Administration and History* 37, no. 2 (Sept. 2005)

Fleming, Thomas, and Carolyn Smyly. "The Diary of Mary Williams: A Cameo of Rural Schooling in British Columbia, 1922–1924." In *Children, Teachers, and Schools*, edited by Barman, Sutherland, and Wilson

Fleming, Thomas, Carolyn Smyly, and Julie White. "Beyond Hope and Past Redemption: Lottie Bowron and the Rural School Teachers of British Columbia, 1928–1934." In *School Leadership*, edited by Fleming

Fleming, W.G. *Ontario's Educative Society.* Vol. 3: *Schools, Pupils, and Teachers.* Toronto: University of Toronto Press, 1971
- *Ontario's Educative Society.* Vol. 5: *Supporting Institutions and Services.* Toronto: University of Toronto Press, 1972

Fletcher, Basil A. *The Next Step in Canadian Education: An Account of the Larger Unit of School Administration.* Toronto: Macmillan, 1939

Fluxgold, Howard. *Federal Financial Support for Secondary Education and Its Effect on Ontario.* N.p.: Ontario Teachers' Federation/Canadian Teachers' Federation, 1972

Foght, Harold W. *The School System of Ontario with Special Reference to the Rural Schools.* Washington, DC: Government Printing Office, 1915
- *Survey of Education in the Province of Saskatchewan, Canada.* Regina: King's Printer, 1918

Forbes, E.R. *Challenging the Regional Stereotype: Essays on the Twentieth-Century Maritimes.* Fredericton: Acadiensis Press, 1989
- "The 1930s: Depression and Retrenchment." In *The Atlantic Provinces in Confederation*, edited by Forbes and Muise

Forbes, E.R., and D.A. Muise, eds. *The Atlantic Provinces in Confederation.* Toronto and Fredericton: University of Toronto Press and Acadiensis Press, 1993

Friesen, Gerald. *The Canadian Prairies: A History.* Toronto: University of Toronto Press, 1984
- *Citizens and Nations: An Essay on History, Communication, and Canada.* Toronto: University of Toronto Press, 2000

Gaffield, Chad. "Children, Schooling, and Family Reproduction in Nineteenth-Century Ontario." *Canadian Historical Review* 72, no. 2 (June 1991)

– *Language, Schooling, and Cultural Conflict: The Origins of the French-Language Controversy in Ontario*. Kingston and Montreal: McGill-Queen's University Press, 1987

Gagné, Mary Lynn. "Print, Profit, and Pedagogy: The School Aids and Text Book Publishing Company." *Saskatchewan History* 10, no. 1 (Spring 2008)

Gagnon, Anne. "'Our Parents Did Not Raise Us to Be Independent': The Work and Schooling of Franco-Albertan Women, 1890–1940." *Prairie Forum* 19, no. 2 (Fall 1994)

Galbraith, John Kenneth. *The Scotch*. 1964; reprint, Baltimore, MD: Penguin Books, 1968

Garner, Hugh. *Cabbagetown*. Toronto: Collins, 1950

Gelman, Susan. "Women Secondary School Teachers: Ontario, 1871–1930." PhD diss., University of Toronto, 1994

Gidney, Catherine, and R.D. Gidney. "Branding the Classroom: Commercialism in Canadian Schools, 1920–1960." *Histoire sociale* 41, no. 82 (Nov. 2008)

Gidney, R.D. *From Hope to Harris: The Reshaping of Ontario's Schools*. Toronto: University of Toronto Press, 1999

– "'Madame How and Lady Why': Learning to Practise in Historical Perspective." In *Learning to Practise*, edited by Heap, Millar, and Smyth

Gidney, R.D., and W.P.J. Millar. "The Christian Recessional in Ontario's Public Schools." In *Religion and Public Life in Canada: Historical and Comparative Perspectives*, edited by Marguerite Van Die and David Lyon. Toronto: University of Toronto Press, 2001

– *Inventing Secondary Education: The Rise of the High School in 19th Century Ontario*. Montreal and Kingston: McGill-Queen's University Press, 1990

– *Professional Gentlemen: The Professions in Nineteenth-Century Ontario*. Toronto: University of Toronto Press, 1994

– "The Salaries of Teachers in English Canada, 1900–1940: A Reappraisal." *Historical Studies in Education* 22, no. 1 (Spring 2010)

– "Schooling and the Idea of Merit: A Framework for Historical Analysis." In *Historical Perspectives on Educational Policy*, edited by Ricker and Wood

Giffen, P. James. *Rural Life: Portraits of the Prairie Town, 1946*, edited by Gerald Friesen. Winnipeg: University of Manitoba Press, 2004

Gleason, Mona. "From 'Disgraceful Carelessness' to 'Intelligent Precaution': Accidents and the Public Child in English Canada, 1900–1950." *Journal of Family History* 30, no. 2 (2005)

Gleason, Mona, et al., eds. *Lost Kids: Vulnerable Children and Youth in Twentieth-Century Canada and the United States*. Vancouver: University of British Columbia Press, 2010

Goldenberg, Carl H. *Municipal Finance in Canada: A Study for the Royal Commission on Dominion-Provincial Relations*. Ottawa, 1939

Goldin, Claudia. "America's Graduation from High School: The Evolution and Spread of Secondary Schooling in the Twentieth Century." *Journal of Economic History* 58, no. 2 (June 1998)

Goldin, Claudia, and Lawrence F. Katz. "Human Capital and Social Capital: The Rise of Secondary Schooling in America, 1910–1940." *Journal of Interdisciplinary History* 29, no. 4 (Spring 1999)

– *The Race between Education and Technology.* Cambridge, MA: Harvard University Press, 2008

Goltz, Eileen. "A Corporate View of Housing and Community in a Company Town: Copper Cliff, 1886–1920." *Ontario History* 82, no. 1 (March 1990)

Goodson, Ivor F., and Christopher J. Anstead. *Through the Schoolhouse Door: Working Papers.* N.p.: Garamond Press, 1993

Goodson, Ivor, and Ian R. Dowbiggin. "Vocational Education and School Reform: The Case of the London (Canada) Technical School, 1900–1930." *History of Education Review* 20, no. 1 (1991)

Gordon, Roth Garthley. "Secondary Education in Rural British Columbia." MA thesis, University of British Columbia, 1935

Gossage, Peter, and Danielle Gauvreau. "Canadian Fertility in 1901: A Bird's-Eye View." In *Household Counts,* edited by Sager and Baskerville

Graham, John F. *Fiscal Adjustment and Economic Development: A Case Study of Nova Scotia.* Toronto: University of Toronto Press, 1963

Gray, James. "Our World Stopped and We Got Off." In *The Prairie West: Historical Readings,* edited by R. Douglas Francis and Howard Palmer. 2nd ed. Edmonton: University of Alberta Press, 1992

Green, George H.E. "The Development of the Curriculum in the Secondary Schools of British Columbia, including Academic, Commercial, Technical, Industrial Arts, and Correspondence Courses." DPaed diss., University of Toronto, 1944

Greenway, H.F. *Housing in Canada.* Vol. 12, Monographs. *Census of Canada 1931*

Gregor, Alexander, and Keith Wilson. *The Development of Education in Manitoba.* Dubuque, IA: Kendal/Hunt, 1984

Guppy, Neil, et al. "Changing Patterns of Educational Inequality in Canada." *Canadian Journal of Sociology* 9, no. 3 (Summer 1984)

Guppy, Neil, and Scott Davies. *Education in Canada: Recent Trends and Future Challenges.* Ottawa: Statistics Canada, 1998

Gushaty, Metro. "An Analysis of the Causes of High School Drop-outs in Southern Alberta, 1947–1951." MEd thesis, University of Alberta, 1952

Haines, William C. "The Secondary School." MA thesis, University of New Brunswick, 1936

Hallman, Dianne M. "'A Thing of the Past': Teaching in One-Room Schools in Rural Nova Scotia, 1936–1941." *Historical Studies in Education* 4, no. 1 (Spring 1992)

Hamilton, Ivan Lorne. "The Extent and Cause of Retardation in the Schools of Rural Manitoba." MA thesis, University of Manitoba, 1935

Hanson, Eric J. *Local Government in Alberta*. Toronto: McClelland and Stewart, 1956

Hare, William. *What Makes a Good Teacher: Reflections on Some Characteristics Central to the Educational Enterprise*. London, ON: The Althouse Press, 1993

Harper, Helen. "Personal and Professional Freedom in the Hinterlands: Women Teachers in Northern Ontario." In *History Is Hers*, edited by Coulter and Harper

Harrigan, Patrick J. "A Comparison of Rural and Urban Patterns of Enrolment and Attendance in Canada, 1900–1960." *Canadian History of Education Association Bulletin* 5, no. 3 (1988)

– "The Development of a Corps of Public School Teachers in Canada, 1870–1980." *History of Education Quarterly* 32, no. 4 (Winter 1992)

Harris, Arthur A. "The Supervisory Activities of the Principal in the Graded Schools in Rural Manitoba." University of Manitoba, Faculty of Education and Education Alumni Association, Research Bulletin, April 1938

Harris, Richard. *Unplanned Suburbs: Toronto's American Tragedy, 1900 to 1950*. Baltimore: Johns Hopkins University Press, 1996

Hawthorne, Dan Robert. "Patterns of 20th Century Attendance: A Systematic Study of Victoria Public Schools, 1910 and 1921." MA thesis, University of Victoria, 1985

Hayday, Matthew. *Bilingual Today, United Tomorrow: Official Languages in Education and Canadian Federalism*. Montreal and Kingston: McGill-Queen's University Press, 2005

Heap, Ruby. "Schooling Women for Home or for Work? Vocational Education for Women in Ontario in the Early Twentieth Century: The Case of the Toronto Technical High School, 1892–1920." In *Gender and Education*, edited by Heap and Prentice

Heap, Ruby, Wyn Millar, and Elizabeth Smyth, eds. *Learning to Practise: Professional Education in Historical and Contemporary Perspective*. Ottawa: University of Ottawa Press, 2005

Heap, Ruby, and Alison Prentice, eds. *Gender and Education in Ontario: An Historical Reader*. Toronto: Canadian Scholars' Press, 1991

Helyar, Frances. "Acadian Teacher Identity in Early Twentieth-Century New Brunswick." *Historical Studies in Education* 23, no. 2 (Fall 2011)

– "Bureaucratic Rationalism, Political Partisanship, and Acadian Nationalism: The 1920 New Brunswick History Textbook Controversy." PhD diss., McGill University, 2010

Heron, Craig. "The High School and the Household Economy in Working-Class Hamilton, 1890–1940." *Historical Studies in Education* 7, no. 2 (Fall 1995)

High, Norman Harvey. "A Study of Educational Opportunity in the Provincially-Controlled Schools of Haldimand County, Ontario." PhD diss., Cornell University, 1950

Historical Atlas of Canada, edited by Donald Kerr and Deryck W. Holdsworth. Vol. 3: *Addressing the Twentieth Century, 1891–1961*. Toronto: University of Toronto Press, 1990

A History of the Ottawa Collegiate Institute, 1843–1903. Ottawa, 1904

Hody, Maud Hazel. "The Development of the Bilingual Schools of New Brunswick." DEd diss., University of Toronto, 1964

Hoerder, Dirk. *Creating Societies: Immigrant Lives in Canada*. Montreal and Kingston: McGill-Queen's University Press, 2000

Horn, Michiel. *The Dirty Thirties: Canadians in the Great Depression*. Toronto: Copp Clark, 1972

Hudson, S.C. *Taxation in Rural Ontario*. Publication 489, Technical Bulletin 4. Division of Farm Management, Agricultural Economics Branch, Dominion of Canada Department of Agriculture. March 1936

Hurl, Lorna F. "Restricting Child Factory Labour in Late Nineteenth-Century Ontario." *Labour/Le Travail* 21 (Spring 1988)

Iacovetta, Franca. *Such Hardworking People: Italian Immigrants in Postwar Toronto*. Montreal and Kingston: McGill-Queen's University Press, 1992

Irving, John A. *The Social Credit Movement in Alberta*. Toronto: University of Toronto Press, 1959

Jackson, Nancy S., and Jane S. Gaskell. "White Collar Vocationalism: The Rise of Commercial Education in Ontario and British Columbia, 1870–1920." In *Gender and Education*, edited by Heap and Prentice

Jakes, Harold E., and Hanne B. Mawhinney. *A Historical Overview of Franco-Ontarian Educational Governance*. Ottawa: Vision Education, Monographs of the Faculty of Education, University of Ottawa, n.d.

Jean, Dominique. "Family Allowances and Family Autonomy: Quebec Families Encounter the Welfare State, 1945–55." In *Canadian Family History: Selected Readings*, edited by Bettina Bradbury. Toronto: Copp Clark Pitman, 1992

Johnson, A.W. *Dream No Little Dreams: A Biography of the Douglas Government of Saskatchewan, 1944–1961*. Toronto: University of Toronto Press, 2004

Johnson, Dana. *Pursuing Higher Education: Going to Secondary School in Ontario, 1800–1930*. Ottawa: Parks Canada, 1984

Johnson, F. Henry. "Changing Conceptions of Discipline and Pupil-Teacher Relations in Canadian Schools." DPaed diss., University of Toronto, 1952

– *A History of Public Education in British Columbia*. Vancouver: Publications Centre, University of British Columbia, 1964

Jones, David C. *Empire of Dust: Settling and Abandoning the Prairie Dry Belt*. Calgary: University of Calgary Press, 2002

– "Schools and Social Disintegration in the Alberta Dry Belt of the Twenties." In *Schools in the West*, edited by Sheehan, Wilson, and Jones

– "A Strange Heartland: The Alberta Dry Belt and the Schools in the Depression." In *The Dirty Thirties in Prairie Canada*, edited by R.D. Francis and H. Ganzevoort. Vancouver: Tantallus, 1980

Jones, David C., Nancy M. Sheehan, and Robert M. Stamp, eds. *Shaping the Schools of the Canadian West.* Calgary: Detselig, 1979

Kalbach, Warren E. *The Impact of Immigration on Canada's Population.* Ottawa: DBS, 1970

Kalbach, Warren E., and Wayne W. McVey. *The Demographic Bases of Canadian Society.* Toronto: McGraw-Hill Company of Canada, 1971

Kendle, John. *John Bracken: A Political Biography.* Toronto: University of Toronto Press, 1979

Keshen, Jeffrey. "Wartime Jitters over Juveniles: Canada's Delinquency Scare and Its Consequences." In *Age of Contention: Readings in Canadian Social History, 1900–1945*, edited by Jeffrey Keshen. Toronto: Harcourt Brace Canada, 1997

King, A.J.C., and M.J. Peart. *Teachers in Canada: Their Work and Quality of Life.* Ottawa: Canadian Teachers' Federation, 1992

Kinnear, Mary. *A Female Economy: Women's Work in a Prairie Province, 1870–1970.* Montreal and Kingston: McGill-Queen's University Press, 1998

– "'Mostly for the Male Members': Teaching in Winnipeg, 1933–1966." *Historical Studies in Education* 6, no. 2 (Fall 1994)

Kirkconnell, Watson. *A Canadian Headmaster: A Brief Biography of Thomas Allison Kirkconnell, 1862–1934.* Toronto: Clarke Irwin, 1935

Kostek, Michael A. *A Century and Ten: The History of Edmonton Public Schools.* Edmonton: Edmonton Public Schools, 1992

Labaree, David F. *The Trouble with Ed Schools.* New Haven, CT: Yale University Press, 2004

Langford, Howard D. *Educational Service: Its Future and Possibilities.* New York: Teachers College Press, 1931

Langley, Gerald James. "The Programmes of Study Authorized for Use in the Northwest Territories to 1905 and the Province of Saskatchewan to 1931, and the Textbooks Prescribed Therewith." MEd thesis, University of Saskatchewan, 1944

Lassonde, Stephen A. "Learning and Earning: Schooling, Juvenile Employment, and the Early Life Course in Late Nineteenth-Century New Haven." *Journal of Social History* 29 (Summer 1996)

– "Should I Go or Should I Stay? Adolescence, School Attainment and Parent-Child Relations in Italian Immigrant Families of New Haven, 1900–1940." *History of Education Quarterly* 38, no. 1 (Spring 1998)

Lawr, D.A., and R.D. Gidney, eds. *Educating Canadians: A Documentary History of Public Education.* 2nd ed. Toronto: Van Nostrand Reinhold, 1978

LaZerte, M.E. "The Selective Nature of Secondary Education." Report of Study No. 21. Canadian Council for Educational Research, May 1942

Leacy, F.H., ed. *Historical Statistics of Canada.* 2nd ed. Toronto: Macmillan, 1983

League for Social Reconstruction Research Committee. *Social Planning for Canada.* 1935; reprint, Toronto: University of Toronto Press, 1975

Learned, William S., and Kenneth C.M. Sills. *Education in the Maritime Provinces of Canada.* New York: Carnegie Foundation for the Advancement of Teaching, 1922

Leonard, Alvin K. "Over-Ageness and Under-Ageness in the Elementary Schools of Ontario." MA thesis, University of Toronto, 1926

Levenstein, Harvey. *Paradox of Plenty: A Social History of Eating in Modern America.* New York: Oxford University Press, 1993

Lewington, Jennifer, and Graham Orpwood. *Overdue Assignment: Taking Responsibility for Canada's Schools.* Toronto: Wiley, 1993

Lindert, Peter H. *Growing Public: Social Spending and Economic Growth Since the Eighteenth Century.* Vol. 1. Cambridge: Cambridge University Press, 2004

Lloyd, Dianne. *Woodrow: A Biography of W.S. Lloyd.* N.p.: Woodrow Lloyd Memorial Fund, 1979

Loewen, Royden K. *Family, Church, and Market: A Mennonite Community in the Old and New Worlds, 1850–1930.* Toronto: University of Toronto Press, 1993

Lowe, Graham S. *Women in the Administrative Revolution.* Toronto: University of Toronto Press, 1987

Lucas, Rex. *Minetown, Milltown, Railtown: Life in Canadian Communities of Single Industry.* Toronto: University of Toronto Press, 1971

Lucow, W.H. "The Origin and Growth of the Public School System in Winnipeg." MEd thesis, University of Manitoba, 1950

Lyons, John E. "Ten Forgotten Years: The Saskatchewan Teachers' Federation and the Legacy of the Depression." In *Schools in the West*, edited by Sheehan, Wilson, and Jones

Lysecki, John E.L. "Education in Manitoba – North of 53." MEd thesis, University of Manitoba, 1936

McBeath, Allan. "A Survey of Education in New Brunswick." MA thesis, University of New Brunswick, 1937

McCordic, William J. *Financing Education in Canada.* Ottawa: Canadian Conference on Education, 1960

MacDiarmid, F.E. "The Administrative and Supervising Functions of a School Principal, Who Is Also Superintendent of Town Schools." MA thesis, University of New Brunswick, 1934

McDougall, J.B. *Building the North.* Toronto: McClelland and Stewart, 1919

McKay, Ian. *Reasoning Otherwise: Leftists and the People's Enlightenment in Canada, 1890–1920.* Toronto: Between the Lines, 2008

McKenna, Mary Olga. "Higher Education in Transition, 1945–1980." In *The Garden Transformed: Prince Edward Island, 1945–1980*, edited by Verner Smitheram, David Milne, and Satadal Dasgupta. Charlottetown: Ragweed Press, 1982

McKibbin, Ross. *Classes and Cultures: England 1918–1951.* 1998; reprint, Oxford: Oxford University Press, 2000

Mackintosh, W.A. *The Economic Background of Dominion-Provincial Relations.* Carleton
Library series. Toronto: McClelland and Stewart, 1964

McLachlan, Elizabeth. *With Unfailing Dedication: Rural Teachers in the West.* Edmonton: NeWest Press, 2001

– *With Unshakeable Persistence: Rural Teachers of the Depression Era.* Edmonton:
NeWest Press, 1999

McLaren, Katherine I. "'The Proper Education for All Classes': Compulsory
Schooling and Reform in Nova Scotia, 1890–1930." MED thesis, Atlantic
Institute of Education, Dalhousie University, 1984

MacLeod, Roderick, and Mary Anne Poutanen. *A Meeting of the People: School
Boards and Protestant Communities in Quebec, 1801–1998.* Montreal and Kingston:
McGill-Queen's University Press, 2004

McManus, Thomas M. "A Survey of Pupil Progress in Edmonton Public Schools."
MED thesis, University of Alberta, 1950

MacNaughton, Katherine F.C. *The Development of the Theory and Practice of Education
in New Brunswick, 1784–1900.* Fredericton: University of New Brunswick Press,
1947

Magnuson, Roger P. *The Two Worlds of Quebec Education during the Traditional Era,
1760–1940.* London, ON: The Althouse Press, 2005.

Mahé, Yvette T.M. "Bilingual School District Trustees and Cultural Transmission:
The Alberta Experience, 1892–1939." *Historical Studies in Education* 9, no. 1
(Spring 1997)

– "Bilingual School Teachers' Cultural Mission and Practices in Alberta before
1940." *Journal of Educational Thought* 34, no. 2 (Aug. 2000)

– "French Teacher Shortages and Cultural Continuity in Alberta Districts,
1892–1940." *Historical Studies in Education* 14, no. 2 (2002)

– "Official and Unofficial School Inspection as Hegemonic and Counter-
Hegemonic Struggle in Prairie Districts before 1940." *Canadian Ethnic Studies*
33, no. 2 (2001)

Mandeville, Donna Lynne. "Who Went to School? School Attendance Patterns
in Three British Columbia Communities in 1901." MA thesis, University of
Victoria, 2002

Mann, George. "Alberta Normal Schools: A Descriptive Study of Their Development, 1905 to 1945." MED thesis, University of Alberta, 1961

Manzer, Ronald. *Educational Regimes and Anglo-American Democracy.* Toronto:
University of Toronto Press, 2003

– *Public Schools and Political Ideas: Canadian Educational Policy in Historical Perspective.* Toronto: University of Toronto Press, 1994

Mark, Clarence Ellsworth. *The Public Schools of Ottawa: A Survey.* Ottawa: Pattison
Printers, 1918

Marsh, Leonard C. *Canadians In and Out of Work: A Survey of Economic Classes and
Their Relation to the Labour Market.* Oxford: Oxford University Press, 1940

Marty, Aletta. *An Educational Creed.* Toronto: Ryerson Press, 1924

Martynowych, Orest T. *Ukrainians in Canada: The Formative Period, 1891–1924.*
Edmonton: Canadian Institute of Ukrainian Studies Press, 1991

Medley, Donald M. "Teacher Evaluation." In *Encyclopedia of Educational Research.*
6th ed. Vol. 4, edited by Marvin C. Alkin. New York: Macmillan, 1992

Meltz, Noah M. *Changes in the Occupational Position of the Canadian Labour Force,
1931–1961.* Ottawa: Queen's Printer, 1965

Millar, W.P.J. "'We wanted our children should have it better': Jewish Medical Students at the University of Toronto, 1910–51." *Journal of the Canadian Historical
Association,* new series, 11 (2000)

Millar, W.P.J., and R.D. Gidney. "'Medettes': Thriving or Just Surviving? Women
Students in the Faculty of Medicine, University of Toronto, 1910–1951."
In *Challenging Professions: Historical and Contemporary Perspectives on Women's
Professional Work,* edited by Elizabeth Smyth et al. Toronto: University of Toronto
Press, 1999

Millar, Wyn, Ruby Heap, and Bob Gidney. "Degrees of Difference: The Students
in Three Professional Schools at the University of Toronto, 1910 to the 1950s."
In *Learning to Practise,* edited by Heap, Millar, and Smyth. Ottawa: University of
Ottawa Press, 2005

Miller, James Collins. *National Government and Education in Federated Democracies:
Dominion of Canada.* Lancaster, PA: author; distributed by the Science Press
Printing Co., 1940

– *Rural Schools in Canada: Their Organization, Administration and Supervision.* New
York: Teachers College Press, 1913

Miller, Pavla. "'My Parents Came Here with Nothing and They Wanted Us to
Achieve': Italian Australians and School Success." In *The Death of the Comprehen-
sive High School? Historical, Contemporary and Comparative Perspectives,* edited by
Barry Franklin and Gary McCulloch. New York: Palgrave Macmillan, 2007

Miller, Selwyn A. "A Comparative Study of Supervision in the Various Canadian
Provinces, with a View to Determining the Optimum Load for Supervisors of
Each Type." DPaed diss., University of Toronto, 1946

Mills, C. Wright. *White Collar: The American Middle Classes.* New York: Oxford
University Press, 1951

Mombourquette, F.A. "Administration of Bilingual Schools with Special Reference
to the Province of Nova Scotia." MA thesis, University of Toronto, 1948

Morgenroth, Kaspar George. "The Development of the Organization and Administration of the Saskatoon School System, 1884–1947." MEd thesis, University of
Saskatchewan, 1949

Morton, Desmond. "The Cadet Movement in the Moment of Canadian Militarism,
1909–1914." *Journal of Canadian Studies* 13, no. 2 (Summer 1978)

Morton, Suzanne. *Ideal Surroundings: Domestic Life in a Working-Class Suburb in the
1920s.* Toronto: University of Toronto Press, 1995

Mosby, Ian. "Making and Breaking Canada's Food Rules: Science, the State, and the Government of Nutrition, 1942–1949." In *Edible Histories, Cultural Politics: Towards a Canadian Food History*, edited by Franca Iacovetta, Valerie J. Korinek, and Marlene Epp. Toronto: University of Toronto Press, forthcoming.

Moss, Mark. *Manliness and Militarism: Educating Young Boys in Ontario for War.* Don Mills, ON: Oxford University Press, 2001

Mowat, Alex S. *School Achievement of Nova Scotia Pupils: Report on an Educational Survey of King's County, NS, made in June 1941.* Report No. 16. Canadian Council for Educational Research, Oct. 1942

National Committee for School Health Research. *Absenteeism in Canadian Schools.* Report No. 3. Toronto, 31 Dec. 1948

– *A Health Survey of Canadian Schools, 1945–46.* Report No. 1. 1947

Newcombe, B.L., and M.V. Marshall. "A Study in Careers." *JEdNS*, Sept. 1944

Nikiforuk, Andrew. *School's Out: The Catastrophe in Public Education and What We Can Do about It.* Toronto: Macfarlane and Ross, 1993

Noël, Françoise. *Family and Community Life in Northeastern Ontario: The Interwar Years.* Montreal and Kingston: McGill-Queen's University Press, 2009

– "The Impact of Regulation 17 on the Study of District Schools: Some Methodological Considerations." Unpublished paper, Canadian History of Education Association Conference, 2010

Norrie, Kenneth, Douglas Owram, and J.C. Herbert Emery. *A History of the Canadian Economy.* 4th ed. Scarborough, ON: Nelson, 2008

Oliver, W.P. "The Negro in Nova Scotia." *JEdNS*, Dec. 1949, and *JEdNS*, Feb. 1964

Oreopoulos, Philip. "Canadian Compulsory School Laws and Their Impact on Educational Attainment and Future Earnings." Statistics Canada Research Paper, May 2005, Cat. No. 11F0019MIE – No. 251

Osborne, Kenneth. *Daniel McIntyre Collegiate Institute: A History.* Winnipeg: [CI Alumni, 1973?]

– *Education: A Guide to the Canadian School Debate – or Who Wants What and Why.* Toronto: Penguin/McGill Institute, 1999

– "'Education Is the Best National Insurance': Citizenship Education in Canadian Schools, Past and Present." *Canadian and International Education* 25, no. 2 (Dec. 1996)

– "100 Years of History Teaching in Manitoba Schools, Part I." *Manitoba History* 36 (Autumn/Winter 1998–99)

– "Public Schooling and Citizenship Education in Canada." *Canadian Ethnic Studies* 32, no. 1 (2000)

Ostry, Aleck Samuel. *Nutrition Policy in Canada, 1870–1939.* Vancouver: University of British Columbia Press, 2006

Ostry, Sylvia. *The Occupational Composition of the Canadian Labour Force.* Ottawa: DBS, 1967

Owen Sound Collegiate and Vocational Institute: 125th Anniversary Auditorium [title of yearbook]. 1980

Paris, R.C.M. "Retardation in a Typical Suburban School." University of Manitoba, Faculty of Education, Research Bulletin, 1940

Parker, Richard. *John Kenneth Galbraith: His Life, His Politics, His Economics.* Toronto: HarperCollins, 2005

Patterson, Robert S. "Voices from the Past: The Personal and Professional Struggle of Rural School Teachers." In *Schools in the West,* edited by Sheehan, Wilson, and Jones

Peabody, George. *School Days: The One-Room Schools of Maritime Canada.* Fredericton: Goose Lane Editions, 1992

Perlmann, Joel, and Robert A. Margo. *Women's Work? American Schoolteachers, 1650–1920.* Chicago: University of Chicago Press, 2001

Perry, George. "'A Concession to Circumstances': Nova Scotia's 'Unlimited Supply' of Women Teachers, 1870–1960." *Historical Studies in Education* 15, no. 2 (Fall 2003)

Perry, J. Harvey. *Taxes, Tariffs, and Subsidies: A History of Canadian Fiscal Development.* Toronto: University of Toronto Press, 1955

Phillips, Charles E. *The Development of Education in Canada.* Toronto: W.J. Gage and Co., 1957

Phillips, Linda M., and Stephen P. Norris. "Literacy Policy and the Value of Literacy for Individuals." In *Citizenship in Transformation in Canada,* edited by Yvonne M. Hébert. Toronto: University of Toronto Press, 2002

Picot, J.E. *A Brief History of Teacher Training in New Brunswick, 1848–1973.* Fredericton: Department of Education, NB, 1974

Pletch, Vera C. *Not Wanted in the Classroom: Parent Associations and the Education of Trainable Retarded Children in Ontario, 1947–1969.* London, ON: The Althouse Press, 1997

Porter, John. *The Vertical Mosaic: An Analysis of Social Class and Power in Canada.* Toronto: University of Toronto Press, 1965

Powers, Jane Bernard. *The "Girl Question" in Education: Vocational Education for Young Women in the Progressive Era.* London, ON: The Falmer Press, 1992

Prentice, Alison. "Multiple Realities: The History of Women Teachers in Canada." In *Feminism and Education: A Canadian Perspective,* edited by Frieda Forman et al. Toronto: Centre for Women's Studies in Education, OISE, 1990

Prentice, Alison, and Marjorie R. Theobald, eds. *Women Who Taught: Perspectives on the History of Women and Teaching.* Toronto: University of Toronto Press, 1991

Pullen, Harry. "A Study of Secondary School Curriculum Change in Canada with Special Emphasis on an Ontario Experiment." DEd diss., University of Toronto, 1955

Purdy, Sean. "'It was tough on everybody': Low-Income Families and Housing Hardship in Post-World War II Toronto." *Journal of Social History* 37, no. 2 (Winter 2003)

Race, Cecil L. "Compulsory Schooling in Alberta (1898–1942)." MEd thesis, University of Alberta, 1978

Reid, Ernest Harvey. "A Comparative Study of Secondary and Higher Educational Interests among the Different Racial Groups of Manitoba." University of Manitoba, Faculty of Education and Education Alumni Association, Research Bulletin, March 1939

Reynolds, Cecilia. "Hegemony and Hierarchy: Becoming a Teacher in Toronto, 1930–1980." *Historical Studies in Education* 2, no. 1 (Spring 1990)

Richardson, William L. *The Administration of Schools in the Cities of the Dominion of Canada.* Toronto: J.M. Dent, 1922

Ricker, Eric W., and B. Anne Wood, eds. *Historical Perspectives on Educational Policy in Canada: Issues, Debates, and Case Studies.* Toronto: Canadian Scholars' Press, 1995

Riddell, W. Craig. "Education, Skills, and Labour Market Outcomes." In *Educational Outcomes for the Canadian Workplace*, edited by Jane Gaskell and Kjell Rubenson. Toronto: University of Toronto Press, 2004

Robbins, John E. *Youth Figured Out: A Statistical Study of Canadian Youth.* Ottawa: Canadian Youth Commission [1947?]

Rousmaniere, Kate. *City Teachers: Teaching and School Reform in Historical Perspective.* New York: Teachers College Press, 1997

– "Go to the Principal's Office: Towards a Social History of the School Principal in North America." *History of Education Quarterly* 47, no. 1 (Feb. 2007)

– "The Great Divide: Principals, Teachers, and the Long Hallway between Them." *History of Education Review* 38, no. 2 (2009)

Russell, Frances. *The Canadian Crucible: Manitoba's Role in Canada's Great Debate.* Winnipeg: Heartland Associates, 2003

[Sadler, Michael E.]. [England] Board of Education. *Special Reports on Educational Subjects.* Vol. 4. "Educational Systems of the Chief Colonies of the British Empire." London: HMSO, 1901

Sager, Eric W. "Women in the Industrial Labour Force: Evidence for British Columbia, 1921–53." *BC Studies*, no. 149 (Spring 2006)

– "Women Teachers in Canada, 1881–1901: Revisiting the 'Feminization' of a Profession." *Canadian Historical Review* 88, no. 2 (June 2007)

Sager, Eric W., and Peter Baskerville, eds. *Household Counts: Canadian Households and Families in 1901.* Toronto: University of Toronto Press, 2007

Salisbury, Albert. *School Management: A Text-book for County Training Schools and Normal Schools.* Toronto: Educational Book Company, 1912

Sandiford, Peter, ed. *Comparative Education: Studies of the Educational Systems of Six Modern Nations.* London: J.M. Dent and Sons, 1918

[Savage, E.G.]. *Secondary Education in Ontario.* London: HMSO, 1928

Savoie, Alexandre J. "Education in Acadia, 1604–1970." In *The Acadians of the Maritimes: Thematic Studies*, edited by Jean Daigle. Moncton: Centre d'études acadiennes, 1982

Savoie, Calixte F. *Mémoires d'un nationaliste acadien.* Moncton, 1979

Seager, Allen. "The Pass Strike of 1932." *Alberta History* 25, no. 1 (Winter 1977)

Seath, John. *Education for Industrial Purposes. A Report.* Toronto: Ontario Department of Education, King's Printer, 1911

Shack, Sybil. "The Making of a Teacher, 1917–1935: One Woman's Perspective." In *Issues in the History of Education in Manitoba: From the Construction of the Common School to the Politics of Voice,* edited by Rosa Bruno-Jofré. Lewiston, NY/Queenston, ON: Edwin Mellen Press, 1993

Sheehan, Nancy M. "Indoctrination: Moral Education in the Early Prairie School House." In *Shaping the Schools of the Canadian West,* edited by Jones, Sheehan, and Stamp

– "The Junior Red Cross Movement in Saskatchewan, 1919–1929: Rural Improvement through the Schools." In *Building beyond the Homestead: Rural History on the Prairies,* edited by David Jones and Ian MacPherson. Calgary: University of Calgary Press, 1985

– "World War I and Provincial Educational Policy in English Canada." In *Historical Perspectives on Educational Policy,* edited by Ricker and Wood

Sheehan, Nancy M., J. Donald Wilson, and David C. Jones, eds. *Schools in the West: Essays in Canadian Educational History.* Calgary: Detselig Enterprises, 1986

Sinclair, S.B. *Backward and Brilliant Children.* Toronto: Ryerson Press, 1931

Sisler, W.J. *Peaceful Invasion.* Winnipeg: Ketchen Printing Co., 1944

Small, Carol. "An Analysis of Principals in Southwestern Ontario, 1920–1969." Directed Research Project, MEd, Faculty of Education, University of Western Ontario, 1996

Smiley, Donald V., ed. *The Rowell/Sirois Report, Book I.* Carleton Library No. 5. Toronto: McClelland and Stewart, 1963

Smith, Albert H. *A Bibliography of Canadian Education.* Toronto: Department of Educational Research, University of Toronto, Bulletin No. 10, 1938

Spence, Ruth Elizabeth. *Education as Growth: Its Significance for the Secondary Schools of Ontario.* Toronto: Spence, 1925

Spencer, Theodore M. "The Supervising Activities of School Principals in Rural Saskatchewan." MEd thesis, University of Manitoba, 1937

Stairs Quinn, Shawna. "'Sympathetic and Practical Men?' School Inspectors and New Brunswick's Educational Bureaucracy, 1879–1909." MA thesis, University of New Brunswick, 2006

Stamp, Robert M. *Becoming a Teacher in 20th Century Calgary: A History of the Calgary Normal School and the Faculty of Education, University of Calgary.* Calgary: Temeron Books, 2004

– "Canadian High Schools in the 1920s and 1930s: The Social Challenge to the Academic Tradition." Canadian Historical Association, *Historical Papers* (1978)

– "Empire Day in the Schools of Ontario: The Training of Young Imperialists." In *Canadian Schools and Canadian Identity,* edited by Alf Chaiton and Neil McDonald. Toronto: Gage, 1977

- *Ontario Secondary School Program: Innovations and Student Retention Rates – 1920s–1970s. A Report to the Ontario Study of the Relevance of Education and the Issue of Dropouts.* Ontario: Ministry of Education, 1988
- "The Response to Urban Growth." In *Shaping the Schools of the Canadian West*, edited by Jones, Sheehan, and Stamp
- *School Days: A Century of Memories.* Calgary: Calgary Board of Education, McClelland and Stewart West, 1975
- *The Schools of Ontario, 1876–1976.* Toronto: University of Toronto Press, 1982

Stanley, Timothy J. "White Supremacy and the Rhetoric of Educational Indoctrination: A Canadian Case Study." In *Children, Teachers, and Schools*, edited by Barman, Sutherland, and Wilson

Staples, R.O. "The Ontario Rural Teacher." DPaed diss., University of Toronto, 1946

Stephenson, Penelope. "'Mrs. Gibson Looked as If She Was Ready for the End of Term': The Professional Trials and Tribulations of Rural Teachers in British Columbia's Okanagan Valley in the 1920s." In *Children, Teachers, and Schools*, edited by Barman, Sutherland, and Wilson

Stone, Leroy E. *Urban Development in Canada.* Ottawa: DBS, 1967

Stortz, Paul J. "The Rural School Problem in British Columbia in the 1920s." MA thesis, University of British Columbia, 1988

Stortz, Paul J., and J. Donald Wilson. "Education on the Frontier: Schools, Teachers, and Community Influence in North-Central British Columbia." *Histoire sociale* 26, no. 52 (Nov. 1993)

Stratton, Walter S. "The Development of Public Secondary Education in the Rural Areas of New Brunswick, 1900–1966." MEd thesis, University of New Brunswick, 1969

Strong-Boag, Veronica. *The New Day Recalled: Lives of Girls and Women in English Canada, 1919–1939.* Toronto: Copp Clark Pitman, 1988

Survey of the Schools of the Greater Victoria Area. 1938

Sutherland, Neil. *Children in English-Canadian Society: Framing the Twentieth-Century Consensus.* Toronto: University of Toronto Press, 1976; reprint with new foreword, Waterloo, ON: Wilfrid Laurier Press, 2000
- *Growing Up: Childhood in English Canada from the Great War to the Age of Television.* Toronto: University of Toronto Press, 1997
- "The Triumph of 'Formalism': Elementary Schooling in Vancouver from the 1920s to the 1960s." In *Children, Teachers, and Schools*, edited by Barman, Sutherland, and Wilson

Sylvester, Kenneth Michael. "Immigrant Parents, Ethnic Children, and Family Formation in the Early Prairie West." *Canadian Historical Review* 84, no. 4 (Dec. 2003)
- *The Limits of Rural Capitalism: Family, Culture, and Markets in Montcalm, Manitoba, 1870–1940.* Toronto: University of Toronto Press, 2001

Synge, Jane. "The Transition from School to Work: Growing Up Working Class in Early Twentieth-Century Hamilton, Ontario." In *Childhood and Adolescence in Canada*, edited by K. Ishwarian. Toronto: McGraw-Hill Ryerson, 1979

Thompson, John Herd, with Allen Seager. *Canada 1922–1939: Decades of Discord.* Toronto: McClelland and Stewart, 1985

Thomson, Gerald. "'Through no fault of their own': Josephine Dauphinee and the 'Subnormal' Pupils of the Vancouver School System, 1911–1941." *Historical Studies in Education* 18, no. 1 (Spring 2006)

Todman, Dan. *The Great War: Myth and Memory.* London and New York: Hambledon & London, 2005

Tomes, Nancy. *The Gospel of Germs: Men, Women, and the Microbe in American Life.* Cambridge, MA: Harvard University Press, 1998

Tomkins, George S. *A Common Countenance: Stability and Change in the Canadian Curriculum.* Scarborough, ON: Prentice-Hall, 1986

Tooze, J. Adam. *Statistics and the German State, 1900–1945: The Making of Modern Economic Knowledge.* Cambridge: Cambridge University Press, 2001

Trueman, Albert W. *A Second View of Things: A Memoir.* Toronto: McClelland and Stewart, 1982

Tyack, David, and Larry Cuban. *Tinkering toward Utopia: A Century of Public School Reform.* Cambridge, MA: Harvard University Press, 1995

Tyack, David, and Elizabeth Hansot. *Learning Together: A History of Coeducation in American Schools.* New Haven, CT: Yale University Press, 1990

– *Managers of Virtue: Public School Leadership in America, 1820–1980.* New York: Basic Books, 1982

Tyack, David B., Robert Lowe, and Elizabeth Hansot. *Public Schools in Hard Times: The Great Depression and Recent Years.* Cambridge, MA.: Harvard University Press, 1984

Urquhart, M.C., and K.A.H. Buckley, eds. *Historical Statistics of Canada.* Toronto: Macmillan, 1965

Van Kleek, Edith. *The Way It Was: Vignettes from My One-Room Schools*, edited by Thelma Jo Dobson. Calgary: University of Calgary Press, 2007

Vermeulen, Hans, and Joel Perlmann, eds. *Immigrants, Schooling, and Social Mobility: Does Culture Make a Difference?* New York: St Martin's Press, 2000

von Heyking, Amy. *Creating Citizens: History and Identity in Alberta's Schools, 1905 to 1980.* Calgary: University of Calgary Press, 2006

– "Shaping an Education for the Modern World: A History of the Alberta Social Studies Curriculum, 1905 to 1955." PhD diss., University of Calgary, 1996

Waiser, Bill. *Saskatchewan: A New History.* Calgary: Fifth House, 2005

Walker, Bernal Ernest. "Public Secondary Education in Alberta: Organization and Curriculum, 1889–1951." PhD diss., Stanford University, 1955

Walker, James W. St G. *A History of Blacks in Canada: A Study Guide for Teachers and Students.* Hull, QC: Minister of State, Multiculturalism, 1980

Warikoo, Natasha, and Prudence Carter. "Cultural Explanations for Racial and Ethnic Stratification in Academic Achievement: A Call for a New and Improved Theory." *Review of Educational Research* 79, no. 1 (Spring 2009)

Warner, John W. "History of Secondary Education in New Brunswick." MA thesis, University of New Brunswick, 1944

Warren, Donald. Essay review: "Beginnings Again: Looking for Education in American History." *History of Education Quarterly* 43, no. 3 (Fall 2003)

Watkin, John Fred. "Extra-Curricular Activities in Alberta High Schools." MA thesis, University of Alberta, 1938

Weeks, Harold. "The Organization, Administration, and Supervision of Business Education in British Columbia." DEd diss., Harvard University, 1943

Weiler, Kathleen. *Country Schoolwomen: Teaching in Rural California, 1850–1950.* Stanford: Stanford University Press, 1998

Weir, G.M. *Survey of Nursing Education in Canada.* Toronto: University of Toronto Press, 1932

Whyte, Donald R. "Rural Canada in Transition." In *Rural Canada in Transition: A Multidimensional Study of the Impact of Technology and Urbanization on Traditional Society,* edited by Marc-Adélard Tremblay and Walton J. Anderson. Ottawa: Agricultural Economics Research Council of Canada, 1966

Wiebe, Rudy. *Of This Earth: A Mennonite Boyhood in the Boreal Forest.* Toronto: Alfred A. Knopf Canada, 2006

Wilbur, Richard. *The Rise of French New Brunswick.* Halifax: Formac, 1989

Wilson, J. Donald. "'I am ready to be of assistance when I can': Lottie Bowron and Rural Women Teachers in British Columbia." In *Women Who Taught,* edited by Prentice and Theobald

Wilson, J. Donald, Robert M. Stamp, and Louis-Philippe Audet, eds. *Canadian Education: A History.* Scarborough, ON: Prentice-Hall, 1978

Wilson, J. Donald, and Paul Stortz. "'May the Lord Have Mercy on You': The Rural School Problem in British Columbia in the 1920s." In *Children, Teachers, and Schools,* edited by Barman, Sutherland, and Wilson. Also in *Children, Teachers, and Schools,* 2nd ed., edited by Barman and Gleason

Wilson, William J. "The School as an Instrument of Urban Reform Education in Winnipeg, 1890–1920." PhD diss., University of Alberta, 1985

Winks, Robin W. *The Blacks in Canada: A History.* New Haven and Montreal: Yale University Press and McGill-Queen's University Press, 1971

– "Negro School Segregation in Ontario and Nova Scotia." *Canadian Historical Review* 50, no. 2 (June 1969)

Woods, D.S. "Education in Manitoba." Manitoba Economic Survey Board, February 1938

Wormsbecker, John Henry Jr. "The Development of Secondary Education in Vancouver." PhD diss., University of Toronto, 1961

Worton, David A. *The Dominion Bureau of Statistics: A History of Canada's Statistical Office and Its Antecedents, 1841–72*. Montreal and Kingston: McGill-Queen's University Press, 1998

Young, Jon, Benjamin Levin, and Dawn Wallin. *Understanding Canadian Schools: An Introduction to Educational Administration*. 4th ed. Toronto: Nelson, 2007

Young, R.A. "Maritimes Rise to War." In *A Country of Limitations: Canada and the World in 1939*, edited by Norman Hillmer et al. Ottawa: Canadian Committee for the History of the Second World War, 1996

Zelizer, Viviana A. Rotman. *Pricing the Priceless Child: The Changing Social Value of Children*. New York: Basic Books, 1985

Index